D1071320

THE GREEK
PURSUIT
OF KNOWLEDGE

THE GREEK
PURSUIT
OF KNOWLEDGE

Edited by Jacques Brunschwig and Geoffrey E. R. Lloyd
with the collaboration of Pierre Pellegrin

Translated under the direction of
Catherine Porter

THE BELKNAP PRESS OF
HARVARD UNIVERSITY PRESS
CAMBRIDGE, MASSACHUSETTS
LONDON, ENGLAND
2003

Copyright © 2000 by the President and Fellows of Harvard College
All rights reserved
Printed in the United States of America

First published as *Le Savoir Grec: Dictionnaire Critique,*
copyright © 1996 by Flammarion

Published with the assistance of the French Ministry of Culture National Book Center

Library of Congress Cataloging-in-Publication Data

Savoir grec. English. Selections.
The Greek pursuit of knowledge / edited by Jacques Brunschwig and Geoffrey E. R. Lloyd;
with the collaboration of Pierre Pellegrin;
translated under the direction of Catherine Porter.
p. cm.
Includes bibliographical references and index.
ISBN 0-674-02155-X (alk. paper)
1. Greece—Intellectual life—To 146 B.C.   2. Thought and thinking—History—To 1500.
I. Brunschwig, Jacques.   II. Lloyd, G. E. R. (Geoffrey Ernest Richard), 1933–
III. Pellegrin, Pierre   IV. Title.
DF78.S2313 2003
938—dc21   2003052247

CONTENTS

TRANSLATORS' NOTE

An informal group of translators based in Ithaca, New York, we agreed in the fall of 1996 to translate the portions of *Greek Thought* originally written in French and Italian. Working largely in bilingual pairs, we met regularly to share problems and search for solutions. A broad group of willing collaborators made our task much easier. We wish to express our gratitude first and foremost to Jacques Brunschwig and Geoffrey Lloyd, coeditors of the original French edition, for their generous assistance and support. We also offer thanks to all the authors who graciously read our drafts, answered questions, and made invaluable corrections and suggestions as needed. Other specialists and consultants helped us at many points along the way: thanks in particular to Charles Brittain, Terence Irwin, Mark Landon, Philip Lewis, Culver Mowers, Pietro Pucci, Hunter Rawlings, Geoffrey Rusten, and Daniel Turkeltaub for their collaboration. The unfailingly helpful staff allowed us to use the excellent collection housed in Cornell's Olin Library with maximum efficiency, and the Department of Classics at Cornell University kindly shared its own well-stocked library. Finally, we are indebted to Jennifer Snodgrass and the editorial staff at Harvard University Press for overseeing this complex project with exceptional patience and professional acumen.

RITA GUERLAC
DOMINIQUE JOUHAUD
CATHERINE PORTER
JEANNINE PUCCI
ELIZABETH RAWLINGS
ANNE SLACK
SELINA STEWART
EMORETTA YANG

INTRODUCTION: ON HOME GROUND IN A DISTANT LAND

Alpha, beta, and the rest, all the way to omega: most of us, on first acquaintance with the Greek alphabet, have toyed with writing our own names with its characters, so close and yet so remote from our own. Their attraction for us is unequaled. Roman inscriptions are lofty and admirable: their letters decorate the pediments of our civic buildings as well as commercial signs. At the extremes of the graphic spectrum, Egyptian hieroglyphics look down upon us from the pinnacle of their forty centuries; Chinese ideograms fascinate us by their symbolism and by the complicated enigma of their design. The Greek alphabet, halfway between the strange and the familiar, is at the perfect distance from our own—of which it is a remote ancestor. It is unfamiliar enough to let us know we have left home. Yet it welcomes us with signals clear enough to avoid complete illegibility. Better than a new dissertation on the eternal modernity of ancient Greece, or one more warning against the myths that nourish such dissertations, the paradoxical kinship of the alphabets offers a limited but illuminating metaphor for the complex relation that ties our present to a past that is also ours, and that continues to inhabit our present, visibly or invisibly.

What we have just said about the Greek alphabet could be repeated, even more justifiably, about everything that has been written with those letters. Despite severe losses, the Greek alphabet has transmitted to us countless texts: poems, myths, histories, tragedies, comedies, political and legal discourses, formal speeches, dialogues, treatises on philosophy, cosmology, medicine, mathematics, zoology, and botany; through direct action, indirect influence, polemical reaction, rereading, and reinterpretation, these texts inaugurated and have nourished the whole tradition of Western thought. Here again, the feelings of familiarity and distance are interwoven. We are on home ground in a distant land; we are traveling without leaving our own room. All our thinking, in one way or another, passes through reflection on the Greeks.

The key to the unparalleled originality of the Greeks may be that their culture, by definition, did not have the Greeks behind it. Of course it did not spring up out of nothing, any more than their alphabet did (its basic elements were borrowed from the Phoenicians); we need not regret that today's historians and scholars, with increasing conviction, are replacing the celebrated "Greek miracle" with unmiraculous Greeks. But however important the Greeks' debt to preceding civilizations, they quickly made their borrowings their own and turned them against their creditors, who represented in their eyes either a civilization turned upside down (the prestigious and astonishing Egypt) or the opposite of civilization (the despotic and barbaric Mesopotamia). Like all those who have followed, the Greeks reflected on the Greeks; but their reflections were like no one else's, simply because they themselves were the Greeks. Their thinking, like God's thinking according to Aristotle, was thinking about thinking.

The Greeks' culture of self-awareness predated the Socratic "Know thyself." Very early, their mythology, newly codified by Homer and Hesiod, gave rise to its own critics (Xenophanes, Heraclitus) and its own interpreters, allegorists or not. The Milesian cosmologies carried on a dialogue; each was intended to resolve a difficulty posed by its predecessor. The intimidating Parmenidean challenge, which threatened to smother physics, elicited almost immediate responses by Empedocles, Anaxagoras, and the Atomists. Socrates, disappointed by the physics of his forerunners, kept his distance from things and turned toward discourse. Plato transposed the ancient myths; he interpreted Socrates, constructing the conditions that made Socrates possible and that would have made his condemnation impossible. Aristotle criticized Plato, as he criticized most of his predecessors, even while he strove to retain what deserved preservation. Epicureans and Stoics, from their own moment in history, mustered enough distance to seek their own masters in a remote past before Plato and Aristotle, in Democritus and Heraclitus. Plato's heritage was diffused and dispersed in a gamut that ranged from skepticism to Neoplatonic metaphysics. Commentary, the critique of texts and the accumulation of glosses, which began astonishingly early, flourished at the beginning of the common era.

But even more striking than the critical turns taken by Greek culture in its successive stages is the work that each of its artisans performed on himself. It would have seemed impossible for Greek scientists, historians, or philosophers to do their work without knowing, or at least without wondering, under what conditions (intellectual as well as moral and political) it was possible to do science, history, or philosophy. To judge by their works, it is clear that the same thing was true for sculptors, architects, musicians, and dramatic poets: their style is manifestly not the result of rote practice or of an empirical tradition based on natural ability. Even shoemaking was taught; even cooks claimed to be conscious auxiliaries of philosophy. Every activity, every perception, every direct relation to an object raised seemingly simple questions that are as disconcerting as those addressed by Socrates to his interlocutors—questions that interpose distance and require the mind to adjust its relation to everything it encounters: "What is it all about?" "What are you really looking for?" "What exactly do you mean?" "How do you know what you have just said?"

The work from which this volume was drawn is titled *Greek Thought*. If it had one central ambition, it was to call attention to this fundamental reflexivity that seems to us characteristic of Greek thought, and which gives it even today a formative value and a capacity to challenge. The essays drawn from that book do not address "Greek science," or "Greek philosophy," or "Greek civilization." Excellent works, both introductory and comprehensive, exist on these subjects, works with which we do not propose to compete. We have not sought to explicate, or even to summarize, the whole of what the Greeks knew, or thought they knew; nor do we tally up what they did not know, the gaps in their knowledge. Similarly, we have not wanted either to repeat or to summarize histories of Greek philosophy; and nothing will be found here that touches directly on Greek art, Greek literature, or Greek religion. Instead we have sought to step back from the products to the processes that gave rise to them, from works to actions, from objects to methods. Of foremost interest to us is the typically Hellenic aptitude for raising questions that are at once "second-order"—in ways that correspond to our modern use of that term—and "first-order." They are second-order in that they relate not to substantive questions that bear immediately on the world, the beings that populate it, the events that take place in it, and the activities that transform it, but rather to the status of those questions and how they should be discussed. At the same time they are first-order or "primary" in a different sense, namely that in the view of many of the most prominent philosophers they must logically be raised first and solved or resolved in one way or another before the substantive issues are addressed. The term "Socratic fallacy" has sometimes been used to designate the idea that one could not say whether a given individual was courageous or not, so long as one was unable to say universally what courage is. Fallacy or not, Greek thought finds in this quest for lucidity its most radical task. Classical knowledge, in the sense in which we are using the term, is not the knowledge indicated by expressions like "knowing that Socrates was condemned to death" or "knowing that the diagonal of a square is incommensurable with its side." It represents, rather, the knowledge denoted in expressions such as "knowing what one is saying," "knowing what one is doing," "knowing what one wants."

This dimension of Greek thought, which takes as its objects not only first-order knowledge, but also life, language, production, and action, strikes us as essential and characteristic, and it is to this dimension that we draw the reader's attention. We look at the Greeks looking at themselves. We evoke not history as they made it and experienced it, but the stories they told themselves about it; not their poetry, but their poetics; not their music, but their harmonics; not their speeches, but their rhetoric. We present their theories about the origin, meaning, and functions of religion. We say nothing about their language itself, but we do offer some of their reflections on the origin, elements, and forms of language.

This book gathers essays on basic topics in philosophy and science. In accordance with contemporary parlance, people we call scientists know things, whereas one must no doubt be a philosopher, and even a sort of philosopher that may be on the verge of extinction, to think that philosophy is a form of knowing. But this division between science and philosophy does not correspond at all to the conceptual frameworks of antiquity; at most it puts in an appearance, with many qualifications, in the Hellenistic era, when specialized knowledge begins to acquire a certain autonomy, though philosophy still claims the right to provide the specialists with their principles and to pass judgment on their methods. Plato clearly subordinates mathematics to dialectics; but the vocabulary in which he expresses that subordination, far from leaving mathematics in its customary category as a science, instead contests that categorization. As for Aristotle, although he was more inclined to see the individual sciences as models according to which the criteria of scientific thought could be elaborated, he grants physics only the status of a "second philosophy." The emergence of philosophy as we have described it is also the emergence of knowledge, and of thought in general. Trying to avoid both the traps of historicism and those of *philosophia perennis,* we seek to put our object in a perspective that inevitably refers to a modern point of observation. In this enterprise we are concerned with measuring the legacy that Greek thought has bequeathed to its posterity, the use that posterity has made of it, and the continuities and discontinuities that this complex relation has engendered between inheritance and heirs—and it is not the least of the paradoxes that, in the inheritance itself, the heirs have found, among other things, the possibility of becoming themselves untrammeled producers of knowledge.

After essays on the central figure of the philosopher and the emergence of epistemology, we offer overviews of the institutional and conceptual frameworks for the extraordinary explosion of desire for knowledge, a desire that Aristotle views as naturally implanted in the heart of all people. Then follows a series of articles on the various branches of knowledge (including some that look to us like pseudo-science today). We have organized them alphabetically rather than adopting the classification—or rather one of the various classifications—that prevailed among Greek thinkers themselves: the theoreticians' agenda, that is to say the ordered set of questions to which any respectable doctrine was obliged to offer answers, from the formation of the world to the origin of humanity, human culture, and institutions, was fixed in its broad outlines at a very early date, and for several centuries manifested an astonishing degree of stability. Yet that agenda was enriched, diversified, and modified in multiple ways, and the classifications proposed rarely failed to become controversial. Certain disciplines, such as logic, did not come into their own until well after the early period of Greek thought; others, like medicine or harmonics, were quickly pervaded by debates on the extent to which they should be attached to or cut off from the common trunk of general philosophical and scientific theories. All things considered, we judged it preferable to fall back on the naïve security of alphabetical order.

Finally, a word about the choice of contributors. As general editors responsible for the overall project that resulted in the original *Greek Thought* volume, the two of us who sign this Introduction are pleased and proud that our association can modestly symbolize the alliance between two major centers of research on the history of ancient thought, Cambridge and Paris; we are even more pleased and proud to have worked all our professional lives, each in our own way, in the conviction that the differences between the Anglo-Saxon and Latin worlds in traditions, methods, and instruments of analysis and research in no way prevent contact, exchange, productive discussion, and the production of a common work. This book bears renewed witness to that shared conviction.

The authors to whom we turned, British or American, Italian or French, have all contributed to the considerable progress that has been made, over the last several decades, in the knowledge and understanding of the intellectual world of ancient Greece. They all have their own personalities, which we have not asked them to suppress; their freedom of opinion and judgment has been intentionally respected. As we have said, the gaze of the moderns looking upon the Greeks looking upon themselves remains obviously, and deliberately, our own gaze, and it measures distances, proximities, gaps, and debts from this standpoint. But this gaze of ours can never be entirely unified: contemporary scholars, sometimes because of the particular fields in which they work, sometimes because of the diversity of their overall approaches, do not all necessarily interpret or appreciate our relation to Greek thought in the same way. No one is in a position to dictate that all these scholars subscribe to the latest trend, or conform to the next-to-latest fashion; if we somehow had such power, we would surely have refrained from using it.

We thank our collaborators for agreeing to write their articles in a style that is not always the one they are accustomed to. We know how wrenching it is, for academics conscious of their scholarly responsibilities, to give up footnotes and erudite references. But we deliberately chose to call upon authors for whom that renunciation would be painful, rather than those whose habits would not have been particularly disturbed.

Finally, we want to thank all those without whom the long and difficult enterprise of producing the original *Greek Thought* volume would have run aground on one or another of the countless reefs that threatened it. Louis Audibert, the literary director at Flammarion, had the initial idea; he followed its realization from beginning to end with incomparable vigilance and care. Pierre Pellegrin played a very effective role in the revision process; he provided the liaison and the coordination that our geographic distance from each other, and from many of our authors, made particularly necessary. And we do not want to fail to thank the technical team at Flammarion, which supported us as much by its high expectations as by the help it offered us toward meeting them.

Jacques Brunschwig, Geoffrey E. R. Lloyd
Translated by Catherine Porter and Dominique Jouhaud

THE CLASSICAL GREEK WORLD

Black Sea

Adriatic Sea

Ionian Sea

Tyrrhenian Sea

Mediterranean Sea

Aegean Sea

THRACE

MACEDONIA

THESSALY

EPIRUS

MAGNA GRAECIA

BRUTTIUM

SICILY

MYSIA

LYDIA

IONIA

CARIA

CHERSONESUS

CHALCIDICE

DORIS

AETOLIA

OZOLIAN LOCRIS

BOEOTIA

ATTICA

ACHAEA

ARCADIA

MESSENIA

LACONIA

Propontis

Bosphorus

Hellespont

Astacus
Chalcedon
Byzantium
Selumbria
Perinthus
Diaolylium
Proconnesus
Cyzicus
Lampsacus
Abydos
Sestos
Aenus
Maronea
Abdera
Apollonia
Stagira
Amphipolis
Olynthus
Potidaea
Mende
Scone
Torone
Pagasae
Phenae
Larissa
Pharsalus
Methone
Pydna
Pella
Therma
Dodona
Ambracia
Corcyra
Epidamnus
Apollonia
Leucas
Ithaca
Cephallenia
Zacynthus
Naupactus
Patrai
Elis
Olympia
Pylos
Sparta
Argos
Mycenae
Corinth
Megara
Athens
Thebes
Chalcis
Eretria
Histiaea
Delphi
Pherae

Sardis
Pergamum
Adramyttium
Antandros
Illium (Troy)
Assus
Methymna
Eresus
Mytilene
Myrina
Phocaea
Cyme
Smyrna
Clazomenae
Colophon
Lebedos
Ephesus
Notium
Miletus
Priene
Halicarnassus
Aphrodisias
Cnidus
Cos
Ialysus
Camyrus
Lindos

Lesbos
Chios
Icaria
Samos
Andros
Tenos
Delos
Naxos
Amorgos
Ios
Paros
Siphnos
Seriphos
Cythnos
Melos
Thera
Astypalia
Rhodes
Karpathos
Crete
Cydonia
Knossos
Phaistos
Gortyn
Hierapytna (Ierapetra)

Lemnos
Samothrace
Thasos
Scyrus
Euboea
Cythera

Taras
Croton
Sybaris
Elea
Posidonia
Naples
Cumae
Locri
Rhegium
Catania
Syracuse
Himera
Acragas

200 miles
200 kilometers
0 50 100 150
0 50 100 150

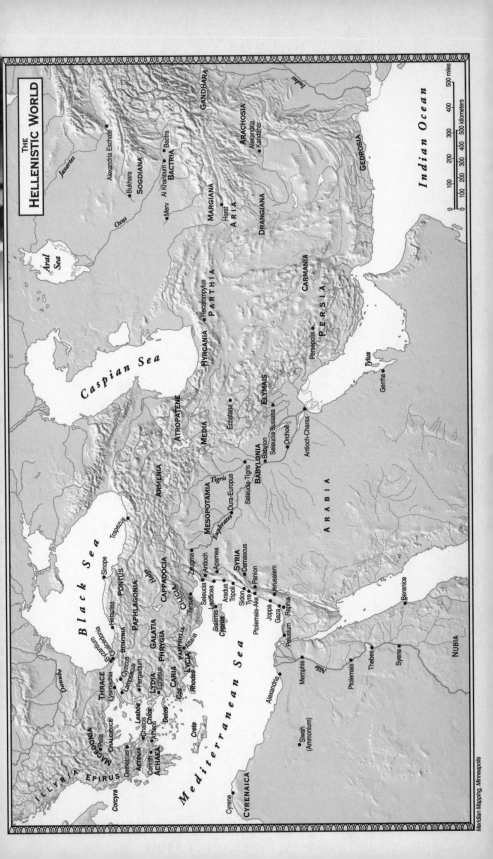

THE
HELLENISTIC WORLD

0 100 200 300 400 500 miles
0 100 200 300 400 500 kilometers

Indian Ocean

GANDHARA

Alexandria Eschate

SOGDIANA
Bukhara
Al Khanoum
BACTRIA
Bactra

Jaxartes

Oxus

ARACHOSIA
Alexandria-Kandahar

Merv

MARGIANA
Herat
ARIA

DRANGIANA

GEDROSIA

Hecatompylus
PARTHIA

HYRGANIA

CARMANIA

PERSIA

Aral
Sea

Caspian Sea

Persepolis

Tylus

ATROPATENE

Gerrha

MEDIA
Ecbatana

ELYMAIS
Babylon
Seleucia-Susiana
Orchoï
Antioch-Charax

ARMENIA

MESOPOTAMIA
Tigris
Dura-Europus
Seleucia-Tigris
BABYLONIA

Euphrates

ARABIA

Trapezus

Black Sea

Sinope

PONTUS
Heraclea
PAPHLAGONIA
Halys

Zeugma
Antioch
Apamea
Seleucia
Laodicea
Aradus
Tripoli
Sidon
Tyre
Ptolemais-Ake
Joppa
Jerusalem
Gaza
Raphia
Pelusium

SYRIA
Damascus
Panion

CAPPADOCIA

GALATIA
CILICIA
Tarsus
Salamis
Cyprus

Byzantium
Chalcedon
THRACE
Lysimachia
Cyzicus
Lampsacus
Pergamum
PHRYGIA
LYDIA
Ephesus
CARIA
Cos
Rhodes

PAMPHYLIA
LYCIA

Attalia

MACEDONIA
Pella
CHALCIDICE
Lesbos
Chalcis
Chios
Delos
Euboea

Demetrias
AETOLIA
ACHAEA
Corinth
Athens

Crete

ILLYRIA
EPIRUS

Corcyra

Danube

Berenice

NUBIA

Alexandria
Memphis
Nile
Ptolemais
Thebes
Syene

Siwah
(Ammonium)

Mediterranean Sea

Cyrene

CYRENAICA

Meridian Mapping, Minneapolis

THE PHILOSOPHER

PHILOSOPHY IS A HISTORICAL PHENOMENON. It emerges out of a need to have a certain kind of answer to certain questions, for instance questions as to the origin of the world as we know it. It obviously would be very frightening to live in a world in which the behavior of things, especially where it affected one's life, seemed completely unintelligible. There were traditional answers available to such questions; in fact, various traditions provided answers. But these answers were in conflict with one another. Thus, as people became aware of the different traditions and their conflict, the traditional answers began to fail to satisfy people's need to feel they have a secure understanding of the world in which they live, of nature, of social and political organizations, of what makes communities and individuals behave the way they do. What were needed were answers of a new kind, answers that one could defend, that one could show to be superior to competing answers, that one could use to persuade others, so as to reestablish some kind of consensus.

It was a long time before attempts to provide such answers led to an established practice and a general enterprise or discipline. But once a discipline of philosophy was established, it naturally came to respond to two different sets of needs or demands: the external ones, which originally gave rise to the practice of philosophy, and also internal demands as to what counted as acceptable or good practice in terms of the discipline. Both demands or needs would ensure that the discipline would change over time. As the culture evolved, the external needs would change, and with it the discipline, to the extent that it continued to be responsive to them. And the internal demands would also force change. New answers would raise new questions, and the answers to those questions could force a revision of the answers to the original ones. Thus the practice of philosophy changed and will continue to change over time, and all the more so as the two sets of demands or needs may come apart or even come into conflict with each other. Indeed, once the discipline develops a momentum or life of its own—achieves a degree of autonomy—its practitioners may become more or less oblivious to the external needs that gave rise to it.

For the reasons given, then, philosophy has changed considerably over time. It is not just the questions and answers that have changed, so have the demands made on acceptable answers. Indeed, the whole conception of the enterprise subtly changes as philosophers try to respond to changing external

1

needs and changing internal demands, and this, of course, affects their philo-sophical practice.

When we study ancient philosophy, we are guided by our contemporary conception of the philosophical enterprise. This makes it easy for us to over-look the fact that the ancient philosophers had a very different conception of their philosophical activity. As a result, we get a very distorted picture of what ancient philosophers were doing and saying. If, for instance, we consult modern accounts to inform ourselves about Euphrates, Apollonius of Tyana, and Dion of Prusa, their existence is barely acknowledged, perhaps only to question whether they were really philosophers. One does not get any sense that they arguably were the most renowned and respected philosophers of their time, the turn from the 1st to the 2nd century. The aim of the following remarks is to provide at least a rough sketch of how the ancients themselves thought of philosophy and its practitioners.

This is a vast topic. A complete treatment would require a discussion of how the conception of a philosopher found its expression in the statues and busts of philosophers set up by philosophers and nonphilosophers, in private and in public, from the 4th century B.C.E. onward, or how this conception was reflected in literature from the late 5th century B.C.E. onward, or in imperial legislation in late antiquity. Much of this evidence also reflects the extent to which the need that the philosophers tried to satisfy by their practice was rec-ognized as a social need. But I will here restrict myself to a sketch in rather abstract terms of the conception the philosophers themselves had of their en-terprise and how it evolved.

It is perhaps best to begin with the very term *philosophos* and its cognates. The term is one of a large family of adjectives, then also used as nouns, formed from *philo-* and some noun, a formation particularly common at the turn from the 5th to the 4th century B.C.E. These terms are used to character-ize a person in whose life the item designated by the noun plays a remarkably large role as an object of positive concern. Thus a *philotimos* is a person who to a remarkable and quite unusual degree is motivated by a concern for honor. Correspondingly, a philosopher would be somebody who, in what he does and how he lives, to an unusual degree is influenced by a concern for wisdom. But obviously one can show a particular concern for wisdom without being a phi-losopher, without being a member of a distinct, identifiable group of people called "philosophers" engaged in a distinct enterprise called "philosophy." In-deed, in their earliest extant uses, the word *philosophos* and its cognates do not seem to refer to a distinct group of persons and a distinct enterprise. If Clement (*Strom.* V.141) quotes Heraclitus correctly, Heraclitus said that men who aspire to wisdom (*philosophoi andres*) need to be inquirers (*histores*) into a good many things. It is clear from fragments B40 and B129 that Heraclitus does not think that knowing a lot of things (*polymathie*) will in it-self make one wise, but he does think that one will not become wise if one does not take the trouble, which people ordinarily do not bother to do, to try to find out about a good many things. Nor does Herodotus (I.30) have philosophy in mind when he has Croesus say to Solon that he must be traveling to distant lands "philosopheōn," out of love for wisdom. Solon does not travel around on business or as a political ambassador; he is engaged in *historia* of the kind Heraclitus recommends to those who aspire to be wise, trying to find out about other parts of the world, other nations, their customs and institutions, and their way of understanding things. Nor does Thucydides want Pericles to say in his Funeral Oration that the Athenians are philosophers when he has him say that the Athenians distinguish themselves among the Greeks in their concern for wisdom *(philosophoumen)*.

The first time we encounter the word *philosopher* in its later, familiar use is in Plato's dialogues. There it and its cognates occur with such frequency that we are tempted to think that term must have come into use in the late 5th century and perhaps was already used by Socrates. In any case, from Socrates onward the term *philosopher* takes on a precise meaning that goes far beyond the vague idea of a person who shows a remarkable concern for wisdom, and philosophers have a definite conception of philosophy, which involves the following assumptions.

First, wisdom is a certain kind of knowledge that is at least the decisive necessary, if not sufficient, condition for having a good life. Thus, to be a philosopher is not just to show an unusual concern for wisdom; wisdom, for a philosopher, becomes a concern that does, and should, override any other concern. Socrates is going to be a paradigmatic philosopher in this, as in other regards. Notoriously, Socrates lets his concern for wisdom override his concern for his craft, for his family, and ultimately for his life. Given how difficult it is to be wise, an overriding concern for wisdom does leave little space for competing concerns. It ideally transforms one's whole life. Philosophy is not something that, as a philosopher, one could pursue as a career, or as one of many interests.

Second, it is not just that wisdom for a philosopher is an overriding concern. A philosopher will also think (until far into late antiquity, when this claim will be challenged by Christians and others) that the only way to concern oneself with wisdom so as to become wise is the philosopher's way.

These two assumptions together amount to the implicit claim that to attain the good life, to become a good person, to be saved, one has to be a philosopher. In this, philosophers from Socrates onward agreed. They differed in how they identified wisdom, in whether they assumed that wisdom was a necessary or also a sufficient condition for the good life, and as to how, as a philosopher, one would strive to attain wisdom. In this way, they differed in their conception of the philosophical enterprise. To be more precise, from Socrates onward we can trace in great detail the evolution of the conception of philosophy, as philosophers came to develop different views as to the nature of the wisdom in question and the way to attain it. But before we can turn to this, we have to return, at least briefly, to the Presocratics.

We tend, with some hesitation, to let philosophy begin with Thales and the Milesians. So did Aristotle and the ancient doxography dependent on Aristotle. But it goes without saying that this way of looking at things is very much the product of retrospective history; it is very much in hindsight that we can see that Thales started a tradition that contributed to the formation of the discipline that came to be known as philosophy. In fact, it is only Aristotle's rather biased, one-sided, and unrepresentative view, expressed, for instance, in *Metaphysics*, that lets Thales appear as such a plausible candidate for the title of the first philosopher. According to this view, wisdom *(sophia)* is theoretical wisdom, which primarily is a matter of grasping the ultimate principles of reality, and Thales and his successors, as if driven by the truth itself, were slowly moving in the direction of Aristotle's position on the principles of reality. But obviously it would be naive to think that Thales set out to found a new discipline, or that he set out to identify the ultimate principles of reality, thereby starting a new discipline. He, among many other things, also tried to develop a new account, and to some extent a new kind of account, of the origin of the world as we know it.

In fact, we have to ask ourselves quite generally to what extent those whom we have come to call Presocratic philosophers did see themselves, and were seen by their contemporaries, as forming a distinct group pursuing a distinct enterprise that would become known as philosophy. What should give us pause is that down to the later part of the 5th century B.C.E. there was not even a word for "philosopher." We have already seen that the term *philosopher*, to refer to philosophers, only came into use just before Plato. It is true that the ancients, when they talked at all about the origin of the terms *philosopher* and *philosophy*, attributed them to Pythagoras (Diogenes Laertius, praef. 12; Cicero, *Tusc.* V.8–9). But for this they clearly relied on a passage in a lost work by Heraclides Ponticus, a follower of Aristotle. And Heraclides, for his claim, had no more to rely on than a story about Pythagoras, obviously part of the already proliferating legend of Pythagoras. Nor was there any other term that could have been used to refer to philosophers. Diogenes Laertius (praef. 12) shows some awareness of the problem that poses itself, even if we, wrongly, assume that Pythagoras introduced the term *philosopher*. He says that philosophers were called "wise" *(sophoi)* or "sophists." It is true that some of the Presocratics, for instance Thales, were called wise or were even canonized as one of the Seven Sages. But not all of them were called this, and those who were shared the honorific epithet with others — poets, rhapsodes, lawgivers, and statesmen. Moreover, philosophers would hardly have thought of themselves as wise. There also was the term *sophist*, used to refer to somebody who, through his own efforts, had acquired some claim to some kind of wisdom. Given that wisdom tended to be regarded as a matter of long, often painful experience, as something that grew on one, if one was able to learn and observe, the very term could invite negative associations, as implying that there was a shortcut to wisdom, perhaps even that wisdom was a matter that one could readily attain through the appropriate instruction. But the term originally had a positive connotation and continued often to have a positive sense even in Plato and later. Herodotus calls Pythagoras a "sophist" (I.29.1; IV.95.2). Diogenes of Apollonia refers to his predecessors as "sophists" (A4 D.K.). And the author of On Ancient Medicine (cap. 20) twice seems to be referring to natural philosophers as "sophists." But it is also true, as Diogenes Laertius pointed out (praef. 12), that the term sophist was not restricted to those we call philosophers. It was used equally for poets (Pindar, Isth. V.28) and for statesmen such as Solon (Isocr. XV.313). That before the latter part of the 5th century there was no special word for philosophers very much suggests that up to that time philosophers did not regard themselves, or were not regarded by others, as a distinct group. This impression is strengthened if we look at the fragments of the Presocratics to see whom they regarded as the proper group of persons they wanted to be compared to and against whom they in some way competed. In particular Xenophanes and Heraclitus repeatedly refer to others by name. Thus Xenophanes refers to Homer, Hesiod, Simonides, Epimenides, Thales, and Pythagoras. Heraclitus refers to Homer and Hesiod, but also to Archilochus, Hecataeus of Miletus, Bias of Priene, Thales, Pythagoras, and Xenophanes. Here the reference class is made up of persons who have a reputation for being wise, or who at least have or make a claim to be heard or listened to, but again it includes, without distinction, poets, statesmen, and those whom we call philosophers.

What these references suggest is that those we call philosophers thought of themselves, and were thought of by others, as being concerned with wisdom in a fairly vague and broad sense, in such a way as to be comparable to or even in competition with poets and politicians and lawgivers. We get some idea of the wisdom they aspired to or came to be renowned for if we look at Thales. Thales came to be regarded as one of the Seven Sages. Indeed, according to Demetrius of Phaleron, it was Thales who was the first to be called "wise" (Diogenes Laertius I.22). Herodotus has three stories to tell about Thales that give us some idea of how Thales' wisdom was perceived: supposedly Thales managed to predict the solar eclipse of May 585, which happened precisely as the Medes and the Lydians were joining battle, and which hence one would be tempted to regard as ominous (Herodotus I.74); Thales advised the Ionians to form one political community with its boule in Teos, given Teos's central location—advice which, if heeded, might have prevented the return to Persian rule (I.170); when Croesus had difficulties crossing the River Halys with his troops, Thales ingeniously solved the problem by diverting the river (I.75).

Wisdom here seems to be seen as something that proves itself in a practical way. There is some emphasis on Thales' political insight. There is little or no emphasis on the theoretical achievement the prediction of an eclipse would involve. If Thales had not supposedly been able to predict the eclipse, and if it had not ominously coincided with the battle, Herodotus hardly would have seen a reason to refer at least indirectly to Thales' attempts to theoretically understand the world. And there is no reason to suppose that Thales himself would have wanted to deny that wisdom has to prove itself in practical ways. There certainly is no reason to suppose that Thales conceived of the wisdom he aspired to as entirely a matter of theoretical insight. And, though Thales' successors may have had a more articulate conception of this wisdom and their concern for it (as, for instance, Heraclitus clearly did), it does seem that they all continued to think of this wisdom as being something of considerable practical relevance, as we see in Empedocles' or Democritus's case. As late a figure as Democritus still thought that it was part of his chosen role to produce not only an atomistic theory but also a very large number of gnomic, "ethical" sayings. It also is telling that Democritus clearly does not yet have a definite conception as to how the theoretical and the practical aspects of wisdom are related, or a conception of the philosophical enterprise in the pursuit of which one would try to develop both a theory of reality and an ethical theory. Indeed Democritus does not produce an ethical theory; he produces wise, moral reflections.

At the same time, we also have to acknowledge that the Presocratics from Thales to Democritus, as part of their general concern for wisdom, tried to provide an account of reality or a theory of nature. And this in the end would solidify into a generally recognized enterprise of which they saw themselves as forming a part. It is in this way that they slowly came to be seen as a separate group. The first extant use of the word *philosophia* seems to be in *On Ancient Medicine* (chap. 20), where it refers to the kind of enterprise in which Empedocles and other inquirers into nature were engaged. But at an early point it would not be so clear that the philosophers for this reason formed a distinct group. After all, Hesiod and Pherecydes of Syros were also offering an account of the world and its origin. Philosophers like Parmenides or Empedocles presented themselves as being poetically inspired. We also have to remember that the clarity with which this tradition comes to stand out as a distinct tradition is in good part a matter of retrospective history and the selective transmission of the evidence. But however clearly the tradition emerges in the 5th century, it also seems clear that it is not a tradition of the pursuit of theoretical wisdom but a tradition of the pursuit of a much more broadly conceived wisdom, of which the attempt to come to a certain kind of theoretical understanding of the world forms just a part, albeit a crucial one.

If, because of our focus on the pursuit of a theoretical understanding of the world, we do not see that those engaged in this pursuit felt committed to a much more broadly understood wisdom with at least a strong practical component, we will find it difficult to understand how Socrates could see himself, and be seen by others, as part of a tradition going back to the Milesians. In fact, it will seem to be a historical accident that philosophy emerged as one discipline with a theoretical and a practical part, rather than as two independent disciplines, one in the tradition of Thales, in pursuit of a theoretical understanding of the world, and the other a discipline, first suggested by Socrates, in pursuit of a practical understanding of how one lives well.

It is notoriously difficult to determine the historical truth about Socrates' position. But to go by the evidence provided by Plato and Xenophon, Socrates identified wisdom with the knowledge of those things that we need to know if we are to live well, namely the good, the bad, and related matters. To be more precise, Socrates seems to have thought that these related matters formed, precisely because they were related, the subject of a systematic body of truths and hence the object of a discipline or art later called ethics or "the art of life." What is novel about this is that, instead of isolated moral reflections of the kind we find earlier among the Presocratics or in poets, or the kind of art attributed, for instance, by Plato to Protagoras (*Protagoras* 318.E5–319.A5), Socrates suggests a systematic discipline based on an insight into the good, the beautiful, the pious, and the courageous, and their interrelations. It is the knowledge and understanding of these matters that constitutes wisdom, precisely because it is the understanding of these matters that is relevant to the kind of life we have. By contrast, if we follow the evidence of, for instance, Plato's *Phaedo* and *Apology*, Socrates turns his back on the tradition of trying to give a theoretical account of reality as it does not contribute to wisdom, because this sort of account is either beyond us or, in any case, does not contribute to wisdom as Socrates conceives of it, to our understanding of the good and related matters.

So at this crucial point in the history of philosophy, when philosophers finally have come to see themselves clearly as a distinct group engaged in a distinct enterprise, when Socrates advances a certain conception of the enterprise that will constitute the historical starting point from which later conceptions of philosophy derive, philosophy is conceived of as a practical enterprise—and this in a twofold sense. First, Socrates' interest in the knowledge that constitutes wisdom is not a theoretical interest but an interest born of the idea that one should put one's mind, if to anything, then to one's life—that there is a whole body of truths to be known about how one should live, if one wants to live well. To the extent that Socrates can assume that the Presocratic interest in wisdom always also had been practical, he can see himself as continuing a long tradition, though in a very refocused form. Second, in spite of his extreme intellectualism—that is to say, his view that the way we act is completely determined by our beliefs, in particular our beliefs concerning the good and related matters—Socrates' life seems to have been characterized by a remarkable degree of asceticism. This strongly suggests that Socrates thought that it is not a matter of pure rational argument which beliefs we espouse and which we fail to espouse, but that, precisely because some of our beliefs are so deeply embedded in the way we feel and behave, our openness to their rational rejection or their rational acceptance, our openness to rational argument, also is a matter of our pattern of behavior and the control we have over our behavior.

From Socrates onward all philosophers in antiquity thought of philosophy as being practical in the sense of being motivated by a concern for the good life and as involving a practical concern for how one actually lives and how one actually feels about things. But they greatly differed in the way they understood this. Most important, few philosophers, like the Stoic Aristo and many Cynics, accepted Socrates' narrow conception of wisdom as a matter of a certain ethical knowledge.

Plato rejected this narrow conception of wisdom and, correspondingly, of philosophy as moral philosophy. And one can easily see why:

I. Socrates, it seems, relied on a substantial notion of the soul as what guides our behavior and whose health and well-being should thus be a primary concern of ours. His extreme intellectualism seems to have been based on a conception of the soul as a mind or a reason, such that our desires turn out to be beliefs of a certain kind.

II. Socrates relied on the assumption that there are, objectively, such things as the just and the pious.

III. Socrates also relied on the assumption that there is, objectively, such a thing as the good, which we can identify by reflecting on how people behave and how they fare.

The first two assumptions, to be sustained, presuppose an account of reality in terms of which we can explain human beings, their constitution, and the role the soul plays in the explanation of their behavior, and which also allows us to explain what kinds of things the just and the pious are supposed to be. As to the third assumption, we may question whether the good is not a global or universal feature in the sense that things quite generally have to be understood in terms of the good, and that the use of the term *good* in the sphere of human affairs has to be understood as just a special case of a much wider use of the term. It is for reasons of this sort that Plato comes to think that ethics has to be embedded in, and supported by, a theoretical account of reality. Correspondingly we get a broader, but still precise, conception of wisdom as involving both a theoretical understanding of reality and a practical knowledge of what matters in life. And with this move philosophy, as Plato conceives of it, looks like a clarification and focusing of the enterprise of the Presocratics, allowing us to distinguish clearly between philosophers, poets, and statesmen.

Just on the basis of what I have said so far, the need for a theoretical understanding of the world might be thought to be entirely due to the fact that our practical knowledge of how to live needs the support of such a theory. This is how Epicureans and Stoics will understand the matter. But the relative priority of the theoretical and the practical parts of wisdom get reversed in Plato and his later followers because of a certain conception of the soul. The soul is conceived of as preexisting and as just temporarily joined to a body. It thus has two lives and two sets of concerns. Its own concern is to live a life of contemplation of the truth. But, joined to the body, it also has to concern itself with the needs of the body. In doing this it easily forgets itself and its own needs, it easily gets confused so as to make the needs of the body its own. To know how to live well is to know how to live in such a way that the soul is free again to clearly see and mind its own business, namely to contemplate the truth. Thus we have an extremely complex inversion of the relative weight of one's theoretical understanding of reality and one's practical knowledge of how to live. It is one's understanding of reality, and the position of the soul in it, that saves the soul by restoring it—to the extent that this is possible in this life—to its natural state, in which it contemplates the truth. Hence a good life will crucially involve, as part of the way one lives, contemplation of the truth. Practicing the right way to live will also be a means to enable the soul to free itself from the body, to see the truth, and to engage in the contemplation of the truth.

Aristotle does not share Plato's dualist view of the soul. Nevertheless he has a view of human beings according to which a distinctly human life is a rational life, and hence a perfect human life involves the perfection of reason. But the perfection of reason involves not just the acquisition of the practical wisdom as to how we live but also the acquisition of the theoretical understanding of the world, both because practical wisdom requires such an understanding and because the mere contemplation of the truth is an end in itself and hence a crucial part of a good life. In fact, Aristotle sometimes talks as if contemplation were the part of a good life that accounted for its goodness. Nevertheless, even in Aristotle the philosopher's concern for theoretical wisdom is practical in the sense that it is a concern for a certain kind of life, namely a life that is perfected and fulfilled because it is dominated by a theoretical understanding of the world. Moreover, even Aristotle recognizes that there is no wisdom without practical wisdom, and that the acquisition of practical wisdom requires a highly practical effort on the part of the philosopher to learn to act and feel about things in a certain way. Our talk of Aristotle's "ethical theory" obscures the fact that, on Aristotle's view, the point of moral knowledge precisely is knowledge and understanding not of facts of a certain kind but of behavior of a certain kind, and that this moral knowledge and understanding cannot be acquired without involving oneself in acquiring the disposition to respond reliably to situations in a way appropriate to them, emotionally and in what one does.

When we turn to Hellenistic times, the priority between theory and practice changes again, decisively in favor of practice. Skeptics question whether any theory is available, and whether, even if it were available, it would help in living wisely. Epicureans and Stoics do assume that both ethical knowledge and an account of the world are attainable. But they are very clear about the fact that the philosopher's concern for ethical knowledge is a concern for the good life, and they both insist that a true account of the world is purely instrumental toward grounding and securing one's ethical knowledge. In the case of the Epicureans, the interest in a theory of nature is a purely negative one. The Epicureans assume that human beings living in a world that they do not understand are prone to be overcome by irrational fears they cannot control and which will not just put a truly good life out of their reach but will ruin the life they have. In particular they are prone to be overcome by the fear that the gods will punish them for their failures, if not in this life, then in an afterlife. They tend to understand natural phenomena as indications of divine anger, threats, or punishments. A moral life is impossible for a person given to such fears. The point of Epicurean physics is to free us from such terrors in order to create the psychological space for Epicurean ethics and a life in accordance with it. The Stoics have a far more positive attitude toward physics, and in particular the part of physics called theology, even if they regard this knowledge as purely subservient to the end of being practically wise. We learn from Stoic physics that the world is governed by an immanent divine rational principle that arranges the world down to the smallest detail so as to be a perfect world. We also know from Stoic physics that we are constructed in such a way as to be naturally guided by reason toward the good, and that, hence, as part of our development, we have to acquire the appropriate beliefs as to what is good, bad, or neither. It is in the light of this understanding of the world, then, that Stoic ethics will tell us what is good, bad, or neither; what it is appropriate for us to do, if we are guided by a concern for the good; and how good action consists precisely in this, doing what is appropriate out of concern for the good.

Now, what is characteristic of Epicureanism and Stoicism is not just the emphasis on ethics but, within ethics, the concern to provide practical guidance and the emphasis on the need to involve oneself practically. I will try to indicate, at least briefly, the nature of this concern in the case of Stoicism. The Stoics revert to Socrates' extreme intellectualism. They deny an irrational part of the soul. The soul is a mind or a reason. Its contents are impressions or thoughts, to which the mind gives assent or prefers to give assent. In giving assent to an impression, we espouse a belief. Desires are just beliefs of a certain kind, the product of our assent to a so-called impulsive impression. Since all that we do depends on our beliefs and, more especially, our desires, all we do ultimately depends on which impressions we give assent to. There are impressions one is justified in giving assent to, and there are impressions one is not justified in giving assent to. Hence, in the ultimate analysis, there is just one way in which we can err or sin, namely in giving assent to an impression that we are not justified in giving assent to. In this sense all sins are equal.

What is so disastrous about them is always the same: they involve assent to an impression that might be false or even is false. But given the logical connection between all beliefs, any false belief, however insignificant it may seem, threatens to destroy the true beliefs incompatible with it that we already have, and thus our chance to become wise. Now, among the impulsive impressions people are prone to give unjustified assent to are those that evoke the so-called passions or affections of the soul, like anger or fear or lust. They all involve the false belief that something is a good or an evil that in fact is neither. On the Stoic view only wisdom or virtue is a good. Thus any passion involves a false belief that is incompatible with a fundamental truth of ethics the mastery of which constitutes a crucial part of wisdom. Therefore a philosophical concern for wisdom involves the eradication of all passion, and this obviously is not just a matter of rational argument. Philosophical wisdom involves an indifference to all things but wisdom and virtue. A corollary of this and of the thesis of the equality of all sins is that all we do requires the same kind of careful attention as to what is appropriate: our eating and drinking, our waking and sleeping, the way we dress, the way we talk. All that we do has to be done wisely. There is thus a vast field of practice for a philosopher who is concerned to acquire a firm and solid knowledge of what matters. For reasons I will return to, this emphasis on the practical side of being a philosopher will become even stronger in later Stoicism. We tend to understand these concerns as reflecting an unphilosophical attitude, because they are untheoretical or even antitheoretical. It is crucial to understand that these concerns, given the Stoic understanding of philosophy, are eminently philosophical; they are, after all, concerns for the cognitive state of the philosopher.

Both Epicureans and Stoics proceed on the assumption that our life crucially depends on our having the right philosophical beliefs, the correct dogmata, concerning certain issues: the existence of God, divine providence, the nature of the soul, the good, the affections of the soul. In this sense orthodoxy comes to be a concern, a matter of anxiety, in a way it had not been before. By contrast, it should be pointed out at least briefly, the Academic Skepticism of Arcesilaus, Carneades, or Clitomachus suggests a life that is wise precisely in being undogmatic, in making do without dogmata. Like Socrates, Arcesilaus and Carneades do not write anything, they do not develop any theories, they do not commit themselves to any philosophical theses they are then going to defend or argue for. They, too, do not fit our ordinary notion of a philosopher, but they were thought of by their contemporaries as philosophers second to none, and, it seems, quite rightly so, even by our standards of philosophical sophistication and resourcefulness, not to mention their argumentative skill and cleverness.

Skepticism seriously dented the optimism with which many philosophers had set out in the hope of attaining the wisdom necessary for a good life. But even independent of Skeptical doubts about the attainability of wisdom, by the turn from the 2nd to the 1st century B.C.E. there were enough reasons to be disillusioned with the course philosophy had taken and what it had achieved. It had not produced any consensus on the questions that seemed crucial. Philosophers, for all their efforts, did not give the impression that they were any nearer to the good life than nonphilosophers. To the contrary, they could easily be seen as quibbling, as wasting their time on pointless subtleties, as being vain and ambitious. Horace writes to Lollius (*Ep.* 1.1.1–4) that he is reading Homer, who is so much better and clearer in telling us what is good and what is bad, what is beneficial and what is not, than Chrysippus or Crantor. Hero of Alexandria pours scorn on the efforts of the philosophers to tell us how to attain tranquillity.

Various diagnoses of the crisis suggested correspondingly different remedies. There was the suggestion that the crisis was due to the personal inadequacy of philosophers, and that personal reform was needed. There was the suggestion that Hellenistic philosophy was inadequate, for instance in its refusal to acknowledge an intelligible realm transcending the physical world, and that one had to return to the ancient philosophers. There was the suggestion that the philosophy of the time just reflected the corrupt culture and society of the time, and that one had to turn to an earlier, less corrupt age for guidance in one's view of the world and for a sounder notion as to how one should behave, perhaps to an age as far back as Homer and Hesiod.

These diagnoses gave rise to different trends. One very conspicuous development, which greatly affected the conception of philosophy and its practice,was the return to the ancient philosophers Pythagoras, Empedocles, Democritus, and in particular Plato and Aristotle, and more specifically to the texts of Plato and Aristotle. These were newly edited, and they began to be commented upon. The study of philosophy increasingly became a study of canonical philosophical texts. New philosophical ideas were developed and expounded in the context of commenting on canonical texts and the problems they raised. This, as we can see in the case of Alexander of Aphrodisias, Porphyry, or Simplicius, often involved a great deal of erudition, which easily became a substitute for genuine philosophical thought. Seneca complained that what was once philosophy had been turned into "philologia" (*Ep.* 108.23).

Another important trend was personal reform. This trend was extremely complex and was motivated by rather different considerations, which we can here distinguish only in the roughest way. Epictetus complained that most so-called philosophers were philosophers only up to the point of saying the sorts of things one expects philosophers to say, without being serious about it in practice (Gellius, *N.A.* 17.19.1). Surely part of what Epictetus meant was that whether one really believed and understood what one said as a philosopher had to show itself in one's life, that there had to be a congruence between doctrine (and preaching) and life, a point insisted on repeatedly at the time. There were two ways this was interpreted in practice. Cynics, it seems, tended to assume that philosophy theoretically amounted to a few simple tenets, for instance the tenet that everything but virtue is completely indifferent. These are easy to grasp but extremely difficult to hold on to in actual life, and it is a Herculean task to actually live in accordance with them. As opposed to what is often said, Stoics in later times did not think that philosophical theory could be reduced to a few theorems, nor did they discourage theory; they did discourage getting lost in theoretical subtleties instead of trying to live up to a highly complex theory in actual life. This was what, for instance, Epictetus insisted on and what Euphrates was praised for (*Epict*. IV.8.17–20). We see how even Stoic ethics was divided into a theoretical part and practical parts (Seneca, *Ep*. 89.14), especially if we take the testimony concerning Eudorus (*Stob. Ecl*. II.42, 13ff W.) to reflect Stoic doctrine. But what is at issue here is not just making one's life consistent with one's views, which is an enormous task, but also arranging one's life and one's disposition in such a way that one is open to the truth and can come to have the right view of things. We find as- cetic tendencies even in the Stoics of the 1st century C.E., for instance in Attalus or in Chaeremon.

Most naturally, though, asceticism fitted the different forms of Platonism. Given that the soul can see the truth unimpeded only if it manages to disen- tangle itself from the body and its concerns, and given that it will free itself from its confusions only if it no longer focuses on the body and its needs but instead looks upward and focuses on the intelligible realm, asceticism seems to be precisely the way to put one's soul in a position to see the truth.

The philosophers of late antiquity considered earlier philosophers like Py- thagoras, Plato, and Aristotle as authorities and their writings as authorita- tive. This is in particular true of Plato, especially since from the late 3rd cen- tury C.E. onward philosophers, almost without exception, claimed to follow Plato. But what did it mean to follow Plato as an authority, and what did one regard as the source of this authority? To follow Plato as an authority meant that one believed oneself to somehow be barred from direct access to the truth, to wisdom, for instance because one lived in an age in which earlier in- sights, an earlier wisdom, had been lost through disregard and corruption; it meant that one believed that Plato had known the truth and thus that one had at least indirect access to the truth through reconstructing what Plato had thought. As to the source of this authority, one did not primarily think that Plato had been such an excellent philosopher that he must have known the truth; one thought, rather—as we can see, for instance, from Numenius— that there was an ancient wisdom that Plato, being the person he was and the excellent philosopher he was, had access to, an ancient wisdom also to be as- cribed, for instance, to Pythagoras, and reflected in Homer. In the light of this, Plato's writings came to have a status rather like Scripture (cf. Origen, *C.C.* VI.17), and all the more so as they are written in such a way as to only hint at the truth and to require complex exegesis. Thus, reconstructing Plato's thought was not seen as the historiographical task of reconstructing what the historical Plato had thought, but as reconstructing the true philosophy—held, among others, by Plato—by means of Plato's writings.

Now it is important to see that if one relied on the authority of Plato in reconstructing the true philosophy, one believed that Plato's writings were merely a means toward attaining the truth that, once attained, would make reference to Plato redundant. One could even believe this if, in reconstructing the true philosophy, one also relied, for instance, on the Chaldean Oracles, which one took to be divinely inspired. So the philosophical enterprise was still thought to crucially involve the development of an appropriate rational theoretical understanding of reality, and a practical attitude toward it based on this understanding, though the means by which one gained this understanding do not correspond to our conception of philosophical method. But the very view Platonists develop concerning reality, following Plato's remarks in *The Republic* about the Good as being beyond being and the intellect (*Rep.* 509 B), put the enterprise of a rational theoretical understanding of reality into question. For the first principle, in terms of which everything else is supposed to be understood and explained, now seems to be beyond intelligibility. This not only affects the conception of philosophy but also raises the question, to what extent can the wisdom philosophers try to attain be achieved without divine cooperation, grace, or intervention, if the grasp of the first principle is beyond our intellect?

This question perhaps was raised first toward the end of the 1st century C.E. by Apollonius of Tyana, a follower of Pythagoras, who aspired to be a divine or holy man. Philostratus in the *Life of Apollonius* (V.37) presents Euphrates as being engaged in a discussion with Apollonius concerning the very nature of philosophy. Euphrates argues for a conception of philosophy "in accordance with nature," that is to say, a philosophy relying on the means nature has provided us with to attain the wisdom that nature ideally means us to attain. And he warns against a conception of philosophy that involves the invocation of God *(theoklytein)*, based on a mistaken conception of the divine that provokes such philosophers to great follies. Apollonius, just like his follower Alexander (cf. Lucian's *Alexander*), does indeed seem to have encouraged the belief in his miraculous powers and the growth of a religious cult (Origen, *C.C.* VI.41). In any case he seems to be the first philosopher we can identify who introduced theurgy into philosophy, that is to say, the idea that certain invocations, perhaps combined with the appropriate ritual practice, could bring God to reveal himself, or bring subordinate divine beings, or even daemons, to reveal themselves and their knowledge. Theurgy, at least a certain conception of it, plays a crucial positive role in Iamblichus's conception of philosophy and that of his followers. One important point, though, is that even if, as a philosopher, one refused to resort to theurgy, one might still believe that it offered a nonphilosophical way to attain the very same wisdom, the very same knowledge, that frees and saves the soul and provides us with the good life. This further undermines the claim philosophers had made that there was no way to become a wise and good person, to have a good life, except the philosopher's way of becoming wise. But then this claim had already long been undermined by the assumption of an original, perhaps inspired, wisdom that philosophers only strove to recover.

Against this background it is easy to see why many early Christians could think of Christian doctrine, in general, as the new true philosophy and of Christian theology, in particular, as the new true theology, replacing the theology of the Stoics, the Peripatetics, and the Platonists. Justin, for instance, is just a particularly striking example among many who regarded Christianity as a philosophy (cf. *Dialogue with Trypho*, II.1). Justin, a philosopher, a Platonist, converted to Christianity but continued to think of himself as practicing philosophy in explaining and expounding Christian doctrine and converting others to Christianity. We should not regard this as a claim to be taken lightly. It is, of course, true that Christians relied on authority for their beliefs, even on the authority of revealed or inspired truth. But this did not distinguish them from pagan philosophers. We also should keep in mind that, though Christian theologians relied on authority, at least originally they seem to have assumed that the understanding they were led to by authority was a philosophical understanding that in the end made reliance on revealed truth superfluous. Origen's dependence on Scripture is striking, but in the case of both Origen and Augustine, at least the earlier Augustine, the theological view we arrive at and the way it is supported looks very much like a philosophical position held on philosophical grounds, and I do not see any reason not to regard Origen as a philosopher in the way this was understood in antiquity.

Christians also came to use the word *philosopher* to refer to monks, and to think of the monastic life as the truly philosophical life (cf. Basil, *De const.* 5; Gregory of Nyssa, *V. Macr.* p. 411, l. 12). Again I think that it would be a great mistake not to take this seriously. If, for instance, we think of Philo's description of the Essenes or Chaeremon's description of the Egyptian priests, both based on a conception of the sage, both misunderstood as referring to historical precursors of monasticism, we realize how indebted early monasticism was to Cynicism, the Stoic focus on the inner life and the attachment to the Good, and often a Platonist worldview in which salvation involved withdrawing from the world, turning inside into the soul, and ascending through the soul, as on a ladder, to its source. In ancient times even pagans would have readily understood that the monk's life is a philosophical life. It rather looked like one form of being serious about being a philosopher.

Now it seems that early Christian authors, like Clement of Alexandria, were tempted by the idea that it was a philosophical understanding of the world, in the light of revelation, that would save the soul and lead to the promised life. But Origen, for instance, in spite of his enormous theological efforts, very clearly rejected this elitist idea. It was the ability, available to everybody, to hold on to the belief in Christ as revealed in his Incarnation and, through him, the belief in God, that saved. Indeed, the invocation of Christ was seen not as an alternative to philosophy but as the only way to the good life.

But once this view became dominant, the philosophical enterprise lost the motivation that had been its main motor: the thought that a good life was a wise life, and that wisdom had to be obtained by philosophical theory and practice. What one now was guided by in one's life was religious belief rather than philosophical belief, and what was now required was religious and religiously motivated moral practice rather than philosophical practice. This meant that philosophers could go on producing theories about the world, or even about how one should act, but these theories no longer were seen as having decisive relevance in life. Their place had been taken by something else. This is not the occasion to discuss the enormous shift involved, but it is reflected in the fact that even today in our ordinary moral thinking and in our philosophical ethics there seems to be little or no place for the exercise of theoretical wisdom in the good life, and in the fact that virtue seems to be identified, with an amazing ease, with moral virtue, as if theoretical wisdom were morally irrelevant.

In this way philosophy was reduced to a theoretical exercise, an exercise one can do well without, without having to fear for one's life or one's soul, an exercise of, at best, marginal relevance to our life. But it is a mistake to think that just because history took this turn, good philosophy has to be something that ultimately is irrelevant to our life, to the life of those we live with and our life with them, and to the life of our communities and societies. And it certainly would be a mistake to project our conception of philosophy as a rather academic enterprise of developing philosophical theories back on the ancients.

MICHAEL FREDE

Bibliography

Burkert, Walter. "Platon oder Pythagoras? Zum Ursprung des Wortes 'Philosophie.'" *Hermes* 88 (1960): 159–177.

Cassin, Barbara, ed. *Nos Grecs et leurs modernes*. Paris: Le Seuil, 1992.

Detienne, Marcel. *Les maîtres de vérité dans la Grèce archaïque*. Paris: Maspero, 1967.

Dixsaut, Monique. *Le naturel philosophe: Essai sur les Dialogues de Platon*. Paris: Les Belles Lettres/Vrin, 1985.

Dumont, Jean-Paul. *Eléments d'histoire de la philosophie antique*. Paris: Nathan, 1993.

Goulet, Richard, ed. *Dictionnaire des philosophes antiques*, vols. 1 and 2. Paris: CNRS, 1989, 1994.

Hadot, Ilsetraut. *Seneca und die griechisch-römische Tradition der Seelenleitung.* Berlin: De Gruyter, 1969.

Hadot, Pierre. *Qu'est-ce que la philosophie antique?* Paris: Gallimard, 1995.

Irwin, Terence. *Plato's Moral Theory: The Early and Middle Dialogues.* Oxford: Clarendon Press, 1977.

Jordan, William. *Ancient Concepts of Philosophy.* London: Routledge, 1990.

Malingrey, Anne-Marie. *Philosophia.* Paris: Klincksieck, 1961.

Nussbaum, Martha. *The Therapy of Desire: Theory and Practice in Hellenistic Ethics.* Princeton: Princeton University Press, 1994.

Ritter, Joachim, and Karlfried Gründer, eds. *Historisches Wörterbuch der Philosophie,* 8: "Philosophie" (contributions by M. Kranz, G. Bien, and Pierre Hadot). Basel/Stuttgart: Schwabe, 1989.

Schofield, Malcolm, and Gisela Striker, eds. *The Norms of Nature: Studies in Hellenistic Ethics.* Cambridge: Cambridge University Press, 1986.

Voelke, André-Jean. *La philosophie comme thérapie de l'âme.* Fribourg: Editions universitaires, 1993.

EPISTEMOLOGY

THE INTELLECTUAL ADVENTURE of Greek thought, considered not simply in terms of the extent of the knowledge acquired but also as a reflection on the nature of knowledge—its origin, objects, methods, and limits—gives the impression of a great profusion of ideas, and also of great disorder and countless theoretical rivalries. The Greeks knew a lot of things, some of which they learned from others and some of which they discovered themselves. They opened up what Kant called "the sure path of science" to certain fundamental scientific disciplines, most notably mathematics. They loved the search for truth and the acquisition of truth with a passion, indeed so exuberantly that they sometimes believed, as Aristotle did, that human beings by nature desire knowledge for itself, seeking no benefit beyond the pleasure it brings. They also believed they knew many things—more, to tell the truth, than they actually did know. They were sometimes cruelly mistaken, and they did not always have valid excuses. They often had—or displayed—too much confidence in their own powers: in spite of their dazzling intuitions, their theories of physical change and matter, their cosmogonies and their cosmologies, what they believed about nature and the origin of animal and human life belongs only quite indirectly to the history of scientific truth. Some among them took as science, and even as models for certain types of science, disciplines that we do not hesitate to categorize as pseudo-sciences. They may have succeeded in creating authentic sciences, but they did not reach agreement on the criteria by which authentic knowledge is recognized (indeed, this is still a problem today).

Did they give insufficient thought to the conditions that must be met if one is to be able to say that one knows something? Quite the contrary. The supreme originality of the Greek philosophers and scholars may well lie in the fact that they raised questions of a sort that would be classified today under the heading of epistemology. They succeeded in asking questions that might be called reflexive (What does it actually mean to know?), critical (Can we really know something? And if so, what sort of thing?), methodological (What means are available to us for answering a question?), or transcendental (How must the world be constituted, and how must we ourselves be constituted if we are to know something about the world?).

But here too, the various responses, and even the questions, offer powerful contrasts. The conquering thrust of Greek knowledge stands out against an initial store of a sort of epistemological wistfulness: from the standpoint of divine knowledge, human faculties are severely limited, not to say worthless. In seeking to transgress these limits, in discovering the invisible enveloped in the folds of space and time, humans run the risk of arousing the anger of the gods, who are protective of their own privileges and quick to chastise hubris, proud excess. Does not the most famous of the Greek philosophers, Socrates, owe the essence of his celebrity to the story of the oracle that designated him the wisest of men, a superiority that he himself interpreted as signifying that he was the only one who did not believe he knew what he did not know? But alongside this pessimism, which moreover will never disappear, we note a large number of expressions indicating real epistemological enthusiasm, derived from and reinforced by the fact that reason is increasingly aware of its own powers. This attitude draws confidence from its own successes, and perhaps too, more fundamentally, from the tacitly and almost universally accepted idea that we humans are not in the world (to quote Spinoza) as an empire within an empire, as an island enclosed in representations that constitute a screen between ourselves and the real: quite to the contrary, we are at home in the world, we are an integral part of it, we are made of the same ingredients as everything else in it, so much so that the immediate problem is not one of knowing how we can attain truth in our words and our thought, but rather how we can miss it. The question of the possibility of error will occupy great minds at least up to the time of Plato, who grapples with it repeatedly and laboriously before he finally answers it in *Sophist*.

The contrast between epistemological pessimism and optimism may be seen as the initial matrix of the great debate between skepticism and dogmatism that traverses Greek philosophy—as it does perhaps, subsequently, all philosophy, if it is true that in some sense skepticism, which is originally a spirit of research and critical examination, is identified with philosophy itself, and if it is true that dogmatism, in the ancient sense of the term, is not to be confused with the use of arguments based on authority but signifies, on the contrary, that after a process of reflection, effort, and inquiry, one has succeeded in developing a well-argued and rationally teachable doctrine.

To come to grips with the mass of Greek texts and documents that incorporate reflection on knowing, it is tempting to sort thinkers and even periods into categories, according to a division that would reproduce those of dogmatism and skepticism. Certain philosophers have been particularly sensitive to the successes of knowing, in its various forms: not particularly vulnerable to the assaults and suspicions of skepticism, they are principally interested in the nature of knowledge. They ask questions such as: What does it mean to know? Are there different types of knowledge, and if so, what are they, and how do they differ? From what other intellectual states is knowledge distinct, and how is it differentiated? What are the mechanisms that come into play in

the acquisition and possession of knowledge? What are the structures of scientific thought? Other philosophers, attracted by skepticism or spurred on by
the challenge it poses, have wondered instead whether human beings are capable of acquiring knowledge. If the answer is negative, what arguments allow us or compel us to doubt or reject the proposition that humans have such
a capacity? What is the nature of the obstacles that oppose it? If the response
is affirmative, what means do we have at our disposal to gain access to knowledge, and to assure ourselves that we have achieved it? These two types of
problems are not entirely independent of one another. If it is true that knowledge cannot be defined in a completely arbitrary way (a statement such as
"He knows that Socrates is a horse, but Socrates is not a horse," for example,
would be unacceptable under any circumstances), one can nevertheless develop a more or less restrictive or generous notion of knowledge; moreover,
such flexibility is nourished by the richness and suppleness of the Greek
terms pertaining to knowing. What one says about the nature of knowledge is
obviously linked to what one says about its possibility and its limits. The
higher one places the bar of knowledge, the harder it is to cross: one can even
place it high enough for it to become impossible to cross, or for it to appear
impossible, and often it takes next to nothing for the loftiest of ambitions to
tip over into total pessimism. This reversal from pro to con can be avoided,
however, either by showing that, at least in certain cases, the bar of knowledge can be crossed, or by challenging the description of knowledge that creates such obstacles and replacing the bar with a different one.

The great questions addressed by the theory of knowledge are thus interrelated, and the theory itself is not autonomous within Greek thought. Only
little by little do we encounter works that focus exclusively on providing an
epistemological justification of their authors' positive doctrines (the lost *Con-
firmations* of Democritus may have been the first work of this type), on analyzing the nature of knowledge in general (Plato's *Theaetetus,* which moreover does not achieve an explicit "solution" of the problem) or the structures
of scientific knowledge (Aristotle's *Posterior Analytics*). In the Hellenistic period, priority is finally granted, within the general ordering of a system, to
works and theories explicitly devoted to the "criterion of truth," such as
Epicurus's *Canon* and the Stoic doctrine of impressions *(phantasia).* One of
the factors that worked against the autonomy of the theory of knowledge was
unquestionably the idea that there has to be a correspondence between the
characteristics of a body of knowledge worthy of the name and the properties
that can be required of the real or possible object of that knowledge: a determinate description of knowledge determines a distinction between the types
of entities that can be known and those that cannot. Everybody acknowledged
in principle that one can know only what is true, and that whoever knows
truth, as Plato put it, "touches upon being" (cf. *Theaetetus* 186d–e); there

were constant exchanges between the theory of knowledge and what can be called ontology (a word that first appeared in the 17th century). The zones of being were divided up as a function of epistemological cleavages (perceptible versus intelligible); conversely, certain ontological divisions entailed important epistemological implications (being versus becoming, necessary versus contingent, supralunar versus sublunar).

The theory of knowledge was thus in constant relations of action and reaction with the theory of being, as a known or knowable object; it was also in relation with the theory of the soul, as a subject knowing or capable of knowing. If knowledge institutes a relation between the soul and being, it attests first of all, in general, to the affinity or kinship that unites them and that makes possible the institution of this relation, and thus, more particularly, it attests to the resemblance that must exist between the elements and structures of each. The idea that "like knows like" made its appearance very early, and—with a few interesting exceptions—was quite commonly accepted, in various forms. This means not only that the resemblance between the elements of being and the elements of the soul is the objective cause of the possibility of knowledge, but also, conversely, that that very possibility is for us the sign of the resemblance. In other words, the theory of knowledge is a privileged instrument of self-knowledge. Greek thought constantly stressed the importance of such knowledge, but also its difficulty, for the knowledge of the self by the self was not viewed as having the transparent immediacy of a cogito: to know oneself, one must know oneself knowing something, and one must reflect on the conditions of that cognitive experience. The set of relations between levels of being, knowledge, and the soul that have just been outlined could be illustrated by the method Aristotle adopts in his treatise *On the Soul*. His study focuses initially on the objects of the soul's cognitive activities and operations (for example, what is felt and thought); from these objects, it turns toward the activities and operations themselves (the act of feeling, the act of thinking); finally, returning from actuality to potentiality, Aristotle is prepared to define the essence of the faculties of feeling and thinking.

I shall not attempt to offer a systematic historical picture here of the various conceptions of knowledge that were presented and supported by the philosophers and the philosophic schools of Greece: the subject is too rich and too complex to be summed up in a brief panorama. Instead, I shall propose a series of gnoseological sketches, in the form of comparative variations intended to show relationships among a certain number of notions belonging to the domain of knowledge and related areas. I shall not dwell on the quite real differences that distinguish the theories; rather, I should like to stress a few fundamental constants that manifest, from one end of the immense historical arc that we call Greek antiquity to the other, a continuity that is often astonishing.

KNOWING AND SEEING

We have to start from the conventional view according to which, in the beginning, the Greeks more or less identified knowledge with sense perception, and
especially with visual perception. Their cognitive vocabulary bears unmistakable traces of this: one of the most common verbs for saying "I know," for example, is *oida*, which comes from the same Indo-European root as the Latin
videre, to see. However, we must note that, grammatically, *oida* is a perfect
form that means not "I see" but precisely "I am currently in the situation of
someone who has seen." What I know is thus not what I am seeing now but
what I have seen, that at which I have been perceptually present, what I remember after ceasing to see it, what I can imagine when I am no longer seeing it, what I can recognize if I happen to see it again, what I can recount or
describe because I have been an "eyewitness" to it.

In contrast to knowledge that is based on direct personal perceptual experience but exceeds experience within a temporal framework and grafts onto its
own passivity the possibility of various active performances, what is the status of the information possessed by someone who has not seen, but to whom
I have narrated or described what I have seen? If knowledge acquired through
direct experience is identified with knowledge as such, what we would call
"hearsay knowledge" has to be viewed quite simply as nonknowledge. This is
the case in a famous passage in Homer, where the poet solicits the aid of the
Muses to be able to list the leaders of the Greek army: "for you are goddesses
and are present and know all things, but we hear only a rumor and know
nothing" (*Iliad* II.484–487). Homer's text contrasts the amplitude of divine
knowledge with the insignificance of human knowledge, but at the same time
it shows what accounts for them both: the knowledge granted to goddesses
and denied to human beings is based on divine presence and human absence
in the face of what is to be known, and on the direct experience of this presence (available to goddesses) and this absence (the lot of humans).

Such a conception implies a rigorous, twofold limitation on accessible
knowledge. What knowing subjects are apt to know is determined by their capacity to see. Human sight is exercised only within narrow limits of place and
time; it is invariably linked to a single point of view that excludes others. In
addition, the realm of knowable objects is limited to that of visible objects.
That is why the philosophical legacy of this conception is to be sought in particular in sensualist or empiricist doctrines. Plato himself, however, in a paradoxical and controversial passage of *Theaetetus*, declares that when a past
phenomenon is in question, for example a crime, only an eyewitness can
know what happened, and if the judge, persuaded by the discourse of the orators, reaches a correct verdict in spite of everything, this will come about
"without knowledge" (*Theaetetus* 201c).

The influence of the visual model on ancient theories of knowledge has sometimes been overestimated; still, this is not a reason to underestimate it. Moreover, the model itself encompassed various possibilities for expansion. If we start from the idea that I know that with which I have the same relation as I have with the people I know because I have met them, people I am capable of identifying and recognizing (this has been called "knowledge by acquaintance"), according to this model of knowledge it is not impossible to conceive of certain objects that are not currently visible for me, in the space and time that I occupy and from the point of view that is mine. Certain exceptional individuals may have the privilege of "seeing" something that, although visible in theory, escapes ordinary sight, something that is hidden away in the subterranean or celestial regions, in the shadows of the past or in the obscurity of the future: the soothsayer is a "seer," the pythoness a "clairvoyant." The visual model may even be transposed to objects that are inherently invisible— abstract and purely intelligible entities, for example; it is tempting to picture the intellectual faculty that grasps them as a sort of "eye of the soul," which exercises its specific form of "vision" on them. This visual metaphor is present in particular in illustrious Greek terms such as *theoria* or *theorein,* which refer first to sight and to spectacles and then, metaphorically, to speculation and intellectual contemplation. In a famous image, attributed to Pythagoras, someone who is going to the Olympic Games not to do business there or to compete, but only as a spectator, is compared to the philosopher, who is a spectator on the world; and it is the latter who is said to enjoy the best sort of life. In the supremely illustrious and influential central books of *The Republic,* Plato bases his theory of knowledge, in its most classic form, on a detailed analogy between vision and knowledge, along with their respective conditions and objects. The analogy must no doubt be understood only as an identity of relations: what vision is to visible things, for example, intellection is to intelligible things, and the truth that illuminates the intelligible is to the light that illuminates the visible. Still, it is easy to move from this idea to that of a resemblance (an analogy in the broad sense) between the terms of these relationships, for example between intellectual knowledge and vision. Such an extension is not necessary, however; Aristotle, in his treatise *On the Soul,* does not hide the fact that he bases his theory of thought on an identity of relations between thinking and feeling, on the one hand, and the object that is thought and the object that is felt, on the other; but he has no intention of claiming that thought and feeling are the same thing—a thesis that he attributes to most of his predecessors and that for his own part he rejects.

KNOWING AND TOUCHING

The visual model of knowledge is sometimes rivaled, on its own ground, by a tactile model. Sight is exercised at a distance, which accounts for its strength (its scope is not limited to the immediate environment) but also for its weakness (at too great a distance it loses its precision, and in the intervening space factors of confusion may arise). Touch has less scope for action, but it makes up for this inferiority with the infallible immediacy of the contact it supposes between the feeling body and the felt body; through touch, the world knocks directly at our door. The tactile world will thus be, par excellence, that of the materialists, who "maintain stoutly," according to Plato, that "that alone exists which can be touched and handled" (*Sophist* 246a). The Democritan theory of simulacra associates sight, which appears to be a sense that operates at a distance, with a particular sort of contact, since it results from the action of tenuous envelopes that are emitted by the felt body and that travel through the intervening space to touch the feeling body.

Touch, which Lucretius exalts as "the sense of the body," has even succeeded in supplying nonmaterialist philosophers with a cognitive model that ignores the corporeality of the entities in contact in favor of the immediacy of the contact itself. Aristotle resorts to tactile images when he defines the type of knowledge that is appropriate for "simple" entities. Since by definition they are "uncomposed," there can be no question of grasping one part of them and missing another part: according to a binary logic, the intellectual grasp of simple entities is accomplished completely or not at all. Touch thus provides a model for a form of knowledge that owes its singular value to the fact that it has as its alternative only ignorance, and not error.

SAVOIR AND *CONNAÎTRE*

Let us open up a discussion here for which visual and tactile models pave the way. The French language, envied by others on this point, distinguishes syntactically between *savoir*, to know as one can know that something is the case (e.g., that $2 + 2 = 4$), and *connaître*, to know as one can know a person (to "be familiar with"). One says *connaître quelqu'un* or *quelque chose*, "to know someone" or "something"; the verb *connaître* is not used with *que* to say "to know that something is this or that." The verb *savoir* is not used with *quelqu'un* or, usually, with *quelque chose*; it is used with *que* to say "to know that something is this or that." Ordinary expressions thus distinguish knowledge of the objectal type from knowledge of the propositional type. In Greek, cognitive verbs are not specialized in this manner: most allow both an objectal and a propositional construction. Certain common syntactic possibilities in Greek blur the distinction even further: a participle may be substituted for a propositional construction (instead of saying "I know that you are telling the truth," one will say, for example, literally, "I know you telling the truth"); and the subject of the completive proposition may appear by anticipation as object of the main verb (instead of saying "I know that Socrates is dead," one will say, for example, literally, "I know Socrates that he is dead").

This absence of a watertight separation between knowledge of things and knowledge of states of affairs has doubtless encouraged the idea that to know that a thing is this or that is to know the thing itself, to know it well enough and in the manner that is required to know that it is this or that; in other words, it is to find in the very nature of the thing, the ultimate object of objectal knowledge, the reasons why it is this or that. This reasoning has led to significant restrictions on the legitimacy of the use of the verb "to know" *(savoir)* in a propositional context: if a given thing is this or that, but without being so by virtue of its nature (for example, if it is so only accidentally, through a temporary encounter, or else relatively, in a certain light, whereas in another light it is not so), one will refuse to say that one knows (or that one "really" knows) that it is so. Strictly speaking, one cannot know that Socrates is seated, since when he stands up he does not cease to be Socrates, nor that he is small, since he is so in comparison to a taller man, but not in comparison to a shorter man.

KNOWLEDGE AND HEARSAY

The visual model leads to denying the status of knowledge to information obtained from an eyewitness by someone who has not himself been a witness to the phenomenon. Such rigorism is not unprecedented, but it would be a mistake to believe that it is a legacy of the "Homeric conception" of knowledge. It has been noted with good reason that Homer's heroes are perfectly prepared to say that they know things that they have not witnessed directly, but that they have learned through an uninterrupted chain of oral and public testimony, the validity of which can be controlled by observing that no counter-testimony, solicited or not, is put forward to contest it. This is the case, for example, in genealogy (*Iliad* XX.203ff).

This example allows us to look at the theoretical inferiority of hearsay knowledge in a more nuanced way: everything depends on the quality of those who have been heard to speak, and on the method available for evaluating their truthfulness. At the lowest level we find vague and unverifiable rumors; at the highest level, we find the transmission of information by one or more witnesses who, one has good reasons to think, have seen the thing themselves, who have no reason to recount it in some way other than the way it happened, and who are in general good enough observers to be worthy of being believed. The model of hearsay knowledge also entails—especially among historians but also among orators—a reflection on the tools available for assessing the testimony. This reflection is extended among the philosophers, who often use the image of a messenger to illustrate various epistemological situations: we still commonly speak, in their wake, of the "testimony of the senses." But this model can be inflected in either a dogmatic or a skeptical direction. How can we be sure, if we view the senses as witnesses, that the messenger delivers his message accurately, since it is clear from the experience of "sensory illusions" that the senses are not always reliable? The Greek philosophers sometimes ambitiously pursued the ideal or the dream of a sensory message that would contain the guarantee of its own authenticity, in the form of a sort of unmistakable and unfalsifiable mark of fabrication; sometimes, too, they settled for a method of verification that entailed evaluating the degree of plausibility of the sense impression, cross-checking it against other sensory evidence, or optimizing the conditions of the experience.

KNOWING AND INFERRING

Oral transmission is not the only way the scope of perceptual knowledge can be extended. In human beings, feeling is sedimented in memory, and this process itself gives rise to experience (in the sense in which one speaks of a "person of experience," someone who has seen and retained a great deal). When experience is reflected, when it is formulated in a universal way, when it grasps the causes of its own successes, it serves as a basis for practical knowledge *(techne)* and for theoretical science *(episteme)*. This natural process, observed even before Plato and described several times by Aristotle as well as by philosophers of the Hellenistic period, comes into play again, methodically, in the inferential process of induction *(epagōge)*. Aristotle attributes the discovery of induction to Socrates; it consists in passing from a number of particular cases that have something in common to a general law that sums them up and encompasses them all (not without risk of error, in instances where the review of particular cases is incomplete).

Another possibility for extending perceptual knowledge consists in reflecting on what one is seeing, and in using it as a sign or index on the basis of which one can attain indirect but authentic knowledge of what is not immediately present before one's eyes: the inhabitants of Ithaca see Ulysses returning to his homeland in the form of an old beggar, but (except for his old dog) they do not identify him; knowing is not seeing, since one can see without knowing who it is that one is seeing. To reach the point of knowing that the beggar is none other than Ulysses, those close to him infer it by relying on signs *(semata):* the scar whose existence is known to the nurse Eurycleia, the possession of secrets that Ulysses alone shared with Penelope, who is questioning him. It is not logically out of the question that a beggar might have the same scar as Ulysses, or that Ulysses might have confided to a traveler something that only Ulysses was thought to know; but by refining the model for identifying and interpreting signs, one can reduce the probability of a coincidence or a hoax to practically zero. The beggar is Ulysses: such is, in sum, the best explanation that can be inferred on the basis of the collected facts.

Philosophical reflection on the conditions and powers of inference through signs occupied an important place in ancient epistemology; it should not be overshadowed by a tendency to focus on observations drawn from the deductive model of mathematics. The Hellenistic schools in particular gave it considerable space in their debates. Their interest is easy to understand if we consider the number, quality, and intellectual and social prestige of the disciplines in which the real or presumed acquisition of knowledge was rooted in observation of facts considered as signs from which nonobservable phenomena could be inferred. The science of nature, in all its dimensions, is a prime example. A very early set of questions came to constitute—and remained, almost unchanged—the agenda for all self-respecting philosophical doctrines; these questions were essentially ones that could be answered only via the method summed up in the dictum proffered by Anaxagoras and strongly endorsed by Democritus: "Sight of the unclear: Phenomena" (opsis tōn adelōn ta phainomena [Anaxagoras, frg. 21a]); in other words, appearances offer a glimpse of the imperceptible. Rational reflection on appearances broadens the scope of vision (in another way entirely from the exceptional powers of the "seer"), to the point of constituting a quasi-vision of what eludes sight. In addition to the natural philosophers, the use of signs is of course quite important to other groups as well: to historians, who reconstitute a buried past on the basis of present indexes; to orators, who do the same thing in tribunals, seeking a more recent past, and also in political assemblies, to predict what is going to happen on the basis of the current situation, or what would happen if a given measure were adopted; to soothsayers, whose purported business it is to interpret signs—and their task is taken very seriously by the Stoics, among others; and, finally, to doctors, who enumerate and define the symptoms of various illnesses in relation to the external conditions of their appearance, and who can establish a prognosis with a certainty that makes people mistake them occasionally for soothsayers.

However, just as there are witnesses and witnesses, there are signs and signs; the same value is not attributed to all types of semiotic inference, and the terms used sometimes distinguish the simple index (semeion) from the probative sign (tekmerion). The characterization of one phenomenon as the sign of another, the unicity and determination of that other, the necessity of the bond that makes it possible to conclude that the latter exists on the basis of the former—all this can be subject to argument. This is why the theory of knowledge acquired through signs takes a very different tack among the rationalists and the empiricists, as the Hellenistic debates attest. One classification, of uncertain origin, distinguishes the so-called commemorative signs from the so-called indicative signs. Commemorative signs allow us to conclude on the basis of an observable phenomenon that another phenomenon is present, one that is also observable in principle but temporarily hidden. The second phenomenon has often been observed concomitantly with the first; for example, smoke is the commemorative sign of fire. Indicative signs are presumed to allow us to conclude on the basis of an observable fact that another fact is present, one that is nonobservable by nature. The latter is presumed to be of such a nature that in its absence the observable phenomenon with which it is associated cannot be produced: for example, perspiration is the indicative sign of the existence of invisible pores in the skin. A rationalist obviously has to believe that indicative signs exist in order to produce doctrines concerning the intimate nature of things and the hidden causes of phenomena; in a sense, this is precisely what being a rationalist means, for only reasoning can assure us that the visible effect could not take place without the hidden cause. The empiricist, on the contrary, will reject this possibility and will simply note, in an almost Pavlovian reflex, that if fire and smoke have often been manifested together, the spectacle of smoke in isolation leads us to think that there is fire somewhere, and that one could verify this by changing the conditions of the observation.

The chief sources of knowledge discussed up to this point, vision and its two extensions, the oral transmission of testimony and semiotic inference, correspond to the three master words of the empiricist doctors: *autopsia,* or direct and personal vision; *historia,* or recollection of the testimony of past or present experts; and *metabasis,* or inferential transfer, passing from knowledge acquired by one of the preceding means to additional knowledge of something that is provisionally out of reach.

KNOWING AND UNDERSTANDING

Having explored some of the extensions of the visual model of knowledge, let us return to the model itself to identify the limits that it was ill-suited to transcend. We may see, hear, or touch many things; we may accumulate impressions and information; we may explore the world on all sides; we may become very "knowing," in a weak sense of the word. Still, all this will not lead us to be "knowing" in the literal sense, if we do not understand what we have seen and heard. Not only does sense experience in general not procure, or not suffice to procure, authentic knowledge but, in addition, particular sense experiences can scarcely lay claim to the status of knowledge if they are not taken up again, one way or another, by the intervention of the intellect. One such intervention is already needed, at minimum, if we are to express such experiences in speech, to tell others what we are seeing and say it to ourselves, categorizing the experience conceptually in a propositional structure ("this is white"); a different sort of intervention is required for more complex elaborations that are necessary to the interpretation of a particular experience ("this is snow") or a general experience ("snow is white"). Thus it is not surprising that one of the first thinkers in whose work we encounter the idea that seeing does not yet amount to knowing, and that piling up information (*polumathie*) does not yet amount to having an intellectual grasp (*noos*) of that information, is Heraclitus, the philosopher of the untranslatable *logos*—both discourse and reason. The eyes and the ears, for example, are poor wit-

nesses for those who have barbarian souls, he says; since a barbarian is someone who does not know Greek, we may take this to mean that sense experience brings no knowledge to someone who is incapable of interpreting the
message it conveys because he or she does not know the language in which
the message is couched. The underlying metaphor has had a long career: the
world is a book that is readable only by those who know the rules for reading
it. To know is to understand, that is, to bring back together (the prefix of the
Greek word for "understand," *sunienai*, has the same meaning as that of the
Latin *comprehendere*), to organize experience according to the structures that
belong to reality, to bring to speech the reason that governs things. To know a
single thing is not to know it; taken to the extreme, there is no knowledge but
total knowledge, and no knowledge but knowledge of everything.

The earliest Greek thinkers, armed only with their naked reason, plunged
headlong into an assault on knowledge of the whole, of the principles on
which everything is based and of all the ensuing consequences. Perhaps their
extraordinary audacity derives from the fact that their conception of knowledge left them no other choice: they had to know everything or know nothing
at all. Not until Aristotle does the principle of a total science begin to give
way to the idea that a science is a structured set of statements bearing on entities that belong to a specific class and to that class alone (numbers, figures,
natural beings), and even Aristotle does not give up the attempt to preserve
the idea of a universal science. He goes about it from various angles, moreover, sometimes proposing the idea of a "science of being as being," a study of
the properties that belong to every being by virtue of the simple fact that it is
a being (and not by virtue of the particular type of being it is), and at other
times advancing the presumably different idea of a "primary" science having
as objects the principles of all things, and that would thus be "universal because primary."

KNOWING AND BELIEVING

These extraordinarily ambitious programs are very probably rooted in an
idea that, quite early, even before Heraclitus, carved out a path for itself in
Greek thought, a path that is perhaps the crucial idea behind all of ancient
epistemology. This idea is that opinion (or belief, for both words can translate
doxa) is not science: believing is not knowing, even if what one believes is
true. In one famous fragment, Xenophanes sketches a formidable argument:
in certain areas at least, "the clear and certain truth no man has seen nor will
there be anyone who knows about the gods and what I say about all things.
For even if, in the best case, one happened to speak aptly of what has been
brought to pass, still he himself would not know it. But opinion *[dokos]* is al-
lotted to everybody (Greek *epi pasin:* may be "to everything")" (frg. 34).

The argument has often been interpreted in a radically skeptical sense: we may stumble across a true opinion by chance, but we have no way to recognize it as such, just as, in a dark room containing an array of vases, only one of which is made of gold, we have no way of being sure that we have picked out the golden vase. In this view, Xenophanes prefigured a celebrated paradox, presented by Plato in *Meno,* that played a stimulating role in epistemological reflection over a long period of time: how can we look for a thing when we have absolutely no knowledge of what it is? How can we identify the thing we have set out to look for, among all those things we do not know? And, supposing we stumble across the thing by chance, how can we know it is the very thing we were seeking, since we did not know it? If we do not want to settle for believing we have found the thing we were seeking, without any good reason for our belief, the wisest course, it seems, is to give up seeking entirely.

The foregoing paradox is the reverse of the idea that we know nothing if we do not know everything. It rules out the acquisition of new knowledge; it blocks the movement that, from a commonsense perspective, seems to be able to lead from ignorance to knowledge on a particular point (on this basis, it represents the application, in the epistemological field, of the difficult problem that continually confronted Greek thought, the problem of the intellectual understanding of movement, of becoming, of the appearance of something new). In response to this paradox, Plato attempts precisely to rescue the idea of total knowledge, by advancing his theory of recollection: the soul, immortal and reborn time after time, has seen all things, has already learned all things; what it does not know it has merely forgotten; it will recover its latent knowledge as soon as a dialectic "midwife" helps it to remember by asking the appropriate questions. To know *(connaître)* is to recognize *(reconnaître),* to recognize what one already knew, what one had forgotten. There is a posteriori knowledge only in appearance; in reality there is only a priori knowledge.

Let us return to Xenophanes' argument. He does not necessarily militate in favor of radical skepticism: it is no doubt possible to acquire an objectively true opinion by rummaging around at random in the basket of opinions; but it is not impossible that one may be able to help "chance" by reflecting on one's experience, "by seeking for a long time," as Xenophanes says, and by using one's reason to reach opinions that are not arbitrary in the least, or necessarily illusory, but at least plausible. Xenophanes seems to be convinced of this when he presents, in his own name, a strikingly new theology and a prudent cosmology. However, the unbridgeable gap between opinion—even true opinion—and science remains: one can say what turns out to be objectively true without being certain that what one is saying is true. What does opinion lack, then, in order to be knowledge? Xenophanes does not answer this question with any precision; perhaps he is saying, in a purely negative way, that a man who has a true opinion does not have knowledge about that about which he has a true opinion; in that case, he is marking a difference without trying to say in what that difference consists. The attempts that have been made since Xenophanes to answer this question have perhaps contributed to naming the difficulty rather than resolving it: thus when one says, in the classic fashion, that knowledge is justified true belief, one would have to be able to say under what conditions a true belief is justified. In *Theaetetus*, a grandiose attempt to answer the question "What is science *[episteme]*?", Plato rejects the identification of science first with sensation, and second with true belief. He then suggests identifying it with "true belief accompanied by an account *[logos]*," but with remarkable honesty he has the dialogue end in failure, or so it seems at first. Despite several attempts, the interlocutors do not succeed in providing the notion of *logos* with a satisfactory content.

KNOWING AND PROVING

We may believe that we can justify an opinion the way we verify a hypothesis: by testing it, by subjecting it to the test of its consequences. But we are then at risk of committing a classic error, an error that was identified as such by the Greeks but that is nevertheless still a threat, the so-called error of "the assertion of the consequent" (if *p*, then *q*; now, *q*; therefore *p*). For example: if there are invisible pores in the skin, then sweat can appear on the surface; now, sweat appears; thus there are pores. But nothing says that a different explanation might not be the correct one: moisture on a carafe is not evidence that the glass is porous. We may perhaps reinforce the plausibility of the pore hypothesis by multiplying the consequences to be examined, by determining that all of these confirm the hypothesis, and that none invalidates it; but refuting the competing hypotheses does not suffice to establish the one that we believe—perhaps owing to a lack of imagination—to be the only one that remains conceivable. The multiplication of tests will never procure the only type of premise that would be appropriate, namely, that sweat can appear not simply *if* but also *only if* there are pores.

To get around the obstacle, we have to reverse our perspective. To justify an opinion, we have to orient the investigation not toward its consequences but toward the principles of which it is itself the consequence. We must seek to put to work the *modus ponens* (or positing mode), which is perfectly valid: if *p*, then *q*; now, *p*; therefore *q*. To know that *q* (that something is this or that) is to know why it is thus (because *p*).

In one passage in *Meno*, Plato gives a cursory presentation of the idea that true opinions are "unstable" and easily escape our soul's grasp (probably because they risk being abandoned as soon as experience seems to invalidate them or skillful discourse seems to refute them); what transforms them into knowledge is "an account of the cause" or "an explanation of the cause" (the word *aitia*, which appears in this formula, designates, as it were, that which is "responsible" for the state of things on which true opinion bears; thus *aitia* is the objective cause of that state of things, and it allows us to explain that things are thus rather than otherwise; it is the "reason for being" of the state of things). This reasoning "binds" true opinions, and transforms them into knowledge by rendering them "stable" (Greek theories of knowledge owe a lot to the fact that the word *episteme*, through its root, evokes the ideas of cessation, rest, stability). Aristotle only extends the indication in *Meno* when he says that "we consider that we have unqualified knowledge *[episteme]* of anything . . . when we believe that we know (i) that the cause from which the fact results is the cause of that fact, and (ii) that the fact cannot be otherwise than it is" (*Posterior Analytics* I.2, 71b9–12). To know something in the sense thus defined, it is necessary and sufficient to prove it, that is, to deduce it from its principles—the clearest and most impressive example of this being mathematical knowledge.

To know that the thing cannot be otherwise than it is, is to know that it is necessary: thus we are touching on an essential ingredient of the Greek notion of knowledge. Essential, but also ambiguous: for if I know that a thing is necessary, what is it that I know, exactly? One distinction, which will become classic, opposes the "necessity of the consequence" to the "necessity of the consequent." It is conceivable, for example, that if a certain number of conditions are met at the same time (a barrel of gunpowder, a naked flame that touches it), a certain effect will necessarily follow (here we are dealing with the necessity of the consequence, a hypothetical or relative necessity). But this does not imply that the explosion itself is necessary (here we would be dealing with the necessity of the consequent, an intrinsic or absolute necessity); for that to be the case, each of the conditions, and their simultaneous fulfillment, would have had to be (intrinsically) necessary—and that is not necessarily the case.

One of the limitations of Greek thought seems to have been the absence of a clear grasp of this distinction (despite certain attempts and approximations): from the reasonable idea that one can know only what is hypothetically necessary, it had a tendency to move on to the less reasonable idea that one can know only what is absolutely necessary. Can we say that we know that an explosion took place on a certain day at a certain hour? No, in contradiction with the customary use of the verb "to know," if we accept the commonsense view that the convergence of factors necessary and conjointly sufficient to set it off was not in itself necessary. Yes, in conformity with the customary use of the verb "to know," if we admit, this time in contradiction with common sense, that the convergence of these factors was itself necessary, and that it derived, for example, from a universal network of linked causes that can be called fate. In each case, we lose on one side what we gain on the other. The mathematical model, here, is both seductive and dangerous, for it seems to allow us a way out of the dilemma. If the premises of a demonstration are either held to be axiomatically necessary, because they are "evident," or else themselves demonstrated on the basis of the axioms, the truth demonstrated is endowed with the two sorts of necessity at once—which makes it difficult to tell them apart. Factual truths will henceforth be reserved to the domain of true opinions; truths of reason will fall in the domain of knowledge.

By a natural extension, once again, only eternal truths will belong to knowledge. It is not necessary, but it is tempting, to think that what is always true is so if and only if it is necessary; that what is sometimes true is so if and only if it is possible; and that what is never true is so if and only if it is impossible. These reciprocal shifts between time and modality are favored, as Jaakko Hintikka has shown, by a particular feature of ordinary language that obtains in English as well as in Greek. Ordinary statements are "temporally indefinite": they are dated only according to the moment of their enunciation. "It is daylight" is true if it is daylight at the moment one says, "It is daylight." But one can pronounce the same sentence, "It is daylight," at midnight as well as at noon; hence the temptation to say that this same sentence, which was true at noon, has become false twelve hours later. By the same token, we shall refuse to call "knowledge" the cognitive situation in which we find ourselves with respect to the truth of "It is daylight" (at the moment when it is true), for it does not have the required "stability." If the identity of the sentence is taken as the marker of the identity of the opinion it expresses, nothing in the concept of opinion is opposed to a case in which an opinion becomes alternately true and false, according to changes in the situation; but knowledge, for its part, as Aristotle says, "cannot be sometimes knowledge and sometimes ignorance." We cannot then, strictly speaking, say that we know that it is daylight: we sometimes have a true opinion about this, sometimes a false one.

To escape from the incalculable consequences of this set of conceptions, we would have to reintegrate into the meaning of the utterance, in an absolute form, the "date stamping" that it receives from the moment of its enunciation. We shall say, for example, that the sentence "It is daylight," pronounced on August 16, 1995, at noon, expresses a certain proposition: "It is daylight on August 16, 1995, at noon," and that it is this proposition, not the sentence, that is true. A different sentence, pronounced after that date, will express the same proposition in a different form: "It was daylight on August 16, 1995, at noon," and the truth value of the single proposition expressed by these two different sentences will remain the same. Conversely, the sentence "It is daylight," uttered on August 16, 1995, at midnight, expresses a different proposition, "It is daylight on August 16, 1995, at midnight," which is false and which will remain the same false proposition in the various expressions that it can be given by different sentences, such as "It was daylight on August 16, 1995, at midnight." This reintegration of the date of enunciation in the signification of the utterance was missed by the Greek philosophers, even by the

Stoics, who however did distinguish between sentences and the propositions that sentences signify. For them, in fact, a temporally indefinite sentence, such as "It is daylight," is the expression of a "complete signified," lacking in none of the determinations that make it possible to assign it a truth value; thus this truth value was itself variable in time.

The distinction between opinion and science, or unqualified knowledge, combined with the ancient principle of knowing like through like, led to the conclusion not only that true opinion lacked something it would need to have if it were to be knowledge, but also that that lack was essential to it, and irremediable. To be sure, Plato had acknowledged in *Meno* that "an account of the cause" made it possible to transform true opinion into knowledge, but in *The Republic* he seems, on the contrary (at least on a first reading), to think that such a metamorphosis is impossible, because opinion and knowledge have to do with two entirely separate domains of objects: opinion, midway between knowledge and ignorance, has to do with becoming, which is itself midway between being and nonbeing; science has to do with immutable being. About particular perceptible things, and, by contamination, about the principles that govern them, if there are any, there can be only opinion (as was the lesson of the splitting of Parmenides' poem into two parts), at best, a plausible opinion (and this will be the lesson of *Timaeus*). Aristotle will have his work cut out for him in his effort to preserve the possibility of a scientific status for physics; even as he continues to acknowledge in principle that there is no science but that of the necessary, he weakens the link between knowledge and necessity by making a place, between the immutable and the unpredictable, for a possible object for a science of nature: that which is produced ordinarily and regularly, most of the time and in most cases (*hōs epi to polu*).

KNOWLEDGE AND INTUITION

The movement of demonstration or proof, which goes back from the propositions to be proved to the premises on the basis of which they can be proved, raises a problem that Aristotle identified clearly. If there were no form of knowledge other than demonstrative knowledge, we would find ourselves caught up in an infinite regression: if, in order to know something, we have to be able to prove it on the basis of something else, which we also have to know, hence to prove again on the basis of something else, and so on, then to know something, we would have to know an indefinite number of things. This regression ad infinitum is ruinous, for the finite mind cannot traverse an indefinite series; thus if one can know nothing except by proving it, one can know nothing at all. There is one way out, which certain mathematicians known to Aristotle had accepted: this consists in turning the demonstrative series back on itself, in a circle, instead of allowing it to extend in a limitless linear fashion. But Aristotle rejects this solution, because it comes down finally to proving a thing by itself. His solution is to admit that "one has to stop," and that it is possible to do so, in the movement back from theorems to their premises: demonstrative knowledge is possible only if it is anchored, at the end of a finite number of stages, in principles that it is neither possible nor necessary to prove. There is proof only if there is some unprovable element; there is demonstrative knowledge only if there is a nondemonstrative mode of knowledge.

The whole question, then, is whether one can posit principles in a manner that is not arbitrary—that is, with some reason to posit one set of principles rather than another set, yet without proving them. The modern idea according to which one can construct axiomatic-deductive systems by arbitrarily designating certain propositions as axioms and certain others as theorems— so long as one can also construct other systems in which the status of these propositions is reversed—is wholly foreign, it seems, to ancient thought: between the principles endowed with explanatory power and the consequences explained by these principles, asymmetry is held to be essential and irreversible. If the ancients had to admit that the position of the principles is arbitrary, the dogmatics would have had to convert to skepticism. The skeptic Agrippa, in order to turn Aristotle's analysis against dogmatism, condemns infinite regression and circular reasoning as Aristotle had, and settles for blocking the ultimate escape route that Aristotle had reserved for himself, by arguing that if there is no reason to adopt a given principle rather than some other one, then the so-called principles are only unfounded hypotheses. This is why the remedy against the peril of skepticism has always been sought in a frantic quest for what Plato was the first to call an "anhypothetic principle" (i.e., one not posited by hypothesis).

But how can one determine the mode of knowing, by definition nondemonstrative, that is appropriate to knowledge of such a principle? On this point, the lesson provided by the mathematical model, the consummate example of demonstrative knowledge, is ambiguous, as a rapid comparison between Plato and Aristotle will show.

To assess the limits of the influence exercised by mathematics on the Platonic theory of knowledge, it suffices to reread the well-known pages of *The Republic* (Books VI and VII) where Plato describes the place he assigns to mathematics in the education of philosophers. In his eyes mathematics has the immense pedagogical advantage of "conducing to the awakening of thought" (*Republic* VII.523a), of "drawing the soul away from the world of becoming to the world of being" (VII.521d). But mathematics can play only an instrumental and propaedeutic role, for it suffers from two essential limitations: on the one hand, it uses (and necessarily so, according to Plato) perceptible objects, figures and diagrams, which it treats as images of purely intelligible realities about which it reasons; on the other hand, it is based on hypotheses that it takes to be known and that it deems to need no justification. Moreover, these two limitations are related to one another: the truth of the propositions that mathematicians take as primordial seems to them capable of being declared "self-evident to all," because this truth is visible, so to speak, on the very figure that they draw. Thus the title of science, which is given to mathematics by common usage, cannot be accepted without some impropriety; the hypothetical character of its principles allows it to claim consistency, but not truth. Only dialectics is truly a form of knowledge, because it calls into question everything that may be called into question, because it does not settle for any evidence procured by some perceptible figure of the intelligible, and because it goes back to the "anhypothetic principle" that will allow it to establish the pseudofoundations of mathematics itself.

This is doubtless not the place to discuss the Platonic identification of the anhypothetic principle with the form of the Good, the enigmatic "greatest thing to learn" (*Republic* VI.505a.2–3). But we can observe that Plato remains rather evasive on the mode of knowing that is appropriate to such an object: it seems that it is a matter sometimes of "seeing" it, "contemplating" it, as a sort of intelligible thing, and sometimes of "rendering an account [of it] to oneself and others," "defining it in one's discourse" by "exacting an account of the essence" and by "distinguishing and abstracting it from all other things" (cf. *Republic* VII.517–520, 532, 534). Plato specifies, however, that "the one who is unable to do this, in so far as he is incapable of rendering an account to himself and to others, does not possess full reason and intelligence [*nous*] about the matter" (VII.534b.4–6), and that this holds true for the good as well as for any other form. We shall thus resist the idea that here *nous* represents a mode of knowing that is intuitive in nature, the only one capable of apprehending, in a mute and quasi-mystical vision, an ineffable and absolutely transcendent object. Moreover, *nous* had been introduced, at the end of Book VI, as the name of that cognitive attitude of the soul that has as objects not the form of the Good alone but all the intelligible forms and their various dialectical relations; and the term *dianoia*, which is explicitly distinguished from *nous*, and which is appropriate to mathematical thought, does not mean "discursive knowledge," as it does in other contexts, but something like "intermediate" or "transitional intellectual grasp" *(dia-noia)* between opinion and intellectual understanding, strictly speaking.

In a sense, Aristotle is Plato's heir when he evokes "the most certain [*bebaiotate*] principle of all" (*Metaphysics* IV.iii.1005b11–12, 17–18, 22–23; 1006a4–5), the principle of noncontradiction. Returning to Plato's term *anhupothetos*, "not based on hypothesis," he specifies that "[it is] the principle which the student of any form of Being must grasp" (*Metaphysics*, IV.iii.1005b14–15). To know it, there is obviously no question of proving it: "If . . . there are some things of which no proof need be sought, they cannot say what principle they think to be more self-evident" (IV.iv.1006a10–11). Against those who, more or less seriously, have spoken in such a way that they seem to reject it, the only way to justify it is to proceed "refutatively," that is, to show by a dialectical path that, starting from the moment when the interlocutor agrees to enter into the sphere of meaningful dialogue, he cannot fail to respect the principle.

However, the principle of noncontradiction (leaving aside exceptions that can always be created for the sake of argument) does not normally enter into a proof as a premise; it functions rather as a fundamental rule of meaningful discourse. Contrary to Plato (and the difference is a significant one), Aristotle grants full-fledged scientific status to the particular disciplines that, like arithmetic or geometry, bear on a specific realm of entities belonging to the same class, like numbers and figures. Each of these sciences, which are demonstrative, has its own principles; they have some principles in common only in the sense that such principles can be applied analogically to more than one science. Dialectics, whose nature is precisely not to bear on any one class in particular, thus seems less apt to justify proper principles than common principles, and the question of how one reaches the point of knowing the unprovable principles of the particular sciences, and what type of knowledge is implied in knowing them, is raised anew in pointed fashion.

Aristotle tries to answer this question in the last chapter of *Posterior Analytics*, a chapter that is as difficult as it is well known. I shall focus here only on the fact that Aristotle designates *nous* as being the cognitive state *(hexis)* that apprehends principles, and that is, on that basis, more exact and more true than demonstrative knowledge itself. It has often been thought (indeed, since ancient times) that in this context the word *nous* designates a true intellectual intuition, a sort of vision of the mind grasping its objects with the same self-evidence and the same immediacy as ocular vision grasping its objects; it would be a question of a faculty specifically adapted to the acquisition of knowledge of unprovable principles. Against this interpretation, it has been pointed out (by Jonathan Barnes) that the chapter at issue raises two separate questions: How do principles become known to us? What is the cognitive state of the person apprehending them? To the first question, Aristotle gives an undeniably empiricist reply: principles become known to us at the end of an inductive process that moves through the classic stages of perception, memory, experience, and science; about intellection, nothing is said. *Nous* comes into play only in the reply to the second question: in the available vocabulary, this is a noun that is appropriate to designate knowledge whose object is a principle, once this knowledge *has been acquired* by way of induction, as described above, just as the noun *science* (demonstrative science) is appropriate to designate knowledge whose object is a proven theorem, once that knowledge has been acquired by way of deduction. If intellectual intuition is conceived as a means for *acquiring* knowledge, we then have to say that *nous* is not an intellectual intuition.

Thus twice in succession, in Plato and again in Aristotle, we have come close to the idea that the supreme instrument of knowing, the one that is capable of making principles known to us and that governs all other knowledge, can be assimilated to a sort of vision of the mind; but then, twice in succession, we have also (it seems) watched Plato and then Aristotle ultimately sidestep that idea. Not until the sort of synthesis of Platonism and Aristotelianism that we find in Neoplatonism, a creative synthesis that is not overly hampered by concern for textual exegesis, do we see the return in force, in the vocabulary of intellectual knowledge and beatific union, of the ancient metaphors of vision and contact. In a certain way, the circuit that we have been trying to trace thus turns out to close.

Jacques Brunschwig
Translated by Catherine Porter and Dominique Jouhaud

Bibliography

Texts and Translations

Anaxagoras. *The Fragments of Anaxagoras.* Ed. David Sider. *Beiträge zur Klassichen Philologie,* vol. 118. Meiseheim am Glan: Verlag Anton Hain, 1981.

Aristotle. *Metaphysics.* 2 vols. Trans. Hugh Tredennick. Loeb Classical Library.

———. *On the Soul.* In *On the Soul; Parva Naturali; On Breath.* Trans. W. S. Hett. Loeb Classical Library.

———. *Posterior Analytics.* In *Posterior Analytics; Topica.* Trans. Hugh Tredennick. Loeb Classical Library.

Long, Anthony A., and David N. Sedley, eds. *The Hellenistic Philosophers.* Cambridge: Cambridge University Press, 1987.

Plato. *Meno.* In *Laches; Protagoras; Meno; Euthydemus.* Trans. W. R. M. Lamb. Loeb Classical Library.

———. *Phaedo.* In *Euthyphro; Apology; Crito; Phaedo; Phaedrus.* Trans. W. R. M. Lamb. Loeb Classical Library.

———. *The Republic.* 2 vols. Trans. Paul Shorey. Loeb Classical Library.

———. *Sophist.* In *Theaetetus; Sophist.* Trans. Paul Shorey. Loeb Classical Library.

———. *Theaetetus.* In *Theaetetus; Sophist.* Trans. Paul Shorey. Loeb Classical Library.

Xenophanes. *Fragments/Xenophanes of Colophon.* Trans. J. H. Lesher. Toronto and Buffalo: University of Toronto Press, 1992.

Studies

Algra, Keimpe, Jonathan Barnes, Jaap Mansfeld, and Malcolm Schofield, eds. *The Cambridge History of Hellenistic Philosophy.* Cambridge: Cambridge University Press, 1999.

Asmis, Elizabeth. *Epicurus' Scientific Method.* Ithaca, N.Y.: Cornell University Press, 1984.

Barnes, Jonathan. *Aristotle's Posterior Analytics*. Oxford: Clarendon Press, 1975; 2nd ed., 1994.

Barnes, Jonathan, Jacques Brunschwig, Myles Burnyeat, and Malcolm Schofield, eds. *Science and Speculation: Studies in Hellenistic Theory and Practice*. Cambridge: Cambridge University Press, 1982.

Berti, Enrico, ed. *Aristotle on Science: The Posterior Analytics*. Padua: Antenore, 1980.

Burnyeat, Myles. *The Theaetetus of Plato*. Indianapolis: Hackett Publishing, 1990.

Canto-Sperber, Monique, ed. *Les paradoxes de la connaissance*. Paris: Odile Jacob, 1991.

Denyer, Nicholas. *Language, Thought and Falsehood in Ancient Greek Philosophy*. London: Routledge, 1991.

Everson, Stephen, ed. *Epistemology*. (Companions to Ancient Thought, vol. 1). Cambridge: Cambridge University Press, 1990.

Fine, Gail. "Knowledge and Belief in *Republic* V." *Archiv für Geschichte der Philosophie* 60 (1978): 121–139.

Granger, Gilles-Gaston. *La théorie aristotélicienne de la science*. Paris: Aubier, 1976.

Hintikka, Jaakko. *Time and Necessity*. Oxford: Clarendon Press, 1973.

Ioppolo, Anna-Maria. *Opinione e scienza: Il dibattito tra Stoici e Accademici nel III e nel II secolo a. C.* Naples: Bibliopolis, 1986.

Lesher, James H. "The Emergence of Philosophical Interest in Cognition." *Oxford Studies in Ancient Philosophy* 12 (1994): 1–34.

Lyons, John. *Structural Semantics: An Analysis of Part of the Vocabulary of Plato*. Oxford: Blackwell, 1966.

McKirahan, Richard D. *Principles and Proofs: Aristotle's Theory of Demonstrative Science*. Princeton: Princeton University Press, 1992.

Robin, Léon. *Les rapports de l'être et de la connaissance d'après Platon*. Paris: Presses Universitaires de France, 1957.

Schofield, Malcolm, Myles Burnyeat, and Jonathan Barnes, eds. *Doubt and Dogmatism: Studies in Hellenistic Epistemology*. Oxford: Clarendon Press, 1980.

Striker, Gisela. "Kriterion tes aletheias." In *Essays on Hellenistic Epistemology and Ethics*. Cambridge: Cambridge University Press, 1966. Pp. 22–76.

Vlastos, Gregory, ed. *Plato: A Collection of Critical Essays, I: Metaphysics and Epistemology*. Garden City and New York: Doubleday, 1971.

SCHOOLS AND SITES
OF LEARNING

PHILOSOPHY, THE PURSUIT OF WISDOM, has had a two-fold origin," Diogenes Laertius writes at the beginning of *Lives of Eminent Philosophers*. "The
one school was called Ionian, because Thales, a Milesian and therefore an
Ionian, instructed Anaximander; the other school was called Italian from
Pythagoras, who worked for the most part in Italy" (I.13). Diogenes further
divides philosophers into ten sects *(haireseis)*; the term designates a coherent positive doctrine, or at least a criterion with respect to the phenomenal
world (I.20).

Diogenes thus classifies philosophers according to the very parameters we
are considering here: schools and sites of learning. Concerning the sites, Diogenes and his sources tell us that philosophy was originally divided among
diverse tendencies that ran from one end of the Greek world to the other,
from Asia Minor to Greater Greece. In fact, philosophy originated in the farthest reaches of the Hellenic universe, and it did not reach Athens until fairly
late. Still, according to Diogenes, whether or not a philosopher belonged to a
particular school depended on the content of his thought; it did not necessarily imply membership in a given institution.

The philologists of the 19th and early 20th centuries saw the origin of the
idea of the university in the philosophical schools of antiquity. Thus they depicted these schools in modern terms, especially the Academy and the Lyceum: as scientific institutions with tenured full, associate, and assistant professors; beginning students and doctoral candidates; classrooms and courses.
These images are often only innocent metaphors, but they have sometimes
introduced distortions into the way we represent the ancient philosophers'
activities.

This phenomenon is limited to the arena of classical studies; medievalists
and historians of education have stressed the differences between the ancient
philosophic schools and modern universities. The latter have an official status
recognized by the state; some form of public approval is required for position-
holders within these institutions; and the course of study leads to a certificate
attesting to the degree obtained. It has been said that if a modern student had
sat long enough at Socrates' feet he would have demanded a diploma, something to show for his efforts. But great teachers such as Socrates did not issue
diplomas. Moreover, in modern universities, membership in an institution

does not mean that one has to subscribe to a particular line of thought; in contrast, in the ancient world, there would have been widespread astonishment if a faithful follower of the Academy had defended, sword in hand, the superiority of Epicurean ethics. The ancient philosophic schools, even the most highly organized, were in principle free institutions, and adhering to them implied, as Diogenes says, the adoption of a firm theoretical position. We may conclude, following the *Oxford English Dictionary*, that the philosophic schools of Antiquity consisted of groups of "persons who . . . are disciples of the same master, or who are united by a general similarity of principles and methods." The word *school* refers only rarely to a specific institution.

It is difficult to generalize about the way the various schools were organized. Sources are often lacking, and the ancient authors rarely bothered to describe the organizational aspects of their activity. Furthermore, a school's organization was directly linked to the doctrine it professed. Today, all departments of philosophy look alike; in ancient times, philosophers had a great deal of freedom to choose the forms through which knowledge would be organized and transmitted. I shall merely indicate a few models, which the individual schools resembled in varying degrees. The simplest distinction we can make is between two types: (1) elementary, atomic structures constituted by a master and one or more disciples, which dissolved when the master died; (2) more complex and hierarchical organizations, with different levels of teachers and disciples, which existed over a considerable span of time. In the history of ancient thought, which lasted more than one thousand years, we find these same two structures over and over, with intermediate nuances.

THE PRESOCRATICS

Greek speculation, in its earliest period, was characterized by an immense diversity of horizons; philosophers lived in different milieux, from Asia Minor to Sicily, and they engaged in controversies across lands and seas. Subsequently, with the growing importance of Athens as the principal city of Greece, philosophic debate was confined to the Athenian city-state alone.

In Greece, philosophy was almost always an urban phenomenon, and it was often linked to important, wealthy city-states. The first "philosophers," Thales, Anaximander, and Anaximenes, flourished in Miletus, a wealthy city-state and very active commercial center in the 7th and 6th centuries, up to its destruction in 494 B.C.E. Anaximander is said to have been Thales' disciple, and a relative. We do not know this for certain, but if we take it as a fact, we have the first instance of family ties between master and disciple, a phenomenon we shall come across frequently in all periods. In those early days, however, the philosophic organization was limited to the master-disciple bond. It seems certain that this was the case with Parmenides and Zeno of Elea; Plato describes them as master and disciple and also as lovers. Diogenes Laertius, for his part, claims that Zeno was adopted by Parmenides; if this is true, here is another example of master-disciple family ties. The Eleatic circle must have been fairly broad if, as Plato tells us, the Stranger of Elea belonged to the group associated with Parmenides and Zeno. Let us note that Plato is not yet using precise terminology to indicate relationships to particular schools.

A philosopher's thinking could also be communicated in written form. Heraclitus seems to have had no direct disciples, but "so great fame did his book win that a sect was founded and called the Heracliteans, after him" (Diogenes Laertius, *Lives* IX.6). Aristotle, too, refers to "those who claim to be following Heraclitus," without thereby designating true disciples. Cratylus must have figured among those to whom Aristotle was alluding, for Plato, in his youth, was one of Cratylus's intimate friends. Cratylus does not seem to have lived in Ephesus or in Ionia, and yet he followed the theories of Heraclitus, and criticized them to a certain extent (*Metaphysics* 987a.32, 1010a.11).

Pythagoras is the only philosopher in connection with whom we can speak of a school. But Pythagoras is a semimythical figure, halfway between archaic religiosity and true philosophy. His sect presents a quite complex set of features, but it may be that the Pythagoreans constituted a political *hetairia* as well as a religious and philosophic association.

A whole series of ritual prescriptions having to do with every aspect of the disciples' daily lives are linked with Pythagoras's name. It was forbidden to eat at least certain parts of the flesh of certain animals. Some behaviors were prescribed, such as setting out on the right foot rather than the left, wearing particular clothing, having certain attitudes toward one's fellow citizens, and so on. These prescriptions recall the mystery cults, and reveal a strong inclination toward the other-worldly and the divine. This set of rules constituted a *bios*, a specific way of life on which the identity of the Pythagorean group was based in large part. Their community was characterized by a series of doctrines on number, on the ordered harmony of the cosmos, and on mathematical sciences such as astronomy and music. It is not clear when this more "scientific" aspect began to be part of the sect's cultural identity, but Pythagoreanism did not exist in written form before Philolaus's era.

The Pythagorean sect was highly cohesive. Pythagorean friendship committed its members to helping one another, even if they were not personally acquainted. Disciples who had been expelled were regarded as dead, for they had been marked as unworthy or as heretics. Still, some sources emphasize a distinction among disciples according to whether they were acusmaticians or mathematicians: this distinction points either to two successive stages in the deepest understanding of Pythagoras's doctrine, or else to an opposition between two groups that had split over the interpretation of his message. The acusmaticians took the sect's prescriptions for living and its taboos as their fundamental tenets; the mathematicians did not reject these injunctions, but for them the doctrine of number lay at the heart of Pythagorism. It seems, too, that the mathematicians considered the acusmaticians, like themselves, to be authentic Pythagoreans, whereas the latter group did not recognize the former.

We know little about how the sect was organized. Its teaching seems to have called for a long period of silence before one was admitted to argue in Pythagoras's presence and with the master himself, but this is not certain. The Pythagorean school cannot be defined as a true philosophic school, even though it may have been taken as a model influencing the birth of the Athenian schools of the 4th century.

SOPHISTS, RHETORS, DOCTORS

From the outset, the Greek world was studded with specialists who went from one city-state to another to proffer their services. The main groups are mentioned by Homer: soothsayers, healers, carpenters, and singers (*Odyssey* XVII.383–384). Many of these groups were organized as hereditary guilds in which fathers transmitted their art to sons.

The Sophists were itinerant teachers; we know that they sojourned frequently in all the Greek city-states, where they taught young men for wages. Gorgias went to Argos and Thessaly, Protagoras to Sicily, Hippias to Sparta and Sicily; each achieved a certain degree of success. Athens drew a large number of learned men, including many philosophers, such as Parmenides, Zeno (if Plato's account is accurate), Anaxagoras of Clazomenae, and a number of Sophists. Like all itinerant craftsmen, the Sophists were paid for their lessons: from three or four to a hundred *mines* for a complete course (one *mine* was worth one hundred drachmas, and one drachma represented the average daily salary of an artisan).

Sophistic teaching covered a very broad range of topics: astronomy, geometry, linguistics and grammar, theology, and literature. The Sophists provided an education of a high level, to increase their disciple's general culture and to make him better able to convince his fellow citizens. Isocrates, for example, recounts a public debate about literature held by the Sophists in the Lyceum before an enthusiastic audience (*Panathenaicus* 18–19); we know that a number of Sophists were concerned with the problem of squaring the circle; many Presocratic themes, Eleatic in particular, were taken up again by Protagoras and Gorgias. Sophistic teaching varied according to its audience. In Sparta, Hippias recited the genealogy of gods and men, and described the occupations worthy of a young Spartan, thus adapting his message to his hearers' tastes; in Athens, on the contrary, a democratic city-state ruled by an Assembly, he focused on rhetoric and dialectics (or eristics). The course must not have been very long, for it was intended as preparation for public life.

The Sophists' activity in Athens came dangerously close to the political sphere: their connections with the leading families—the source of most of their disciples—and the innovative content of their teaching aroused public hostility, especially in democratic circles. Around 433, Diopeithes decreed that anyone who did not believe in the gods or who presented arguments *(logoi)* about celestial spaces should be taken to court. Plutarch, who relates this episode, sees it as an attempt to discredit Pericles by bringing charges against his master Anaxagoras *(Life of Pericles* 32). In the years that followed, Protagoras, Diagoras, Theodorus "the Atheist," Socrates, and others faced— or were at least threatened with—similar charges. The Athenian people's distrust slowly faded, but it resurfaced periodically, generally in connection with important political events, such as Alexander's death.

When they arrived in a city, the Sophists sought to win clients by demonstrating their abilities in public. In a world where official degrees and diplomas were unknown, such exhibitions of personal competence were necessary. They took place in sites where the biggest crowds gathered, such as the sanctuary in Olympia or the theater in Athens. The Sophists would read a prepared speech or would improvise at the public's request. Sometimes, however, a Sophist already well-known to the public did not need to establish his talents (Plato, *Protagoras* 310b). Sure of his audience, he would withdraw to some private place, usually the home of a wealthy citizen, where he would have enough room to bring together his own disciples; there he would give his lessons, for a fee, to his host and others. We know that the Sophists were welcomed in the greatest houses of Athens, for example those of Callias, Euripides, and Megacleides. But they could also hold their meetings in gymnasiums or public squares, and from ancient comedies we learn that Sophists held forth in the Lyceum, in the Academy, and at the entrance to the Odeon.

In *Protagoras* (314e–316a), Plato describes the behavior of the Sophists in action. One walks about, surrounded by his most important disciples, who are followed by their juniors; another, seated on a chair, speaks to listeners seated on stools arranged in a half-circle; a third receives his disciples from a reclining position and engages in dialogue with them while stretched out on his bed. These same scenes reappear virtually unchanged in descriptions of many other, later groups. Teaching does not presuppose the use of particular instruments; oral teaching and debate were the rule, and the Sophists were proud of being able to produce lengthy speeches and to answer specific questions and engage in dialogue with their interlocutors. The rhetorical part of their teaching must have consisted in learning entire texts by heart, or in mastering rhetorical schemas for later use.

Isocrates recounts an incident that allows us to glimpse life in one school of rhetoric. The master writes an argument *(logos)*, then corrects it while rereading it with three or four disciples; he then asks one of his former students to do the same thing, summoning him from home (apparently the latter had left the school and was leading the life of an ordinary citizen [*Panathenaicus* 200]). Theophrastus followed similar practices in his school, and maintained that his public readings were useful in helping him correct his own work.

Thus the institutional characteristics that typified the activity of philosophers began to crystallize. Sites devoted to teaching began to appear: the homes of the wealthy, city squares, public gymnasiums. The latter, according to Vitruvius (*De architectura* V.xi.2), had arcades where philosophers could stroll about with their disciples, and exedras furnished with benches, to facilitate discussion. The choice of a teaching site was often related to the type of philosophy being taught: Socrates chose public streets and squares so as to demonstrate his availability to all his fellow citizens and to show his lack of interest in remuneration, for speakers could only be sure of collecting money from the public in an enclosed teaching space. The Cynics did the same thing, in every era, and they always tended to prefer the public display of "natural" behaviors to the transmission of complex doctrines. In contrast, the Academicians, the Peripatetics, the Stoics, and other groups taught in enclosed spaces well-equipped with scientific instruments and libraries, and in the homes of wealthy and powerful individuals.

It may be useful to compare the teaching of philosophy with that of medicine. In Greece, medical training was concentrated in a few city-states, such as Cos and Chios; it had no official status, and no diplomas were awarded. In the beginning, the trade was passed on from father to son. We know the names of various members of Hippocrates' family: they were all doctors at the Macedonian court, and the family tradition was maintained up to the Hellenistic period. But there came a time when disciples from outside the family were accepted; Hippocrates' famous *Oath* includes the terms of a sort of contract according to which the disciple agrees to consider the master's relatives and friends as his own, and to provide them with help and assistance.

Medical schools consisting of a master and his disciples were organized in a fairly straightforward way. The teaching involved lessons and exercises; the disciples observed the master at work, helped him, and became accustomed to using instruments. All our sources take pains to make accurate lists of disciples of famous masters, whether they are talking about doctors, philosophers, or rhetors; such lists attest to the worth of the people selected. The master's lessons were eventually written down, and they constituted the doctrinal patrimony of the school, as was the case later on for schools of philosophy. Thus the teachings of the Cnidus school were compiled in a text called *Cnidian Sentences,* which has been lost; the Cos school produced the *Hippocratic Corpus.* An analysis of the latter text shows that complete doctrinal orthodoxy was not required; the various authors represented in the *Corpus* often put forward divergent theses simultaneously. These writings also include manuals of medical rhetoric and dialectics, to be used in meetings among colleagues in order to assure oneself of employment; they propose rhetorical and eristic schemas along with basic medical notions to be used in debates.

PLATO'S SCHOOL

Socrates' disciples did not create true schools. Even the Megarians, the best organized, did not have real schools; instead, they had independent masters who brought groups of disciples together, sometimes for long periods.

Plato, in contrast, established a school. According to Diogenes Laertius, whose account of Plato's life is not entirely clear, Plato taught at the Academy when he returned from his first trip to Sicily; later he lectured "in the garden at Colonus," adjacent to the Academy (*Lives* III.5–7). Thus we have two sites for the school, either in the Academy or in a garden on Plato's property. Since the school had no institutional organization, and since it consisted only of a spontaneous group of friends, its location might well have varied for practical reasons. The type of teaching and the research carried out in the school did not actually require much equipment.

Plato's school marked the history of philosophic thought for centuries to come, from both theoretical and institutional standpoints. But the school was constituted from elements that came out of earlier traditions. A passage from Philodemus provides a good description of Plato's role: "He functioned as an architect, and set problems" (*Academicorum Index*, Plato Y.4–5). However, unlike the Pythagoreans, Plato did not impose any doctrinal orthodoxy. He may have gotten the idea of setting up a community devoted to philosophy during his stay in Sicily, from his contacts with the Pythagoreans, but the Academy was organized very differently, owing in particular to the absence of dogmatism. Olympiodorus writes in his *Life of Plato* (61) that Plato succeeded in freeing himself from the Pythagorean practice of doctrinal secrecy and from an unquestioning acceptance of the master's word as well as from Socratic irony; indeed, he maintained courteous relations with his own students. The school's lack of orthodoxy meant that Plato's chief disciples could criticize fundamental points of his metaphysics. The unity of the school was based on the fact that the disciples set themselves common problems to discuss: Being, the Good, the One, Science; these were quite different problems from those addressed elsewhere—in Isocrates' school, for instance.

The establishment of a philosophic school by an Athenian was the pretext for countless jokes on the part of comic writers; Plato was ridiculed, represented with a furrowed brow (Amphis) or depicted as strolling about and talking to himself (Alexis). In *The Shipwrecked*, Ephippus parodies the "lively little fellows" who were Plato's disciples, and Epicrates tells how the master and his pupils were defining nature and carving it up into genres, when a Sicilian doctor was heard making clamorous objections. Rather than allowing the discussion to be disrupted, Plato politely asked his disciples to start over. Plato's role, even in this description, is precisely that of the master who sets problems and directs the disciples' investigation.

The Platonic school had no internal literature at first, for Plato insisted that the doctrinal core of his thinking could not be written down (Epistle VII 344c); the absence of a doctrinal corpus created problems for the life of the school. At the same time, there was a literature addressed to those outside the school, intended to spread knowledge of Plato's philosophy beyond the circle of his disciples. Philodemus asserts that "his writings brought countless people to philosophy" (*Academicorum Index* I.12–14). Aristoxenus, for his part, tells how Plato gave a talk one day on the Good before an uninitiated public, without much success (*Elementa harmonica* II.1). This event is echoed by an amusing line from a comedy: "I have more trouble understanding these things, O Master, than Plato's notion of the Good" (Amphis, *Amphicrates* frg. 6K).

The complete training of a Platonic philosopher, compared to that of a Sophist, took a long time; Aristotle, for example, spent twenty years at the Academy. Life in the school gradually became an end in itself.

The value of the teaching offered by a Sophist, a rhetor, or a philosopher was measured above all in the number and quality of his pupils. Isocrates was proud to have had famous Athenians, noted statesmen, generals, and even foreigners as students. Philodemus of Gadara and Diogenes Laertius preserved the list of Plato's disciples, including Xenocrates, Crantor, Archesilaus, Telecles, Cacydes, Carneades, Antiochus of Ascalon, Zeno the Stoic, Chrysippus, Diogenes of Babylon, Antipater, and Panaetius.

Plato's will makes no allusion either to the garden or to the school. According to Diogenes, Plato chose to be buried near the Academy. Pausanias describes his tomb, and points out that it is located beyond the Academy proper. The custom of burying a master on the grounds of his school was characteristic of the chief philosophic schools of Athens. The hypothesis according to which the school was a religious guild dedicated to the cult of the Muses has been ruled out. We do not know whether Plato thought that his community would survive after his death. It did so, however, thereby distinguishing itself from earlier groups, which had disintegrated when the master left or died.

FROM PLATO'S DEATH TO THE FIRST CENTURY B.C.E.

At the end of the 4th century, the four great schools that would forever link the name of Athens to that of philosophy were established within the city-state. But Athens was not the only home of philosophers: many of the minor Socratics set up schools elsewhere, for example at Megara, Elis, Olympia, and Eretria. The Platonics traveled widely—to Atarnea, in the Pontus region, and to the court of Macedonia; Epicurus did the same thing. But it is telling that both Aristotle and Epicurus, after beginning their activity elsewhere, decided to go back to Athens to establish their own schools in a city-state whose importance guaranteed a huge audience for their doctrines. Zeno of Citium opened his school in the same city for the same reasons. Thus the four principal Hellenistic philosophic schools were created in Athens, two by Athenian citizens and the other two by foreigners.

The schools now took on their ultimate form. A special vocabulary was instituted in the philosophic community: in addition to the venerable term *diatribē*, the term *schole* was used to designate the course of study, lessons, and seminars. This meaning of the word was unknown in the time of Plato and Aristotle; then, it designated "free time." According to Philodemus, the school was called *hairesis*, "choice," in the sense of the selection of a philosophic doctrine; sometimes the analogous term *agoge* was used instead. The terms *kepos* (garden), *peripatos* (stroll—here in the sense of the place where people walked), and *exedra* were also common. One could thus designate a school by alluding to the activities that took place there, the doctrines espoused, or its physical structure.

Dicaearchus (frg. 29) spoke out against the tendency of philosophy in his day to become institutionalized; he argued that one could do philosophy anywhere—in public squares, in fields, or on the battlefield—without any need for a chair, textual commentary, or set hours for lessons or for strolling about with one's disciples. Menedemus of Eretria is criticized in some sources for his indifference to the conditions under which he taught. He required no special order or seating arrangement; his disciples could choose to sit or walk about while listening, and their master had the same options (Diogenes Laertius, *Lives* II.130).

On Plato's death, his community did not fold; his nephew Speusippus succeeded him as head of the school (Philodemus, *Academicorum Index* VI.28–29). This succession can probably be attributed to the fact that, as a family member, Speusippus could inherit the garden where most of the common activity took place. There is no contradiction here, since family ties were often intertwined with school ties. Speusippus himself seems to have held most of his meetings in the garden. The ancient sources are quite specific about the sites where the various scholarchs directed common activities. Speusippus had statues of the Muses erected in the garden, with a dedication crediting them as the sources of the school's philosophic doctrines. As the head of a school, Speusippus became the most prominent figure of the community, but we do not know whether that gave him the authority to influence the thinking of other, older members. The fact remains that when Speusippus took over, Aristotle went off to establish a school outside of Athens; Xenocrates may have done the same thing. Speusippus defied his uncle's taboo on writing down the fundamental doctrines. The titles of his dialogues and notes taken during his lessons have been preserved.

When Speusippus died, the youngest disciples chose his successor by vote. In the selection process, voting alternated with designation by the previous scholarch. Xenocrates won by a small margin over the other candidates, it seems; he had seventy votes, which suggests that the community must have been fairly large. Xenocrates' primary residence was the school (Diogenes Laertius, *Lives* IV.6). Polemon, too, spent most of his time in the garden of the Academy, so much so that the disciples built huts so they could live near him, near the place of the Muses *(mouseion)* and the exedra where he gave his courses. Polemon, Crates, and Crantor seem to have lived in the same house, the first two as lovers; all three were buried in the garden, following the school's custom. After the death of Polemon, the third head of the Academy, we hear no more about Plato's garden.

With the establishment of other philosophic schools, problems of membership and orthodoxy began to arise. Who could legitimately claim to be "Platonic" or "Epicurean"? In the case of the Academy, membership did not depend on strict obedience to the founder's doctrine. Indeed, Plato's dialogues were conceived so as to allow various interpretations; as for Speusippus and the other directors, their works never had a canonic role. To be an Academician, at this stage of the school's history, meant rather that one belonged to a group that had historical continuity and an identity maintained throughout its various theoretical evolutions. Compared with that of the Pythagoreans or the Epicureans, this identity appeared fairly weak. The very fact that the ancient authors could distinguish among several phases in the Academy's history shows clearly that it was not conceived as having a rock-solid unity; however, it was not diversified, either, to the point where it would split into opposing factions.

Aristotle did not establish a school. As a metic, he could not own property in Attica; however, he may have taught in a rented private house. The surviving Aristotelian texts make it clear that his courses could not have been held in a gymnasium; he needed a site specifically devoted to teaching, because he used instruments and books.

The Peripatetic school typically focused on collecting and cataloguing empirical data, as Aristotle's *History of Animals* and Theophrastus's *History of Plants* attest. The Peripatetic school also collected 158 city-state constitutions, classified by political regime, as well as the names of the winners of the Pythian Games, as attested by an inscription from Delphi where both Aristotle and Callisthenes are mentioned. The school used lists, anatomical tables, geographical maps, models of the heavenly sphere, and star charts. Its goal was not to prepare anyone for political life; rather, it offered a choice of lifestyle and a path to happiness—a *bios*. The corpus of Aristotle's lessons formed the school's conceptual patrimony, just as the *Hippocratic Corpus* did for the Cos school. Aristotle also wrote a series of works for the public, to incite people to take an interest in philosophy, but these have been lost.

Aristotle did not go hunting for disciples; neither he nor Plato showed evidence of the embarrassing tendency toward self-celebration that characterized both the Sophists and the doctors. The subsistence of the philosopher and his school, in both cases, depended not on salaries paid by the disciples but solely on the personal patrimony of the group members, or of the school. In fact, Aristotle's will reveals that he was a rich man, and the fortune of the Peripatetics was legendary in ancient times.

There is no mention of Aristotle's school in the text of his will. On Alexander's death, Aristotle had been subject to attacks by the popular party and was forced to emigrate; it is probable that he gave no thought to the survival of his school after his own disappearance. The birth of the Lyceum (peripatos) as an institution dates from the time of Theophrastus, Aristotle's principal disciple (321–287); Demetrius of Phaleron, Peripatetic and Athenian statesman, who governed Athens at the time, granted Theophrastus, whose student he had been, the right to own real estate in Athens. Theophrastus bought a garden where he organized the Aristotelian school, modeled on Plato's. The school did not bear its founder's name, since Theophrastus was seeking to carry on the community Aristotle had started.

Theophrastus's will provides a good deal of information about this community. His goal, in founding it, was to make theoretic life (bios theoretikos) a reality: "The garden and the walk and the houses adjoining the garden, all and sundry, I give and bequeath to such of my friends hereinafter named as may wish to study literature and philosophy there in common" (Diogenes Laertius, Lives V.52–53). It was forbidden to sell the property or to make private use of it; the group was to use the garden as if it were a temple (which means that it was not one), in a spirit of familial concord. The possessions included a sanctuary devoted to the Muses with several statues, a small portico, a larger one with geographical maps in stone, a garden, a peripatos, and some houses. Theophrastus, too, had himself buried in a corner of the school and had a funerary monument erected, as the Academicians had done. The ten disciples who benefited from the property were guaranteed a certain material comfort. Here, too, there were close family ties: the beneficiaries included direct heirs, testamentary executors, some of Aristotle's nephews, and friends of long standing. We find the same interweaving of school and family ties as in the medical schools.

The fall of Demetrius of Phaleron led to the final persecution of the philosophers by the popular party. A certain Sophocles of Sunium proposed a law forbidding any philosopher from directing a school without the Assembly's permission, on pain of death. All the philosophers had to flee Athens, but they came back the following year, when a Peripatetic, Philon, charged Sophocles' law with illegality, and won. From then on, Theophrastus lived peacefully, surrounded by large numbers of disciples.

The wills of the other Peripatetic scholarchs have also survived. Strato succeeded Theophrastus, and he left the school to Lyco, along with his library and some furniture (but excluding, for unknown reasons, the manuscripts of Strato's own lessons). He asked the other disciples to cooperate with Lyco, and, like Theophrastus, provided for his own funerary monument, probably to be erected on the school's grounds. Lyco in turn left the school to a group of disciples, charging them with electing a scholarch capable of governing the community and making it grow. His library was left to one disciple, while another was given the task of producing a faithful edition of Lyco's own lessons; this too, as we shall see, was the customary practice. Like his predecessors, Lyco arranged for his own funerary monument and statue.

These wills show that the Peripatetic scholarchs were men of means; the texts were handed down, in all probability, because they were kept in the school as evidence of the tradition of the institution. Athenaeus (547d–e) preserved a fragment from Antigonus of Carystus in which the latter described the situation of the school in Lyco's day. Antigonus criticizes the practice of common monthly banquets in which even former members of the school participated; we are told that there was an official position on the "good behavior" of the members, who were concerned with collecting funds for their shared expenses, and, in case of necessity, with providing from their own personal funds, according to the custom of the Athenian "liturgies"; in addition, he cites the office of "curator of the cult of the Muses." The poorer disciples were exempt from these liturgies. The school met either in the *kepos* or in a rented house in Athens.

After Theophrastus and Strato, the school underwent a rapid decline. The ideal of the theoretic life was insufficient to establish an orthodoxy; in addition, the Aristotelian method encouraged the fragmentation of philosophy into erudite studies and detailed investigations focused on specific topics. In time, a legend grew up attributing the school's decline to the loss of Aristotle's works over the centuries; however, the legend has no basis in fact.

Epicurus came back to Athens to found his school in another garden, following Theophrastus's example, the same year that the law of Sophocles of Sunium was brought to trial. Epicurus established his garden outside the city walls, not far from the Academy. As an Athenian citizen, he had more legal rights in the area of real estate than Theophrastus had, and his community was established on a firm footing: Epicurus left his garden to his natural heirs, on condition that they make it available to Hermarchus and his disciples, and, after them, to their chosen successors. The goal of his school was to give all philosophers the means to carry on their philosophic activity, provided that they followed Epicurus's doctrines; the subsistence of its oldest members was ensured. Philodemus recorded excerpts from Epicurus's letters in which he required that, out of a spirit of friendship, the richest members had to pay an annual quota and had to give financial aid to members in difficulty (frgs. 74, 76, 92, 97, 99, 120, 121, 123).

Epicurus named a director and defined a philosophic orthodoxy. Hermarchus was assigned to take care of Epicurus's library, which included the teachings of Epicurus himself, collected in a series of books *peri physeos,* "on nature." Here, too, family and philosophic bonds were interwoven: the sons of prominent members were given jobs in the school, and their daughters were married to the best disciples. Monthly meetings were held, and a funerary cult of Epicurus and his family was also instituted. Unlike the other schools, Epicurus's seems to have been open to all social groups, including courtesans and slaves.

Unlike the Aristotelians, the Epicurean community was infused with a practical ideal: in the place of scientific research and erudition, Epicurus proposed a particular way of living and philosophizing, the only way that could enable man to free himself from pain and find happiness. Epicurus placed great stress on the need to learn the principal doctrines by heart and meditate on them. In *Letter to Herodotus,* he declared that he had written a brief summary of his thought so that readers could memorize it and use it at any point in life.

Internal relations within the school were maintained in an atmosphere of collaboration and emulation. Certain members were obviously more advanced than others, but there was no hierarchy, and a spirit of friendship permeated all relationships. Seneca informs us (*Letter* 52.3–4) that Epicurus identified several ways of leading his disciples to the truth, according to their various temperaments: one advanced on his own, another needed help, a third had to be pushed. In his treatise *Peri parresias,* Philodemus stressed the intensity of the group relations: to be sure, the leader was the best of all, but each one felt responsible for the progress of the others. This led to the practice of public self-criticism of one's own errors, and to public denunciations of others' mistakes. One day, according to Plutarch, Colotes was so excited by Epicurus's speech that he kneeled down before him; the master, judging the act contrary to his doctrine, knelt down in turn, in order to reestablish equality and friendship *(philia)* between them (frg. 65, Arrianus). The Epicureans customarily wore rings bearing the master's likeness, and had pictures of the school's founders in their homes.

On the institutional level, the importance of the Stoic school is not comparable to the enormous influence it had on Greek philosophic life. Zeno and his successors Cleanthes and Chrysippus had no private garden in which to create a community. Zeno gave his lectures in a public place, the Stoa Poecile (or painted portico) on the Agora, one of the most heavily frequented spots in Athens; thus his site contrasts with the more secluded locations of the other schools. His teaching met with success, and the Athenians awarded him great honors. Diogenes Laertius (*Lives* VII.10–12) reports a decree of the Prytaneis in honor of Zeno, after his death: he was offered a crown of gold and a tomb in the Ceramicus at state expense, as a reward for practicing philosophy, ex-

horting young people to virtue, and living in conformity with his own doctrines. The earlier hostility toward philosophers seems to have died out.

Zeno's group survived its founder's death, and Cleanthes took over as head
of the school. The functions of a Stoic scholarch are not very clear; the position may have merely entailed a certain cultural preeminence among Zeno's
fellow disciples. The school's somewhat loose organization led in time to several schisms: Ariston founded his own school in the Cynosarges gymnasium,
outside the city to the south; two of his disciples are known to us. Cleanthes'
successor, Chrysippus, completely reorganized Stoic doctrine (hence the saying "but for Chrysippus, there had been no Porch" [Diogenes Laertius, *Lives*
VII.183]); he wrote more than seven hundred works. Whereas Zeno and
Cleanthes were metics in Athens, Chrysippus was a naturalized citizen, but
this did not lead him to establish a philosophic community in an independent
garden (Plutarch, *De Stoicorum repugnantiis* 1034a). He continued to teach
at the Stoa at regular hours, and perhaps also at the Odeon, near the theater
of Dionysus. The Stoics were not rich, and they lived mainly by teaching
their own disciples, for pay (Quintilian, *Institutio oratoria* XII.7.9). This does
not seem to have shocked the Athenians, who were accustomed to such practices.

A few details about these practices have been passed down. Cleanthes was
paid in advance, after some discussions with his students. Chrysippus recognized that selling wisdom was a way of life suited to the philosopher, and he
pointed out ways of requesting one's pay gracefully, avoiding arguments.
Stobaeus recounts a debate among the Stoics that took place because some of
them were concerned that the practice of teaching for pay reduced them to
the level of the Sophists (II.7.11m).

The problem of the unity of the Stoic school is particularly vexed. Even the
ancients had noted that Stoicism allowed for a certain autonomy of thought.
However, the various Stoic positions were expressed in a common vocabulary,
which attested to membership in the same school (the case of Herophilus's
medical school was analogous), and the need to respond to adversaries' objections led to a continual reformulation of basic definitions. The dynamic unity
of Stoicism sufficed to allow the identification of a Stoic philosophy.

It is impossible to follow the vicissitudes of all the schools and groups of
philosophers of this period: they were loosely organized and often short-lived
communities, dependent on the presence of a master in a certain place. Still,
we can trace the evolution of the principal schools after their founding.

Original philosophic production did not constitute, as we might be inclined
to think today, the only important aspect of Greek philosophers' activity. Like
the neo-Thomists or the Marxists of the 20th century, these philosophers carried on their work in three directions. They expanded on the theoretical inspiration of the school's founder in areas the latter had neglected; they looked
after the critical edition of the master's work and the interpretation of his

writings; they entered into polemics with the other schools. Even more than with theoretical development, they were concerned with the training of disciples and with the practice of their own particular philosophy as a way of life.

Once accepted as an integral part of ordinary cultural life, philosophy began to split off into sects, under the somewhat skeptical eye of the public. In the 1st century B.C.E., Diodorus of Sicily wrote a highly polemical text claiming that the Greeks practiced philosophy to earn money; in his view, this accounted for the perpetual innovations, the new schools, and the polemics that produced confusion and uncertainty among the disciples. In fact, the best-known schools seemed to make it a point of honor to contradict one another (Diodorus, II.29.5–6). In compensation, in the imperial era, wealthy young people got into the habit of frequenting the major philosophic schools in turn, thus showing a certain impartiality; they were implicitly rejecting each school's claim to be the only good one.

As we have seen, the Peripatetics never had a philosophic orthodoxy. After Lycon, the Lyceum seems to have undergone a rapid decline. Several sources (Cicero, *De finibus bonorum et malorum* V.13–14; Plutarch, *De exilio* 14; Clement of Alexandria, *Stromateis* I.14.63) allow us to reestablish the list of his successors (Ariston, Critolaus, Diodorus of Tyre, and so on), though in most cases we know nothing of their philosophical orientations. Only for Critolaus is there evidence of an intention to remain faithful to Aristotle's teachings (Wehrli, frgs. 12–15). Athens had entered into an alliance with Mithridates, owing to a decision by the tyrant of the period, the Epicurean Aristion; the city was attacked by Sulla, and the Academy and the Lyceum were destroyed during the siege. A certain Apellicon is mentioned among other Peripatetics involved in Athens's alliance with Mithridates. Apellicon seems to have been in possession of Aristotle's writings at the time, but the fate of the latter's works is not clear. There is evidence, however, that in the first or second half of the 1st century B.C.E., Andronicus of Rhodes, working either in Rome or in Athens, produced an edition of Aristotle's courses, dividing them into treatises. Starting from the time of their publication, these texts played a major role in the history of European thought.

The evolution of the Academy after Polemon was quite complex. As we have seen, the problem of orthodoxy in the Platonic school was complicated by the fact that the dialogues presented quite diverse philosophical positions. Arcesilaus inaugurated the Academy's "skeptical" period, which was marked by a radical theoretical shift. However, the school did not change its name. Arcesilaus is said to have admired Plato and to have owned his library (Diogenes Laertius, *Lives* IV.32; Philodemus, *Academicorum Index* XIX.14–16). This probably means that he intended to be faithful to Plato's writings. What we know about the way the school functioned shows that it followed the practices of its time. We have lists of disciples and precise indications about where the various masters taught. We know that Lacydes (late 3rd century) taught at the Academy, in the Lacydeus garden, and that Carneades, Carneades the Younger, and Cratetes of Tarsus taught in the gymnasium or in the exedra. What we know about the succession of scholarchs in the period is rather complicated and unclear; there were numerous schisms and regroupings. Such shifts occurred in particular around the time of a new scholarch's election, when it was customary for disgruntled members to leave the group (a practice begun by the Academicians in Speusippus's day).

In the Academy, the masters entrusted their favorite disciples with the task of pulling together their notes and ensuring the publication of their courses, as was done in the Peripatus. This was the origin of some malicious anecdotes of a type also attested in the medical schools: for example, Arcesilaus was accused of altering, inventing, or burning Crantor's courses. Pythodorus transcribed Arcesilaus's lessons; Zeno of Sidon and Diogenes of Tarsus transcribed those of Carneades. The latter's notes were reread in public (as was the case for those of Isocrates and Theophrastus), and we know that Carneades severely reproached Zeno for his editorial work, while he praised Diogenes for his.

At the time Athens was reconquered by Sulla, the current scholarch, Philon, left for Rome, where his teaching met with success. His disciple Antiochus of Ascalon left Athens for Alexandria during that period, then returned to Athens to teach at the Ptolemaion (a gymnasium with its own library). It is not clear whether he succeeded Philon or whether he started a new school called the Ancient Academy in reaction against the Skeptics' Academy; the sources are ambiguous (Philodemus, *Academicorum Index* XXXIV.33; Cicero, *Brutus* 307; Plutarch, *Lucullus* 42). In any case, Antiochus did have a school, and he was succeeded by his brother and disciple Ariston, Cicero's master and a friend of Brutus.

The school had been in a process of disintegration for some time. The abandonment of its initial site, the countless modifications of its doctrines, the quarrels over the appointment of scholarchs, and the establishment of autonomous schools were all factors in the Academy's gradual disappearance from view. Ariston's disciples Cratippus of Pergamum and Ariston of Alexandria became Peripatetics. The former taught Horace, Brutus, and Cicero's son, also named Cicero, who obtained Roman citizenship for his master, while a decree of the Areopagus urged Cratippus to remain in Athens to teach. In Philon's day, a certain Aenesidemus, who may have been a former Academician, criticized the philosophy taught in the Academy, charging that it was nothing but Stoicism in disguise; he gave renewed impetus to Skeptic philosophy.

Epicureanism and Stoicism seem to have survived longer. When St. Paul arrived in the Areopagus in Athens, around 52 C.E., he found only Stoic and Epicurean philosophers (Acts 18:18). Hermarchus and Polystratus were Epicurus's first successors, and in Cicero's day Zeno of Sidon and Phaedrus were scholarchs. Diogenes Laertius points out that, unlike the other schools, which had vanished, the Epicurean school had had an uninterrupted line of scholarchs up to his own day (*Lives* X.11). Two epigraphs by the emperor Hadrian make it clear that the school in fact still had its original site in Epicurus's garden, on the road leading to the Academy. Hadrian granted money for the construction of a gymnasium as well as funds to meet the philosophers' material needs; however, confronted with their pressing demands for subsidies, on several occasions he urged the Epicureans to return to the ideal of a modest life that their master had advocated. The imperial decree was to be preserved in the school, along with Epicurus's writings and works.

Compared with the intellectual atmosphere of the other schools, especially the Academy, with its complex doctrinal evolution, Epicurus's garden seems somewhat monotonous. Numenius of Apamea (2nd century C.E.) praised the school's unshakeable faithfulness to its master's thought. Not that there were no internal debates; however, to judge by notes written by Philodemus of Gadara, they focused chiefly on the interpretation and development of Epicurus's seminal ideas and those of his intimate friends. Some critics challenged the school's traditions and claimed to be referring directly back to Epicurus; such moves were characteristic of all schools in all periods. The importance of Epicurus's writings for the school's identity led his disciples to study the master's works philologically, as doctors studied Hippocrates' writings.

After Chrysippus, the importance of the Stoic school seems to have declined in Athens. We know the names of his successors, Zeno of Tarsus, Diogenes of Babylon, and Antipater of Tarsus, and we have a few fragments of their work. We know that Antipater went against tradition in his old age and taught in his own home rather than in the Stoa. Later, Panaetius took over the school, having first been *proexagein* (the term is unclear; it may designate someone who gave preparatory courses) under Antipater; a certain Paranomus played the same role under Panaetius. The latter appears to have gone back to teach at the main Stoa. In this school, too, theoretical innovations were presented as interpretations of Zeno's thought, but opposing arguments were probably quite common as well. Successors to Zeno continued to be named until the end of the 2nd century C.E. (*Inscriptiones atticae* II.1155). We find no references to property belonging to the school.

Alexandria was one of the greatest scientific centers of the Hellenistic period. The Ptolemaic sovereigns encouraged study and research, under the influence of the Aristotelians Theophrastus, Straton of Lampsacus, and Demetrius of Phaleron (Diogenes Laertius, *Lives* V.37, 58, 77). The influence of the Peripatetic philosophy was present in a general way, but conceptual links between Peripatetic philosophy and Alexandrian science are hard to find. The term *Peripatetic* was applied at that time to any educated person and to all biographers—even those with anti-Aristotelian leanings—who came from Alexandria (Hermippus, Satyrus, Sotion, and others). In contrast, Stoic philosophy had little influence on Alexandrian cultural life.

The great Library founded by the Ptolemaics contained more than four hundred thousand volumes, including the works of Plato and Aristotle. Galen tells us that the kings had ordered the confiscation of all books transported by ships docking in Alexandria; the books were to be returned only after they had been copied (*Galeni in Hippocratis epidemiarum librum iii commentaria iii*, p. 606). The Museum was located next to the royal palace. Like the Athenian schools, it included a *peripatos*, an amphitheater, and a great room for banquets attended by all its members. It was common property, and someone named by the king was in charge of maintaining a cult to the Muses (Strabo, XVII.I.8). Members of the group were exempt from paying taxes (*Orientis Graeci Inscriptione Selectae* 714), and they were supported by revenues from the Museum's own property. Their activity was more philologic and scientific than philosophic; according to Philon of Byzantium, even technological research was encouraged.

This community of scholars kept strictly to itself, not mixing with local culture, despite the great tributes to the ancient wisdom of the Egyptians paid by Herodotus, Plato, and Aristotle. Alexandria always remained a Greek city situated outside the confines of Egypt proper.

The Ptolemaics welcomed various philosophers to their court, such as the Stoic Sphaerus, the Cyrenaics Theodorus and Hegesias, and the Epicurean Colotes, who dedicated his treatise *On the Point That It Is Not Possible Even to Live According to the Doctrines of Other Philosophers* to Philadelphus. But there were no real philosophic schools until the 1st century B.C.E., when the schools in Athens were destroyed by Sulla. Antiochus of Ascalon, as we have seen, spent some time in Alexandria, but the Platonics Eudorus, Ariston, Cratippus, and Aenesidemus also taught there regularly, along with a certain Potamon, the founder of eclecticism, who chose from each sect the maxims that he liked best. His school did not last very long (Diogenes Laertius, *Lives* I.21).

In this period, Alexandria was also a very important center for teaching medicine. The school of Herophilus, a disciple of Praxagoras of Cos, had prospered there for centuries. This was a private institution, probably located in Herophilus's own house. Alexandria's kings supported the school's practice of dissecting cadavers and of vivisection, contrary to Greek tradition. Herophilus in fact used criminals released from the royal prisons (von Staden, Testimonia 63a). He trained paying disciples in his own home, as was done in the Hippocratic school: his teaching included practical exercises and readings from the master's texts. Herophilus wrote his own manuals, which constituted the conceptual and practical basis for his school throughout its long and complex history.

After Herophilus, the school took particular philological interest in the works of Hippocrates, producing glossaries, commentaries (some written by order of the Ptolemaic kings), critical editions, doxographic works, and polemics against the other schools. The rival Empirical school, and later Galen, produced the same sorts of works. The Empirical school was founded in the 3rd century B.C.E. by Philinos of Cos; it challenged Herophilus's precepts. In the 1st century B.C.E., Herophilus's school gave rise to other schools, such as the one that was established in Laodicea, near the temple of the god Men Karou.

GREECE AND ROME FROM THE FIRST CENTURY B.C.E. TO THE THIRD CENTURY C.E.

Rome's attitude toward philosophy was at first reminiscent of that of Athens, but with more rigor. In the 2nd century B.C.E. a series of decrees led to the expulsion of the Greek philosophers from Rome, and the Roman world opened up only slowly to philosophy. The most famous episode has to do with three philosophers sent by Athens as ambassadors to the Roman Senate in 155 B.C.E.: the Academician Carneades, the Stoic Diogenes, and the Peripatetic Critolaus (no Epicureans among them). The three of them alarmed Cato to such an extent that he promptly had them expelled (Plutarch, *Lives*, "Cato," m22).

But the ruling classes began to protect philosophers. Panaetius stayed in the home of Scipio Aemilianus in Rome and accompanied him to the eastern Mediterranean (Cicero, *Academica* 2.ii.5). This first example typifies the situation of philosophers in Rome: generally speaking, noble Romans went to hear the Greek philosophers in their own homeland, or took them as spiritual counselors or teachers for their children. Many other examples can be cited: Tiberius Gracchus took the Stoic Blossius of Cumae as his adviser; Philodemus of Gadara lived in Calpurnius Piso's villa in Herculaneum. The noble Romans of the day, like noble 5th-century Athenians, often opened their homes to philosophers. In "On the Virtues and the Opposing Vices," Philodemus justified accepting benefits in exchange for teaching as the best way of life for a sage (XXIII.22–30). We have seen that Philon of Larissa went to Rome, and Lucullus turned his home into a "Greek foyer," even while showing a decided preference for Antiochus of Ascalon (Plutarch, *Lucullus* 42). The quality of life of a philosopher established in the home of a noble Roman depended on the latter's goodwill, and the philosopher's existence could easily become parasitic, as is evident from caricatures penned by Petronius, Lucian, and Aulus Gellius. Philosophers would flock to the doors of rich young citizens and wait all morning for the men (who had been up all night) to wake up and receive them.

There were no authentic philosophic schools in Rome. The greatest authors of the 1st century B.C.E. and the 1st century C.E., such as Cicero, Seneca, and

Musonius Rufus, were men involved in politics who devoted only their leisure hours to writing philosophical texts in Latin. Lucretius himself, about
whom we know very little, belonged to the highest class. Certain authors,
such as Brutus, Caesar's assassin, and the emperor Marcus Aurelius, continued to write in Greek.

The custom of having philosophers as friends and clients persisted under
the empire; the Cynics and the Stoics were the first to develop such a practice.
Augustus protected the philosopher and doxographer Arius Didymus, who
was an invaluable imperial adviser. Thrasyllus, the editor of Plato's dialogues,
lived uneasily in Tiberius's court (Tacitus, *Annals* VI.20–21). Philosophers
continued to be expelled, for instance Epictetus under Domitian, at the end of
the 1st century C.E.: Epictetus took refuge in Nicopolis, where he opened a
school with full legal standing. His lessons were transcribed and published by
his disciple Arrian.

During that period, schools of philosophy proliferated throughout the
Greek world, especially in Athens, Alexandria, Tarsus, Aegae, and Pergamum;
in the West there were schools only in city-states of Greek origin, such as
Naples and Marseilles. The teaching of philosophy in schools remained a pre-
dominantly Greek affair, although among the Roman nobility there were
philosophic circles like that of Quintus Sextius, often evoked by Seneca;
Quintus Sextius gave up his political career to establish a brotherhood, a
blend of Stoicism and Neopythagoreanism (Seneca, *Epistulae* 98.13; *Naturales quaestiones* VII.32.13).

The end of the Academy and of the Peripatetic school did not spell the end
of the associated schools of thought. Independent masters surrounded by disciples, some of whom became masters in their turn, carried on the spirit of
those communities. M. Annius Ammonius, Plutarch's master, is one example.
Born in Egypt, then a resident and magistrate in Athens in the 1st century
C.E., he lived on into Domitian's era, teaching Platonic philosophy. The renaissance of Platonic thought, connected with Middle Platonism, probably originated in groups of this sort.

As an example of the activity of one of these teachers, we can recall what
Aulus Gellius said about Calvenus Taurus, his teacher of Platonic philosophy
in Athens. Taurus taught in his own home, where his visitors included important people. His teaching was largely based on readings of the Platonic texts
(Aulus Gellius, XVII.20); his disciples often took credit for deciding what to
read (I.9.9–10). The more intimate disciples were invited to closed meetings,
philosophical suppers where food was scarce but talk was plentiful. They discussed *problemata*, questions of physics and dialectics: for instance, "At what
moment does a dying person die?" "What does it mean to get up?" "Why
does oil congeal easily, while wine does not?" (VII.13; XVII.8). We have an
abundant literature concerning *problemata* of this type, passed on in the
names of Aristotle, Alexander of Afrodisias, Plutarch, and others. The philos-

ophy of this period is above all exegesis, and even the authors who protested vigorously against this tendency, such as Epictetus (*Diatribai* II.21.6e, 23, 27) were in the habit of constantly interpreting the texts of past authors in their own pedagogical practice.

The first to follow this path, as we have seen, were the Epicureans, but they were soon followed by the other schools. The purpose of the commentaries was the clarification and systematization of the masters' doctrines; this was particularly necessary in the case of Aristotle and Plato, but there are even hostile commentaries written against works by masters of the other schools. Even the history of the previous interpretations was taken into account in this period. Manuals and introductions to the founders' works began to be written, such as those Albinus and Alcinous produced about Plato.

Athens's prestige as the seat of the chief philosophic schools of the Hellenistic period and as the place of residence of private teachers associated with the various schools led Marcus Aurelius, in 176 C.E., to establish teaching chairs in Athens for all branches of knowledge, at the expense of the empire, as a gift to humanity as a whole. Chairs of Stoic, Platonic, Epicurean, and Peripatetic philosophy were created: positions were awarded for life, pay was very high, and candidates were selected by a vote of the best citizens (Lucian *Eunuchus*, V.3). The initial selection of philosophy professors was made by Herodes Atticus (Philostratus, *Lives of the Sophists* 2). The object was to teach the various types of philosophy to the young, who tended, as we have seen, to frequent the major philosophic schools in turn.

We know very little about these schools, although we have the names of some of the Peripatetic philosophers, such as Alexander of Damascus, who had met Galen in Rome and consulted with him before going to Athens. The most important name associated with these schools is that of Alexander of Aphrodisias, who alludes to being named master of philosophy by the emperor (*De fato* 1). He declares that he is head of Aristotelian philosophy by virtue of this charge, which gives him special preeminence; his first product was a polemical text against the Stoics. What characterized the "chair" was the cultural preeminence the master enjoyed among his disciples, and the polemical role the master played vis-à-vis other schools. The few minor works we have by Alexander include instructional texts; there may also be some texts by his disciples. We do not know how the school ended; the last mention of it indicates that Eubulus, a teacher of Platonism, had contacts with Plotinus.

There were chairs of philosophy in other cities as well: Galen completed his studies in the four schools in Pergamum, while Apollonius of Tyana did the same thing near Aegae. Both undertook their philosophical studies in their youth, at about age fourteen, and pursued them for only a few years.

In the Greco-Roman age, medical teaching continued as before to be conducted privately, in the school of a master. There were centers in which the teaching was carried out by many instructors, as in Ephesus, Pergamum, and Alexandria, but these were never official schools, nor did they specialize in the various branches of medicine. Teaching continued to involve both lessons and clinical practice. There were forms of common life, such as dining together (Galen, *De tremore, palpitatione, convusione et rigore* 7). The masters often compiled their lessons in written form, or else the disciples transcribed them. But there were some masters who limited themselves to oral teaching. The disciple who went off after the training period to practice medicine in a city often took with him a written compilation of his master's lessons. Sometimes the schools were possessive about the masters' writings and refused to show them to anyone outside the group.

Reading the Hippocratic texts was part of a doctor's education, and thus there were many written commentaries, corresponding to the oral commentary on the texts produced inside the school. We have a number of written commentaries by Galen: these are works with a practical aim, directed at disciples who already had acquired a basic knowledge of medicine. Galen sought to establish the authenticity of the Hippocratic texts, and the correct reading of difficult passages, in a conservative spirit; he shunned erudition and philology as ends in themselves (he referred to them as "Sophistics"), and for this reason he did not concern himself with the history of interpretations of the text. In this respect the medical commentaries differ from those produced in the philosophical schools, though they are otherwise very similar.

THE NEOPLATONIC ERA

In the middle of the 3rd century, Plotinus carried on and renewed the tradition of the philosophical schools. According to Porphyry *(Life of Plotinus)*, the master lived in a patrician residence, where he founded a genuine school made up of a somewhat complex group, including faithful disciples and less diligent dignitaries. One of the latter, Amelius, seems to have collaborated with his master in teaching; he was assigned to write a commentary on *Timaeus* (Proclus, *In Platonis Timaeum commentaria* II.300.25), polemical texts against rival schools, and refutations of the objections of unpersuaded disciples. Plotinus also tutored quite young disciples, aiming to turn them into accomplished philosophers. His teaching was based on exegeses of the texts of Plato and Aristotle, which were read and discussed during meetings of the school, along with the principal commentaries. Plotinus encouraged his disciples to raise objections, but one can detect the beginnings of a certain intolerance toward the dialogic method.

In his teaching, Plotinus treated his pupils with cordiality. On four occasions during his lifetime he experienced a mystical union with divinity. His books were written in a single draft, without even being recopied, as if they were already present in his mind. Polemics against the other schools were generally left to his disciples, though Plotinus himself wrote refutations. His group gave banquets and lectures to celebrate the birthdays of Socrates and Plato.

Plotinus's school was the only true philosophic school that Rome ever knew. Other philosophers established quite similar schools elsewhere, such as the school of Aedesius at Pergamum (Eunapius, *Vitae sophistarum* VII.1–2). Except for these schools, Neoplatonic philosophy was concentrated in Athens and Alexandria.

The school that Plato had founded in Athens did not survive past the 1st century B.C.E. However, its prestige lasted for centuries, and in the 4th century C.E. it was reestablished as an institution. Athens remained an extremely important center of literary and philosophical studies in this period, and virtually all of its cultural life remained in the hands of pagans; Christian students made up only a small though combative minority (Gregory of Nazianzus, *Orationes* XLIII.14–24). This was the climate in which Plutarch of Athens, descendant of an aristocratic family connected with the Mystery tradition, undertook to reestablish Plato's school in his own home, located south of the Acropolis in an affluent residential neighborhood. As in Alexandria, Neoplatonic philosophy was the privilege of the well-to-do. Damascius's *Life of Isodorus* provides many details.

Plutarch once again gave rise to a foundation, a quite wealthy institution that grew over time, thanks to numerous bequests: in Proclus's time, its income amounted to 1,000 *nomismata* per year. The foundation, like those of the 4th century B.C.E., sought to ensure financial independence for philosophers. In an outburst of enthusiastic archaism, Damascius declared that Plato's garden was still part of the school's property; according to him, this property had been maintained without interruption for ten centuries. While this is not credible, it may be that the Platonists had acquired a garden that was, or was thought to be, on the grounds where Plato had taught.

The school's goal was to read Plato's dialogues, comment on them, and spread Platonism among its disciples. The master played the role of guide in reading and studying. His best disciples lived with him and were treated as his sons, according to ancient custom. The characteristic vocabulary of the schools reappeared: disciples *(mathetai)*, meetings *(sunousia)*. There may have been a second, subordinate master, as Amelius was for Plotinus, but we cannot be certain. Teaching was provided strictly in the form of lectures, and Plutarch of Athens rarely allowed a student to ask questions and interrupt his explanations. Still, a certain tradition of discussion and dissension persisted within the school, such as the disagreement that pitted Domninos against Proclos. A mystical, theurgic tendency linked to the mystery cults paralleled the philosophic teaching and sometimes overtook it; this was the case for Aegae, in contrast to Damascius. Owing to its real estate holdings, the school was able to subsist until the beginning of the 6th century, whereas the schools founded by Plotinus in Rome, Iamblichus in Syria (early 4th century), and Aedesius in Pergamum did not outlive their founders. We have a fairly reliable list of the successive heads of Plutarch's school up to Damascius.

The rebirth of the Athens school came about in a hostile environment, at a time when Christianity was showing its most sectarian face. Philosophers had to stay indoors or find a deserted place to sacrifice to their gods (Marinus, *Life of Proclus* 11.e.29). Proclus could still cherish the illusion that the domination of Christianity and the persecution of pagans would come to an end, but Damascius appears more pessimistic, despite all his efforts to strengthen the Athenian school, and Simplicius speaks of the complete destruction of culture and philosophy. Damascius's intransigent anti-Christian stance led to the prohibition of his teaching.

In 529 a decree of the emperor Justinian banned, among other things, the teaching of philosophy (Malagas, *Chronographia* XVIII). The closing of the school was definitive: Plato was no longer taught in Athens. A few years later, we are told (Agathias, *Histories* II.28–32), several philosophers, including Damascius and Simplicius, decided to emigrate to Persia, to the court of Chosroes (king of Armenia) or to the city-state of Carrhae. The following year, a treaty between the two empires allowed the philosophers to return to their homeland and live there in peace; we do not know if they had permission to teach. Philosophers must have been viewed as important figures if they were singled out for special attention in a treatise between two great emperors of the time. Damascius may not have returned to Athens, however; he seems to have died in Syria. As for Simplicius, the author of important commentaries on Aristotelian physics, we know relatively little. He participated in the expedition to Persia, and after the 532 treaty was able to devote himself to writing commentaries, as a private citizen, either in Athens or in Carrhae. After his death, there is no further evidence of pagan philosophers in Athens.

In Alexandria, a long line of professors taught Platonic philosophy, for example Ammonius Saccas (who was Plotinus's master), Origen, and many others. Philosophy teachers in Alexandria are thought to have been paid on occasion from the public treasure, though the evidence for this is scanty and uncertain; they may simply have been paid by their own disciples. A certain Anatolius, senator and philosopher, is said to have been chosen by his fellow citizens to reestablish the school in Athens. A Christian who later became bishop of Laodicea, he may have been Iamblichus's teacher. In the 3rd century, relations between the pagan and Christian communities were somewhat tense, since philosophic teaching remained the privilege of the pagans and the upper classes, while the Christianized masses looked on the practice of philosophy with suspicion. These relations grew worse in the following century.

The mathematician and philosopher Hypatia, a disciple of Plotinus at a century's remove, conducted her teaching in public; she fell victim to the hostility of a violent Christian crowd, stirred up by the patriarch Cyril, and was massacred in front of the door to her house. Supported by imperial power, the Christians made the pagans' lives increasingly difficult; physical conflicts between the two groups were not uncommon (Damascius, *Life of Isodorus* pp. 77.1–17; 255. 2–3; Zacharias Scholasticus, *Life of Severus* p. 23.26).

The last pagan philosopher of the Alexandrian school was Olympiodorus, who defended pagan doctrines quite courageously. After him, there were only Christian masters in Alexandria, foremost among them Philoponus, who defined himself as a grammarian *(grammatikos)* rather than as a philosopher. In addition to publishing treatises by Ammonius (435–526), adapting them as he saw fit, Philoponus wrote a polemical treatise against the pagans, *Against Proclus on the Eternity of the World,* in the same year that the Athens school was closed. Elias, apparently a disciple of Olympiodorus, and David were also Christians. So was Stephanus, who was named professor of philosophy at the imperial court of Byzantium after Heraclius acceded to the throne. Stephanus appears to have been the last of the Neoplatonic Alexandrian philosophers.

CARLO NATALI
Translated by Catherine Porter and Jeannine Pucci

Bibliography

Texts and Translations

Antigonus of Carystus. *Fragments.* Ed. and trans. Tiziano Dorandi. Paris: Les Belles Lettres, 1999.

Diogenes Laertius. *Lives of Eminent Philosophers.* Trans. R. D. Hicks. 2 vols. Loeb Classical Library.

Galeni in Hippocratis epidemiarum. Ed. G. C. Kühn. Leipzig: B. G. Teubner, 1821–1833.

Hadrian. In Simone Follet, "Lettres d'Hadrien aux Epicuriens d'Athènes." *Revue des études grecques* 107 (1994): 158–171.

Inscriptiones atticae aetatis quae est inter Euclidis annum et Augusti tempora. Ed. U. Koehler. 5 vols. Berlin: G. Reimer, 1877–1895.

Philodemus. *Agli amici di scuola* (PHerc. 1005). Ed. and trans. A. Angeli. Naples: Bibliopolis, 1988.

———. *Storia dei filosofi: Platone e l'Academia* (PHerc. 1021 and 164). Ed. and trans. Tiziano Dorandi. Naples: Bibliopolis, 1991. (See also the selections in Konrad Gaiser, *Philodems academica.)*

———. *Storia dei filosofi: La Stoa da Zenone a Panezio* (PHerc. 1018). Ed. Tiziano Dorandi. Leiden and New York: E. J. Brill, 1994.

Plato. *Epistles*. In *Timaeus; Critias; Cleitophon; Menexenus; Epistles*. Trans. R. G. Bury. Loeb Classical Library.

Porphyry. *Plotinus*. Trans. A. H. Armstrong. Loeb Classical Library.

Studies

Burkert, Walter. *Weisheit und Wissenschaft: Studien zu Pythagoras, Philolaos und Platon*. Nuremberg: H. Carl, 1962.

Cambiano, Giuseppe. *La filosofia in Grecia e a Roma*. Rome and Bari: Laterza, 1983.

Clay, Diskin. "Individual and Community in the First Generation of the Epicurean School." In *Syzetesis: Studi sull' epicureismo greco e romano offerti a Marcello Gigante*. 2 vols. Naples: G. Macchiaroli, 1983. Pp. 255–279.

De Witt, Norman Wentworth. "Organization and Procedure in Epicurean Groups." *Classical Philology* 31 (1936): 205–211.

Donini, P. L. *Le Scuole, l'anima, l'impero: La filosofia antica da Antioco a Plotino*. Turin: Rosenberg and Sellier, 1982.

Evrard, Etienne. "A quel titre Hypatie enseigna-t-elle la philosophie?" *Revue des études grecques* 90 (1977): 69–74.

Fowden, Garth. "The Platonist Philosopher and His Circle in Late Antiquity." *Philosophia* (Athens) 7 (1977): 359–383.

Fraser, Peter Marshall. *Ptolemaic Alexandria*. Oxford: Clarendon Press, 1972.

Gaiser, Konrad. *Philodems Academica: Die Berichte über Platon und die alte Akademie in zwei herkulanensischen Papyri*. Stuttgart-Bad Canstatt: Fromman-Holzboog, 1988.

Garbarino, Giovanna, ed. *Roma e la filosofia greca dalle origini alla fine del II secolo a.C.: Raccolta di testi con introduzione e commento*. Turin: G. B. Paravia, 1973.

Glucker, John. *Antiochus and the Late Academy*. Göttingen: Vandenhoeck and Ruprecht, 1978.

Goulet, Richard, ed. *Dictionnaire des philosophes anciens*. Vols. I–II (A–D). Paris: CNRS, 1989–1994.

Griffin, Miriam T., and Jonathan Barnes, eds. *Philosophia togata: Essays on Philosophy and Roman Society*. Oxford: Clarendon Press; New York: Oxford University Press, 1989.

Haase, Wolfgang, and I. Temporini. *Aufstieg und Niedergang der Römischen Welt*. Vol. 36 ("Philosophie"), vol. 37 ("Wissenschaft"). Berlin and New York: Walter de Gruyter, 1987–1994.

Hadot, Ilsetraut. *Le problème du néoplatonisme alexandrin: Hiéroclès et Simplicius*. Paris: Institut d'études augustiniennes, 1978.

Hadot, Pierre. *Qu'est-ce que la philosophie antique?* Paris: Gallimard, 1995.

Jouanna, Jacques. *Hippocrates*. Baltimore: Johns Hopkins University Press, 1998.

Lynch, John Patrick. *Aristotle's School: A Study of a Greek Educational Institution*. Berkeley: University of California Press, 1972.

Marrou, Henri-Irenée. *A History of Education in Antiquity*. Trans. George Lamb. New York: Sheed and Ward, 1956; New American Library, 1964.

Meyer, Ben F., and E. P. Sanders, eds. *Jewish and Christian Self-Definition*. Vol. 3: *Self-Definition in the Graeco-Roman World*. London: SCM Press, 1982; Philadelphia: Fortress Press, 1983.

Müller, Reimar. *Die Epikureische Gesellschaftstheorie*. Berlin: Akademie-Verlag, 1972.

Natali, Carlo. *Bios theoretikos: La vita di Aristotele e l'organizzazione della sua scuola.* Bologna: Il Mulino, 1991.

Staden, Heinrich von. *Herophilus: The Art of Medicine in Early Alexandria.* Cambridge and New York: Cambridge University Press, 1989.

Taormina, Daniela Patrizia. *Plutarco di Atene: L'uno, l'anima, le forme.* Rome: University of Catania, 1988.

Trabattoni, Franco. "Per una biografia di Damascio." *Rivista di Storia della Filosofia* 40 (1985): 170–201.

OBSERVATION AND RESEARCH

To WHAT EXTENT did ancient Greek philosophers and scientists engage in systematic empirical research? How far, in particular, did they attempt controlled experimentation? In what circumstances, and for what reasons, did they undertake programs of detailed observation? At what point, and again for what reasons, were the value and importance of such programs explicitly recognized in self-conscious methodologies?

To begin to answer these questions we need, first, to make certain conceptual distinctions. First, we should distinguish between observation and deliberate research, although the one no doubt shades into the other. It is not our task here to attempt to analyze everything that any Greek philosopher or scientist can be said to have observed, in the sense of carefully perceived. Rather, what we are concerned with is the practice of observation: it is deliberate and systematic observation that entitles us to use the term *research*.

The behavior of animals, the habitats of plants, and the configurations of constellations have always been possible subjects of interest, and in the first two cases, especially, the ethnographic literature demonstrates that many modern societies, including many without any advanced technology whatsoever, possess detailed and often quite recondite knowledge, acquired through careful observation. We should guard against two assumptions here: first, that such observations are always carried out with practical interests mainly, if not solely, in mind, and second, that the knowledge, once acquired, is never subject to revision. Of course the uses of plants as foods and medicines are of interest to every society. Often, however, their symbolic associations, values, and significance are an added focus of attention. The stars may be studied to help determine the seasons or the weather, but their groupings may also carry powerful symbolic associations. Again, although the stock of knowledge may be represented as stable, that may be misleading. What is known or believed about plants or animals may, in the process of transmission from one generation to the next, be subject to modification. How far any such modification is recognized *as such* will vary. But just as an understanding of the uses of plants as medicines is slowly built up from observation and experiment in the loose sense of trial-and-error procedures, so continued experience may serve as a source of critical reflection on even well-entrenched beliefs.

Similar factors are at work in early scientific research, but the extra factors that scientific research involves are that the scientist is engaged in the acquisition of systematic understanding and in the resolution of theoretical issues. These issues may take the form of specific problems, such as whether the earth is flat or round, whether plants exhibit gender difference, whether the seat of cognitive activity is the brain, the heart, or some other organ. However, some detailed scientific programs of research do not serve to resolve clearly formulated problems but present themselves as more purely descriptive in aim. They may, for example, be directed to establishing a classification. Yet even when the research is said to be carried out with a view merely to establishing the data, theory enters in, in determining what counts as the significant data. Every classification presupposes a conceptual framework of some kind. Clearly in some actual classifications, symbolic considerations or practical human interests may be the dominant factor.

Aristotle correctly points to a distinction between the observations carried out by fishermen in the course of their work and those that are undertaken specifically for the purposes of establishing data about fish. That is a valid distinction between possible motives in the conduct of observation. However, when Aristotle proclaims his own interest to be in the investigation of animals for its own sake, he too has, of course, *theoretical* concerns, for instance in determining the genera and species of fish. Moreover, we should recognize that the quality of the observations conducted is not determined solely by the expressed intentions of the observer. The fishermen whom Aristotle consulted sometimes appear to have known more than he did about the facts of the matter—about the actual behavior of fish—although their observations were not undertaken for the purposes of scientific research.

The distinction between observation and theory is a relative, not an absolute one. No observation, no research, is undertaken *without* some theoretical interest, without some theoretical framework, and the interaction between theory and observation will be of particular concern to us in this study. The theoretical framework often provides the key both to the domains of phenomena explored and to the way in which they were investigated, and this in two distinct ways. First, there is the question just mentioned, of the motivations of research: how far is there a clear intention to investigate the phenomena for the purposes of understanding? But then second, and more specifically, theoretical frameworks will be crucially relevant to the way in which the problems addressed are formulated. As we shall see time and again, in Greek science a program of research is directed to the resolution of quite specific problems. Part of our task here, then, will be to identify those problems, to consider why they were the specific focus of attention, and to explore the ways in which the conduct of observations was affected by the particular theoretical issues being investigated.

These references to the theoretical framework of observation lead me to my final preliminary conceptual point, namely the distinction between the *practice* of observation and research, and the *explicit recognition* of their importance. It is one thing for a scientist or philosopher to engage in detailed investigations of animals, plants, minerals, stars, musical concords, or diseases. It is another to have an explicit methodology that allots a determinate role to empirical data in scientific study. A further part of our task will be to consider at what point, and for what reasons, Greek philosophers and scientists developed such methodologies. In other words, when was the importance of observation and research self-consciously recognized?

I have spoken so far of Greek philosophers and scientists in general terms. I am concerned, here, not just with whose primary interests lay in metaphysics, let alone in moral philosophy, but also with those who engaged in any of the different domains of what the Greeks called *phusikē*, the study of nature. This includes, at one end of the spectrum, what we should call the exact sciences, notably astronomy, acoustics or harmonics, and optics. These are called the "more physical of the mathematical studies" by Aristotle in *Physics*, 194a7ff. At the other end of the spectrum we must also include not just what we call the life sciences (biology, botany, and so on) but also medicine. Naturally, we must pay due attention to the fact that the primary concerns of different types of investigators—doctors, astronomers, writers on music, philosophers, and so on—differ in important ways. Nevertheless all have a contribution to make in answering the principal questions we have posed.

Special difficulties are presented by the unevenness of the source material. We have comparatively rich sources for medicine in the 5th and 4th centuries B.C.E. Aristotle, Galen, and Ptolemy are represented by considerable bodies of extant work. However, our sources for the early Pythagoreans, for the 5th-century atomists, and for some of the major Hellenistic biologists are very thin, and we have to depend on the often tendentious reports and interpretations of other writers. We have to make the best use of the evidence we have but acknowledge the tentative nature of our conclusions, given the biases and lacunae in our sources.

In what must be a highly selective survey, I shall divide the discussion into three main sections on broadly chronological lines: the evidence for observation and research in the period before Aristotle, the theory and the practice of observation and research by Aristotle himself, and the role of observation and research in philosophy and science in the post-Aristotelian period.

PRESOCRATIC NATURAL PHILOSOPHERS

At first sight it might appear that there is little positive, but a good deal that is negative, to say about either the theory or the practice of observation and research, so far as the Presocratic natural philosophers are concerned. The first point would relate to their practice. Neither in their general cosmological theories nor in their reported specific explanations of detailed natural phenomena does much attention seem to be paid to the collection and evaluation of empirical data. Second, in certain prominent epistemological doctrines, reason is privileged, and perception downgraded, in such a way that one might speak not just of an indifference to empirical research but of an attitude of positive hostility toward it.

Both points are certainly valid to some extent. However, both stand in need of qualification. First, so far as epistemological theory goes, it is true that in the tradition represented by the Eleatic philosophers, Parmenides, Zeno, and Melissus, the evidence of the senses is condemned as misleading. Parmenides warns, in frg. 7, against being deceived by the senses and ordinary belief: "Do not let habit, born of experience, force you to let wander your heedless eye and echoing ear or tongue along this road" (that is, the Way of Seeming). Again Melissus, in his frg. 8, develops a reductio argument that starts from the common assumption that the evidence of sight and hearing is acceptable, but ends with their rejection. They tell us that things change, whereas it is clear, Melissus believes, that change is impossible. This is on the usual Eleatic grounds, that nothing can come to be from what is not.

These anti-empirical views are echoed, though in modified form, by several later philosophers, and the downgrading of perception was to be a well-developed theme, with many variations, in Plato. However, there is another side to the picture. Several of the Presocratic philosophers produce dicta that show that they explicitly set at least some store by what we may call research. Thus Xenophanes at one point insisted that "the gods have not revealed all things to men from the beginning: but by seeking men find out better in time" (frg. 18). Both Empedocles and Anaxagoras are critical of the deliveries of perception, but accord them a role nevertheless. Anaxagoras is reported to have said that "through the weakness [of the senses] we are unable to judge the truth" (frg. 21). Yet in a further famous dictum (frg. 21a) he advocated using the "things that appear" as a "vision" of things that are obscure. We are told that that principle was approved by Democritus, who elsewhere (frg. 125) insisted that the mind derives its data from the senses, even if he also categorized the senses as yielding only "bastard" knowledge by contrast to the "legitimate" knowledge we have of such principles as atoms and the void (frg. 11).

But what may we say about the actual performance of the early natural philosophers in observation and research? Their general cosmological doctrines are usually based on certain recurrent models or analogies, representing the cosmos as a whole as a political state, as a living creature, or as an artifact. Neither those doctrines nor the overall theories concerning the basic constituents of physical objects that go with them make much use of direct empirical observation. In the case of Presocratic element theories, the same familiar examples are cited over and over again—interpreted differently according to the theory concerned. These same "data" were indeed treated as evidence *for* those theories, despite the fact that it must have been well known to the theorists who cited the data that their interpretation was contested.

Thus it was commonly supposed that air changes to cloud, then to water, then to earth and indeed to stones. This sequence is referred to in connection with the theories of both Anaximenes and Anaxagoras, and it even reappears in Melissus's refutation of change. Yet Anaximenes interpreted the sequence in terms of his principles of rarefaction and condensation: each of the changes is an instance of condensation, while air also "rarefies" to become fire. However, Anaxagoras cited the same "data" in connection with his theory that "in everything there is a portion of everything." His view of the changes would be that air already contains cloud, water, earth, stones, and indeed every other kind of thing, and that all that happens in change is that the proportion of the different kinds of things change in the objects we see. Even Melissus, when he argues from the position of his opponents in order to refute their ideas about change, puts it that "earth and stones seem to come to be from water."

This example indicates that the criteria by which Presocratic physical theories were judged relate to their simplicity or economy or to the force of the abstract arguments used to justify them, rather than to the richness of the empirical data they encompassed. In the main, the Presocratic philosophers made few attempts to *extend* the data available to them by empirical research; nor did they, as a general rule, try to *decide between* rival interpretations of the same known or assumed data by experiment.

There are, however, exceptions to what remains the general rule. Thus Xenophanes (one of the philosophers cited above whose epistemological doctrines incorporate a recommendation to engage in research) is one such exception. According to an admittedly late source, Hippolytus, Xenophanes cited the evidence of what we should call fossils to support his view that the relations between land and sea are subject to fluctuation and that what is now dry land was once covered by sea. Not only are shells found inland and on mountains, but also the impressions of certain living organisms turn up in the quarries of Syracuse, on Paros, and on Malta. Whether or not Xenophanes himself engaged in his own research in this connection, he was evidently at some pains to marshal what are no mere common-or-garden observations in support of his theory.

But the best example of more sustained empirical research in pre-Platonic philosophy relates to certain investigations in the field of harmonics attributable to some of the Pythagoreans. Admittedly the stories that purport to record Pythagoras's own experiments, leading to the discovery of the intervals corresponding to the concords of octave, fifth, and fourth, are late fabrications. Indeed many of the stories relate to tests that would not, in fact, have yielded the results claimed. However, the tradition of empirical investigation of the musical harmonies certainly antedates Plato, since in *The Republic* he criticizes this approach to the problems. At *Republic* 530d Socrates first agrees with the view, which he ascribes to the Pythagoreans, that harmonics and astronomy are "sister sciences." But he then goes on to criticize as "useless labor" the attempt to measure audible sounds and concords against one another. Evidently others besides the Pythagoreans are involved. But he objects to the Pythagoreans too, for "looking for numbers in [the] heard harmonies, and not ascending to problems." For Plato himself, the chief aim of the proper study of harmonics that he has in mind in *The Republic* is to train the young potential philosopher-kings in abstract thought: for that purpose empirical research is otiose, even a distraction. The Pythagoreans themselves, however, on this testimony, appear to have engaged in some detailed investigations of an empirical nature in connection with their examination of the underlying relationships of musical scales and harmonies.

Here, then, we have evidence of a more deliberate program involving observation and research. But we must be clear that the reasons for undertaking it are quite distinctive. We hear from a variety of sources, Aristotle especially, that the Pythagoreans maintained that "all things are numbers," though the interpretation of that dictim is far from clear and indeed disputed. Aristotle represents some of them, at least, as committed to the belief that numbers *constitute* things: they are (as Aristotle would have put it) the matter of which other things are composed. It may, however, be more likely that the Pythagoreans, or most of them, were committed only to the much weaker doctrine that the underlying relationships of things are *expressible numerically:* on that view the concord of an octave is expressible by the ratio 1 : 2, but not constituted by that ratio as its matter. However, whichever interpretation of the dictum itself is to be adopted, it is clear that the doctrine that "all things are numbers" provided the chief stimulus to investigate the musical scales and harmonies. The aim of those investigations was undoubtedly to illustrate and support that general doctrine. So we may be clear that the first sustained empirical research in Greek philosophy had distinct theoretical aims.

The term often used for natural philosophy in early Greek texts is *peri phuseōs historia*, the inquiry concerning nature, but the kind of *historia* involved often relied heavily on abstract argument. That term, *historia*, itself was, however, often used in other contexts where research is the key characteristic of the inquiry. Two fields, especially, exemplify this in the period before Plato, namely the domain *we* call history, and medicine. Clearly the writings of Herodotus and Thucydides in each case represent the results of a very considerable effort of research. Whether the subject is past events, as in Herodotus, or contemporary ones, as in Thucydides, different accounts had to be collected and evaluated. Herodotus often intrudes in his text in the first person singular, reporting the results of his own personal observations or recording his personal opinion as to the veracity or verisimilitude of the stories he relates (although he does not always state the *basis* on which he formed his judgments). Thucydides, in turn, constantly exercises his critical skills in the assessment of the evidence both of human witnesses and of material remains, drawing, from time to time, on what we should describe as archaeological data in his reconstruction of the period leading up to the Peloponnesian War.

But while the practice of research in the domain of history provides an important part of the intellectual background of philosophy and science, it is the second field, medicine, that is more directly relevant to the development of positive attitudes toward empirical research in science. There can be no doubt that a prominent tradition in clinical medicine, as exemplified in some of the Hippocratic treatises from the 5th and 4th centuries B.C.E., both stressed the need, in principle, for careful observation and put that principle into practice. This is true, in particular, in the context of the assessment of individual case histories, though the chief preoccupation of Greek doctors was not so much diagnosis as prognosis, the foretelling of the outcome of the disease. We have, however, to investigate the contexts and motives for the efforts at observation and research we find, and assess their strengths and limitations.

We may begin with the evidence for an explicit recognition of the need for careful observation in relation to individual clinical cases. A chapter of the first book of *Epidemics* sets out an impressive list of the points to be attended to (chap. 10, Littré): "Then we must consider the patient, what food is given and who gives it . . . the conditions of climate and locality both in general and in particular, the patient's customs, mode of life, pursuits and age. Then we must consider his speech, mannerisms, silence, thoughts, habits of sleep and wakefulness, and dreams, their nature and time. Next we must note whether he plucks his hair, scratches or weeps. We must observe his paroxysms, stools, urine, sputum and vomit . . . Observe, too, sweating, shivering, chill, cough, sneezing, hiccough, the kind of breathing, belching, wind whether silent or noisy, haemorrhages and haemorrhoids. We must determine the significance of all these signs."

More famously still, the opening chapter of the treatise on *Prognostic* describes what to look for in examining a patient's face (the Hippocratic facies). The doctor should observe the color and texture of the skin, and especially the eyes, where he should study whether "they avoid the flare of light and weep involuntarily," whether "the whites are livid," whether the eyes "wander, or project, or are deeply sunken," and so on. Moreover this treatise not only tells the doctor what to look out for, but sets out some of the inferences to be drawn from particular signs. Thus this on urine (chap. 12): "Urine is best when there is a white, smooth, even deposit in it the whole time up to the crisis of the disease . . . Sediment like barley-meal in the urine is bad . . . Thin white sediment is a very bad sign, and it is even worse if it resembles bran . . . So long as the urine is thin and yellowish-red, the disease is not ripened . . . When a patient continues to pass thin raw urine for a long time and the other signs indicate recovery, the formation of an abscess should be expected in the parts below the diaphragm. When grease forms patterns like cobwebs on the surface of the urine, this constitutes a warning, for it is a sign of wasting."

Such accounts as these about how to conduct a clinical examination display a remarkable appreciation of the variety of points to be considered, and an acute sense of the need for thoroughness and attention to detail. Moreover the principles they set out were not just idealized recommendations, but were—sometimes at least—closely followed in practice. Several books of *Epidemics*, notably the first and the third, contain detailed reports of individual case histories, recording the progress of a particular patient's disease, generally day by day, over quite long periods. In some cases there are occasional observations up to the 120th day from the onset of the disease. The entries under each day vary from a single remark to an elaborate description running to some nine or ten lines. Thus in case three of the first series set out in *Epidemics* III we find this entry for the fourth day: "Fourth day; vomited small quantities of yellow bilious matter and, after a while, a small quantity of rust-coloured material. There was a small haemorrhage of pure blood from the left side of the nose: stools and urine as before: sweating about the head and shoulders; spleen enlarged; pain in the region of the thigh; a rather flabby distension of the right hypochondrium: did not sleep at night; slight delirium." In this case observations continue daily until the twenty-first day and further occasional entries are made up to the fortieth, when—exceptionally—this patient reached a crisis and recovered. I say exceptionally, for it is one of the striking features of the case histories in *Epidemics* that their authors had no compunction in setting down the details of the diseases of patients whom they failed to save. In books one and three, indeed, the majority of those recorded end in death.

Evidently the authors of these case histories successfully practice the principles recommended in the theoretical texts we considered earlier. The observations of the progress of individual cases are certainly carried out with great care and thoroughness. The reports contain few explicitly interpretative comments, and no overall theory of disease is presented. The terms used in the descriptions are, to be sure, to a greater or lesser degree "theory laden": although these treatises do not propose, nor even presuppose, any schematic doctrine of humors, references are nevertheless made, on occasion, to the "bilious" or "phlegmatic" material in the patients' discharges.

The principal aim of these case histories is clearly to provide as exact a record as possible of the cases investigated. But we can and should be more precise than this about the writers' aims. In particular we may remark that they have a distinct motive for carrying out and recording their observations *daily*—over and above a laudable desire to be thorough—in that they adhere to the common Greek medical doctrine that the courses of acute diseases are determined by what were called "critical days." These were the days on which marked changes took place in the patient's condition—whether for better or worse. Establishing the periodicity of the disease was crucial for diagnosing it, as the terminology of "quartan," "tertian," "semitertian," and so on indicates.

Moreover, particular attention is sometimes paid, in the case histories, to whether pains or exacerbations occurred on the *odd* or the *even* days from the onset of the complaint. Elsewhere in *Epidemics* (for example, I.12, Littré) we find detailed tables setting out the supposed critical periods for diseases that had crises on even days, and for those on odd days. In the Pythagorean Table of Opposites, reported by Aristotle in *Metaphysics* (986a22ff), odd is correlated with right, male, and good, and even with left, female, and evil. So the expectation that exacerbations may occur on even days may be said to correspond to Pythagorean assumptions. However, it is not necessary to see the medical writers represented in *Epidemics* as themselves all Pythagoreans, nor do they straightforwardly endorse a correlation between even days and evil. We have to bear in mind that the fundamental distinction between odd and even is common to all Greek arithmetic. Moreover, as noted, even days are sometimes associated with crisis and recovery, not with exacerbation and death. It is rather the case that the classification of numbers into odd and even provides part of the general background to the investigation of periodicities in the medical case histories: the doctors believed that they *might* be significant and they accordingly paid them particular attention in recording the changes to their patients' conditions.

The doctrine of critical days, and an interest in determining the periodicities of diseases, form the general theoretical framework guiding these detailed observations. Some of the conclusions presented in these treatises take the form of sweeping generalizations, as for instance when general theories of critical periods are put forward. But many of the conclusions stated are explicitly qualified. The writers state what happened "for the most part" or "in the majority of cases," and exceptions are often noted. It is not the case that these writers conducted their observations merely to confirm general rules that they had already formulated in detail. Rather, those detailed rules are, in the main, generalizations arrived at on the basis of their particular observations, including, no doubt, many others besides those recorded in the case histories as we have them.

The undertaking and recording of careful observations in the context of clinical medicine provide our best early examples of sustained observation and research. But as we have seen, there are particular reasons for this, for the observations were, in part, stimulated by the theory of critical days. Elsewhere the performance of the writers represented in the extant Hippocratic treatises presents a different picture. The medical writers were evidently often just as speculative as the natural philosophers. As in Presocratic philosophy, so too in many Hippocratic works, theories of the constituent elements of the human body or of material objects in general are proposed with little direct empirical support. The physiological processes inside the body are inferred on the basis of what are assumed to be analogous processes outside it. The anatomical structure of the body, similarly, was rarely investigated directly. Although very occasional references are to be found in 5th- and early 4th-century medical texts to the practice of animal dissection, that technique was not systematically deployed before Aristotle. Anatomical structures were inferred from external observation of the body, from what became visible during wounds or lesions, from what was known of animal bodies from sacrifices and butchery, or from analogues with non-living objects. None of this detracts from the claims that may be made for the ability of many Greek doctors as observers, but we must recognize that there were considerable variations in the extent to which those skills were exhibited in different contexts.

ARISTOTLE

Before Aristotle we have seen that the evidence for the practice of empirical observation and research is limited to particular fields and to particular theoretical concerns. It is Aristotle who provides the first general methodology that secures a distinct and important role for the collection and evaluation of what he calls the *phainomena*—though, as we shall see, his use of that term cannot be held to correspond to what we would describe as empirical phenomena. Aristotle's methodological principles were worked out, in part, in opposition to the views of Plato, and it will be convenient for us to begin this section by examining the similarities and differences between these two major philosophers.

Aristotle agrees with Plato that the particular, qua particular, is not a proper object of scientific knowledge or understanding. Proper understanding relates to universal truths. However, where Plato often represents particulars as merely imitating forms, or participating in them, Aristotle's ontology proposes a very different account of the relationship between forms and particulars. In the doctrine he sets out in *Categories*, primary substances, such as this or that individual human being, are what basically exists. Qualities, quantities, and so on depend, for their existence, on there being substances that exhibit the qualities and quantities in question. But the primary substances of *Categories* are analyzed, in *Physics* and elsewhere, in terms of a combination of form and matter. An individual human being is a *sunholon*, a composite whole, consisting of form and matter. But form and matter are not the components in the sense of constituents of the composite whole. Rather they are better described as aspects of the individual substance. We may ask, concerning an individual substance, what it is made of—its material cause—and what makes it the substance it is—its formal cause, and two further types of question will take us to what brought it about (the efficient cause) and the good it serves, its goal or end (the final cause).

But whereas, for Plato, the particulars are often imagined as falling short of the forms, for Aristotle they exemplify the forms, for his forms are seen as answering to the question of what makes the individual substance the substance it is—what makes the individual human being, say, the human being it is. In the doctrine of recollection set out in *Phaedo* Plato certainly allowed that this process may be initially stimulated by *perception*, for example of the ways in which particulars resemble or are unlike the qualities they represent. Thus a pair of equal objects may initiate the process of recollection leading to the apprehension of the form, equality, itself. But for Aristotle the particular substances are what primarily exists, and although the scientist is concerned with forms and with the other types of causes, it is not as if these can be recollected.

The important conclusion that immediately follows from this is that the attention paid to empirical data is not directed at individuals qua the *individuals* they are. The scientist's interest, for Aristotle, lies in the universal, not in particulars as such. The starting point of inquiry is often described as the *phainomena*. But this term covers not only what appears directly to the senses but also what is commonly thought or believed—what appears in the sense of what appears to be the case. When Aristotle wishes to specify perceptible phenomena, he does so by adding the phrase "according to perception" to the term *phainomena*.

Moreover, the collection and evaluation of "what appears" are important not just to establish the data and to set out what is commonly believed, but more particularly to identify the problems that require solution. Aristotle frequently prefaces his own discussion of a subject area with a survey of earlier views. This is done not so much to gain a historical perspective on an issue, let alone for the sake of a historical account itself, as to set out the chief difficulties, *aporiai*, that require resolution and elucidation.

Aristotle has, then, an ontology that takes particulars as basic, and an epistemology that insists that the proper objects of scientific understanding are the forms those particulars possess. He has, too, a general methodology that advocates the review of the common opinions on a subject, as well as the empirical data, before turning to the chief theoretical problems that occupy him. That methodology is put into practice with remarkable consistency throughout his work, including not just his treatises on physical subjects but also those, for example, on politics. Naturally the degree to which the *phaenomena* in question correspond to what we should call observational data varies. Thus in the work called *Physics* Aristotle is largely concerned with problems in what we should call the philosophy of science, such as the nature of time, place, and infinity and the question of the kinds of causes that should be admitted. Here he proceeds by way of abstract argument more often than by way of direct appeal to the results of observations. He pays due attention, to be sure, to the same familiar, real or supposed, data of experience that had figured in earlier, Presocratic deliberations, and he certainly subjects those earlier discussions themselves, and the common opinions, to an extensive, acute, and often damning critique. But as a whole the empirical data marshalled in *Physics* mostly amount to little more than some well-known facts or what were taken to be such.

The situation is quite different in the zoological treatises, where the *phaenomena* reviewed are often observed data, and where Aristotle has often been at pains to extend those data with the findings of his own original research. In a manner that recalls the work of the historians, he and his collaborators collected and evaluated the view of a wide variety of people who could be expected to have special knowledge concerning one or another aspect of animal life or behavior. He repeatedly refers to what he has been told by hunters, fishermen, horse rearers, pig breeders, eel breeders, doctors, veterinary surgeons, and midwives, among others. He draws, too—more surprisingly from our point of view, but quite consistently from his—on literary sources, including, for instance, Herodotus, whom, however, he sometimes treats with disdain as a mere "mythologist."

To this secondhand evidence are added the results of his own and his collaborators' independent research, though he often remarks that the facts are difficult to ascertain, that observation is difficult, that further research is necessary. He does this, for example, in his famous discussion of the generation of bees. Here he first puts forward a set of theories that largely reflect his own a priori preconceptions. Thus one of the factors that leads him to conclude that the worker bees are male is his belief that there is a greater probability of males' being better equipped with offensive and defensive weapons than females. Yet at the end of his discussion he writes (*On the Generation of Animals*, 760b27ff): "This then seems to be what happens with regard to the generation of bees, judging from theory [*logos*] and from what are thought to be the facts about them. But the facts have not been sufficiently ascertained, and if they ever are ascertained, then we must trust perception rather than theories, and theories too so long as what they show agrees with what appears to be the case [*phaenomena*]."

In one domain, in particular, Aristotle can be considered a major pioneer. I have noted that dissection was very rarely used before him, and Aristotle himself implies that his fellow Greeks felt a certain squeamishness on the question. Thus he remarks in *On the Parts of Animals* (645a28ff) that "it is not possible to look at the constituent parts of human beings, such as blood, flesh, bones, blood vessels and the like, without considerable distaste." Human postmortem dissection, in fact, was still not on the agenda. Yet so far as animals were concerned, Aristotle was successful in overcoming his own expressed inhibitions, for he provides clear evidence that he and his associates undertook extensive and careful dissections of some scores of different animal species.

The motives for this were not research for its own sake. On the contrary, Aristotle explains with the greatest care and emphasis that the investigation of the parts of animals is not directed primarily at an inquiry into the material constituents but into their forms and final causes. As always, there are clear *theoretical* issues at stake: the understanding of the structures and functions of the parts of animals. The research is guided throughout by his notion of the different causes to be investigated, and within the four causes, the essence (or formal cause) and the good (final cause) are of greatest importance. The method of dissection was, then, used primarily to reveal the operations of those two causes, though, to be sure, his use of the technique brought to light much that he was in no position to have anticipated. While animals are said to be inferior objects of study when compared with the divine heavenly bodies, he remarks that the latter are remote and difficult to observe. So animals have the advantage that "we have much better means of obtaining information" about them, and "anyone who is willing to take sufficient trouble can learn a great deal concerning each of their kinds [viz. both animals and plants]" (*On the Parts of Animals*, 644b28ff). Once he appreciated how he could proceed to that investigation, and given that he had the motive to do so—to reveal the essences and the good—the possibility of an altogether more systematic program of research opened up, and Aristotle himself progressed far in its implementation even while much work, of course, remained for his successors.

The impressive observations Aristotle carried out, in zoology especially, are guided, as I said, by the conceptual framework provided by his doctrine of the four causes. But I must add that his particular theoretical preconceptions influence both his program of research and many of his reported findings, and there are certainly limitations, in places severe ones, to the observational work he conducted. We can see the role of his theoretical preconceptions in such an example as his analysis of the internal parts of animals. His work here is guided by his doctrine of the different vital faculties, or faculties of soul, such as reproduction, digestion, perception, locomotion, and so on. Thus in his inquiry into the internal parts of the main groups of bloodless animals he appears especially concerned to answer such questions as how and where food is taken in, how and where residues are discharged, where the controlling principle of the animal is located, what modes of perception it enjoys (does it smell? does it hear?), and how it moves. His work on the digestive tract of many species is thorough. But without any idea of the role of what we call the nervous system, either the sensory or the motor nerves, he has only superficial remarks to make about the way in which perception and locomotion occur. In the latter case, while he discusses the arrangement of the organs of locomotion with some care, he pays little attention to the internal musculature of the animals concerned.

Not dissecting human subjects, he mistakes certain basic features of human anatomy. Thus he holds that the heart has three chambers and that the brain is largely empty. The former idea corresponds to his belief that there should, ideally, be a single control center (the middle chamber) and the latter to his conviction of the paramount importance of the heart, an idea that left the brain with a very subordinate role. However, so far as his views of the importance of the heart go, he appealed to empirical investigations of the development of the eggs of hens to support the conclusion that the heart is the first organ in the body to become distinct in the growing embryo.

Again he represents males as essentially stronger and longer lived than females; when he finds species of animals that are exceptions, he does not modify his general belief but treats the animals in question as inferior. What is *natural*, in many cases, corresponds not to what is the case in a majority of instances but to the norm or ideal set by the higher animals, especially by the species deemed to be supreme among animals—namely, humans. Thus, believing that right is inherently stronger than and superior to left, and yet recognizing that right-left distinctions are not always strongly marked in animals, he claims nevertheless that in humans the right is especially right-sided. Again he defines upper as the direction from which food is taken in, and accepts the consequence that plants, fed from their roots, are functionally upside down. In humans alone, indeed, the upper parts are directed toward the upper part of the universe. In humans alone, he is prepared to say (*On the Parts of Animals*, 656a10ff), the natural parts are *according to nature*.

Aristotle's work thus exemplifies, in striking fashion, the *inter*dependence of theory and observation. The observations are conducted not for their own sake but for the help they give in the resolution of theoretical issues. Aristotle was not the only researcher, in ancient or in modern times, whose observations are often marshalled directly to support his preconceived theories. He accuses others of not being patient in the conduct of their research, and of assuming the conclusions they wish to reach before they have verified whether the data support them. Yet the same is sometimes true of his own work. At the same time, we cannot fail to be impressed by the range of the empirical studies he undertook. While theoretical preconceptions override observational exceptions on many occasions, the latter are sometimes allowed to contradict and so to modify the former. Above all, as I noted, he often stresses that not all the relevant evidence has been collected, and he is prepared to suspend judgment on detailed issues until further research has been undertaken. His is the first *generalized* program of empirical inquiry into natural science, undertaken for the sake of the causal explanations that such an inquiry can yield.

RESEARCH IN PHILOSOPHY AND SCIENCE AFTER ARISTOTLE

In the period after Aristotle, the separation of many of the branches of science from general philosophy becomes more marked. The main dogmatic philosophical schools of the Hellenistic period, the Epicureans and the Stoics, based primarily in Athens, both emphasized the importance of the study of nature—but only within limits. "Physics" included, especially, element theory, but also detailed explanations of natural phenomena, particularly those that continued to be considered strange or frightening, such as eclipses, earthquakes, thunder and lightning. But for both these schools, "physics" was undertaken as a means to an end, not as an end in itself. Some knowledge of physics was necessary to secure peace of mind, *ataraxia*, without which happiness is impossible. But the end of philosophy, its goal, was essentially moral, to secure that happiness, and once satisfactory explanations on the primary physical problems had been reached, it was pointless, indeed distracting, to continue inquiry.

The Epicureans, especially, rejected much of the work of the natural philosophers as useless, even as no better than mythology. Epicurus insisted that when several explanations of a single phenomenon (such as eclipses) seem possible, then *all* should be accepted and kept in play. As a principle that has a laudable undogmatic, indeed antidogmatic, ring. But the Epicureans' own actual proposed explanations were often fanciful and not only insufficiently critical but also ill-informed. Epicurus itemized some four or five different theories of eclipses, all of which were to be entertained as possible; yet these do not include the real explanation, which had not been in any doubt to practicing astronomers since the middle of the 5th century. With rare exceptions, such as the independent-minded middle Stoic Posidonius, in the 1st century B.C.E., the major Hellenistic philosophers undertook no detailed empirical research themselves.

In the specialized sciences the situation is very different. The development of these inquiries in the Hellenistic period is in part a history of the development of demonstration. At the same time there are also important developments in the range of empirical work conducted. In what has to be a drastically selective survey, we will concentrate here on four fields especially: astronomy and optics among the exact sciences, and anatomy and physiology among the life sciences. A more extensive account would have to include far more, notably the empirical investigations in harmonics in the work of Aristoxenus, Ptolemy, and Porphyry; those in geography in Eratosthenes, Hipparchus, Posidonius, Strabo, and Ptolemy; those in botany in Theophrastus; those in pharmacology in Dioscorides; as well as many developments in clinical medicine in a long list of distinguished medical writers.

One by-product of the conquests of Alexander was that the Greeks gained greater access to Babylonian astronomy. Some knowledge of Babylonian observational work in that domain is attestable in the 4th century, possibly also in the late 5th century, but this related largely to such basic data as the values of the fundamental periods of the planets, sun, and moon. But the two major astronomical theorists, Hipparchus (2nd century B.C.E.) and Ptolemy (2nd century C.E.), drew extensively on Babylonian records. Ptolemy, for instance, chose the first year of the reign of Nabonassar (845 B.C.E.) as the beginning of his system of dating and cited several specific lunar eclipses observed by Babylonian astronomers in the 8th, 7th, and 6th centuries.

But if Greek astronomy in the Hellenistic period exploited the results of Babylonian work to good effect, the Greeks also engaged in careful astronomical observation on their own account. Some of the contexts in which they did so are largely unconnected with the chief issue in astronomical theory, the construction of models to account for the movements of the planets, sun, and moon. Thus first Hipparchus and then Ptolemy produced detailed star catalogues. That of Hipparchus is not extant, and its contents have to be inferred, largely from the evidence that Ptolemy provides. However, it appears to have contained some 850 stars. The coordinate system that Hipparchus used was a mixed one. Some of our data relate to equatorial coordinates (the right ascension or declination of the star) or to mixed equatorial and ecliptic ones (the so-called polar longitude). There was as yet, it seems, no single definite system of spherical coordinates for stellar positions.

By the time we get to Ptolemy himself, however, each star is located by ecliptic coordinates (celestial longitude, measured east or west along the ecliptic, and celestial latitude, north or south of the ecliptic). The extent to which Ptolemy merely copied out Hipparchus's catalogue, with adjustments for the variations of the positions of the stars in his own day, is disputed. But it is clear, first, that he drew heavily on Hipparchus (it would have been foolish not to have done so) and, second, that he added to the earlier catalogue, including some 1,020 stars. Whoever takes the credit for the data on which the extant catalogue in VII and VIII of the *Syntaxis (Almagest)* is based, we may say it provides clear evidence of sustained observation. It has been estimated that the mean error in longitude is about 51' and that in latitude about 26'. Ptolemy further describes the instruments he uses for these and other observations—the dioptra, the meridional armillary, the plinth or quadrant, the parallactic ruler, and the armillary astrolabe, all of them, with the exception of the last, quite simple—and more important, he remarks on the difficulties of their accurate construction and use.

The motivation for the construction of a star catalogue is more descriptive than theoretical. However, it provides, of course, a clear map of stellar positions, an essential prerequisite for the determination of planetary positions, the chief issue in astronomical theory and the key also to the practice of astrology. Moreover, the careful observation of the positions of stars in the band of the ecliptic led Hipparchus to a momentous consequence—the discovery of the phenomenon known as the precession of the equinoxes, the slow retrograde motion of the equinoctial points with respect to the fixed stars. Comparing his own results for the position of the star Spica in Virgo with those recorded by his predecessors, Hipparchus was led to investigate whether there was a systematic shift either just in the stars close to the ecliptic, or in all stars. He was aware, of course, of the inaccuracy of much of the observational work done before him, and, like Ptolemy after him, suspected systematic errors in some of his instruments. Yet he concluded that there is indeed such a shift and that the whole of the outermost celestial sphere rotates at a rate of around one degree in 100 years (that was the figure Ptolemy himself adopted, though it may have been the lower limit for precession in Hipparchus's calculation).

This ranks as one of the most striking ancient examples in which an observational program undertaken with no specific theoretical issue in mind yielded a result that was utterly unexpected—and in which that result was accepted despite the radical revision it implied in the previously held view of the absolute fixity of the sphere of the outermost stars. Indeed, so strong did that conviction remain, in common belief, that Hipparchus's discovery was often ignored or dismissed. Ptolemy, to be sure, accepted precession and devoted a detailed discussion to its verification. But many later commentators, including otherwise well-informed scholars, such as Proclus and Philoponus, expressed their frank disbelief that precession occurs—despite the fact that with the passing centuries the comparison between earlier and later stellar positions should have suggested, more and more forcefully, that it does.

The other main context for detailed observational research in astronomy was, of course, in relation to the main theoretical issue that had preoccupied Greek astronomers from the 5th century B.C.E. onward, the construction of geometrical models to account for the apparently irregular motions of the moon, sun, and planets. By Ptolemy's day, the preferred models employed eccentric circles and epicycles, or combinations of them, and Ptolemy himself introduced certain theoretical elaborations, notably the equant, the point other than the earth or the center of the eccentric with relation to which uniform motion is to be measured. That assumption came to be criticized as, in effect, breaching the fundamental principle that the motions *are* uniform.

Ptolemy's ambition was not just to provide general, qualitative solutions to the problems of planetary motion—that is, to resolve the geometrical problems in general terms. He aimed to give an exact quantitative account, determining, for each planet, the degree of eccentricity, the size of the epicycle or epicycles in relation to the deferent, and the planet's apsidal line, as well as the speeds of revolution—the periodicities—of the epicycle and deferent. If Ptolemy's own report is to be believed, Hipparchus himself had been unable to give a satisfactory detailed account of the planets, though his models for both moon and sun were fully quantitative. It would appear, then, that Ptolemy was himself responsible for the first complete theory of planetary motion, providing detailed solutions from which the exact position of the planet at any time in the past, present, or future can be determined.

For this purpose he cited a number of specific observations in his exposition of each individual planet. Yet in part, no doubt, to keep that exposition as simple and as clear as possible, he cited close to the *minimum* number of observations needed to extract the specific parameters of the motion of each planet. Evidently these are chosen with a view to getting the eventual results he proposes—and the general quality of his observational work has again in this context (as in relation to his star catalogue) been impugned. There can be little doubt that he allows himself adjustments to specific observed positions, just as he does in the roundings he repeatedly makes in the purely mathematical part of his calculations. By the standards of accuracy applicable to later astronomical theory, his procedures are slapdash. Yet his overall success in arriving, in most cases, at results that give good approximations to the observed planetary movements is considerable. The very fact that he saw himself as forced to introduce certain complexities into his theoretical models (especially for Mercury and the Moon) in order to obtain an adequate fit between theory and observation may be taken as testimony to the attention he paid to the latter. Although within the *Syntaxis* itself he does not present all the data he uses or feels he needs to take into account, it is only because of that need that he was induced to modify and elaborate the models he proposed.

In optics, the second field I have chosen for consideration, there are theoretical disputes both about the nature of light and the directionality of vision. In the former case, one school of thought held that light should be interpreted as the transport of particles through the void, while another held, rather, that it corresponded to the transmission of a certain tension in a continuous medium. In the latter, there were those who argued that the light ray proceeds outward from the eye to the object, others who held that it goes from the object to the eye. None of these physical debates directly affects the empirical investigations of such questions as the laws of reflection and refraction. Once again it is Ptolemy who provides the fullest evidence for those investigations, though we may be sure that both reflection and refraction, as such, were known before him.

The treatise he devoted to the subject, *Optics*, is extant only in a Latin translation of an Arabic version, and at points we have reason to question the accuracy of the text as we have it. It is clear, however, that the original contained detailed accounts both of the experimental verification of the laws of reflection and analyses of refraction, including attempts to determine the variation in the extent of refraction, for different angles of incidence, for different pairs of media, namely from air to water, from air to glass, and from water to glass.

This provides the occasion for some general remarks about the role of experimentation in Greek natural science, where it has often been argued that one of the greatest shortcomings of the Greeks lies in a failure to appreciate the value of experimental methods. It is clear, first of all, that in many fields in which Greek scientists were interested, experiment is impossible. This is the case in astronomy, for instance, where there can be no question of intervening directly to test hypotheses via specially contrived situations. The same is broadly true also of meteorology and geology. The Greeks were in no position to investigate thunder and lightning, or earthquakes, by creating such phenomena artificially, even in miniature. Rather, their usual procedure was to appeal to some real or supposed analogue, as Anaximanes is reported to have done in the case of lightning, which he compared to the flash of an oar in water. But any such procedure begged the question of whether the phenomena compared are indeed similar in the relevant characteristics.

In the investigation of the physical elements, some limited experimental procedures are occasionally invoked. Aristotle, for instance, claims that sea water, on evaporation, turns into fresh. He also suggests that wine does so, a result that may prompt reflection not so much on Aristotle's ability as an observer as on the procedures he employed, and on the conceptual framework within which the results were evaluated. The main drawback to the effective deployment of the experimental method in relation to his physical theory lies in the vagueness of the definitions of the simple bodies, earth, water, air, and fire themselves. They are identified with combinations of the primary qualities, hot, cold, wet, and dry, but what we encounter as earth or water or air or fire is never the *pure* simple body, always to a greater or lesser extent a mixture. Thus the "water" that Aristotle claims came from wine on evaporation might well be what he took the vapor from heated wine to produce on recondensing: if he conducted any such test, the condensate would no doubt have been a colorless, more or less tasteless fluid that would pass as easily as "water" as naturally occurring samples.

Yet in some cases, as the evidence in Ptolemy's *Optics* shows, detailed experimental investigations, using apparatuses devised for the purpose, were carried out. Ptolemy measures the actual refraction he says he has observed between his pairs of media and sets out his results for angles of incidence at 10-degree intervals from 10 to 80 degrees. In all three cases the first result is introduced with the qualification "nearly," and they are all stated in terms of degrees and half degrees. He thus appears to make some allowance for approximation. Yet the more surprising feature is that *all* the results tally exactly with a general law that takes the form of the equation $r = ai - bi^2$, where r is the angle of refraction, i the angle of incidence, and a and b are constants for the media concerned.

Evidently *Optics* presents results that have already been adjusted to match the underlying general theory. I shall cite cases of experimental procedures where no such adjustments have been made when we come to anatomy and physiology in the next section. But we may remark at this stage that a common, even though far from universal, feature of such testing procedures as the Greek scientists used is that they are appealed to not so much as neutral ways of *deciding between* alternatives antecedently deemed to be more or less equally plausible, but rather as an extension of the use of evidence to *corroborate* a particular theory or set of results. In this regard, experiment is used not so much as an—ideally—neutral testing procedure but as testimony to support a distinct point of view.

The two remaining fields we should consider are closely related and may be taken together, namely anatomy and physiology. I have already discussed the development and use of dissection in Aristotle, where it was limited to animal subjects but was the chief factor enabling Aristotle to reach a far clearer picture of many internal structures than his predecessors had had. Two scientists working chiefly at Alexandria at the turn of the 4th and 3rd centuries B.C.E., Herophilus and Erasistratus, took the next step of dissecting human subjects. Indeed reports suggest that they also carried out vivisections on humans—on "criminals obtained out of prison from the kings," as Celsus puts it. Clearly this research depended heavily on the support of those kings, notably the first two Ptolemies. It appears, however, that after Herophilus and Erasistratus the use of human subjects for postmortem anatomical research declined, even though in the 2nd century C.E. Galen suggests that osteology was still taught at Alexandria using humans.

The extension of the technique of dissection to human subjects was one factor that contributed to the very rapid development of anatomical knowledge in the immediate post-Aristotelian period. Herophilus and Erasistratus, between them, were responsible for a large number of important discoveries, the most significant of which was that of the nervous system. The term used for nerve, *neuron*, had originally been used indiscriminately of a wide variety of structures, including tendons and ligaments. The role of what we call sensory and motor nerves in the transmission of sensation and the control of the muscles was, accordingly, totally ignored. Aristotle, as we saw, believed that the heart is the seat of the controlling principle in the body, but his account of the connections between it and the organs of sensation is desperately vague and unclear.

Whether or not Herophilus and Erasistratus were stimulated by a sense of the inadequacy of Aristotle's work in this area is not clear. We have, in any case, to reconstruct their work from the quotations and comments in later sources such as Galen. But the *general* problem of where the controlling principle is to be placed, whether in the heart or the brain, was one of the most commonly debated issues in the work of both medical writers and philosophers. The problem goes back at least as far as the mid-5th-century philosopher Alcmaeon, who, like Plato after him, opted for the brain as control center. Alcmaeon may even have investigated the back of the eye with a probe in order precisely to establish its connection with the brain, but the idea that he dissected the brain or any other part of the body has to be discounted as going well beyond what our evidence suggests. While he may have described a

OBSERVATION AND RESEARCH • 87

channel, *poros*, at the back of the eye, it was certainly not yet identified as what came to be called the optic nerve.

It was the step of identifying certain structures as sensory nerves and others as motor nerves that marks the discovery of the nervous system as such. It was here that Herophilus and Erasistratus achieved the breakthrough. Although Galen criticizes Herophilus's work as incomplete and explains that Erasistratus carried out detailed investigations only in certain areas toward the end of his life, that should not be taken to diminish the importance of their fundamental realization of the role of the two main types of nerves.

Nor were their anatomical investigations confined to the single problem of the transmission of sensation and movement. Herophilus, for instance, was responsible for, among other things, the first clear description of the four membranes of the eye, and for the identification of the ovaries as female testicles. Erasistratus is credited with the discovery of the four main valves of the heart, controlling the flow of materials into the right and the left side. Galen reports that he identified the various ventricles of the brain, and two of the specific structures in the brain, the torcular Herophili and the calamus scriptorius, were described and named for the first time by Herophilus.

Much of this work was, no doubt, done on animals, and the extent of the use of human subjects was not necessarily very great. Yet their inclusion enabled comparisons to be made directly between humans and other animals, as opposed to merely inferring human structures on the basis of real or supposed analogies with other species. Herophilus's comparison between human and animal livers is reported by Galen, as is Erasistratus's between human and animal brains. And Herophilus would not have arrived at his name for the duodenum had he not measured the length of that structure in humans (for the name he coined implies its twelve-fingers' breadth).

This effort in research was not just descriptive in character. Apart from the issue of the control center in the body, there were theoretical debates on such physiological processes as respiration and digestion. Thus Erasistratus may have used vivisection to support his account of digestion, which he interpreted in purely mechanical terms: the stomach and digestive tract do not "concoct" the food but transform it into usable nourishment by grinding it down. He was, too, convinced that the arteries normally contain air and that the blood that flows from them in a lesion comes from neighboring veins through invisible capillaries. But whatever theoretical issues were at stake, it is clear that he had a highly developed sense of the need, importance, and difficulty of empirical research. Thus Galen quotes him as follows: "Those who are completely unused to inquiry are, in the first exercise of their mind, blinded and dazed and straightforwardly leave off the inquiry from mental fatigue and an incapacity that is no less than that of those who enter races without being used to them. But the man who is used to inquiry tries every possible loophole as he conducts his mental search and turns in every direction and so far from giving up the inquiry in the space of a day, does not cease his search throughout his whole life. Directing his attention to one idea after another that is germane to what is being investigated, he presses on until he arrives at his goal."

Despite what may seem to us the brilliant successes of Herophilus and Erasistratus, the method of dissection remained controversial, for a variety of reasons. Animal, and especially human, vivisection was condemned, almost universally, as cruel and immoral. But postmortem dissection was also rejected by two of the main Hellenistic medical sects (the so-called Empiricists and Methodists), on the grounds that the evidence it yields is not relevant to the understanding of the living creature, only of the dead one. Similarly, animal vivisection was of no use for determining vital processes, since it depended on a violent intervention on the living creature. In addition many doctors argued that medicine was a matter of curing the sick, and the doctor should not be concerned with explaining the how and why of the workings of the body, only with how to remedy malfunctions. No doubt, too, a respect for the dead was a general inhibiting factor militating against the use of human subjects (though we may reflect that in other contexts the ancients sometimes showed little compunction for desecrating the dead, when the dead were their defeated enemies). However, for whatever combination of reasons, human dissection certainly declined (as I noted) after Herophilus and Erasistratus themselves.

Yet Galen in the 2nd century c.e. certainly carried on the tradition of anatomical research even while he worked almost exclusively on animals. We must also point out that dissection and vivisection, in his hands, were not just tools of research. Sometimes their role was rather as *publicity*, as support for the claims to having knowledge that was superior to that of rivals. Medicine was always highly competitive, and one way a doctor could make a name for himself was with his ability as an anatomist. Galen reports occasions when dissections were carried out in public, with rival experts claiming to predict the results and even taking bets as to who had got it right. Thus he describes how he discomfited some Erasistratean opponents by challenging them to establish their claims that the arteries naturally contain air. On a further famous occasion an elephant was dissected in public in Rome, with Galen (on his own account) again outdoing all his rivals with his predictions of what the dissection would reveal. In such contexts it is clear that dissection was used neither for teaching, nor for research, but rather for display.

Yet we must also acknowledge that Galen's own anatomical descriptions show clear signs of careful observation and well-directed research. Building on the work of his predecessors he was able to take the investigation of the nervous system a good deal further than they. He undertook systematic experiments to determine the effects of severing the spinal column at different points, either by cutting right through it or by making a half section. He sets out the results in the treatise *On Anatomical Procedures*, where he identifies the precise role of the nerves entering the spinal column between each of the pairs of vertebrae from the sacral to the cervical. Here we have experimental vivisections used to determine functions, with no interference from theoretical preconceptions.

The history of dissection in antiquity illustrates very clearly the complex interaction of observation and theory. In some cases the idea of investigating animal bodies using such a technique was stimulated by a particular theoretical dispute, as when the issue was the control center—the heart or the brain? In others, dissections were carried out not so much to confirm or refute a particular theory as to enable the formal and final causes of the parts of animals to be clarified. In that case, in Aristotle especially, dissection becomes a more general method, and its findings might include new discoveries that corresponded to no particular theoretical preoccupation. Those findings might, indeed, lead to the reformulation of the problems themselves—as later happened with the discovery of the nervous system. Dissection was always guided by theories and assumptions of some sort, but once one of those assumptions was a realization that the problems themselves might be more complex than had generally been believed, the investigation was more open to the unexpected. Thus the use of the method could and did generate what were effectively new problems, leading in turn to new programs of research. We cannot say precisely what Herophilus and Erasistratus were *looking for* when they identified the valves of the heart as valves, but once their role in controlling the flow into and out of the two sides of the heart was established, the question of the relations between the arterial and venous systems and the possibility of communication between them produced major new issues for physiological debate—issues that were, indeed, to remain unresolved throughout antiquity.

We may now, in conclusion, briefly take stock of the findings of our survey. The need to conduct observations and carry out research may seem an obvious feature of the work of anyone seriously engaged in natural scientific inquiry. Yet the history of the idea and the practice of observation and research in Greek antiquity indicates that both took time to develop, posed conceptual and practical difficulties, and remained controversial. First among the difficulties were the doubts expressed about the reliability of perception and the strong preference, expressed by prominent philosophers from Parmenides onward, for taking reason and argument alone as trustworthy guides to the truth. But even among those who did not adopt an ultrarationalist position, the mere recognition that perception is of some value was not, by itself, enough to stimulate deliberate research. That had always to be motivated either by some particular theoretical problem to be resolved or by a general framework of explanation dictating the detailed examination of a variety of phenomena—for example (as in Aristotle's case), to identify the problems and to discover the formal and final causes underlying the appearances.

Often we find observation used merely to confirm or refute a particular thesis: once that goal was achieved, further investigation ceased. Often, too, observations, including those conducted in relation to experimental situations, were cited directly to support a particular preconceived opinion. Antiquity provides many instances of hasty or superficial observations, where the researcher has concluded, all too swiftly, that the data confirm his theory, interpreting those data in the light of the theory or even adjusting the results to provide such confirmation. (Of course, such jumping to conclusions is far from confined to *ancient* science.)

However, when a particular theoretical or conceptual interest existed, sustained observations were carried out in such fields as clinical medicine, zoology, astronomy, and optics, and these observations included some that not only did not confirm but even tended to conflict with the preconceived opinions of the researchers. Hippocratic clinical observations often did not fit *any* neat schema of critical days. Aristotle, too, had to admit exceptions to many of his generalizations in zoology, even though he sometimes resorts to secondary elaborations to explain away the apparent counterevidence. Hipparchus's discovery of precession went against the grain of his own assumptions as well as those of all his contemporaries. While observations were always carried out in the light of *some* theory, there are cases where, once the data had been collected, the nature of the problems was transformed—as with the discoveries of the nervous system and the valves of the heart. Thus while theory guides research, there was also important feedback, when the observations themselves led to the formulation of new problems and the generation, in turn, of further programs of research.

The value and importance of empirical research never became universally accepted principles of natural science, neither before Aristotle nor after him; neither by the philosophers nor by the medical writers nor by those engaged in particular inquiries in the exact or the life sciences. But that did not prevent particular investigators, in particular contexts and in particular periods, from advocating such research in principle—often in the face of hostile attitudes and criticisms from rationalists, pragmatists, and skeptics—nor from implementing those principles in practice. The ancient world provides many examples where an excellent methodological principle is advocated but the advocates themselves hardly live up to the claims they make for the methods. While some recommendations of the value of empirical investigations were no more than the wishful statement of high-sounding ideals untranslated into practice, that was not always the case. The sustained programs of research actually carried through, with great determination, by some of the Hippocratic doctors, by Aristotle, by Herophilus, Erasistratus, Hipparchus,

Ptolemy, and Galen, indicate that high-sounding principles were not just idealized recommendations but indeed, in their case, implemented in full measure in practice.

Geoffrey E. R. Lloyd

Bibliography

Bourgey, Louis. *Observation et expérience chez Aristote*. Paris: Vrin, 1955.

———. *Observation et expérience chez les médecins de la collection hippocratique*. Paris: Vrin, 1953.

Burkert, Walter. *Lore and Science in Ancient Pythagoreanism* (revised translation by E. L. Minar of *Weisheit und Wissenschaft*, Nuremberg: Hans Carl Verlag, 1962). Cambridge, Mass.: Harvard University Press, 1972.

Kudlien, Fridolf. *Der Beginn des medizinischen Denkens bei den Griechen*. Zurich: Artemis Verlag, 1967.

Le Blond, Jean-Marie. *Logique et méthode chez Aristote*. Paris: Vrin, 1939.

Lloyd, Geoffrey E. R. *Magic, Reason, and Experience: Studies in the Origin and Development of Greek Science*. Cambridge: Cambridge University Press, 1979.

———. *Methods and Problems in Greek Science*. Cambridge: Cambridge University Press, 1991.

Neugebauer, Otto. *The Exact Sciences in Antiquity*, 2nd ed. Providence, R.I.: Brown University Press, 1957.

———. *A History of Ancient Mathematical Astronomy*. 3 vols. Berlin: Springer Verlag, 1975.

Van der Waerden, B. L. *Science Awakening*, 2nd ed. Oxford: Oxford University Press, 1961.

DEMONSTRATION AND THE
IDEA OF SCIENCE

THE NOTION OF DEMONSTRATION is closely linked to one, and in many respects the most important, concept of science in Greco-Roman antiquity. It will, accordingly, be convenient to deal with these together. However, it must be stressed at the outset that the idea that scientific knowledge should be based, ideally, on demonstration is far from being the *only* concept of science proposed in antiquity. Moreover the notion of demonstration itself took different forms in the work of different writers and in different contexts. The definition we find in Aristotle's *Posterior Analytics,* that demonstration proceeds by strict deductive argument from premises that are themselves indemonstrable, was, as we shall see, worked out in part in direct contradistinction to other, less formal and less rigorous, ideas.

So far as our extant evidence goes, attempts to give strict demonstrations antedate the formulation of the explicit concept by several decades. The first sustained deductive argument in philosophy (the first such in European literature) comes in *The Way of Truth,* the philosophical poem written by Parmenides and thought to date from around 480 B.C.E. Where this resembles and where it differs from later styles of demonstration are alike suggestive.

Parmenides' main substantive conclusions about the nature of reality are set out in frg. 8, and they take the form of a series of tightly knit deductive arguments. Several of these are in the form of a reductio, and most appeal, directly or implicitly, to an exclusive choice between alternatives assumed to be exhaustive; we shall consider some examples in due course. However, the whole deductive chain depends on a starting point that Parmenides evidently takes to be undeniable. In frg. 2, where he distinguishes between two possible ways of inquiry, he states that "it is and it cannot not be." This itself is supported by arguing that the opposite, the other "way," namely that "it is not and it needs must not be," must be rejected. That has to be rejected on the grounds that "you could not know what is not, at least, nor could you declare it" (that is, assert it as true). As frg. 3 goes on to say: "It is the same thing that can be thought and can be."

The sense of the verb *to be,* the subject we must understand, and the precise nature of the alternatives presented are all disputed issues. But that does not affect the main point, which is that, at the outset, Parmenides was evidently attempting to establish a starting point that all would have to accept.

One way to understand this is to take it that he is claiming that for any *inquiry* to get anywhere it must be an inquiry into something. It must have a subject matter. One cannot conduct an investigation into the totally nonexistent. If an inquiry is to take place at all, it must be into "what is." But as for our rejection of "it is not," we must remark first on the complete indeterminacy in the statement of the two ways, and second that it appears that Parmenides forces a choice not between strict contradictories but between contrary propositions. The contradictory to "it cannot not be" (i.e., it is necessarily the case that it is) is not "it needs must not be" (it is necessarily the case that it is not) but rather "it is not necessarily the case that it is."

More important still, the basis of the subsequent deductive chain of argument is not a set of clearly identified *axioms*. Even if Parmenides no doubt would have insisted that his statement that "it is and it cannot not be" must be accepted as true, his starting point evidently does not take the form of anything like an axiom set or set of indemonstrables.

However, once the starting point is taken as secure, Parmenides gives an articulated argument, in frg. 8, recommending a whole series of highly counterintuitive conclusions, for example that it is ungenerated and indestructible, not subject to movement nor change, and both spatially and temporally invariant. Again, many points of detail, some of them important ones, are obscure or controversial. But the main structure of the argument is generally agreed, and that it has a rigorous deductive form is not in question. Parmenides sets out what he is going to establish at frg. 8.2ff and then proceeds to demonstrate each point in turn in a carefully constructed sequence of arguments. Thus the first conclusion, namely that it does not come to be, is shown by a reductio (frg. 8.20ff): "If it came to be, it is not." But—as had been shown—"it is not" must be denied. And so we must reject coming-to-be. Similarly, movement and change in turn are rejected, since they presuppose a coming-to-be, namely that of the new situation created by the supposed movement or change. But coming-to-be had just been ruled out by the earlier argument. And so movement and change have also to be rejected.

To these reductio arguments we can add others that take other forms. Thus as an extra consideration telling for the conclusion that "it is ungenerated," Parmenides produces an argument that appeals to what we might call the principle of sufficient reason. At frgs. 8–9f the demand is: "What need would have raised it to grow later, or earlier, starting from nothing?" If no cause can be adduced, no explanation given, as to why the universe came to be at one time rather than at any other, then we may consider this an argument for rejecting the notion that it came to be at all. The relevance of this argument is not confined, of course, to such earlier Greek cosmogonical theories as Parmenides himself may have had in mind.

The *aims* of *The Way of Truth* are clear: Parmenides sets out to establish a set of inescapable conclusions by strict deductive arguments from a starting point that itself has to be accepted. Those are features it shares with later demonstrations. However, the terminology in which he describes what he is doing is a very limited one. This is not just a matter of his not having any terms to describe the various argument schemata, such as reductio, that he uses. He has no word for deduction, nor for premise, let alone axiom. True, he offers what he calls a "much-contested *elenchos*" (frg. 7.5ff) and that has sometimes been taken to be translatable as "proof." However, it seems more likely that the primary sense here is that of "refutation"—as in later Socratic *elenchos*, where, in Plato's dialogues, Socrates exposes the inconsistencies of his interlocutors' beliefs. As for the sequence of conclusions set out in the body of The Way of Truth, they are simply introduced with the remark that there are many signposts, or marks, *sēmata*, on this way, indications, that is, that it is ungenerated, indestructible, and so on.

The immense impact that Parmenides had on subsequent Greek philosophy derives as much from his methods as from his conclusions. Certainly so far as the latter are concerned, the later Presocratic cosmologists responded directly to the challenge posed by Parmenides' denial of change and coming-to-be. They accepted his principle that nothing can come to be from the totally nonexistent, but postulated that what is is itself a plurality. Change and coming-to-be can then be interpreted in terms of the interactions of already existing things. But the pluralists, too, use indirect proofs, or reductio, even if not all their deductive arguments were directly modeled on those of Parmenides.

In Parmenides' own Eleatic followers, Zeno and Melissus, however, the range of dilemmatic arguments deployed increases. Zeno, especially, attempts to establish a monistic ontology by the systematic rejection of all rival pluralist positions. He appears to have proceeded by considering, and refuting, all possible ways of construing "the many." Whatever notion of *division* is invoked to distinguish the various items that constitute the plurality, the idea will turn out to be incoherent, undermined by its own self-contradictions. For example, the "many" will turn out to be both "limited" and "unlimited," both "large" and "small." As in Parmenides himself, we have arguments that appeal to terms that are themselves left highly indeterminate—as indeed is also the case with the terms *one* and *many*, where Zeno evidently takes it that to refute the latter is to establish the former.

Deductive argument used for constructive or destructive purposes is thus commonly deployed in Greek philosophy from the middle of the 5th century B.C.E. onward. From about 430 we have further explicit evidence for sustained deductive argument in mathematics. Our first extant set of mathematical proofs is the work of Hippocrates of Chios. His work on the quadratures of lunes is reported at some length by Simplicius, who tells us that he drew on the account of the 4th-century historian of mathematics, Eudemus. Though, as so often, some of the details are obscure, and the extent of the reworking of Hippocrates' arguments in the process of transmission is unclear, there is no reason to doubt that the substance of the four main proofs given represents the work of Hippocrates himself. These proofs establish the quadratures of lunes with an outer circumference equal to, greater than, and less than, a semicircle and that of a lune together with a circle. In each case Hippocrates identified a lune that *can* be shown to be equal to a rectilinear area and proved the equality.

These proofs are impressive not just for the extent of the mathematical knowledge displayed but also for the general rigor of the demonstrations. For instance, Hippocrates does not just *construct* lunes with outer circumferences greater and less than a semicircle, but in both cases he provides proofs of these inequalities. However, if the quality of the proofs is high, the lack of technical vocabulary to describe the procedures used is as remarkable in Hippocrates as it had been in Parmenides. Later Greek mathematicians were generally careful to specify the nature of the indemonstrable primary premises on which their demonstrations were based, for example, definitions, postulates, and axioms or common opinions. However, in the quadrature proofs Simplicius reports that Hippocrates took as his "starting point" *(archē)* the proposition that similar segments of circles are to one another as the squares on their bases, and this was evidently in no sense an axiom or indemonstrable. It was indeed a proposition that (we are told) Hippocrates *showed* by *showing* that circles are to one another as the squares on their diameters (though *how* he showed that is, unfortunately, not recorded).

In this context, then, it looks as if Hippocrates worked with a concept of starting point or principle that is relative to, and serves as the foundation of, a particular sequence of mathematical arguments. The question of whether he also had the notion of the *ultimate* starting points for the *whole* of geometry revolves around the evaluation of the evidence for his work on the elements. Our chief source here is Proclus's sketch of the early history of mathematics in his commentary on book I of Euclid's *Elements*. Here we are told that the first person to have composed a book of elements was Hippocrates, and Proclus identifies several other mathematicians between Hippocrates and Euclid (including, for example, Archytas and Theaetetus in the 4th century) who "increased the number of theorems and progressed toward a more systematic arrangement of them."

So far as Euclid's own *Elements* goes, there can be no doubt that *its* aim was the systematic deductive presentation of the whole of mathematics, starting from three types of primary indemonstrable premises, which he calls definitions, postulates, and common opinions. Moreover the term *elements* itself was undoubtedly used in mathematics, as well as in philosophy, before Euclid himself (whose work is traditionally dated around 300 B.C.E.). Thus Aristotle reports in *Metaphysics* (988a25ff) that "we give the name 'elements' to those geometrical propositions, the proofs of which are implied in the proofs of all or most of the others."

The questions then arise of how systematic and comprehensive Hippocrates' work was, and whether it was clearly based on ultimate starting points identified as elements, and in both cases we are unfortunately reduced to conjecture. Proclus takes Hippocrates as the originator of the tradition that culminates in Euclid, but how far was he justified in doing so? The proofs used in the quadratures of lunes reported by Simplicius certainly presuppose, as I noted, an extensive knowledge of elementary geometry, corresponding to much of the content of Euclid, books I–IV and VI. We should certainly not rule out the possibility that Hippocrates attempted an overall deductive presentation of a substantial body of theorems. However, caution is indicated so far as the development of explicit concepts corresponding to the notion of axioms is concerned.

There is good reason for hesitation on that score in the evidence we have of the hesitant development of the vocabulary of axiomatization in the period between Hippocrates and Aristotle. The testimony of Plato is particularly significant in this respect. Plato several times refers to the use that geometers make of what he calls "hypotheses." In *Meno* (86e ff) this is a matter of investigating a complex problem by "hypothesizing" that it is equivalent to some other problem and exploring that. There, while much of the detail of the interpretation of the passage is disputed, it is clear that the "hypothesis" is in no sense an ultimate starting point or assumption. In *The Republic* (510c ff), however, Plato again cites mathematical examples to illustrate what is here a different notion of "hypothesis." Mathematicians, we are told, "hypothesize" "the odd and the even, the figures and the three kinds of angles and other things like these in each inquiry. They do not give an account of these either to themselves or to others, as if they were clear to all, but beginning with them they go through the rest consistently and end with what they set out to investigate."

It is not clear whether either of these texts in Plato reflects an *actual* use of the term *hypothesis* in earlier mathematics. But whatever the original terminology, Plato indicates that certain basic assumptions, taken as clear, were employed as the starting points for mathematical deductions. Plato himself complains that the mathematicians do not give an account of those starting points. *His* ideal is that hypotheses should be related to the supreme Form of the Good, the "unhypothesized beginning," from which (he claims) the whole of the intelligible world—including the geometers' hypotheses themselves—can be in some sense derived. But while his account of *their* procedures points to the role of certain principles in mathematics, the precise character of these principles is still left, in certain respects, unclear. He mentions "odd and even," "the figures," and "the three kinds of angles." But it is an open question whether, for example, these are to be construed as—or to in-clude—definitions (like the definitions of odd and even in Euclid VII, Defini-tions 6 and 7) or existence assumptions (corresponding to Aristotle's hy-potheses) or—as seems possible in the case of the figures—as assumptions concerning the possibility of carrying out certain constructions (like the first three of Euclid's postulates). Plato thus provides confirmation that mathemat-ics used starting points of some kind, on which deductions could be based, but his work is also evidence of a certain indeterminacy in the conception of those foundations. A fortiori, then, we should be cautious about ascribing a clear concept of the axioms, let alone clear ideas concerning the different kinds of possible indemonstrable starting points, to Hippocrates of Chios in the latter part of the 5th century.

Our conclusions concerning Hippocrates may, then, be summarized as fol-lows. The evidence of the work on quadratures established his mastery of an impressive body of elementary geometry and his skill in the practice of rigor-ous deductive argument. There is some evidence that the systematization of geometry that culminates in Euclid's *Elements* begins with him. But it is very doubtful that he had a clear, explicit concept of the axioms or of other kinds of indemonstrables as such.

The further question then arises of whether the notion of deductive argu-ment was developed independently in mathematics and in philosophy, or whether it appeared first in one of these two fields and was then taken over by the others. To answer this we have to tackle the much more difficult problem of the status of the ascriptions of certain mathematical proofs to Thales and to Pythagoras and the dating of the discovery of such famous mathematical the-orems as that of the incommensurability of the side and the diagonal of the square.

Several of our late antique sources, among the commentators on Euclid and the Neopythagorean writers, ascribe a number of important theorems to both Thales and Pythagoras. Proclus, for instance, uses terminology that suggests that he is confident that Thales not only discovered certain theorems but also found their proofs. Yet the reliability of this evidence is very much in doubt. Aristotle is always hesitant in his remarks about Thales, who seems to have left no writings. Thus Aristotle conjectures the reasons for Thales' choice of water as his principle (of "Images of the world"), presumably because no definite evidence on the point was available in Aristotle's own day. Again Ar-istotle does not attempt to reconstruct Pythagoras's own contributions to phi-losophy of mathematics in his history of early thinkers in *Metaphysics* and elsewhere, contenting himself with an account of what the "so-called Pythag-oreans" believed, where he probably has in mind thinkers of the mid-5th cen-tury at the earliest.

In these circumstances it does not seem very likely that even Eudemus, in the late 4th century, let alone any much later writer, had access to reliable, specific evidence concerning Thales. As regards Pythagoras, the further complicating factor is the general tendency, in many late writers, to ascribe important discoveries and inventions to the heroic founders of Greek philosophy. The fulsome accounts of Pythagoras's mathematical research that we find in some who considered themselves his followers owe more to their pious desire to revere the founders of their group than to the available historical data.

Yet certain theorems, and their proofs, may well antedate Hippocrates of Chios. I have already remarked on the extent of the geometrical knowledge implied by his work on quadratures. It is extremely unlikely that *all* the theorems he knew were his own discovery. In the case of the theorem that states the incommensurability of the side and diagonal of the square, we can be sure that that was known to mathematicians of Theodorus's generation (around 410). We know this from Plato's *Theaetetus* (147d ff), where Theodorus and his associates are represented as studying incommensurables from that which corresponds to the square root of 3 onward—presupposing the case corresponding to the square root of 2 as already familiar. The question is how long before Theodorus that incommensurability was known—and to know the proposition is, in this case, to know its proof, for we are not talking of having a rough idea that the side and the diagonal have no common measure, but of being in a position to show that they do not. While we have no means of settling the issue decisively, any more than we can be confident about *which* of several possible proof methods was the one first used to establish the theorem, the most likely conjecture is that this was a discovery dating from around the middle of the 5th century.

It may be noted in parenthesis that although some have seen this discovery as leading to a "foundation crisis" in mathematics, the reverse is rather the case. The fact that this provides such a fine example of a mathematical proposition that is demonstrable, and indeed was demonstrated, must have encouraged mathematicians in their bid to secure such proofs. As we see from *Theaetetus*, mathematicians of Theodorus's period, building on that first discovery, set to work to investigate more complicated cases. Incommensurabilities, so far from inhibiting mathematical inquiry, became the basis for what may even be called a research program. While the original discovery of the incommensurability of the side and diagonal of the square would have posed a problem for ontology—that is, for the view that physical objects are constituted by numbers as their matter—that is a separate issue. Besides, although Aristotle sometimes ascribes such a view to Pythagoreans, this is not so much a direct statement of their position as an inference concerning what Aristotle himself believed their position entailed. So far as mathematical study itself goes, the discovery of incommensurability may well have encouraged, rather than discouraged, the search for demonstrations.

Our review of the available evidence leaves *open* the possibility that the first strictly deductive arguments aiming at demonstrations were indeed those in Parmenides' *Way of Truth*. At the same time, we cannot rule out the further possibility that in mathematics, too, in approximately the same period, similar arguments had also begun to be developed. In general terms, the style of argument in both domains is, not surprisingly, similar. Thus we find that reductio, or indirect proof, is as important in early mathematics as it is in philosophy from Parmenides onward. At the same time, we cannot represent mathematics as entirely dependent on proof forms that can also be exemplified in philosophy. Mathematics certainly comes to develop its own, specifically mathematical, modes of demonstration, especially that based on the method of exhaustion, generally ascribed to Eudoxus in the late 4th century. This was a mathematical procedure that exploited the assumption of the infinite divisibility of the geometrical continuum. It enabled the areas of curvilinear figures (such as a circle) to be determined by successively closer rectilinear approximations, and was of general applicability and, from the 4th century onward, the geometrical proof procedure par excellence. While the *ambition* to provide demonstrations was common to both mathematics and philosophy, the demonstrative techniques employed in either domain were, to some extent at least, independent of one another.

Demonstration provides the basis for claims to certainty, and as such it had a fundamental role in both philosophy and mathematics from the mid-5th century onward. But the ambition to prove theories and conclusions came to be a dominant preoccupation in many areas of natural science as well. It is now time to consider the range of competing models of scientific understanding that were made explicit in the period before Aristotle. While one such model took it that knowledge depends on demonstration, others adopted laxer requirements for science. The evidence from the extant Hippocratic treatises of the late 5th and early 4th centuries is particularly interesting in this regard, since it shows both how some medical theorists sought to adopt or adapt the models provided by mathematics and philosophy, and how others resisted those tendencies and offered an alternative analysis of the status and proper methods of medicine.

The treatise known as *On Ancient Medicine* is a work that dates from the late 5th or, more likely, the early 4th century. The author attacks those who practiced medicine on the basis of what he calls a "hypothesis," a term he uses in the sense of "postulate" or "assumption." To be sure, it is not just *any* use of any kind of assumption that he has in mind. Certainly he himself uses a variety of concepts that we might characterize as assumptions. Rather, the use the writer particularly objects to is when a small number of such assumptions are taken as the basis for an entire theory of medicine. He criticizes his opponents especially for "narrowing down the causal principle of diseases," treating all diseases as if they were the outcome of just one or two factors such as "the hot," "the cold," "the wet," and "the dry." He compares the medical use

of such assumptions to the methods used by some of the natural philosophers—those who investigate "things in the heavens or under the earth."
While he does not mention mathematics, mathematical deductive arguments
based on a limited number of starting points might be a further analogue to
the methods he criticizes in medicine, and the evidence we have noted before
from Plato suggests that the term *hypothesis* may have been used in mathematics at least before Plato himself.

Reconstructing the precise method attacked in *On Ancient Medicine* is difficult, and we are not in a position to name particular theorists whom this author may be taken to have definitely had in mind. Yet it seems that his principal objection is to treating medicine as if the whole subject could be deduced
from a small number of starting points or principles. We have seen before
that a well-defined notion of axioms may not antedate Aristotle himself. At
the same time, both mathematics and philosophy provide examples of systems of deductive arguments based on a small number of starting points of
some kind. It is some such ambition, to systematize the whole of medicine
and treat it as a deductive structure derivable from a limited number of principles, that the author of *On Ancient Medicine* resists. He does so in the name
of a rival view that insists that certainty and exactness are not possible in
medicine, which is a matter, rather, of experience, of practice, of a trained eye.
In the author's own view medicine is certainly a skill, a *technē*—where there
are recognizable distinctions between good and bad practitioners—but it is
a skill for which a better analogy would be seamanship than speculative philosophy.

This is not the only treatise that throws light on the growing dispute,
within medicine, between two main competing conceptions of the subject. On
the one hand, there are those whose ambition it was to assimilate medicine, as
far as possible, to an exact science, who claim that it can achieve, even has
achieved, certainty. One such is the author of the work *On the Art* who, recognizing that medical practice is fallible, explains this not in terms of the
shortcomings of medicine itself, nor of its capacity to achieve cures, but rather
in terms of the inability of patients to follow orders. Again there are several
writers who claim that they can show, indeed have shown, the necessity of
their conclusions, even on such problematic topics as the fundamental constituents of human bodies or of physical objects in general, or on the causes,
and cures, of diseases. Thus we find dogmatic theories on those subjects
presented in such works as *On the Nature of Man*, *On Regimen*, and *On
Breaths*. True, some of these authors appeal to what we may call empirical evidence, as *On the Nature of Man* refers to the effects of drugs in inferring the
presence of certain humors in the body. But while, in refutation, the combination of evidence and deductive argument in that work provides an impressive
basis for the demolition of rival, monistic views, the attempts to show the necessity of the alternative pluralist theory are, naturally, quite inconclusive.

Yet the ambition to secure fundamental principles from which the whole of physiology and pathology can be derived is widespread.

On the other hand, resistance to the view that medicine can possibly be held to be deducible from a small number of postulates is represented not just by the author of *On Ancient Medicine* but by the undogmatic and anti-dogmatic tendencies to be found in many of the more purely empirical works. Many medical writers emphasize the conjectural nature of the art of medicine, not just in relation to the application of general principles to particular cases, but in the matter of the nature of the general principles themselves. One such treatise is *On the Places in Man,* which observes that there is a good deal of variability in medicine and remarks on the difficulties, in practice, of determining the right moment for intervention. The work *On Diseases* goes further. Exactness is not attainable either on the question of the differences between one physique and another, one illness and another, or on the issue of the timing of the doctor's own interventions. Medicine as a whole, this author states, has no demonstrated beginning or principle that is correct for the whole of the art of healing.

We thus find already in the period before Aristotle the main battle lines drawn up for what was to be the major ongoing epistemological and methodological dispute throughout ancient Greek medicine and even science as a whole. Against those who were for treating medicine as a deductive, exact science, there were those who insisted on its inexactness. Against those who sought necessity, there were those who considered that probability is the most that can be attained. Against those who thought that for understanding to be scientific it had to be certain, there were those who argued that medicine, for instance, is based on experience and must, to some extent, employ guesswork or conjecture, and yet it can still be claimed to be a rational inquiry, a *technē*, with its proper principles and methods.

We shall follow the fortunes of this debate in Aristotle and beyond, but for some of the background to the demand that science be demonstrative Plato provides crucial further evidence. His analysis of the concept of proof is a good deal more sophisticated than that of any earlier writer. In several of the dialogues, notably *Gorgias, Phaedo, The Republic,* and *Phaedrus,* the notion of proof, *apodeixis,* is elaborated in contradistinction to that of mere persuasion (where the key Greek term is *peithō* and its cognates). The latter is often associated with rhetoric, and it is the need to contrast true philosophy, and dialectic, with mere rhetoric that provides some of the stimulus to elaborate a strict concept of proof.

Certain contexts in which persuasion is used attract Plato's special attention. In the law courts and assemblies, what the judges or the people as a whole may be persuaded of may or may not be true, may or may not be the best policy. Sophists, and those who taught the art of public speaking, often aimed at, and were content with, achieving persuasion alone, whether or not that went with the truth—or so, at least, Plato claims. Like Aristophanes and others, Plato condemns those who made the worse, or weaker, argument seem the better or stronger, and more especially those who taught others how to manipulate arguments thus. If rhetoric and sophism are, at best, amoral, and often positively immoral, dialectic is the sincere search for the truth for its own sake. This might take the form of question and answer—as in the Socratic *elenchus*—but if so, it was not a question of refuting a thesis for refutation's sake but of doing so to discover the truth. Here it is not a matter of persuading a mass of jurors, or a lay audience, but of gaining the agreement of the person whose ideas are under examination. Moreover the procedure is not directed at the person himself but at the subject under discussion. If there is a competitive element in the correct method, it is a rivalry to get to the truth.

Plato does not offer a formal definition of *apodeixis*, but he explains his views on dialectic and on the accounts that philosophers should be expected to be able to give in justification of what they claim to know. In *The Republic*, especially, "dialectic" is contrasted with the procedures of the mathematicians and is rated higher than theirs on two counts in particular. First, the mathematicians make use of visible diagrams, while dialectic is a totally abstract study. More fundamentally, the mathematicians (as already noted) are said to give no account of their hypotheses but to take them "as evident to all." The dialecticians, by contrast, can and should do so, proceeding upward from their starting points to higher and higher hypotheses until they arrive at what Plato calls an unhypothetical first principle, to be identified with the Form of the Good, the Form in virtue of which all the other Forms acquire both their being and their knowability.

Much in this description is obscure, but it is obvious that with the unhypothetical first principle we are dealing with no mere axiom of the kind that came to be used in mathematics—in Euclid, for example. This is no mere proposition accepted as self-evidently true. It is rather, one supposes, a principle deemed to be essential to the correct conduct of any inquiry. Presumably Plato's point is, or includes, the idea that the order and regularity of the intelligible world exhibit *goodness*. As we can see from *Timaeus*, the account that Plato requires in cosmology is teleological, in terms of the beneficent interventions of the divine Craftsman who brings order into chaos. Moreover, in more general terms, for something to be revealed as ordered is, for Plato, for it to be revealed also to be good. Thus the Forms, as principles of order, may be said to depend (in a sense) on this supreme Form, the Form of the Good, since without it they would not be the principles of order that they are.

Difficult as it is to interpret this notion, we can understand the *claims* made on behalf of a dialectic thus founded on the principle of Goodness. The dialectician who *has* grasped the Form of the Good will be in a position to give an account of his recommendations and explanations in every field of study.

Once the whole complex, articulated structure of the Forms is apprehended as the structure it is, certainty will be attainable—even if Plato is careful not to imply that Socrates *has* attained it, let alone that he himself had. The *ambition* to attain it is, however, clear. The method based on a principle that is itself unhypothetical is a method that can *secure* its results, not just in relation to the Good itself, but with regard to all the Forms seen to depend on it.

Moreover, this account of the highest form of study inevitably has repercussions on Plato's evaluation of other inquiries. We have remarked that mathematics is ranked below dialectic in *The Republic*. In *Philebus* (55ff) we have a more complex stratification of the various branches of knowledge. At the top comes dialectic, of course. But below that mathematics is subdivided into a higher, purer study—the philosophical study of numbers in themselves, for instance—and a lower, applied one—the arithmetic used in practical calculation. Lower still, there are arts such as architecture, music making, navigation, and medicine, but these are distinguished and graded according to the extent to which they make use of numbering, weighing, and measuring. Thus architecture, which does so to a considerable degree, is rated higher on this score than music making, said to be based not on measurement so much as on guesswork. It is notable that while Plato is prepared here to accommodate medicine as *a* branch of knowledge, it is one of the lowliest, as being an essentially conjectural discipline.

Aristotle is at once clearer and more systematic than Plato, and it is Aristotle who may be said to provide the first *explicit* definition and explanation of an axiomatic deductive method of reasoning. In *Posterior Analytics* (71b11ff) he defines demonstration, *apodeixis,* as deductive, specifically syllogistic, in form, and he insists that it should proceed from premises that must be true, primary, immediate, and explanatory of the conclusions. They must be explanatory, since the knowledge or understanding that demonstration yields is, strictly, not of mere facts but of their explanations or causes.

Thus Aristotle is clear on three fundamental points. First, deductive argument is wider than demonstration, for deductive arguments may be valid or invalid, and valid deductions can be drawn from premises irrespective of whether those premises are true or false. For demonstrations, the deductions must be valid *and* the premise true as well as primary and explanatory. Second, not all true propositions can be demonstrated. The primary propositions from which demonstrated conclusions follow must themselves be indemonstrable—to avoid an infinite regress. For what premises could they be demonstrated from? Third, the primary indemonstrable premises needed for demonstrations will take different forms. Aristotle specifies definitions, hypotheses, and axioms. By definitions he has in mind not nominal definitions of terms but real definitions—that is, accounts that correspond to the realities of the subject matter investigated. He explains his notion of hypothesis in terms of the assumptions, such as that of the existence of objects defined.

Thus in his mathematical example, the definition of a point tells us what "point" signifies, but the corresponding hypothesis is the assumption that there are such. Finally there are the axioms, both general laws setting out the principles on which all communication is based (the laws of noncontradiction and of excluded middle) and axioms specific to particular inquiries. Again Aristotle's example is a mathematical one, the equality axiom that states that if equals are taken from equals, equals remain. Aristotle takes it that any attempt to *prove* this would itself have to presuppose the principle in question.

If we bear in mind the indeterminate nature of the "starting points" assumed in extant mathematics or in philosophy before Aristotle, including even in Plato himself, we can see that the distinctions that Aristotle introduces between the different types of indemonstrable, and his analysis of their role in demonstration, achieve a remarkable clarification of the issues. At the end of the *De Sophisticis Elenchis* (183a37ff, 183b34ff) he writes of his own originality in having given the first formal analysis of deductive argument, and we may agree that there is no reason seriously to dispute his claim.

Here, then, is a powerful procedure by which not just truth but certainty can be attained, secured by valid deductive arguments proceeding from self-evident primary premises. Many of Aristotle's examples in *Posterior Analytics* are mathematical, and although Greek mathematical reasoning is not syllogistic in form, it was, of course, in that domain that the practice of axiomatic deductive reasoning could and did have its main area of application. Yet Aristotle's own scientific activity was rather in the field of natural philosophy, especially zoology, and questions arise as to whether such an ideal of demonstration is applicable there and, further, whether Aristotle thought it was.

Certainly there are examples drawn from physics, from meteorology, from astronomy, from zoology and botany, along with mathematical examples, in *Posterior Analytics*, and these clearly indicate that at the time that work was composed, at least, Aristotle was hopeful of applying some of its ideas in those fields too. There is, to be sure, no problem in seeing Aristotle as endeavoring to implement some of the ideals *for explanation* that are set out in *Analytics*, in practice, throughout his work, even if he rarely, if ever, presents his results in clear syllogistic form, that is, in a fashion that exhibits transparently their syllogistic structure. But there is a fundamental difficulty concerning the indemonstrables that are appropriate to, and possible in, physics.

The general axioms of reasoning are, of course, applicable in physics as in all communication. But nothing *follows from* them. They will not figure in demonstrations except in the rare case where the demonstrator wishes to show some logical principle directly linked to them. But Aristotle never gives a clear zoological or botanical example of an axiom *specific* to those domains (on a par with the equality axiom in mathematics), and indeed it is hard to supply any plausible example of one. Definitions, to be sure, are an important topic of investigation in the physical treatises. Yet these are not then used as the indemonstrable primary premises from which are deduced demonstrated conclusions corresponding to the ideal requirements of *Posterior Analytics*. Moreover many of the key terms used in his physical works are explicated in ways that acknowledge that no simple univocal definition can be given of them. They are "said in many ways." Such is the case not just with the abstractions discussed in *Physics*, such as the notions of time, space, continuity, and the like, but also with some of the fundamental concepts on which his physical theories are based. This applies, for instance, to element theory. The primary opposites, hot, cold, wet, and dry, are explicated roughly in the work *On Coming-To-Be and Passing-Away* but are recognized, in *Parts of Animals*, to be "said in many ways."

The mismatch between the practice of the physical treatises and the ideal model of demonstration set out in *Posterior Analytics* poses a problem that remains at the center of scholarly controversy. On one line of interpretation, *Posterior Analytics* should be seen not as recommending that proper science be formal, but simply as showing how a formal description of proper science can be given. Yet this still leaves plenty of problems concerning the securing of indemonstrables that are appropriate to the concerns of proper science. On another view, the object of this treatise is to explain how a science can be *taught*, and Aristotle is accordingly not exercised with how the scientific investigator goes about his own researches. The actual procedures of the physical treatises might more often be better described as dialectical than demonstrative. On a third view, Aristotle may have modified his ideas as his own scientific activities developed, including his views on the *ideals* that are suitable to such investigations, as well as his views on their actual practice.

This is not the place to enter into the details of these disputes. But one fundamental point may be made that goes to the heart of the question. This is that there is, in any case, no question of *Posterior Analytics* presenting the *only* theory or concept of demonstration, *apodeixis*, in Aristotle. When we turn to the rest of his work we find him using and developing a variety of different notions of demonstrations, in different contexts. He sets out a second carefully worked-out theory of demonstration in *Rhetoric*, where he uses the term *enthymeme* for what are, precisely, rhetorical demonstrations. Not only does their form differ from the demonstrations analyzed in *Posterior Analytics*—they do not, for instance, proceed from indemonstrable primary premises and indeed do not conform to the rules for the valid modes of the syllogism—but, furthermore, Aristotle explains that they will be useful not to establish incontrovertible conclusions but rather for the purposes of securing conviction in relation to what is unclear or disputed.

There should be nothing surprising in this further theoretical analysis of a rhetorical mode of demonstration in Aristotle's *Rhetoric*. We should bear in mind that from its very beginning, Greek forensic and deliberative oratory had repeatedly presented what the orators themselves call demonstrations, of the facts of the case, of the guilt or innocence of the parties concerned, of the rights and wrongs of the policies under discussion. While, as we saw, the chief effort of Plato was to *deny* that rhetoric as usually practiced achieved more than mere persuasion, the terminology both he and Aristotle used for the highest kind of demonstration in philosophy is the *same* as that which the orators themselves used of *their* claims to have proved points beyond reasonable doubt. Aristotle indeed duly acknowledged that there is *rhetorical* demonstration, even though in his account of it he is far from just describing the usual procedures of the orators, which he would fault on a number of grounds.

It is not that the physical treatises of Aristotle exemplify rhetorical demonstration as he defines it. Yet in the scattered methodological remarks we find in *Metaphysics* as well as in the zoology and elsewhere, there is a clear recognition that demonstration may be more or less strict, indeed more or less necessary, depending on the subject matter in hand. Whether or not we say that Aristotle's position on the topic of demonstration in physics changed, we must agree that we find a variety of views expressed on the styles of demonstration possible and appropriate on different problems and in different areas. The actual practice of his scientific investigations is, then, a good deal more flexible, and looser, than the requirements of *Posterior Analytics* might lead one to expect. Finally it must be added that if he had attempted to set out demonstrations in the *Posterior Analytics* style in the physical and zoological works, on the vast majority of occasions this would hardly have improved the investigation. To have insisted on indemonstrable primary premises that are true, immediate, and necessary, on many of the problems he was concerned with, would have bought surface clarity only at the cost of artificiality and arbitrariness.

The theory of rigorous demonstration that was set out in *Posterior Analytics* came closest to implementation in practice not in Aristotle's own physical works, but in the mathematical work of Euclid. As noted, Greek mathematics was never cast in syllogistic form—nor indeed can most mathematical reasoning be so cast without great strain. But the work that above all exhibited what the comprehensive presentation of a systematic body of knowledge set out in strict deductive form looked like in practice was Euclid's *Elements*. Just how far Euclid may have been directly influenced by Aristotle, and how far he was following and elaborating the models provided by earlier mathematics, is uncertain. Like Aristotle he adopts a triadic classification of indemonstrables, though his triad does not match Aristotle's exactly. His definitions and common opinions correspond to the definitions and axioms in Aristotle well enough, and one of his common opinions is the equality axiom cited also by Aristotle. However his third kind of indemonstrable is the postulate, and these clearly differ from Aristotle's hypotheses. The first three of his postulates in *Elements*, book I, relate to the possibility of carrying out certain constructions (for example, to draw a straight line from any point to any point), and the other two assume certain truths concerning geometrical construc- tions that form the basis of what *we* call Euclidean geometry, namely that all right angles are equal, and that nonparallel straight lines meet at a point.

But the question of indebtedness is a subsidiary issue. What is both uncon- troversial and of first-rate importance is that *Elements* thereafter provides *the* model for the systematic demonstration of a body of knowledge, a model in- fluential (as we shall see) not just in mathematics but far beyond it. Of course by modern standards of axiomatization, that in Euclid's mathematics is far from perfect. Among minor points of criticism are that he includes certain re- dundant definitions (for example, that of rhomboid). Among more important ones are that several of his key terms remain undefined and unexplicated, as, for instance, his notion of measure, where, as with the notion of proportion, *Elements* seems to draw on a variety of traditions and has not resolved all the problems of consistency that they pose. Moreover the very notion of at- tempting explicit definitions of all the fundamental terms in geometrical discourse itself appears odd to a modern view, at least insofar as it seems su- pererogatory to provide such in the case of *primitive* terms. *Their* sense is precisely what the geometry developed on their basis explicates—in a man- ner more appropriate than any formal definition could achieve.

At this point, interestingly, the thrust of possible modern criticisms con- trasts with that of some ancient objections to *Elements*. Some ancient com- mentators complained not that Euclid had done too much, but that he had not done enough—not that he tried to be too explicit, but rather that he had taken as axioms propositions that should have figured as theorems to be proved. A sequence of later writers, including Ptolemy and Proclus, com- plained that the parallel postulate should have been demonstrated. They sometimes themselves attempted proofs, though their offerings all suffer from circularity. With the benefit of hindsight we can now see the wisdom of treating this as a postulate in the context of the geometry Euclid constructed on its basis. Whether this was Euclid's own contribution is unclear, but since Aristotle reports that attempts to prove assumptions concerning parallels are open to the charge of circularity, the notion of adopting the postulate con- cerned as a postulate can hardly have antedated Euclid by many years.

Neither Euclid nor anyone else in antiquity seriously envisaged the possi- bility of non-Euclidean geometries. Euclid almost certainly assumed that *Ele- ments* presents not just a consistent set of mathematical truths but a set that corresponds to the reality of spatial relationships in the world. Most Greek mathematics, indeed, adopts a confidently realist position about the relation- ship between mathematics and physics, even when some theorists allowed that certain physical phenomena are capable of different mathematical ac- counts. But that did not stop Euclid taking as a postulate a proposition that he may well have known others would have attempted to prove. However, if the adoption of the parallel postulate was controversial, no one was in any doubt concerning the impressive strengths that the argumentative structure of *Elements* as a whole exhibits. First there is the economy and clarity with which individual theorems are established, using direct or indirect proofs, especially reductio and the method of exhaustion. Second there is the careful articulation of the whole into a single comprehensive system.

After Euclid, proof in the style of *Elements,* proof *more geometrico,* as it was later to be called, became a potent ideal imitated in a wide variety of disciplines. Thus Euclid's own optics, parts of music theory, parts of theoretical astronomy, and statics and hydrostatics were presented in this style, with first the setting out of the postulates, common opinions, axioms, definitions needed, then the deductive demonstration of a body of theorems. There can be no doubt that much of the work so produced ranks among the most remarkable achievements of Greek science. This may certainly be said of Archimedes' statics and hydrostatics, for instance, where, in the first case, he explores the consequences of a set of postulates concerning balances and proceeds to the proof of the law of the lever, and, in the second, demonstrates, again on the basis of appropriate postulates, the principle named after him: that solids heavier than a fluid will, if placed in the fluid, be carried down to the bottom of the fluid, and they will be lighter in the fluid by the weight of the mount of fluid that has the same volume as the solid.

However, certain constraints on scientific work must also be acknowledged to have come from the concentration on the Euclidean ideal. In mathematics itself, the preoccupation with the strict demonstration of results may well have had an inhibiting effect, if not on mathematical inquiry itself, at least on what mathematicians chose to publish as their results. The exception here that proves the rule is Archimedes' *Method.* Quite exceptionally for a Greek mathematical text, this work discusses discovery as well as demonstration and presents a method that, Archimedes says, is heuristic without being demonstrative. The method is called a mechanical one, and it depends on two interrelated assumptions, first that a plane figure can be thought of as composed of the parallel lines that it contains, and second that it can be thought of as balanced against some other area or set of lines at a certain distance (the distance being imagined as a balance from which the figures are suspended). Now it is not clear from what Archimedes himself says, and it is disputed in modern scholarship, whether his reason for refusing to think this method a demonstrative one was the use of the mechanical assumption (which breached the categorical distinction between physics and mathematics) or that of indivisibles (which breached the assumption of the geometrical continuum), or indeed of both. But that point need not concern us here; the point that does is that Archimedes allows informal methods no more than a heuristic role and insists that the results thereby obtained must thereafter all be proved strictly using reductio and the method of exhaustion.

The inhibition that Greek mathematicians generally, and not just Archimedes, felt about presenting results other than in strict demonstrative form must have acted as a break on investigation. Archimedes' heuristic method remained unexploited by later Greek mathematicians (indeed all but ignored), and if that was partly because the treatise that described it was not generally known, that is not the whole story, since some of the theorems in his *On the Quadrature of the Parabola* implicitly depend on a similar method. The problem was the more general one of the reluctance to rely on informal methods.

I remarked that it was not just in mathematics and the exact sciences that proof in the Euclidean manner became the ideal. Our next topic should be the imitation of these methods in the natural sciences, such as physiology, psychology, and even medicine. By far the most outstanding example of this comes in the work of the 2nd-century C.E. medical writer Galen, and it will be convenient to concentrate our discussion on him.

Galen's reputation, in antiquity, did not depend just on his preeminence as a physician, since he was also considered a notable philosopher and he certainly made impressive original contributions to logic in particular. Unfortunately his masterpiece in that field, the fifteen-book work *On Demonstration*, is not extant, but it is clear from his own and other references to it that it contained a comprehensive analysis of the subject. In the short treatise *That the Best Doctor Is Also a Philosopher*, Galen gives three types of reasons to support the thesis that gives the work its title. First, the doctor should be morally upright and in particular free from avarice. Second, the doctor will need to study natural philosophy in order to base his medical theories on the correct physical principles, for example the theory of the elements. But third, the doctor should also be trained in scientific method, especially in demonstration. It is not just that doctors should, in his view, have a clear grasp of elementary logic and be able to distinguish valid and invalid inferences. Galen wants far more, namely that the doctor should be able to present scientific demonstrations on theoretical points throughout his work.

This is not just an abstract, theoretical claim, for Galen evidently puts it into practice on many occasions in his own biological treatises. Negatively and destructively he often criticizes his opponents' arguments as invalid, inconsistent, based on ambiguous terms, and so on. For this purpose and for his own constructive demonstrations he draws not just on Aristotelian, but also on Stoic, logic, using in particular Stoic formalizations where the variables expressed as numbers stand not for terms but for schemata. Thus both the Stoic elementary propositions later known as Modus Ponens and Modus Tollens are referred to: "if p, then q; but p; so q," and "if p, then q; but not q; so not p."

In many cases the points he claims to demonstrate are fairly straightforward consequences of hypotheses that state generally accepted principles. But he also attempts demonstration of some of his fundamental physiological and psychological doctrines. Thus in the work *On the Doctrines of Plato and Hippocrates* he sets out to prove his modified version of Plato's tripartite psychology (a theory maintained also, he would claim, by Hippocrates). According to Galen there are three main faculties of the soul (or life force), namely the appetitive, the spirited, and the rational. The first is to be located in the liver, the source of the veins; the second is placed in the heart, the source of the arteries; and the third in the brain, the source of the nervous system.

These are positions that he claims are demonstrable, and he himself proceeds to demonstrate them. Interestingly enough he distinguishes between the ease and certainty of the demonstrations of the locations of the higher two faculties of the soul, and the relative complexity of the arguments that establish that the appetitive function is to be placed in the liver. In the case of the rational faculty he proposes the simplest of syllogisms: "where the beginning of the nerves is, there is the governing part. The beginning of the nerves is in the brain. Therefore the governing part is there." Here the key step is, of course, that which establishes the origin of the nerves in the brain, and for this he refers to his own and earlier anatomical investigations. Thus if the carotid nerves leading up to the brain are ligated, the animal immediately loses consciousness. This provides the connection Galen needs, and with this secure he moves to state the whole proof as outlined above. His method is similar in the case of the role and function of the heart, but he concedes that no direct procedure, using ligation, is possible in the case of the liver. However, he believes he can establish well enough that the veins originate there, and that the nutritive and appetitive functions have their origin there too.

Galen thus frequently uses his knowledge of argument schemata to help in the construction of the proofs of physical, physiological, and psychological theories. Many of his arguments can readily be presented in rigorous formal terms: he presents some of them in that form himself. But the chief question that arises relates to the problem that I have already mentioned in connection with Aristotle. Valid deductive arguments lead to true conclusions if and only if the premises are themselves true. If the premises are accepted by an opponent, then he has to accept the conclusions as well; if the premises are agreed to provisionally as working hypotheses, we can say that we have dialectical arguments recommending the conclusions. However, the fundamental problem is that for strict demonstration we need ultimate primary premises that are themselves indemonstrable, and the question is, what will count as such in such domains as physiology or pathology?

We can agree that definitions will play some such role, but they will hardly be adequate for the task on their own. To supplement them, Galen appears to hold that some very general physical and pathological principles have the status of axioms. One such is the doctrine that nature does nothing in vain, which he treats as a regulative principle of physiological explanation. If that is denied, no proper explanations of the functions of the parts of the body can be given. The principle itself cannot be proved, but it provides the foundation for the investigation of nature. Similarly in pathology Galen frequently cites the principle he ascribes to Hippocrates, that opposites are cures for opposites, and indeed some such doctrine will certainly be needed for the purposes of his medical demonstrative arguments.

Yet in both cases these principles have serious shortcomings *as axioms*. The view that nature does nothing in vain was rejected by many philosophers and scientists, notably by both the pre- and the post-Aristotelian atomists. Moreover the particular version of the doctrine that Galen adopts is especially controversial, since in his view (at least as he sometimes expresses it) the doctrine states not just what is generally true but what is true without exception. Unlike Aristotle, who allows that some of the parts of the body do not directly serve a good purpose but are the residues or by-products of physiological processes, Galen sometimes writes as if there were no such exceptions—difficult as that doctrine is to sustain in practice, in the face of such evident problems as that of the presence of pathogenic substances in the body.

Again the trouble with the doctrine that opposites are cures for opposites is that it leaves quite unclear what will count as "opposites." As Aristotle pointed out, hot, cold, wet, and dry, for instance, were "said in many ways" and their application to foods, drugs, processes was in fact highly disputed. A substance might appear hot to the touch but not *be* hot, depending on the theory invoked in its analysis. What counted as "repletion" and "evacuation" was equally massively indeterminate. So while most Greek medical theorists may indeed be said to have accepted, in one form or another, the idea of attempting to counteract opposites to achieve a cure, the *content* of that doctrine varied considerably from one theorist to another.

Neither medical science nor physiology had, in Galen's day, the remotest chance of actually securing primary premises that are both indemonstrable and true, from which to derive *incontrovertible* conclusions. Galen's concern with the validity of arguments, his own and those of his opponents, is entirely admirable. Yet his further ambition to construct medicine and physics as far as possible on the model of mathematics and the exact sciences seems, in the state of the sciences at the time, extravagant. His obsession with logically rigorous formalized demonstrations is all the more paradoxical in that, if we consider the ways and means that might be thought appropriate to establishing the types of anatomical and physiological conclusions with which he is concerned, the best method would often rely on the very kind of empirical procedure, namely dissection, that Galen himself used so skillfully. What we still call *anatomical demonstrations,* for example to exhibit the structures and functions of particular nerves or the processes of digestion, are amply represented in such works as *On Anatomical Procedures.* Yet Galen still rates these empirical procedures as inferior to the strictly logical demonstrations he yearns for in physiology and pathology.

A long line of prominent philosophers and scientists stretching from Parmenides down to Galen and beyond exemplify the recurrent Greek concern with rigorous demonstration. In large part this concern reflects the desire for certainty, and in some cases it is clearly a negative reaction to the perceived weaknesses of merely persuasive argument. This was associated by Plato with the practices of orators in the law courts and assemblies, where indeed persuasive argument was commonly and most effectively deployed and sometimes even represented by the orators themselves as demonstrative.

Here then was one ideal for philosophy and science. Yet it was not the only conception of their goal, even if it was the dominant one in the work of several prominent theorists. I mentioned an alternative, empirical conception of the proper methods of scientific inquiry in the pre-Aristotelian medical literature. It is now time to review briefly, in conclusion, some of the later evidence for those who adopted a view of science that did not place the emphasis on the types of rigorous demonstration exemplified in the Euclidean tradition.

For this purpose we should first turn back to some points in Aristotle himself. We have seen that he set out, in *Posterior Analytics*, a very strict theory of demonstration but in practice, in the physical treatises, rarely if ever presents arguments that strictly conform to that theory. We noted, too, certain texts that suggest the possibility of looser styles of demonstration appropriate to certain problems in physics and elsewhere. While for the highest form of demonstration necessity and universality are definite requirements, physics deals, as he often stresses, with what is true always *or for the most part*. It is clear from the inclusion of propositions that state truths that hold "for the most part" in *Posterior Analytics* that Aristotle's aim, there, was to present a theory of strict demonstration that would also encompass them, although he encounters difficulties in so doing. But conclusions based on premises that state generally accepted or well-founded but not certain premises are given a recognized place in Aristotle's analysis in that they provide the basis of his account of what he calls dialectical reasoning. In practice, too, and not just in theory, much effort is devoted, in the physical treatises, to the critical evaluation of what was commonly believed, where Aristotle sometimes rejects but sometimes accepts, in modified form, what others also held.

Thus while Aristotle's own preference for demonstration over any merely dialectical procedure is clear, the latter provides the basis not for an alternative model for the highest science, but at least for supplementing the models that insist on demonstration in either its stricter or its laxer modes. After Aristotle, however, there were those who rejected with some vigor the whole concept that scientific inquiry, to be legitimate, had to yield results that could be claimed as incontrovertible.

Once again our main evidence comes from some of the medical writers, even though in the immediate post-Aristotelian period much of the work of important medical theorists is lost and their views have to be reconstructed from later reports. However, the evidence we have in both Celsus and Galen enables us to infer the main lines of a wide-ranging methodological and epistemological dispute about the status, aims, and proper methods of medicine, a dispute that continued from the late 4th century B.C.E. down to Galen's own day. The medical writers labeled "dogmatists" were not a well-knit sect. Rather, that term was used of any theorist who sought causal explanations of hidden phenomena in physiology or pathology. But more important for our purposes here are the views of two other rather more clearly defined groups regularly contrasted with the dogmatists. These are the Empiricists (starting with Philinus of Cos around the mid-3rd century B.C.E.) and the Methodists (who took their origin from the work of Thessalus and Themison around the 1st century B.C.E. and the 1st century C.E.). In both cases these theorists rejected the whole endeavor to give causal explanations of such physiological processes as respiration and digestion, and in both cases the method of dissection was criticized as irrelevant to the study of the living, normally functioning individual.

The alternative aim that the Empiricists and Methodists presented as the true goal of medicine is a pragmatic one. There is no need to inquire into how we breathe, Celsus reports the Empiricists arguing, but only what relieves labored breathing. There is no need to find out what moves the blood vessels, only what the various movements signify. The inquiry into obscure causes and natural actions is superfluous because nature cannot be comprehended. This was a view with which the Methodists, too, generally agreed, even while they reformulated the grounds for it, arguing not that it is impossible to comprehend nature, but rather that it is useless to do so. That is an issue on which judgment should be suspended.

The traditions of rationalist, dogmatic medicine were thus seriously undermined, and reasoning itself was viewed with some suspicion. In theorizing, the Empiricists held, it is always possible to argue on either side of the question, but then it is far from clear that victory in the argument goes to the person who has the better grasp of the subject. Both groups held that the aim of medicine is not theoretical knowledge but achieving cures. What counted was not book learning but practical experience. The Empiricists' method was to try to determine how to treat the particular case in hand on the basis of similarities with past cases. They proceeded on the basis of analogies, or as they put it, they used the "transition to the similar." Some of their opponents criticized them on the grounds that they would be at a complete loss if faced with an entirely new type of disease. But the Empiricist response to that might well have been that it was no good attempting to *deduce* a cure from a would-be universal principle, in such cases, since that would beg the question of *whether* the new disease could indeed be treated as an instance of some such general principle or otherwise brought under an existing general law.

The Methodists shared the pragmatic aims of the Empiricists but went

much further than them in rejecting not just research into hidden causes but
the basic assumption of most traditional Greek medical theory, namely the
possibility of identifying and classifying kinds of diseases. That is, they rejected the fundamental notion of disease entities. What the patient suffers
from, and what the doctor has to try to cure, are what they called "common
conditions," *koinotētes,* the "lax," the "restricted," and the "mixed." These
were not single diseases but rather, as their name suggests, general states. In
evaluating a patient's state the doctor would need to take into account the
whole condition and arrive at a plan for therapy only on the basis of a full assessment of that. Although extant Methodist writings, such as the gyneco-
logical work of the 2nd-century C.E. writer Soranus, still use traditional terms
for diseases, we should not be misled by this into supposing that their authors
endorsed these. Rather, the terms were used for the sake of a lay audience
who would have some idea of what they referred to, even if their understanding had to be reeducated to an acceptance of the very different approach to
questions of pathology that the Methodists themselves adopted.

A tension between the demand that science should be exact, yield certain
results, give demonstrations that proceed from self-evident premises via valid
deductions to undeniable conclusions, and a quite different view of science
that allowed a place for the probable, for conjecture, for empirical experience,
characterizes both the practices and the theories of Greek science from its
early beginnings down to the 2nd century C.E. and beyond. We can see this
tension in play *within* many of the sciences that I have so far not had occasion
to mention. A good example is provided by music. In music theory there were
those who took their stand by the experience of practicing musicians: their
aim was to describe the perceived phenomena of actual musical performances,
where indeed the great variety of modes in Greek music provided plenty of
scope for analysis. At the opposite end of the spectrum, there were writers
for whom music theory was a branch of mathematics, whether or not they
agreed specifically with Plato's recommendation, in *The Republic,* that the
study should concern itself solely with which numbers are essentially concordant with which. On one view, reason was not just a better guide to the underlying laws of harmony, it was the sole criterion. Thus when it became
evident that the numerical relationship corresponding to the interval of an
octave plus a fourth, namely 8 : 3, is neither multiplicate (like 2 : 1 or 3 : 1)
nor superparticular (like 3 : 2 and 4 : 3), the reaction of some theorists was to
conclude that whether or not such an interval *sounded* like a concord, it could
not *be* one, since it did not meet the requisite arithmetical condition for such.
To that Theophrastus commented that what music theory studies is not number but sounds, even if the relationships between concordant sounds are expressible numerically, as ratios between integers.

In astronomy, too, there are, on the one hand, broadly descriptive studies and, on the other, the attempt to create geometrical models to account for

the apparently irregular movements of the sun, moon, and planets. In some cases we have extant treatises that limit themselves to the purely geometrical analysis, for example, of interacting spheres in motion. One such is Autolycus of Pitane's work *On Moving Spheres* and another is Theodosius's *Sphaerica*. Neither of these carries the study forward to the point where a direct application is made to observed phenomena. No empirical data as such are brought to bear, and the discussion remains geometrical throughout. Similarly Aristarchus's work *On the Sizes and Distances of the Sun and Moon* is largely a hypothetical discussion of how the proportions of these sizes and distances can be worked out on the basis of certain assumptions.

However, much of Greek astronomical theory is not just geometrical, even while it uses geometry in the development of models to explain the movements of the sun, moon, and planets. The position of Ptolemy is especially revealing and will provide our last concrete example of the recurrent tension in Greek science between the desire for certainty and exactness and the need to accommodate imprecision in the detailed application of theory to empirical data.

In the opening chapters of *Syntaxis* Ptolemy contrasts mathematics (under which heading he includes the astronomical study he is himself about to engage in) with both theology and physics. Those two studies are both conjectural: not much knowledge can be acquired about the gods, and physics deals with unstable phenomena. Mathematics, by contrast—the claim is—yields certain results, based as it is on indisputable geometrical reasoning. Similarly in his astrological treatise, *Tetrabiblos*, the attempt to make predictions concerning events on earth is contrasted with the prediction of the movements of the heavenly bodies themselves, with the latter being far less certain.

Mathematical astronomy itself, these remarks imply, can yield exact conclusions. Yet in practice the application of Ptolemy's models to the particular movements of each of the planets, the sun, and the moon is permeated by approximations of one type or another. True, the geometrical reasoning is exact. So far as the geometry goes, nothing could detract from the claim that these are indeed Euclidean-style demonstrations. However, as soon as empirical data are brought into play—as they must be if the models are to be determinate quantitative models for each of the heavenly bodies, as opposed to merely impressionistic qualitative ones—there are elements of inexactness. These spring both from the acknowledged inexactnesses of particular observations (owing to the errors of instruments or observers or to the difficulties of observation) and from features of the calculations, the frequent adjustments that Ptolemy makes within the purely arithmetical parts of his computations, as, for instance, when he converts chords to arcs or vice versa. The outcome is indeed a set of fully determinate models, with definite parameters enabling the movements of the planets, moon, and sun to be predicted. Yet the elements of appreciation throughout are manifest.

The notion of demonstration thus lies at the heart of a methodological and epistemological dispute that runs through Greek philosophy and science from their very beginnings, a dispute often articulated around the contrast between reason and perception or, more generally, experience. Some Greek scientists opted resolutely for one of these two broad criteria to the exclusion of the other. That pushed the science they did toward either pure mathematics and logic or a pragmatism stripped of general theory. Some demanded strict demonstration in the geometrical manner, while others insisted on a relaxation of the requirement that science be demonstrative, allowing proper science to include—or even to consist in—conjecture. In between the two extreme positions there were those who sought a compromise, allowing both reason and experience a role, though in a variety of combinations. The fundamental dilemma that surfaces in many of the greatest works of ancient science and is, of course, far from being confined to ancient science is that the purer the science, the more it approximates pure mathematics in form, but then the further removed it will be from the very data that the science purports to explain. The tension was between the aim to make science exact and demonstrative and the need for it to be applicable. While some chose the goal of exactness at the cost of applicability (Archimedes) and others (among the medical writers) abandoned demonstrativeness for the sake of practice, the works of Galen in anatomy and physiology, and of Ptolemy in astronomical theory, exhibit the tensions that arise from the uneasy match between the desire for certainty and the actual recognition of the elements of approximation in many of the results obtained.

GEOFFREY E. R. LLOYD

Bibliography

Berti, Enrico, ed. *Aristotle on Science: The Posterior Analytics.* Padua: Antenore, 1981.

Burnyeat, Myles, ed. *The Sceptical Tradition.* Berkeley: University of California Press, 1983.

Détienne, Marcel, and Jean-Pierre Vernant. *Cunning Intelligence in Greek Culture and Society.* Trans. Janet Lloyd. Repr. Chicago: University of Chicago Press, 1991.

Gentzler, Jyl, ed. *Method in Ancient Philosophy.* Oxford: Clarendon Press, 1998.

Gotthelf, Allan, and James G. Lennox, eds. *Philosophical Issues in Aristotle's Biology.* Cambridge: Cambridge University Press, 1987.

Irwin, Terence H. *Aristotle's First Principles.* Oxford: Clarendon Press, 1988.

Knorr, Wilbur R. *The Evolution of the Euclidean Elements.* Dordrecht: Reidel, 1975.

Kullmann, Wolfgang. *Wissenschaft und Methode.* Berlin: De Gruyter, 1974.

Lloyd, Geoffrey E. R. *Magic, Reason, and Experience: Studies in the Origin and Development of Greek Science.* Cambridge: Cambridge University Press, 1979.

Mignucci, Marco. *L'argomentazione dimostrativa in Aristotele.* Padua: Antemore, 1975.

Mueller, Ian. *Philosophy of Mathematics and Deductive Structure in Euclid's Elements.* Cambridge, Mass.: MIT Press, 1981.

Netz, Reviel. *The Shaping of Deduction in Greek Mathematics.* Cambridge: Cambridge University Press, 1999.

Schofield, Malcolm, Myles Burnyeat, and Jonathan Barnes. *Doubt and Dogmatism.* Oxford: Clarendon Press, 1980.

Tannery, Paul. *Pour l'histoire de la science hellène,* 2nd ed. Paris: Gauthier-Villars, 1930.

ASTRONOMY

THE EARLIEST USE of astronomy among the Greeks appears in the poems of Homer and Hesiod (8th century B.C.E.). By that time the Greeks, like many other agricultural societies, had identified and named certain prominent stars and star groups (Arcturus, the Pleiades, and so on). We can see especially from Hesiod's *Works and Days* that the heliacal risings and cosmical settings of these (their first appearance and last disappearance just before dawn) were used to mark important points in the agricultural year, such as the time to begin plowing or harvesting. In the absence of a settled calendar, such an "astronomical calendar" was very necessary, and this traditional Greek astronomy was eventually codified in a kind of almanac (which, like modern almanacs, also contained weather predictions). Even after the development of scientific astronomy, these *parapegmata* continued to be popular, and examples were produced by some of the most eminent Greek astronomers. The early Greeks had also recognized the existence of planets and named some of them, but they had not yet recognized that the morning star and the evening star are the same planet, Venus.

Although a number of astronomical topics (such as the causes of eclipses) were discussed by the philosophers of the 7th and 6th centuries B.C.E. (supposedly beginning with Thales), their speculations should be described as cosmological rather than astronomical. But by the 5th century some astronomical truths had been enunciated, although they were not yet universally accepted even by the educated. Thus in the early 5th century Parmenides of Elea, in his remarkable philosophical poem, stated that the earth is a sphere and that the moon receives its light from the sun. In the next generation Empedocles correctly inferred that the cause of a solar eclipse is the moon passing in front of the sun. But equally important in the development of Greek astronomy during and perhaps even before the 5th century is the transmission of knowledge from Mesopotamia, where observational astronomy had been systematically practiced and recorded since the 8th century, and where astronomical systems were already being developed. This is apparent in the work of Meton, the first Greek who can properly be called an astronomer.

Meton is dated by his observation of the summer solstice at Athens in 432 B.C.E. Although not very accurate (it is a day in error), it marks the beginning of a new stage in Greek astronomy, for Meton made the observation by means of an instrument, simple but large and effective, that he had constructed for the purpose. Meton is also famous for his introduction of the nineteen-year luni-solar cycle, in which the solar year and the (true) lunar month are reconciled by the intercalation, in a fixed pattern, of a thirteenth month in seven years out of the nineteen. This is an obvious example of Mesopotamian influence, for a similar cycle had been in use in Babylon for some time. However, Meton was still operating within the framework of traditional Greek astronomy, since both his observations and his cycle were directed toward the composition of a *parapegma* almanac.

It is not until the next generation that the most original and profound Greek contribution to astronomy appears. This is the idea of using a geometrical model to explain the apparent motions of the heavenly bodies. Perhaps inspired by the success of geometry in revealing "truths" by deductive methods, some Greeks of the early 4th century sought to apply it to the heavens, particularly the often puzzling behavior of the planets. Later sources attribute to Plato the requirement that the apparent movements of the planets should be explained by uniform and orderly motions. Although no such passage appears in his works, it is consistent with views that he does express; but in this he is probably following the lead of others, notably his contemporary Eudoxus, a mathematician of the first rank, who in addition to his profound contributions to geometry also devised the first geometrical model to explain the motions of the heavens.

By the time of Eudoxus the picture of the universe generally accepted among educated Greeks was as follows: the earth is in the center, spherical and motionless; at the outer edge is a sphere on which the fixed stars are located, which rotates about the earth once daily; in between are the sun, the moon, and the planets, which also rotate about the earth, but with different motions and in different directions. The planets were particularly difficult to fathom. In the late 5th century the philosopher Democritus was still unsure as to their number, and their motions were puzzling, since they sometimes reversed direction (becoming "retrograde"). Eudoxus's explanation for this was brilliant in its combination of ingenuity and simplicity. He proposed that each body was carried by one or more spheres rotating uniformly about the earth as their common center (hence it is known as a homocentric system), but with different poles, these spheres all being connected with one another so that the motion of the outer was transmitted to that of the inner. Thus the outermost sphere of the fixed stars revolves round the earth once daily, about the poles of the equator, carrying with it the spheres of the sun, moon, and so on. The sun, for instance, is fixed on a sphere whose poles are those of the celestial ecliptic, and which rotates once annually in the direction opposite to the daily rotation. The moon required additional spheres to account for its deviation in latitude from the ecliptic. For the planets the great problem was accounting for their retrogradations. Eudoxus discovered that if one examines the motion of a point located on the equator of a sphere rotating with uniform velocity, this sphere in turn being fixed on another sphere with different poles, rotating with the same velocity but in the opposite direction, the combined motion of the point will be a figure eight (called by the Greeks a *hippopede*, or horse-fetter, which had that shape), the length and breadth of which is determined solely by the distance between the poles of the two spheres. Accordingly he supposed that each planet had such a combination of two spheres (now visualized as a *hippopede*) superimposed on the equator of the sphere carrying it around the ecliptic. This would in principle produce the variation in speed, and even the retrogradation, observable in the planets, as well as a deviation in latitude. The period of rotation on the *hippopede* was necessarily the "synodic period" of the planet (the time in which it returned to the same position with respect to the sun), while the period of rotation on the sphere carrying it was the "sidereal period" (the time in which it returned to the same fixed star).

As a theoretical construct Eudoxus's system was extraordinary, but when confronted with some easily observable astronomical facts it was clearly defective. First, no homocentric system could account for the variation in brightness of Mars and other planets, the most obvious explanation for which is a variation in their distance from the earth. Another defect was that the system could produce retrogradation for Mars only by the assumption of a grossly wrong synodic period. Although Aristotle adopted it in a modified form (which is the only reason we know anything about it), it was soon superseded by other geometric models. It is nevertheless of great interest as the first attempt by a Greek to apply mathematics to astronomy, in which the principle was established that any explanatory model must employ uniform circular motion. It is also important as an indication of the state of the Greeks' astronomical knowledge in the early 4th century: for instance, the planets enumerated by Eudoxus are the same five, with the same names, that became canonical (and are indeed the only planets known to antiquity), Saturn, Jupiter, Mars, Venus, and Mercury. Since these had all been known in Mesopotamia long before, the question of Babylonian influence arises. This influence is even more certain in another astronomical work by Eudoxus, a description of the heavens, as visible in Greece, in which he grouped all the fixed stars into the constellations that are still in use today. This work is a combination of traditional Greek nomenclature and mythology with Babylonian elements (most obviously in the twelve constellations of the zodiac). It is impossible to separate Eudoxus's own contributions from earlier elements, but the substance became definitive when it was cast into poetic form by Aratus in the early 3rd century: his poem *Phaenomena* was immensely popular both in the Greek and later in several Latin versions, and indeed was the principal source of most educated laymen's knowledge of the heavens.

The surviving astronomical works from the late 4th and the 3rd century, mainly treatises of elementary "spherics," do not do justice to the intense interest in both theoretical and practical astronomy that characterized the period after Alexander's conquests led to the rapid expansion of Greek culture to new areas. However, the two seem to have been kept separate, observational astronomy being directed toward the traditional areas of the *parapegma* (involving determination of the times of equinox and solstice, and observations of the positions of fixed stars relative to the horizon), while theoretical astronomy was concerned only with constructing geometric models to explain the motions of the heavenly bodies. During this period were proposed the two models that came to dominate classical Greek astronomy: the eccentric and epicyclic hypotheses. In the eccentric model the planet or other body is supposed to rotate with uniform motion on the circumference of a circle placed eccentrically to the earth. In the epicyclic model the body rotates uniformly about the center of a small circle ("epicycle") that in turn is carried with uniform motion about a larger circle (the "deferent") whose center is the earth. It is obvious that either of those models will produce a variation in the distance of the body, and it is easy to show that each will also, under suitable assumptions (which include the rotation of the center of the eccentric about the earth), produce retrogradation in a planet. The ingenious Greek geometers must have soon discovered that under such assumptions the eccentric and epicyclic models are fully equivalent in a mathematical sense, and it was no doubt in the context of this kind of mathematical transformation that Aristarchus of Samos (ca. 280 B.C.E.) came to formulate his famous heliocentric hypothesis, according to which the sun is the center of the universe and the earth, like all the other planets, revolves about it, while rotating daily on its own axis (the latter rotation had already been envisaged by Heracleides of Pontos in the 4th century). While this might have been acceptable from a purely mathematical viewpoint, it was at odds with ancient physics, and also entailed that the fixed stars must lie at an unthinkably enormous distance (since their relative positions remained unchanged during the earth's annual orbit). As a result, the heliocentric hypothesis was never taken seriously by ancient astronomers.

For all their versatility, the epicyclic and eccentric models were used only as a tool of astronomical explanation and demonstration. This can be seen in the elegant use of them by the mathematician Apollonius of Perge to show how one could, in theory, derive the "stationary points" of a planet (the points on its orbit where it begins and ends its retrogradation). Neither Apollonius nor anyone else at this period seems to have been interested in actually doing the calculation for a real planet at a real time. That would have involved far more in the way of information about its motions and position, and also in methods of calculation, than any Greek possessed at that time. The great change in this respect, and the evolution of Greek astronomy from an explanatory to a predictive science, came with Hipparchus, whose working life was spent in Nicaea and Rhodes from about 150 to 125 B.C.E.

Although all but one of Hipparchus's numerous monographs are lost, enough can be learned from mentions of his work in Ptolemy's *Almagest* and other treatises to reconstruct the outlines of his revolutionary innovations in Greek astronomy, and to be sure that, besides his own extraordinary contributions, both observational and theoretical, he owed a great debt to Babylonian astronomy. By the time of Hipparchus the Mesopotamian astronomers had not only compiled an archive of systematic observations going back 600 years, but they had also developed elaborate and ingenious mathematical tables for calculating and predicting the positions and resulting phenomena of the moon and the other heavenly bodies. Some of both the observational and computational material, inscribed on clay tablets, has been recovered from the site of Babylon in the past century. The mathematical tables have no underlying geometrical model: instead they are based on very precise period relations (of the type "720 retrogradations of Venus occur in 1,151 years"), combined with simple arithmetical functions (for instance, a body might be supposed to move between a minimum and maximum velocity in steps of equal increments). The calculations were greatly simplified by the use of the sexagesimal place-value system (comparable to our decimal system, but with a base of 60) that had been developed in Mesopotamia many centuries earlier. While stray elements of Babylonian astronomy are found in the Greek world before Hipparchus, he is the first Greek who displays an intimate acquaintance with both the observational and the computational aspects of it. We have no information about how he obtained this knowledge, but it is so wide and deep that we must suppose some kind of personal contact with the astronomer-scribes of Babylon. From his source he derived, for instance, a complete list of all eclipses observed at Babylon going back to the 8th century.

Both Babylonian observations and Babylonian methods can be traced in Hipparchus's work. But he did not simply copy what he found. For example, all the mean motions of the moon that he used are identical with those derivable from the Babylonian lunar ephemerides, but we know that Hipparchus used eclipse observations, both Greek and Babylonian, to confirm them. Moreover, he took from the Babylonians the idea of computing astronomical positions by means of tables, but he adapted it to the Greek idea of representing the phenomena by geometric models. That meant that he had to determine the size of the moon's epicycle, for instance, and then, from that and some observed position, compute tables that would allow the lunar position to be determined at any given time. To this end he developed a method, using three (Babylonian) eclipses, of finding the lunar eccentricity (this can be expressed as an abstract mathematical problem: given three points on the circumference of a circle, and the angles that they make at the center of the circle and some other point within the circle, determine the distance between the center and that other point). No Greek or Babylonian before him had done anything of the kind. In his calculations he was aided by the Babylonian sexagesimal system for fractions, but he had to invent trigonometry by himself (he is the calculator of the first trigonometrical function in history, a "chord table" that is closely related to our sine function).

As a pioneer in the reform of Greek astronomy, to make it the predictive mathematical science it eventually became, Hipparchus made enormous progress but did not complete all that, in his view, needed to be done. He produced working theories, based on eccentric and epicyclic models, for both sun and moon, using Babylonian period relations and both his own and Babylonian observations; thus he was able, for the first time among the Greeks, to compute eclipse phenomena. In the case of solar eclipses this confronted him with the problem of lunar parallax, for which he needed to determine the distance to the moon. Although his predecessors had investigated this (the only surviving treatise of Aristarchus is on the sizes and distances of sun and moon), their work had been largely conjectural or else based on methods that could not lead to a secure result. Hipparchus was the first to calculate an essentially correct lunar distance, of about sixty earth radii (his estimate of the solar distance, like almost all before the invention of the telescope, was far below the true value). He did extensive investigations of the fixed stars; not only did he criticize the descriptions of them by Eudoxus and Aratus (ironically, the work in which he did this is the sole treatise of Hipparchus that has survived, only because it was connected with Aratus's popular poem) but he also determined the positions of a large number of stars in numerical coordinates for the purpose of inscribing all the constellations on a star globe. In the course of his investigations he discovered the phenomenon of the "precession of the equinoxes"—that the fixed stars are not in fact fixed with respect to the celestial equator, but appear to perform a motion in longitude along the ecliptic so slow that it could be detected only by comparing observations hundreds of years apart. Hipparchus confirmed this phenomenon (which in modern times is explained by the very slow rotation of the earth's axis) from a number of different types of observation, but was unable to fix its amount precisely. In planetary theory his work was also left unfinished. The planetary models of his Greek predecessors had all been based on a single "anomaly," or factor causing nonuniform motion, the period of which was the planet's return to the sun—hence it is known as the synodic anomaly. Hipparchus must have known from his study of Babylonian planetary ephemerides that those who compiled them had recognized two anomalies, the synodic and the sidereal (the period of which was the planet's return to the same point in the ecliptic). He was able to demonstrate that the theories of his Greek predecessors could not account for the phenomena resulting from the two anomalies, but did not himself produce any alternative theory for the planets. He did, however, present period relations for the mean motions of all five planets (which we now know were derived from Babylonian sources), and he compiled a list of all the planetary observations he could extract from Babylonian and Greek sources, reduced to a common calendar, for the use of his successors.

No successor capable of properly appreciating and developing Hipparchus's achievements appeared for almost three hundred years, but certain aspects of his work were enthusiastically seized on. In particular, the enormous expansion in the Greco-Roman world of horoscopic astrology (which depends on the computation of the positions of the heavenly bodies at birth or some other critical time) in the century after Hipparchus is intimately connected with the change of direction he had introduced into Greek astronomy. It was mainly for this purpose that planetary tables were constructed, based on epicyclic and eccentric models, and indeed taking account of both the anomalies that Hipparchus had demonstrated, but in a fashion that was neither mathematically consistent nor logically defensible (although they did produce results acceptable to the astrologers). We know of these strange hybrids primarily from Indian astronomy of the *siddhāntas* (which was derived from the Greek astronomy of this post-Hipparchan period), since the original Greek works were lost, except for a few fragments, after Ptolemy's *Almagest* made them obsolete. Indeed, the period between Hipparchus and Ptolemy is one of the most obscure in the history of that science among the Greeks.

Ptolemy, whose great astronomical work, known as the *Almagest*, was completed about 150 C.E., set out to reform what he clearly regarded as the dismal state of the science of astronomy in his time. While he had the highest regard for the achievement of Hipparchus and recognized the value of the Babylonian observations, he disapproved of the Babylonian computational techniques that Hipparchus had continued to employ alongside Greek geometrical methods, and that were still common among the practicing astronomers and astrologers of his own time. He rigidly excluded these arithmetical methods from his treatise, which was designed to present the whole of mathematical astronomy (as the Greeks understood the term) in a logical and comprehensible fashion, starting from first principles. *Almagest* is a masterpiece of clear and orderly exposition that deserved the dominance it rapidly achieved in the field of scientific astronomy. I shall merely summarize here the main points in which it corrects or completes what Hipparchus had done.

For astronomical problems involving the observer's position on the earth's surface (for instance the calculation of the time taken for an arc of the ecliptic to rise at a given terrestrial latitude), which Hipparchus had solved by a combination of approximative and descriptive methods, Ptolemy employed the full rigor of spherical trigonometry (which had been developed only in the generation before Ptolemy, by Menelaus). In lunar theory Ptolemy, using the method developed by Hipparchus for finding the lunar eccentricity from three eclipses, achieved a more accurate result than his predecessor, showing where Hipparchus had made computational errors. But he also demonstrated that while the model proposed by Hipparchus works well for lunar positions near conjunction or opposition with respect to the sun, at intermediate positions great discrepancies with observation could appear. To account for these he introduced a modification, which was in some respects an unhappy one: although it satisfied the requirements of observation with respect to the longitude, it also produced a variation in the distance of the moon from the earth far greater than it really is, and ignored the fact that the visible variation in the size of the moon's disk refutes this feature of his model. In the theory of parallax, although Ptolemy's estimates of the distances of the sun and moon are not very different from those of Hipparchus, his methods of computing the resulting parallaxes are, apparently, much more rigorous, which ought to mean that computations of solar eclipses based on Ptolemy's tables were more reliable.

Ptolemy's catalogue of fixed stars, while relying heavily on data derived from Hipparchus, was organized in a new way, using the coordinates of celestial longitude and latitude (whereas previously most observations of star positions had been based on the declination, the distance of the star from the celestial equator). This organization was designed to take account of the motion of precession, since the catalogue could be reduced to later epochs simply by adding a constant value to the longitudes. Ptolemy determined the value of precession as 1 degree in 100 years (a value that Hipparchus had suggested as a lower limit).

Ptolemy's most original contribution to astronomy was in the theory of the planets. Like some of his predecessors, he represented the two anomalies by a combination of eccentric (to take account of the sidereal anomaly) and epicycle (for the synodic anomaly). But by careful analysis of different types of observations he came to the conclusion that the eccentricity that produced correct longitudes for a given planet also produced variations in the planet's distance from the earth that were about twice too great. He solved this dilemma by introducing the "equant" point: while retaining the same eccentricity, he supposed that the uniform motion of the planet's epicycle was counted not about the center of the epicycle on which it rode, but about another halfway between the center and the eccentric point representing the earth. This innovation was frequently criticized during the Middle Ages and into the Renaissance, since it seemed to violate the principle of uniform circular motion. However, it was undeniably successful in representing the phenomena: it has been shown that the longitudes derived from an equant model with the proper eccentricity differ from those derived from a Kepler ellipse of the same eccentricity by an amount well below 10 minutes of arc, which represents the limit of accuracy of ancient observations. Unfortunately, introduction of the equant greatly complicated the process of deriving the eccentricity from observations, since a problem that had previously been soluble by an adaptation of the method that Hipparchus had devised for the lunar eccentricity had been transformed into one that was no longer soluble by Euclidean methods (it amounts to solution of an equation of the eighth degree). Ptolemy overcame this difficulty by assimilating the insoluble problem to the soluble one, finding a preliminary eccentricity that he then used to find "corrections" to the observational data, from which a new eccentricity was derived, producing new corrections, and so on. This is the most ingenious use of an iterational mathematical procedure from antiquity, and fortunately it does converge on the correct result. Ptolemy's theory of the planets was completed by the construction of geometrical models to represent the planetary latitudes, very complicated because of the constraints of the geocentric imperative, but undoubtedly far superior to anything that had preceded.

Although *Almagest* is the earliest save one of Ptolemy's astronomical works, the structure he built in it is little changed in his later work. His *Ready Tables* introduced some improvements in organization over the tables presented in *Almagest*, but the underlying astronomical constants and models are the same except in the latitude theory, which is improved and simplified. The latitude theory is also improved in his *Planetary Hypotheses*, but the great importance of that work is the influence it had on cosmological views during later antiquity and the Middle Ages. This work, the ostensible purpose of which is to allow the reader to produce a working model of the universe, adopts the Aristotelian principle that nature does nothing in vain: hence there is no space wasted in the universe, which entails that the "spheres" of the planets (actually shells enclosed by spheres in which the mechanism of epicycle and eccentric operate) are contiguous. This enabled Ptolemy to compute the precise distances of all heavenly bodies, starting from the known lunar distance, right out to the sphere of the fixed stars. For good measure he added the sizes of all the bodies (based on estimates of their apparent diameters). The result is a universe that is very small by modern standards (Ptolemy's distance from the earth to the fixed stars is about the same as the modern computation of the distance from the earth to the sun). But the picture it presents is the one that was almost universally accepted right down to the end of the Middle Ages, in both Islamic and Christian lands (with minor modifications to accommodate the account in Genesis). It is recognizable, for instance, in Dante's *Divine Comedy*.

Although Ptolemy intended *Almagest* to be definitive only for his own time and looked forward to improvements on it in the work of his successors, those did not appear at all in later antiquity and appeared only in limited areas in the Middle Ages. Yet there were some serious shortcomings in the work, even by the standards of antiquity. Because of his too great reliance on Hipparchus's solar theory, both the position and the mean motion he attributed to the sun were in error, an error that increased over time. We have already noticed that his lunar model produced far too great a variation in the distance to the moon. Because Ptolemy used lunar eclipses to establish the position and mean motion of the moon, the error in the solar mean motion and position was also transmitted to that body (although fortunately this had very little effect on eclipse computations). Ptolemy's value for precession is also too low by an amount precisely corresponding to the error in the solar mean motion. The parameters embodied in his planetary theory, on the other hand, could hardly have been improved in his time, except in the case of Mercury, where the poor quality of the observations open to him led him to propose an unnecessarily complicated (and very inaccurate) model.

Despite these imperfections, *Almagest* was so superior to anything preceding it that it soon established itself as the standard work on astronomy, a position it occupied for over a thousand years in both Europe and the Middle East. In antiquity no advance was made beyond it, for the works of Pappus and Theon in 4th-century Alexandria are mere commentaries on Ptolemy. *Almagest* was translated into Persian and Syriac in late antiquity, and into Arabic (more than once) in the 8th and 9th centuries, and it contributed to the flowering of astronomical studies in Islamic lands. There, indeed, significant improvements were made to the solar and lunar elements, but the rest was accepted largely unchanged. Star catalogues, such as that of al-Ṣūfī, were essentially copies of the *Almagest* catalogue with the longitudes increased by a constant for precession; and despite criticisms of the equant and proposals of alternative models, almost all planetary tables down to the beginning of the modern era were based on Ptolemy's elements. It was not until the 16th century, with the work of Copernicus, Tycho Brahe, and Kepler, that Greek astronomy, as formulated by Ptolemy, finally became obsolete.

G. J. TOOMER

Bibliography

Delambre, Jean-Baptiste Joseph. *Histoire de l'astronomie ancienne.* 2 vols. Paris, 1817.

Grasshoff, Gerd. *The History of Ptolemy's Star Catalogue.* New York, Berlin, and Heidelberg, 1990.

Heath, Thomas Little. *Aristarchus of Samos.* Oxford, 1913.

Jones, Alexander. "The Adaptation of Babylonian Methods in Greek Numerical Astronomy." *Isis* 82 (1991): 441–453.

———, ed. *Astronomical Papyri from Oxyrhynchus.* Philadelphia, 1999.

Neugebauer, Otto. *A History of Ancient Mathematical Astronomy.* 3 vols. Berlin, Heidelberg, and New York, 1975.

Tannery, Paul. *Recherches sur l'histoire de l'astronomie ancienne.* Paris, 1893.

Toomer, G. J. "Hipparchus and Babylonian Astronomy." In *A Scientific Humanist: Studies in Memory of Abraham Sachs.* Ed. Erle Leichty et al. Occasional Publications of Samuel Noah Kramer Fund, 9. Philadelphia, 1988.

Toomer, G. J., ed. and trans. *Ptolemy's Almagest.* London and New York, 1984. Rev. ed., Princeton, 1998.

COSMOLOGY

WITH VERY FEW EXCEPTIONS, the Greeks who wrote about the natural world took the earth to be stationary, as human intuition suggests: we learn the difference between moving and staying in place by taking our place on the earth as the fixed point of reference. But if the earth is at rest, it follows that the stars, planets, sun, and moon are in motion relative to the earth, and observation coupled with some simple inferences suggest that they move around the earth, probably on circular paths.

It can hardly fail to be observed that the sun and the moon move on different paths, and that by contrast all the stars move without changing their own relative positions, on paths different from those of the sun and the moon. Closer observation shows that there are five other heavenly bodies whose paths vary with respect to the "fixed" stars: they soon got the name *planētai*, "the Wanderers."

A crucial consequence of the decision that the earth is stationary is that the whole system of stars, planets, sun, and moon came to be thought of as a finite whole. At first there was some hesitation about the relative distances of the heavenly bodies from the earth, but by the time of Plato and Aristotle there was general agreement that the stars are farthest from the earth. Since the constellations of stars keep their own relative positions, forming unvarying patterns and never varying perceptibly in size or brightness when the sky is clear of cloud, they were taken to rotate around the earth as a unity, equidistant from the earth, and to form the boundary of the whole system.

Thus there was room for doubt about what, if anything, lies outside the boundary of the fixed stars. There were those who claimed that outside the boundary there is either unlimited empty space or else nothing whatever, not even space. Others claimed that there are unlimited numbers of other worlds, invisible to us, in the space beyond the boundaries of our world, just as there are other cities beyond our own city walls.

Both camps were agreed, however, on certain features of our own world: that it is a system characterized by durability in time (though not necessarily forever), and by regularity. The regular movements of the heavens provided the standard for measuring the seasons, with all their qualitative differences, and they divided night from day. The wonderful regularity of the whole system justified its being called cosmos—a word that signified beauty and good order.

To distinguish those who believed our world to be all that there is from those who believed there is something outside our world, Greek writers distinguished between the concepts of the world *(cosmos)* and the universe *(to pan)*; we shall preserve this distinction in what follows. "Cosmos is a system composed of heaven and earth and the natures contained in them": this definition, quoted from the pseudo-Aristotelian treatise *On the Cosmos* (391b.9), was more or less standard. The universe, on the other hand, consists of our cosmos together with whatever else exists, if anything does.

Later writers, led by Aristotle, recognized that there was a new beginning in thought about the natural world in the Ionian Greek city of Miletus, on the Aegean coast of Asia Minor, in the 6th century B.C.E. Three Milesians were mentioned: in chronological order, Thales, Anaximander, and Anaximenes. Nothing that they wrote survives; we know of them only through quotations in much later authors. What seems clear is that they broke away from the earlier stories about nature that we characterize as myth, in which the leading characters are anthropomorphic gods and goddesses.

According to Aristotle, whose brief words about his earliest predecessors founded the Greek tradition of the historiography of philosophy, the break with "myth" was quite sharp. If we knew more, we might be able to reconstruct a more gradual story of a transition from religious to naturalistic ways of thinking—very probably at the same time as a transition from Near Eastern to Greek conceptions of the world. There are traces of the intermediate stages in the few surviving fragments of Pherecydes of Syros, a contemporary of the earliest philosophers recognized by Aristotle. But although in general Near Eastern mythology may be recognized as the source out of which Greek natural philosophy grew (especially among the Ionian Greeks, who were in constant touch with their Near Eastern neighbors), direct connections are hard to prove. The Greek tradition outlined by Aristotle, prejudiced or not, is clearer.

Hesiod had written, in *Theogony*, a story of the birth of the world, more or less after the pattern of sexual generation: "Out of Chaos, Erebos and black Night came to birth, and from Night again there came forth Aether and Day, whom she bore after lying with Erebos. And Earth first bore the starry Heaven, equal to herself, to cover her about" (123–127). The Milesians, so far as we can judge from the scanty evidence, still spoke of the origin and growth of the world, but in nonanthropomorphic terms. Thales, famously, held that the world originated from water ("because the seed of all things is moist," said Aristotle); Anaximander wrote that from the primitive Boundless came something like "a seed of the hot and the cold"; Anaximenes made air the primitive substance and introduced compression and rarefaction of air as the mode of generation of the different world masses. Other metaphors besides biological growth appear. Anaximander attributed something of the regularity and balance of natural change (summer and winter, perhaps) to "justice"—not the justice of Zeus, but an internal relation between the contending powers themselves. Anaximenes compared the air that generated the differentiated world to "psyche"—the life force of animals. All three produced descriptions of the earth and the heavens, and meteorological phenomena, but the interpretation of the evidence is too controversial to be discussed here.

What is perhaps the most important achievement of the Milesians is that their work started a tradition of criticism: unless the later sources from whom we learn about the Milesians found patterns of development where there were none, each later thinker knew the work of his predecessor, found weaknesses in it, and substituted something he thought better on rational grounds—a more fundamental starting point, a more persuasive analogy, a more plausible explanation.

The next generation of thinkers of this style continued the critical tradition. Xenophanes of Colophon (still in Greek Asia Minor, near Ephesus, although he migrated to the Western Greek world) and Heraclitus of Ephesus are the first two whose work survives in relatively substantial quantities. Both criticized their great forerunners: "Homer and Hesiod attributed to the gods everything that is a shame and a reproach among men: stealing, adultery, deceit of each other" (Xenophanes, frg. 11). "The teacher of most men is Hesiod. This man they take to know most things—who did not know day and night; for they are one" (Heraclitus, frg. 57). Examples could be multiplied. The point is this: if we apply our human understanding to the traditional stories, they fall short; we must seek something more consistent with our best conceptions of what is rational. The powerful gods of tradition should be better, not worse, than men. Day and Night should be personified as self-subsistent individuals: they are conceptually linked, as being inseparable parts of a single unit of time. The critical tradition reached a high point with the 5th-century philosopher Parmenides of Elea (on the west coast of southern Italy), who conclusively changed the course of philosophical speculation. But before attempting to assess his contribution, we must briefly go back in time.

The Greek communities of the Aegean region produced the recognized pioneers of Greek cosmology. But in the 5th century the cities of southern Italy and Sicily also produced philosophical heroes. It seems that migration from East to West brought this about. At some point Xenophanes left the Aegean and moved to Italy. More significant was the move of Pythagoras from Samos in the Aegean to Croton in south Italy, some time in the second half of the 6th century. Although Pythagoras himself wrote nothing, and extraordinarily little is actually known on good authority about his life and teaching, his influence on subsequent philosophy was very great. "Those called Pythagoreans," to use Aristotle's phrase, came to be recognized as a group with certain highly distinctive views both about the physical world and about religion and morality. In cosmology, their importance was very great, in many ways, but especially through the eponymous Pythagorean of Plato's cosmo-logical treatise, *Timaeus.*

Pythagoras, or his followers, introduced mathematics into cosmology. It is true that Thales is said to have predicted an eclipse of the sun and the dates of the solstices (probably learning from Babylonian records), and that Anaxi-mander had given mathematical values to the distances of the sun, moon, and stars from the earth—probably 27, 18, and 9, respectively (he was highly unusual in supposing the stars to be the nearest of the heavenly bodies). But Pythagorean theory elevated mathematical structure to the status of the pri-mary element, instead of the Milesian primitive material (water, the Bound-less, or air).

Pythagorean theory is wrapped in mystery, and it is impossible to trace its chronological development. But it is not implausible to guess that one of the earliest bases on which theoretical edifices were built was the discovery that musical consonances were expressible in numerical ratios. The ratio of the oc-tave is 1 : 2; the fifth is 3 : 2; the fourth is 4 : 3. It was a striking discovery that the string of a musical instrument stopped at these intervals produced sounds that were recognizably "in tune." Moreover these four numbers, 1 + 2 + 3 + 4, add up to 10. "The whole cosmos [say the Pythagoreans] is arranged ac-cording to attunement *[harmonia]* and the attunement is a system of three concords, the fourth, the fifth, and the octave" (Sextus, *Math.* 7.95). At some stage the components of the cosmos, stars, sun, moon, five planets, and earth, since they total only nine, were supplemented in Pythagorean theory by a tenth, the "counter-earth." Earth and counter-earth circled around the central fire—hence the Pythagoreans were unique among early philosophers in dis-placing the earth from the center of the cosmos.

At the beginning of the 5th century Parmenides' criticisms of all cosmolog-ical theories of growth changed the course of philosophical thought. He chal-lenged the cosmologists to give a rational account of change: previous theo-ries claimed that "what *is*" comes to be out of "what *is not*"—but one cannot think or speak intelligibly about what *is not.* To put it in the simplest terms, the effect of this was to generate theories in which physical change is ex-plained as a rearrangement or restructuring of enduring elements. The first elements to be proposed were materials, such as the earth, water, air, and fire of Empedocles, or the atoms of Democritus. Next came the eternal Forms of Plato, which stood as eternal models while the changing physical world "shared in" or "copied" them. They were succeeded by Aristotle's immanent forms: change in general was the actualization of a form previously present in potentiality.

Parmenides himself, although the argument of the first part of his poem (like Xenophanes and Empedocles, he wrote in epic hexameters) challenged the very idea of change and difference, added a cosmogony of his own, based on a fundamental duality of night and light. Quotations are scarce; they include a line that appears to be the first statement that the moon shines with borrowed light, as well as a complex astronomical theory and an account of the origins of the human race. After Parmenides but before Plato, three different cosmological theories were put forward that clearly attempted, in different ways, to respect Parmenides' ban on "coming to *be* out of what *is not*." In this period Greek cosmology began to develop in two basically different directions. The first led to the view that our world is unique, and is under the direction of divine forces; this culminated in the work of Plato, Aristotle, and the Stoics. The second was the way of the Atomists, Leucippus, Democritus, and Epicurus, whose universe contained many worlds, put together without the aid of gods by the unguided motions of atoms in the void.

Through the whole of the period when Greeks dominated the philosophical and scientific thought of the Western world, the "one world" theorists had the support of those who applied mathematical reasoning to the cosmos. Plato, Aristotle, and the Stoics made use of the calculations and theorems of geometrical astronomy. The Atomists, on the whole, could make little use of the results of the exact sciences. In the absence, particularly, of knowledge of fundamental laws of motion, they could not easily match their atomic theory of matter with astronomical measurements. As Cicero once put it: "That turbulent hurly-burly of atoms will never be able to produce the orderly beauty of this cosmos" (*De finibus* 1.20).

Empedocles of Acragas in Sicily, and Anaxagoras of Clazomenae were the first to meet Parmenides' challenge—the former in epic verse and in the Italian style, the latter in prose and in the Ionian manner. Anaxagoras began his book with a description of the beginning of the world: "All things were together, infinite in both number and smallness." Instead of the Milesians' single originative substance, Anaxagoras substituted a mixture of all things, so finely and completely mixed that nothing was distinguishable in the overwhelming clouds of air and aether. At some point in time, the primitive mixture was disrupted by a cosmic force of Mind, which began a process of rotation and thus progressively separated out the ingredients from each other. Earthy things went to the middle, lighter things to the boundary of the whirl, where they can still be seen in part as they carry the heavenly bodies around. Mind alone was distinct in kind from all the rest: the heavenly bodies were earthy in substance, nothing but white-hot stones.

Anaxagoras spent many years in Athens, where his ideas became well known. The biographers report that he was prosecuted for the impiety of his materialist theory of the sun and moon. His theory of Mind as the creative agent in the cosmos, however, may have had more real importance for the philosophy of nature. Although Plato expressed disappointment that Anaxagoras made little use of the theory in his cosmology (*Phaedo* 98b), the idea that the cosmos is the product of Mind, rather than a natural growth or an accident, was there to stay: it received the fullest development in Plato's *Timaeus*, it was modified by Aristotle, and it was exaggerated by the Stoics.

Empedocles, like Anaxagoras, held that cosmic growth and change is brought about by the rearrangement of things unchanging and permanent. But he drastically reduced the range of the basic materials, to the quartet that became standard: earth, water, air, and fire. He increased the causes of cosmic change from one to two: a force that attracted unlike constituents to each other, called Love, and an agent of separation, called Strife. Both forces are at work in our world, but on the large scale their dominance eternally alternates, from a period of total unity, under the rule of Love, to a period or a moment of total disruption, through Strife, after which the rule of Love begins again. The surviving fragments contain fascinating images of the formation of the cosmos, including a theory of the first formation of vegetation and of animal species, limited to viable kinds through the survival of the fit.

The atomic theory is associated with the names of Leucippus, about whom very little is known, and Democritus of Abdera. It is another attempt to meet Parmenides' challenge by constructing a changing world out of eternally unchanging elements—*atoma*, "uncuttable" bits of identical matter, too small to be perceived individually, making up compounds whose perceptible properties result from the size, shape, and motion of the atoms and the extent of void space between them. In this theory there are no motive agents like Mind, or Love and Strife; the atoms collide and rebound or get linked up together as chance or "necessity" dictates. As has been mentioned already, a cosmos for the Atomists is just one compound among many in the infinite void: like all compounds, worlds come into being and are dissolved again into their component atoms. The first beginning of a cosmos is a "whirl" *(dinē)* of atoms in some region of space, which sorts the atoms by size and shape ("mechanically," as we might say) so as to form an earth, seas, air, sky, sun, moon, and stars. The end comes when the motions no longer hold things together in due order.

Most, perhaps all, of the theories mentioned so far regard the earth as a flat disk, and correspondingly suppose that the direction of free fall is perpendicular to the surface of the earth, and therefore in parallel lines. It is a problem for the theories to explain why the earth itself does not fall, as a piece of earth falls when released from a height. What supports it? Most answered that it somehow floats on a cushion of air, because of its great area.

Plato's *Phaedo* first makes the important move to a completely spherical cosmology. The earth, says Socrates in the dialogue (108–109), is round, and being in the middle of the heavens it needs no support from air or any other such force to prevent it from falling—the homogeneity of the heavens and the equal balance of the earth are sufficient. The picture is elaborated in *Timaeus*, where we have again a spherical cosmology. The earth is at the center of the sphere of the heavens, and all the earthy material in the universe tends toward this center, all the fiery matter toward the perimeter, with the two intermediate elements, water and air, between them. The four elements stand to each other in continuous geometric proportion—but Plato does not specify the quantities involved (whether volumes, or intensity of quality, or whatever).

The four elements, which themselves consist of particles shaped like four of the five regular solids, make up the body of the world: its soul (for it is a living creature) is the stuff of which the heavenly bodies are made. In a long and elaborate fantasy Plato describes an armillary sphere constructed out of two circular "soul-strips," one representing the equator of the sphere of fixed stars, the other, inclined (as the ecliptic is) at an angle to the first, being split into rings representing the motion of the seven "wandering" bodies. The whole system, including its axis, turns with the motion of the fixed stars, but the rings of the planets, sun, and moon also turn with their own motion around the axis, in the reverse direction, and the earth, at the center, rotates around the spinning axis so as to counteract that motion and thus remain stationary.

The cosmic "animal" thus described is neither eternal nor self-generated: it is made by a divine Craftsman (*dēmiurgos*), copying an eternal model. Like all good craftsmen, he aims at the highest possible degree of beauty in his work but is limited by the capabilities of the material with which he works. There are thus two explanatory factors to be reckoned with in the detail of the physical world: the perfection aimed at by Mind, and the limitations imposed by the "Necessity" of the material. At once, a controversy arose about Plato's meaning: were the Demiurge and his creation to be taken literally, as Aristotle took them? Or were they a device of literary exposition, as Plato's successors Xenocrates and Speusippus held? The controversy continues. But whether myth or science, *Timaeus* was a dominant influence for many centuries.

In Plato's account of the heavens in *Timaeus*, the movements of the sun, moon, and planets are sketched in symbols that make little claim to astronomical accuracy. Each moves on a circle of the world-soul, itself composed of "Sameness," "Difference," and "Existence." Sameness no doubt symbolizes the regularity of their motions, Difference their independence from the stars and from each other, and Existence their eternity. In his last dialogue, *Laws* (821), Plato rebukes people for attributing wandering motions to some of the heavenly bodies, calling them *planetai*, and indicates that although the planets depart from the uniform rotation of the stars, they nevertheless move with a strict regularity of their own.

It was the aim of contemporary astronomers to compose a model of the heavens that would describe with accuracy the motions of all the visible heavens. Eudoxus of Cnidos, who created a school at Cyzicus known for its mathematical astronomy, spent time at Plato's Academy in Athens. Whether Plato was acquainted with the detail of his astronomical work when he wrote *Timaeus* is controversial, but there may well be a reference to it in *Laws*. In any event, there is no doubt that Plato's greatest pupil, Aristotle, studied the theories of Eudoxus and his pupil Callippus, and made them the basis for his own account of the heavens.

Aristotle's whole system is constructed out of concentric spheres, with the earth, itself spherical, occupying the center of the whole. The essence of the model is as follows. The fixed stars are assumed to be set rigidly in the outermost sphere of the heavens, which turns at a constant speed about its north-south axis once daily. Each of the planetary bodies has its own set of spheres. The innermost sphere of each set carries the planet. The outermost sphere moves on the same axis and with the same speed and direction as the sphere of the stars. This sphere carries with it the poles of a second sphere, concentric with the first, rotating about its own, different axis also at a constant speed. The axis of the second sphere is inclined to that of the first so that its equator, as it rotates, passes through the middle of the signs of the zodiac (i.e., along the ecliptic circle). Each of the planetary bodies has a sphere that shares the position and direction of motion of this second sphere; if the planet were fixed on the equator of this second sphere, it would rotate daily around the earth along with the fixed stars but change its position with relation to the zodiacal signs a little each day.

But the planets are observed to deviate from regular motion on the ecliptic circle. To account for the deviation, Eudoxus posited a third and fourth sphere for each planet, nested inside the first two, with different axes and velocities. The planet is assumed to lie on the equator of the fourth, innermost sphere. The third and fourth spheres are so arranged that the planet follows a path (relative to the ecliptic) known as a *hippopede*, or horse-fetter, roughly equivalent to a figure eight.

Each sphere rotates at a constant velocity, but they differ from each other. For the sun and the moon, Eudoxus postulated only three spheres each, the third being to account for the recession of the nodes. Callippus, a more obscure figure who adopted and modified Eudoxus's model of concentric spheres, added two spheres each to the sun and the moon, to account for their anomalies, and one further sphere to each of Mars, Venus, and Mercury.

All that is visible to the observer, of course, is the light of the heavenly bodies: the spheres are invisible. The heavenly bodies themselves do not move at all; they are carried around by the motion of the sphere in which they are set. The stars are all set in the single, outer sphere of the whole universe; each of the planetary bodies is set in the equator of the innermost sphere of its set of spheres.

The seven sets of spheres are nested inside each other, in the order Saturn, Jupiter, Mars, Venus, Mercury, sun, moon. In Eudoxus's scheme, there are no eccentric spheres and no epicycles, as in later astronomical theories. Consequently it was assumed that all the heavenly bodies remain at a constant distance from the earth; it is a weakness in the system that it has no way of explaining differences in the brightness of the planets at different times. This, then, was the astronomical model taken over by Aristotle. What he undertook to do was to turn it into a *physical* theory, in which the spheres were not geometrical postulates but material bodies.

The astronomical model, as we have seen, used the motion of the sphere of the fixed stars as the base on which the other motions were overlaid. For the construction of a physical theory, this created a difficulty concerning the motions of all the planetary bodies except the outermost one, since the sets of planetary spheres are implanted in each other. Jupiter's set, to take an example, is inside the set of Saturn's spheres. But the motion of the innermost of Saturn's spheres—the sphere that carries Saturn on its equator—is obviously not identical with that of the sphere of fixed stars; its function is precisely to justify Saturn's deviation from that motion. The outermost sphere, however, of the next planet (Jupiter) must move with the motion of the fixed stars. Consequently the physical theory must return to this base, by interpolating a set of spheres whose motions *cancel out* the special motions of Saturn. Let S^1, S^2, S^3, S^4 be the spheres that explain Saturn's motions; S^4 is the one that carries Saturn. Then we postulate, inside S^4, a sphere S^{-4}, which rotates on the same axis and at the same speed as S^4, but in the reverse direction. Its motion is thus identical with that of S^3. We postulate S^{-3} and S^{-2} in similar fashion. Now S^{-2} has the same motion as S^1—i.e., the motion of the fixed stars. The first of Jupiter's spheres, J^1, has its poles fixed inside the sphere S^{-2}.

Aristotle took over Callippus's modifications of the Eudoxan system and held to the thesis of a complete and separate set of spheres for each planetary body. The total amounts to fifty-five, no counteracting spheres being required for the moon, since there are no heavenly bodies beneath it.

We have now described the structure of the concentric spheres. But physical spheres must have physical *body*. So Aristotle is faced with the question: what are the heavenly spheres made of? They can hardly be made of any of the four familiar elements, earth, water, air, or fire, because each of these (he claims) has a characteristic natural motion that is in a straight line: earth and water toward the center of the universe, air and fire toward its circumference. The motion of the heavens, according to Aristotle's view in *De caelo*, requires us to posit a fifth element whose natural motion is not rectilinear but circular, and whose nature is not changeable, like the four sublunary bodies. Since he regards it as superior, in more than one sense, to the other four elements, he names it the first body, but it is generally referred to as aether.

There are indications that Aristotle rather tentatively gave a role to aether in the sublunary world as well as in the heavens. Cicero knew something to this effect, from his acquaintance with some of the works of Aristotle that are now lost: "He [Aristotle] thinks there is a certain fifth nature, of which mind is made; for thinking, foreseeing, learning, teaching, making a discovery, holding so much in the memory—all these and more, loving, hating, feeling pain and joy—such things as these, he believes, do not belong to any one of the four elements" (*Tusculan Disputations* 1.10.22). It is hardly likely that Aristotle *identified* the mind with aether, but it is possible that at some time he wrote of the soul, or some of its faculties, as being based in an element different from the usual four. There is some confirmation of this in his own more cautious words in *De generatione animalium* 2.3 (736b29–737a1). The semen of animals contains a "vital heat" or "breath"—which is analogous to the element of the stars.

The evaluative strain in this passage is significant. The extra element is called "divine" and is associated with the ranking in "honor" of the soul that is based on it—this refers, no doubt, to a *scala naturae* that puts man, the rational animal, at the top and grades the lower animals according to their faculties. Aether is not merely the element endowed with the natural faculty of moving in a circle, which is the main emphasis in *De caelo*. It is also eternal, and therefore divine, and free from the corruption of the earthly elements.

Aristotle was committed to a dualism as sharp as Plato's distinction between the intelligible and unchanging Forms and the perceptible and perishable material world. The heavens are the realm of a matter that moves eternally in circles, is incorruptible, unmixed, divine. With the possible limited exception of the material base of the animal soul, everything in the cosmos inside the sphere of the moon—the sublunary world—is made of different materials, all of them rectilinear and therefore finite in motion, perishable, liable to mixture and interchange among themselves. This was a dualism that lasted, notoriously, until the time of Galileo.

Plato's cosmos was created, according to Aristotle's view of *Timaeus*, at some particular time, but he took the view that there could be no beginning of the heavenly motions without setting up the incoherent concept of a beginning of time. There were no creator gods, therefore, but there were sustaining gods. Aristotle's theology, set out rather elliptically in *Physics* 8 and *Metaphysics* 12, claims that the eternal rotation of the heavenly spheres is the work of god, or gods: in *Metaphysics* 12.8 Aristotle allocates a Mover to every sphere; sometimes he puts all the emphasis on the supreme God, the Unmoved Mover of the outer sphere of the heavens.

He writes (in *Metaphysics* 12.7) with reverence about the life of God—a life of thought, better than the best that humans can enjoy only for a short time. God does nothing directly to cause the motions of the heavens: he moves the spheres "as one being loved." This implies that the spheres themselves are beings with souls, capable of feeling a desire to share the eternal activity of divine thought. Aristotle says remarkably little about this animistic aspect of his cosmology, which was much developed in postclassical times.

It is interesting that Aristotle's pupil and successor as head of the Peripatos, Theophrastus, raises critical questions about his master's theology in the work that survives under the title *Metaphysics*. If the Mover is one, how do the heavenly spheres come to have different motions? If more than one, how are they harmonized? Why does love of an unmoved god impel the spheres to move? What is especially desirable about rotary motion? Perhaps such questions suggest something of the exploratory nature of Aristotle's theology.

Theophrastus continued Aristotle's interest in the philosophy of nature and added much to the already large library of Peripatetic work in this area. A substantial amount survives: small treatises on winds, on stones, and on fire, and two large collections, *The History of Plants* and *The Causes of Plants*. One of his most influential works survives only in fragments, *The View of the Physicists (Physikōn Doxai)*; a good deal of our knowledge of early Greek cosmology comes directly or indirectly from this work. The Peripatetic school continued its interest in some of these fields for at least one more generation, with Theophrastus's successor Strato of Lampsacus. Aristotle's denial of the existence of empty space—indeed the whole structure of his theory of place—was questioned and modified by both Theophrastus and Strato.

In the 4th and later centuries, the character of the Greek cosmologists underwent great change. The most important development was the rapid advance of mathematical astronomy; the key names in this area are Aristarchus, Archimedes, Apollonius of Perga, and Hipparchus. Hipparchus's work, in the 2nd century B.C.E., formed the basis for Ptolemy's *Almagest* (2nd century C.E.), which became the standard textbook on astronomy for many centuries.

In passing, we must note that Aristarchus of Samos was the one serious astronomer in the Greek period who entertained the thesis that the heavens are at rest and the earth moves in a circular orbit around the sun. Unfortunately we are told very little of what Aristarchus made of this thesis, and there are surviving bits of his work that make no use of it at all; it may have been no more than an exploratory hypothesis.

In post-Aristotelian cosmology, Epicurus offered the most radical opposition to Plato and Aristotle. Although he came from an Athenian family, Epicurus lived most of his early life in Samos and the Ionian cities of the mainland. There he became acquainted with the atomic theory of Democritus, adopted it, modified it in some respects, and set up a school in Athens to disseminate it to his followers. The contrast with Plato and Aristotle could hardly have been more complete. In place of a unique, finite, eternal cosmos, Epicurus posited an infinite number of worlds, coming into being and passing away like any other material compounds. Instead of divine creation or maintenance, Epicurus attributed the birth of the worlds to the accidental collisions of atoms whirling about in the infinite void. Instead of a unified material continuum, Epicurus posited atoms and void space. Instead of a spherical earth, Epicurus reverted to the flat earth of earlier cosmologists, and instead of the centrifocal theory of motion of Plato and Aristotle, he claimed that the natural motion of all atoms is downward, parallel fall.

We have two primary sources for Epicurean cosmology: a brief summary in Epicurus's own *Letter to Herodotus (Ep. Hdt.)* and a much fuller account in Lucretius's poem *De rerum natura (DRN)* especially the fifth book. Both begin, almost in the manner of a geometrical textbook, with a set of basic propositions.

First, the universe consists of "body and void." The existence of body can be known through the direct evidence of the senses; the existence of void can be known indirectly, as being necessary to explain the observed fact of motion. Body exists in the form of eternally unchangeable atoms.

Second, the universe is infinite. The argument for this is that anything finite has a limit, and a limit is discerned by contrast with something else (Aristotle had claimed that this is a requirement for *contact*, but not for limit). Since there *is* nothing other than the universe, the universe has no limit and consequently must be infinite (*Ep. Hdt.* 41; *DRN* I.1007).

Third, atoms exist in an inconceivably large, but not an infinitely large, number of shapes. If they were not so many, it would be impossible to account for the observed differences between compounds; if they were infinite, atoms would have to vary infinitely in size also, and some atoms would be so large as to be visible, which is contrary to what is observed to be the case. This last proposition needs an extra premise to support it: namely, that atoms do not vary continuously in shape but differ by finite quanta—*minimae partes*, as Lucretius calls them.

Epicureans asserted that all atoms have a natural tendency to move downward. We can observe that every perceptible object that has weight moves downward when its fall is unimpeded, and there is no reason to deny this same tendency to atoms. Aristotle's theory of the natural upward motion of fire and air is rejected. But what does "downward" mean? Aristotle had argued that it meant toward the center of the universe, but the infinite universe of the Epicureans had no center. Epicurean metaphysics allowed for no forces acting on the atoms except by collision; there was no room for a theory of attraction at a distance. So it was not possible for them to adopt the idea later put forward by the Stoics, that matter was attracted to its own center, so that downward motion could be regarded as the manifestation of this attraction toward the center of the cosmic mass. Epicurus and his followers were left, as it seemed, with no option but to take up the assumptions of the builder who uses a plumb line, that all falling bodies fall in parallel lines at right angles to the earth's surface—therefore that the earth's surface is, generally speaking, flat. The flat earth was a commonplace of the 5th century and earlier, but after Plato and Aristotle it became hard to accept. Lucretius does his best with it by poking fun at the idea of upside-down creatures on the other side of the world, which he took to be a consequence of the geocentric theory of motion.

It is hard to know what degree of obstinacy and obscurantism, if any, was required to maintain this reactionary position at the end of the 4th century B.C.E. Aristotle's argument for the sphericity of the earth had largely depended on his own centrifocal theory of the natural motions of the elements (De caelo 2.14.297a8–b23), and we have seen that the Epicureans rejected that theory. But Aristotle already knew of astronomical reasons for believing the earth to be spherical, particularly the observation that as one moves on a north-south line, different stars appear in the zenith (ibid. 2.14.297b23– 298b20). This could be explained by the Epicureans only on the assumption that the stars are rather close to the earth: the effect is like that of walking across a large room under a painted ceiling. Other astronomical problems, such as the shape of the earth's shadow on the moon during an eclipse, could be accounted for by a disk-shaped earth as well as by a sphere.

Given, then, that atoms are endowed with a natural tendency to fall downward through the void, and that "downward" means in parallel straight lines, it appears that some extra assumption is needed to explain how it comes about that atoms form compounds. One might suppose that collisions could occur by virtue of differences of speed among the falling atoms: but that is ruled out a priori. The reason given by Epicurus is that differences of speed are explained by differences of resistance of the medium through which motion takes place. But the void offers no resistance whatever, hence there is no reason why any atom should fall faster or more slowly than any other. All of them move at a speed described in the phrase "as quick as thought."

That is not to say that compounds cannot move at different speeds. All variations of speed are possible, between the two limiting cases of the speed of motion of individual atoms, "as quick as thought," on the one hand, and rest, on the other. In a compound, atoms are to be thought of as moving, individually, at standard atomic speed without intermission, but remaining within the boundaries of the compound. A stable compound is one in which the component atoms move backward and forward, up and down, and side to side, colliding with each other within the same space. The compound itself moves when the algebraic sum, so to speak, of the motions of the individual atoms has some positive value in one direction or another. The limit of speed is reached when all the component atoms are moving in the same direction—a state of affairs achieved only by thunderbolts, apparently.

But if differences of speed cannot account for collisions between atoms, what can? To deal with this difficulty, the Epicureans introduced their most famous physical thesis—the swerve of atoms (parenclisis in Greek, clinamen in Latin). The swerve is fully described by Lucretius (*DRN* 2.216–293), but there is no mention of it in the extant fragments of Epicurus himself. However, ancient writers had no hesitation in attributing it to him.

The swerve served two purposes in the Epicurean system: to explain the possibility of collisions between atoms, and to account, in some way, for the voluntary motions of animals, including humans. Among modern writers there is no agreement even about the basic mechanics of the swerve, so to speak. Do all atoms swerve, or only some of them? Presumably all of them may do so, since otherwise there would be an unaccountable difference in kind between the swervers and the nonswervers. But how often do swerves take place? Opinions differ widely; the answer depends largely on one's interpretation of the swerve's role in voluntary motion. Does an atom, when it swerves from the straight downward path, take up a straight motion at an oblique angle to the vertical? Or does it swerve momentarily, like a car changing lanes on a motorway? Each answer has its advocates. Some things are clear. The swerve of an atom has no cause in events previous to its occurrence; it is in principle unpredictable and random. Moreover in its cosmological role it is not to be thought of as the beginning of the world, or of any world. We are not to think of an uninterrupted downward rain of atoms that is at some moment for the first time disturbed by the occurrence of a swerve: rather, atoms have fallen, swerved, and collided for all eternity.

Epicurus avoids the dualism of Aristotle's theory of motion; rectilinear motion is the rule, and the observed circular motion of the heavenly bodies is explained by a variety of mechanisms, such as the effects of winds—much as the straight flow of water has the effect of causing the waterwheel to rotate. But Epicurean astronomy is not, on the whole, to be taken seriously. Its object is to promote peace of mind: that means, above all, to reassure humankind that the gods are in no way concerned with the operations of nature in this or any other cosmos. To be troubled with such things would be inconsistent, Epicurus claims, with the supreme happiness and tranquillity that are part of what it means to be a god. Sense perception cannot tell us exactly how the heavens move. But by analogy with rotating objects within our earthly experience, we can make suggestions about the behavior of the heavenly bodies. So long as our suggestions are possible and do not conflict either with perception or with our a priori beliefs about the gods, we must accept all of them. Epicurus does not even attend to consistency: he suggests, for example, that the moon's light may be reflected from the sun but also that the sun may be extinguished and rekindled each day.

Like Plato and Aristotle, the Stoics held that the cosmos in which we live is the only one in the universe. It is spherical in shape, with the stars, planets, sun, and moon moving in circular paths once daily around the earth, which is stationary at the center. Their cosmos, like Aristotle's, is a corporeal continuum, with no void space inside it, and matter itself is continuous, not atomic. This much is enough to place the Stoics squarely in the same camp with Platonists and Aristotelians, against the Atomists. But differences arise at once, and they are of great significance.

One major difference is that whereas Aristotle believed our cosmos to be everlasting, the Stoics held that it has a birth, a death by conflagration *(ekpyrōsis)*, a rebirth, and so on forever. Both Aristotle and the Stoics believed that our cosmos is unique, but the Stoics added that it has a limited lifespan that is endlessly repeated. Sometimes the surviving reports of Stoic doctrine distinguish between *kosmos* and *diakosmēsis*—i.e., between the ordered world and its ordering. This marks an important distinction. When the present cosmos perishes, it will not pass out of existence altogether, to be replaced by an entirely new one. The same material persists, but the *order* changes. So although in a sense the Stoics and Epicureans were in agreement that our world will come to an end, the Epicurean theory of the birth and death of quite different worlds was of a different sort altogether from the Stoic theory.

Plato in *Timaeus* had combined the similes of biology and the crafts in describing the origin of the cosmos—leaving posterity to doubt whether either simile was to be taken literally. The Stoics chose the biological model, but used it in a way that was almost mystical. Whereas Plato described a Craftsman God working on a material to make the cosmos, which then took on its own life, Zeno takes God to be identical with the cosmos in its initial state (about which I shall say more shortly). God is the principle of life. At first there is nothing else, then God creates a difference within himself, such that as the principle of life he is "contained" in moisture. This is the living "sperm" that produces the cosmos according to the "formula" of which it is the bearer; God is the *spermatikos logos*. God is at the same time material fire and providential intelligence.

It is as if the Stoics deliberately combined numerous elements from earlier theories. The emphasis on fire recalls Heraclitus; the cosmogonic role of a transcendental divine intelligence recalls Anaxagoras, as well as Plato; and the embryological model of the seed goes back at least that far, if not even to Thales and Anaximander themselves, the founders of the Greek cosmological tradition. The careful analysis of the sperm into a moist vehicle and an active "formula," or *logos*, is found also in Aristotle's *De generatione animalium*.

The decision to view the cosmos as a living creature may be regarded as the foundation of Stoic cosmology. We can guess at the reasons that made it an attractive picture. Like living organisms, the cosmos is a material body endowed with an immanent power of motion. It consists of different parts, which collaborate toward the stable functioning of the whole, each part performing its own work. The relation of the parts to each other and to the whole exhibits a kind of fitness, not always obvious in detail but unmistakable in the large picture. This sense of fitness suggests rationality: it is an easy inference that the cosmos itself is possessed of reason, and since reason is a property confined to living creatures, this again suggests that the cosmos is a living being.

The cosmos is permeated by Reason *(Logos)*—this is the most distinctive claim of the Stoics, with ramifications into every field of their thought. It is far more than the epistemological claim that it is possible to understand the workings of the cosmos rationally. It amounts, in fact, to a very large metaphysical theory. Being thoroughgoing materialists, the Stoics had to give a corporeal form to the Logos. Since nothing less than divine power could move and control something so vast as the cosmos, they identified the Logos with God. And as we have seen in the passage quoted above, they assumed that the Logos was something that can have no origin itself but must be the origin of everything else. Thus far the Stoic notion is preserved rather exactly in the first verse of St. John's Gospel: "In the beginning was the Logos, and the Logos was with God, and the Logos was God."

It may be that the notion of "seed-formula" *(spermatikos logos)* saved or prevented the early Stoics from working out a detailed cosmogony in the manner of book 5 of Lucretius's poem. The surviving reports tell us very little about their cosmogonical ideas, beyond the generation of the four elements. As these reports (inadequate though they are) make clear, it was a crucial thesis of the theory that when the cosmos is periodically consumed by fire and becomes a single fiery mass, the seed-formula is preserved intact. The seed-formula for the cosmos as a whole, and for each one of the natural kinds specifically, is present from the beginning; the formula is eternal, the generative force is immanent. So there is no need, as there is in the Atomic theory, for an account of the gradual emergence of more complex forms from simple elements.

The end of the world—or, more exactly, of the present phase of the world—comes about through conflagration; the technical term is *ekpyrōsis.* This argument follows a long tradition, stretching back into mythology, that told of the periodic destruction of the world either by fire (the myth of Phaethon) or by flood (the myth of Deucalion). The tradition was mentioned in Plato's *Timaeus* (22d–e), and this is enough in itself to account for its being known to the early Stoics.

They had reasons for preferring fire to flood. It was a thesis of Stoic physics that the heavenly bodies, and especially the sun, consumed fuel in the form of "exhalations" from the world below them. If parts of the sublunary cosmos were thus assimilated by the fiery sun, it was reasonable to assume that the same might happen to the whole cosmos in due course. But quite apart from this argument, the Stoics could hardly do other than choose a fiery rather than a watery end for the life of the cosmos. The end of the cosmos was to be the beginning, the seed, of the next phase: the active power in the seed was heat, rather than moisture. In Stoic theory, this heat was identified with God; living creatures (including the whole cosmos) thus contain an innate providential agency that accounts for their well-adapted structures and capacities.

But why, we may ask, did the Stoics adopt a cyclical theory of destruction and rebirth at all? Why could they not follow the path of Plato, who held that God would not destroy his own creation, or of Aristotle, who held that the cosmos is eternally the same, without beginning or end? We can make some reasonable guesses. It must be observed, first, that Aristotle was the exception in Greek cosmology. From the myths of Hesiod through all the rest of the earlier history of natural philosophy, there was speculation about the origin of the world. It was less universally agreed that the world would come to an end: Lucretius treats this as a surprising thesis. All the same, many previous philosophers did theorize that our world would come to an end. Another reason for the end of the world order in conflagration is also reported. God is a living being, composed of body and soul, and his soul is always growing. Thus there will come a time when he becomes nothing but soul. If one thinks of the conflagration in this way, it can be seen not as the death of the cosmos but as its fullest life.

The cyclical theory is connected with the astronomical idea of the Great Year. The ordinary year is determined by the position of the sun relative to the earth; a year has elapsed when the sun and the earth return to the same relative position. Astronomers speculated about the length of time that elapses between two moments at which the sun, the moon, and the five known planets were all in the same relative position (*Timaeus* 39d). This period, of which different estimates were made, was the Great Year. It appears that the period between one conflagration and the next was supposed to be one Great Year.

This could hardly be otherwise if the Stoics were to claim, as they did, that events in one world were precisely repeated in the next. Socrates will defend himself against Anytus with the same words, and will be condemned by the same jury, every time the cosmic wheel turns full circle. One does not have to accept that the stars exercise a causal influence on the affairs of men: it is enough that the exact description of an event must include all its features, including the position of the sun, moon, and planets when it occurs, so that if it is to be exactly repeated those features of it must be the same. The notion that all events are exactly repeated in each successive cosmic period was thought very striking, particularly by opponents of Stoicism. The reasons for adopting this bizarre theory are not reported by our sources. They must lie in the Stoic theory of causation, coupled with the premise that divine Providence organizes the cosmos for the best. For if this world is the best, succeeding worlds could differ from it only at the cost of being worse, and no reason could be given for the existence of a worse world. So each cosmos must be exactly the same as the last one.

Zeno created the concept of "designing fire" *(pyr technikon)*. The notion of an innate heat in animals was familiar from earlier biology, and Zeno extended it to the heavenly bodies, presumably because of the life-giving heat of the sun. Chrysippus appears to have given the doctrine a new form, with the concept of *pneuma*, or breath. This, too, had an earlier history, especially in Aristotle's biological works, and Zeno had identified it with the psyche in animals. In nonphilosophical contexts, the word can mean either "breath" or "breeze"—the noun is from the verb *to blow*. (Latin *spiritus* and English *spirit* are later translations.) Chrysippus made a cosmic principle out of it, and it became one of the most characteristic Stoic ideas.

Pneuma is a mixture of hot and cold, fire and air, and it pervades the entire universe, down to its smallest parts: the Stoics developed a new concept of "through-and-through mixing" to describe the total union of pneuma with the rest of the substance in the world. All physical body, in Stoic theory, is divisible ad infinitum: the doctrine of total mixture asserted that two bodies may be mixed in such a way that no particle, however small, lacks its portion of either body. By mixing with the whole world, pneuma exercises control over everything. It is the vehicle of (perhaps more strictly, it is identical with) God's providence. It seems to follow from this doctrine that two bodies can occupy the same place, at least in the case where one of the bodies is pneuma. The Stoics differed entirely from Plato and Aristotle in this matter. Plato might say that a physical body "has a share of" or "participates in" a Form, but the Form itself was an immaterial being. Aristotle's secondary categories of being, such as qualities, were dependent on and inherent in bodily substances but were not bodies themselves. Both Plato and Aristotle held that the psyche is not itself a bodily thing. The Stoics held that only a body can act on another body or serve as an efficient cause of a body's actions or passions. Hence such beings as souls or qualities were all to be regarded as bodies—not perhaps capable of existing independently but nevertheless corporeal. All such things consisted of pneuma in its various aspects.

As the active ingredient in all things in the world, pneuma is responsible for the "tension" that holds all the world and everything in it together. The guiding idea in this doctrine is that there is a difference between an identifiable thing and a formless heap of matter. It is most obvious, of course, in a living being, but even a lake or a rock has a principle of unity that differentiates it from a mere quantity of water or mineral. The Stoics said that inanimate things were held together by their "holding power" *(hexis)*, plants by their nature *(physis)*, and animals by their soul *(psyche)*, and each was identical with the pneuma that permeated them and held them in tension. In one graphic description, it is "pneuma that turns back toward itself. It begins to extend itself from the center toward the extremities, and having made contact with the outer surfaces it bends back again until it returns to the same place from which it first set out." This theory has important implications for the theory of natural motion.

The Stoics, like Aristotle, held that there is no void space within the cosmos: matter fills the whole region within the exterior spherical boundary within any interstices. This decision probably arose from the need to preserve the unifying tension imparted to the whole by pneuma. Void intervals would interrupt and endanger the unity. At the same time, the Stoics differed from Aristotle in positing a void space stretching in all directions outside the boundary of the cosmos, and some of their reasoning is preserved in this case. If the substance of the cosmos is periodically consumed by fire, it requires space for expansion; before the *ekpyrōsis* this space must be empty, and it must stretch to infinity, since there is nothing that could limit it.

The thesis that there is infinite void space outside the cosmos carries an extremely important corollary. No sense can now be made of the notion of the center of the *universe*. The center would have to be picked out either by being equidistant from the boundary of the universe everywhere, or by some distinction of quality within it. But if the universe has no boundary, the first cannot apply, and the second is ruled out because there can be no qualitative distinction between any point in the void and any other. Hence Aristotle's dynamic theory, which uses the center of the universe as its focal point, must be rejected: the focal point must be the center of the cosmos itself.

The Stoics applied their theory of *hexis* or "holding power" to the cosmos as a whole. Any identifiable object in the Stoic material continuum was said to be characterized by a holding power that gave it stability and identity. The holding power was provided by the all-pervasive pneuma, whose motions prevented the object from collapsing and dispersing. This must apply to the cosmos as a whole, as well as to its individual contents: the corporeal continuum that composed the cosmos was permeated by a force that drew all of its contents toward *its own* center. This is the closest that classical Greek cosmologists came to a theory of gravity. But centripetal motion in the geocentric cosmos could not by itself explain the motion of the heavenly bodies. If the earth stands still, as they assumed, then the heavens go round in circles, and this circular motion appears to have been explained in purely animistic terms: the heavenly bodies *choose* to move in this way.

The total interpenetration of the divine pneuma through the whole physical world raised in an acute form the problem of freedom of choice in rational beings. There was much debate about it, reflected, for instance, in two surviving works—Cicero's *De fato* and Alexander of Aphrodisias's work of the same title. This divine power is a causal agent, is directed toward maintaining the good order of everything in the cosmos, and is, literally, everywhere. Determinism is total. How, then, can human beings choose freely to act as they do? What sense can be made of moral praise and blame? The Stoics' arguments are too complex to summarize satisfactorily. Briefly, the solution offered by Chrysippus appears to be that it is enough that an action be *our* action—that is, that some essential part of the causing of the action be brought about by us. If our contribution can itself be traced to other causes, that does not affect the issue: the action is still ours, and it is rational that we should be regarded as the agent. Cleanthes summed up the position thus: "Lead me, Zeus and Destiny, wherever you have ordained for me. For I shall follow unflinching. But if I become bad, and am unwilling, I shall follow nonetheless."

DAVID FURLEY

Bibliography

Barnes, Jonathan. *The Presocratic Philosophers*. London: Routledge, 1979.

Brague, Rémi. *Aristote et la question du monde*. Paris: Presses Universitaires de France, 1991.

Cornford, Francis M. *Plato's Cosmology*. London: Routledge, 1937.

Dicks, D. R. *Early Greek Astronomy to Aristotle*. London: Thames and Hudson, 1970.

Duhem, Pierre. *Le système du monde*. Part 1: *La cosmologie Hellénique*. Paris: Hermann, 1913.

Furley, David. *The Greek Cosmologists*, vol. 1. Cambridge: Cambridge University Press, 1987. Vol. 2 forthcoming.

Guthrie, W. K. C. *History of Greek Philosophy*. 6 vols. Cambridge: Cambridge University Press, 1962–1981.

Heath, T. L. *Aristarchus of Samos: The Ancient Copernicus*. Oxford: Clarendon Press, 1913.

Koyré, Alexander. *From the Closed World to the Infinite Universe*. Baltimore: Johns Hopkins University Press, 1957.

Long, A. A., and Sedley, David. *The Hellenistic Philosophers*. Cambridge: Cambridge University Press, 1987.

Solmsen, Friedrich. *Aristotle's System of the Physical World: A Comparison with His Predecessors*. Ithaca, N.Y.: Cornell University Press, 1960.

Sorabji, Richard. *Matter, Space, and Motion*. London: Duckworth, 1988.

———. *Time, Creation, and the Continuum*. London: Duckworth, 1983.

Vernant, Jean-Pierre. *The Origins of Greek Thought*. Ithaca, N.Y.: Cornell University Press, 1982.

Vlastos, Gregory. *Plato's Universe*. Seattle: University of Washington Press, 1975.

GEOGRAPHY

"To DRAW OR WRITE about the earth": the Greek origin of the word *geography* suggests a potentially misleading familiarity. While the contemporary field of geography readily acknowledges Herodotus, Eratosthenes, Strabo, and Ptolemy as its precursors, suggesting a continuity of thought, objective, and methods, it is important not to confuse the Greeks' knowledge of geography with that of their successors. This is particularly true since geography has been troubled throughout its history by arguments over its identity and boundaries as well as its goals and methods. Is its task to describe the earth, to produce an inventory of places and peoples? Does it constitute, for example, an explanatory principle for the movements of history? Or does it aim to construct models of space, maps, diagrams, and tables of facts?

The recent concern in the history of science with questions of cultural anthropology has led to research into the nature of Greek geography and, in turn, to an expanded understanding of the field and its influence. As a result, geography appears to be less a formal discipline with a separate identity than a field of knowledge and experience, manifesting multiple and parallel approaches to the environment of the earth.

Starting with Eratosthenes of Cyrene, who became librarian at Alexandria around 245 B.C.E., geography—the term first appeared about that time—was organized around the project of mapmaking and developed, a posteriori, a genealogy of authors: Anaximander, Hecataeus, Eudoxus, Dicaearchus. The absence of Herodotus, of Hippocrates' treatise *On Airs, Water and Places*, and of authors of travel narratives and periegeses (descriptions taking the form of real or imagined voyages)—for example, Scylax—is significant. Eratosthenes himself appears to be the founder of Hellenistic geography, and in their polemics Hipparcus of Nicaea, Polybius, and Strabo each claim him as a forebear. In the 2nd century C.E., Marinus of Tyre and Ptolemy perpetuate this tradition. These few names indicate the ambiguous nature of what we view as "Greek geography": a shifting field of knowledge where cosmology, astronomy, geometry, history, ethnography, and medicine come together; a meeting place where travel narratives, abstract descriptions, maps, and commentary on maps converge.

One can give this geography some historical depth by distinguishing its successive phases. The oldest emerged in the cities of Ionia, with Anaximander (mid-6th century B.C.E.), Hecataeus of Miletus, and then Herodotus (around 450 B.C.E.). This phase corresponds to the development of colonization in the Mediterranean and Black Sea areas, and to one of the founding projects of Greek historiography. The second phase is that of Hellenistic geography, which existed in the philosophical schools of Athens: in Plato's Academy, with the works of Eudoxus of Cnidos, and in Aristotle's Lyceum, with the works of Dicaearchus of Messana. The study of geography later moved to Alexandria, the capital of the kingdom of the Lagides and the major intellectual center, thanks to the creation of the Library and the Museum. Eratosthenes' map incorporated a mass of new information gathered during Alexander's expedition to Asia. Similarly, Roman expansion led to new geographical development in the work of the historian Polybius, as well as in Strabo's writings at the beginning of the Christian era.

This sort of historical outline requires a great deal of prudence, however. The links connecting the objective factors involved in the broadening of the spatial horizon with the advance of geography are far from mechanical: the ways facts are integrated, interpreted, and diffused belong to a complex process. Moreover, the genealogy leading from Anaximander to Ptolemy creates an illusion of progress that is both linear and cumulative. This genealogy is the product of one interpretation of the history of Greek geography, going back to Eratosthenes himself. But while the succession and cumulative progress of knowledge may apply to cartography, it cannot be said to constitute a global model of the evolution of geographical knowledge. Paradoxically, in fact, mathematical cartography turns out to have had only very limited influence on the contemporaneous geographical consciousness. Texts, more than maps, were the principal bearers of geographical knowledge: in addition to the practical difficulty of transferring images onto metal or wooden panels or onto papyrus, there was the problem of the esoteric nature of Hellenistic maps, which were more like geometric diagrams than figurative maps of the world. The scientific basis of these maps, like the language they used, was incomprehensible to the overwhelming majority of readers, including cultivated and literate authors such as the 2nd-century geographer and traveler Pausanius, who mentions only once the works of "those who claim to know the dimensions of the earth."

If one of the tasks of the history of geography is to determine what the concurrent visions of the world in Greek society might have been, it should be recognized that the geography of the *Odyssey*, Herodotus's ethnography, the geo-ethnographic view of the tragic poets, and the literary geography of the Alexandrian poets, such as Callimachus and Apollonius of Rhodes, all had much greater influence than the works of either Eratosthenes or Ptolemy. The latter influenced only a small, elite group of scientists in erudite circles. Neither geographer had a school. It was only in the Islamic world, and later during the European Renaissance, that the usefulness of Ptolemy's *Geography* was understood.

It is impossible to separate "scientific" geography from the whole collection of renderings, including literary and anachronistic ones, that constituted the worldview of that time. For "history of geography" we should substitute "history of parallel geographies," subtly woven together through alteration, polemics, and the circulation of information.

MODELING / REPRESENTING

One of the most remarkable aspects of Greek geography lies in the early emergence of cartography. Maps themselves symbolize a powerful intellectual endeavor on the part of human beings to set themselves apart from the terrestrial environment and to construct, through reason and imagination, a point of view from above and beyond the earth.

Greek maps are distinct from the cosmological charts found in Egyptian and Mesopotamian civilizations, which offered a schema for understanding the whole world in a single graphic rendering, integrating earth, sky, and the divine powers that personified them. From the time the first map appeared in Greece with the diagram of Anaximander of Miletus (6th century B.C.E.), maps moved away from mythico-religious thinking and, a fortiori, from the cosmogonical models found, for example, in Hesiod's *Theogony*. From that point on, Ouranos (the Heavens), Ge (the Earth), and Okeanos (the Oceans) are secularized, intellectual objects, subject to the principles of geometry, which constitutes one of the dominant paradigms of Ionian science. In addition, maps deal with the *oikoumene*, "the inhabited world," as opposed to the Earth as a cosmological entity. Miletus, as the departure point for numerous colonial expeditions, particularly around the Black Sea, was undoubtedly one of the places where geographical information converged, and where tales about the experiences of navigators and founders of cities were collected. But so far as we can judge, Anaximander's map was not intended for travelers or for colonial expeditions. It was not an aid to navigation of the Black Sea coast but a sketch of the whole inhabited world, projecting onto the earth's surface a shape and an a priori organization that were thus made available to mathematical calculations and the geometric study of forms and symmetries.

The first map sparked the imagination of later geographers, who stressed the audacious genius of its creator, but we can say nothing about its content without extrapolation. However, with the creation of this map, traditionally designated as the first one, we find certain essential elements of Greek cartography coming together: the link with strong cosmological hypotheses, leading to the projection of lines on the earth's surface (which in Anaximander's map was flat), a structure related to the organization of the heavens conceived as a finite sphere on which the earth occupies the exact geometrical center; an effort to give drawings a geometrical cast, charting a graph of the earth through a process of mental calculations; a close connection between the sketch and a treatise bearing on a number of related ideas. Like Anaximander, who wrote a treatise titled *On Nature* (an intellectual project typical of Ionian science and going beyond the framework of geography), Eratosthenes supplemented his map with a treatise called *Geographika,* in which he explained how the map was constructed, and he also included a history of the discipline, a critique of the map's predecessors and descriptive developments. In Ptolemy, by contrast, we find a perfect concordance between the cartographic project and the treatise. There is nothing to suggest that this geometrized Greek cartography ever took on the appearance of medieval maps of the world, with their rich iconography. The esoteric nature of the early drawings, and the necessity of mastering complex knowledge both to produce them and to read them, meant that they were destined for a small circle of specialists in philosophical schools or in a great center of learning like Alexandria. It must be stressed that these maps of the inhabited world were of a strictly theoretical nature; according to all available sources they were not used by travelers, administrators, planners, or anyone else.

Anaximander was not a geographer but a "physician" in the Greek sense. His intent was not to draw a "geographical map" but to devise a visual model of the earth encompassing both the cosmos and meteorological phenomena. When, in 423 B.C.E., the comic poet Aristophanes presented *The Clouds* in Athens, he satirized intellectuals and Sophistic schools, and the map of the world appeared among instruments of astronomy and geometry: an abstract contrivance, of no use to the city-state, and linked to pure speculation, with no political value. The schools of Plato and Aristotle continued the tradition of scientific study, and the works of Eudoxus of Cnidos and Dicaearchus are similarly important milestones between the Ionians and Alexandria. By the 3rd century B.C.E., the cosmological model has changed. The earth is henceforth conceived as a sphere whose geometric organization mirrors that of the heavenly sphere: meridians, parallels, equator, tropics, poles. The *oukemene* (inhabited world) occupies one portion of the northern half of the sphere. The habitable zone lies between the equator and the Tropic of Cancer. Geometrization still predominates with the drawing of the major lines of reference, like the parallel of Dicaearchus, which crosses the entire inhabited world from the colonies of Heracles all the way to India, passing through the Mediterranean, Attica, Rhodes, the Gulf of Issus, and the Taurus Mountains.

We are acquainted with Eratosthenes' work today largely thanks to Strabo, who often used it in polemics. With Eudoxus and Dicaearchus on the one hand and Eratosthenes on the other, we move from Athens to Alexandria, from the city-state par excellence to a new city, the capital of a Hellenistic kingdom; from private philosophical schools where most activity is oriented toward teaching to a royal foundation where intellectuals work with state subsidies. Alexander's expedition and the flood of new information on Asia it produced constituted another major breakthrough. The fall of the Persian empire opened the doors of the Orient to the Greeks. It also allowed for the expansion, not to say the complete revision, of knowledge that had evolved very little since the time of Herodotus (mid-6th century B.C.E.) and Ctesius, a doctor who had been a hostage at the court of King Artaxerxes II (early 4th century B.C.E.). The new era essentially offered unprecedented resources to research, and the Library at Alexandria played a critical role.

Eratosthenes was the first cartographer to work in a library. He grasped the intellectual implications of the influx of new sources that demonstrated, by their number, their contradictions, and their very novelty, the need to correct the old maps. While his geodesic work, such as the famous measurement of the meridian arc between Alexandria and Syena, is in the tradition of speculative thought on the part of geographer-philosophers, particularly of the Academy, Eratosthenes' map and his geographic work appear to be uniquely Alexandrian creations. This is reflected in the importance of Euclidean geometry (*Elements* was published in Alexandria around 300 B.C.E.), with its heuristic potential for graphing parallel and perpendicular lines following from the orthogonal projection chosen by Eratosthenes (in which meridians do not converge toward the poles), and even more in the new methods of intellectual inquiry based on the accumulation of written documents from different lands and of different genres.

By compiling and critiquing his sources, Eratosthenes was able to determine where regions were located and extrapolate their shapes. However, he was not a traveler himself. Establishing the arc of the earth's rotation represented an experimental procedure, but this was not typical of his work in geography. Unable to determine all the positions in latitude and longitude through astronomical calculations (which would remain problematic until precise clocks were perfected in the 18th century), Eratosthenes had to use voyagers' accounts; in other words, he had to translate estimated distances, which varied widely, into a system of measurable disjunctions, gaps that could then be transferred to points on the map.

Thanks to all these theoretical calculations, it was possible, starting with partial sources collected in the Alexandrian Library, slowly to construct the view of the entire inhabited world, and to build up a body of knowledge about the most remote regions a priori, by taking a critical approach to eyewitness accounts. Maps were part of this development, providing visual and mathematical coherence each step of the way. They provided a consistent means for verifying the effects of a local decision on the overall structure, and for making the necessary responses and adjustments suggested by modifying the placement of a parallel or a base meridian. The map is completely oriented toward geodesic work and the schematization of space in relative and measurable geometric form.

Eratosthenes' work marks the beginning of a tradition of the map as the working tool of the geographer, a device that allows for easy transmission from one geographer to another, and for control over, even correction of, one's predecessors' work. Hence we see Hipparchus of Nicea, in his work *Against Eratosthenes*, criticizing the work of the Alexandrian cartographer, whom he reproaches for a lack of mathematical rigor and for his makeshift fashion of establishing positions based on data from travelers. Later, in the first two books of his *Geography*, Strabo echoes these criticisms in order to defend Eratosthenes against Hipparchus's fierce attacks.

Following Eratosthenes, cartographers built on the work of their predecessors. The earlier work provided the starting point, the framework, and the space in which to apply a variety of critical methods that enabled the mapmaker to bring it up to date, to complete and perfect it. This was Ptolemy's position in the 2nd century C.E. vis-à-vis the work of his predecessor, Marinus of Tyre.

The author of treatises on astronomy, mathematics, and optics, Ptolemy made a number of contributions to geography with his astrological geography *(Tetrabiblos)*, his *Canon of Remarkable Cities*, and finally his *Geography*. The last work, in the form in which it has come down to us, consists of eight books. Book I and part of Book II are devoted to a theoretical description of mapmaking methods, in particular the representation on a flat surface of the convergence of longitudinal lines toward the poles. The second part of Book II and Books III and IV are in the form of a catalogue of 8,000 points expressed in degrees of longitude and latitude, making it possible to transfer these points onto regional maps with perpendicular representation.

Ptolemy's importance lies in the dual nature of his work as both theory and inventory. The only text by a cartographer to survive (despite all the problems involved in passing down maps and despite the many stages the writing of the text may have been through), Ptolemy's work gives geography a strong definition, oriented toward defining the purpose of maps: the mimesis, or representation, of the inhabited world in its totality, in contrast to chorography, the mapping or description of a particular region according to its natural configuration. This fundamental distinction will play an essential role in geography during the European Renaissance. A veritable inventory of the places of the world at the height of the Roman empire, Ptolemy's *Geography* also provides, in its tabulations, an impressive body of geographical positions readily transferable to maps. This was the only means of protecting the coordinates from the distortions inherent in the manual reproduction of texts and drawings. These 8,000 positions no doubt result in large measure from the manipulation of fictional data; the role of conjecture and approximation and of completely unverifiable data is masked by the authoritative and persuasive effect of the lists of coordinates that obscure all traces of their source. These tables of positions later played an important role in the geography of ancient Islam, which continued the Ptolemean tradition, and in the European Renaissance, where they made it possible for cartographers to recreate the maps of Alexandrian scholars before modernizing their topographic content.

From Anaximander to Ptolemy, Greek cartography appeared to be a highly specialized process and technique. Other accounts acknowledge the circulation of round maps, derived undoubtedly from Ionian prototypes, and both Plutarch, at the end of the 1st century C.E., and Lucian, in the 2nd century, hint at the existence of archaistic maps, freed of the complex mathematical equipment of the Alexandrian production.

DESCRIPTION / INVENTORY / EXPLANATION

Although mapmaking did have a theoretical objective and dealt with the entire inhabited world, governed by the geodesic order and cosmological hypotheses on the similarity of the heavenly and earthly spheres, it was by no means the only tool available to the field of geography. The difficulties of reproducing and transmitting drawings, like the high degree of specialization needed for making them, limited the influence of maps. Moreover, mapping maintained a series of complex links with verbal discourse, which extended its influence beyond the highly specialized circles in which it was used. The map imposed a new order, implicit or not, on geographical description, introducing a form of spatial organization that shaped the corresponding written text. Between map and treatise there is a complex system of interaction: the former provides for visualization and mnemonic images, while the latter affords the indispensable means for conveying knowledge about countries and peoples — itineraries, descriptions, place names, ethnographic digressions, myths, natural science, and so on. Often, the descriptions give the cartographer the material he needs, while the maps can implicitly shape the written description.

Anaximander's map began a tradition in which geographic description — as we understand it today — is supported by prior evidence of a global form that provides a narrative model: the circular voyage. It is tempting to correlate this first map with the *Periegesis* of Hecataeus of Miletus (late 6th century B.C.E.). This work is presented as a tour of the earth, an intellectual journey around the Mediterranean, describing the three continents of the inhabited world (Europe, Libya, Asia); in a sort of catalogue of countries, it lists all the places and peoples on the route. Each stop offered the possibility of integrating a variety of information (ethnographic, for example). Once a principle of global order was established, it was possible to insert new places, to digress and deal with new developments, without disturbing the structure of the whole. This circular model, which resembles a circumnavigation of the Mediterranean coast, also allowed for inland excursions toward the lands and peoples in the interior of a continent. The circumnavigations and other *periodoi ges* (trips around the earth) thus appear to be an odd compromise between the navigators' accounts — adopting the latter's narrative rules, their metonymic logic, sometimes even their detailed topographic information — and maps, which offered a global structure based on an intellectual and ecumenical itinerary, using material from real voyages without being bound by the limits of those voyages. Maps also provided the opportunity to move from real but limited voyages to intellectual, global journeys, virtual tours of the earth.

The history of *periploi* (circumnavigations) and *periegeses* in Greece is crisscrossed by this dialectical tension between, on one hand, the actual tour, the account of the voyage, and, on the other, its intellectual reconstruction within a descriptive model in which circularity is a measure of completeness and comprehensiveness. It is not just by chance that the ancient sources use the expression "circling the earth" for texts and maps. *Periegeses* and *periploi* are both genres associated with discovery and exploration (as in the voyage attributed to Hanno, involving navigation along the Atlantic coast of Africa, or the journey made by the Alexandrian admiral Naearchus, who directed the Greek fleet from the mouth of the Indus to the mouth of the Euphrates), and also with commercial itineraries (the *Periplus of the Erythraean Sea*), and with the first forms of ecumenical geography (the journey of Scylax of Caryanda, *Stadiasmus Maris magni*, the *Periegesis* of Denys).

Whereas Hecataeus of Miletus sought to present the world's places and peoples in an orderly fashion, using Anaximander's map to organize the accounts of travelers and to integrate parts of the voyage into an ideal circle (an enterprise similar to the one he undertook with Greek mythology and which he rationalized in his *Genealogies*), Herodotus's purpose was quite different. Just as *Histories*, in dealing with the recent past and the causes and course of the conflict between the Greeks and the barbarians, differed from the genealogies of Hecataeus, who went further into the distant past and explored an area of conjectural knowledge, the representation of space Herodotus presented differs from the Hecataean model and also from Anaximander's geometric rationalism. However, both models have left traces in Herodotus's text, despite the historian's ironic tone with reference to the excessive symmetry of the Ionian map.

In his contribution to a major question of meteorologics, the location of the sources of the Nile, Herodotus allows himself a surprising degree of cartographic extrapolation. He interprets north-south symmetry on both sides of a base axis, making the Nile, to the south, the equivalent of the Danube, to the north; thus he can find sources of the first corresponding to those of the second (which are located in the Celtic countries, near the city of Pyrenees). So too, when he sets out to explain the sequence of peoples in Asia Minor, or in Scythia, Herodotus resorts to geometry and to a type of description in terms of shapes and orientation that assumes the existence of geographic maps.

The most important innovation in Herodotus's geography, however, lies in the close connections he makes with historical research. Places, and the people inhabiting them, fall within the same intellectual order as events of the past: they are objects of inquiry, understood through the convergence of observation and hearsay, and through the exercise of a critical mind that defines the

field of the plausible without always explaining its criteria. Where Ionian rationalism had drawn a circle around the inhabited world with a compass,
Herodotus opened up vague boundary areas, where human knowledge stops
short of the ocean's edge. These boundary areas are places of alterity and excess, of natural wonders or happy, almost godlike people: the long-lived Ethiopians, Indians, Arabs living in lands of spices. This landscape of the outer
limits of the human world remained rooted in the ancient imagination and
probably contributed more to creating a picture of the world than did all the
geometry of Alexandria. It continued into the Middle Ages and the Renaissance, thanks largely to the rediscovery of Latin encyclopedias.

In Greece, geography could be said to be limited to the inhabited world, in
other words, to the *oekoumene*, a limit that even Eratosthenes respects. In
Herodotus's work, this area is the theater for the conflict between the Greeks
and the Persians. The Persian Wars played an essential role in developing a
conception of cultural identity that set the Greeks apart from the Barbarians.
The Persian Wars established a cultural and political opposition between peoples that in turn raised questions for the Greeks about their own identity, by
leading them to recognize in themselves certain characteristics that are reversed in the mirror image offered by another people.

The ethnographic framework established in Herodotus's work is one aspect
of intelligibility in the conflict, and it is also an object of obvious fascination
and curiosity. But despite the overlapping discussions of Egyptians, Persians,
Ethiopians, or Scythians, which appear at times as digressions in the text, the
link with the Persian Wars is never entirely lost. Herodotus's *Histories* are set
in a space that has been schematically charted within the Ionian tradition. The
stakes in the conflict might be termed geopolitical, in that they resulted from
the dangerous proximity between the Persian empire and the Greek city-
states of the coast of Asia Minor; the latter's revolts unleashed the hostilities
and brought war to the land and seas of Greece itself. Herodotus describes
Aristagoras, the Milesian ambassador at Sparta, equipped with a geographic
map that he uses to try to persuade King Cleomenes to fight for the liberation
of the subjugated cities and to conquer the Persian empire itself, including the
treasures of Susa. In the process, the historian conveys brilliantly the scales of
distance and power, the forces in conflict, the role of the sea separating Greece
and Persia, and the formidable ethnic coalition arrayed against the Greeks.

We lack the milestones that would allow us to trace the evolution of geographic literature up to the 4th century B.C.E. Ethnography and "barbarian
customs" appear frequently in titles of works attributed to the logographer
Hellanicus of Lesbos, who seems to have made a specialty of local and regional history. The physician Ctesias, in his works on Persia and India, also
dealt with historical, ethnographic, and political data; his work remained
without peer until the expedition of Alexander the Great. We can assume that
ethnographic preoccupations were manifested in the collection of *Constitu-*

tions attributed to Aristotle. The *Periodos ges* by Eudoxus of Cnidos had a scientific and cartographic orientation, and it probably included descriptive information as well.

Herodotus inaugurated a tradition in which geographic knowledge is closely linked to history: it constitutes a framework for history, helps make history intelligible, and provides an introduction to ethnography, which characterizes foreign peoples. In its ecumenical aspect, geography was naturally associated with the genre of universal history. Ephorus supplemented his *History* with a cartographic diagram that was preserved for us by a Christian writer, Cosmas Indicopleustes. It is a simple rectangle with the four cardinal points marked, as well as the peoples living at the frontiers: Celts, Scythians, Indians, and Ethiopians. With Polybius (2nd century B.C.E.), we rediscover this dimension of ecumenical geography in a monumental *History*, which sets out to cover the genesis of the Roman empire and attempts to make sense of the dramatic events that the author himself has experienced. There is a notable geographic dimension to this work. Book XXXIV takes the form of a treatise on geography that is relatively autonomous within the overall structure. The description it offers incorporates information acquired from Alexandrian mapmaking and on occasion takes up highly polemical debates (Polybius defends the geographic competence of Homer, who anchored Odysseus's navigations firmly in the Mediterranean, against Eratosthenes, who relegated them to the ocean and to the domain of pure fiction).

Polybius's historical work influenced both his conception and his practice of geography. He was keenly aware of how much the world had grown as a result of the Roman conquests, and he recognized the need for a reconfiguration of Eratosthenian geography. Roman expansion was one of the major historical events of the epoch, and geography gave Polybius a tool for ordering history. He adopted a broad, quasi-cartographic view that led him to grasp the simultaneity of events in different theaters of action; the temporal order of his work as a chronicler thus coexists with a geographic order that allows him to present events in Asia Minor, continental Greece, North Africa, Spain, and elsewhere. The descriptions of the different theaters of action—cities or battlefields—constitute an important dimension of his story and fit nicely with the Polybian conception of "pragmatic history," where experience prevails over book learning. Polybius himself was a traveler, indeed an explorer, and he portrays himself as an Odysseus turned historian.

Strabo is close to Polybius in many respects. His historical work (which has been lost) took up where *Histories* left off. But in contrast to his predecessor, he devoted a separate work to geography. In calling his treatise *Geography*, Strabo established himself as a successor to Eratosthenes and set himself apart, as had Polybius, from the genre of "circumnavigations." His text is one of the major surviving accounts of Alexandrian geography. The first two books continue the Eratosthenian model: they present a summary of the his-

tory of Greek geography (though Strabo breaks with his predecessors in rein-
stalling Homer as the founder of the line), a critical examination of these predecessors, and a discussion of Eratosthenes' theses, the general frameworks
of the Alexandrian map and the polemics sparked by Hipparchus, and the
scientific knowledge required to enter into the debates. But Strabo's *Geography* is not a cartographic treatise. It is not meant for the same public as
Eratosthenes' work, since Strabo wanted to be of service to Roman statesmen
and provincial administrators who needed information on population, economics, and natural resources. His text was meant as a description of the
Roman empire, from the Iberian Peninsula (Book III) to Egypt and Libya
(Book XVII).

However, despite its introduction and the intent to serve the empire, in its
detailed descriptions this *Geography* resembled a complex and heterogeneous
literary construction, reworking sources of information from various periods.
The description of Greece itself is taken in large part from the "Catalogue of
Ships" in Book II of the *Iliad* and from Homer's Alexandrian commentators.
For other regions, Strabo borrows whole segments of *periploi* (Artemidorus),
and he lists the places spread along the coastline. In India, Strabo seems to
forget the harshly critical cast of his earlier statements; he relies on the testimony of Megasthenes, Daeimachus, and other Hellenistic sources who presented a picture of India and its people that combined aspects of wonder with
ethnographic observation. At the same time, for Iberia and for Gaul Strabo
relied largely on the Stoic Posidonius, who combined ethnographic observations with a particular interest in natural resources and economics.

A collection of regional descriptions from a variety of genres and sometimes from different epochs, Strabo's work is representative of a field of inquiry that goes beyond what we ordinarily mean by "geography." Literary
criticism, mythology, history, *mirabilia* (marvels), ethnography, and cartography are all aspects of the spectrum of geographic knowledge, unified only by a
relation to space. Against this dizzying inventory of places and peoples and
their characteristics, one can posit a few powerful ideas that introduce a coherent worldview. Strabo was interested only in the territory under Roman
authority or along its borders. His was a geography of the inhabited world.
For Strabo, topography and climate may determine the degree of civilization
of people, but acculturation tempers the deterministic model: Rome plays a
clear civilizing role.

Was Strabo a precursor of the 19th-century European universal geographies? He illustrates an encyclopedic tendency in geography, now freed of the
mathematical framework of the Alexandrians, a geography that became a
means of understanding political reality, the human and civilized world, identified with the Roman empire. The encyclopedic tendency reappears in a minor text of the 2nd century C.E., the *Pariegesis of the Inhabited World*, by
Denys of Alexandria, who offered students in the schools, in the brief form of

a mnemonic poem, a mental map on which the world of gods, the world of heroes, and the world of men were superimposed.

GEOGRAPHIC KNOWLEDGE

From the Presocratics to Ptolemy, Greek geography offers a combination of distinct intellectual projects. While it is true that this long tradition entailed an accumulation of layers of knowledge about the inhabited world, certain specific aims must be kept in mind.

Some scholars looked to geography for a principle of cause and effect, capable of explaining human phenomena. Climatic determinism, destined to survive in the tradition of modern geography, was the object of the Hippocratic treatise *On Airs, Water, and Places* (second half of the 5th century B.C.E.). This manual for the itinerant physician presented a set of correspondences between the environment (topography, climate, hydrography) and the health of the population. Local observations were recorded in a larger deterministic system, governed by the equilibrium or disequilibrium of the relations between hot and cold, dry and wet; these relations were viewed as one of the causes of human disease, and also as a factor explaining cultural and physical differences among peoples living in neighboring regions. In this model, Greece and Asia Minor occupied the temperate center, where extremes are balanced. The Stoic Posidonius used the distribution of climatic zones on the earth as an explanation for physical variations among people living in different regions. Astral determinism also offered an explanatory grid for physical and cultural variations (Ptolemy's *Tetrabiblos*).

Another tradition is that of meteorology, the science of natural phenomena occurring on earth and in sublunary space. Beginning with the Presocratics, questions arose about earthquakes, the Nile River floods, winds, and rain. This tradition inspired Aristotle's *Meteorologics,* a treatise devoted to the classification of these phenomena and to research into their causes. Members of Aristotle's school, such as Straton of Lampsacus and Posidonius *(On the Oceans),* followed this line of inquiry. Even Eratosthenes had been interested in geophysical phenomena such as the tides, earthquakes, and volcanoes.

Cartography may well be the tradition whose coherence and objectives were most strongly marked by Greek thinkers, starting with Eratosthenes. Resting on a set of astronomical premises and geometric theorems, the discipline emerged as a theoretical activity practiced by philosophers who sought to model the world, from the celestial sphere to the graphic projection of the inhabited earth. Mathematical order, symmetry, and the isomorphism of the heavenly and earthly spheres were at the heart of their investigations. Contrary to what one finds in ancient China, Greek maps were not used to govern, improve, or manage territory. They were not instruments distributed to all levels of the local administration; rather, they represented the activity of a small number of celebrated thinkers working in private philosophical schools (Athens and Rhodes) or in the cultural institutions of Hellenistic rulers (Alexandria and Pergamum). Maps were, above all, the working instruments of cartographers, scholars committed to collecting results, hypotheses, calculations, and attempts at geometric formalization.

For travel by land or sea, travel accounts always superseded maps. For giving shape to the geographic horizon, Homer, Herodotus, and the tragic and Hellenistic poets played a role beyond that of the scientists and thinkers of Alexandria. Their representations, though often archaic, were at least consistent with the literary culture taught in schools. What we term geography today is the result of the convergence of a number of intellectual domains: philosophy, astronomy and mathematics, historiography, physics, and ethnography. All these disciplines are inextricably linked to the exploration of a world that is defined primarily by its human populations and the political and historical issues at stake in their coexistence.

CHRISTIAN JACOB
Translated by Elizabeth Rawlings and Jeannine Pucci

Bibliography

Aujac, Germaine. *Strabon et la science de son temps*. Paris: Les Belles Lettres, 1966.

Harley, Brian, and David Woodward, eds. *The History of Cartography*, vol. 1: *Cartography in Prehistory: Ancient and Medieval Europe and the Mediterranean*. Chicago: University of Chicago Press, 1987.

Janni, Pietro. *La mappa e il periplo: Cartografia antica e spazio odologico*. Rome: Università di Macerata, 1984.

Nicolet, Claude. *Space, Geography and Politics in the Early Roman Empire*. Ann Arbor: University of Michigan Press, 1991.

Pedech, Paul. *La géographie des grecs*. Paris: Presses Universitaires de France, 1976.

Prontera, Francesco, ed. *Geografia e geografi nel mondo antico: Guida storica e critica*. Bari: Laterza, 1983.

———. *Strabone: Contributi allo studio della personalità e dell'opera*. Perugia: Università degli studi. Vol. 1, 1984; vol. 2, ed. Gianfranco Maddoli, 1986.

Van Paassen, Christian. *The Classical Tradition of Geography*. Groningen: J. B. Wolters, 1957.

HARMONICS

EVERYWHERE PRESENT in everyday life as well as religious and political life, music was for the ancient Greeks not only the most beautiful of the arts but also the object of the highest philosophical speculation. A mass of textual, visual, and archaeological documents bears witness to the Greek predilection for musical activity: literary, papyrological, and epigraphical evidence; figural representations on ceramics or in relief sculpture; vestiges of the stringed, wind, and percussion instruments that have survived in significant numbers; and, above all, some fifty scores (on papyrus or in inscriptions) give us a rich and varied picture of the musical life of the ancient Greeks. But as much as music was a fervently practiced art, it was also a skill and a science the nature, object, and method of which are defined in writings that are both technical and theoretical. More broadly, music entered the political realm: in Sparta and, to a lesser degree, in Thebes and Mantinea, music and politics were so tightly linked that laws were established governing musical practice and musical education.

The Athenian citizen, for his part, was expected to know how to sing and play at least the *lyra* (an instrument for amateurs, as opposed to the kithara, which was used only by professional musicians). After spending years learning how to read, write, and do arithmetic, Athenian children went for three years to a *kitharistes*, who served both as a teacher of the *lyra* (despite the title) and as a teacher of music in general. The *kitharistes* taught by example, using memory as his principal tool.

Nothing in that era suggests that musical education went further than rudimentary lessons in vocal and instrumental practice. The ancient sources give no indication that a student was expected to acquire theoretical knowledge of any depth. In Book VII of his *Politics*, Aristotle makes it clear that the goal of musical education was not at all to train accomplished musicians—and still less virtuosi—but only to complete the student's general education with basic skills in music. If it is true that the transmission of music was and remained a fundamental given in Greek civilization, it was limited, in the case of amateurs, to the inculcation of ideas entirely oriented toward the practical performance of music and did not even include written notation: school scenes on Attic ceramics show the teacher face to face with his pupils, *lyras* in hand. The scrolls that are sometimes shown on their laps contain poetic texts but never musical scores. In Athens, Thebes, Sparta, and Mantinea, musical city-states par excellence, citizens could neither read nor write music.

To find traces of more advanced musical instruction that includes instruction in music theory as well as stringed instrument technique, we have to go to Ionia, to Magnesia ad Meandrum, and especially to Teos, site of one of the most powerful professional corporations of artists known to antiquity, the Dionysian *technitai* (artists). An inscription dating from the beginning of the 3rd century C.E. describes the sequence of studies to be carried out in a school founded by a generous donor named Polythrous. A *kitharistes* was hired for an annual salary of 600 drachmas, to teach certain young men the art of playing the kithara, with and without plectrum (a technical specialization not included in the ordinary course of study), but in addition—and this is a crucial innovation—he also taught musical theory, *ta mousika*. The text stipulates that examinations in music were to be given annually.

In Magnesia ad Maeandrum, according to a 2nd-century C.E. inscription, the year-end awards given the best pupils included prizes for *melographia* and *rhythmographia*, as well as prizes for kithara playing, *kitharoedia* (singing to kithara accompaniment), and arithmetic. The references to "melodic writing" and "rhythmic writing," probably in the form of musical dictation, strongly imply a passage from the level of advanced mastery of a technically difficult stringed instrument to a higher level involving musical theory.

The term *ta mousika* warrants some explanation. This plural neuter is not equivalent to *he mousike*, music, a term that very often refers to general musical culture, including not only music as such but also what was later called the quadrivium. *Ta mousika* implies a plurality that is still concrete and applied, that has not quite reached full theoretical knowledge of the subject or of the various disciplines that constitute the subject. According to the great theoretician Aristoxenus of Tarentum, only the second sort of knowledge defines the *mousikos*, the authentic musician. Furthermore, inscriptions tell us that some musicians, having the same education as the young men of Teos, went from one city-state to another giving talks on the topic of *ta mousika*, addressing a public made up not of specialists but of amateurs interested in the subject. Thus we find a decree in the city of Tanagra, dating from 171–146 B.C.E., honoring a certain Hegesimachus of Athens, described by the text as *mousikos hyparkhon*, "a professional musician by trade," and his son, who over a period of several days gave talks during which they used musical instruments and discussed the instruments themselves. In so doing, according to the inscription, they demonstrated the excellence of their *techne*, in other words, their technical skills as musicians. The term *techne*, quite different from *episteme*, is undoubtedly one of praise. It is found in a large number of honorific inscriptions marking free performances or lectures given not only by musicians but also by physicians and orators. Nevertheless, it clearly delineates the boundaries of the knowledge that has been put on display: theoretical knowledge, unquestionably, and to some extent scientific, but no more than that; it is still anchored in musical practice (that of a specific instrument, for example) and not inhospitable, in all likelihood, to considerations involving the history of music, all of which was excluded from the compass of the musical *episteme*.

This distinction between *techne* and *episteme* has direct consequences for the form of the musical treatises that have come down to us—approximately fifty of them, covering a period of about ten centuries (from the end of the 6th century B.C.E. up to the 5th century C.E.). Indeed, there are two distinctly different types of authors: on the one hand, there are musicographers, and on the other, theoreticians. The first wrote fairly short works for the most part, with titles that indicate clearly enough the limits of their ambitions: thus Cleonides and Bacchius the Old produced works called *Eisagōge* (Introduction) or *Encheiridion* (Manual), and the Pythagorean writer Nicomachus of Gerasa wrote a brief work that is only a draft prefiguring a scientific treatise. Theoreticians, for their part, give us works like *Peri mousikes* and *Peri harmonikes* (On Music, On Harmonics), the implicit underlying feminine term being *epistemes*, science.

In the texts, these two types of studies diverge significantly. After a rapid and superficial approach to the subject, the musicographers quickly enter into purely technical considerations, in a language stripped of any literary pretensions. Concepts are studied one by one, in the form of successive definitions, in increasing order of difficulty and complexity as each new element is added and combined with the others. The aim is to impart progressively, through a series of affirmations that belong neither to criticism nor to research, a sort of musical catechism that the student will eventually have to memorize from beginning to end. The *Introduction* by Bacchius the Old even proceeds by way of question sets (as if the teacher were examining the student) and model answers:

"How many kinds of consonant intervals are there in the perfect system?"
"Six."
"What are they?"
"They are the fourth, the fifth, the octave, the octave plus the fourth, the octave plus the fifth, the double octave."

The theoreticians of music, for their part, were all associated with one or another of the great philosophical schools of antiquity. There was no theoretician who was not a philosopher; conversely, there was no philosophical school that did not construct its own doctrine of musical science. Ancient Pythagoreanism is illustrated by the treatises of Philolaus (only fragments of which survive, unfortunately), then of Archytas of Tarentum; Aristoxenus, author of the oldest work on harmonics that we have, was first a student of the Pythagoreans before he became a follower of Aristotle's teachings; Theon of Smyrna was a Platonist; Philodemus of Gadara identified himself with

Epicureanism, and in his *Peri mousikes* he challenged the musical doctrines of the Stoic Diogenes of Babylon; even the Skeptics, with Sextus Empiricus, had their own ideas about the nature and function of music, essentially aimed at dismissing all the other philosophical schools.

These treatises, which are reasonably lengthy, have some common features. They always integrate into their respective musical systems the fundamental ideas of the school from which they come, principles and methods included. All of them reflect, starting in their very first paragraphs, on the nature of musical science and its place in the system of learning and knowledge: How does it relate to mathematics, physics, or even metaphysics? What are its criteria? How does it operate, and in what form? Unlike the musicographers, the theoreticians are always careful to contest and refute opposing theses with solidly supported arguments, either to challenge particular points or else to undermine an entire doctrine starting with its basic assumptions.

A third group has to be distinguished both from the musicographers and from the theoreticians: those who are broadly categorized, despite their differences, as "Harmonists," and who left no known works. We find their theories only in the form of polemical summaries by their adversaries, chiefly Plato and Aristoxenus. Insofar as one can judge by these indirect and partial accounts, their theoretical teaching did not include any philosophical reflections. Their basic focus was on musical practice, whether in terms of playing an instrument, like the *aulos*, or in terms of musical notation. One of the illustrious representatives of this tendency (since there is no way in this context to speak of a particular school) was the 4th-century Athenian kitharist Stratonicus. He is said to have had students in harmonics, and to have been the first to devise a musical diagram.

It is difficult to assign to Plato a position of his own among the musical currents of antiquity, not only because he did not leave any specialized treatise on music but also because his thinking on harmonics and musical practice does not really constitute a doctrine as such. Largely inspired by the Pythagorean system of calculating intervals, to which he subscribed, ironic in his opposition to the Harmonists who built their theories by "fiddling" with the strings of their instruments, Plato opened the way for those who would later be called Neoplatonists (such as Theon of Smyrna and Aristides Quintilianus) rather than actually constructing his own science of music.

The history of the philosophico-musical literature of Greek and Roman antiquity is also the history of a persistent schism, one that lasted nearly ten centuries. It opposes—irreconcilably, despite the efforts of the great Alexandrian astronomer Ptolemy, among others—the Pythagorean and Neopythagorean schools to Aristoxenus of Tarentum and his successors. The quarrel erupted in the second half of the 4th century, when Aristoxenus wrote his major work, a magisterial treatise on harmonics known under the traditional but probably erroneous title of *Harmonika stoikheia* (Harmonic Elements).

Before Aristoxenus, musical and harmonic science was the province of the Pythagoreans and—with the reservations noted above—the Harmonists. For someone like Philolaus or Archytas, music was "sister" to mathematics and astronomy, as a science of numerical relations governing the musical intervals, of which they are both the essence and the expression. The central idea is that the universe is structured according to a perfect order, an order defined by numbers and by which the human soul must be penetrated if it is to participate in this perfection itself. Music, and especially harmonics, are among the manifestations of this order: starting from the observation (at first experimental, with the earliest observations on a single-stringed instrument called a *monochordon*) that consonant intervals correspond to simple numerical relations in the superpartial form of the ratio $(n + 1) / n$, the Pythagoreans in a sense reversed this proposition: harmonious intervals are consonant *because* they may be expressed as (or because they simply *are*) remarkable numerical relations. In this system of thought, it goes without saying that musical science, reduced here to harmonics and acoustics, stems from "physics," understood as a science of the order governing the entire universe, and that this science used the tools of mathematics to express itself. Consequently, any melody perceptible to the ear can be deemed beautiful only inasmuch as it is the audible expression of an abstract perfection, which transcends it. The disciple's efforts, then, will be to abstain from any musical practice blemished by imperfection, which would be capable of altering the harmony of his soul. Whence the injunction, thought to go back to Pythagoras himself, to play only the *lyra*, whose seven-stringed *accordatura* reflects the order of the seven planets, among other things in order to participate in the order of the world. Starting from such principles, the musical treatises of the first Pythagoreans have titles like Philolaus's *Peri physeos* (On Nature), or *Peri arithmetikes* (On Arithmetic).

With Aristoxenus of Tarentum the era of music in thrall to mathematics quickly came to an end. A close follower of Aristotle, who throughout his work had called into question several aspects of the Pythagorean theses even though he had not formulated a complete doctrine of his own, Aristoxenus established, for the first time in antiquity, a musical science independent of mathematics, an autonomous science ruled by its own principles and endowed with a method suited to its own nature, to the objects it studies, and to its own goals, based on two criteria directly related to its own specific features: the ear, *aisthesis*, and rational thought, *dianoia*. There were to be no more calculations of intervals: the object of harmonic science was now to be musical sound itself and not mathematical entities.

The split between the two doctrines was thus absolute. It bore on the roots and the very foundations of the science of harmonics. In historical terms, the schism was complete around 325 B.C.E. From then on, everything was marked by the irremediable opposition between Pythagoreanism (or, to a lesser degree, Platonism) and Aristoxenism. Thinkers had no choice but to take sides and ally themselves with one of these formidable doctrines or the other; they had to defend its principles and conclusions anew, and to struggle against the opposing school, unless they positioned their arguments on strictly technical grounds, just as the more modest musicographers had done in their didactic writings.

The only significant attempt to reconcile the two doctrines is found in the *Harmonika* in three books by Ptolemy, written in the 2nd century C.E. This voluminous text is of crucial importance in the history of Pythagorean musical thought. Without ever calling into question Pythagorean acoustics and physics, with which he openly identified, and still less the mathematical nature of the science of intervals, which he never tired of calculating, Ptolemy comes across here as a figure both remarkable for his independence and admirable for the critical spirit that he develops toward his subject. In spite of his protestations of obedience, he in fact strives to point out everything in Aristoxenus that, as he sees it, represents an intelligent and authentically musical contribution to harmonics, especially anything that has to do with auditory sensation, which he then uses as a criterion as reliable as *dianoia*.

But there was never any real syncretism. The last theoretical writings in Latin, by St. Augustine and by Boethius (ca. 480–524), who wrote *De institutione musica*, and later the *Harmonics* in Greek by the Byzantine author Manuel Bryenne (around 1320), still remained dependent on one tradition or the other. Boethius, very much in the Pythagorean camp, and Manuel Bryenne, a strictly orthodox Aristoxenean, are the last champions of the two causes.

Around the edges of the purely theoretical treatises, we know of works that are undoubtedly derived from an early source—of which, unhappily, there are almost no surviving fragments—dealing with instruments: *Peri organon, Peri aulon, Perio aulon treseōs* (On Instruments, On Auloi, On Piercing of Auloi), attributed to writers who are notoriously Pythagorean (such as Euphranor) or Aristoxenean (beginning with Aristoxenus himself). In these texts, which one might view at first glance as technical works, since they seem to originate in the *techne* of instrument making, what is at issue goes far beyond the practical realm. The aim is to undermine the opposing doctrines and to shore up one's own theses, starting from instrumental realities, which serve both as the experimental basis and as material proof in support of a doctrine. This is why the set of surviving fragments of these works are included in philosophico-musical treatises.

In spite of the considerable divergences that set theoreticians against one another across ten centuries of musical literature, a sort of consensus arose concerning the place assigned to harmonics within the various disciplines that make up the *mousike episteme*, and (more surprisingly) concerning the various elements included in *harmonikē*. This term must not be understood in the modern sense of the word *harmonics*, which is the science of chords and their sequences. Indeed, even if we have some evidence that the ancients used a sort of polyphony, this was never the object of the slightest attempt at codification, either by musicographers or by theoreticians.

The oldest classification of musical disciplines in which *harmonikē* appears goes back to Lasus of Hermione, who taught in Athens during the 6th century. This classification has not come down to us directly; it is mentioned by the Latin author Martianus Capella in his *Nuptials of Philologia and Mercury*, written between 410 and 439 C.E. Lasus distinguishes three major components of musical knowledge (technical, practical, and performative), themselves subdivided into three branches. *Harmonikē* is the first branch of the technical component, where it precedes rhythmics and metrics.

The second classification that will leave a lasting mark on Greco-Roman musical theory is that of the theoretician Aristoxenus. It is no longer a matter of oral teachings here, since Aristoxenus is the author of the oldest treatise on harmonics that has survived almost intact. For him, harmonics is the first of the musical sciences, by its importance in the order of the acquisition of knowledge: "The science of *melos* is complex; it is divided into several parts. Among them, we have to consider the science called 'harmonic [*harmonikē*],' which comes first in rank and has an elementary value. In fact, it is the first of the theoretical disciplines: from it stems everything relating to the theory of systems and tones; and it is fitting to ask nothing more of anyone who has mastered this science, because that is its goal; all the subjects at a higher level that are studied once the poietic science makes use of systems and tones do not belong to harmonics, but to the science that encompasses both harmonics and all the sciences that study the entire set of musical questions. And it is the possession of this latter science that makes the musician" (*Harmonic Elements* 1.11–2.7).

Aristoxenus's magnum opus, *On Music*, has not survived. In it he must have written at length about his conception of the various elements that constitute a musical knowledge worthy of the status of *episteme*. To attempt to restore it, we are obliged to extrapolate from the introduction and from the remaining portions of his *Elements of Rhythm*, as well as from the indications he left in the treatise on harmonics and in the fragments of works cited by other writers.

There is no doubt that harmonics and rhythmics are theoretical sciences, clearly distinct from the science of instruments *(organikē)* and from musical practice. The writer introduces the notion of "poietic science," which includes both the art of musical composition and that of poetic writing (both governed by strict rules). In any event, the documentation remains so sparse that one cannot seriously envision proposing an Aristoxenean flow chart for musical science.

The problem of the transmission of texts does not arise with the third and

last classification, that of the *Peri mousikes,* written in the 3rd century C.E. by
the theoretician Aristides Quintilianus, who was influenced as much by the
Pythagoreans and the Platonists as by Aristoxenus. This is the most complete
treatment by far that we have. For the first time, as respect for the Pythagorean tradition required, there is a section on physics in the theoretical part,
which deals with arithmetic and physics properly speaking. The phenomenon of sound as such is examined, along with acoustics, before the arithmetic calculation of intervals is formulated. It goes without saying that the
Aristoxenean school rejects even the very existence of this physical aspect of
the musical sciences. The second, or technical, section takes up the tripartite
subdivision that goes back to Lasus, was adopted by Aristoxenus, and was
shared by all the schools: harmonics, rhythmics, and metrics. The second major subdivision is "practical," or "educational." It includes, on the one hand,
composition (melody, rhythm, poetics), and on the other, execution (reminiscent of Lasus), which regroups the organic (instrumental playing), the odic
(chant, or song) and the hypocritic (dramatic action).

What was the object of "harmonics"? If we consider the entire corpus of
musical, theoretical, and musicographic literature of antiquity, it seems that
all the schools, beyond the basic quarrels that divided them, were more or
less in agreement on the various elements encompassed by harmonics, even
though there was never any agreement as to its nature and methods. All the
writers listed these elements in the opening lines of their works. They num-
bered six or seven, depending on whether *melopoiia,* musical composition,
was included or not. Everyone also agreed that harmonics was the science of
melos, or musical sounds (in contrast to meters or rhythms), considered as by
nature perfect in organization; the role of the science of harmonics is to discover and then to articulate the laws that govern the structured relations
among these elements. The seven traditional sections of works on harmonics are presented in the following order: (1) sounds; (2) intervals; (3) systems; (4) genera; (5) tones, or *tropoi;* (6) *metabolai;* (7) musical composition
(melopoiia). This terminology, except for the first two terms, is unique to
Greco-Roman antiquity. It warrants a few words of critical explanation.

(1) Sounds: These are the *phthongoi,* sounds belonging specifically to music, as distinct both from noise (Theon of Smyrna gives thunder as an example) and from spoken sounds. For Pythagorean thinkers, sound should initially be defined as a physical, or acoustic, phenomenon: it is produced by a
shock of air, and its pitch depends directly on the speed of its movement.
The more rapid the movement propagated through air or fluid (according to
Nicomachus), the higher the resulting sound will be. Aristoxenus leaves these
questions to the physicists. Harmonic science is concerned with distinguishing musical sound from the sound of the speaking voice; in language, the
voice proceeds by continuous movement, without isolating pitch levels, while

musical sound is "the stopping of the voice on a single pitch," in a strictly discontinuous movement of the voice. Thus for Aristoxenus and his followers, musical sound cannot be identified with any movement whatsoever.

In the Aristoxenean theory of sound, there are a certain number of consequences bearing on the theory of language and, consequently, on the art of oratory. In the 1st century C.E. Quintilian returned to Aristoxenus's theses on the movements of the voice in his *De musica* in order to derive instructions of a practical nature.

(2) Intervals: Although musicographers and theorists unanimously call intervals *diastemata*, they do not agree on much else. They still recognize that an interval is made up of two sounds that are produced successively or simultaneously, whether they are identical or different in pitch. The names and definitions of intervals is another matter altogether. In the ancient terminology of Philolaus the Pythagorean, as reported by Nicomachus, the fourth is called *syllaba*, the fifth *dioxeia* (literally, "climbing toward the sharp"), and the octave, *harmonia*. This vocabulary was quickly abandoned, it seems, even by the Pythagoreans, to be replaced by the generally agreed-upon terms *dia tessarōn*, *dia pente*, and *dia pasōn*, to indicate the fourth, the fifth, and the octave. These terms derive directly from the playing of stringed instruments. The notions of "string" and "note" are confused by then: *chordōn* (*chorde* is the Greek term for string) is implicit in each of the three terms: "across four [strings]," "across five [strings]," "across all [strings]."

As soon as we come to intervals smaller than the *ditonos* (our major third), the terminologies diverge. The tone is called *epogdoon (diastema)* by the Pythagoreans, but *tonos* by the Aristoxeneans. The fact is that the terminology in this instance is a direct reflection of the way in which each school describes and defines intervals. The Pythagoreans, as we have seen, expressed intervals through numerical relations, while Aristoxenus considered them only in terms of how they were perceived by the ear and how they could be defined by careful reflection.

According to the old Pythagorean school, the octave is the relation 2 to 1; the fifth, the relation 3 to 2; the fourth, the relation 4 to 3; and the tonic (the "difference" between the fifth and the fourth), the relation 9 to 8. How were these numerical relations established? By the so-called experiments on the monochord, mentioned throughout Pythagorean and Neopythagorean literature: if a string stretched between two pegs is pressed, or stopped, at its midpoint, the sound it produces is one octave higher than the sound produced by the string left unstopped. Stopped at three-quarters of its length, the sound produced is the fourth above; at two-thirds, the fifth above, and so on. These observations, which were tried out on a graduated monochord (in more and more complex fashion over time), were verified or extended by arithmetic calculation: by combining a fourth and a fifth: $(4/3) \times (3/2) = 2/1$, we obtain the relation to the octave. To discover the numerical relations of the tonic, one proceeds by "subtraction" (actually by division) of the two same relations: $(3/2) : (4/3) = 9/8$.

The relation 9/8 is *epogdoon*, because it introduces the number 8 *(octo)* and another number that goes beyond it by one unit, or one-eighth. The fourth, 4/3, is for the same reason called *epitrite*. The octave is quite naturally "double," *diplasion*. The common point for all these relationships is that they have the superpartial *(epimore)* form $(n + 1)/n$: their numerator (as one would say today) is one integer larger than their denominator.

As soon as one gets to the subdivision of the tone, the differences between schools become absolute. In fact, while Aristoxenus declared that the human voice and musical instruments were capable of producing an accurate half-tone (identified as such by the ear), the Pythagoreans for their part believed that an accurate half-tone could not exist. Why? Because, as the Pseudo-Euclid said, "There is no middle in the double relation" (for which it would actually be necessary to find the square root). How does one proceed then to "find" a half-tone?

It is necessary to "remove" a *ditonos* from a fourth, since the fourth, as everyone acknowledged, is composed of two tones and a half. This produces the following equation:

$$4/3 : (9/8)^2 = 4/3 : 81/64 = 256/243$$

This half-tone, multiplied by itself, is not equivalent to the *epogdoon* interval of the tone. It is smaller than the true half-tone, as may be seen by a very simple calculation, which consists in looking for the "difference" between the tone 9:8 and the *leimma* expressed by the ratio 256:243:

$$9/8 : (256/243) = 2187/2048$$

This new half-tone is called an *apotome*. To designate the two half-tones obtained in this way with a single word, the term *diesis* is used; it means "division" or "passage," depending on how it is interpreted.

The partisans of the Aristoxenean school rebelled against a method that resulted in using calculations to create intervals that no voice and no instrument could produce and that the ear could not identify. According to Aristoxenus of Tarentum, this was an outrage against nature and against the phenomenon of music itself. Thus when he used the term *diesis,* he was designating the quarter-tone or the third-tone as they are used in vocal and instrumental practice.

(3) *Systemata,* or systems, involve two intervals and at least three sounds in a succession governed by precise rules. The system of reference that informs the logic of harmonics is the tetrachord, or fourth, which remains the

basic unit throughout the ten centuries of Greek and then Latin musical literature. The limits of this system are fixed, with each boundary note separated
from the other by two and half tones, while the two intermediary sounds
may change position according to the genus to which the system belongs.
Two tetrachords can be conjunct or disjunct, depending on whether a disjunctive tone remains between them or the upper note of the lower tetrachord
is also the lower note of the upper tetrachord. In the first case, the system
covers a seventh; in the second, it extends to the octave. The maximum reach
of the system of tetrachords combined among themselves, by conjunction
and disjunction, is two octaves, which thus create the great "perfect system" *(systema teleion)* that was completed during the Hellenistic period. It
is made up, from low to high, of an "added" note, called for this reason
proslambanomene, then of tetrachords, each of which has a particular name.
As is clear from the accompanying figure, the third tetrachord is sometimes
disjunct, if its lower note falls one tone higher than the highest note of the
mesōn (middle tetrachord), and sometimes conjunct, if the two tetrachords
share a common note.

(4) Three genera (singular, genus) were known in antiquity: the enharmonic, the chromatic, and the diatonic. They depend on the place occupied by
the two "mobile" degrees within tetrachords. Their structure assumes three
principal forms (from high to low), according to the ancient theoreticians:

Diatonic: tone–tone–$\frac{1}{2}$ tone
Chromatic: tone $\frac{1}{2}$–$\frac{1}{2}$ tone–$\frac{1}{2}$ tone
Enharmonic: ditone–$\frac{1}{4}$ tone–$\frac{1}{4}$ tone

As is apparent here, the lower intervals of the tetrachords have a tendency
to become "compressed." When the sum of the two lower intervals is equal to
or smaller than the "rest of the fourth" (Aristoxenus), the genus is then

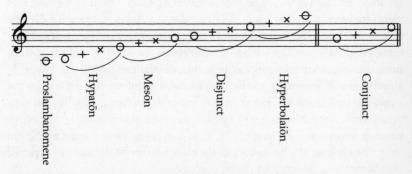

The "perfect" system with five tetrachords

"compressed"; this was particularly appreciated in vocal and instrumental musical practice. In good theory, or at least in Aristoxenean theory, no subdivision of the fourths is allowed in which the median interval is larger than the upper interval.

Beyond the three principal genera, both Greeks and Romans knew and practiced variants that they called *chroai,* a vivid term that may be translated by "shades" or "colorations," recalling its link with *chrōma,* color, as well as the chromatic (genus). On reading the theoretical texts, we understand that the instrumentalists must have made considerable and even abusive use of *chroai.* Aristoxenus is vituperative on the subject of their anarchic misuse, which leads him to try to normalize their use starting from general principles such as the exclusion of a median interval larger than either of the two others. The Neopythagorean treatises did not have this concern, probably because the issue was not closely tied to practice. On the contrary, as if carried away by their vertiginous calculations, they ended up proposing scores of ever more numerous variants, with intervals that were increasingly difficult to link with any musical reality: this is especially the case with Ptolemy in his *Harmonika,* in the 2nd century C.E. However, musicians seem to be in agreement in allowing six "shades" (not counting the enharmonic genus), namely, in addition to the three genera listed above,

Soft diatonic: tone $\frac{1}{2}-\frac{3}{4}$ tone$-\frac{1}{4}$ tone
Hemiolic chromatic: tone $\frac{3}{4}-\frac{3}{8}$ tone$-\frac{3}{8}$ tone
Soft chromatic: tone $\frac{5}{6}-\frac{1}{3}$ tone$-\frac{1}{3}$ tone

(5) Tones or tropes *(tonoi, tropoi):* Contrary to a very widespread misunderstanding (derived, it must be said, from erroneous interpretations of Greek texts by certain late Latin theorists), these have nothing to do with "modes," which would presuppose distinctions that were never made in the Greek and Roman worlds. The *tropoi* (called *harmoniai* up to Plato and Aristotle's time, when they still encompasssed only an octave) are the various ways of spacing the great perfect system, in any genus, starting from a thetic base note that varies from one *tropos* to another. The progression takes place from half-tone to half-tone and is articulated around five principal *tropoi.* From low to high, these are the Dorian, the Iastian, the Phrygian, the Aeolian, and the Lydian, the names explicitly referring to the presumed ethnic origins of the *tropoi.* At a fourth below, the *tropos* is called *hypo-* and, at a fourth above the principal *tropos,* it is called *hyper-.* The spacing of intervals evolved gradually over centuries, with some differences of opinion here and there as to the respective place of one interval or another, or as to the appropriate name for a given tone. The survival of Mixolydian, in the place where one would have expected the Hyperdorian, is evidence of this evolution.

In the classical period, or when a later author takes the ancients as his model (this is true of Plutarch when he looks to pre-Aristoxenean sources as his models), there is no mention of either *tropos* or tone; instead, we simply find adverbs ending in -*sti*: *dōristi, iasti, phrygisti, lydisti,* and so on. This ancient terminology is still found in Aristophanes as well as in Book VIII of Aristotle's *Politics,* but it ceases to have currency in Aristoxenus's *Harmonic Elements,* in the last quarter of the 4th century. There, for example, Aristoxenus speaks of *lydios tonos* and no longer of *lydisti.*

To close this controversial chapter on Greek *tropoi,* let me add that their tripartite classification coincides with the distinction between the three "regions of the voice" *(topoi tēs phōnes),* low, medium, and high *(hypatoeidēs, mesoidēs, andnetoidēs),* a distinction accepted in all the schools of harmonics.

(6) *Metabolai* correspond more or less to our modern modulations. There is a *metabolē* when we pass from one system, genus, or *tropos* to another, from conjunction to disjunction, and this is true whether the borrowing is temporary or, on the contrary, it entails a complete structural change. Here we are entering into the realm of the laws that regulate what Aristoxenus names, in terminology that recalls that of his master Aristotle, musical alteration *(alloiōsis),* but without really impinging on the use of the elements of harmonics. At this stage of musical science, the phenomenon is described and designated by name, but its practice has not yet been codified; this codification will depend directly on the choice and usage (according to Aristides Quintilianus) of the composer or practitioner. But the analysis of metabolai is actually located at the threshold of the seventh and last part of harmonic science, a part that, for this reason, does not appear in certain treatises: *melopoiia,* or melodic composition.

(7) *Melopoiia* stems in fact as much from musical theory as from its practical application. In the classifications proposed by Lasus or Hermione or Aristides Quintilianus, it enters into the executive or practical element, since it presumes actual usage, a *chresis.* However, in writings on harmonics, *melopoiia* does not consist in defining laws of composition or music writing; quite the contrary. In Aristides Quintilianus, who has the most to say on this subject, the chapter devoted to it is limited to defining the "figures of melody" *(schemata tes melodias)* in analytic and descriptive terms. A given melodic line is deployed in three different ways. In the *agōge,* conduct, it proceeds by ascending or descending movement. When the melody skips steps, alternating movements toward lower notes with movements toward higher ones, there is *ploke,* interweaving, or *melos keklasmenon,* broken melodic line. Finally, *petteia* designates a stationary line, whether the note is held or repeated on different syllables. It is used frequently in all the surviving ancient scores.

These, then, are the constituent parts of harmonic science. The Platonic school and the Pythagoreans do not stop here; they are convinced that music produces specific effects on the soul and body (which is not the case for any of the other arts), effects that warrant description and explanation in an effort to codify musical practice more effectively. This is what they call the *ethos,* a concept that deals not only with *tropoi* but also with instruments and the type of musical work. It is because the Phrygian *tropos,* particularly well adapted to the aulos, is soft, and thus debilitating to the human soul, that Plato and the Pythagoreans banish its use, along with the wind instruments that correspond to it. In contrast, they recommend the Dorian for its virility, suited to stimulating human energies.

Aristoxenus denies that music could have moral effects, but despite the austerity for which he was famous in antiquity, he still acknowledges that certain genera, such as the enharmonic, are more noble and more beautiful than others. For him, the only applicable aesthetic categories are those of the beautiful and the ugly. Those of good and bad remain outside harmonic science as he conceives it.

Our overview of the constitutive parts of harmonics may be perplexing in that it lacks (in our own contemporary terms) anything having to do with musical notation. However, in the most scientific treatises as in the short didactic manuals, there is not the slightest development on this question, which is studied along with the very first rudiments of music in the modern world. Worse still, and even more surprising, is the fact that no theoreticians, no musicographers ever cite any passage borrowed from some work by a great composer, nor do they ever provide musical examples of the sort that are so frequently found in our works of basic music theory, harmony, and orchestration. The break between theoretical reflection and musical practice remains absolute throughout antiquity.

This exclusion of notation has a deep-seated reason, which Aristoxenus explains at length, and not without a certain venom, in the preamble of the second part of his treatise. It is not only true, he says in substance, that the notation of a melody is not, as some would have it, the ultimate end of harmonic knowledge, but it is not even a component of that knowledge. Likewise, the notation of meter is neither the goal nor an integral part of metrics. He invokes two main arguments to defend his view. First, by relying on the acuteness of his ear, a notator is capable of writing the musical signs of a melody that he hears and that turns out to be in the Phrygian mode, even though he has no true, that is to say theoretical, knowledge of the Phrygian, for in order to write down the music he perceives, he has only to identify the spread of the intervals, without attaining a true grasp of the *melos.* Second, this grasp comes about through an intellectual understanding of the *dynamis* of sounds, systems, and genera—that is, of their function within the sonic space.

Aristoxenus's diatribe attests to the existence in Greece of schools of music—or rather of harmonics—where, after a course of study meant to inculcate the necessary musical notions, pupils received instruction in melodic and rhythmic notation. We have proof of this, moreover, in the recently published papyrus of Oxyrhynchus no. 3705: it is the exercise of an apprentice notator, where an iambic line, always the same one, is given several musical renderings. The teacher has deliberately sprinkled errors throughout the notation, either in the signs themselves or else in the choice of notes (in which case there is a violation of the complex laws that govern the relations between the accentuation of Greek words and the pitch level of the musical sounds that can be attributed to them).

As an art, a skill, and a science, music has always occupied a privileged, indeed primordial, place in Greek civilization: the abundance of written testimony, direct and indirect, amply attests to this. The Roman world never produced theoreticians as great as those of ancient Greece: the musicographical works of the Latin authors are very heavily indebted to the Greek thinkers, whom they did not, however, always understand.

In contrast, from the 6th century B.C.E. to the 5th century C.E. Greece saw a constellation of musicians (teachers of music, Harmonists, and musicographical and philosophical specialists) who worked endlessly to advance musical knowledge in all its forms. The manuscript tradition has preserved only a small part of their works. While our knowledge of harmonics and its evolution may be satisfactory, the loss of treatises on "*organikē*" and, above all, manuals of musical composition is only in part compensated for by the survival of scores and of vestiges of musical instruments, thanks to which we have succeeded in grasping only the particular and material expression of the two traditions of musical knowledge from which they arise. However, we can hope to discover new papyri analogous, for example, to papyrus Hibeh 54, which will bring us fragments of these lost treatises.

But, in a phenomenon unique in ancient civilizations, Greece has left us written, figured, and archaeological traces of the kind that give us, if not a complete image, at least a significant glimpse of the science of music and its history; the most precious of these are the roughly fifty scores that have been spared from the ravages of the centuries. If, after two thousand years of silence, we are today in a position to decipher, transcribe, and even play them, let us not forget that we owe this not so much to the musician-philosophers as to a humble musicographer named Alypius, who left us tables of musical signs, in both vocal and instrumental notations, used in the entire set of scores that antiquity has bequeathed to us. Musical notation may not have warranted the status of science; it is nevertheless notation that has enabled Greek music to be reborn, after twenty centuries of silence.

ANNIE BÉLIS
Translated by Emoretta Yang and Catherine Porter

Bibliography

Texts and Translations

Aristides Quintilianus. *De musica.* Ed. R. P. Winnington-Ingram. Leipzig: Teubner, 1963.

———. *On Music in Three Books.* Ed. and trans. Thomas J. Mathiesen. Music Theory Translation Series. Ed. Claude V. Palisca. New Haven: Yale University Press, 1983.

Musici Scriptores Graeci: Aristoteles, Euclides, Nicomachus, Bacchius, Gaudentius, Alypius et melodarium veterum quidquid exstat, recognovit prooemiis et indice instruxit Carolus Janus. Leipzig: Teubner, 1895; repr. Hildesheim: Olms, 1962.

Ptolemy. *Die Harmonielehre des Klaudios Prolemaios.* Ed. Ingemar Düring. Göteborgs Högskolas Arsskrift 36 (1930): 1; repr. Hildesheim: Olms, 1982.

Studies

Barker, Andrew. "Harmonic and Acoustic Theory." In *Greek Musical Writings,* vol. 2. Cambridge: Cambridge University Press, 1989.

Bélis, Annie. *Aristoxène de Tarentum et Aristote: Le "Traité d'harmonique."* Etudes et commentaires, vol. C. Paris: Klincksieck, 1986.

———. "Les Hymnes à Apollon." In *Corpus des inscriptions de Delphes,* vol. 3. Paris: De Boccard, 1992.

———. *Les musiciens dans l'Antiquité.* Paris: Hachette Littératures, 1999.

———. *La musique dans l'Antiquité grecque et romaine.* Paris: La Découverte, forthcoming.

Chailley, Jacques. *La musique grecque antique.* Paris: Les Belles Lettres, 1979.

Gevaert, Fr. Aug. *Histoire et théorie de la musique de l'Antiquité.* 2 vols. Gand, 1875, 1881; repr. Hildesheim: Olms, 1965.

Lohmann, Johannes. *Mousiké et logos: contributions à la philosophie et à la théorie musicale grecques.* Trans. Pascal David. Mauvezin: Trans-Europ-Repress, 1989.

Michaelides, Solon. *The Music of Ancient Greece: An Encyclopedia.* London: Faber and Faber, 1978.

West, M. L. *Ancient Greek Music.* Oxford: Clarendon Press, 1992.

Compact Disc

De la pierre au son: Musique de l'Antiquité grecque. Ensemble Kerylos, dir. Annie Bélis. Reference K617-069.

HISTORY

HISTORY IS THE CRITICAL OR ANALYTICAL STUDY OF THE PAST, not simply the recording of the past or a concern for tradition. Although many societies have shown an interest in their past, the development of a critical historical literature is a rare phenomenon. Only three societies in world history have independently created such an attitude to their past: these are the Jews, the Greeks, and the Chinese. All other traditions of historical writing are dependent on one or more of these.

Each of the three traditions has its own characteristics. The Jewish tradition began with the concept of the covenant of God with His chosen people, and the story of His concern for their destiny, their sufferings as a result of their disregard for His laws, and their triumphs over adversity because of His protection. The priestly authorities who in the 6th and 5th centuries B.C.E. compiled an authoritative account of Jewish history had access to a wide variety of sources, legal, poetic, prophetic, and narrative; they showed great skill in combining these, and paid special attention to documentary evidence. But subsequent Jewish historiography from the age of the Maccabees onward is weak and largely derivative on the dominant Hellenistic Greek tradition, and the true successor to Jewish historical writing is the tradition of church history, developed in the Roman empire, from Eusebius to the Renaissance.

Chinese historical writing began with the Annals, written to record and defend the activities of a government supposedly obedient to the principles of Confucius. The first sign of a critical attitude is found in the work of Sima Qian, hereditary grand historian of the Qin dynasty in the late 2nd century B.C.E.; his work is distinguished by a vivid narrative style and a critical approach to the moral failings of the rulers of China that was in turn based on his sense of betrayal and isolation after he was sentenced to castration for involvement in a court intrigue. Although the organizational method that he evolved had great influence, his critical approach was less often imitated, and most later Chinese historical writing simply sets out to record public events or glorify the emperor.

The Greek tradition is for us the most difficult to understand, since it represents the origin of modern Western attempts to organize and explain the past; there is no clear break between the Greek view and our view of the function of historical writing, and many of our fundamental attitudes are based on reinterpretations of the Greek attitude to the past. The knowledge of the

Greeks is our knowledge, and its investigation involves our own conception of the purpose and methods of history today.

HISTORY AS LITERARY GENRE

The survival of ancient Greek and Roman texts through their use in rhetorical schools and copying by hand in the monasteries of Europe through the Middle Ages has for historical texts resulted in a more or less continuous *catena*, or chain of historical narratives. "Natural selection" resulted in the survival, for the most part, of only one of the available histories of a particular period, and the process of selection was largely determined on stylistic grounds rather than in relation to the authority of the texts. Thus Herodotus and Thucydides survived because they were fundamental literary prose texts; Xenophon's Attic style ensured his survival over more serious narratives. Arrian's account of Alexander the Great, written nearly five hundred years after the events, was preferred to earlier and more authoritative accounts. The *Historical Library* of Diodorus, a superficial compilation of the late 1st century B.C.E. that reproduced in a pleasant and undistinctive style a variety of earlier authors, ensured the disappearance of those texts. Of the great works of the Hellenistic age, only Polybius survives in part. The same process of selection occurred with the historians of Rome, where, for instance, the Greek writer Dionysius of Halicarnassus is responsible for the decimation of much early Roman historical writing.

Therefore, to understand the nature of Greek historical writing, both that which survived to influence the Western tradition and that which did not, it is necessary to recreate as far as possible the entire corpus of Greek historiography as it once was. The 19th century was much concerned with the factual accuracy of surviving historical accounts and the lost narratives on which they were based. This science or art of "source criticism," established by B. G. Niebuhr (1776–1830), focused attention on the need to rebuild the context of our historical narratives from a factual point of view, and the publication in 1891 of the papyrus of the Aristotelian work on the constitutional history of Athens demonstrated how much of the lost genre of local history might be recovered. It was in 1909 that the young Felix Jacoby published his famous article "On the Development of Greek Historiography," in which he laid out both a new theory of the interrelations between the various historical genres of the Greeks, and a program for the publication of all the "Fragments of the Greek Historians" on generic principles. This publication, the basis of all study of Greek history today, was begun in 1923 and was largely completed (except for antiquarian history, biography, and geography) by his death in 1958. Despite occasional attempts to undermine the vision of Jacoby, his program of 1909 still stands as the most successful and complete account of Greek historical writing.

The origins of Greek history lie in the undifferentiated sphere of early Greek prose writing, which was as much myth about the geography of the world and the customs of other peoples as a record of the unfolding of historical events. The earliest prose genres were therefore genealogy and mythography, closely followed by geography: these were exemplified in the two known works of the late 6th-century author Hecataeus of Miletos, and many 5th-century writers can be found practicing a variety of genres. The first true historian was Herodotus, who combined in one work the ethnographic interests of Hecataeus with the epic narrative of a war between East and West. His work incorporated most of the themes of Greek history that were later separated out, and he introduced many of its more distinctive literary conventions, such as the absence of documents, the inclusion of speeches, the complex interplay of digressions from the main theme. After Herodotus, historical writing developed according to two main currents.

The first was local history of individual cities and peoples. Once thought to be earlier than general history of the Herodotean type, this was shown by Jacoby to be a development from the late 5th century, and to be essentially a breaking down of the grand themes of Herodotus to create a history adapted no longer to the conflict between civilizations, but to the interests of individual city-states. It was local history that introduced, or at least privileged, two new elements, the retelling of local myth and the use of archives: "These men made similar choices about the selection of their subjects, and their powers were not so very different from one another, some of them writing histories about the Greeks and some about the barbarians, and not linking all these to one another but dividing them according to peoples and cities, and writing about them separately, all keeping to one and the same aim: whatever oral traditions were preserved locally among peoples or cities, and whatever documents were stored in holy places or archives, to bring these to the common notice of everyone just as they were received, neither adding to them nor subtracting from them" (Dionysius of Halicarnassus, *On Thucydides* 5). Local history was later developed and adapted to the new needs of the Hellenistic world: it could remain as the history of individual communities or city-states, but it could also include religious, ethnographic, and geographic elements in relation to the newly conquered territories, such as Babylon, Egypt, and India. This ethnographic type of history always remained conscious of its debt to Herodotus.

Thucydides was contemporary with the earliest group of these historians and occasionally criticized or used them. But his form and his methodology were essentially based on a critical dialogue with Herodotus. On the one hand, he accepted the theme of a great war; on the other, he rejected absolutely the methods of Herodotus. He denied the possibility of a detailed history of the past, believing that only broad generalizations could be made; instead he asserted the importance of a narrative of contemporary affairs,

written by a protagonist as the events were happening. Even under these circumstances he was insistent on the difficulty of discovering the true facts. In a
famous and obscure programmatic statement (*History of the Peloponnesian
War* 1.22) he claimed to reject invention in speeches in favor of a close adher-
ence to what was said (a claim that he perhaps found impossible to adhere to
as his work progressed). He arranged his narrative according to an idiosyncratic chronology of campaigning seasons, which privileged military events,
just as his use of the artificial device of paired speeches privileged political decision making.

The power of Thucydides' vision of human affairs established the idea of a
history devoted to politics and war, telling the story of a great event or a period that possessed unity as the sphere of action of an individual or group of
individuals. The age of Philip, the story of Alexander the Great, the account of
the age of the Diadochoi or the rise of Rome, provided later historians with a
thematic unity that provided a natural starting point and conclusion. But
Thucydides' narrative had in fact been unfinished and was continued by
Xenophon and others as contemporary memoirs to whatever point seemed to
them significant. From this arose the idea of a universal history, whether of
the Greek world or of the "inhabited world" *(oikoumene)* in general. These
histories might be essentially narrative accounts of politico-military events,
or (the more they included the non-Greek world) they might approximate
back again to the Herodotean model. Toward the end of the Hellenistic period
such grand historical encyclopedias tended to be more derivative, more superficial, and more complete in their coverage of a narrative, which might include
myth as well as history.

In such a way it is possible to understand the development of a complex
and varied historical literature determined according to the changing rules of
a literary genre. Each element within the picture can be located in the broader
spectrum, whether it is chronography, mythography, or the local history of a
particular city, such as Athens. From an undifferentiated beginning of works
in prose devoted to describing and analyzing the world inhabited by men and
their actions, there were gradually separated out a variety of special types responding to particular needs and interests. But this interpretation is essentially a literary one, based on form and theme; it scarcely distinguishes between an almost entirely fictional personal narrative, like the *Persicha* of
Ctesias, and serious attempts, like that of Polybius, to understand one's world.

HISTORY AS SCIENCE

It is of course possible to view history from a quite different perspective. The
essential characteristic of history according to the canons of 19th-century
positivism is that it tells a true story; and the history of the science of history is the story of the development of the importance of truth as an aim for

history, and of the methods by which the historian may arrive at the truth. Again we may take as representative of this approach to the ancient historians the name of a contemporary scholar and student of historiography, Arnaldo Momigliano. For him history was an art that aimed at the truth. Its development was the story of successive generations of writers who shared this aim, and who attempted with greater or lesser success to realize it. He was not interested in those who failed this austere test of relevance to the continuing study of history today.

The criterion of truth was proclaimed in the first sentence of the first Greek historical work, Hecataeus's book *Genealogies:* "Hecataeus the Milesian speaks thus: I write these things as they seem true to me; for the stories told by the Greeks are various and in my opinion absurd" (*FGH* 1, frg. 1). But Hecataeus's interest in the truth led to a misguided attempt to recover historical events from mythical narratives by removing the incredible or supernatural elements. This rationalization of myth produced a story that could be believed rather than one that was true, but such was the power of heroic myth that Greek conceptions of truth never escaped from the hope that there was something that was true in their mythic past. Both Herodotus and Thucydides clearly believed in the historical truth of selected elements of mythology, and failed to realize that their selection of facts merely reflected the prejudices of their age. Subsequent historians, too, thought it possible to write a narrative that extended back into the mythic past, or to interpret the religious myths of other peoples as part of a historical narrative. The result was a blurring of the line between myth and history that maintained the principle of historical truth while involving a fatal elision between myth and history.

With the development of oral history and anthropology it has become possible to view Herodotus as providing a methodological model. His attempt to record the oral traditions of a wide variety of Greek and native peoples, however uncritical and selective it may seem, compares favorably with many discussions of non-European peoples in the early modern age. He can rightly be seen as the founder of a form of history that was not bound by concepts of political narrative but attempted to view societies as a whole, through the interrelationship of religious, social, and geographic factors; his apparently naive reproduction of individual stories can also be compared with the recording techniques of modern oral historians, who must exclude interpretation from the basic recording of their data. Already in the 16th century Herodotus was admired for his ability to transcend cultural boundaries and record the customs of foreign peoples, and respect for his abilities increased as European writers attempted to come to terms with alien worlds like those of South America, the Ottoman empire, and Japan. As 19th-century excavations and explorations revealed the material basis of the cultures of ancient Egypt and the Near East, respect for Herodotus's account of these peoples increased:

his narrative, however flawed, remains the basis of Persian history, and his Hellenistic successors, Manetho and Berossus, still provide the narrative framework for Egyptian and Babylonian history. Thus Herodotus's inclusiveness and curiosity created a methodology—based on the natural social forms of human geography, myth, religion, narrative history, and customs—whose flexibility across cultural boundaries has resulted in his becoming a model for modern anthropologists and historians of culture. His very failure to consider any form of causation other than the natural course of events and culturally inherent conflicts, which once seemed to suggest a prescientific attitude to history, can now be seen as an appropriate response to the unimportance of causal models for the understanding of social and cultural history. Modern critics attack Herodotus not for his unscientific attitude to history, but for his contribution to the creation of the concept of the otherness of non-Greek cultures: Herodotus is seen as the inventor of "orientalism," the idea of a conflict between East and West, described in terms of the victory of freedom and courage over despotism and luxury, which is thought to vitiate much of Western historiography in relation to the non-European world. Herodotus the *"philobarbaros"* has become Herodotus the orientalist: however unfair this characterization, it demonstrates the respect of the modern world for Herodotus as the founder of Western historiography.

If Herodotus established the Western canons of "katastematic history," of societies at rest, it has always been easy to see Thucydides as the originator of "kinetic history," of societies in motion and in conflict. His invention of the idea of different levels of causation is exemplified in the account of the origins of the Peloponnesian War, with its immediate and underlying causes. Thomas Hobbes called him "the most politick historiographer that ever writ"; he was obsessed with the decision-making process in fully conscious political societies; he attempted (with less success) to understand the economic basis of imperialism and warfare. He described the collapse of social systems under the impact of plague and revolution. His insistence on the need for contemporary recording of events makes him the founder of all sociology and political science. Finally, his attitude to evidence and his concern for the need for true knowledge of the facts have made him the model for the concept of modern scientific history, as formulated by 19th-century positivist historians. In certain passages he can even be seen to have anticipated the insistence on documentary evidence and archival research that was the contribution of Leopold von Ranke to 19th-century historical research methods.

Thucydides certainly provided the model for the main tradition of Western historiography, with its interests in political and military history, factual accuracy, and causation. Polybius is his worthy successor in these respects, introducing another central concept in Western historical thought, the theme of *grandeur et décadence,* the rise and decline of a great imperial power. If this tradition is now viewed more critically, it is because of the crisis of positivism and the fact that we no longer see power as the crucial factor in the formation of human society.

More controversially, Momigliano tried to see the local historians of antiquity as the forerunners of the antiquarianism that was so dominant a feature of the Western historical tradition from the 16th to the 18th century. But systematic antiquarianism derives from the Roman antiquarian tradition, not local history, whose works did not survive to influence the antiquarians of modern Europe. Although it is true that the Aristotelian *Constitution of Athenians* is the earliest surviving treatise on constitutional antiquities, it was not discovered until after the publication of Mommsen's *Römisches Staatsrecht,* which was the culmination of the fusion of legal and historical studies in the 19th century. The need for a model precedes its discovery, and the historian only finds what he is looking for.

The problem of antiquarianism highlights one of the two weaknesses revealed by the methodological analysis of Greek historiography. Greek historiography is bound by tight literary conventions that encourage the use of (usually invented) speeches and formal descriptions of places and events but discourage and even prohibit the citation of documents. Compared with Jewish historical writing, Greek historians seem little interested in the written evidence for their statements; on the rare occasions when a document is cited in Thucydides, this is usually adduced as an indication that that particular section of his narrative is unfinished. Only in local history and in the Aristotelian tradition is documentary evidence prominent; Greek historical writing is often more literary and more rhetorical than the scientific interpretation would allow.

A second weakness in Greek historiography is the comparative absence of interest in biography and in the study of human personality as a motive force in history. The later development of a biographical literature under Roman influence, with the *Parallel Lives* of Plutarch, has indeed disguised the absence of a true biographical tradition in earlier Greek literature; the evidence analyzed by Momigliano in his controversial book *The Development of Greek Biography* (1971) serves merely to reinforce this conclusion. Personal motivation of course abounds in Greek historians, but the comparative neglect of human biography is an aspect of the insistence on communal decision making in Thucydides and the tendency to consider the individual in terms of social context rather than personality.

HISTORY AS MYTH

New questions about the nature of Greek historiography are raised by modern developments in historical writing. History is now seen as a form of discourse related to an ideology, designed to establish a view of the past that corresponds to present preoccupations; alternatively, modern historians seek to change the present through a reinterpretation of the past. The relativity of all observation and of all theory in the human sciences implies the relativity of all historical narrative. The basic evidence is no longer a fact but the interpretation of an event, in which the human agent is implicated from the start; as Thucydides saw, different protagonists in a battle will experience different battles, but the historian no longer feels able to determine which battle is the true one. The historian is simply the last in a chain of witnesses: he can no longer play God with his adjudication.

This new view of the nature of history implies a new interpretation of Greek historiography. It is not necessary to assert the preeminence of rhetoric in history, for relativity does not imply the dominance of persuasion over truth. Rather we should explore the relationship of history to myth in our own age and in antiquity. Here Greek historical writing provides a model, and its development can be seen in the light of the changing function of ancient myth.

The origins of Greek historical writing lie in the fascination of the Greeks for the heroic age, as described in myth and epic poetry. In the 7th and 6th centuries myth came to be used as a means of structuring the past and validating the present; one of the dominant forms of myth in ancient Greece was the "charter myth," a narrative of past mythic events that offered an explanation for a present situation or justified present activities. The "Return of the Sons of Hercules" was a myth created to explain the Dorian presence in the Peloponnese, and it may well owe its popularity in Spartan tradition to a parallel need to justify the conquest of the Messenians in the 7th century. It is hard to know in such situations where oral tradition ends and free mythic creation begins. But the rationality of such narrative is demonstrated by its function as a means of relating past and present; in a later age it was possible for Greek historians simply to adapt these myths to the purposes of historical narrative by ignoring the folktale motifs and the aspects of divine intervention. In Herodotus, Io ceases to be a cow driven mad by a gadfly through the envy of Hera and becomes simply a girl seduced by a Phoenician trader, whose abduction was the starting point for the hatred between East and West; the eponymous Europa was no maiden transported by Zeus disguised as a bull but a daughter of the king of Tyre, seized in retaliation by Greek pirates. These rationalizations were what Hecataeus meant by his claim to find truth in the stories of the Greeks; Thucydides can similarly transmute the stories of the age of heroes into a historical narrative.

Myth is history, and the earliest historians were myth makers or myth writers. Herodotus moves easily from the mythic prefigurations of the Trojan and Persian Wars to point out "who it was in actual fact who first injured the Greeks" with the equally mythic story of the origins of the Lydian dynasty.

Myth and truth are intermingled, and the narrative techniques of the myth maker combine with those of the "enquirer" or historian. Even the end point of his history, the account of the Persian Wars, is the product of a generation of poetic praise and oral tradition, on the basis of which Herodotus sought to create a new prose epic to glorify a new age of heroes, those who had defeated the modern Trojans. Pleasure and truth are equally important to the myth maker, as Thucydides pointed out.

But even Thucydides, with his claim that his work is not a "display piece for instant listening, but a possession for all time," could not escape the mythic origins of Greek historiography. His own story began in the interpretation of myth and was itself a new myth for the age of the polis. His methods and techniques were designed to explain the methods and principles behind the world he inhabited. There decisions were taken in mass assemblies, symbolically represented in narrative by paired speeches, and warfare was a series of set battles fought on specific days and won or lost according to set rules, not a continuing activity involving a whole generation of Greek protagonists and affecting their daily lives in every aspect. Thucydides' conception of the amorality and tragic quality of the events he describes is a mythic interpretation of the world of the polis, and it created a model not for all history but for those aspects of later history that could be related to the political and military concerns of the polis.

Each later historian created his own *mythos* for the events he wished to describe, and his activity was conditioned by the ideology of the world he inhabited. Histories of periods conceived as unities, histories of great expeditions like that of Alexander, histories of the rise and fall of empires, histories of native peoples, can be seen as each involving its own mythic discourse; these discourses interconnect, without establishing rigid generic rules and without offering any progression toward a perfect form of positivist history. The Greek tradition does not offer us a complete set of models of discourse for all possible forms of history; it is imperfectly formed in certain aspects and incomplete in others. But the great variety of these discourses creates for us a series of alternative models, which can free us from the conception of history as a single mode of discourse, and on which we can base our own conceptions of the various *mythoi* of history. History is not separable from myth: like myth, it is a story that aims at the truth rather than one that is true.

OSWYN MURRAY

Bibliography

Jacoby, Felix. *Die Fragmente der griechischen Historiker*. Berlin and Leiden, 1923–1958. Cited as *FGH*.

——. "Über die Entwicklung der griechischen Historiographie und den Plan einer neuen Sammlung der griechischen Historikerfragmente" (1909), repr. in his *Abhandlung der griechische Geschichtsschreibung*. Leiden, 1956. Pp. 16–64.

Momigliano, Arnaldo. *The Classical Foundations of Modern Historiography*. Berkeley, 1990.

———. *Contributo alla storia degli studi classici e del mondo antico*. 14 vols., Rome, 1955–.

Strasburger, H. "Die Wesensbestimmung der Geschichte durch die antike Geschichtsschreibung" (1966), repr. in *Studien zur Alten Geschichte*, vol. 2. Hildesheim, 1982. Pp. 963–1014.

LANGUAGE

As an explicit field of investigation, language in ancient Greece was a relative latecomer. Its beginnings go back to the second half of the 5th century B.C.E. when, with rhetoric emerging as a profession, Protagoras and Prodicus initiated inquiry into "the correctness of names." In the next century Plato and, especially, Aristotle made significant contributions, but the study of language as distinct from logic began to flourish in systematic ways only during Hellenistic times (ca. 300 B.C.E. onward). Ptolemic Alexandria, with its Museum and Library, provided the patronage to support such notable scholars as the Homerists and librarians Zenodotus and Aristarchus, the poet and encyclopedist Callimachus, the polymath Eratosthenes, and the grammarian Dionysius of Thrace.

Other cultural centers apart from Athens became prominent at this time too, including Pergamum, whose library was second only to that of Alexandria. The literary and linguistic investigation of older literature now deemed "classical" (especially Homer) stimulated closer reflection on the Greek language than had been practiced hitherto. Simultaneously, Stoic philosophers, centered largely in Athens, were making innovative contributions to the study of language as a part of their work in "dialectic." It is to this period and these cultural events that we can attribute the identification of grammar and philology as determinate fields of inquiry.

Hellenistic interests in the study of language are certainly important. Yet it would be misleading to give the impression that language had been previously neglected in Greek perceptions of what we may broadly call anthropology. The truth is, rather, that self-consciousness about language can be traced right back to our earliest literary record of the Greeks, the epic poetry of Homer. The poet of the *Iliad* (II.867) characterizes the inhabitants of Miletus and other Ionian cities by the term *barbarophonoi*, foreign speaking. *Barbarian* in this composite word does not convey the ethnic slur that it would acquire later, but rather refers to people who are distinguished by language from the Greeks. Homeric epic, quite apart from its semantic content, is a linguistic tour de force. It was the product of a centuries-long oral tradition, and much of its vocabulary differs significantly from the dialects of everyday speech. As Hellenic civilization developed, its people, especially in Athens, became acculturated to a subtle recognition of the lexical, rhythmical, and stylistic differences between literary genres. Thus Aristophanic comedy derives much of its effect from parodying the high style of epic and tragedy. It also delights in the invention of absurd words, mockery of intellectual discourse, and sudden shifts between gross colloquialisms and high-sounding phrases.

Such sensitivity to language was scarcely grounded in any formal understanding of grammar and linguistic structure. Just as one does not need knowledge of musical theory to have a keen musical ear, so the great products of Attic literature in the 5th century B.C.E. were appreciated by people whose scientific grasp of language was rudimentary. Yet Sophoclean tragedy and Thucydides' history, to mention but two examples, manifest extraordinary virtuosity in diction and style. Both authors were almost certainly influenced by the Sophists Protagoras and Prodicus, foreigners to Athens but particularly successful as teachers in that community; Aristophanes alludes to their newfangled ideas about grammar in *Clouds*, his comedy attacking intellectuals. Protagoras and Prodicus gave lectures to persons who were eager for instruction in both the interpretation of poetry and the practical skills of persuasive speech. There is then a connection, and clearly not an accidental one, between the beginnings of linguistic study and a culture already attuned to complex literary forms. But Greek sensitivity to language not only predates the work of the Sophists; it also helps to explain why and how that work developed.

PRETHEORETICAL INTERESTS IN LANGUAGE

In spite of their political and dialectical divisions, the Hellenic peoples looked to their common language as the strongest mark of their ethnic identity. Herodotus, an elder contemporary of Thucydides, conjectured that the Greeks were coeval with the age of their language; their ancestors, such as the Pelasgians, will have spoken "a barbarian tongue" (I.57). Herodotus was an indefatigable traveler and inquirer. He carefully noted the names of places and objects, not just Greek names but also the way things were called in other languages. He registered numerous linguistic observations: the hybrid of Egyptian and Ethiopian spoken by the Ammonites (II.42), the affinity between the Carian and Caunian languages (II.172), the negative connotation of the term *Ionian* for the first Greeks (II.143), the conclusion of all Persian names in the same letter (II.139). It is to Herodotus that we owe the lovely story about the Egyptian king Psammetichus (II.2): he deprived two infants of hearing any speech in order to determine, by the first articulate sounds that they uttered, the identity of the oldest language. When they were heard to say "bekos," the Phrygian word for bread, he gained his answer.

Herodotus was highly atypical in his explicit interest in languages other than Greek. We may assume, however, that his educated contemporaries would have shared his realization that languages have histories, that lexical differences between languages are entirely compatible with shared meanings, and, above all, that language is a prime determinant of human and cultural identity. No doubt too they were sharply observant, as he was, about the alphabetic properties of words. All of these points are important as assumptions or tendencies that influenced the earliest theoretical investigations into language.

Still more important, and in evidence as early as Homer, are a number of presuppositions about the linkage between speaking and thinking. I say "speaking" rather than "language" to do justice to the Greek intuition that a speech act is not simply or even primarily the utterance of articulated sounds but the expression of a thought that "says something" or "makes sense" *(legein ti)*. To make the point sharply, though anachronistically, one could say that before theoretical investigation began, *parole,* the semantics and affects of discourse, received more attention than *langue,* the lexical instruments of expression.

For Homer, as for all succeeding Greek authors, speaking is both the primary form of social life and the chief vehicle of thought or internal reflection. Not only are the *Iliad* and *Odyssey* packed with speeches, but Homer also uses direct speech as his way of narrating the most significant moments of both epics: for instance, the quarrel between Achilles and Agamemnon; the failure of the embassy to persuade Achilles to return to the fray; the final meeting of Priam and Achilles; and the encounters between Odysseus and Polyphemus, Eumaeus, Penelope, and her suitors. What is most significant about these episodes, for understanding Greek presuppositions about language, is the poet's capacity to engage his audience with three functions of discourse—true or false storytelling, antithetical argument or mutual attempts at persuasion, and the expression of strongly felt emotions. This is not to say that those who experienced Homer and other poets were inattentive to their language as *langue.* Aristophanes' *Frogs* displays remarkable interest in the lexical and metrical differences between the tragedies of Euripides and those of Aeschylus. Thucydides (III.82) writes a most powerful account of the way words were manipulated in the revolution at Corcyra. But before Hellenistic times *onoma,* "name," is the closest the Greeks came to having a generic term for "word." Inquiry into semantic, epistemic, and rhetorical issues advanced much more rapidly at first than the study of grammar and syntax.

Because language was widely regarded as the vehicle of thought, it was taken to be the principal difference between humans and other animals, and more implicitly as a capacity that humans share with gods. Probably because of their anthropomorphic divinities, Greek mythology makes little use of talking animals. (The horses of Achilles are an exception, but they were immortal!) The standard epithet to distinguish nonhuman from human animals was *alogos,* "lacking speech" and hence also lacking reason or thought. When the chorus of Sophocles' *Antigone* illustrates the "wonders" of man, they celebrate the learning of language along with the development of technology, agriculture, and medicine. (Similarly Plato, *Protagoras* 322a.)

These presuppositions about the cultural significance of language are emphasized by Isocrates in his treatise *Antidosis* (253ff), written in the middle of the 4th century B.C.E. to defend himself as an expert teacher of persuasive discourse. His remarks can be assumed to chime with opinions widely held by his audience: "In our other properties . . . we have no advantage over other animals; in fact we are inferior to many of them in speed, strength and other provisions. Yet because we have been engendered with the capacity for mutual persuasion and for indicating our intentions to ourselves, not only have we escaped from the life of beasts, we have also come together and established communities and made laws and discovered crafts—indeed practically everything we have devised has been secured for us by discourse. For it is this that has legislated concerning right and wrong, and without these prescriptions we would not be able to live together. Through it too we blame those who are bad and praise the good, educate the undiscerning and assess the wise. For we regard appropriate discourse to be the best index of a sound mind."

Although Isocrates has his professional axe to grind, his observations about "discourse" match Greek preconceptions that stretch right back to Homer. It would be possible to translate *logos*, his word for "discourse," as language. My only reason for not doing so is to avoid giving the impression that Isocrates is concerned here with linguistics *as distinct from* the social, psychological, and semantic functions of speech. Taking him as representative of the general Greek interest in language at the time of Plato, we may now consider the technical contribution of early Greek philosophy to the subject.

THE STUDY OF LANGUAGE IN GREEK PHILOSOPHY FROM HERACLITUS TO PLATO

Heraclitus and Parmenides, the two giants of early Greek philosophy, did not investigate language from perspectives we would term grammatical or syntactical. Each of them, however, did a great deal to ensure that topics intimately tied to language (for instance, truth and falsehood, reason in argument, naming and predicating) would be fertile ground for subsequent philosophers.

Heraclitus uses the term *logos* to signify both his "account" of the nature of things, and the "rationale" that governs natural processes. He intends his auditors to regard his *logos* as the objective truth. In a series of aphoristic sentences (such as "The way up and down is one and the same," D-K 22.B.60) he seeks to articulate the union of opposites, which the partial perspectives of everyday life tend to conceal. Although Heraclitus does not say so explicitly, one has the impression that his sentence structure and choice of words are intended to provide a direct reflection of extralinguistic reality. Two examples will make the point: "Immortal mortals, mortal immortals, living their death, dying their life" (D-K 22.B.62). The probable point of this aphorism is to challenge, as powerfully as possible, conventional ideas about the distinction between permanence and temporality. "For the bow, the name is life, but its work is death" (D-K 22.B.48). In this cryptic sentence, Heraclitus exploits his hearers' knowledge that one of the Greek words for a bow has the same alphabetic structure as the word for life *(bios)*; what differentiates the words is their accented syllable. Ignoring the latter point, Heraclitus draws a contrast between the name of the bow and its destructive function. He uses the pun to draw attention to the extralinguistic connection between life and death.

Heraclitus also makes use of the striking expression "barbarian souls" (D-K 22.B.107). The point he wants to make here is that "vision and hearing are misleading witnesses" to persons who are incapable of *interpreting* his words about the true nature of things. He composes his riddling sayings as challenges that are semantic, structural, and ontological: to understand the real pattern of things, you need to be an exegete of Heraclitus's cryptic yet truthful discourse.

Parmenides makes much more sober uses of language. Most striking in his argument is the identity he seeks to establish between what can be spoken and what can be thought. In a remarkable stretch of sustained argument, he undertakes to establish the predicates that are the only true and speakable ways of characterizing "what is"—that it is without origin and ending, complete, motionless, temporally present, one and continuous (D-K 28.B.8). Parmenides does not call these "predicates," but he appears to have an implicit understanding of the distinction between a referring expression ("what is") and a description (the "name" of something attributable to "what is"). In a later part of his argument he underlines the link between thought and language by characterizing erroneous opinions as "the naming of two forms" (in contrast with the one "being" he has laid out for consideration). His manner of stigmatizing error in terms of unwarranted "naming" draws on the assumption that names are normally given to things in the belief that the things so named are real. This assumption predates philosophy in the Greek world, but what is it about a name that makes it correct? This question was explicitly thematized a generation or so later by Protagoras and Prodicus. What is known about their work, much of it reaching us via Plato's ironical pen, is rather sketchy. But the evidence is sufficient to show the main tendencies of linguistic study around the year 400 B.C.E.

"Correctness of names" (*orthotes ton onomaton* or *orthoepeia*) is the closest early Greek thinkers came to identifying language as a determinate field of study. What did it involve? Protagoras is credited with dividing the "classes of names" into "males, females, and things" (Aristotle, *Rhetoric* III.5.1407b6). He is also said to have distinguished different types of sentences (*logos*; variant accounts of the details are given, Diogenes Laertius IX.53–54). In making these observations, Protagoras's purposes seem to have been prescriptive rather than purely descriptive. We have reports that he criticized Homer for committing a fault of gender at the beginning of the *Iliad* by making *menis*, "wrath," feminine (its standard gender in Greek) rather than masculine, and for "commanding" the Muse, instead of invoking the goddess by means of a sentence with the form of a "wish" (D-K 80.A.28–29). In the dialogue Plato named for him, Protagoras charges the poet Simonides with self-contradiction (339c). On the basis of these examples, Protagoras took incorrectness of names to involve a faulty match between language and the designation intended by its user.

Prodicus is also a participant in the discussion of Simonides' poem. Socrates, who undertakes to defend Simonides, appeals to Prodicus as the expert in distinguishing the meaning of apparently synonymous terms. The purpose of his appeal is to remove Protagoras's charge of self-contradiction. Socrates' efforts are a deliberate travesty, but they are broadly in line with Prodicus's principal concern—to avoid ambiguity by drawing fine distinctions between words of closely similar meaning. We are told that "he tried to attach a specific sense to each individual name" (D-K 84.A.19). The function of Prodicus's analysis of language, like the critical comments of Protagoras, was normative. Each of them wanted to legislate for language that would be correct, not by the standards of actual usage but as a better instrument for designating thoughts and their intended reference. This emerges particularly clearly from Protagoras's complaints about the feminine gender of *menis*. What he finds unsatisfactory is the disparity (common enough in Greek) between the gender of the word and the masculine connotations of the thing it names.

Our best evidence for the question concerning "correctness of names" is Plato's dialogue *Cratylus*. The subject for investigation is whether, as Cratylus maintains, the correctness of a name consists in its "natural" connection to the thing named or, alternatively, whether "convention and agreement" are the sole basis of linguistic correctness, as Hermogenes proposes. (Independently of Plato we know that Democritus endorsed the convention option, and that the opposite thesis—names as "natural outgrowths"—was defended by the author of the Hippocratic treatise *De arte* II). Plato's discussion, masterminded by Socrates, proceeds by first canvassing the naturalist option. Numerous words are analyzed with a view to showing that their letters and syllables "imitate" incessant change, which is Cratylus's Heraclitean conception of nature. However, the undertaking fails when Socrates points out that there can be no one-to-one correspondence between linguistic sounds and meaning: thus, the letter *l* (lambda), which has been presumed to signify softness, is an element of the word *sklerotes*, which means hardness (435b ff). Convention, then, is certainly one factor in the way names correctly function, though mimetic correspondence between names and things must not be completely excluded either. On the basis of this compromise, Plato seems to advise his readers to reject the study of names as a proper route to the investigation of reality. So Socrates concludes: "We should seek to learn and investigate things *from themselves* and not from their names" (439b.6).

Cratylus is a complex dialogue. On the one hand, it reflects the principal points of contemporary debate about language with its allusions to Protagoras, Prodicus, and persons who are "expert in dividing up the elements of words" (424c, which may allude to the sophist Hippias; cf. *Hippias major* 285d). On the other hand, in spite of his reservations about everyday language as a reliable sign of the nature of things, Plato clearly makes independent linguistic observations of his own. Rather than attempting to sift these out specifically, it seems best to highlight the dialogue's most significant contributions.

In the sphere of phonetics, historical linguistics, and morphology, *Cratylus* probably gives a fair idea of linguistic study at this date. Syllables are distinguished from individual letters, and the latter are divided into vowels and consonants (393e, 424c). There is a clear recognition that "names" and larger linguistic units are compounded out of simple "elements" (*stoicheia*, 422a). Like Herodotus, Plato is well aware that languages change through time. It is suggested that any "natural" correctness names now have must be derived from "primary names"—an original language, established by the gods or by a superhuman name giver (389d, 425d). Numerous etymologies are advanced. Most of these depend on a mimetic relationship between sound and meaning, but we also find attempts to derive divine names from verbs whose *sound and meaning* suit the name (for instance Apollo from *apolluon*, "one who destroys").

In the field of syntax, Plato makes the first recorded attempt to distinguish between "names" *(onomata)* and other expressions, which he calls "things said" *(rhemata):* "Diphilus" is a (proper) name, but with the addition of a second iota and a change of accentuation, we get *Dii philos,* meaning "beloved of Zeus" (399a), which is what we today would call an adjectival expression. Little is made of this distinction in *Cratylus,* but in the later dialogue *Sophist* (262e) Plato invokes it to argue that a sentence *(logos)*—an expression of truth or falsehood—requires the combination of an *onoma* and a *rhema* (e.g., "Theaetetus is sitting"). His concept of *rhema* is the closest anyone before Aristotle came to distinguishing predicative expressions from names or subject terms.

Noteworthy though they are, these observations of *Cratylus* are overshadowed by the dialogue's contribution to semantics. Before Socrates elaborates his string of etymologies, he outlines a theory of "natural names," which is put forward as valid for all languages (389d). The requirement of a "naturally correct name" is to communicate and discriminate reality. Particular names are correct if (1) they satisfy this general function of naming and (2) they satisfy it in ways that are specific to the thing named. Names are "assigned to" letters and syllables, but they are not reducible to their alphabetic properties.

The same name can be expressed by different combinations of letters. What Plato here calls names the Stoics would later call *lekta*—meanings that transcend the particular languages in which they are expressed. For Plato the correctness of a name has more to do with epistemology and logic than with linguistics. When he talks about the Form that a correct name must instantiate, we are reminded that what primarily interested him was not language but the identification of Forms (extralinguistic and nonphysical entities) as the ultimate referents and foundation of true discourse about the world.

ARISTOTLE AND EPICURUS

Plato and his intellectual contemporaries may have had a more technical understanding of language than our evidence for the first half of the 4th century B.C.E. records. The justification for thinking so is the scope of Aristotle's observations. Although Aristotle was a massive innovator in the sphere of logic, he can scarcely have invented all the terminology and formal distinctions to be found in those of his works that study language most directly—*Categories, On Interpretation, Topics, Rhetoric,* and *Poetics.* What we learn there is not only Aristotle's approach to language but also the probable extent of linguistic knowledge in Greece prior to Alexandria, Stoicism, and the explicit development of grammar.

Like Plato, Aristotle was primarily interested in language as the vehicle of thought. The meaning and the truth or falsehood of "what is said" concerned him much more deeply than grammar, morphology, or syntax. He is often criticized for having conflated logic and linguistics. But although a Roman schoolboy at the time of Cicero would learn more formal grammar than Aristotle knew, his instinctive feel for the structure of language is more advanced than anything attested before his time. He regarded the way people talk about the world as material that a philosopher must include in reviewing the basic data of inquiry. More than any other Greek philosopher before the Stoics, he developed a precise terminology for expressing his methods of analysis; for instance, the distinction between "form" and "material," "potentiality" and "actuality," "essential" and "accidental," "without qualification" and "in some respect." Via his medieval disseminators, these distinctions have colored modern language in such expressions as per se, per accidens, simpliciter, sine qua non, and the like.

So far as technical features of language are concerned, Aristotle takes account of the vocal movements necessary to generate particular vowels or consonants (*Poetics* 20). He distinguishes between "voice" ("a sound that signifies something") and other kinds of uttered sounds (*De anima* II.3). He regularly differentiates between linguistic "signs" and "significates" (though the Stoics were the first to canonize this terminology): vocal utterances "signify" or "symbolize" thoughts and the "things" (states of affairs) that thoughts betoken (cf. *On Interpretation* 1). Language, considered as utterance, is comprehended by the term *lexis* (expression), and is distinguished from thought (*dianoia; Poetics* 19). The parts of *lexis* comprise, at their simplest, letters and syllables, and a *logos* (phrase), at their most complex. Other parts include individual words, which Aristotle enumerates as particles, conjunctions, names, verbs, and the "inflection" *(ptosis)* of the latter pair (*Poetics* 20). In defining the verb *(rhema),* he emphasizes its function of signifying time (*On Interpretation* 3).

From a Stoic and later grammatical perspective, this classification of *lexis* is confusing and incomplete. It is confusing because it groups together sentences, phrases, individual words, and single letters or syllables. It is incomplete because it omits certain parts of speech. Aristotle's terminology also suffers from vagueness, as when he describes verbs that are not constituents of sentences as "names" (*On Interpretation* 16b19). "Name" *(onoma)* for him is still an imprecisely collective term, although it has become much closer to "noun" than in its earlier Greek usage. Nonetheless, Aristotle's approach to formal properties of language is considerably more systematic than anything of which we have earlier evidence. He makes acute remarks about the gender of names, and about compound and other types of names (*Poetics* 21). His observations about inflection show that he understands the difference between semantics and morphology (*On Interpretation* 16a32).

To his credit perhaps (given earlier practices), he shows little interest in etymology. Previous efforts in this area (as Plato's *Cratylus* indicates) had been premised on a "natural" relation between the elements of language and features of the world. Aristotle opts firmly for convention as the basis for linguistic "symbols" (*On Interpretation* 1): "Letters and vocal sounds are not the same for everyone, but the mental states of which they are primarily the symbols are the same for everyone; and the actual things of which these mental states are likenesses are also the same." On Aristotle's teleological view of mental life, we perceive or think things by having their perceptible or intelligible forms present to consciousness. That apprehension is probably what he means here by characterizing mental states as "likenesses" of actual things. On his view, what underwrites meaning is isomorphism between the structure of reality and the structure of the thoughts to which we give linguistic expression.

He begins *Categories* by distinguishing between homonyms, synonyms, and paronyms. Modern scholars are sometimes disturbed because Aristotle treats these concepts as referring to "things" and not "terms." Aristotle's ancient commentators too, writing against the background of later developments in grammar, were puzzled about his procedure: Is *Categories,* they asked, a treatise about terms, meanings, or things? Their standard response was that it combines all three, and this is surely the most promising way to do justice to Aristotle's very powerful essay. *Categories* is about language, in the sense that its findings cast light on, and are informed by, the distinction between isolated words and sentences, subject terms, and predicates, the difference between names and definitions. But the "categories" themselves are not expressions but *"things* said," i.e. the kinds of "being" that expressions signify. The aim of this work and its companion piece *(On Interpretation)* is not the elucidation of language as such but investigation of reality through reflection on the way we talk about it.

Aristotle's bias toward logic rather than linguistics was continued by his successor Theophrastus, who made important refinements to Aristotle's analysis of syllogisms and also contributed to rhetorical theory. However, the formal study of language as distinct from logic does not appear to have advanced in the post-Aristotelian Lyceum. The chief centers of innovative philosophy at this date (ca. 300 B.C.E.) were elsewhere—the Garden of Epicurus and the Stoa frequented by Zeno of Citium. At face value the Epicureans, in contrast with the Stoics, "reject dialectic [including the formal study of language] as superfluous" (Diogenes Laertius, X.31). But although our focus here will be on Stoicism, Epicurus had views on language that are far too interesting to be passed over without brief comment.

On the question of language's origin, Epicurus developed a theory nicely suited to the empiricism characteristic of his anthropology in general. In place of a primeval name giver, whether human or divine (Lucretius, V.1028–1090), Epicurus proposed that at a certain stage of human development, "people's own natures underwent feelings and received impressions which varied peculiarly from tribe to tribe, and each of the individual feelings and impressions caused them to exhale breath peculiarly, according also to the racial differences from place to place" *(Epistula ad Herodotum* 75–76). In their primary form, then, vocal utterances were an involuntary response to experience. What turned them into "the names of things" was "utility," by which Epicurus refers to the principle he regularly invokes in explaining social developments: early peoples discovered that the sounds they were instinctually uttering could serve their needs for communication. Subsequently, the primitive languages within each group were refined "on a collective basis," with a view to avoiding ambiguity and improving concision. In addition, new terms were deliberately introduced by intellectuals to designate things beyond the immediate data of experience.

This theory is striking in its economy, and also in its subtle recourse to both nature and artifice as explanatory factors. Although Epicurus emphasizes the peculiarity of each linguistic group and the experiences of its members, we should hardly suppose, as some interpreters have done, that he envisaged a primary stage in which each individual had his own private language. The variations to which Epicurus is so sensitive differentiate between linguistic communities and not between the members of one community. What facilitated the development of each language, he seems to presume, is the unity of experience of each group, together with their common environment and physiology.

Earlier theorists had taken the "naturalness" of language to involve a mimetic correspondence between words and things. Epicurus shows no interest in such attempts at etymology. For him language is an anthropological fact, with its differences explicable by the different circumstances of different cultures. As for the naturalness of a given language's means of expression, here too his empiricism stands him in good stead. Since language originates as an uncontrived response to feelings and sensory experiences, basic meanings must be ascertained by identifying "the primary concept corresponding to each word" (*Ep. Hdt.* 37–38). By "primary concept" he almost certainly refers to what Epicureans regularly call *prolepseis*. These "anticipations," mediated by repeated experience and memory, provide Epicurus with his answer to the question of how words can signify things: they symbolize (as Aristotle too had supposed) the thoughts that persons naturally come to have as a result of the way the world impinges on them. Epicurus seems to have supposed that careful attention to the empirical foundations of language would enable persons to discover primary meanings, uncontaminated by convention and metaphor. For him the key to understanding language was neither logic nor grammar but the study of physical reality.

HELLENISTIC SCHOLARSHIP AND STOICISM

Epicurus was born in Samos, but he inherited Athenian citizenship from his father. The leading Stoic philosophers, starting with Zeno, were all immigrants to Athens. They came from cities in Cyprus (Zeno and Chrysippus) or Asia Minor (Cleanthes, Antipater) or even further afield (Diogenes of Babylon). If their first language was Greek, which is possible but not certain, it will hardly have been in the Attic dialect. The beginnings of Stoicism coincide with the rapid diffusion of Hellenic language and culture into Egypt and Asia as a consequence of Alexander the Great's conquests and the division of his spoils into the kingdoms governed by his successors. The Hellenistic world, as this epoch is conventionally called, was most dramatically symbolized by the foundation of new cities, most notably Alexandria, which became the capital of the Ptolemaic kingdom. Athens, though reduced to political insignificance, remained the center of philosophy. But it was Alexandria, thanks to Ptolemaic patronage, that attracted the literary scholars and scientists whose work was facilitated there by the foundation of the great Library and Museum.

Both institutions need to be seen in large part as symbols of cultural ecumenicism. The Ptolemies, to be sure, had the worldly ambitions of every monarch, but the scholarly work they supported was grounded in their desire to preserve, refine, and propagate those works of literature that collectively defined Hellenic identity. Since Homer was indisputably preeminent, Hellenistic scholars devoted particular attention to producing improved texts of the epics and to commenting on their language and content. Starting with Zenodotus, a tradition of scholarship developed that culminated in the 2nd century B.C.E. in the work of Aristarchus of Samothrace, the greatest of all Alexandrian literati. He edited and commented on the texts of Herodotus as well as Homer and other archaic poets.

Aristarchus was complimented with the title "eminent grammarian" *(grammatikotatos)*, but he was not primarily a student of language or grammar in a technical sense; rather, as we would say today, he was a philologist and exegete of literature. The chief pioneers of linguistic study in the Hellenistic world were the Stoics. However, it is important to recognize that they, too, were keenly interested in Homer. Their founder, Zeno, wrote a work entitled *Homeric Problems* in five books. Virtually nothing is known about its content, but if we can draw conclusions from the evidence surviving from the later Stoic Chrysippus's work on Homer, the Stoics were primarily interested in precisely the kind of linguistic exegesis being practiced in Alexandria (H. von Arnim, *Stoicorum Veterum Fragmenta* III.769–777). It is this philological focus that will have distinguished their work on Homer from investigations of his poems that earlier philosophers, especially Aristotle, had already made.

In contrast with Epicurus, who professed to despise conventional *paideia*, the Stoics were concerned from the beginning to invoke the Greek poets in support of their own doctrines. In doing so, they not only aligned their school with traditional culture but also did so in ways that suggest a deliberate policy of assimilation. Many factors were doubtless at work here. These include the Stoics' status as arrivistes to Athens, the new fashion for ecumenicism, and, at a deeper level, the rationale of Stoicism itself. As the most systematic of Greek philosophies, Stoicism was grounded in the claim that the world is rationally organized through and through. The rationality of human nature, they taught, manifests itself in our capacity to speak, and especially in our capacity to express patterns of thought whose logical structure mirrors the structure of nature itself.

This faith in the universality of reason, as manifested in language, must be accounted a major factor in the Stoics' practice of proposing etymologies for numerous words, particularly the proper names and epithets of the many divinities in the Greek pantheon. By interpreting the "original meaning" of these terms, they wanted to show that Homer and Hesiod were the transmitters of primeval myths whose authors understood the world correctly, as etymology could reveal. Thus they took the name Hera to signify air *(aer)* and Cronos to signify time *(chronos;* Cicero, *De natura deorum* II.64–66). Most of their etymologies, like these examples, were as fanciful as those presented by Plato in *Cratylus,* but the rationale behind them, as distinct from the linguistics involved, was genuinely scientific: language is an intelligent construction, and analysis of language provides prime evidence of how people think and what they believe. Contrary to what is often said, the Stoics did not claim that Homer and Hesiod were "allegorical" exponents of Stoicism. Their interest in these early poets was "etymological"; they used them as sources for the *original meanings* of those who had told myths about the gods.

Zeno wrote a book titled *On Hellenic Education.* Together with the points just mentioned, the title of this work (which is all that survives of it) helps us to place the Stoics' work on language in its proper intellectual context. Their contributions to this field should be approached from multiple perspectives. For some of their findings they were clearly indebted to Plato and Aristotle. But they were also responding to interests similar to those awakened in Alexandria, while at the same time pursuing a study that reaches to the core of their philosophy.

Although our evidence for the Stoics' work on language is fragmentary and transmitted largely secondhand, it is sufficient to show that they were the primary innovators in most areas that were developed by the Greek and Roman grammarians of later antiquity. Among the most important innovations of the Stoics we may note the following: definition of *five* "parts of speech"—proper name, appellative, verb, conjunction, article—to which a sixth part, adverb, was later added (Diogenes Laertius, VII.57); identification of at least three of the "oblique" cases or types of inflection—accusative, genitive, and dative (ibid. VII.64–65)—and possibly the vocative as well; adumbration of the concept of conjugation, classifying four "times of action" for verbs—present, imperfect, perfect, and pluperfect (Priscian, VII.I.8.39). In addition, the Stoics took account of the differences between transitive, reflexive, and intransitive predicates (Diogenes Laertius, VII.64), foreshadowing the grammatical distinction between active, middle, and passive verbs. These categorizations were extended by those who later wrote on grammar specifically. Yet the Stoics did not think of themselves explicitly as grammarians. They wrote as students of language quite generally or, rather, as students of what they called "logic" or "dialectic." An appreciation of this point is essential if we are to grasp the general thrust of their work in this area.

They were the first Greek theorists to make a formal distinction between the "vocal" and the "semantic" aspects of language, or between "signifiers" and "significations" (Diogenes Laertius, VII.43). Signifiers, consisting of spoken or written symbols, are corporeal (ibid. VII.55). They range from the simplest "elements" (letters and syllables) to complete words, phrases, and, finally, sentences (combinations of at least a noun and a verb). The signification of a sentence is something of a quite different order. It is neither the utterance nor the thing referred to (which must be a body or bodily state, according to Stoicism), nor the individual thought of the speaker or hearer (also a bodily state, for the Stoics), but an "abstract" or "incorporeal" thing called a "sayable" (*lekton;* ibid. VII.63). *Lekta* are "meanings." They are what someone who says or writes, "Socrates is reading a book," means to say, and they are what someone who understands those words understands on hearing or reading them.

Considerable difficulty (partly due to defective evidence) attaches to any modern attempt to give a complete analysis of the Stoic theory of meaning. It appears that they regarded nouns, taken in isolation from sentences, as signifying not *lekta* but "qualities"—"common" ones in the case of appellatives like *man*, and "peculiar" ones in the case of proper names (Diogenes Laertius, VII.58). However, in "complete *lekta*," which are the semantic correlate of sentences, the function of nouns is to "complete" the "predicate" (signified by a verb), by supplying it with an "inflection" *(ptosis)*. Thus in the expression "Socrates is reading a book," the respective functions of the words *Socrates* and *a book* are to provide a "nominative" and "accusative" inflection for the predicate *is reading* (ibid. VII.64). We would call those functions subject and object, but the Stoics instead treated them in terms we are accustomed to call grammatical rather than semantic.

The *lekton* exemplified above is what the Stoics called an *axioma*, conventionally translated "proposition." Its defining characteristic is to be either true or false. In addition, the Stoics distinguished other kinds of *lekta*—questions, commands, imperatives, oaths, exclamations, and vocatives—that do not possess a truth value (Diogenes Laertius, VII.65–68). They also systematically analyzed types of propositions, including "hypothetical ones," which are of cardinal importance in their logic (ibid. VII.71–76). All of these *lekta* are identified in logical or semantic terms, and never by the grammatical form of the words through which they are expressed.

This point again illustrates the fact that the Stoics, notwithstanding their pioneering work in language, did not draw modern boundaries between grammar, semantics, and logic. Although they were interested in inflection, the main focus of their linguistic work was in semantics as distinct from morphology and accidence. Even such syntax as we may attribute to them—for instance, distinguishing between different kinds of predicates—has to do with meaning, or *lekta*, rather than formal grammar. That having been said, there is no question that they enormously advanced the study of complex speech acts, especially the forms of expression by which statements and inferences are made.

One writer of later antiquity (*SVF* II.146) attributes to the Stoics a theory about "primary utterances," pristine terms, as it were, from which subsequent words are derived. The original names, according to this report, will have been "mimetically" related to "things," as in the theory presented by Plato in *Cratylus*. As for later words, they were formed on principles of "resemblance," "affinity," or "contrast" with things (so Augustine, *Contra dialecticos* 6)—the latter being illustrated by the notorious *"lucus a non lucendo"* ("a *grove*, from the *absence of* illumination"). This material is difficult to control, and impossible to assign to individual Stoic philosophers. Chrysippus was certainly prepared to invoke etymology to make philosophical points, as in his bizarre claim (*SVF* II.884) that the movements made by the face when one pronounces the first person pronoun *ego* signify that the chest is the center of consciousness. Yet he also insisted that language, at the level of expressions *(lexeis)*, is irreducibly ambiguous (*SVF* II.152). Whatever he may have thought about the "natural" relation of original languages to things, the focus of his semantic theory is not on the phonetic properties of words but on *lekta*. Since *lekta* are not words but meanings, they transcend any particular language, just like tokens of Plato's "Form of name." They explain how language can mediate a speaker's thought to a listener, and, further, how translation between languages is possible.

So far as the philosophy of language goes, the Stoics represent the highpoint of Greco-Roman antiquity. Although there is little contemporary evidence to go on, their findings and methodology concerning diction were certainly influential on Alexandrian philology. As investigators of "classical" texts, Alexandrian scholars were chiefly interested in trying to codify the rules of Hellenism (i.e., the standard of good Greek), to explain rare or obscure terms, to pronounce on questions of authenticity, orthography, and the like. Thus grammar, in something close to its modern sense, was born as the symbiosis between Stoicism and Alexandrian scholarship.

This point can be amplified by reference to the Pyrrhonean philosopher Sextus Empiricus. He provides an excellent conspectus of what Greek grammar signified during the earlier years of the Roman empire. In his treatise *Against the Grammarians*, Sextus cites several definitions of grammar. He also gives detailed accounts of its subject matter in ways that enable us to distinguish between common assumptions and controversies. Particularly controversial, it seems, was the question of whether grammar should be regarded as aiming at the formulation of precise rules, like the study of musical harmony, or whether instead its rationale was more conjectural and empirical. Dionysius the Thracian, an exponent of the latter conception, defined grammar as "experience in what is said *for the most part* by poets and writers of prose" (Sextus, *Against the Grammarians* 57). Other grammarians opted for a stricter conception of grammar as a "diagnostic art" seeking "the greatest possible precision" (ibid. 76).

Modern scholars (following the Roman grammarian Varro in his work *De lingua Latina* VII.I–X) frequently refer to this controversy as one between "analogists" and "anomalists": analogists sought to establish grammatical rules, which could serve as the standard for evaluating deviations from a norm, whereas anomalists were concerned with analyzing language as a phenomenon resistant to such determinate codification. This controversy may well be anachronistic so far as Alexandria and Stoicism are concerned, but it is plausible to suppose that Alexandrian philologists like Aristarchus were more sympathetic to the analogical approach than Stoic philosophers will have been.

Sextus Empiricus divides the study of grammar into three parts—historical, technical, and special (*Against the Grammarians* 91–96). The first and the last of these directly reflect the scholarship initiated in Alexandria, for they deal with commentary on texts and legends (the historical part) and the language of prose and verse (the special part). What we today call grammar is subsumed under the technical part. Its subdivisions, as enumerated by Sextus (97–247), comprise, first, "elements" (individual letters, together with their quantity and accent); second, "syllables" (including their quantity); third, complete words and parts of speech; fourth, orthography; fifth, Hellenism; sixth, etymology. What is glaringly absent from this list, it may seem, is syntax. But an explanation for its absence is not hard to find. The list of topics corresponds very closely to the study of "utterance," as canonized by the Stoics (Diogenes Laertius VII.56–59). And they, too, as we have seen, did not identify syntax as a topic to be studied under this heading. In fact the first grammarian to study syntax systematically was probably Apollonius Dyscolus, whose work may have been unknown to Sextus Empiricus, his near contemporary. Sextus's treatise *Against the Grammarians* confirms the impression that it was the Stoics who primarily stimulated the field of investigation called grammar. As philosophers, they were distinctive in showing so much interest in the phenomenal aspects of diction. Yet in spite of this, they would probably have agreed with Plato and Aristotle that language is primarily worth studying for the light it can shed on the *things* we talk about.

ANTHONY A. LONG

Bibliography

General Works

Baratin, Marc, and Françoise Desbordes. *L'analyse linguistique dans l'antiquité classique.* 2 vols. Paris: Klincksieck, 1981.

Fraser, P. M. *Ptolemaic Alexandria.* Oxford: Clarendon Press, 1972.

Manetti, Giovanni. *Le teorie del segno nel'antichità classica.* Milan: Bompiani, 1987.

Pfeiffer, Rudolf. *History of Classical Scholarship,* vol. 1: *From the Beginnings to the End of the Hellenistic Age.* Oxford: Clarendon Press, 1968.

Pinborg, Jan. "Classical Antiquity: Greece." *Current Trends in Linguistic Theory* 13 (1975): 69–126.

Schmitter, Peter, ed. *Sprachtheorien der abendländischen Antike.* Tübingen: Gunter Narr, 1991.

Steinthal, Heymann. *Geschichte der Sprachwissenschaft bei den Griechen und Römern.* Berlin: Dümmlers Verlag, 1890.

Specialized Works

Atherton, Catherine. *The Stoics on Ambiguity*. Cambridge: Cambridge University Press, 1993.

Ax, Wolfram. *Laut, Stimme, und Sprache: Studien zu drei Grundbegriffen der antiken Sprachtheorie*. Göttingen: Vandenhoeck and Ruprecht, 1986.

Blank, David L. *Ancient Philosophy and Grammar: The Syntax of Apollonius Dyscolus*. Chico, Calif.: Scholars Press, 1982.

———. *Against the Grammarians*. Oxford: Clarendon Press, 1998.

Brunschwig, Jacques. *Papers in Hellenistic Philosophy*. Trans. Janet Lloyd. Cambridge: Cambridge University Press, 1994.

Everson, Stephen, ed., *Companions to Ancient Thought*, vol. 3: *Language*. Cambridge: Cambridge University Press, 1994.

Frede, Michael. *Essays in Ancient Philosophy*. Minneapolis: University of Minnesota Press, 1987.

Kerferd, G. B. *The Sophistic Movement*. Cambridge: Cambridge University Press, 1981.

Lamberton, Robert, and J. J. Keaney, eds. *Homer's Ancient Readers: The Hermeneutics of Greek Epic's Earliest Exegetes*. Princeton: Princeton University Press, 1992.

Long, A. A., ed. *Problems in Stoicism*. London: Athlone Press, 1971; repr. 1996.

Long, A. A., and D. N. Sedley. *The Hellenistic Philosophers*. 2 vols. Cambridge: Cambridge University Press, 1987.

Schenkeveld, D. M. "Language," in Keimpe Algra et al., eds., *The Cambridge History of Hellenistic Philosophy*. Cambridge: Cambridge University Press, 1999.

Schmidt, R. T. *Die Grammatik der Stoiker*. Braunschweig and Wiesbaden: Friedrich Vieweg and Sohn, 1979.

Schofield, Malcolm, and Martha Nussbaum, eds. *Language and Logos: Studies in Ancient Greek Philosophy Presented to G. E. L. Owen*. Cambridge: Cambridge University Press, 1982.

Sluiter, Ineke. *Ancient Grammar in Context*. Amsterdam: VU University Press, 1990.

LOGIC

A BASIC PRINCIPLE must be noted before we begin to deal with the origins of logic in Greece: we shall be examining not the way logic is used, but the theory of logic. It is one thing to follow rules, grammatical rules, for instance; it is something else again to theorize the correct use of those rules. Most people apply the rules of their own language correctly; however, they are rarely able to supply the general rules that justify the way they use language. The same thing holds true for logic. Almost all philosophers use it, sometimes well; few of them have developed a theory of logic. In what follows, when I speak of "logic" I shall be referring to the theory of logic; when I ask who were the earliest philosophers who concerned themselves with logic, the question will bear on those who developed a theory of logic.

We shall also have to adopt a viewpoint that implies the adoption of a theoretical stance, one that is decidedly less obvious than the preceding observation. What are we to understand by "logic"? We cannot answer this question through recourse to history, by considering the meaning that the ancient authors gave expressions such as *"he logike (techne)"* or *"he dialektike (techne),"* because of the variety of meanings these expressions have, and especially because authors such as Aristotle, even though they may be universally recognized as logicians, have no word that corresponds to our word *logic.* My own theoretical choice, which may not be accepted by everyone, is to use the word *logic* to refer to a theory of inference that is rationally capable of distinguishing between correct and incorrect types of argumentation.

An important consequence of this choice is that every self-respecting logical theory has to bear on types of inferences, not on isolated arguments; criteria making it possible to group similar inferences together must therefore exist. In other words, any theory of inference must include an understanding of the logical form or structure of inferences, a basis on which they can be organized according to schemas of inference. The notions of logical form and schemas of inference would require a more precise (and more complicated) characterization, but the idea must be familiar to anyone who has dealt with logic at all. Let us consider the two following inferences (where the horizontal line separates the premises, above, from the conclusion, below):

(1) All men are mortal
All Athenians are men

All Athenians are mortal

(2)   All quadrupeds are donkeys
      All whales are quadrupeds
      _____
      All whales are donkeys

We see clearly that the first inference is correct, and it is easy to be convinced that the second is correct as well, even though its premises and its conclusion are false, unlike those of (1). This simple observation shows that if (1) and (2) are correct, this does not depend on the truth or falsity of the propositions at stake but on the fact that the propositions exhibit the same logical form: in the case in point, a series of relationships that are described by the predicative linking verb *are* and specified by the quantifier *all*. *Are* and *all* thus constitute part of the logical form of these inferences, whereas *man, Athenian, mortal, quadruped, donkey,* and *whale* are irrelevant to the determination of the validity of (1) and (2). The moral of this story is that logic begins where a theory of inference based on recognition of its logical form comes to light, at least in a rudimentary manner.

When did logic begin? If we take the word in the sense I have just suggested, we cannot say that it began with Plato. In his writings we find neither a conscious distinction between logical form and content nor a theory of inference. The doctrine of division, which represents his major effort to develop a formal analysis of the relationships between concepts, is not a theory of inference, as Aristotle understood quite clearly, and it does not aim to bring to light structural relationships among concepts. It has often been thought that the doctrine of division was the direct antecedent of the Aristotelian theory of syllogisms. But Plato's division is not identical to Aristotle's syllogism, nor is it even similar in logical form. The most charitable interpretation of their relationship is to say that division is the psychological antecedent of the syllogism; reflection on division may have led Aristotle to discover the syllogism, rather as reflection on Ptolemy's system may have led Kepler to construct his theory.

Efforts to discover the Platonic ancestry of the Aristotelian syllogism in the last part of *Phaedo*, where the relationships between individuals and Forms are described, seem more promising, at least at first glance. There Plato maintains, for example, that if A is the contrary of B, what participates in A does not participate in B. It is possible to translate this position into a logical thesis that, appropriately manipulated, would exhibit a logical structure similar to the Aristotelian syllogism. Nevertheless, while such isolated observations may be logically impeccable, they can have offered Aristotle only food for thought, on the same basis as the deductions of the mathematicians.

The use of a fully formed logical theory first appears with Aristotle. He perceives clearly that the validity of an inference depends not on its content but on the structure of the propositions it includes. At the beginning of his

Prior Analytics, he distinguishes among three types of premises corresponding to arguments: demonstrative or scientific, dialectical, and syllogistic arguments. Truth is necessary in the first type: to make deductions that produce scientific knowledge, one must start with true premises. The same does not hold true for dialectical arguments, in which what counts is that the premises are propositions accepted by the adversary and capable of being generally approved by those who witness the debate. In the case of a simple syllogism, inference pure and simple, the only thing that counts is the logical structure of the premises, independent of their truth or falsity. This view implies a distinction between logic and epistemology: the predicative structure of the propositions included in inference is the only thing that counts for logic; taking their truth or their plausibility into account belongs to the realm of applications of logic to particular sectors of knowledge, in this case science and dialectics.

This, then, is a broad overview of the chronological framework of the birth of logic in Greece. But it would be a distortion of historical truth to limit ourselves, in this connection, to references to Plato and Aristotle. To be sure, Aristotle's logical reflection was born in the context of Platonic philosophy, especially if by this we mean not only the countless debates carried out by the characters in Plato's dialogues but also the discussions to which his writings gave rise within the Academy, where Aristotle, we must not forget, spent twenty years. However, other factors surely contributed to the birth of logic.

Let us recall, first of all, the extraordinary development of Greek mathematics. We know very little about pre-Euclidean geometry, though we know enough to say that it was organized along strictly deductive lines. Inferences played a decisive role and produced startling results, such as the demonstration of the incommensurability of the diagonal with the side of a square. How can one fail to feel the need to verify the steps in such a demonstration systematically, to assure oneself that this powerfully counterintuitive result was not the conclusion of faulty reasoning?

Let us turn next to the Sophistic movement and its sustained interest in language and in the function, sometimes positive and sometimes misleading, that it plays in argumentation. Authors such as Eubulides and Diodorus Cronos were formed in this melting pot of linguistic discussions. Eubulides was a disciple of Euclides, a namesake of the mathematician and the founder of the so-called Megarian school. We know little about Eubulides, but he deserves to be counted among the logicians: he is credited with inventing some famous paradoxes, including the Liar Paradox and the paradox of the Sorites. Let us suppose that everything I say is false. What would then be the truth value of the proposition: "What I am saying is false"? A little reflection shows that if the proposition is thought to be true, it has to be taken as false, and if it is taken as false, it is true, which is contradictory. Similarly, a grain of wheat is certainly not a heap (*sōros*) of wheat, whereas a billion grains of wheat surely form a heap. But it is difficult to deny that if *n* grains do not make a heap, $n + 1$ grains do not make one either: no magical grain can transform into a heap what is not yet a heap. Thus, a billion grains do not make a heap, contrary to the initial assertion based on experience.

We do not know how Eubulides formulated these paradoxes; the versions that survive come from later authors, Stoics in particular. Nor do we know why Eubulides invented the paradoxes. Some scholars have supposed that, following an Eleatic inspiration, he wanted to show the contradictory character of experience; others have thought that he invented the paradoxes to attack Aristotle (and indeed he had criticized him quite impolitely). But his interest was perhaps guided by the taste for discovering disconcerting aspects of language. In fact, contrary to one view that has come down from the ancient tradition, Eubulides' paradoxes are not merely head scratchers or curious playthings: they conceal fundamental difficulties in logic and in some of the basic notions of which they make use, the concept of truth in particular. Aristotle does not seem to have been conscious of their subversive import; only the Stoics tried to study them, with the idea that to neutralize them it was necessary to give up something important in our philosophical conceptions.

Diodorus Cronos is a very complex figure. According to most historians, he belonged to the Megarian school, as did Eubulides. Others think he belonged to the dialectical school, separate from the Megarian school but with connections to it. His disciple Philon may also have belonged to that school; Diodorus engaged in polemics with Philon on the subject of the truth conditions of conditional propositions, as we shall see.

Diodorus's fame rests on the so-called Master argument, thanks to which he thought he had proved that only what is already or what will be is possible. Unfortunately, our sources have given us incomplete information about the structure of the argument. According to these sources, Diodorus viewed the following three propositions as incompatible:

(i)   Everything that has happened is necessary;
(ii) From the possible the impossible does not follow;
(iii) That is possible which is not and will not be.

Since, according to Diodorus, one must accept (i) and (ii), one must reject (iii) and thus conclude that possibility cannot concern something that in fact is not at any moment: if tomorrow it does not turn out to be the case that I go to the movies, then it is impossible for me to go to the movies tomorrow. The reason that these three propositions are incompatible is not clear; all the reconstructions intended to explain it end up introducing new premises more or less surreptitiously. What seems certain, however, is that the ancients viewed Diodorus's inference as logically correct; they sought to respond to him by rejecting one or the other of his premises, so as to avoid the paradox of a reduction of the possible to the factual. We know, for example, that Cleanthes denied the necessity or the irrevocability of the past, while Chrysippus rejected the logical thesis according to which from a possible an impossible does not follow. Certain historians also supposed, but without compelling arguments, that the famous ninth chapter of Aristotle's *On Interpretation* (or, more accurately, "On Expression"), where determinism and the logical status of propositions having to do with future contingent events are discussed, was a response to Diodorus's Master argument. The existence of these sophisticated debates in Aristotle's day suffices to show that we must not view the Platonic Academy as the only site that nourished a logical culture and a conscious interest in the formal aspects of argumentation.

Aristotle's logic is included in a group of works traditionally designated as the *Organon*, that is, "the instrument"—understood primarily as the instrument for philosophy. *Organon* comprises six treatises: *Categories, On Interpretation, Prior Analytics, Posterior Analytics, Topica*, and *Sophistical Refutations*. These works are unanimously judged to be authentic, except for *Categories*, about which doubts have been raised in the modern era. In contrast, although Andronicus denied the authenticity of *On Interpretation*, that text is accepted as authentic today. It is also agreed that *Sophistical Refutations* does not constitute an autonomous treatise but is, rather, the last book of *Topica*.

Unfortunately, it is very difficult to establish an absolute and relative chronology of Aristotle's texts on logic. Most of them are thought to have been youthful works, written while he was a member of the Academy or shortly thereafter. But some scholars believe that *On Interpretation* is a late work, if it is true that that work contains a polemic against Diodorus Cronus that could only have been written toward the end of Aristotle's life. However, these hypotheses are by no means held unanimously, and it is more prudent to suspend judgment in the absence of compelling evidence. Similarly, the relative chronology of these texts has not been definitively established. Certain parts of *Topica* that contain no reference to the theory of the syllogism must have been composed before *Prior Analytics*. There is thus a nearly unanimous tendency to consider *Topica* to be the first treatise of *Organon*, by virtue of the fact, too, that the work seems to be an immediate reflection of the forms and content of the discussions that must have taken place within the Academy; in contrast, the question of the chronological relationship between *Prior Analytics* and *Posterior Analytics* has been the source of endless argument.

We cannot go into the details of these discussions here. By choosing to identify logic with the theory of inferences, I shall refer in particular to *On Interpretation*, which includes many indications concerning the conception of the proposition, and to *Prior Analytics;* I shall occasionally mention *Posterior Analytics*, where the theory of science is presented, and *Topica*, a text chiefly devoted to dialectics, that is, to techniques that allow one to win arguments.

Aristotle proposes at least two complementary characterizations of the notion of proposition. One consists in defining it in terms of predication: a proposition is the attribution, affirmative or negative, of something to something. In this sense, Aristotle is only following the line set forth by Plato, who in *Sophist* distinguished between the act of naming and the act of predicating, the proposition being the result of the latter. But Aristotle also proposes another, more complex characterization of propositions. In *On Interpretation*, he considers the proposition to be a particular type of *logos*, a term generally translated—rather badly—by "discourse." A *logos* is a verbal expression of which certain parts, taken separately, have a meaning, without being affirmations or negations. "Pierre is a man" is a discourse, because its components, *Pierre* and *man* have meaning without being propositions.

Discourses can be *apophantic* or *nonapophantic*. The former are those that can be called true or false; in contrast, in the case of the latter one cannot properly speak of truth or falsity. Aristotle cites the example of prayer; to this others have added discourses such as orders or exhortations, drawing on a typology that, according to Diogenes Laertius, goes back to Protagoras. Some have seen this Aristotelian distinction as an anticipation of the modern distinction between performative and nonperformative speech acts. Without attempting to pass judgment on these sorts of connections (which are always risky), it goes without saying that Aristotle identifies propositions with particular types of apophantic discourses; affirmation and negation—that is, the attribution or the denial of attribution of a predicate to a subject—are viewed as propositions.

At least two observations on this subject are called for. First, it is clear that Aristotle considers the predicative structure to be the basic structure of propositions, and that he interprets this structure in terms of relationships between a predicate and a subject. These two theses have been challenged in modern times. In fact it is not at all self-evident that a proposition such as "It is raining" must be understood according to the model "Dion is running," even though the Greek language, unlike French or English, can understand "It is raining" as the equivalent of "Zeus is raining." Furthermore, since Frege, we have tended to think that the best logical analysis of a proposition such as "Socrates loves Callias" is not to make *Socrates* the subject and *loves Callias* the predicate; we prefer to view the predicate of this proposition as *loves,* and to see this predicate as having two subjects, *Socrates* and *Callias*. It is then much easier to account for inferences containing relational propositions. Aristotle is conscious of the specificity of relational predicates, but he does not succeed in analyzing them in terms different from those used for nonrelational predicates so far as their function in propositions is concerned.

The second observation has to do with the relation between affirmation and negation, the minimal units of apophantic discourse. Although Aristotle seems, in *On Interpretation*, to subordinate negation to affirmation, he does not seem to have had the idea—one that is widespread among the moderns and fairly self-evident on its own terms—that negation is a compound proposition, achieved starting from an affirmation through the addition of an operation of negation; this idea was put forward by the Stoics. From Aristotle's viewpoint, negation seems to be as primitive and as elementary as affirmation. Not only is predication customarily defined as a liaison or separation of terms, that is to say affirmation or negation, but it also brings into correspondence with this operator two states of affairs, positive and negative, respectively, that make the corresponding propositions true or false.

If we set aside singular propositions concerning contingent future events, everyone agrees that, according to Aristotle, every proposition is true or false—that is, in modern terms, every proposition has a truth value (this is what we call the principle of bivalence). By interpreting a well-known passage of *Metaphysics,* perhaps somewhat audaciously, we may say that this value is true if the state of affairs expressed by the proposition is the case, and that it is false if the opposite state of affairs is the case.

The details of the Aristotelian doctrine are less banal. For Aristotle, a proposition always has a truth value, but it does not necessarily *always* have *the same* truth value. Let us consider, for example, the proposition:

(3) Callias is running.

The verb *is running* contains a temporal reference that we can make explicit, from Aristotle's perspective, by adding to (3) a reference to the present, thanks to an expression such as "now." Aristotle analyzes the truth value of (3) as follows: "Now," which is contained implicitly in the proposition, refers to the moment when (3) is uttered; if at this moment Callias is in fact in the process of running, (3) is true; otherwise, (3) is false. But if we refer to two acts of utterance that are separate in time, (3) may be true at one moment and false at another. The truth value of an Aristotelian proposition thus cannot be understood, in Frege's manner, as the extension of the proposition. One must say, rather, that truth value is the value of a function of time, applied to a particular propositional content. This perspective is meaningful only if we acknowledge the existence of authentically temporal propositions such that the reference to temporal indicators such as *now, before,* and *after* cannot be reduced to objective dates. Moreover, we cannot tell whether Aristotle had the idea of propositions that are atemporal in their content. Whereas we would be inclined to say today that the proposition $2 + 2 = 4$ leaves out the temporal dimension, there is some evidence that Aristotle would have preferred to say that $2 + 2 = 4$ is a proposition that is *always* true.

If an elementary proposition is an affirmation or a negation, it is clear that its primary components will be nouns and verbs. Aristotle distinguishes between proper and common nouns, or, in a more appropriately logical formulation, between singular and universal terms. These are distinguished by the function they fulfill in predication: a universal term can serve as a predicate but also as a subject; a singular term cannot serve as a predicate (except in the case of predications of identity). Aristotle expresses this thesis by saying that every universal term is, by its nature, suited to be the predicate of several distinct individuals. This of course does not mean that at least two individuals have to fall under the extension of a term if we are to be able to call it universal. It means, rather, that only universal terms are capable of fulfilling the role of being true of several individuals. Even a term that is true of nothing, such as *tragelaphos* ("goat-deer"), or even one that cannot be true of anything, such as "different from oneself," is universal, because if it were true of something, it could be true of at least two distinct individuals.

A nontrivial question connected with the distinction between universal and singular terms is that of reference in each case. It is not difficult to imagine that singular terms refer to the individuals to which they apply. But the delicate question, in Aristotle's perspective, is knowing to what universal terms refer. Aristotle's polemic against Plato, with regard to the existence of Forms, allows us to rule out the possibility that he considered ideal individuals as the correlates of universal terms. From his standpoint, no ideal man exists who represents that to which the term *man* refers: there is no individual who is the objective counterpart of man, as Callias is the correlate of the name Callias. However, Aristotle's critique of Plato does not rule out the possibility that the term *man*, if it is not an individual's proper name, can be the proper name of an attribute, the one that consists in being human. If we suppose that this attribute is shared by several individuals, the way a jointly owned apartment is shared, we might offer the hypothesis that "man" represents the attribute that Callias and Socrates share with other human beings, and which is identically present in all of them. In this light, the difference between Plato's position and Aristotle's would be reduced to the fact that the former's Forms are ideal individuals, existing independently of the things of our world, whereas the latter's attributes are entities that are identically present in several individuals, and that cannot exist unless at least one of those individuals exists. But from the semantic viewpoint, the two philosophers would have the same perspective: universals, no less than singular terms, are the proper names of entities that exist in the world.

Although this conception may appear seductive, it is difficult to believe that it is Aristotle's, at least in the most mature phase of his ontology. In book Z of *Metaphysics*, he seems to maintain that the *ousiai* of individuals—that is, their substantial forms—are different for different individuals. Different *ousiai* belong to Socrates and to Callias, even though they are both men, so that the being-human of the one is not the being-human of the other. There is thus not a single reality to which the term *man* corresponds. If this is the case for universals like *man*, that is, for terms that refer to the *ousiai* of individuals, it is perhaps legitimate to extend that conclusion to all universal terms, such as *white, good, three cubits high*.

On this basis, then, we may presume that for Aristotle universal terms are not really referential. Referring to something, capturing it, is a function reserved to singular terms: to put it crudely, "Callias" or "Socrates" may be viewed as labels of objects. In contrast, according to this hypothesis, the defining characteristic of universal terms is that they are (at least in principle) true of a multiplicity; that is, they play the role of predicates. They denote nothing, even though they are true of individuals, and even though they are radically distinct, in this sense, from singular terms. Naturally, they have a meaning. But for a universal term to have a meaning does not imply that it has a denotation, because its task is to be true of an individual, not to indicate one.

The problem that this interpretation raises is the problem of understanding what guarantees the legitimacy of true predications. If truth consists, according to Aristotle, in stating things as they are, and if there is nothing that corresponds to the term *man*, on what basis can we legitimately maintain that "Callias is a man" is true, and that "Socrates is a lizard" is false? Aristotle does not lean in the direction of a response that might appear natural and that has been adopted quite often in the modern era, namely, the psychological response: universal terms, from this standpoint, refer to concepts that represent the ways in which we classify reality. "Callias is a man" is then a true proposition because we all agree to classify Callias as a man, and not as a lizard.

Aristotle operates instead on the terrain of ontology, unfortunately without ever clearly explaining his point of view. To attempt a clarification on the basis of some rather tortuous texts, let us consider two individuals a and b, of whom it is true to say F—for example, that they are men. If a and b are men, in them are present two distinct and different *ousiai*, respectively the being-man of a and the being-man of b. Let us call these two *ousiai* Fa and Fb. It is legitimate to suppose that Fa and Fb are not distinguished by the fact of being man: Socrates is not human in a different manner from Callias, and the one is not more human than the other. What makes the difference between Socrates' being-man and Callias's being-man is not being-man taken in itself, but simply the fact that one being-man belongs to Callias and the other to Socrates. One may view the two *ousiai* as two absolutely identical spheres that can be distinguished from each other only because they occupy different parts of space.

From this viewpoint, the relation that unites attributes with universal terms becomes clearer (or at least less obscure). The universal terms have as their meaning what might be called the f-ness of Fa, of Fb, and so on: they represent the various properties of things, without regard to the relations that these properties have with different individuals. Thus no universal term denotes anything at all, given that the f-ness of Fa, of Fb, and so on, does not exist independently of the fact that it is the f-ness of Fa, of Fb, and so on. Still, the attribution of a universal term to an individual is neither arbitrary nor the simple result of an epistemic operation of classification based on psychological categories.

The distinction between universal terms and singular terms allows Aristotle to classify propositions as singular or universal; to avoid confusion, let us call the latter "general" propositions. Singular propositions are those that have a singular term, such as *Callias*, as their subject; general propositions have a universal term, such as *man*, as their subject.

The introduction of this latter type of proposition allows Aristotle to introduce a supplementary division: general propositions may be universal, particular, or indefinite. Universal propositions are those whose subject is determined by a universal quantifier (such as *all*, or *none*, in the case of negative propositions); particular propositions are the ones whose subject is specified by a particular quantifier or, as one says today, existential, such as *some*. Probably for the first time in the history of Western thought, we are witnessing here the introduction of quantifiers as relevant components of the logical structure of propositions; this alone would suffice to make Aristotle one of the great logicians.

Since every proposition can be affirmative or negative, we thus obtain four types of general propositions: affirmative universal ("Every man is mortal"), negative universal ("No man is mortal"), affirmative particular ("Some man is mortal"), and negative particular ("Some man is not mortal"). For convenience, I shall adopt the medieval usage here and call affirmative universals *a* propositions, affirmative particulars *i* propositions (from the first two vowels of the Latin *affirmo*), negative universals *e* propositions, and negative particulars *o* propositions (from the two vowels of the Latin *nego*).

Indefinite propositions constitute a separate and much less clearly defined category: they are propositions with a universal subject in which no quantification is specified, such as "Man is white" and "Man is not white." Observing that indefinite propositions imply the corresponding particular propositions, Aristotle seems to reduce the former to the latter. It is clear, moreover, that "Man is not white" is not the logical negation of "Man is white," owing to the fact that the first does not necessarily have a truth value opposed to the second.

Aristotle devotes considerable effort to examining the relationships that come into play between the types of propositions identified by his classification. Thus he states that the negation of an affirmative singular proposition reverses its truth value: of the two propositions "Socrates is white" and "Socrates is not white," one is true and the other false. But one cannot say the same thing about a pair of singular propositions in which two contrary or incompatible predicates are attributed to the same subject, such as "Socrates is healthy" and "Socrates is ill": in such instances, according to Aristotle, it is not always the case that one of the two propositions is true and the other false. But one cannot infer from this argument that, according to Aristotle, every singular proposition must have an existential import—in other words, that the subject term refers to something that exists. In fact, Aristotle maintains that when Socrates does not exist, the proposition "Socrates is not healthy" is true: thus for him there are true singular propositions whose subject does not denote an existing object. It does not seem legitimate, either, to maintain that existential import is for him a necessary condition of the truth of affirmative singular propositions, whereas this would not be the case for negative singulars: in a controversial passage of *On Interpretation*, Aristotle asserts that if "Homer is a poet" is true, one cannot deduce from this that Homer exists. He thus imposes no general condition of existence on the truth of singular propositions: everything depends on the type of predicate considered. Predicates of the type *healthy/ill* are such that to be able to affirm them truthfully of an individual, one must presuppose that that individual exists; this is not the case for the predicate *poet*, which according to Aristotle may be attributed legitimately to an individual, even if that individual does not exist. Singular propositions, whether they are affirmative or negative, thus do not have existential import, generally speaking.

Probably for epistemological reasons, Aristotle's interest is focused chiefly on quantified general propositions and their relationships. His doctrine on this point is traditionally called the theory of the *logical square*. He calls propositions *a* and *o* and propositions *e* and *i* contradictory, and he asserts that they cannot either both be true or both be false. The logical relation between propositions *a* and *e*, called *contraries*, is different: they can both be false, but they cannot both be true. Aristotle does not assign a label to propositions *i* and *o*, which the later tradition will call *subcontraries;* they can both be true, but he does not say explicitly that they cannot both be false, though this thesis is implicitly contained in the one according to which the contraries cannot both be true, since the contradictories are precisely the subcontraries. The tradition has also made explicit, under the name of *subalternation*, a supplementary relation that connects propositions *a* and *i*, and *e* and *o*, respectively. Aristotle is perfectly aware of the law that governs this relation: from the truth of the universal proposition that of the corresponding particular proposition follows; in other words, from *a* there follows *i*, and from *e* there follows *o* (the inverse, naturally, is not true).

The doctrine of the logical square, broadly accepted in the Middle Ages and in the modern era, has been severely criticized by contemporary logicians. To understand these criticisms, let us first observe that, once the rule of contradictories is accepted, the other rules follow all together: for example, one cannot accept the rule of contraries and reject that of subalterns; a counterexample invalidating the one would affect all the others. Next, let us note that the doctrine supposes a precise interpretation of the nature of the quantification. In particular, a proposition *i*, such as "Some Athenian is noble," must be understood as affirming that there is at least one individual who is Athenian and noble. Similarly, "Some Athenian is not noble" must mean that there is at least one individual who is Athenian and who is not noble. The contradictory of this last proposition, "Every Athenian is noble," will thus be true if and only if there exists no individual who is Athenian and not noble. The consequence of this is that when no individuals of a certain type exist, everything that one says about their totality is true. For example, let us suppose that no witches exist; in this case, the assertion "Every witch is wicked" is true, since in the hypothesis according to which no witches exist, there are not any witches, either, who are not wicked. For a symmetrical reason, its contrary, "No witch is wicked," is also true. It is thus not logically correct to maintain that two contrary propositions cannot both be true. Moreover, "Some witch is wicked," the subaltern of "Every witch is wicked," is false if no witches exist: it would be true only if there were at least one individual who was a witch and wicked; now, by hypothesis, there is not one. The law of subalternation is thus not always valid, and, consequently, the entire doctrine of the logical square is to be rejected.

This critique is based, clearly enough, on two distinct presuppositions. The first is the recognition of *empty* terms, which are true of nothing at all. The second concerns the analysis of quantification: every true particular proposition affirms the existence of an individual who exemplifies the subject term, and every universal proposition entails the negation of that existential implication.

Defenders of the Aristotelian conception customarily reject the first of these presuppositions. In fact, if one excludes empty terms, if every term has at least one exemplification, the logical square is exempt from counterexamples, and its rules are valid. At first glance, the defense appears to be efficacious. If logic is a serious thing, why worry about witches, elves, or magic mountains? An ideal city-state governed by logicians would banish such entities, which may inhabit the imagination of children but not the reflections of philosophers and wise men. Still, the fact remains that Aristotle grants language the possibility of using empty terms: one of his favorite examples is the *tragelaphos*, the "goat-deer." Furthermore, it cannot be affirmed that empty terms are derived only from fables. To prove that there exists no natural number inferior to zero, that is, to prove that that expression is empty, is an exercise that mathematicians can carry out; to establish that there exists no human being anterior to the Neanderthal is a false scientific conclusion. If we were to limit Aristotle's logic to nonempty terms, we would limit its applicability, and we would render it even more incapable than it is of accounting for scientific inferences.

The effort to avoid the impasses of the logical square has led some to search for a different way out. Through reliance on the texts in which Aristotle maintains that in certain cases, affirmative singular propositions, unlike negative ones, have an existential import, this thesis has been generalized, leading to a conclusion that every affirmative proposition has such an import and no negative proposition does. From this point on, the logical square is safe from modern objections. From this perspective, "Every witch is wicked" becomes false, and thus no longer constitutes a counterexample to the rule of subalternation. Nevertheless, this solution entails at least two difficulties. First, we cannot see clearly whether for Aristotle all affirmative singular propositions have an existential import or only some of them, as we had understood earlier. The generalization of the thesis of *Categories* runs up against the obstacle of *On Interpretation*. Furthermore, in *Analytics*, Aristotle applies systematically to syllogistic schemas the so-called proof by exposition, which requires that the terms contained in the premises, whether affirmative or negative, possess an exemplification. Thus it does not appear legitimate to attribute to Aristotle the idea that only affirmative propositions have an existential import, if we suppose, barring proof to the contrary, that his doctrine is coherent.

There may be one last way to save the Aristotelian conception, one that has not been explored until now. It consists in abandoning the second presupposition of the modern critique, that is, the thesis according to which all particular propositions have an existential import. From this standpoint, there is no longer any reason to assert that "Every witch is wicked" is true and that the corresponding particular proposition is false. Naturally this cheap rescue operation has its price, which cannot be spelled out in detail here (in particular, it becomes difficult to determine the truth conditions of particular propositions). Let me suggest this direction for research, emphasizing simply that Aristotle's theory does not allow us to assimilate his idea of quantifiers readily to that of the moderns, even though the attempt has often been made.

The heart of Aristotle's logic is his doctrine of inference. The Aristotelian word for "inference" is *sullogismos,* which we must be careful not to translate as "syllogism," because Aristotle normally uses the term not to designate the particular inferences whose theory he is developing, namely, syllogisms, but to designate the general class of inferences of which syllogisms are a privileged type, for, according to him, every logically correct inference can be reformulated as a syllogism.

The Aristotelian definition of inference is presented with particular care at the beginning of *Prior Analytics;* it calls for two important observations. Aristotle first posits as an essential condition that the conclusion of an inference be different from its premises; this means that he rules out inferences of the type "A, thus A," which are nevertheless legitimate from the modern viewpoint, and even welcome, owing to the very fact that their banality guarantees their correctness. Aristotle seems on the contrary to maintain that an inference must always lead to something new. Furthermore, we must not read the Aristotelian definition with our eyes fixed on the modern conception of the notion of logical consequence—the one that, at least since Tarski, has referred to the notion of truth. There is nothing of the sort in Aristotle: he says neither that the truth of the conclusion necessarily follows that of the premises, nor that if the premises are true, the conclusion is also true. He simply maintains that if the premises *are posited,* a conclusion necessarily follows, which no doubt means that the positing of the premises is a sufficient condition of the positing of the conclusion. "Positing" must not of course be understood in a psychological sense: it is not because one asserts the premises that one is compelled to assert the conclusion; Aristotle is well aware that this is not at all the case. It is rather a question of an ideal positing, through which a set of premises finds itself isolated. If this isolation occurs and if the premises are appropriate, one is legitimately authorized to posit the conclusion after the premises. In this sense, the premises are the sufficient conditions, not of the existence of the conclusion, for the latter does not exist when it expresses a false proposition, but of the fact that it comes after the premises in the process that leads from the premises to the conclusion. In this perspective, the Aristotelian notion of inference, unlike the modern notion, makes a reference that cannot be eliminated to the notion of cause.

Aristotle formulates the inferences whose theory he is developing by means of letters that take the place of the general terms of their constitutive propositions. There has been much discussion about the meaning of these letters. It is probably not appropriate to speak in this connection of *variables* in the modern sense, as has been done (in the proper sense, a variable x is what is bound by a quantifier, "for every x" or "for some x," which these letters never are). What comes closest to Aristotle's letters is the idea (theorized by Quine, among others) of *dummy letters,* which can be indefinitely substituted for the concrete terms of ordinary language.

One type of Aristotelian inference thus has a form of which the following schema would be an example:

(4)   A belongs to all B
       B belongs to all C
       _____
       A belongs to all C

in which A, B, and C take the place of general terms, and in which the expression "A belongs to all B" translates the characteristic way in which Aristotle expresses an affirmative universal, logically equivalent to "every B is A." This schema always includes two premises, in which a common term, the *middle,* appears twice, whereas the other two terms (the *extremes*) are the ones that appear in the conclusion. More precisely, the *major* extreme is the predicate of the conclusion, and the *minor* is the subject.

According to the type of relation that the middle term has with the extremes in the premises, syllogisms are grouped into *figures*. Aristotle considers three of these: in the first, the middle term is the subject of the major term and the predicate of the minor term; in the second, the middle term is the predicate in both premises; in the third, the middle term is the subject in both. Schema (4) is thus an example of the first figure. Here is an example of the second:

(5)   A does not belong to any B
      A belongs to all C
      _____

      B does not belong to any C

Here is an example of the third:

(6)   A belongs to all C
      B belongs to all C
      _____

      A belongs to some B

The figures are not schemas of inference but ways of categorizing such schemas. Aristotle recognizes four types of valid syllogisms in the first figure; they are traditionally called *modes* and given the following names: Barbara, Celarent, Darii, Ferio. The second figure also has four valid modes: Cesare, Camestres, Festino, Baroco, and the third has six: Darapti, Felapton, Disamis, Datisi, Ferison, Bocardo. (4) is in the Barbara mode, (5) in the Cesare mode, and (6) in Darapti.

These bizarre names have a mnemotechnic function. Their vowels indicate, in order, the types of premises and conclusion that characterize the inference. For example, Barbara, the first mode of the first figure, has propositions of the *a* type as its premises and its conclusion.

Aristotle divides the inferences he is theorizing into two major groups: perfect syllogisms and imperfect syllogisms. The members of both groups are syllogisms and satisfy the definition, but the former, unlike the latter, are self-evident and thus require no justification of their validity. Imperfect syllogisms require justification of their validity: Aristotle calls this process "reduction" *(analusis)* and articulates it as a deduction of these syllogisms from perfect syllogisms. Once derived in this way, an imperfect syllogism is perfected; in this sense, it becomes self-evident. The perfect syllogisms fulfill, in a way, the function of axioms in the theory, although they do not satisfy the condition of independence characteristic of axioms.

Aristotle considers syllogisms exemplifying the first figure to be perfect, and those exemplifying the other figures imperfect. His idea is fairly simple: let us isolate a group of inferences that are certain and incontrovertible, and let us show that those that can give rise to doubt depend on those that are incontrovertible, so that denying the latter implies rejecting the former. What is less clear is the identification of perfect syllogisms with those exemplifying the first figure. Aristotle appears to associate the perfection of the latter with the fact that they rely directly on the definition of universal predication. But his thesis is not entirely clear.

To derive the modes of the second and third figures starting from those of the first figure, Aristotle basically uses three methods. The first depends on the use of rules for conversion of propositions, which are discussed in a chapter of *Prior Analytics*. The conversion of a proposition is the substitution of its predicate for its subject and vice versa. The problem lies in establishing under what conditions this substitution preserves truth, and, when it does not, whether one can obtain the same result by weakening the quantification of the proposition. The conclusion of the investigation is that universal negatives can be converted *simpliciter*, as was said in the Middle Ages—that is, by simple substitution between predicate and subject. "A belongs to no B" is converted into "B belongs to no A," *salva veritate* (truth remaining intact). Similarly, affirmative particular propositions can be converted *simpliciter*: if "A belongs to some B," it is legitimate to infer that "B belongs to some A." In contrast, universal affirmative propositions can be converted only *secundum quid*, that is, by weakening the quantification: from "A belongs to all B," we can move to "B belongs to some A." Finally, Aristotle rightly notes that negative particular propositions cannot be converted, in the sense that no possible conversion always preserves their truth.

Aristotle is able to prove, by applying the rules of conversion, that most of the second- and third-figure modes depend on the first-figure modes. In the second figure, the conversion of the negative premises of Cesare and Camestres makes it possible to get Celarent, and that of the negative premise of Festino makes it possible to get Ferio. In the third figure, Darapti, Datisi, Felapton, and Ferison are reduced by conversion of the minor premise, the first two being reduced to Darii and the next two to Ferio. Disamis is also reduced to Darii by conversion of the major premise.

Conversion is not applicable to Baroco in the second figure, nor to Bocardo in the third figure: in fact, conversion produces no valid first-figure mode. Aristotle then falls back on the method of reduction to the impossible. Let us suppose that Baroco and Bocardo are invalid. Hence, in one case at least the premises will be true and the conclusion false; in other words, the premises and the negation of the conclusion will both be true. But this cannot be, because the negation of the conclusion, together with one of the premises, gives rise in Barbara, the first mode of the first figure, to the negation of the other premise. Since the invalidity of these two modes is impossible, they have to be counted among the valid modes.

Thus all syllogisms of the second and third figure are reduced to syllogisms of the first figure, and in this sense they are justified. However, Aristotle mentions a third type of proof for syllogisms of the second and third figure; he calls this type exposition *(ekthesis),* and uses it as an auxiliary proof. The interpretation of this type of proof is controversial; we cannot go into the details here. It will suffice to say that if exposition plays a secondary role in syllogistic reductions, it takes on capital importance in proofs of the laws of conversion; the rule of conversion of negative universals, on which the proof of the other rules relies, is proved by exposition.

Aristotle does not stop at proving that all the second- and third-figure modes he is considering are valid, once the validity of the first-figure modes has been recognized. He shows, too, that all the other combinations of premises, in the three figures, do not give syllogistic conclusions. Let us consider for example the following pair of propositions:

(7)   A belongs to all B
      B belongs to no C

The position of the middle term, B, might lead us to believe that we are dealing with the antecedent of a first-figure mode, and that we can establish a connection between A as predicate and C as subject. Aristotle proves that this hypothesis is false, owing to the fact that, whatever predicative relation we establish between A and C, truth is not preserved. In other words, it is always possible to find a case in which the propositions of (7) are true and the presumed conclusion is false. For example, if we substitute "animal" for A, "man" for B, and "horse" for C, we get the following pair:

(8)   Animal belongs to all man
      Man belongs to no horse

This pair of propositions is true. But if we were to suppose that from (7) it follows, for example, that A belongs to no C, the substitutions that gave us (8) would lead to "Animal belongs to no horse," which is false. Thus we cannot affirm that from (7) it follows that "A belongs to no C." Thanks to other substitutions of terms, it is easy to prove in a similar fashion that (7) and "A belongs to all C" are true at the same time. From (7), then, no proposition follows having A as its predicate and C as its subject. We have to conclude that (7) is not a valid syllogistic antecedent.

Aristotle thus proves not only that his system of inferences is valid but also that it is syllogistically complete, given that his schemas constitute the only valid modes in the three figures. In truth, Aristotle is defending a much more ambitious thesis. He judges that every correct inference can be expressed, in the final analysis, thanks to one of the syllogistic modes of his three figures. Actually, this claim is trivially false, as Augustus De Morgan proved more than a century ago: a perfectly legitimate inference such as:

All horses are animals

All horses' heads are animals' heads

is absolutely incapable of being reformulated as an Aristotelian syllogism.

Even though Aristotle explicitly defends the thesis of the strong completeness of his system, we probably should not take his claim too seriously, since in other passages he shows that he is aware of inferential schemas that are correct but irreducible to the syllogistic form. Such is the case, for example, with what is called *Modus Ponens*, which can be formulated as follows:

(9) If A, then B
     A

     B

Quite clearly, an inference of this sort (in which the letters represent propositions, not terms) cannot be transformed into a syllogism; nevertheless, Aristotle recognizes its legitimacy. His idea, which is developed by the ancient commentators, is that an inference such as (9) must be considered not as an inference properly speaking but rather as a rule for governing and constructing inferences. Let us suppose that we want to prove B, but that we have no proof of B. If we know, or at least if we admit, that A implies B, we can consider the proof of A sufficient to be able to affirm B. Schemas such as (9) are thus assigned a role in syllogistic without being granted the status of inferences, properly speaking, that would be placed on the same level as syllogisms.

We cannot conclude this presentation of Aristotle's position without alluding, however briefly, to his modal logic. A proposition such as "Every man is mortal" is a nonmodal or *categorical* proposition. However, the same proposition can be qualified as necessary or as possible, depending on whether one adds to it expressions such as "it is necessary that" or "it is possible that."

Alongside his nonmodal or *categorical* syllogistic, Aristotle devoted a great deal of effort to the parallel development of a modal syllogistic—that is, a theory of inferences including propositions supplied with modal specifications. His problem is the following: given a valid categorical syllogistic schema, what becomes of the conclusion if the premises are specified as necessary or possible? If, for example, the premises are both necessary, Aristotle rightly establishes that the conclusion is also necessary. But what happens if one of the premises is necessary and the other possible, or if one is modalized and the other not? Aristotle analyzes all possible cases very meticulously. But unlike what happens in his categorical syllogistic, here his investigation does not always meet with success: many of his theses appear odd and not very convincing. For example, he maintains that in Barbara, if the major premise is necessary and the minor is categorical, the conclusion is necessary, whereas if the major is categorical and the minor necessary, the conclusion is categorical. To explain this odd point of view, we may suppose that Aristotle interprets "necessarily A belongs to every B" as meaning "every B is necessarily-A"; the modal operator in this case bears only on the predicate of the proposition. Consequently, by virtue of the fact that B belongs to all C, one may legitimately deduce that necessarily-A belongs to all C. Aristotle's viewpoint thus becomes entirely legitimate.

However, this interpretation does not account for other affirmations on Aristotle's part, particularly in his analysis of conversion, which appear to imply, on the contrary, that the modal operator applies to the categorical proposition as a whole. Hence there is an oscillation in the understanding of the modal operator, and this systematic ambiguity disrupts the foundations of the theory, thus greatly diminishing the interest of the Aristotelian system of modal inferences.

Aristotle does not usually define modal operators. He certainly does not appear to have the idea that modern semantic theories seem to suggest, namely, that a proposition is necessary if it is true in all conceivable situations or, as they say, in all possible worlds, whereas it is possible if it is true in at least one of these worlds. Some interpreters think that his idea of necessity is connected to time: A is necessary if it is always true. The difficulty of this conception is that, on this basis, a proposition is possible if it is true at one moment at least, which seems to run counter to the intuition, apparently shared by Aristotle, that there are possibilities that are never realized. The perspective that seems most in harmony with the texts is that of a syntactic characterization of modality: a proposition is possible if from the supposition that it is true no contradiction follows. Along the same lines, although Aristotle never says this explicitly, a necessary proposition could be defined as a proposition whose falsity would lead to a contradiction. But Aristotle does not systematically develop this line of interpretation of modalities, the seeds of which are nevertheless present in his work.

Let us consider one more problem related to the logic of modalities, a problem that, although marginal in Aristotle's logic, has been and remains at the heart of a vast historical and theoretical debate: the problem of contingent future propositions and their relation to determinism. Let us consider a contingent proposition concerning the future: "Tomorrow there will be a naval battle," to use Aristotle's example. Tomorrow, this proposition will surely have a truth value: if the event takes place, the proposition is true; if the event does not take place, it is false. Let us suppose that tomorrow there really is a naval battle: then today it is already true to say that tomorrow there will be a naval battle. But if it is true to say this already today, tomorrow there cannot not be a naval battle. The future is therefore in reality not contingent; it is already determined.

The interpreters do not agree on the response Aristotle would have made to this difficulty to maintain the contingency of the future. The most broadly accepted thesis is that he would deny that a contingent future proposition had a truth value before the event to which it referred took place or not: before the battle occurs, it is neither true nor false to affirm that tomorrow there will be a naval battle. Since the event in question is contingent, the truth conditions of the propositions that speak of it ahead of time are not given; these propositions thus have no truth value, and the objection of the determinist is completely disarmed. The disadvantage of this solution is that one must then admit that Aristotle set limits to certain logical principles, in particular to the principle of bivalence, according to which every proposition is true or false: in effect, he is now acknowledging propositions that are neither true nor false. The general definition of the proposition as the site of truth or falsity would have to be reconsidered and corrected.

Moving on to Stoic logic, we shall focus again on the notion of inference, and it is necessary to begin by describing the Stoic notion of proposition (which the Stoics call *axiōma*). According to them, the proposition is a *lekton*, a term that corresponds to a fundamental notion and that is difficult to translate (it is generally translated by "expressible" or "sayable"). Sextus characterizes it fairly clearly: a *lekton* is what we understand when we hear a meaningful verbal expression pronounced. One might say that *lekta* are the contents of our words, and it is no accident that the *lekton* is often identified with the *semainomenon*, the signified. In fact, the Stoics distinguished—much better than Aristotle did—between three levels of reality: the level of things, *tunchanonta* in their language; the level of signifiers or verbal expressions; and finally the level of *lekta*. To highlight the differences, the Stoics stressed that signifiers and things are corporeal entities, whereas *lekta* are incorporeal. Thus it becomes clear that *lekta* cannot be assimilated to concepts, which are themselves material in that they are affects of the soul, which is a corporeal reality. *Lekta* are rather the contents of our concepts, and to illustrate the distinction, despite the risk of anachronism, one could evoke the Fregean distinction between *Vorstellung*, representation, which is something that belongs to the conscious subject and that is proper to that subject, and *Sinn*, which is what the various representations have in common when one is thinking of the same thing. These representative contents recall the Stoics' *lekta*, and it is not without reason that some authors have related the *lekta* to the Fregean notion of *Sinn*, meaning.

According to the Stoics, *lekta* are either imperfect or perfect. Imperfect *lekta* correspond to the terms that are the constituents of propositions, while perfect ones correspond to the content of propositions; they are what is signified by a proposition. The underlying idea seems to be that propositions have a complete meaning, in contrast to their simple constituents. As for Aristotle, every proposition, for the Stoics, is either true or false; some defend this thesis so rigorously that they accuse Aristotle of not defending it enough, since, as we have seen, he eliminates contingent future propositions from its scope.

For the Stoics, propositions are either simple or complex, depending on the presence or absence of connectors *(sundesmoi)*. Simple propositions (which could be called *atomic* in modern terminology) are either definite, indefinite, or intermediary. Definite propositions are those whose subject is a demonstrative or "deictic," such as "This one is a man." Indefinite propositions, such as "Someone is walking," do not refer to a specific individual. Intermediary propositions, such as "Socrates is a man" or "Man is mortal," are different from the other types in that they do not have a deictic as their subject, unlike definite propositions, but they are not indeterminate like the indefinites. Sextus Empiricus, who presents this doctrine, reports that according to the Stoics the truth of an indefinite proposition implies the truth of a corresponding definite proposition. He also seems to suppose that the truth of an intermediary proposition implies that of a corresponding definite proposition, but this thesis seems to be disproved by the position attributed to Chrysippus, according to which "Dion is dead," pronounced after Dion's death, is true, even though the corresponding deictic, "This one is dead," has no truth value, as we shall see later on.

The theory of complex propositions that has been handed down is better articulated. The Stoics distinguished among several species of complex propositions, or, to use modern jargon again, *molecular* propositions; one of their principal merits is that they elaborated a theory of relations among propositions that logically precedes the Aristotelian theory of relations among terms. They considered first of all disjunctive propositions, in which *or* is the principal connector. Disjunctive propositions are either exclusive (one of the two propositions that constitute them is true and the other false) or inclusive (nothing prevents both propositions from being true); in their theory of inference, as we shall see, the Stoics make greater use of the first type than of the second. But the distinction is blurred by the fact that they seem to characterize exclusive disjunction in stronger terms than the terms, today called truth-functional, in which I have just introduced it: they seem to require, for disjunction to be true, not only that one of its constituents be true and the other false, but also that they be mutually incompatible. If we give this term a modal value, we have a strong definition of disjunction that goes beyond the purely truth-functional conception. The Stoic definition of conjunctive propositions, in contrast, comes closer to a truth-functional presentation: in a conjunctive proposition, the principal connector is *and,* and a conjunctive proposition is true if and only if all its constituents are true.

But the sort of complex proposition that most interested the Stoics is the conditional proposition, of the type "If it is raining, then the earth is wet." There are at least two reasons for this. First, this type had been extensively discussed in the tradition to which the Stoic school was most directly attached. In addition, the truth conditions of conditional propositions were linked, for the Stoics, to the notion of the validity of the arguments. The polemic over conditionals had begun with a discussion between Diodorus Cronus and his disciple Philon. The latter had maintained that a conditional is true either if its antecedent is false or if its consequent is true. According to this criterion, "If the Earth flies, then there is sunshine during the day" is true, and "If there is sunshine during the day, then the Earth flies" is false. This conception comes curiously close to the modern notion of *material implication,* but the analogy cannot be carried too far. From the viewpoint of material implication, a conditional such as "If I am speaking, then $2 + 2 = 4$" is not only legitimate but also true. Its legitimacy depends on the fact that the connector "if . . . then" is conceived in a truth-functional fashion: in other words, any two propositions may be the constituents of a conditional, on the sole condition that they be true or false. This is not of course what happens in ordinary language, where other conditions are required to construct a meaningful conditional. The ancients probably presupposed these conditions of ordinary language without analyzing them.

Diodorus maintained, against Philon, that a proposition such as "If it is night, then I am speaking," true according to Philon when I am actually speaking, must in reality be judged false, because there is a moment when it is night and when I am not speaking. This observation shows that Diodorus's notion of the conditional is stronger than Philon's, and that it is qualified in terms of time: for a conditional to be accepted as true, it does not suffice that it not be the case that its antecedent is true and its consequent false; it is also necessary that that situation *never* occur. In other words, a conditional is true, according to Diodorus, if its consequent is true every time the antecedent is true.

In a well-known passage of his *Hypotyposes,* Sextus Empiricus presents two additional types of conditionals, arranged by increasing strength. After Philon's conditional and Diodorus's, there is a third type, which Sextus attributes to "those who introduce connection": it is true only if the negation of the consequent is *incompatible* with the antecedent. A fourth conditional has as its distinguishing feature that its consequent is potentially contained in the antecedent. The testimony of Diogenes Laertius suggests that the definition in terms of connection should be attributed to the Stoics. For them, he says, a conditional such as "If it is day, then Dion is walking" is false, because the negation of the consequent, "Dion is not walking," is not incompatible with the antecedent "it is day." Conversely, a conditional such as "If it is day, it is light" is true, because the negation of its consequent is incompatible with its antecedent. The notion of incompatibility must then be understood as a modal notion: a conditional is true if the conjunction of the negation of the consequent and its antecedent is *impossible*. This interpretation of the Stoic conditional brings to mind the definition of *strict implication*, introduced by Lewis in modern logic. But one must stress the difference that affects the conception of the modal operator of impossibility here. In modern schools of semantics posterior to Lewis, the notion of impossibility is a logical notion connected to that of a possible world: a proposition A is (logically) impossible if it is not true in any possible world, a possible world being a world in which the only invariants are determined by the laws of logic and mathematics. From this point of view, it is difficult to believe that a conditional such as "If it is day, it is light" can be deemed true: there is no logical impossibility in conceiving of days without light. But the Stoic notions of necessity and possibility were linked to physical notions rather than logical ones; furthermore, Stoic metaphysics, which conceives of the development of the world as identical to that of the *logos*, did not encourage any differentiation between physical and logical. The definition of the modal operators transmitted by our sources confirms this interpretation: the notion of possibility is defined here with reference to the presence of favorable external conditions. Once again in a polemic against Philon, the Stoics maintained, for example, that it is impossible for a piece of wood at the bottom of the sea to burn, because the external circumstances prevent the realization of this possibility that otherwise the wood would have in its own right. Their notion of possibility is thus largely conditioned by physical possibility, and there is no reason to think that it would be otherwise for the other modalities. In any event, it is clear that the Stoic conditional is stronger than Diodorus's: Diodorus merely imposes an invariance of truth with respect to time, whereas the Stoics extend that demand to all possible situations.

Why did the Stoics feel the need to fall back on such a strong conception of the conditional? The question is related to that of the validity of arguments. In general, an argument is characterized in extremely abstract terms: it is simply a matter of a series of propositions, the last one of which is called the *conclusion*, whereas the others, called *premises*, have the function of allowing access to the conclusion. According to Sextus Empiricus, for the Stoics, arguments are either nonconclusive or conclusive. Conclusive arguments may in turn be true or not true, depending on whether the propositions that constitute them are true or not, and true arguments are either demonstrative or nondemonstrative. As was the case with Aristotle, the truth of the constituent propositions is not a necessary condition of the validity of the arguments, which proves that the Stoics, too, had a *logical* theory of arguments.

The crucial point is of course the distinction between conclusive and nonconclusive arguments. The Stoic position, at least starting with Chrysippus, is simple and clear: an argument is conclusive if the conditional that has as its antecedent the conjunction of its premises, and as its consequent its conclusion, is true. Given this, we can understand why the Stoics preferred a type of conditional that was stronger than Philon's or Diodorus's. Naturally, the adequacy of such a definition of conclusive arguments, or to put it in modern terms, of logical validity, depends heavily on the notion of necessity that specifies the conditional. In all plausibility, it is a question of a physical and not a logical necessity; this obviously compromises the legitimacy of identifying the Stoic position with the modern position insofar as the notion of validity in terms of universal necessity is concerned.

The Stoics divided conclusive arguments into those that were conclusive "but not according to the method" and those that were conclusive "according to the method." We do not have a formal definition of the first group; we can only make conjectures on the basis of the examples preserved. It is reasonable to suppose that an argument that is conclusive but not according to the method is an argument that satisfies the general definition of conclusive arguments, but without exemplifying a logical schema. Let us consider the following argument:

(10) Coriscos is a man
_____

Coriscos is an animal

This argument is valid because, at least in one sense, the negation of its conclusion is incompatible with its premise. But if we were to formalize it, we would get the logical schema "A, thus B," in which "A" and "B" hold the places of any two propositions, a schema that in general is not valid, nor always conclusive. This means that (10) is correct only in function of the content of the two propositions in question.

According to our conjecture, arguments that are conclusive according to the method must be those that are particular cases of logical schemas. The Stoics divided the latter into *syllogistic* arguments (a term that has a very different meaning for them than it does for Aristotle) and arguments that were *reducible to syllogistic arguments.* It is plausible that the arguments called syllogistic in one branch of the tradition are those that, elsewhere, are called *anapodictic* (indemonstrable) and that have a role more or less comparable to that of the axioms of a logical theory. But they are not axioms properly speaking (nor are they rules of inference), because it is normally required of the axioms of a theory that they be independent, that is, that they not be derived from other axioms, which is certainly not the case with the Stoics' undemonstrable arguments. We may believe that these were chosen on the basis of their immediate and incontrovertible character.

The first undemonstrable corresponds to what modern logicians, following the example of their medieval forebears, call the *Modus Ponens* (or more precisely, the *Modus Ponendo Ponens*). The following argument is an example:

> If it is raining, the earth is wet
> It is raining
> _____
> The earth is wet

The Stoics expressed the corresponding schema by means of numbers that took the place of propositions and that had a function analogous to that of the schematic letters of Aristotelian syllogistic, with one difference: the latter, as we have seen, take the place of general terms, not of propositions. Thus the Stoic schema had the following form:

> If the first, the second
> The first
> _____
> The second

It is easy to observe that in this case "the first" and "the second" take the place of the propositions that constitute, respectively, the antecedent and the consequent of a conditional.

The second undemonstrable corresponds to the *Modus (Tollendo) Tollens*, which consists in concluding the negation of the antecedent of a conditional on the basis of the negation of its consequent:

> If the first, the second
> Not the second
> _____
> Not the first

The third undemonstrable is based on a conjunctive proposition. If we posit its negation, and if we affirm one of its components, then our conclusion must be the negation of the other, that is:

> Not (the first and the second)
> The first
> _____
> Not the second

The last two undemonstrables concern disjunction: the first of them at least requires the strong notion of exclusive disjunction to be considered valid. It is the fourth undemonstrable that makes it possible to conclude the negation of one of the members of the disjunction on the basis of the positing of the other:

> The first or the second
> The first
> _____
> Not the second

Finally, in the last undemonstrable, one infers one of the members of the disjunction on the basis of the negation of the other:

> The first or the second
> Not the first
> _____
> The second

The correctness of this last inference does not formally require exclusive disjunction; inclusive disjunction is sufficient. But for the uniformity of the system, it is probably appropriate to think that the *or* of the first premise has, as in the fourth undemonstrable, an exclusive sense.

According to the Stoics, all arguments that are conclusive "according to the method" are reducible to the five undemonstrables; this reduction constitutes the inverse of a deduction of the former on the basis of the latter. The idea resembles the one we have seen at work, in Aristotle, in the reduction of syllogisms of the second and third figure to syllogisms of the first figure. The difference is that the Stoic undertaking is much more formal, in the sense that the Stoics seem to have formulated a series of rules that govern these deductions. They called these rules *themata*, and we know that there were five of them, but we do not have explicit formulations for all five. Without going into detail here, we can get an idea of the type of rules represented by the *themata*, and of their function, by considering, for example, the following two inferences, which are examples of the first undemonstrable:

> (11) If A, then (if A then B)
>   A
>   _____
>   If A then B

and

(12) If A then B
    A
    ———————
    B

The third *thema* explicitly authorizes us to replace, in (12), the premise "if A then B" by the premises of which it is the conclusion in (11). In this way we obtain the following inference, which is reduced, by the inverse route, to the first undemonstrable:

(13) If A, then (if A then B)
    A
    ————————————
    B

The Stoic attitude toward modal logic is particularly innovative, especially if one considers the contribution of Chrysippus, the school's great logician. On the definition of the modal operators, the Stoics were opposed to Philon and Diodorus, but I prefer to consider here the Stoic response to Diodorus's Master argument. This response is not unified. We know that Cleanthus had attacked the most "physical" premise of the argument, the one that concerns the necessity of the past. Chrysippus, on the other hand, denied the validity of the "logical" premise according to which from the possible no impossible follows. He invoked the following counterexample. Let us consider the conditional

(14) If Dion is dead, this one is dead

and examine its antecedent. When Dion is living, the proposition is false, but it can become true: it becomes true as soon as Dion dies; "Dion is dead" is thus a possible proposition. As for the consequent of (14), "this one is dead," during Dion's life it is never true. But what happens when Dion dies? Unlike "Dion is dead," "this one is dead" does not become true, because "this one" is a deictic that, referring to a person, cannot be the subject of a proposition except in the presence of the person in question. Once Dion is dead, the proposition "this one is dead" is "destroyed"; it no longer possesses the truth value "true." This proposition can never become true; it is impossible. We thus have a case of a possible from which an impossible follows.

Without going into detail here, let us simply note that Chrysippus's argument requires a distinction between what is never true (impossible) and what is always false (necessary). "This one is dead" is never true, although without being always false, since at the moment when Dion dies, the proposition is destroyed and has no more truth value. We are perhaps in the presence of a prefiguration of the "lacunary" semantics that arouse so much interest among contemporary logicians. We cannot rule out the possibility that this distinction between impossibility and necessity, in which the first is a weaker notion than the second, allowed Chrysippus to claim that one could accept the possibility of true predictions relative to future events, even while rejecting the determinism that, according to some, this possibility would imply, according to Cicero's testimony in his *De fato*. But the Ciceronian texts are controversial, and no interpretation has won unanimous acceptance.

If Cicero is to be believed, Chrysippus was not the only one to cast doubt on a well-supported logical thesis in order to avoid determinism: Epicurus, denying the validity of the principle of bivalence for future contingent propositions, had done much worse. His idea seems to be that a contingent proposition in the future can be declared true only when its truth conditions are given, that is, the situations that make it possible to attribute to it a truth value. To go back to Aristotle's example, one cannot attribute a truth value to "Tomorrow there will be a naval battle" before one of two situations comes about: either the one that irrevocably determines the event or the one that the event itself constitutes. In this sense, the proposition is at present neither true nor false, and the principle of bivalence does not apply to it. Consequently, one cannot conclude from the truth of propositions concerning the future that the realization of the corresponding events is necessarily not the case.

Although plausible, this solution to the problem of determinism, which according to some goes all the way back to Aristotle, gave rise to ridicule and hostility among ancient authors. Cicero speaks of it scornfully, and the ancient Peripatetics carefully avoided attributing it to their master, Aristotle. Boethius reacted violently to the idea, put forward by certain Stoics, that Aristotle would have recognized limitations on the principle of bivalence in the case of future contingent propositions.

I shall conclude this brief presentation of ancient logic by mentioning one other characteristic feature of the Stoic position, found most notably in Chrysippus. As we have seen, the Megarian school was distinguished by its interest in logical paradoxes. Not only was the invention of the most important of these attributed to Eubulides, but in addition, Diodorus committed suicide, it is said, because he could not bear the shame of having been unable to solve a paradox that had been proposed to him in public. This unverifiable anecdote reflects the interest and the tension that the introduction of paradoxes had aroused, as well as the difference in attitude toward them between the Megarian and Stoic traditions, on the one hand, and the Platonic and Aristotelian traditions, on the other. Galen sets out the latter effectively: logical paradoxes have to be studied to provide the apprentice philosopher with the means to avoid being embarrassed by false experts. To master paradoxes, all one needs is a certain skill and familiarity with the laws of correct logic.

The Stoics, especially the most ancient ones, studied paradoxes very closely. In the catalogue of Chrysippus's works that has been preserved, many treatises are devoted to sophisms; many titles, in particular, have to do with the Liar Paradox. The few allusions found in Cicero do not allow us to understand very well what solution he may have proposed for this paradox. He seems to have suggested that the crucial proposition "I am lying" is a proposition endowed with meaning, and yet that it is not capable of being qualified as true or false. If this was Chrysippus's point of view, it is easy to see that it implied a revision of one of the foundational principles of Stoic logical theory, namely, the thesis according to which every proposition is true or false. In this sense, Chrysippus's attitude is much closer to the modern perspective than the Platonico-Aristotelian tradition is. To escape from paradoxes, it does not suffice to refine one's logical competence and to ferret out linguistic and structural errors; one must resign oneself to revising certain intuitions concerning the fundamental notions of logic, for example, the notion of truth. Chrysippus seems to have embarked on this path because he was aware that at least some paradoxes, far from being captious arguments destined to embarrass the naive, convey the obscurity of certain fundamental notions and thus require, if they are to be resolved, a revision of our way of approaching them.

After the apogee of ancient Stoicism, the creative thrust of Greece in the domain of logic began to decline. On one side, the Peripatetics exhausted themselves in challenging the Stoic innovations, seeking to show that their good aspects were already present in Aristotle and that the rest was false or devoid of interest. On the other side, the Stoics seemed unaware of the rival school, and they went on trying to give new foundations to logic as it had been developed by the first masters of the school. Their efforts succeeded in creating a sort of logical *koine*, which was crystallized in manuals and which was used even by the Stoics' critics. But the taste for innovation was fading, even if brilliant intuitions come to light here and there. One of these is certainly the solution of the problem of logical determinism that appeared in the framework of Neoplatonism, with the distinction between what is true in a determinate fashion and what is true in an indeterminate fashion. The proposition "Tomorrow there will be a naval battle" is true or false before the conditions that determine whether or not the event occurs are given. However, before those conditions are realized, the proposition is true only in an indeterminate fashion; the possibility that the contrary event will occur remains open. It is only tomorrow, when the event in question occurs or when the conditions that determine it irrevocably are met, that the proposition receives a determinate truth value: at that moment, the possibility of the contrary no longer exists. Although it is presented by authors such as Ammonius and Boethius as an interpretation of Aristotle's position, this perspective is particularly innovative, and it has important implications for the notion of possibility and the semantics of propositions.

The discussion reported by Ammonius about the possibility of quantifying the predicate of a proposition is equally interesting. Aristotle had denied the legitimacy of such a quantification; Ammonius devotes many pages to challenging an attempt to develop it in a systematic fashion. His faithfulness to the master leads him astray here: by accepting this perspective, he would easily have arrived at a conception of relational propositions comparable to the modern conception, with immediate advantages for inferences that include such propositions. But these are only details, and they betray a lack of innovative spirit and logical creativity. A new forward thrust does not come until the heyday of the Middle Ages, when scholars gather in the legacy of antiquity and develop it in profoundly original ways.

MARIO MIGNUCCI
Translated by Catherine Porter and Jeannine Pucci

Bibliography

Ackrill, John L., ed. *Aristotle: Categories and De Interpretatione, Translated with Notes and Glossary.* Oxford: Clarendon Press, 1963.

Becker, Albrecht. *Die aristotelische Theorie der Möglichkeitsschlüsse: Eine logisch-philologische Untersuchung der Kapitel 13–22 von Aristoteles Analytice Priora I.* Berlin: Jünker and Dünnhaupt, 1933.

Blanché, Robert. *La logique et son histoire, d'Aristote à Russell.* Paris: Armand Colin, 1970.

Bochenski, Innocentius M. *A History of Formal Logic.* Trans. and ed. Ivo Thomas. 2nd ed. New York: Chelsea, 1970.

Brunschwig, Jacques, ed. *Les Stoïciens et leur logique.* Paris: Vrin, 1978.

Döring, Klaus. *Die Megariker: Kommentierte Sammlung der Testimonien.* Amsterdam: Grüner, 1972.

Döring, Klaus, and Theodor Ebert, eds. *Dialektiker und Stoiker: Zur Logik der Stoa und ihrer Vorläufer.* Stuttgart: Steiner, 1993.

Frede, Michaël. *Die stoische Logik.* Göttingen: Vandenhoeck and Ruprecht, 1974.

Hintikka, Jaakko. *Time and Necessity: Studies in Aristotle's Theory of Modality.* Oxford: Clarendon Press, 1973.

Hülser, Karlheinz. *Die Fragmente zur Dialektik der Stoiker.* 4 vols. Stuttgart: Frommann-Holzboog, 1987–1988.

Kneale, William, and Martha Kneale. *The Development of Logic.* Oxford: Clarendon Press, 1962.

Lear, Jonathan. *Aristotle and Logical Theory.* Cambridge: Cambridge University Press, 1980.

Lukasiewicz, Jan. *Aristotle's Syllogistic from the Standpoint of Modern Formal Logic.* 2nd ed. Oxford: Clarendon Press, 1957.

Mates, Benson. *Stoic Logic.* 2nd ed. Berkeley: University of California Press, 1961.

Mignucci, Mario. *Il significato della logica stoica.* 2nd ed. Bologna: Pàtron, 1967.

Mignucci, Mario, ed. *Aristotele: Gli analitici primi. Traduzione, introduzione, commento.* Naples: Loffredo, 1969.

Muller, Robert. *Les Mégariques: Fragments et témoignages.* Paris: Vrin, 1985.

Nortmann, Ulrich. *Modale Syllogismen, mögliche Welten, Essentialismus: Eine Analyse der aristotelischen Modallogik.* Berlin: De Gruyter, 1996.

Patzig, Günther. *Aristotle's Theory of Syllogism.* Trans. Jonathan Barnes. Dordrecht: Reidel, 1968.

Ross, W. D., ed. *Aristotle's Prior and Posterior Analytics: A Revised Text with Introduction and Commentary.* Oxford: Clarendon Press, 1949.

Thom, Paul. *The Logic of Essentialism: An Interpretation of Aristotle's Modal Syllogistic.* Boston: Kluwer, 1996.

Vuillemin, Jules. *Nécessité ou contingence: L'aporie de Diodore et les systèmes philosophiques.* Paris: Editions de Minuit, 1984.

Weidemann, Hermann, ed. *Aristoteles: Peri Hermeneias, übersetz und erläutert.* Berlin: Akademie Verlag, 1994.

MATHEMATICS

To THE ANCIENT GREEKS we owe the notion of mathematics as a form of theoretical knowledge, a body of propositions arranged in a deductively ordered sequence. In this conception, the project of geometry is not the manipulation of figures in physical constructions but the understanding of their properties in pure thought. The transition from *praxis* to *theōria*—from mathematics as *technē* (techniques for dealing with practical activities) to mathematics as *epistēmē* and *gnōsis* (a form of pure knowledge)—occurred only once in human history, namely, among the classical Greeks. No earlier mathematical tradition gives evidence of such a theoretical dimension, and where one encounters mathematical theory among later traditions, it is in the context of some manner of borrowing from the ancient Greek precedent, either through translation of texts or through personal contacts. But already at the time of Plato, ca. 370 B.C.E., as we see in mathematical passages such as *Republic* 510c–d, this shift, with the accompanying emphasis on deductive reasoning in mathematics, could be taken as given and cited as a paradigm toward the rigorization of epistemology in general.

In the following account I shall attempt to trace out the developing relation of the two strands, the technical and the philosophical. It is well to bear in mind, however, that our principal documents, the Greek mathematical treatises, patterned on the model of Euclid's *Elements*, are directed toward the exposition of technical subject matter. Although executed with a sophisticated sense of the demands of demonstrative method, they are not formal foundational efforts as such and only rarely and obliquely address issues of an explicitly metamathematical sort. In this regard, their situation is hardly different from that of textbooks in any mathematical field today, but it must condition any project that seeks to reconstruct the character and origins of the theoretical sensibility itself among the ancients.

ORIGINS

In the modern conception of mathematics, practical forms like commercial arithmetic and surveying geometry are taken to be but a prelude to the essential forms of mathematics. The progression from such applied forms to the corresponding abstract fields may be viewed either as pedagogical or as conceptual. But it is reasonable to see a chronological element as well: that the earliest forms of mathematical activity in any given culture would be of this practical sort, only later developing from this into theory.

Remarkably, those Greeks who speak of the origins of mathematics pass over the essential issue of the timing, manner, and intent of the earliest reorientation from practice toward theory. Instead, they are more concerned with the origins of mathematical technique, that is, the first discoveries of specific technical results. One typical account assigns the first geometry to Egyptian surveyors, compelled to reestablish property markers after the Nile floods; Proclus maintains this, and passages from Herodotus and other early authorities indicate the likely tradition Proclus here relied on. In just this way, according to Proclus, the precise knowledge of numbers *(tōn arithmōn akribēs gnōsis)* took its start among the Phoenicians' activities in commerce and exchange. At the same time, Proclus projects certain interpretive conceptions of his own, for he observes: "It is not at all surprising that the discovery both of this (sc. geometry) and the other sciences *(epistēmai)* commenced from need *(chreia)*, since everything in *genesis* proceeds by moving from the incomplete *(ateles)* to the complete *(teleion)*. It is thus reasonable that the transformation *(metabasis)* would occur from perception *(aisthēsis)* to reckoning *(logismos)* and from this to mind *(nous)*."

Despite Proclus's Neoplatonist gloss, his view of theory as developing out of practice seems reasonable, and there is some evidence, albeit quite slender, corroborating it. Presumably, the oldest forms of arithmetic inquiry grew out of practical activities, such as commerce. Still, Proclus's citation of the Phoenicians as the precedent for the Greeks raises questions, since we possess little information on how the early Greeks did arithmetic, and that does not necessarily point to borrowings from the Levant.

Two different numeral systems were already current among the Greeks before the middle of the 5th century B.C.E., as attested in inscriptions. The more primitive system, sometimes called acrophonic, since some of its numerals are formed from the initial letters of the corresponding number words, follows the base-ten additive principle, much like the Egyptian hieroglyphic system and the Roman numeral system. This mode quickly becomes unwieldy for representing large numbers, however, and has little value for the execution of arithmetic operations. It appears that such numerals served their primary function as recording symbols, where the computations could be performed via abacus. More than a dozen specimens of abacus survive from the classical period to support this view.

Alternatively, in what is sometimes called the Herodian system, the Greeks represented numbers via the letters of the alphabet: to represent each of the initial values from 1 to 9, they used in sequence the first nine letters (with the archaic *digamma* inserted in sixth position); for the next range, by tens from 10 to 90 they used the next nine letters (with archaic *goppa* in ninth position), and for the hundreds, the remaining nine letters (with archaic *sampi* last).

This scheme is extended to higher numbers by special marks: for thousands, a stroke is prefixed to the corresponding digit symbol, from 1 to 9, while for multiples of 10,000 the symbol M (for *myrias*) is written with the appropriate numeral as superscript. For still higher values, a variety of schemes were introduced, but, as one would expect, the contexts demanding these were rare and specialized. For instance, Theon of Alexandria (4th century C.E.) requires third-order myriads (signified by the symbol MMM) to work out his computation of the volume of the earth in cubic stades.

Modern critics, familiar with the so-called Hindu-Arabic numerals that utilize a more powerful place system, typically underestimate the computational capacity of the Greeks' alphabetical scheme. But in practice, the arithmetic operations are performed in this system little differently than in a place system. It would be difficult to insist that Greek arithmetic, whether practical or theoretical, was hindered in any way by this alphabetical mode during the span of twelve centuries when it was prevalent. Since the Greek alphabet is certainly derived from the Phoenicians, one might naturally suppose that the alphabetical numeral system traced back to the same source. This is Proclus's view, as we have seen, perhaps for this very reason, and it may be correct. But confirmation from old Phoenician inscriptions is wanting. When the same alphabetical mode (in Semitic characters) is attested in Semitic inscriptions, it is in the Hellenistic period, apparently under the influence of Greek precedents.

In terms of the most elementary forms of arithmetical training, the Greeks appear to have been directly influenced by Egyptian models. Plato cites with approval the Egyptian practice of employing games to teach children the arithmetic procedures (*Laws* 819b). Certain computational methods, attested in Greek papyri from the Hellenistic period onward, are hardly distinguishable from those in the oldest surviving Egyptian papyri from the middle of the second millennium B.C.E. Most striking is the technique of computing with fractions, where values are expressed in terms of sums of unit-fractional parts; for instance, the equivalent of $\frac{2}{7}$ is written as 4′28′ (that is, $\frac{1}{4} + \frac{1}{28}$). This same mode persists among the Greeks, even after the introduction of a more flexible general mode of fractions (of form p/q).

A correspondingly early link with Mesopotamian numerical methods is difficult to discern. Already within the Old Babylonian dynasties (early second millennium B.C.E.), a sexagesimal place system was developed for carrying out the arithmetic operations. This powerful innovation, however, seems long to have had no circulation outside Mesopotamia and to have reached the Greeks not before the 2nd century B.C.E. Even then, the Greeks adopted it only within the special field of astronomical computation (see below), which doubtless was the context of its transmission to them. Some special areas of number theory have counterparts in Mesopotamian documents. In particular, a remarkable tablet from the Old Babylonian period (Plimpton 322 at Columbia University) lists numbers related to fifteen cases of so-called rational triples (integers a, b, c such that $a^2 + b^2 = c^2$) in a manner that indicates awareness of a general rule for their formation. Among the Greeks the same numbers, including their formation rules, are found in Euclid, Diophantus, and the Neopythagorean arithmetics, and may well have been known in the classical period, perhaps through transmission from Eastern sources. But the time and manner of this transmission, if such is the case, has not been determined.

A similar ambiguity attends speculation on the origins of geometry. A powerful set of geometric techniques are documented in Mesopotamian sources. And it happens that geometric identities of the same form are set out in Euclid's Book II (e.g., propositions 5 and 6), and they are applied in Euclid's *Data* and Diophantus's *Arithmetica*. Such coincidences suggest a Mesopotamian source for this part of the early Greek geometry, as Solomon Gandz, Otto Neugebauer, and B. L. van der Waerden have argued. Acceptance of this proposal, however, has been far from unanimous.

How is the question of transmission to be resolved? It would seem reasonable that geometric techniques of this kind were transmitted to the Greeks by Egyptian teachers—who in their turn were indebted to an even earlier transmission from the older Mesopotamian tradition. Encountering this tradition in Egypt in the 5th century, Greek scholars would naturally take it to be a native tradition.

PYTHAGOREANS AND ELEATICS

In describing the earliest phases of Greek mathematical theory, both ancient and modern commentators typically turn to Pythagoras and his school. It is maintained, according to the account in Iamblichus, that when the Samian, expelled from his home city for political reasons, completed travels in Babylon and Egypt, he established his base at Croton in Magna Graecia and there founded an ascetic community devoted to studies in philosophy, theology, politics, cosmology, and mathematics. Proclus credits Pythagoras for founding the philosophical curriculum on mathematics and for abstracting geometry from its concrete manifestations. But he is here apparently only glossing a line taken from Iamblichus: "Pythagoras converted the philosophy of geometry into the figure of a liberal education, by examining its principles from above and investigating its theorems both immaterially [*ahylōs*] and conceptually [*noērōs*]" (ed. Friedlein, 65.16–19). However prominent a reputation the Pythagoreans have come to acquire, the most reliable evidence of early Greek mathematics does not easily sustain such a view. In the case of Proclus's testimony, for instance, this commentator, who has no reason at all to underrate the Pythagorean role, assigns to Pythagoras only two geometric findings: "He discovered the subject of the irrationals and the construction of the cosmic figures." But even this is dubious, since it anachronistically assigns to Pythagoras what appear to be later studies of the irrationals and the construction of the regular solids.

The prominence of the Pythagoreans thus appears to be a historical construct fostered by Neoplatonists like Iamblichus and Proclus, who conceived the Pythagoreans as prototypes of their own Neoplatonism. Surveying the testimonia most likely to be based on the oldest accounts, such as Aristotle and Eudemus, one can attribute to the Pythagoreans a relatively modest core of mathematical study: a central core of arithmetic studies, together with a few related studies in geometry and its applications in cosmology and the theory of nature.

In arithmetic the Pythagoreans inquired into the properties of number, such as odd and even numbers, figured numbers (e.g., triangular and square numbers), and the like. Certain results of this sort appear to have been examined via quasi-geometric configurations in which the units of the numbers are figured as points (or marks, such as the letter *alpha*), perhaps inspired by the pebble counters *(psēphoi)* used in the abacus.

The early Pythagorean arithmetic also embraced studies of ratios and their application to the harmonic intervals, for instance, that the interval of the octave *(dia pasōn)* is expressible by the ratio 2 : 1, the fifth *(dia pente)* by 3 : 2, the fourth *(dia tessarōn)* by 4 : 3, and the whole tone by 9 : 8. These are plainly set out in a fragment from Philolaus (late 5th century B.C.E.), although they are likely to relate to earlier studies, perhaps by Pythagoras himself. In the more elaborate scheme developed by the Pythagorean Archytas of Tarentum early in the 4th century B.C.E., the consonant intervals are associated with epimoric ratios (that is, those of form $n + 1 : n$), and he establishes that subdivision of any such interval (most notably, the whole tone interval 9 : 8) into equal half intervals is impossible arithmetically.

However modest this body of arithmetic results may seem, one must recognize that they already partake of that important transition we are examining: these are researches into *arithmētikē* in the theoretical sense, the properties of numbers purely as such, rather than of numbers taken to be the measures of bodies or objects of one sort or another.

For the Pythagoreans, arithmetic became a template for inquiring into cosmology and the theory of nature. Their view is encapsulated by Aristotle in the slogan, "All is number." But its meaning, if indeed one may rightly assign it to the Pythagoreans, is ambiguous. On some accounts, it has been interpreted to entail a form of "number atomism" in which pebble configurations of the type illustrated above might be extended into representations of all physical bodies. Some such notion may be intended in an obscure testimonium relating to the Pythagorean Ecphantus. But Aristotle seems to have in mind a more general concept: that the structural relations among things can be expressed in terms of numerical ratios. One might suppose that such an association of mathematics within reasoning about nature might sponsor concerns over the logical coherence of mathematical claims and their validation. But Aristotle's examples of Pythagorean applications of mathematics do not support this view, for much of Pythagorean speculation is mere numerology: the *tetraktys* (the number 10 figured as a triangular array, $1 + 2 + 3 + 4$) symbolizes health and perfection, 4 represents justice, and so on. Aristotle even seems to ridicule certain applications of this scheme, as when he criticizes the Pythagoreans for introducing a hypothetical planet to bring the number of heavenly bodies up to ten.

In the historical sources, a few direct attributions of geometric results are made to Pythagoreans. To them, according to Proclus, Eudemus assigns the theorem that the sum of the angles in a triangle equals two right angles. Proclus and others know of traditions that ascribe to Pythagoras himself the theorem that in any right triangle the square of the hypotenuse equals the sum of the squares of the two sides adjacent to the right angle. But in Plutarch this attribution occurs in the context of a dubious anecdote: that Pythagoras sacrificed an ox in celebration of the discovery of the "famous figure" (*periklees gramma; Moralia* 1094b). Plutarch himself is uncertain whether the anecdote relates to the theorem on the hypotenuse or to the technique of area application. Even worse, Pythagoras would hardly have celebrated any such discovery in this way, given that his reform of Greek cultic practice focused on the abolition of animal sacrifice.

A few testimonia assign to Pythagoreans the construction of regular polygons, in particular the pentagon (a symbol of special significance in the group), as well as the regular dodecahedron. Following the pattern of Euclid's construction of the pentagon, one sees the connection to the "area application" technique which, as we have seen, Eudemus assigns to the "Pythagorean Muse," and through this a possible link to older Mesopotamian methods.

One special field of early geometry deserves further comment. Some time after Pythagoras, researchers in his following became aware of the phenomenon of the "irrational" (*arrhēton*) among geometric magnitudes. According to one later tradition, a certain Pythagorean was penalized by death in shipwreck for making this knowledge public, and some have argued this Pythagorean to be Hippasus of Metapontum, elsewhere reported to have perished by drowning for claiming the discovery of the construction of the dodecahedron as his own. This inference is not assured, however, and even so, the manner and timing of the first discovery of the irrational would remain, as they have, a subject for vigorous debate.

Kurt von Fritz has proposed that the irrational was first recognized by Hippasus through the construction of the regular pentagon (namely, the figure that forms the faces of the regular dodecahedron), for the diagonal d and side s of the pentagon satisfy the extreme and mean ratio, that is, $s + d : d = d : s$, so that $s + d$ and d can be made, respectively, the diagonal and side of a larger pentagon. The construction can be extended in the same proportion either in the upward direction (by successively adding the side and diagonal to form the new diagonal), or alternatively, downward (by subtracting: $d : s = s : d - s$, and so on). In the latter case, one realizes that the possibility of continuing the sequence, to produce ever smaller pentagons, conflicts with any supposition that the initial ratio $d : s$ could equal a ratio of integers; for the successive reduction of integers is necessarily bounded by the unit, and so cannot continue indefinitely. This subtractive procedure, called *anthyphairesis* (or the Euclidean division algorithm, in modern parlance), is the foundation of Euclid's arithmetic theory (Books VII and X), being his means for constructing the greatest common measure of given integers or of given commensurable magnitudes. Prima facie, then, it would not seem unreasonable that this same method underlay the early studies of the ratio of the side and diagonal of the pentagon.

However attractive this reconstruction may seem, it lacks support in the sources. The earliest extant accounts relating to the irrational, in mathematical passages in Plato and Aristotle, never mention the pentagon in this regard but invariably focus on the diagonal and side of the square as the paradigmatic case. For instance, Plato speaks of the "rational and irrational diameters of the pentad" (*Rep.* 546c), meaning 7 and $\sqrt{50}$, respectively, and one may infer in this an oblique reference to a numerical procedure for generating an indefinite sequence of such values—the so-called side and diameter numbers, described by the later Neopythagorean writer Theon of Smyrna (ca. 100 C.E.), that is, $(1,1)$, $(2,3)$, $(5,7)$, . . ., (s,d), $(s + d, 2s + d)$, and so on. As the very terminology reveals, the ancients realized that each pair $s : d$ provides an approximation to the ratio of the side and diameter of the square (i.e., $1 : \sqrt{2}$), although no proof—at best only the ingredients for one—is transmitted in the accounts surviving from Theon, Iamblichus, and Proclus. Associated with this, also indicated in Plato's terminology, is that the limiting value $1 : \sqrt{2}$ is "irrational" (*arrhētos*).

No explicit proof of this incommensurability survives in early sources. But Aristotle alludes to a proof in which the hypothesis of rationality reduces to an impossibility: that the same numbers will be even and odd. A proof of this form is presented among materials appended to Book X of Euclid's *Elements*.

It seems reasonable that the earliest encounter with the irrational followed a pattern comparable to the proof known to Aristotle. It could not have been *discovered* according to this logical format, however, since reasoning by contradiction begins with the explicit statement of the proposition as already known. A geometric configuration seems possible in which the subdivision of the square, as in Plato's *Meno* 82b–85b, leads to ever smaller squares, always preserving the same ratio as the initial side and diameter. Supposing numerical values for both the initial side and diameter, one finds that both these values are even, as are the sides and diameters of *all* the smaller squares derived from them by successive halving. One would realize, however, that any finite number permits of being bisected only finitely many times. A geometric reasoning of this sort would elicit, as if by accident, an awareness of the paradox entailed by assuming numerical values for the side and diameter, and through this realization one could begin to consolidate the reasoning in light of an explicit concept of the "irrational."

Toward the close of the 5th century the knowledge of irrationals was extended. Archytas's theorem that no epimoric interval can be bisected by a numerical term—that is, that no integer is the mean proportional between two numbers that have the ratio $n + 1 : n$—entails a geometric corollary: that the line constructed as mean proportional between lines in an epimoric ratio must be incommensurable with those lines. Although we cannot say whether Archytas actually proposed such a geometric corollary, the manner of its construction and proof would generalize immediately to the theorem that the mean proportional between any two lines whose ratio is not a ratio of square numbers is incommensurable with those lines. Some scholia assign this theorem (an equivalent to Elements X.9) to Plato's younger contemporary Theaetetus. Indeed Plato (Theaetetus 147c–148a) describes how the young Theaetetus inferred a form of the same theorem as he contemplated a more limited result presented by his teacher Theodorus of Cyrene: that the dynamis (that is, square) of 3 feet, for instance, and that of 5, and so on, each has a side that is incommensurable with the unit foot; by stopping at 17 (for reasons unstated in the account) Theodorus left open the description of the whole class of incommensurables entailed by this construction, the project completed by Theaetetus.

Reconstructions of Theodorus's procedure abound, for Plato presents no technical details of the proof beyond the enumeration of the cases. However, inferring from a dramatic episode of this sort, the actual history of these researches is problematic, since Plato's dialectical intent (showing how Theaetetus articulates the general definition under the suggestion of Theodorus's recitation of cases) is clear. Since the discovery of incommensurability most likely arose in the context of the special case of the side and diameter of the square, it is not unreasonable that the first extensions of this discovery would likewise have involved special cases. If Plato's passage does not warrant assigning to Theodorus a role within this transitional research, however, then we have no documentation for assigning any name to it at all.

In view of this limited basis of Pythagorean mathematics, some accounts have looked elsewhere for the emergence of a deductive sensibility. One approach, initiated by Paul Tannery (1887) and modified by Helmut Hasse and Heinrich Scholz (1928), supposes that the discovery of irrationality provoked a "foundations crisis" that stimulated research into the logical basis of geometric theory, culminating in the rigorous methods of limits and proportions instituted by Eudoxus. A variant of this view, set out by Árpád Szabó, locates the stimulus toward rigor, as well as the intuition of the "anti-empirical," in the Eleatic paradoxes. To Parmenides, according to this account, one must assign the development, indeed the very invention, of indirect reasoning. For by inferring the inadmissible, that "what-is-not is," from hypotheses about the reality of change, difference, plurality, inhomogeneity, and the like, Parmenides presumed to establish the invalidity of those hypotheses, that is, that "what-is" must be eternal, immutable, altogether homogeneous, and one. Similarly, Zeno argued that the conventional suppositions about plurality and motion lead to contradictions: if there is a plurality, then being is at once infinitely great and infinitely small (frg. B1-2); if there is motion, then the finite stretch would require infinite time to traverse (the "dichotomy" and the "Achilles"), the moving body would be at rest (the "arrow"), and the double speed would equal the half speed (the "moving rows"). In these paradoxes, not only is the technique of *reductio ad absurdum* forged into an instrument for reasoning, but also the fundamental concepts of mathematics—number, magnitude, infinite divisibility—come under scrutiny. Accordingly, Szabó attempts to construct a path from the early Pythagorean arithmetic studies, under the pressure of Eleatic criticisms, to the expounding of dialectical method by Plato, ultimately to the theoretical synthesis in Euclid's *Elements*.

Hypotheses of this type must be judged on their intrinsic plausibility, for explicit support from mathematical documentation in the pre-Euclidean period is lacking. It is remarkable, however, that none of the ancient discussions of early mathematics, including the accounts in Proclus and the Neopythagoreans, assigns to the Eleatics any role in the development of mathematics as such. Moreover, if Szabó finds it most appropriate to focus on early arithmetic for the first systematization of patterns of proof, it is a puzzle that the major development of theory actually occurs in geometry. Indeed, the arithmetic works nearest to the tradition of Pythagorean arithmetic—the introductions by Nicomachus and Iamblichus—display no proof structure at all.

Such accounts all share the notion that the impulse toward formulating, scrutinizing, and tightening proofs must have come from outside the mathematical field. It is true that a mathematical tradition might adhere to practical techniques without producing a systematic structure of validation (as witness the Egyptian and Mesopotamian traditions). But this need not always be the case. If we can imagine, for instance, how certain Greek geometers, examining the familiar construction for doubling the square, could suddenly realize the paradox involved in supposing that both the side and diameter had integer values, then the project of working out a proof would follow simply from the impulse to make sense of this discovery. Thus, some form of proof structure, however tentative, could be occasioned as a consequence of the earliest exploration of incommensurables.

Organizing the larger domains of geometry did not occur all at once. It was the result of an evolution that spanned at least a century and a half between the Pythagoreans (if we place the beginning of this movement with them) and Euclid, and the interactions with more general philosophical inquiries seem always to have been subtle and bilateral. Moreover, explaining the rise of proof in mathematics via the impetus of Presocratic speculations in philosophy must assume that the emergence of theory and proof in the latter context is well understood. This is far from clear, however. Inquiries into Presocratic modes of reasoning, most notably by G. E. R. Lloyd, have grounded its characteristic emphasis on techniques of validation in the special political circumstances of classical Greece (e.g., the emergence of the polis and the relatively open forms of political interaction entailed by it). Within such an environment the simultaneous emergence of concerns over justification in mathematics and philosophy would seem as plausibly assignable to a parallel response to such political and social stimuli, as to a specific unilateral influence of the one discipline on the other. In any event, it seems that the proper investigation of this question must assimilate the methodological developments in all areas—mathematics, science, medicine, and philosophy—without presupposing a predominant influence by any one of them on the others.

IONIANS

Other than Pythagoras, Proclus names only six figures as being distinguished for geometry in the period before Plato: Thales of Miletus; Ameristus, brother of the poet Stesichorus; Anaxagoras of Clazomenae; Oenopides of Chios; Hippocrates of Chios; and Theodorus of Cyrene. This bare outline can be filled out in a few instances by means of testimony from other commentators.

According to Proclus, Thales was first to recognize that the circle is bisected by its diameter, that the base angles of isosceles triangles are equal, and that the vertical angles formed by the intersection of two lines are equal. But in the case of the theorem that two triangles having two of their angles and the included side equal are congruent (I.26), which, according to Proclus, Eudemus said was necessary for Thales' reported determination of the distance of ships at sea (ed. Friedlein, 352), one sees that the attribution is conjectural even on Eudemus's part. Moreover, in the light of the triangulation techniques employed in Egyptian teachings, which Thales presumably would have known, a more efficient method based on similar triangles was available to him. Proclus (and Eudemus, for that matter) are also misleading in these instances in suggesting that Thales had somehow *proved* forms of the corresponding Euclidean propositions. Thales' understanding probably did not go beyond the awareness of certain geometric properties and measuring techniques.

Proclus assigns to Oenopides the constructions of the line perpendicular to a given line from a given point "as being useful for astronomy" (*Elements*

I.12) and the construction of an angle equal to a given angle (I.23). Oenopides also figured the inclination of the ecliptic via the construction of the fifteen-sided regular polygon (Theon of Smyrna, ed. Hiller, 198). Hippocrates is noted for his reduction of the problem of cube duplication to finding two mean proportionals (cited by Proclus, ed. Friedlein, 213; and by Eratosthenes, as reported by Eutocius, *In Archimedem*, ed. Heiberg, III.88). On Hippocrates' quadratures of the lunes (figures bounded by two circular arcs) we possess a long fragment from Eudemus, as presented by Simplicius in his commentary *Physics* (ed. Heiberg, 60–68).

Hippocrates' quadrature of lunes indicates a fully developed geometric format. Regrettably, the substantial fragment preserved by Simplicius from Eudemus's *History* includes Simplicius's own glosses, contaminating the older text with citations of Euclid. Beyond that, it would be impossible to determine how Eudemus himself (or a prior authority) had modified Hippocrates' treatment. Nevertheless, this fragment reveals a high level of technical expertise as well as a fully articulated scheme of demonstration, with a regularized geometric terminology. In the first and simplest of the four cases examined, a right isosceles triangle is inscribed in a semicircle, and on its base a circular segment is drawn similar to each of the segments formed between the semicircle and the legs of the triangle. Then, since this larger segment equals the sum of both of the smaller segments, adding to each the part of the triangle lying above the larger segment, one finds that the lune (bounded between the two circular arcs) equals the triangle.

The constructions of the next two cases are more complicated, and each includes the proof that the outer bounding arc of the lune is greater or less, respectively, than a semicircle. In the final case, the lune, taken together with a given hexagon, is shown to equal the circle circumscribed about the hexagon.

This fragment thus displays the basic geometric manner fully actualized: figures are constructed and their properties are stated and proved in proper logical sequence. Certain necessary results are explicitly postulated on the basis of prior proved results (e.g., that similar segments of circles are to each other as their bases in square; cf. *Elements* XII.2); many results are assumed in the course of the proofs—e.g., the so-called Pythagorean theorem on right triangles and its extension. One presumes that the exposition of these results could be accepted from Hippocrates' own collection of "Elements," cited by Proclus, which must have embraced much of Euclid's account of rectilinear and circular figures in *Elements* Books I, III, and VI.

As Eudemus observes, Hippocrates' constructions are of interest for their connection to the circle quadrature. Not only are the lunes, as figures bounded by circular arcs, comparable to the circle itself, but also the fourth case of lune, where it is equatable with a given rectilinear figure, would yield a quadrature of the circle, since their difference, the hexagon, is a given rectilinear figure. Hippocrates' position on the circle quadrature is difficult to construe. But in his fourth construction Hippocrates has indeed *reduced* the problem of circle quadrature to that of squaring a particular lune. His handling of the problem of cube duplication is precisely in this manner: not solving it as such, Hippocrates instead reduces it to another problem, that of finding two mean proportionals between given lines. This reductive strategy for dealing with more difficult problems itself may be considered an important methodological development, as a preliminary form of the method of analysis.

In sum, by the close of the 5th century B.C.E. the field of geometry known to Hippocrates already has taken the form of a deductively ordered science. It has matured well beyond the elementary level to include many results and methods more advanced than anything suggested in the contemporaneous nontechnical literature, such as the mathematical passages in the Presocratics or Plato.

Proclus's account of the early group of geometers notably omits any mention of Parmenides or Zeno, Democritus, or any of the Sophists. As discussed above, the Eleatic critiques of the common conceptions of plurality, magnitude, and motion in principle ought to have had implications for the emergence of mathematical theory. Apparently, the mathematical authorities consulted by Proclus did not describe them as influencing the historical development of the field. The doxographers assign several mathematical writings to Democritus, and he is cited for two geometric theorems (that the pyramid and cone equal a third of the corresponding prism and cylinder, respectively). The most significant fragment of mathematical bearing, however, deals with the following paradox. Does the parallel sectioning of a cone yield consecutive sections that are equal or unequal? If unequal, then the surface of the cone would be irregular and jagged, but if equal, then the cone would not differ from the cylinder, in being composed of equal circular sections. Although the conception adumbrated here of sectioning figures into parallel indivisible components becomes a powerful heuristic method for finding their measures, as one encounters it with Archimedes, for instance, and also with Cavalieri, Kepler, and others in the 17th century, this fragment does not indicate that Democritus made any technical use of it.

As for the Sophists, Antiphon and Bryson are criticized by Aristotle for fallacious arguments on the circle quadrature. Antiphon supposed that by inscribing a regular polygon in the circle and then successively doubling the number of sides, eventually the polygon would merge with the circle, as its sides became indistinguishable from the corresponding arcs. Bryson compared the circle with the sequences of inscribed and circumscribed regular polygons, arguing that since each polygon is quadrable, then the quadrable figure that is greater than every inscribed figure and less than every circumscribed figure would equal the circle. These arguments, although defective as solutions of the circle quadrature, turn on conceptions of limiting polygonal sequences that become significant in the work of Eudoxus, Euclid, and Archimedes.

Ultimately, the notion that the Eleatics or Democritus or the Sophists played a central role in the development of early Greek mathematics rests entirely on modern interpretations and reconstructions. The various fragments and testimonia bearing on the issue indicate that mathematical conceptions did occasionally get taken up within the philosophical speculations of these thinkers, as they elaborated their major theories of being, knowledge, and perception. But Proclus, our most extensive source on the early history, makes no claim that such inquiries directly influenced the historical development of mathematics, and nothing in the extant mathematical literature would justify that claim. It is the case, however, that the paradoxes we have mentioned from Democritus, Antiphon, Bryson, and others, as well as the Eleatics, indicate that the subject matter of geometry was drawn into the philosophical discourse for dialectical scrutiny. In effect, geometry becomes susceptible in this period to the same intellectual stresses that affect the development of philosophy more generally. Following proposals by G. E. R. Lloyd, one may look toward the general political environment within the classical Greek poleis, and particularly that of 5th-century Athens, as fostering this trend toward explicit justification strategies in philosophy on one side, and in geometry on the other.

MATHEMATICS AND THE ACADEMY

In the latter half of his survey of Euclid's precursors, Proclus begins with Plato, described as having stimulated mathematical study through his frequent inclusion of mathematical passages in his works and his effort "everywhere to awaken wonder about this subject among students of philosophy." Proclus next names three contemporaries of Plato, Archytas of Tarentum, Theaetetus of Athens, and Leodamas of Thasos, who "increased the theorems and put them into a more systematic arrangement." He then provides notes on ten other geometers, of whom Eudoxus of Cnidus and his followers are most prominent, and concluding with Plato's associate Philip of Mende (presumably the same as Philip of Opus), who "at Plato's instructions took on the project of researching those things that he thought would contribute to Plato's philosophy."

The clear impression of Proclus's account is that the entire development of geometry in the century before Euclid was dominated by Plato's institution, for he remarks that "all these pursued their collaborative researches with each other in the Academy." Modern accounts tend to follow the same line of interpretation. But the fact that this very view is one that we would naturally expect from Proclus's Neoplatonism recommends caution. It can be supported from Plato's friendship with Archytas, whose work seems to underlie a geometrical passage of *The Republic* (528b–d) and the harmonic doctrines of *Timaeus*, and Plato apparently held Theaetetus as an intimate friend, remembered as a central character in *Theaetetus* and *Sophist*. But the situation with Eudoxus is less clear: although the later testimonia describe him as a disciple of Plato's, Eudoxus established in his own right a prominent school of technical studies at Cyzicus that was hardly a mere offshoot of the Academy. But Proclus is surely right in assigning special significance to the work of Theaetetus and Eudoxus, for, as the following summary indicates, their discoveries stimulated researches fundamental for a major part of Euclid's *Elements*.

Theaetetus was most noted for advancing the study of irrational lines. By definition, lines are "commensurable" when they have a common measuring line, that is, when they have a ratio expressible in terms of integers; equivalently, the squares on these lines have a ratio of square integers. Taking any two lines whose squares are commensurable to each other but whose lengths are not (that is, lines whose squares have a ratio in integers that are not both squares), Theaetetus showed that certain combinations of the lines—specifically, their geometric, arithmetic, and harmonic means—are not commensurable with the given lines in square. Theaetetus's work does not survive, but Euclid's Book X transmits a theory of irrational lines that develops from it.

The paradigm case of lines that do not fit into this condition are the diameter and side of the regular pentagon inscribed in a circle of unit radius; these satisfy the conditions of Euclid's fourth class of irrationals, the major and minor, respectively. The actual case of the side of the pentagon, proven to be a minor irrational, is given in XIII.11. This theorem bears directly on the construction of the regular dodecahedron (*Elements* XIII.17). From certain testimonia one infers that Theaetetus wrote on the construction of the five regular solids, a presumptive source for Euclid in Book XIII of the *Elements*.

The theory of irrationals presupposes a general theory of the divisibility of integers, such as that presented in Euclid's Book VII. The basic conception here is that of relatively prime numbers, being those that possess no common measure other than the unit. For determining the greatest common measure of given integers, Euclid employs the procedure of continued subtraction of terms and remainders (termed the Euclidean division algorithm in modern textbooks), whose Euclidean term is *anthyphairesis*. On this basis one can establish the basic theory of numerical proportion and from this, important general theorems on divisibility, such as that relatively prime numbers are the least of those having the same ratio (VII.21); that any number relatively prime to two numbers is relatively prime also to their product (VII.24); that any prime number that measures a product of two numbers measures one or both of those numbers (VII.30).

Bridging the theory of numbers and the theory of irrationals is the procedure of *anthyphairesis*, which in Euclid's Book X becomes the condition for determining the greatest common measure of commensurable magnitudes. From a passage in Aristotle's *Topics* (158b29) one infers that this procedure (here called *antanairesis*) was adopted for defining proportionality among magnitudes and for proving that a line drawn parallel to the sides of a parallelogram divides its area and base proportionately. The appearance of this definition indicates awareness that a theory of proportion established in terms of integers would not be adequate for the purposes of studying ratios of geometric magnitudes, given the existence of incommensurable magnitudes.

Sensitivity for foundational issues especially marks the work of Eudoxus. His primary work is in the measurement of curvilinear figures, like the circle and sphere, to which the basic results obtained for rectilinear figures do not immediately apply. One knows, for instance, that Hippocrates assumed that circles are to each other as their diameters in square. But a valid proof of this theorem would require some form of limiting procedure, such as that implied in the paradoxes of Antiphon and Bryson, in which sequences of regular polygons can be taken in relation to the circle. By a special manner of demonstration (termed misleadingly in modern accounts the method of exhaustion) Eudoxus showed that, by hypothesizing the negation of the property for the given figures, one could construct certain rectilinear figures that, although they are known to have the property in question, by being taken sufficiently close to the given figures, must also satisfy the negation. In this way, one obtains a logically correct proof based strictly on finitistic lines. The Euclidean theorems that circles are as the squares on their diameters (XII.2), that spheres are in the third power of their diameters (XII.16–18), and that pyramids and cones are one-third of the prisms and cylinders, respectively, having the same altitude and base (XII.5–7, 10), appear to represent the basic mode adopted by Eudoxus.

Similarly Euclid's Book V, presenting the general geometric theory of proportions, seems to develop out of a new theory proposed by Eudoxus. On the model of the exhaustion technique, one sees that a theorem on proportions can be established in the indirect manner, by assuming the negation and constructing commensurable magnitudes that, while having the property in question, nevertheless must also satisfy the negation. In the Euclidean version this conception is regularized in a modified form (V.Def. 5): four magnitudes are said to be in proportion, i.e., $A : B = C : D$, when for any integers m, n it is the case that mA and mC are simultaneously greater than nB, nD, or equal to them, or less than them. By this definition, one both finesses the difficulties posed by the existence of incommensurable magnitudes and also excludes the problematic case of indivisible magnitudes. Modern critics invariably praise this definition as an astute forerunner of the modern definition of "real number," as worked out by R. Dedekind and C. Weierstrass in the 19th century. Certainly Eudoxus must receive credit for the underlying conception of the Euclidean definition, possibly formulated in an indirect manner comparable to the proofs by exhaustion in *Elements*, Book XII. But the proofs of the propositions in Book V are sometimes badly managed, so that one would hardly assign this particular form of the theory to Eudoxus. Presumably Euclid's treatment is based on a form of the theory revised by disciples in Eudoxus's circle.

In the more advanced fields, geometry in the 4th century benefited from the introduction of several new methods whose power would become apparent later at the hands of such as Archimedes and Apollonius. One such method was that of "analysis," which was foreshadowed in Hippocrates' method of the reduction of problems, as he reduced the cube duplication to the finding of two mean proportionals; it relates also to a certain geometric method "by hypothesis" that Plato mentions in *Meno* (86e–87b). The earliest extant specimen of geometric analysis as such relates to the problem of the finding of two mean proportionals, as solved by Eudoxus's disciple Menaechmus. If to the given lines A, B one assumes the two mean proportional lines X, Y, as known, then since $A : X = X : Y$ it follows that $X^2 = AY$, and since $A : X = Y : B$, it follows that $AB = XY$. The former condition, viewed as a locus for X, Y, describes a given parabolic curve, while the latter describes a given hyperbola. Thus, since the two curves are given, their intersection is given. In the formal construction of the problem, one would then invert this reasoning into a "synthesis": given A, B, one constructs the parabola and hyperbola articulated in the analysis, and their intersection yields the desired lines X, Y. The fragment does not elucidate in what sense the two curves are "given."

Menaechmus's curves can also be produced as planar sections of the cone (in addition to the parabola and hyperbola, there arises a third case, the ellipse). The first explicit mention of any of these curves as a conic section appears in the pseudo-Aristotelian *Problems* (XV.7), where the shape of the gibbous moon is said to resemble "a section of a cone." The first extensive elaboration of the properties of the conic sections appears to come from Euclid only shortly after this passage.

Other cases of special curves, besides those of Eudoxus and Menaechmus, are attested from this period. Archytas finds the two mean proportionals via the mutual intersection of given solid surfaces (a cone, torus, and cylinder), entailing a certain space curve as the common section of the torus and cylinder. Dinostratus, brother of Menaechmus and fellow disciple of Eudoxus, introduced another form of kinematic curve, generated by the composition of a linear and a circular motion. This curve was employed toward the solution of the circle quadrature, whence it received the name *quadratrix*. Since, however, this application of the curve requires lemmas not introduced before Archimedes, it seems that Dinostratus used it for other purposes, such as the trisection of the angle. Both in its formation and its use, the curve provides a precedent for the Archimedean spiral.

Such technical advances in geometry stimulated efforts, notably with Aristotle, to assimilate them into the general philosophical account of scientific knowledge. The method of analysis, for instance, is cited, if somewhat misleadingly, as a fruitful mode of heuristic reasoning (*Nicomachean Ethics* 1112b11–24), analogous to deliberative procedures seeking stated ends via accessible means. In *Prior Analytics* Aristotle articulates and classifies the modes of syllogistic reasoning, and demonstrates their relations in accordance with a standard geometric expository format. In *Posterior Analytics*, he inquires into the basic structure of scientific knowledge, in effect, extending the established format of geometry to other domains. Noteworthy is his distinction between propositions susceptible of proof and certain kinds of prior premises whose validity must be postulated.

But among modern critics far greater attention has been directed toward another metamathematical issue: the status of the infinite. Aristotle carefully distinguishes two cases, the "actual" or completed infinite versus the "potential" or progressive infinite. In one analysis of Zeno's paradox of the dichotomy, for instance, Aristotle rejects the notion that one can actually have marked off (whether physically or mentally) an infinite number of intervals (sc. the half, the quarter, the eighth, and so on) in finite time, but asserts that one can continually mark off parts only in succession (*Physics* 263a4–b9). As this distinction between "potential" and "actual" infinites corresponds precisely to that between Eudoxus's finitistic proofs via exhaustion and the presumptive infinitist arguments suggested by Antiphon's construction, one accordingly reads in many modern accounts that the ancient Greeks were stricken by a *"horror infiniti"* to abolish any applications of the infinite in their mathematics. But this view seriously misrepresents the Greek tradition. Infinitely small magnitudes, for instance, figure not only in the paradoxes of Zeno but also in the geometric reasonings known to Democritus (and presumably also Hippocrates), and were fruitfully exploited by Archimedes and others later. What the ancients recognize, however, is that infinitist conceptions are restricted to a heuristic role that, however valuable for research, does not extend into the context of formal demonstrations. It is this formal tradition, stemming from Eudoxus to Euclid and the comprehensive treatises following his model, that dominates within the extant literature. If a greater portion of the informal accounts survived, however, our view would be drastically modified.

EUCLID

Beginning with Euclid, active during the first half of the 3rd century B.C.E., we enter what one may call the "golden age" of Greek geometry. According to Proclus, Euclid "collected the *Elements*, by arranging many of the things of Eudoxus, bringing to completion many other things of Theaetetus, and converting still others, proved rather loosely by his predecessors, to irrefutable proofs." This places Euclid squarely in the tradition of technical exposition of the preceding century, honing the prior treatments of the domains inaugurated by Theaetetus, Eudoxus, and their disciples. Set in the context of what we know of these prior efforts, *Elements* appears to fit this description precisely.

(1)   The body of constructions of rectilinear plane figures and the properties of congruent triangles, forming the nucleus of Book I, is already substantially present in the reports about Oenopides and Hippocrates, while constructions and properties dealing with circles (Book III) and similar triangles and quadrilaterals (Book VI) are also associable initially with Hippocrates, whose collection of "elements" may well have set the first precedent for these parts of Euclid's *Elements*.

(2)   From the Pythagoreans come the constructions of the "application of areas" (the end of Book I, Book II, and the end of Book VI) and possibly also the constructions of the regular polygons (Book IV).

(3)   The general theory of proportions of geometric magnitude (Book V) is founded on the researches of Eudoxus.

(4)   The arithmetic books include a masterfully organized account of the divisibility of integers, which is based on the concept of relative primality (Book VII) and may develop from Theaetetus's researches; the more loosely organized parts on geometric progressions, the divisibility of square and cubic numbers, and the like (Book VIII and the opening of Book IX) may derive ultimately from Archytas, while appended results on odd and even numbers and a construction of "perfect" numbers (end of Book IX) may owe to Pythagoreans.

(5)   The imposing theory of irrational lines, constituting the largest book (Book X, about a quarter of the bulk of the entire *Elements*), stems from researches begun by Theaetetus and continued, it appears, by Eudoxus and his followers.

(6)   The general theory of solid geometry, forming the solid analogue of the plane geometry of Books I and VI, was in its infancy in Plato's time (as *Rep.* 527 indicates), but achieved its first major advances through Archytas and Eudoxus.

(7)   To Eudoxus one may also assign the method of "exhaustion" exploited for measuring circles, cones, and related figures (Book XII).

(8)   Finally, the constructions of the five regular solids are assignable to Theaetetus (Book XIII).

In each instance, there must have been considerable distance between the initial researches here indicated and the final versions in *Elements*. Book IV on the regular polygons could hardly, as such, be a Pythagorean treatise, even though a scholium makes that claim. Similarly, Book V is not, as such, by Eudoxus (the defects in several of its proofs would alone suffice to disqualify it), nor are Books X and XIII, as such, by Theaetetus. Indeed, Book X combines with some inconsistency two different accounts of the theory of irrationals. In all cases, one must assign to the figures named by Proclus in the followings of Theaetetus and Eudoxus the editing, revising, and extending of these fields.

What this leaves for Euclid's role is difficult to say. The inconsistency of technical performance—the ostensibly "Theaetetan" Books VII, X, and XIII are generally well executed, but although Book XII is also well done, Book V is notably flawed, despite their both allegedly being from Eudoxus—would suggest Euclid's access to an ensemble of completed expositions. But *Elements* is not likely to be merely a transcript of prior treatises. At the same time, Euclid himself is probably not the actual discoverer of very many of its theorems or constructions. One might suppose that the uniformity of expository style (e.g., in terminology and format of proofs), to the extent there is such uniformity, would be due to the editor. But even here one must be cautious, for the refining and homogenizing effect of later editors must have been considerable; indeed, it is impossible to know for sure how much of the extant text is free of influence from the edition produced by Theon of Alexandria (mid-4th century c.e.).

While Euclid's editing appears to have retained certain defects of his sources, one can discern nuances of logical refinement that could well be Euclid's own. The project of assembling treatises on the different fields of geometry into a corpus covering the whole domain commits the editor to a specific order of exposition. At various points there arises the need to establish results without recourse to technical methods that are being deferred. When one perceives this process in *Elements*, one can surmise Euclid's responsibility for the special form of proof, since we assume he was first to order the treatises in this way. Two examples may be cited.

First, with the theory of proportions deferred to Book V, Euclid is restricted to methods of congruence in his treatment of plane figures in the first four books, where, accordingly, certain propositions receive quite intricate proofs, even though considerably simpler proofs are possible via similarity principles.

Second, in Book I the condition for parallels is formulated as a special postulate (post. 5) in an unusual form: that when two lines are cut by a third line such that the interior angles formed on one side of the line are together less than two right angles, then the two lines will converge on that side of the line.

This principle, being in effect the converse of prop. 28 (that when two lines are cut by a third such that the interior angles on the same side equal two right angles, then the lines are parallel), is invoked for the first time in the proof of prop. 29, establishing that when two parallel lines are cut by a third the interior angles on the same side of that line equal two right angles. This is, in fact, merely the contrapositive formation of the postulate. A body of commentary attempting to prove the postulate is reported by Proclus, who presents arguments of his own and Ptolemy's; one finds traces of such efforts even before Euclid, in passages from the Aristotelian corpus. It emerges, then, that Euclid took the bold move of proving his key proposition on parallels (I.29) by framing its equivalent (in post. 5) as a postulate. Neither Euclid nor any other of the ancients, of course, perceived the depth of this tactic: that it was necessitated by the independence of the postulate from the others, being the criterion for the Euclidean form of plane geometry, as distinct from the non-Euclidean geometries (the so-called elliptical and hyperbolic geometries) based on its negation.

Among the theorems dependent on the parallel postulate is I.32: that the angles of a triangle sum to two right angles. This theorem, as we have seen, figured in the Pythagorean geometry, although the earlier treatment would not have handled the assumptions about parallels in Euclid's manner. Indeed, Aristotelian passages on parallels mention that if the parallel principle is violated, then so also would the angles of the triangle have a sum different from two right angles (e.g., *Prior Anal.* 2.17.66a11–15). Further, the theorem in I.16 (that the exterior angle of a triangle is greater than either of the nonadjacent interior angles), which Euclid proves without recourse to the parallel postulate, would have no place in the older system, since it would be trivial in the light of I.32.

Another Euclidean work, *Data*, is a companion to *Elements*. It covers the same basic domain as the first six books of *Elements*, the properties of rectilinear and circular plane figures, but adopts a special format suiting it specifically for applications within analyses.

Pappus includes Euclid's *Data* among about a dozen works that constituted a standardized corpus of analysis *(topos analyomenos)*. Euclid's lost *Porisms*, as well as his lost *Surface Loci*, were also included in this set. Presumably, his lost treatise *Conics* would also fall within it, for although Pappus does not cite this work in this context, he does cite the treatise that superseded it, Apollonius's *Conics*. These lost works have proved elusive for reconstruction, despite some detailed efforts based on Pappus's rather substantial notes on *Porisms* and *Surface Loci*. The former includes results that inspired the efforts founding projective geometry, as by Desargues and Pascal in the 17th century. Both works may have related to the extension of the field of conics.

Euclid compiled important works in the geometric sciences. In astronomy, *Phaenomena* provides a geometric account of the basic phenomena of risings and settings of segments of the ecliptic. In harmonics, Euclid's *Section of the Canon* explores the limits of the commensurable division of harmonic intervals, thereby codifying the earlier studies by Archytas; indeed, Tannery has suggested that this tract was actually not by Euclid but by a disciple of Archytas. In optics Euclid produced two treatises—*Optics*, on the phenomena of direct vision, and *Catoptrics*, on phenomena pertaining to vision via reflected rays. Here too there may have been precedent studies, as perhaps by Plato's associate Philip of Opus (the ancient testimonia are inconclusive). Any forms of these precedents in writings from the 4th century, however, were effectively superseded by the Euclidean versions, which remained models of exposition in their respective fields for centuries, long after they were overtaken by more advanced research.

ARCHIMEDES

Today often considered the finest mathematical mind from antiquity, and frequently ranked with the likes of Newton, Gauss, and Einstein as among the most gifted of mathematical physicists ever, Archimedes (fl. ca. 250 B.C.E., d. 212), had already become a legend for his scientific achievements, both theoretical and practical, among the ancient commentators.

Archimedes' basic project in geometry was continuous with the work of Eudoxus: to determine the measurements of geometric figures via the "exhaustion" technique. On the model of Eudoxus's theorem on the circle, Archimedes established that any circle equals half the product of its radius and its circumference, and that the ratio of the circumference to the diameter of the circle (sc. the constant we represent by π) is less than $3\frac{1}{7}$ but greater than $3\frac{10}{71}$. Similarly, Archimedes found the area of any parabolic segment to equal $\frac{4}{3}$ the triangle having the same altitude and base as the segment (*Quadrature of the Parabola*, prop. 24). This result is of particular interest, Archimedes himself observes, in that it marks the first case where a curved figure in the class of the circle or the conics has been found equal to a rectilinear figure.

For these proofs Archimedes states a special principle of continuity (now sometimes called the Archimedean axiom), which fills a perceived gap in the Eudoxean proofs, namely their assumption of a "lemma" (that any finite magnitude, on successive bisection, can be reduced to less than any preassigned finite magnitude of the same kind). This Archimedes reformulates in a manner more flexible for application in proofs (that of two finite magnitudes, the lesser, by being added to itself a suitable, finite number of times, can be made to exceed the greater). One infers that Archimedes does not have before him the Euclidean treatment of this material, since Euclid's definition of "having a ratio" (*Elements* V, def. 4), his proposition on the bisection (X.1), and his applications of these in the "Eudoxean" propositions of Book XII would have rendered Archimedes' lemma superfluous.

Determining centers of gravity involves a form of weighing of the figures, as if on a balance. In *Method* Archimedes exploits this notion for the measurement of areas and volumes, in what he terms his mechanical method. Archimedes also first articulated the basic principle of hydrostatics: that floating bodies displace their equal in weight, while submerged bodies displace their equal in volume. The principle underlies his solution of the legendary problem of the crown: to determine whether a given artifact was made of pure gold, or of an alloy of gold mixed with silver. Hitting on the principle of the solution, it is said, Archimedes charged naked from the baths crying, "Eureka!" But his writing *On Floating Bodies* presents these principles in a less impassioned frame. There Archimedes determines the conditions of stability for buoyant spherical segments and paraboloid segments. Although such results might in principle have applications in the design of ships, Archimedes appears to have applied his analysis to those particular solids whose volume and center of gravity, being known, permitted their solution. It emerges as an exercise in pure geometric theory rather than practical application.

ALEXANDRIANS AND APOLLONIUS

Archimedes' work stimulated active research by a group of talented geometers in the decades to follow. It will be possible here to cite only a few areas of research and the geometers specifically engaged in them.

Eratosthenes of Cyrene, noted as director of the Alexandrian Library and a scholar of diverse interests, was a correspondent of Archimedes' and engaged in a variety of mathematical studies, including efforts in number theory and geometry. Among these was his work in mathematical geography, for which he introduced a modified estimate for the measurement of the earth, 250,000 stades (equivalent, approximately, to 25,000 miles) by comparing the elevation of the sun at the time of the summer solstice at Syene and Alexandria.

Just as Archimedes had employed his mechanical method for the measurement of figures, a result of a closely related sort is due to Dionysodorus: the measure of the torus (or anchor-ring, in modern nomenclature), the solid formed by the revolution of a circle about an axis parallel to its plane, is expressed in terms reminiscent of a more general method proposed in Pappus and equivalent to the barycentric rule stated in the 17th century by Paul Guldin. In this case, the volume would equal that of a cylinder whose base equals the figure (the circle) whose revolution gives rise to the solid, and whose height is the distance traversed by that figure's center of gravity.

An interesting study of isoperimetric figures is due to Zenodorus, who showed, inter alia, that the circle is greatest in area of all plane figures having the same perimeter, and that the sphere is greatest in volume of solids having the same surface area. The treatment, while well crafted over all, suffers some major gaps: it does not adequately cover the entire domain of possible figures, for instance, but compares the circle only to the rectilinear plane figures and the sphere only to regular and conical solids; and it omits any proof of the existence of the maximal figures. One finds in Archimedes' work results of a closely related sort.

An Archimedean solution for the angle trisection appears to have inspired an effort by Nicomedes to solve this problem by means of a special curve, called the conchoid. Other applications of this curve, defined via a sliding ruler *(neusis)* construction, correspond to *neusis* constructions in Archimedes' *Spirals*.

To Diocles is due an interesting study on burning mirrors. This writing is lost in Greek, save for fragments excerpted by the commentator Eutocius, but a version survives through its medieval Arabic translation. Among its propositions is a practical construction of the parabola via its focus-directrix property and a proof that the parabolic contour directs solar rays all to a single point, while a spherical contour directs rays not to a point, but to a given segment of its axis. A few ancient authorities assign to Archimedes constructions of burning mirrors, as well as a general study in the theory of catoptrics. But the effort of Diocles, nearly contemporary with Archimedes, by virtue of its omitting any mention at all of related work by him, would relegate the later testimonia to misattribution.

Chronologically, one might include in this group of Archimedes' successors Apollonius of Perga, whose principal field was the study of conic sections and the solution of problems via geometric analysis. However, as these areas are important for, but not central to, Archimedes' work, one might better view Apollonius in the succession of Euclid, also notable for studies in conics and analysis.

In his eight-book treatise *Conics*, Apollonius consolidates the field of the elements of the conics, considerably extending it beyond the prior treatises of Euclid and Aristaeus (now lost). Apollonius generalizes the definition of the curves as sections of an arbitrary cone (not an isosceles cone, as in prior treatments). His account of their basic properties, as developed in Books I and III, in effect provides the analogue of Euclid's account of the circle in *Elements* Book III, including such results as the construction of tangents and the properties of intersecting chords and secants. Apollonius notes how these results are applicable toward the solution of conic problems, e.g., the three- and four-line locus, the finding of conics in accordance with specified incidence conditions (passing through given points, or having given lines as tangents), and so on. The actual solutions of these problems, however, do not appear in *Conics* itself but must have constituted separate treatises. Book IV on intersections of conics provides basic material for diorisms (finding criteria of solvability of problems). The remaining four books are more specialized in aim: Book V on drawing normal lines to conics, Book VI on constructions relating to similar conics, Books VII and VIII on conic problems. Of these, Book VIII is lost, and the other three survive only through their Arabic translation.

In his survey of the analytic corpus, Pappus describes six other works by Apollonius, in addition to *Conics*. Although all are lost in Greek, one of them, *On Cutting of a Ratio*, is extant in its Arabic translation, and scattered fragments of a few others are also preserved in Arabic sources.

Although modern accounts of Greek mathematics typically suppose that the restriction to planar constructions served as a normative principle already in research antedating Euclid, the explicit statement of this principle occurs only once in the extant literature, in a tentative observation by Pappus. One does see such a restriction implicit, however, in these efforts by Apollonius, if not before. Its presence indicates the maturity of the geometric discipline at his time, when the multiplicity of solutions permitted the ordering and ranking of the various methods.

LATE ANTIQUITY

With the work of Apollonius and his contemporaries early in the 2nd century B.C.E., we reach the highpoint of the discipline of geometry, as initially marked off by the pre-Euclidean contributors and consolidated by Euclid. A scattering of interesting results are preserved in the later commentators, such as Pappus (early 4th century C.E.) that may be attributable to research in the intervening period, but by and large the interest directed toward geometry from the 2nd century B.C.E. on would more accurately be called scholasticism than research. Although for this very reason the later period is typically described as one of decline, there were several areas where important work continued to be done.

Mathematical astronomy witnessed a major development involving astute applications of geometric theory as well as advances in observational and computational expertise. The field of "spherics"—in its simplest geometric form, the study of the properties of triangles described on the surface of a sphere—represented by the earlier treatises of Autolycus and Euclid, was further developed, first in the *Sphaerica* of Theodosius (ca. 2nd century B.C.E.) and subsequently in the *Sphaerica* of Menelaus of Alexandria (early 2nd century C.E.). With regard to the geometric description of planetary motions, the provisional models of Eudoxus and Callippus were set aside in favor of schemes involving eccentric and epicyclic motions, far better suited to the phenomena at issue. The geometric properties of the eccentric and epicyclic models were studied by Apollonius, who recognized their equivalence and determined, for instance, the geometric condition for stationary points and retrogrades. In extending these methods, Hipparchus of Rhodes (2nd century

B.C.E.) profited from the receipt of observational data and parameters (e.g., measures of the periods of planetary motions) from the tradition of arithmetical astronomy then thriving at Babylon. The Hipparchean system, fortified by refinements both in data and theory, was further elaborated by Ptolemy of Alexandria (mid-2nd century C.E.) in *Mathematical Syntaxis*, which (under its Arabo-Latin title, *Almagest*) continued as the definitive treatise in geometric astronomy throughout the Middle Ages and the Renaissance.

To calculate planetary positions from the geometric theory, one requires the appropriate computational methods, such as arithmetic algorithms and trigonometric tables. Although precedents for trigonometric calculations are found in Aristarchus and Archimedes, credit goes to Hipparchus for producing a table of chords suitable for general use. This also marks the introduction among the Greeks of the sexagesimal arithmetical algorithms, which, like the basic quantitative parameters, were derived from the Babylonian precedent. Although the fact of this borrowing seems not to be in question—it is even remarked on by later Greek authorities—the precise manner of the transfer has not been clarified.

Arithmetic treatment of geometry carried through in the manual on practical geometry, *Metrica*, by Hero of Alexandria (mid-1st century C.E.). Here the computational mode is strictly in the alphabetical numeral system, long conventional among the Greeks, although it is enriched by algorithms for fractional and root computations. Hero's treatment benefits from the geometric discoveries of Archimedes—he includes Archimedes' estimate for π (i.e., $3\frac{1}{7}$), his measuring rules for the circle, parabola, ellipse, conical and spherical surfaces, and the sphere and the cylindrical segments, as well as Dionysodorus's rule for the torus (indeed, Hero is our unique testimony to the latter). It is clear, however, that the basic notion of a metrical form of geometry is not new with Hero: we have precedents in pre-Euclidean mathematical passages, as well as in surveying practice among both the Greeks, and the Egyptians and Mesopotamians before them.

But arithmetic theory receives a major technical advance in the work of Diophantus of Alexandria (ca. 3rd century C.E.) whose *Arithmetica* is an ambitious treatise in thirteen books expounding methods of solving arithmetical problems. In his exposition Diophantus presupposes the theory of Euclid and basic identities (including the solution of quadratic relations) that are established geometrically within the Euclidean tradition. But his own format is exclusively arithmetic, displaying certain features that would inspire the founders of algebraic method (e.g., Viète and Fermat) in the early modern period. Throughout the hundreds of problems examined in this treatise, Diophantus applies a consistent format: problems, although stated in general, are solved in the context of specific numerical values. The solving method is reminiscent of analysis among the geometers, in that the solving number is assumed and the conditions it is to satisfy are then formulated as an equation relating the several powers of the unknown. A nomenclature and symbolism are introduced extending up through the ninth power of the unknown. For instance, to find two numbers whose sum is given and the sum of whose squares is given (I.28), Diophantus posits the given numbers to be 20 and 208, respectively, and sets the difference of the two numbers sought as twice the unknown ($2x$), whence the greater is $x + 10$, the lesser $10 - x$, and the condition on the sum of their squares leads to the relation $2x^2 + 200 = 208$. One thus finds x to be 2, whence the numbers are 12, 8. Although this is a relatively simple example of Diophantus's art, it reveals his basic procedure as well as his understanding of more general aspects of his problems, and even a flair for nontrivial approaches suited to the special features of given cases.

In 4th-century Alexandria technical study was cultivated within the academic curriculum, as we see in the work of Pappus. His commentaries on Ptolemy and Euclid were much consulted by later commentators, such as Theon and Proclus. His eight-book anthology, *Collection*, reflects an active, competitive environment in more advanced geometric studies. This compilation includes a rich body of material, in many cases preserving unique evidence of important areas of the later development of geometry.

Theon of Alexandria (mid- and late 4th century) followed Pappus as teacher of technical studies at Alexandria. He issued new editions of Euclid's *Elements* and *Data*, which all but superseded the pre-Theonine versions. In Theon's astronomical work he was assisted by his daughter Hypatia (late 4th century, d. 415), who became the leading figure among the Neoplatonists in Alexandria. Her notorious death by lynching at the hands of Christian fanatics left a deep impression not only on later historians of the church, who deplored the incident, but even more on the legendizing about ancient science and religion in the modern age. Among her technical works were commentaries on Diophantus and Apollonius, which unfortunately do not survive.

In the later centuries, technical studies become more an adjunct of the philosophical curriculum than a course pursued for its intrinsic merit. In Athens at the Platonic Academy, Proclus included mathematics in his commentaries on Plato (particularly on *Timaeus* and *The Republic*). His commentary on Euclid's Book I, as we have seen, preserves much historical information, as well as ample philosophical glosses relating Euclid's propositions to Neoplatonist interests.

Ammonius in Alexandria (late 5th to early 6th century), a follower of Proclus, devoted his principal work to lectures and commentaries on Aristotle. But he encouraged technical interests among his disciples, the principal among them being Eutocius, Philoponus, and Simplicius. Eutocius (fl. early 6th century) apparently took over leadership of the school for a relatively brief period after Ammonius's death. But Eutocius is significant more for his commentaries on Archimedes and Apollonius, and his new edition of the first four books of *Conics*, the basis of the extant tradition of that work. While Eutocius's mathematical expertise is not to be exaggerated, his technical comments are usually sound, and he incorporates invaluable historical material, including the reconstruction of a lost section of Archimedes' *Sphere and Cylinder* (together with related fragments from Diocles and Dionysodorus) and an anthology of accounts of the cube duplication, preserving the substance and, in several instances, the texts of eleven different contributors, including Archytas, Menaechmus, Eratosthenes, Nicomedes, and others.

Philoponus, a contemporary of Eutocius, compiled commentaries on Aristotle, initially based on the lectures of Ammonius. These include some mathematical material of interest, e.g., on cube duplication and circle quadrature, as the particular passage gives occasion. But his major work is in theology and cosmology, as in his polemical attacks against the Aristotelian cosmologists for their doctrine of the eternity of the world.

Simplicius produced an extensive set of commentaries on Aristotle, of which those on *Physics* and *De caelo* preserve several important fragments of early mathematics, most notably, the account of early circle quadratures, including Hippocrates' treatment of the lunules, and the account of Eudoxus's system of concentric spheres.

Anthemius of Tralles (early 6th century) and Isidore of Miletus (early to middle 6th century) bring the focus of technical studies to Constantinople. Anthemius, noted for his designs of mechanisms, was appointed chief architect in the reconstruction of Hagia Sophia (532–537). His expertise in geometry is represented in his extant tract on burning mirrors, and his being the dedicatee of Eutocius's commentaries on Apollonius. Isidore also combined practical activities (e.g., as Anthemius's assistant at Hagia Sophia) and scholarly efforts. In the latter regard, he was esteemed as a lecturer on geometry, composing a commentary on Hero's *Vaults* (not extant), a set of results on regular solids (extant as part of the so-called Book XV of *Elements*), and a revision of Eutocius's commentaries on Archimedes.

It would appear that, by contrast with the philosophically oriented curriculum at Alexandria, the Constantinople school emphasized practical and technical study. This may reflect a growing antagonism toward pagan philosophy within the Christian establishment from the time of Justinian onward. But a few centuries later, when the excesses of the iconoclastic movement gave way to orthodoxy in the late 9th century, a revived commitment to philosophical study carried with it an interest in the mathematical classics. Under humanists like Leon "the Philosopher," new editions of Euclid, Archimedes, Apollonius, and their commentators were compiled, and these ultimately became the basis of what now survives of this tradition. Their effort assured the transmission of the finest specimens of formal exposition, particularly in elementary geometry. Their coverage of more advanced fields and of informal treatments was spotty by comparison, and this has left an unbalanced impression of the primacy of formalist concerns over heuristic methods in ancient mathematical research. But in both these respects the Byzantine humanists fostered the advancement of mathematical studies in Arabic and Latin scholarship in the Middle Ages and the Renaissance. Possessing only the finished architecture, as it were, of ancient mathematics, the later geometers were compelled to recreate the scaffolding, or what they took to be the secret methods perversely withheld by the ancients.

WILBUR KNORR

Bibliography

Bowen, A. C., ed. *Science and Philosophy in Classical Greece.* New York and London, 1991.

Burkert, Walter. *Lore and Science in Ancient Pythagoreanism.* Trans. Edwin L. Minar, Jr. Cambridge, Mass., 1972.

Fowler, D. H. *The Mathematics of Plato's Academy.* Oxford, 1987.

Heath, T. L. *History of Greek Mathematics.* 2 vols. Oxford, 1921.

Jones, Alexander. *Pappus of Alexandria: Book 7 of the Collection.* 2 vols. New York, 1986.

Klein, Jacob. *Greek Mathematical Thought and the Origin of Algebra.* Cambridge, Mass., and London, 1968.

Knorr, W. R. *The Ancient Tradition of Geometric Problems.* Boston, 1986.

———. *The Evolution of the Euclidean Elements.* Dordrecht and Boston, 1975.

———. *Textual Studies in Ancient and Medieval Geometry.* Boston, 1989.

Kretzmann, Norman, ed. *Infinity and Continuity in Ancient and Medieval Thought.* Ithaca, N.Y., 1982.

Lloyd, G. E. R. *Magic, Reason, and Experience.* Cambridge, 1979.

Mueller, Ian. *Philosophy of Mathematics and Deductive Structure in Euclid's Elements.* Cambridge, Mass., 1981.

Neugebauer, Otto. *A History of Ancient Mathematical Astronomy.* 3 vols. Berlin and New York, 1975.

Szabó, Árpád. 1969. *The Beginnings of Greek Mathematics.* Trans. A. M. Ungar. Dordrecht and Boston, 1978.

Tannery, Paul. *Mémoires scientifiques,* vols. 1–3. Paris and Toulouse, 1912.

Van der Waerden, B. L. *Science Awakening.* Groningen, 1954.

Zeuthen, H. G. *Die Lehre von den Kegelschnitten im Altertum.* Copenhagen, 1886; repr. Hildesheim, 1965.

MEDICINE

AT THE END OF HIS TREATISE *On Youth, Old Age, Life, and Death,* Aristotle wrote: "But as to health and disease, not only the physician but also the natural scientist must, up to a point, give an account of their causes. . . . Facts show that their inquiries are, to a certain extent, at least coterminous. For those physicians who are cultivated and learned make some mention of natural science, and claim to derive their principles from it, while the most accomplished investigators into nature generally push their studies so far as to conclude with an account of medical principles" (480b21). Actually, Presocratic "physicists" exhibited an interest in medicine that has never been contested, so much so that some of them, such as Empedocles, Alcmeon of Croton, and Archelaus, were considered physicians as well as philosophers. Parmenides himself, according to some ancient sources, founded a "school" of medicine. Among the objects of most intense study for the ancient natural philosopher were the various vital phenomena, to the point that "physicists" were sometimes inclined to view these phenomena as models that explain the entire universe. According to Aristotle, if the natural philosopher must concern himself with the principles of health and sickness, it is because neither of the two can be "the properties of things deprived of life" (*On Sense and Sensible Objects* I.436a19). The very meaning of the term *physics* changed, of course, between the time of the Presocratics and Aristotle: for the latter, physics was no longer a comprehensive science claiming to explain the creation of the entire cosmos. Aristotelian physics is the theoretical science of living beings, those that contain in themselves the principle of their own motion. In other words, living beings constitute the paragon of physical reality.

The two passages from Aristotle cited above suggest three historical and epistemological observations. The first concerns the grounding of medicine in physics—in the ancient sense of the word—and points toward what is specific to Greek medicine. As Aristotle noted, medicine has a place only among living creatures and for their benefit. Nevertheless, biology and medicine are not related to physics in the same way. Biology (which is not quite the proper term for describing ancient speculation about living creatures) is just one part of physics, and therefore of philosophy, and has never claimed to be anything else. Among physicians, however, beginning in the 5th century B.C.E., there was disagreement over how much medicine should depend on philosophy, a question Aristotle no doubt had in mind when he wrote the texts

264 THE GREEK PURSUIT OF KNOWLEDGE

quoted above. The Hippocratic treatise *On Ancient Medicine* is critical of medicine's adoption of the methods of Presocratic natural philosophers, while in the preface of his treatise on medicine Celsus, a Latin encyclopedist of the early Christian era, contrasts physician-philosophers such as Pythagoras, Empedocles, and Democritus with Hippocrates, "who separated this branch of learning from the study of philosophy" (*De medicina*, Prooemium 8). The second observation concerns the history of natural philosophy: it was not until Aristotle's day, when physics had dropped its claims of embracing all science, that the connection between the study of vital phenomena and the practice of medicine became meaningful. In addition, we should recall that even for Aristotle, who came closer to it than anyone else, our modern notion of biology had no exact equivalent among the ancients. In Aristotelian physics, the elements (fire, air, water, earth) that constitute matter belong to the same category as the living, inasmuch as they contain the principle of their own movement, and the entire cosmos is considered to be alive. Michel Foucault demonstrated that at the beginning of the 19th century a concept of biology could develop—Lamarck was one of the first to use the term; indeed, he introduced the word in French—only when life itself had been grasped as a specific way of being. A second condition was also necessary: biology, in the modern sense, requires the proper demarcation of the boundaries of the living world. Aristotle satisfied the first of these conditions but not the second. Finally, the relationship between biology and medicine was not understood in the same way by physicians and natural philosophers. While physicians unquestionably looked to physicists for theoretical models, the latter only rarely modified their systems in light of medical discoveries.

Until now, medical historians have emphasized the *unity* of Greek (or Greco-Roman) medicine as compared to medical theory and practice in other cultural spheres, particularly those of Babylon and Egypt. These historians, who have often acknowledged the hegemony of Hippocratic medicine, have, as a result, underestimated the diversity of ancient medicine. Tracing ancient medical science to what might be called its historic and theoretical center should allow us to take into account these two aspects of Greek medicine, its specificity and its fullness.

ALEXANDRIAN MEDICINE: HEROPHILUS

During the first half of the 3rd century B.C.E., Herophilus of Chalcedonia practiced and taught medicine at Alexandria. I might have chosen to focus on someone less brilliant, on a physician more representative of the medicine of his time, but there are advantages in choosing a scholar as exceptional as Herophilus. Although we have only a few fragments and some testimony cited by later authors, we know somewhat more about him than about his less renowned colleagues, particularly owing to the important work of Heinrich

von Staden. Moreover, Herophilus's high standing gave him particular importance in one of the key transformations in Greek medicine, the birth of
medical schools.

Before practicing medicine himself, Herophilus studied with Praxagoras
of Cos, possibly in Alexandria but more likely in Cos, Hippocrates' homeland. However, he eventually settled in Alexandria, where he practiced and
taught medicine. While Athens was still the philosophical capital of the Greek
world, Alexandria was its scientific center. The famous Library, established
and funded by the dynasty of the Ptolemys, brought together veritable research institutes of every known discipline, centered around the Museum.
While there is no proof that Herophilus was a court doctor appointed by the
king, or even that he was connected to the institution of the Museum, we
know that he had political connections, because he was the first to practice, on
a large scale, not only human dissection on cadavers but also, according to
Celsus, human vivisection on condemned prisoners taken from the king's
dungeons. No doubt the exceptional position of Alexandria, a Greek city recently founded in Egypt, permitted a partial lifting of the prohibitions having
to do with human cadavers; some scholars have suggested that dissection
probably seemed less shocking in a culture where the dead were embalmed.
As for vivisection, it was possible only because explicit permission had been
granted by the Ptolemaic kings, who had a strong desire to see Alexandria
recognized as the intellectual capital of the world. Scholars have proposed numerous hypotheses regarding the possible influence of Egyptian medicine on
Herophilus and the other Greek physicians in Alexandria. From earliest antiquity, Egyptian doctors were famous; Persian and Hittite kings had personal
physicians who were brought from Egypt. Herophilus and his colleagues may
have benefited from certain drugs used by the pharaohs' doctors from time
immemorial, but the medicine Herophilus practiced was unmistakably Greek
and showed no signs of Hellenic-Egyptian syncretism.

It is often said, incorrectly, that Greek medicine was "rational" whereas
Egyptian medicine was "magical." Thanks to some papyri which have come
down to us from as far back as the 20th century B.C.E., we have fairly detailed
information about pharaonic medicine. These composite texts contain a mix
of invocations to the gods and magic formulas, but they also demonstrate frequent recourse to reason and observation. They offer a description of the vas-
cular system and an explanation of diseases based on the flow of morbid humors in the body that closely resemble what is found in the corresponding
texts of the *Hippocratic Corpus*, but the Egyptian papyri were written fifteen
centuries earlier. Given the well-known competence of Egyptian physicians,
pharmacologists, surgeons, and obstetricians, it is clearly unacceptable to classify Egyptian medicine with the magico-charlatanism that has existed everywhere and throughout history.

Nevertheless, the differences between Egyptian and Greek medicine are enormous, and they emerge clearly when we look at the training of future physicians. The Egyptian doctor was trained in the temple, where he learned to observe his patients' symptoms and to use them as the basis for applying certain formulas from manuals, some of which—but only some—were clearly magico-religious. In his *Politics*, Aristotle mentions that Egyptian physicians were not authorized to depart from the treatments prescribed in the manuals until four days after the onset of the disease, and that a doctor transgressed this rule at his own risk, for he would then be held responsible for any negative consequences. In contrast, as a young man, Herophilus studied with a teacher in one of the medical "schools" where, as in our own university hospitals today, both treatment and training took place. He probably had to pay for his training, but he was then entitled to membership in the medical circle, a "brotherhood" in the strictest sense. The text of the well-known Hippocratic oath, which probably dates from the beginning of the 4th century B.C.E., imparts a religious cast to the new doctor's obligation to become a member of his teacher's family: "I swear by Apollo physician, by Asclepius, by Hygeia, by Panacea and by all the gods and goddesses . . . to hold my teacher in this art equal to my own parents; to make him partner in my livelihood; when he is in need of money to share mine with him; to consider his family as my own brothers, and to teach them this art, if they want to learn it, without fee or indenture; to impart precept, oral instruction, and all other instruction to my own sons, the sons of my teacher and to indentured pupils who have taken the physicians' oath" (Hippocrates, *The Oath* 299). Texts such as this one bear crucial traces of a history that requires analysis.

In Greece, alongside the customary medicine of bone setters and charlatans, a form of religious medicine was also practiced, in the sanctuaries of Apollo and later in those of Asclepius, such as the one at Epidaurus. We have a good deal of information about these practices from texts as well as from archaeological material, particularly votive steles. They reveal, for example, that patients sometimes sought "incubation," which involved sleeping in the temple so that the course of action they should adopt might be revealed while they slept. But we also have information going back at least to Homeric times about a form of lay medicine that differed markedly from its magico-religious counterparts; its practitioners were considered technicians. Thus the Greek army, sent to fight Troy, had its own physicians in addition to the necessary carpenters, ships' pilots, and cooks. In its idealization of the harsh virtue of primitive times, Plato's *Republic* tells us that this ancient medicine was almost exclusively devoted to traumatology. Starting in the 6th century B.C.E., medical centers appeared, for example, in Cyrene in what is now Libya, and in Croton, in southern Italy. However, from the 5th century on the center that was best known, owing to the exceptional fame of Hippocrates, was on the island of Cos, where Herophilus was trained a little less than a century after the master's death. In addition, itinerant physicians traveled throughout the Mediterranean world, practicing their art, competing with local physicians and among themselves; in most cases, however, they did not teach.

ANTECEDENTS: THE *HIPPOCRATIC CORPUS*

The conditions Herophilus encountered had developed slowly, as a careful reader of the oath might have guessed. Hippocrates became a doctor because he came from the family of the Asclepiades, in other words, from those who claimed to be descendants of Asclepius, initially a demigod of medicine who was later fully "deified." Asclepius's two sons, Podalirus and Machaon, were physicians in the Greek army during the Trojan War. The two largest medical "schools" of the classical age, in Cos and in Cnidus (a city situated on the continent of Asia opposite the island of Cos), where most of the treatises of the *Hippocratic Corpus* were produced, were family associations; both claimed Podalirus as their ancestor. Although not all of the Asclepiades' male descendants were destined to study medicine, medical science was passed down within families: Hippocrates' grandfather, father, sons, and grandsons were all physicians. It is quite likely that, two hundred years earlier, Herophilus could not have become a doctor. It was during Hippocrates' time, and perhaps even thanks to him, that people outside the family were permitted to come to Cos to study; this probably happened later at the other centers as well. The oath recalls the old tradition by symbolically integrating outsiders into their teachers' families.

Such an important transformation must be viewed in light of a fundamental fact of Greek intellectual history: the birth of physics, or natural philosophy, in the polis. While the social structure of the pharaonic monarchy was able to keep the practice and teaching of medicine under the control of the priests, it must have been increasingly difficult for Greek medical families to retain their privileged position. Beginning in the 6th century B.C.E., within the context of free inquiry and competing hypotheses that prevailed during the composition of a number of treatises on nature, "physiologists" assumed the right to oversee the processes of disease, asserting that they alone were capable of explaining them. As for the city-states, they sought to recruit competent physicians, "competence" now entailing not only the reputation of a famous family but also the rational examination of doctrines and therapeutic methods. Plato and Aristotle tell us that the city-states required candidates to take serious examinations to become public doctors, a position that was specific to the polis. Hence the transmission of knowledge and experience strictly within families was bound to conflict with the public ideals of the city. In this new world, medicine could either become sectarian, in the strictest sense of the word—for the city-states had suppressed, without entirely eliminating, the cultic societies and other more or less secret associations—or it could go public. The *Hippocratic Corpus* bears more than one trace of this debate, which profoundly affected medicine in Hippocrates' day.

Indeed, it is by understanding the way medicine was adapted to a political environment, in which philosophy was the dominant intellectual consequence, that we can better assess one of the great contradictions running through the *Hippocratic Corpus,* embodied in the contrasting treatises of Cos and Cnidus. The contradiction may have been overstated by some interpreters, but it was certainly not invented by them. The author of *On Regimen in Acute Diseases,* a treatise dating from the end of the 5th century B.C.E., probably belonged to the Cos "school"; in other words, the author was probably a follower of Hippocrates or of one of his immediate successors. In that treatise, three distinctive features of the rival "school" of Cnidus are described: the physicians of Cnidus used a rigid and very detailed classification of diseases (for instance, they recognized four sorts of jaundice and three types of tetanus); they used only a very small number of remedies (the treatise mentions milk, whey, and purges); they referred to a work called *Cnidian Sentences,* which the author says had been collectively revised. For modern interpreters of the *Hippocratic Corpus,* the Cnidian school represents the outcast wing of classical Greek medicine, denounced as archaic and empirical, as opposed to the medicine of Cos practiced by Hippocrates himself, which some scholars see as the forerunner of 19th-century experimental medicine inspired by the work of Claude Bernard.

Thus Book II of the treatise known by the title *Diseases* in the *Hippocratic Corpus,* regarded as Cnidian in origin, has two principal characteristics. This treatise is a catalogue of illnesses presented in order, "from head to toe": diseases of the head, nose, neck, chest, and so on. For each of the diseases— many varieties of which are listed in succession—the presentation follows the same order: identification (in other words, the name of the disease: tetanus no. 1, tetanus no. 2), semiology, therapy, and prognosis. This order is most scrupulously adhered to in the second part of the treatise, which appears to be older than the first. Thus the treatise must be viewed as a well-organized work, and not simply as a collection of notes or patients' charts, examples of which can also be found in other parts of the *Corpus.*

Let us take, for example, one of the chapters in the work: "Another jaundice: there are mild fevers and a heaviness of the head . . . in some cases, the fever actually goes away; the person becomes yellow—powerlessness of the body, and he passes thick yellow-green urine. Wash this patient in hot water and give him drinks. When he seems to you to be better, and his color is better, administer a medication to his nostrils; afterwards, have him drink a medication that acts downwards. Let him eat very soft foods and drink diluted sweet white wine. If he does these things, he recovers" (*De morbis* II.39).

On the basis of a collection like this one we can sketch the professional and intellectual portrait of a physician of Cnidus. He does not limit himself to following recipes: he must determine precisely the moment when the different phases of the cure must be initiated ("when he seems to you to be better"), and in this it is clear that *De morbis* II and *Cnidian Sentences* do not function at all like the collections of treatments rooted in magic. Behind such texts as these we detect long experience in treatment and a considerable accumulation of observations. Nevertheless, the doctor in the case described is a practitioner who applies knowledge that he has had no part in generating and the basis of which is never explicitly presented. This empirical and authoritarian medicine is well adapted to transmission through the family line, but its practitioners must have had difficulty "coming to terms" intellectually under questioning by philosophers.

Doctors thus came to follow the example of philosophers and rhetoricians. This is the source of another distinction that runs through the *Hippocratic Corpus*. Until recently, some of the treatises—for example, *On Winds* and *On Art*—were regarded as exercises in rhetorical virtuosity and attributed to some Sophists with a passing knowledge of medicine, for whom the term *iatrosophists* was coined. Jacques Jouanna has shown that there is no reason to think that these treatises were not written by physicians who believed in the theses that they were defending. Thus the author of *On Winds* really believed that all sickness had a single cause, namely, the air. He used rhetorical techniques appropriate to his audience: he was not addressing colleagues, but speaking to lay people whom he sought to convince. Perhaps such a discussion should be put in the context of the institution of public doctors, since *On Winds* and *On Art*, both of which have a clearly apologetic tone in that they defend medicine against its critics, are obviously addressing citizens whose opinion, in the end, will determine the actions taken by the city. These treatises from the *Hippocratic Corpus* contrast with others, of various sorts, written for specialists, physicians, and "natural philosophers." Let us examine three types.

Treatises such as *Fractures*, which explains the steps to take in treating fractures and dislocations, may be called technical. We may call another group of works documentary: the seven books of *Epidemics* are a collection of patients' records, written by different authors in different eras. For example: "Meton was seized with fever and painful heaviness in the loins. *Second day.* After a fairly copious draught of water, had his bowels well moved. *Third day.* Heaviness in the head; stools thin, bilious, rather red. *Fourth day.* General exacerbation; slight epistaxis twice from the right nostril; an uncomfortable night; stools as on the third day . . . Fifth day, violent epistaxis of unmixed blood from the left nostril; sweat; crisis. After the crisis, sleeplessness; wandering; urine thin and rather black. His head was bathed; sleep; reason restored. The patient suffered no relapse, but after the crisis bled several times from the nose" (*Epidemics* I, Case vii.196–208).

In Book II of *Diseases* we are far from the type of description provided by the foregoing example. Here, the physician, probably one of the itinerants mentioned above, supplied examples not of illnesses but of patients. This collection of cases was intended for use by the physician himself and by his colleagues in the school. The *Hippocratic Corpus* also includes "speculative" treatises that specifically address the problem of the connection between medicine and philosophy.

Herophilus was thus associated with the Hippocratic tradition of medicine, a tradition grounded in rationality but claiming both practical and theoretical autonomy vis-à-vis philosophy. Starting with Celsus, if not before, it was standard practice for historians and doxographers to treat certain figures in pairs: Hippocrates was paired with Diocles of Carystus, who wrote the first treatise on anatomy, in the 4th century; Praxagoras of Cos was paired with Chrysippus, of Cnidus, and Herophilus with Erasistratus. The latter, somewhat younger than Herophilus, was the other great figure in Alexandrian medicine and was probably a student of Chrysippus, just as Herophilus was a student of Praxagoras. This suggests that Erasistratus chose to be trained in the Cnidian school, the rival to Cos; by that time, the Cos school seems to have lost the empirical and archaic character that it had in the time of Hippocrates.

The expression "Hippocratic tradition" does not refer to a duly constituted doctrine, for the treatises of the *Hippocratic Corpus*, even when we consider only those texts from Cos written before the middle of the 4th century B.C.E., are highly divergent. But this doctrinal diversity is framed, as it were, by a few "invariables" that appear to be more significant than the actual content of the theories offered in the collection. Hippocratic doctors had a common understanding of illness and of the way the body functions; traces of this shared view first appear in the writings of the Pythagorean doctor Alcmaeon of Croton (6th century B.C.E.). Using a political metaphor, Alcmaeon defined health as the balance between the elemental qualities that make up the body (hot, cold, dry, wet, sweet, bitter . . .), while in sickness a single one of these qualities was believed dominant. Considered for years to be the chief legacy of Hippocratic medicine, the theory of humors originated in the speculations of the Presocratic natural philosophers. Several systems of humors are found in the *Hippocratic Corpus*, but the most famous—and the one that survived, through the work of Galen, right up to the beginning of the 19th century— came from Hippocrates' son-in-law, Polybius, in his treatise *On the Nature of Man.* Polybius describes the body as the site of the interlacing flows of blood, the warm and humid spring humor; yellow bile, the hot and dry summer humor; black bile, the dry and cold autumnal humor; and phlegm, the cold and wet winter humor. Pathology described the deviant behavior of these humors, of which we may have too much or too little; they may overflow, leaving a vacuum to be filled by others, or they may become concentrated in certain organs, causing inflammation or decay.

Medical knowledge was thus primarily directed at prognosis: owing to his experience, the physician could predict the course of the illness and its various phases. Particular attention was given to what were known as the "critical days" and to the cycle of symptoms, particularly of fevers (resulting in certain medical expressions in use right up to the 20th century to designate fevers that recur regularly, for example every three or four days). Yielding to the temptation of arithmetic logic, as some philosophers did, the authors of a few of the treatises in the *Hippocratic Corpus* sought to establish a numerical basis for the rhythms of human life and of the universe: according to the treatise *Flesh*, the number seven, through its multiples and divisions (3 + 4), provided the key to understanding the evolution of diseases as well as the growth of the fetus. Treatment basically consists in helping to provoke a crisis, during which the body's equilibrium is reestablished; for example, the remedy for an excess of a given humor is a discharge of that humor. The most important factor is timing: the doctor's intervention must come at the right moment, neither too soon nor too late.

Despite the often harsh criticism that certain treatises in the *Hippocratic Corpus* level against philosophy and its theoretical imperialism, we can see a deepening commonality between Hippocratic physicians and the philosophers, whom skeptics later call Dogmatists, a label that "rationalist" physicians inherited: the truth of the symptom lies not in what is seen but in *hidden causes* that the doctor has to discover, just as science must try to reveal the hidden network of causes that governs all phenomena. Herophilus falls squarely within this perspective, and several ancient sources tell us that he sought the explanation of disease in humoral pathology. Moreover, he helped strengthen this rational approach to medicine through his contribution to the development of the medical arts.

THE NEW FACE OF MEDICINE

Herophilus was above all a skillful anatomist, owing to his extensive practice of dissection and human vivisection. His contemporary, Erasistratus, also practiced dissection on a wide scale, and possibly human vivisection as well, though this is not confirmed. Their immediate successors, however, abandoned human dissection, and it was almost never practiced again in the West until the end of the Middle Ages. In "linear" histories of medicine that ascribe to each name a set of "discoveries" adding up to everything known to modern medicine, Herophilus is credited with discovering the distinctions between sensory and motor nerves, the hemispheres of the brain, and the ovaries and Fallopian tubes, although he had no awareness of the process of ovulation. In addition he also described, quite precisely for his time, the system of veins and arteries that his teacher, Praxagoras, seems to have been the first to identify clearly—though Herophilus continued to believe that the arteries carried blood mixed with "breath"—and he was responsible for a thorough study of the pulse that made him famous in antiquity. By differentiating between the strength, size, and rate of the pulse, and by resorting to analogies in music, he was one of the first to introduce a concept of rhythm into the life sciences. Herophilus explored other areas as well, in particular physiology—he studied respiration in detail—and psychiatry; his analysis of dreams won him praise from Freud.

One aspect of the search for hidden causes involved opening up cadavers and the bodies of living human beings. A North African doctor of the 4th century B.C.E., who condemned the practice of vivisection on humanitarian grounds, reports that Alexandrian physicians, including Herophilus, dissected cadavers to discover the causes and circumstances of death. It seems likely, therefore, that dissection, far from being practiced by Herophilus in the name of some experimental empiricism, was actually, in his view, a means of uncovering "intermediate" causes, those that lay between "obvious" but nondetermining causes such as, according to Celsus, "heat or cold, hunger or surfeit" (De medicina, Prooemium, 11) and fundamental hidden causes that can be discovered only through reasoning. It appears that Herophilus fulfilled the program of the rationalist physicians better than any of his predecessors. When Celsus redefines the objectives of the form of rational medicine that originated with Hippocrates, he seems to include the contributions of the Alexandrian anatomists: "They, then, who profess a reasoned theory of medicine propound as requisites, first, a knowledge of hidden causes involving diseases, next, of evident causes, after these of natural actions also [as he says later, Celsus means physiological functions like respiration and digestion], and lastly of the internal parts" (De medicina, Prooemium, 9).

This question of causes is crucial, and it goes beyond medicine. In the Alexandrian world, Aristotle's influence was powerful: Strato of Lampsacus, successor to Theophrastus as head of the Lyceum, was the teacher of King Ptolemy II Philadelphus, and by and large the Alexandrian scientific establishment continued to pursue Aristotle's encyclopedic project. Moreover, the rising influence of the Stoics was reflected in the fact that etiology was one of the central questions of philosophy. In this respect, Herophilus's theoretical stance is more complex than it appears. Its complexity surfaces in the contradictory doxography concerning Herophilus, in which some writers hold that he meant to infer from observable phenomena the hidden causes that govern them (this is the position of the rationalists or Dogmatists), while others report that he meant to describe perceived phenomena and declared the hidden causes inaccessible (the position of the Empiricists). After demonstrating that these extreme interpretations are mistaken, Heinrich von Staden offers what is probably an accurate interpretation of Herophilian epistemology: like Aristotle, Herophilus starts with the observation of perceptible phenomena in order to arrive at their causes; however, recognizing that real causes often elude the doctor in physiology and pathology, he settled for *hypothetical* causes.

Old and new elements are combined in a most striking way in Herophilus's work. The most radical innovation in Herophilus's medicine, compared with that of Hippocrates, resides in the practice of dissection itself. Herophilus and perhaps his teacher Praxagoras before him illustrate the distinction Aristotle made between theoretical physicians—whom he credited with knowledge of physics—and ordinary therapists (*Politics* III.11): they brought into the intellectual arena the theoretical physician—we would say the biologist—who was absent from the *Hippocratic Corpus*. However, when it came to treating patients Herophilus remained faithful to the old Hippocratic tradition of the humors and to traditional pharmacology and surgery.

Erasistratus divided medicine into two principal branches: the first, called scientific, included anatomy, physiology, and the investigation of causes; the second, called stochastic, dealt with diagnosis, prognosis, and treatment. Physicians in Alexandria allowed the two traditions to coexist. They sought to further the development of a life science that saw pathologies simply as deviations from normal conditions, explained by the same causes as normal states. Their project was undoubtedly an ancient one, but Aristotle had given it an especially appealing form. In this theoretical enterprise, Aristotle's influence was so strong that physicians did not hesitate to adopt not only his fundamental principles—for example, finality—but also his errors: Praxagoras endorsed Aristotle's cardiocentrism.

The discoveries of the anatomists of Alexandria and their successors refined and improved the Aristotelian explanations but did not overturn their theoretical framework. However, all this theoretical development seems to have had only minimal influence on treatments: Erasistratus frequently recommended bleeding, and Herophilus relied on the pulse more than the authors of the *Hippocratic Corpus* might have done, but the fundamental aim was to restore the balance among the humors through diet, exercise, or traditional drugs (purges, diuretics, or emollients). Medical practice thus remained Hippocratic. Though surprising at first glance, this coexistence of Aristotelian biology and Hippocratic treatment is easily explained: the anatomo-physiological discoveries of the physicians of Alexandria, as remarkable as they are, were not readily applicable to treatment. The gap between theory and practice in medicine could not be grasped as such by the practitioners themselves. As a result, there was a widespread effort to reevaluate the *Hippocratic Corpus* that amounted almost to a rewriting: not only was Hippocrates represented as a rationalist doctor who closely resembles his followers in Alexandria, but also a tradition was established—perhaps beginning with Herophilus himself, and certainly with his disciple Bacchius—of writing commentaries on the principal treatises of the *Corpus*. This blend of Aristotelianism and Hippocratism grew in an unprecedented way in the 2nd century C.E. through the work of Galen, who adopted Aristotelian finalism and at the same time ensured the influence of the humoral theory for centuries to come.

MEDICAL SCHOOLS AND NOSOGRAPHIES

Within a short time this new way of conceptualizing medicine, if not of practicing it, introduced a number of theoretical and institutional innovations. Medical schools have been mentioned a number of times in this essay; I have placed the term in quotation marks at the first mention of a school when I refer not to a school per se but to a group that left its mark in the *Hippocratic Corpus*. In fact, scholastic organization was a fundamental aspect of ancient *philosophical* life. The first school worthy of the name, besides the Pythagorean brotherhood that was a mix of philosophy and religion, was Plato's Academy. As a hierarchical and institutional reality, endowed with what we today would call an institutional identity, the school of philosophy was a place of immense affective investment for its students. The relationships among the students and between the students and the head of the school (the scholarch) resembled family ties, and with them the strength and complexity of Oedipal relations. Even if, in some cases, at the Academy in particular, the master did not impose a true *orthodoxy*, his doctrine became an obligatory point of reference. Whenever one speaks of a "school" to designate the physicians gathered at Cos, at Cnidus, and, even though much less is known about them, at Croton or Cyrene, the term is used broadly and, in the last analysis, incorrectly.

Beginning with Herophilus, on the contrary, the students of a given master formed associations called sects—the term we use to translate the Greek term *hairesis*, meaning choice or preference and from which we get the word *heresy*. Their purpose was to defend and spread the master's doctrine and practice, which they sometimes helped to articulate, clarify, or expand. It is difficult to evaluate the influence that the philosophers exercised in this regard over the physicians, but it was certainly of some importance. Thus people spoke of the Herophilians, or "the people around Herophilus." However, it would be an exaggeration to say that Herophilus gave these medical sects their definitive forms, particularly the rigid institutional structure that they assumed in the following century and maintained until the decline of the ancient world. Herophilus's school, which was founded on a coherent doctrinal system but remained relatively informal from an institutional point of view, combined the old and the new.

Herophilus's school lasted more than two centuries in Alexandria, then moved to Asia Minor, occupying a site surrounding an ancient temple near Laodicia. It was probably there that it acquired stronger institutional structures, possibly because of the proximity of the temple, but more probably to conform to the new model that had become dominant. In theory, the Herophilians adhered to the tradition of rational medicine bequeathed by Hippocrates, and thus were categorized among the Dogmatists. They also preserved and expanded the rich pharmacopoeia perfected by their master, and most of them stayed faithful to pulse-taking as the primary basis of diagnosis. However, the practice of dissection appears to have ceased very early. Herophilus's school experienced something common to all schools, of philosophy as well as of medicine: betrayal. One defector, Philinus of Cos, founded the Empiricist sect, and in so doing inaugurated a new era in medicine.

Early medicine, beginning with the end of the Hellenistic period, is ordinarily thought to have been dominated by competition among the three major schools: Dogmatist, Empiricist, and Methodist. To these is sometimes added the Pneumatist school, so-called because it insisted on the importance of breath (pneuma) and explained illness as a result of the pneuma's becoming too cold or warm, too fast or slow, too heavy or light; the Pneumatists attempted to cure patients by correcting these problems, substituting heat for cold, and so on. In reality, these sects are not simply different instances of the same model.

There really was no Dogmatist (sometimes called rationalist) school—because no doctor ever called himself a "Dogmatist." The term was used first by their adversaries, and later by historians and doxographers. As we have seen, the historical and the critical traditions both placed Herophilus in the school that traced its roots back to Hippocrates himself. The Empiricists, however, did constitute a school in the strict sense of the word, by virtue of their rivalry with Herophilus's disciples, who constituted a "proto-school," a rivalry all the more bitter since the founder of the empirical sect was a defector from the Herophilian ranks. The Empiricists' argument with the Dogmatists was essentially epistemologic, and Galen, with some malice, claimed that they often agreed on the treatment of a particular patient, disagreeing only on the underlying method; this, in the end, is consistent with what we have already noted about the composite character of Hellenistic medicine. For the Empiricists, hidden causes are unknowable and only experience can reveal the proper treatment of a particular illness. According to this view, medicine is no longer a science. Of course, it is not simply a matter of the experience of a single individual, for the Empiricists recognized the validity of what they called *historia*, the cumulative experience of predecessors as transmitted through oral teaching and in written observations. Similarly, experience gained from one case could be extended, since the Empiricists did not exclude analogies, which allowed them to apply to one organ what they had observed in another, or to apply to a given drug the results of experiments undertaken with a different one. The influence of Skeptic philosophy on Empiricist physicians, whether that of the Pyrrhonians or of the Skepticist Academy of Arcesilas, seemed self-evident to many commentators. The question of influence is actually a very difficult one, and, like many others, it is far from being resolved: the history of the Empiricist school remains to be written, and whoever takes on this difficult task will confront a number of obstacles, not least of which is the tenacious prejudice of modern historians toward Empiricist physicians.

A careful reading of the records, particularly those of Galen, reveals important differences among Empiricist physicians. Philinus took an extreme position by refusing to consider even what tradition calls obvious causes, for example, wounds and overeating. Thus, though all Empiricists officially adhered to the same mandate to reject all rational arguments in medicine, there were vastly different interpretations of this stance. If a physician like Serapion of Alexandria (3rd to 2nd century B.C.E.), whom Celsus cites as a founder of the Empiricist school, condemned all use of reasoning in matters of medicine, certain later Empiricists, like Heraclides of Tarentum (1st century B.C.E.), were not as strict. They advocated a sort of reasoning that they called epilogism, as opposed to the analogism of the Dogmatists. Epilogism, besides its defensive value for Empiricism vis-à-vis its adversaries, might allow for the discovery of hidden phenomena and relationships, but only the kind that, under other circumstances, could be *observed*. Thus they still refused to proceed by inference from observation of perceptible things to something that could be known by reason alone. With Menodotus (1st to 2nd century C.E.), Empiricism ended up employing inductive reasoning in a way that appears very modern.

The Empiricists have to be taken quite seriously. They were neither Sophists seeking to achieve a dialectical tour de force—to build a medical system that did not depend on reason—nor reactionaries longing for the prerational time of archaic medicine. These physicians were responding to contemporary or prior nosological attitudes in tones that were both positivist and rational. It was never a question of encouraging physicians to act in some irrational, animal-like way, but of rejecting what philosophers called demonstration *(apodeixis)*. The Empiricists have been widely criticized for their rejection of anatomy and especially of dissection. Was this not simply a clear indication of the contradiction, already referred to, between the theoretical virtuosity of the new medicine and its inability to apply the benefits of this virtuosity to treatment?

The third of the medical schools of antiquity, the Methodist school, was founded by physicians who were just as anti-Dogmatist as the Empiricists but who were not satisfied with the Empiricist critique of Dogmatism. The ancients themselves disagreed about the identity of the founder of the Methodist school. Some considered it Themison of Laodicia (1st century B.C.E.) and others Thessalus of Tralles (1st century C.E.). Although we have some groundbreaking works, such as *De medicina methodica* by Prosper Alpinus (1611) and *L'histoire de la médecine* by Daniel Leclec (1723), until recently there has been little interest in a system of medicine that has been the object of sharp attacks since ancient times, particularly by Galen. There is undoubtedly important work waiting to be done: entire texts by Methodist physicians are available to the historian of Methodism, including works by Soranus of Ephesus (1st to 2nd century C.E.) and Caelius Aurelianus (ca. 5th century C.E.), although we have no statement of the doctrine itself by a Methodist doctor.

Like the Empiricists, the Methodists thought that the physician should not try to explain diseases by inferring hidden causes from what can be observed. However, they adopted a different attitude toward hidden realities: while the Empiricists believed that such realities did not exist, the Methodists did not take a position on this point, saying that hidden realities, whether they existed or not, were of no consequence for the physician. They held certain Dogmatist notions, but gave them a somewhat different meaning. For example, for the Dogmatists, *endeixis* (indication) was the ability of certain phenomena to *indicate* particular entities or connections that were imperceptible. As Galen said: "Although they [the Methodists] were especially interested in phenomena [like the Empiricists], they differed on the use of the indication"; the Methodists' indication is not the same as the Dogmatists' (*On Sects* 14) "in that it comes from what is apparent" whereas the Dogmatists drew indications from causes that were not manifest. Actually, the use of the term *indication* by the Methodists applied to only one situation, that of a remedy indicated by a pathological condition, whereas in Dogmatist philosophy, at least in one famous case, the soul could be indicated by movement. The use of the term *indication* by Dogmatists and Methodists is more a case of homonyms than of shared concepts.

The principal difference between Methodists and Empiricists lies in the fact that for the former the treatment of a pathology is not determined experimentally (either by firsthand experience or by induction from what can be observed). The central idea of Methodism is that symptoms themselves are indicative of treatment, in the way that thirst indicates its own remedy, drinking. But how are the symptoms to be read? Through a unique and universal conceptual construct, that of "self-evident communities."

This is a complex doctrine, one that is not well understood and that changed during the history of the Methodist school. For instance, the number of communities varied, especially when some Methodists introduced "therapeutic communities." Let us limit ourselves here to the doctrine that seems to have been the most widely recognized. According to this doctrine, there are three communities *(koinotetes)*: the strict *(stegnon)*, the loose *(roōdes)*, and the mixed *(epiploke)*. In the body, every pathological condition comes from a state of constriction or slackening, or a combination of the two. This suggests that the body itself can be described in terms of condensation and rarefaction.

The Methodists thought that they could overcome in this way both the practical and the epistemological hurdles posed by phenomenism. Galen explained this well: symptoms could be similar and yet require different treatment; conversely, it could be necessary to employ the same remedy for seemingly different symptoms. There are interesting examples: the same therapy ought not to be used for the same affliction "as in the case of phrenitis, for example the feeling of tightness in the diaphragm, or the feeling of slackening," whereas one would employ the same treatment for pleurisy and phrenitis "if they both result from constriction" (Pseudo-Galen, *De optima secta*, ed. Kühn, I.163). However, for the Methodists it was not only "self-evident communities" that indicated the remedy to be used (a condition of tightness would call for a loosening). They also took into account phases in the evolution of disease, but according to a predetermined "chart" applicable in every case: all sickness has a beginning *(arche)*, a development *(auxesis, epidosis)*, a high point *(acme)*, and a decline *(parakme, anesis)*.

Where do the self-evident communities come from? According to Galen, "They were not 'apparent' in the sense of being obvious to the senses. Not every condition (of tightness, etc.) can be perceived by the senses, but the condition was 'apparent' if it could be grasped in and of itself, even if it was not observable" (*De optima secta*, ed. Kühn, I.175). The author added that for the Methodists, "apparent" *(phainomenon)* is more or less synonymous with "obvious" *(enarges)*. Put another way, apparent communities avoid two charges: that of being perceived by the senses, with all the uncertainty implied by acquiring knowledge through sensory perception, and that of being rationally established on the basis of "indicative signs."

From the descriptions of Methodism, we have the general impression that we are dealing with an absurd, if not grotesque, speculation, an impression attributable largely to the low opinion of it held by Galen, who is our principal source. Adopting the theory of apparent communities led the Methodists to espouse paradoxes that were shocking to their contemporaries. They said, for example, that it was useless to be concerned with symptoms and circumstances—age, sex, environment, and so forth—in determining treatment. In fact, the Methodists attempted to establish a genuine empiricism by rethinking the role of sensory perception in medical theory and practice. They refused to choose between pure empiricism, which proved to be intolerable, and a priori rationalism; they understood that the Dogmatist approach combined heterogeneous realities, and that no real connection was possible between the general causes imagined by theoreticians and medical practice.

One of the principal features of the new medicine that developed after Herophilus can be found in changes that appear in the accounts of pathological conditions. This is particularly noticeable toward the end of the 2nd century B.C.E.—the beginning of the period of nosographies, which continued for several centuries. The new approach involved defining nosological entities and classifying them by types and species, leaving the doctor to decide, on the basis of the combination *(syndrome)* of the patient's symptoms, what illness he was treating. Although it is difficult to identify the steps in a typical account by the authors of these nosographies, some of the same headings often reappear: a description of symptoms, a report of other physicians' opinions on the illness, an account of the treatment applied, and often an explanation of symptoms based on the "medical system" of that particular author. This process is very different from the one found in *Epidemics* in the *Hippocratic Corpus*: medicine has been described as passing from a description of patients—for individual cases are meaningless unless all the specific symptoms manifested under specific circumstances are brought together—to a description of illnesses, as in proceeding from prognosis to diagnosis. To be sure, we need to recall that in the *Hippocratic Corpus* there were treatises describing diseases—I cited an example from *Diseases* II above—and that the Hippocratic prognosis was, in some ways, a diagnosis; but the change was profound nevertheless. In the nosographies, diseases are defined in terms of one major distinction that has survived into our own time: the distinction between acute and chronic illness, which was probably introduced by Themison.

However, ancient physicians themselves did not seem to have grasped how new the medicine they practiced really was. Just as we have seen this "new" medicine claim descent from Hippocrates, as the practitioners' habit of writing commentaries on the *Hippocratic Corpus* plainly shows, the authors of nosographies constantly denied there had been any change. As Galen writes in his minor work *Quod optimus medicus sit quoque philosophus* (That the Good Physician Is Also a Philosopher): "Failure to know how to classify illnesses by species and genus results in mistakes in treatment; this is what Hippocrates taught when he urged us to follow the rational method."

RATIONAL BUT NOT SCIENTIFIC MEDICINE

Rational medicine, first introduced by Herophilus, saw little change until the end of antiquity. It retained many of the features common to prescientific speculations, particularly the expansion of theory, which served to mask its impotence in actual practice.

From a contemporary point of view, early medical theory offered two very different aspects. Beginning in the 3rd century B.C.E., a remarkable amount had been learned about the human body through observation and experience, sometimes by chance, as when a bodily injury revealed hidden functions and structure, and contrived experience, as in the case of anatomy, the practice of human and animal vivisection. The human skeleton was well understood, with only a few minor exceptions that surprise us today, but these probably resulted from animal experiments. Muscles, though unknown to Aristotle (who explained movement by a system of tendons), were also recognized. The major systems were well identified. Distinction was made between veins and arteries in the circulatory system, although the idea of actual circulation of blood had not emerged; the ancients believed that the blood that circulated in blood vessels collected in the body to make flesh, and had to be continually produced by food; this was the gist of Aristotle's theory. At the same time, the description of the nervous system, which distinguished between sensory and motor nerves as revealed by experiments in vivisection, showed a marked advance in Hellenistic medicine. The central nervous system was thoroughly described, but without any idea about how it worked. There were huge advances in the anatomy of the lungs, but again without the slightest idea of the purpose of respiration; most physicians believed that it primarily served to cool off the body. Functions remained obscure, obviously, as we noted in the cases of cerebral and respiratory function: digestion was generally thought of as either steeping or grinding, and the glands were not thought of as organs of secretion but as spongy growths intended to absorb excess liquid in the body.

The therapeutic consequences of these discoveries were relatively small, and while, as we have seen, physicians remained generally committed to the old Hippocratic pharmacopoeia, it was because the positive discoveries that they had made about the human body could not bring about a revolution in treatment. However, it seems that by Galen's time important advances had been made in surgery and in areas as delicate as odontology or ophthalmology, though trepanation and the setting of fractures and dislocations had been practiced since Hippocrates' day. As for medication, although fairly effective antipyretics for reducing fever had been in use for a long time, there was nothing at all like a disinfectant, for the simple reason that there was no concept of infection.

Another aspect of ancient medical theory is found in the relationship between medicine and what we call biology. The obstacles encountered by physicians attempting to translate the new knowledge in anatomy and physiology into remedies did not stop them from basing their treatments on theoretical considerations that were in turn based on certain assumptions about the human body and its functions. Erasistratus explained fever as the partial obstruction of blood vessels owing to some residue that impeded the normal flow of blood.

Galen, synthesizing the Hippocratic humoral theory, Aristotelian finalism, and the physiology in Plato's *Timaeus*, developed a network of correspondences between organs, functions, humors, and the outside world that came to dominate Western and Arabic medicine up to the Renaissance. Consequently, the speculative, theoretical aspect of medicine remained similar to philosophical speculation.

Since early biology remained speculative—a part of physics understood as "natural philosophy"—it was never able to benefit from the many advances over Aristotelian descriptions afforded by the observations and experiments of anatomists. Bachelard and others have shown that an intellectual construct of this type is not open to rectification or refutation resulting from experiments that could always be simplified and integrated. At the very most, an untenable position such as cardiocentrism was abandoned even by Aristotelians like Galen. Physicians continued to construct systems of general explanations—what might be called medical biology—that obviously never found practical application. The critics, first Empiricists and then Methodists, tried to stop this speculative folly. Nevertheless, such folly was characteristic of ancient medicine and gave it a very different conceptual orientation from that of modern science.

PIERRE PELLEGRIN
Translated by Elizabeth Rawlings and Jeannine Pucci

Bibliography

Texts and Translations

Aristotle. *On Sense and Sensible Objects.* In *On the Soul; Parva naturalia; On Breath.* Trans. W. S. Hett. Loeb Classical Library.

Celsus. *De medicina.* Trans. W. G. Spencer. Loeb Classical Library.

Galen. *De optima secta ad Thrasybulum Liber.* In *Opera omnia.* Ed. and Latin trans. C. G. Kühn. 20 vols. Leipzig: 1821–1833; repr. Hildesheim: Olms, 1964–1965.

———. *Three Treatises on the Nature of Science.* Trans. Richard Walzer and Michael Frede. Indianapolis: Hackett, 1985.

Hippocrates. Trans. W. H. S. Jones. Vols. 1 and 2. Loeb Classical Library.

Studies

Bourgey, Louis. *Observation et expérience chez les médecins de la collection hippocratique.* Paris: Vrin, 1953.

Grmek, Mirko D. *Diseases in the Ancient Greek World.* Baltimore: Johns Hopkins University Press, 1989.

Grmek, Mirko D., ed. *Western Medical Thought from Antiquity to the Middle Ages.* Cambridge, Mass.: 1998.

Lloyd, Geoffrey E. R. *Early Greek Science.* New York: Norton, 1971.

———. *Greek Science after Aristotle.* New York: Norton, 1973.

———. *Magic, Reason, and Experience: Studies in the Origin and Development of Greek Science.* Cambridge and New York: Cambridge University Press, 1979.

———. *Science, Folklore, and Ideology: Studies in the Life Sciences in Ancient Greece.* Cambridge and New York: Cambridge University Press, 1983.

Pigeaud, Jacky. *La maladie de l'âme et du corps dans la tradition médico-philosophique antique.* Paris: Les Belles Lettres, 1989.

Staden, Heinrich von. *Herophilus: The Art of Medicine in Early Alexandria.* Cambridge and New York: Cambridge University Press, 1989.

PHYSICS

Any history of the sciences that would extend back to antiquity must encounter what one might call the "homonymic obstacle." Is it possible to include Aristotle's biology and Claude Bernard's in a single history, as linguistic usage suggests, since the names of modern sciences are often either those of ancient disciplines (mathematics, astronomy, medicine) or they have had names of Greek or Latin origin attributed to them (biology, linguistics)? Asking this formidable question forces us, first of all, to distinguish among different types of continuity: the theoretical permanence of mathematics is hardly comparable to the identity, problematic in itself, of the object of the life sciences, or to the common therapeutic aim of doctors ancient and modern. But homonymy is most deceptive in the case of physics, so profound was the Galilean rupture. Homonymy entails ambiguity: when our atomic theory was conceptualized by modern physics, for example, it was, properly speaking, *through wordplay* that it acquired Democritean antecedents. Moreover it was explicitly *against* ancient—or rather, Aristotelian—physics that Galilean physics, the first of the sciences in the modern sense of the term, developed (if we leave aside the uncertain case of mathematics). No other science has required such theoretical parricide in order to come into being. And yet the absence of conceptual continuity between ancient and modern physics does not exclude perhaps more fundamental modes of insinuation. Through their research in physics the ancients were led to formulate epistemological principles without which the modern sciences, particularly physics, could not exist. But these principles—determinism, or sufficient cause, for example—do not belong to ancient physics as such and were quickly adopted, at least from the time of Aristotle, by a specialized discipline known in the Hellenistic period as logic. In contrast, some concepts and schemas operative in ancient speculation in these areas have proven to be of incontestable heuristic value for modern scientists. This is largely due, however, to the intellectual history of the latter, and it is difficult to say how modern physics might be different if the ancients had not forged notions like that of continuum or reversibility.

The noun *physics* derives from the Greek *physike* (literally, natural things), which implies science *(episteme)*, discipline *(methodos)*, art *(techne)*, and so on. In the philosophical schools of the Hellenistic period, physics was a part of philosophy, along with logic (or dialectics) and ethics, according to a tripartite division that apparently goes back to the ancient Academy. This is the product of a reductive movement the principal stages of which we must now examine.

THE INQUIRY INTO NATURE

Philosophy itself actually started out as physics. No one has yet seriously challenged the idea, which comes to us directly from the ancients themselves, that with the so-called Milesian school in the 7th century B.C.E. a new way of considering the universe appeared, namely, philosophy. Properly speaking, then, philosophy has not always existed everywhere and at all times, and it is legitimate to investigate its relationships with earlier, contemporary, and later attempts at explanation, whether competing or complementary.

Philosophers as concerned with the history of philosophy as Aristotle and his immediate successors acknowledged philosophical antecedents outside the sphere of Greek culture. We must remember that we owe to these philosophers not only most of the accounts we possess concerning the Presocratics but also the interpretive framework within which we are compelled to read these accounts. We know from Herodotus that the Greeks were fascinated by the great empires of the Near East, pharaonic Egypt in particular. But what Socrates, in the intellectual autobiography Plato supplies for him in *Phaedo*, termed the "inquiry into nature" *(historia peri physeōs)* comes into being with Thales of Miletus and his successor Anaximander. The expression is neither a Socratic nor a Platonic innovation, since the Hippocratic treatise *On Ancient Medicine* uses it to designate the work of "Empedocles and others who wrote on nature." Moreover, ancient historians and doxographers credited most Presocratic philosophers with works entitled "On Nature" *(Peri physeōs)*. Some wrote nothing else; some, like Empedocles, may have composed other texts. It is by no means certain that the texts actually bore this title, if only because the notion of "title" may be a later one; a work was usually designated in antiquity by its opening words. But this is not critically important, since the fundamental unity of Presocratic philosophy remains.

What is this nature *(physis)*, this object of study of the first philosophers, who were called physicists *(physikoi)* or physiologists *(physiologoi)* by Aristotle for this very reason? It derives from the root *phy-*, whose original meaning seems to have been increase, grow, be born, and, transitively, cause to grow, engender. The word existed in Greek before Thales; it is likely that Anaximander turned it into a philosophical term, or perhaps one should say grounded philosophy in it. The *Odyssey* uses it to designate the nature (in the sense of properties) of a plant that protects Odysseus against the witchcraft of Circe. But it was probably its philosophical use that made it a common Greek expression. Among the earliest Presocratics the word has three main senses, which occur both separately and concurrently in the texts. *Physis* designates first of all the primordial substance from which everything is derived.

It is therefore a principle, or *arkhe*, which is the second key term in the philosophy of the *physiologoi*. But *physis* is also the process of growth and differentiation of things out of their original substance. This is closest to the original meaning of the root *phy-*. Last, *physis* is the result of the process of growth and coming into being. This is the sense that the usual translation of *physis* as nature captures best; the Latin *natura*, from *nasci*, be born, shows the same semantic breadth as *physis*. In this latter sense *physis* denotes the characteristic properties of a thing, of a collection of things, or even of all things. Thus the *physikoi* attempted to construct explanatory models for the production of natural phenomena (including human beings and their societies) from primordial nature, by means of qualities (hot, cold, moist), entities (water, air, fire), and processes (condensation, rarefaction). These secular and rational models derive their persuasive force from reason, and, analogically, from everyday experiences such as evaporation, desiccation, or putrefaction.

To grasp the originality of this *physical* philosophy, historians are (fortunately) in the habit of comparing it with what preceded it. An overview of the plentiful literature devoted to this question is offered in the masterful studies that Jean-Pierre Vernant, Pierre Vidal-Naquet, their colleagues, and their students began to publish in the 1960s. They have definitively shown that the birth of "physical" philosophy must be traced back to the profound alteration, still largely enigmatic and profoundly consequential, that was the advent of the original social formation we know as the Greek city-state (polis). Philosophical—in other words, physical—explanations of the universe are consonant with *political* power, which is exercised within the framework of laws usually established by the citizens or their representatives, through the persuasive power of public speeches. Mythological explanations of the order of things, on the contrary, are based on an *authority* that they both legitimize and reinforce. Myth, divine or heroic tales full of violence, sex, prohibition, and transgression, provided ancient Greek society with a foundation that man tampered with at his peril. Thus mythological accounts of the universe are particularly well suited to ruling dynasties whose sovereigns can claim that their power is divinely sanctioned.

But accepting this analysis does not obviate the need to develop or qualify it further. Scholars comparing mythological and physical explanations of the universe generally rely for the former on Hesiod's *Theogony*, and to a lesser extent on his *Works and Days*. In Hesiod's account, Chaos and Earth, primordial powers along with Love, together engendered Erebos and Night, who gave birth to the Upper Air and Day. But Earth also coupled with Sky, whom she had herself engendered, and one of their offspring, Cronos, brought the rule of his father Sky to an end, castrating him before being himself dethroned by one of his children, Zeus, who established the current order of the universe. Humankind lived in harmony with the gods until Prometheus, who had the job of dividing the food between the two, secretly favored humans. As an act of vengeance Zeus deprived humankind of fire, which the philanthropic Prometheus stole back for them, suffering accordingly. Anaximander's account is completely different. From a primordial substance described as "infinite," pairs of opposites—hot/cold, dry/moist—are "ejected"; a preponderant role seems to have fallen to moist. It is disputed whether this "ejection" results from a "mechanical" interaction of material particles, or manifests the generative power of the infinite, sometimes described as a living being. Living creatures are born from the desiccation of a moist substance that is possibly terrestrial, humankind being the final product of an evolution from aquatic animals.

As the first of the *physiologoi* whose system can be described with some precision, Anaximander is often taken to be paradigmatic of this earliest phase of physics. But echoes of several other systems have come down to us: according to one, everything derives from water through condensation and rarefaction; for another, everything derives from air; for a third, from fire; still others, whose traces are preserved in the *Hippocratic Corpus,* hold that everything is derived from other primordial substances, compound or simple. This diversity, an object of mockery from a fairly early date—at least from the time of Socrates—calls for two remarks. On the one hand, it is emblematic of the new spirit that marked the advent of physics. No longer appealing to authority, physical explanations originated in the imagination, broadly construed, of those who conceived them. They were *hypotheses* put forward for acceptance, and also for criticism, by everyone endowed with reason. This is a characteristic, likewise inherited from the Greek polis, that ancient philosophy upheld to the end, even after authoritarian regimes had put an end to political freedom in the city-states: philosophy was deployed in the free confrontation of diverse systems and opinions, where no single orthodoxy held sway. In contrast, in bringing all these explanations together under the heading of "inquiry into nature," the ancients were certainly aware that what they held in common theoretically—their explanation of the origin of things in terms of transformations of a primordial substance from which all things ultimately derive—was far more characteristic of them than the ways in which their accounts diverged.

The following discussion will depart from Jean-Pierre Vernant's schema on two points: one has to do with myth itself, and the other with the structure of the physical explanation of the universe. The works of Hesiod, written toward the end of the 8th century B.C.E., are perhaps not the ones best suited to illustrating the distinction that Vernant seeks to make. Comparing Hesiod to the Babylonian myth related in the poem *Enuma Elish,* Gérard Naddaf notes several interesting points of contrast between the two texts. In the first place, the Hesiodic myth lacks the essential characteristic of correspondence to a ritual that allows, through symbolic reenactment of the heroic mythos, for both the periodic renewal of world order and the reinforcement of royal prerogative in cyclical—that is, immutable—time. From this viewpoint the function of the Hesiodic account, written after the great dynasties such as that of Mycenae had disappeared, is more literary than social; it reads as a narrative sequence of "reigns": Ouranos, followed by Cronos, followed by Zeus. To be sure, there is the occasional "return of the repressed" in the Hesiodic myth; for example, having defeated the coalition led by Cronos and dispatched its members to Tartarus, Zeus must deal with Typhon, a monster attempting to restore primeval chaos. Typhon's desperate attempt is a reminder that primordial chaos was suppressed but not eliminated. At the same time, the actual "creator" element in Hesiod's cosmogony is remarkably impersonal: the universe arises through the interaction of relatively abstract entities (Chaos, Earth, Eros). This is not the case later on in Hesiod, when the gods' accounts take center stage.

Reading the fragments of the first *physiologoi* with these remarks concerning Hesiod in mind, one notes that the undeniable differences between the poet and the philosophers are accompanied by a remarkable convergence. Scholars disagree as to whether certain Presocratics conceived of the universe as having infinite extension in time and space. Did Anaximander, Heraclitus, and Anaxagoras believe that the cosmogenesis they described was indefinitely repeated in time whenever the cosmos returned to its primordial stage? In any case, all pre-Aristotelian physics remained imprisoned in a *narrative structure* that it shared with the Hesiodic account: the creation of the world took place in linear time and in a necessary order, while the events in this *(hi)story* arose out of the automatic and necessary interaction of the properties of the elementary entities at work in cosmogenesis.

The *physiologoi* do seem at least to have overcome the rupture between primordial and contemporary time created by myth, through a prefiguration of the idea of "laws of nature," just as modern physicists would come to abolish the Aristotelian rupture between supralunary and sublunary worlds. It has even been suggested that in these rules, which are valid for every point in the universe, one should see an intellectual reflection of the law of democracy, which applies equally to all citizens, while the mythological rupture between primordial and present time reflects the insurmountable difference of status between divine rulers and their subjects. In fact this is overly simplistic. Many of the Presocratic cosmogonies articulate different *periods* that can hardly be viewed as governed by the same rules. According to the Milesians, the universe had a period of dawning in which the phenomena we see before us were not yet visible, and it was Empedocles who designated most clearly the difference between cosmic phases governed by different principles (Love and Hate). Nevertheless, even for physicists who distinguished among periods, at any given moment all reality obeyed the same laws.

Perhaps most fascinating of all in these meager vestiges of the earliest physicists—and this may be attributable to some resonance with our own unconscious desires—is this claim of complete apprehension of reality as a whole. Milesian Nature, from which all beings arise and to which all beings return, is indeed that great mother-without-father, inexhaustible and benevolent, the need for which all children have experienced. The physicist makes his first appearance in search of the principle or principles underlying all things, yet this search takes place within the framework of a Nature that is, ultimately, the sole reality. In this sense the Milesians' concept of Nature was the opposite of the modern one, since nature is defined for us by what it is not. Therefore for them there is no phenomenon that is not natural, and the inquiry into nature encompasses all things. For many centuries the treatises that bore this title (or that acquired it later on) were constructed along the same lines: the author begins by examining the formation of the cosmos, starting from a principle or principles that he has chosen; then he describes the genesis of living creatures and explains their characteristics and endowments, with humankind generally coming at the end of this description, and he finally considers the formation and history of human societies. These analyses have in common the fact that they appeal only to the "mechanical" action of factors utilized in the genesis of things. Here perhaps is their principal difference from earlier mythical cosmogonies, including Hesiod's: the cosmos of the earliest physicists is devoid of intentions, of passions, and of choices. The gods themselves are natural entities and are therefore subject to the laws of nature. Theology is thus a part of physics, and Anaximander, for example, transfers traditional attributes of divinity, such as ingenerability, incorruptibility, immortality, and eternity, to *physis*.

THE ELEATIC SCHOOL AND THE
ATTEMPTS TO RESTORE PHYSICS

The first radical challenge to ancient physics, at the beginning of the 5th century B.C.E., came from Parmenides of Elea and his school, called Eleatic after the city in which it was founded. Throughout antiquity and even beyond, philosophers have had to respond to Parmenides' critique. Situating oneself in relation to Parmenides was considered almost an obligatory phase of philosophical inquiry very early on, and quotations from his poem *On Nature* are thus sufficiently numerous to give us a fairly accurate idea of some of his views. Parmenides criticizes first of all the philosophical nonchalance of the earliest physicists, who saw nothing problematic in deriving all living things from a single principle. Thus the "infinite," which Anaximander takes as a first principle, is indeterminate—this is also the sense of *apeiron*, translated as infinite—and is therefore not a being, even though at the same time it is an engenderer of all things. It may issue from a woman's mouth, but this is paternal discourse, in other words, discourse that prescribes and forbids in the name of the principle of reality, which Parmenides addresses to the adherents of the ancient physics. "I shall not allow you to say nor to think that being comes from non-being" (frg. 8.7–9), says the goddess who instructs the poet, before demonstrating to him the absurdity of the speech "of mortals." Why is a living being born at one instant rather than another, in one place rather than another?

The Eleatic school profoundly altered the shape of physics. For Parmenides, the all-encompassing science became an impossible science. The manner in which the second part of Parmenides' poem is to be understood will no doubt continue to be debated for a long time to come; it proposes, paradoxically, a cosmology of the same type as those of his predecessors, which the philosopher has just severely criticized. Should we see it as a "physics lesson," similar to Alceste's "poetry lesson" to *les précieux* in Molière's *Le misanthrope*, in which Parmenides proves that in the domain of the "false" he is just as capable as the rest, and perhaps more so? Or as an example of what one should not do? Or of a physics belonging to the sphere of appearance and opinion, and not that of truth? In any case, physics lost its status as a rigorous science. Parmenides' greatest victory is clearly visible in later Greek philosophy: henceforward no one would question that intelligibility belonged to what is eternal and immutable, while what is perishable or mutable belonged at best to the realm of opinion.

After Parmenides, no one dared return to the old inquiry into nature. But philosophers did attempt to make physics once again possible. Aristotle saw that the atomist hypothesis of Leucippus and Democritus reintroduced the possibility of plurality and movement while maintaining the central tenets of Eleatic philosophy: that that which is, in the strictest sense of the term, is complete, homogeneous, ingenerable, and incorruptible, and that being and nonbeing are unable to mix or to derive one from the other. But instead of positing a single entity, the atomists imagined an infinity of particles that are whole, indivisible (this is what "atom" means), eternal, and in constant movement in an infinite void that is "nonexistent." Aggregations of these atoms, spontaneously generated, produce the various entities (cf. Aristotle, *On Coming-To-Be and Passing-Away* I.8.325a23ff).

The same could be said for the systems of Empedocles and Anaxagoras: the Eleatic prohibition against the derivation of being from nonbeing is fundamental. "Of all mortal things none has birth, nor any end in accursed death, but only mingling," Empedocles wrote (frg. 350, in Kirk et al.). Everything is made from new combinations that are eternally unmade, and that arise from four fixed elements: Air, Fire, Water, and Earth. Remarkably, the word that has to be translated here as birth is *physis*, the central term of the ancient physics overthrown by the Eleatic school. Anaxagoras, probably a contemporary of Empedocles, also stated that "nothing comes into being nor perishes, but is rather compounded or dissolved from things that are" (frg. 469, Kirk et al.).

All these "restored"—i.e., post-Parmenidean—physical systems share with the Milesian school a "mechanism" that is strongly criticized by both Plato and Aristotle. It is by virtue of their properties, which we would call physico-chemical, that elementary particles come together to form the compounds we see in the world around us. Thus the sole conditions that must be satisfied for two atoms to join together are that they have forms making them suitable for it and that they encounter each other, which is purely a matter of chance. But in an infinite time and space, *all* combinations must necessarily arise.

"IN SOCRATES' TIME"

In the first book of his treatise *On Parts of Animals*, after he has explained that the Presocratics did not arrive at a correct analysis of natural phenomena, because they had no conception of substance that would allow a finalist explanation, Aristotle adds: "In Socrates' time an advance was made so far as the method was concerned; but at that time philosophers gave up the study of Nature and turned to practical [virtue], and to political science" (I.i.642a29).

When the Athenians accused him of, among other things, looking into what took place in the heavens and beneath the earth—of pursuing an inquiry into nature—Socrates answered that he had no interest in these matters, which "he did not understand." The accusation may have been simply anachronistic, since in the autobiography of Socrates found in Plato's *Phaedo* we see Socrates turning to the speculations of ancient physicists before expressing disappointment and turning away. From this position (and it is unimportant for our purposes whether we are following an actual chronology or one reconstructed after the fact), Socrates is solely concerned with making his fellow citizens better, in the ethical sense of the term. His complaint against the earlier physicists is that their accounts were exclusively based on what the Aristotelian tradition would term material and efficient causalities. Hence the famous example in *Phaedo* (98c), where the cause of Socrates' being seated at that particular moment in prison would have been ascribed by the earlier physicists to his body's being made of bones and sinews articulated in a particular manner. For Socrates, the true cause of his being in prison was that, owing to a certain conception of duty and justice, he preferred to submit to the verdict of Athenian judges rather than evade it. Socrates levels an additional charge at the authors of physical treatises that appears in Plato's *Apology*—notably in the ironic passage where Socrates states that he has no intention of disparaging the man who, wiser and cleverer than he, possesses sure and certain knowledge concerning nature—but that is more fully reported by Xenophon. In the latter's account, Socrates states several times that the science of nature is greater than the powers of the human spirit, or that it is by design that the gods have left us in the dark on this subject.

It is difficult to know exactly to whom Aristotle was referring when he mentioned philosophers "in Socrates' time." He may well have meant both those who counted themselves in some manner disciples of Socrates, that is, the Socratics (but does this include Plato?), and people like the Sophists, whose relations with Socrates were more tenuous, and also, finally, more complex. The role of the Sophists in the history of Greek physics needs to be reexamined, for although it was undoubtedly the conditions surrounding the exercise of power in the polis, and notably in democratic regimes like that of Athens, that principally fostered or even directly provoked the rise of the Sophistic movement, the theoretical foundations as well as the uncertainties of the pre- and post-Parmenidean physicists seem to have decisively influenced the content, as well as the method, of the Sophists' teaching. Certain Sophists, Hippias for example, claimed to teach disciplines, such as astronomy, that were directly related to physics. Texts such as Gorgias's *On Not Being,* as well as the relativistic accounts of the doctrines of Protagoras offered by both Plato and Aristotle, seem to indicate that the Sophists were particularly alert to divergent views among the earlier physicists. Thus they helped to deepen the divide between physics and what would later be called practical philosophy. In the famous Sophistic distinction between that which is by nature and that which is by convention, the intelligent causality that is human free will is seen as operating in the sphere of the conventional. Here Socrates and the Sophists could easily find common ground. From this perspective, Aristotle was right: the Socratics (Cynics, Cyrenaeans, and, to a lesser extent, Megarians) abandoned physics to take up practical philosophy, and also logic.

This second criticism of ancient physics was perhaps even more devastating than that of the Eleatic school. Ancient *physis* was, in effect, dismembered: human beings, who remained part of it at least as living creatures subject to the constraints of all living organisms, claimed exemption from theoretical explanations that applied to all things, on the one hand, and claimed the right to impose their own laws on their environment, on the other. This paved the way for a conception of nature nearer to our own, in which men could proclaim themselves "lords and masters," while the ancient unified view would persist in a solitary and nostalgic existence, flowering now and again among widely diverse authors.

Where is Plato in all this? The position of the most celebrated of Socrates' disciples relative to this sidelining of natural philosophy—which had become of little interest in the world of men, as well as inaccessible to human thought—is not easy to pin down. At first glance it seems hard to imagine that Aristotle would include the author of *Timaeus* among the philosophers "in Socrates' time" who had abandoned natural philosophy. Here, too, Gérard

Naddaf has proposed an appealing hypothesis: Plato was undertaking on his own behalf a project similar to that of authors of inquiries into nature, but for a purpose that was principally ethical and based on new premises.

From *Phaedo* on, Plato's critique of the speculations of ancient physicists manifests an ethical dimension. To say that Socrates was sitting in prison owing to his muscles and sinews is to ignore the ethical reasons that led him to prefer death to flight. This view is presented much more pointedly in *Laws:* because they offer mechanistic explanations of the formation of the universe, inquiries into nature are accused of corrupting youth by turning them away from belief in the gods. For Plato, a morality that was sound, and therefore effective, had to be based on the True, whence the detour in *The Republic* through the changeless world of Forms, dominated by the Form of the Good. In Naddaf's view, Plato's aim, at least from the time of *Timaeus* (written later than *The Republic*), was to demonstrate that a true morality was in accordance with the order of the universe. Acquaintance with this universe became indispensable to any philosopher who sought to introduce the new morality into the city-state. Plato intended to write his own "inquiry into nature" in a trilogy of dialogues: *Timaeus*, which describes the formation of the universe and its inhabitants, including man; *Critias*, which traces the history of civilization up to the sinking of Atlantis and the Athenian army (only the beginning of this dialogue survives, and we do not know whether Plato completed it); and *Hermocrates*, which was never written, but which was intended to tell the story of the renewal of civilization—our own—after the cataclysm. This last enterprise was finally completed, Naddaf suggests, in the third book of *Laws*. In doing so, Plato followed the rules of the inquiry-into-nature genre, which tended to begin with a cosmogony *(kosmogonia)* and proceeded to the creation of animals *(zoogonia)*, man *(anthropogonia)*, and finally society *(politogonia)*.

But the basic conception of this enterprise is completely new: Plato was the first philosopher to propose an inquiry into nature that is creationist rather than evolutionist. The strongest evidence for this radical departure is that some of Plato's immediate successors tried to bring it into line with conventional approaches. Xenocrates, for example, is thought to have declared the creationist theory of *Timaeus* to be a mere pedagogical fiction. This creationism, discernible in the finalism of *Phaedo* when it maintains that the true explanation of things resides in the *intention* of their creator, also has a strong ethical component: morality is sound inasmuch as it is based on an order of the universe that was expressly intended by God. This idea, according to which the order of the world was optimally devised by a divine intelligence, was upheld before Plato, notably by Diogenes of Apollonia, a disciple of Anaxagoras. It is surprising that the Socrates of *Phaedo* does not allude to it; perhaps he would have had to revise his global condemnation of the inquiry into nature, and perhaps that was precisely what he wanted to avoid. But between maintaining that the order of the world derives from an intelligent principle and declaring that this order was established by a divine being also preoccupied with the moral destiny of humankind, there is a step that Plato appears to have been the first to take. This is why the physico-teleological proof of the existence of the divinity in Book X of *Laws* may be considered the culminating point of both Plato's inquiry into nature and his reformulation of ethics.

One may wonder why Plato found it necessary to provide both a cosmological and a theological moral foundation, when in *The Republic* the Idea of the Good was sufficient to engender morality and construct the ideal constitution. The discussion at the beginning of *Timaeus* is explicitly described as continuing from "yesterday's discussion"; the reference (as we know from the summary provided) is to the organization of the ideal city-state in *The Republic*. This sequence has been deemed so bizarre, given the widely divergent perspectives of *The Republic* and *Timaeus*, that some modern scholars have made the unlikely claim that there must have been a second, lost version of *The Republic*. To justify the trilogy being inaugurated, Socrates claims at the beginning of *Timaeus* that the earlier treatment was like a painting whose figures he would like to see become animate; he particularly desires to see how the ideal city would function in war. According to Luc Brisson in the introduction to his translation, "*Timaeus* begins with a summary of the ideal Constitution as described in *The Republic* . . . , followed by the story of Athens' ancient victory against Atlantis, because Plato is trying to establish 'in nature' the ideal Constitution described in *The Republic*" (p. 10). This should no doubt be viewed as one of the events in the "realist conversion" that scholars perceive in Plato's final years.

This Platonic rehabilitation of the inquiry into nature, in the form of a creationist cosmogony and anthropogony, does have its complexities. The principal one is to be found in ten much-discussed passages in *Timaeus* in which Timaeus downplays his own discourse, saying that he can make no claims as to the truth of statements about that which is "firm and discernible by the aid of thought" (29b); he can only hope to produce statements "inferior to none in likelihood," a "likely account" (29d). The discourse of physics, because it has to do with sensible reality, which is fleeting and obscure, cannot take on the rigor of scientific discourse. These statements must have influenced Xenocrates in his reading of *Timaeus* mentioned above. In any event, the passages in question support the hypothesis that Plato's inquiry into nature does not have its end in itself, but that its aim is in the last analysis ethical. The actual study of nature does not suffice, according to Plato, to belie Parmenides' condemnation of natural science. Therefore, strictly speaking, Plato may be included among the philosophers who, "in Socrates' time," turned away from physical inquiry—Aristotle said *theoria physika*. The (second) restoration of physics belongs to Aristotle.

ARISTOTELIAN PHYSICS

Aristotle's natural philosophy marks the high point of the physical thought of the ancients. It was Aristotelian physics that medieval thinkers were at pains to understand and develop; it was also Aristotelian physics that was attacked by 17th-century physicists. In his review of earlier doctrines—as he did in other areas, but perhaps to a greater extent with physics—Aristotle tried to show that each harbors a grain of truth, viewed from the proper perspective. Aristotle was not an eclectic, however; his method of theoretical reappropriation of earlier doctrines is virtually the opposite of eclecticism—which naturally makes the Stagirite suspect as a historian of philosophy. Aristotle devoted a fascinating but little-known treatise, *On Coming-To-Be and Passing-Away,* to putting the great problems of Presocratic philosophy "in perspective."

Neither a complete science nor an impossible one, physics for Aristotle is the science of a domain of existence. Entities that possess the principle of motion in themselves are called "natural," the term *motion* being understood in its global Aristotelian sense of change across all categories affected by movement. A living plant has in itself the principle of its own growth; the element Fire has in itself a tendency to move toward the periphery of the universe. A table, on the other hand, has the principle of its becoming-a-table located in something other than itself, i.e., in the craftsman manipulating his tools. From a certain viewpoint, all entities in this world are natural, including tables, since they are made of wood, which is, or once was, a natural object. But this point of view is not *essential:* being made of wood is not a table's essential characteristic. What defines a table is its use, and this is due more to the carpenter than to the tree from which the table is made. The study of physics is then limited to certain entities that Aristotle enumerated in the first lines of the treatise *Meteorologica:* entities in motion and their elements, including heavenly bodies, living creatures, and "meteorological" phenomena, which encompass objects we ourselves would term meteorological—rain, hail, rainbows—and also tides, the sea, currents, earthquakes, and phenomena such as comets, shooting stars, and the Milky Way (which Aristotle located in the atmosphere.)

This theoretical science of self-moving entities takes Parmenides' criticism into account. First of all, the system of physical beings, the cosmos, is finite, closed, and eternal. To be sure, Aristotle refrains from representing all the transformations that occur in it as simple *alterations* of one or more substances that are always the same, as did, according to Aristotle, those philosophers who held that the universe derived from a single, fundamental reality. Here he is alluding to the Milesians, not without putting them through the Caudine Forks of Aristotelianism. Contrary to what the Stagirite claims, Anaximander's infinity cannot be reduced to a *material* in the Aristotelian sense, since, far from being a passive object, infinity is the generator of all things. Even in Aristotelian physics, then, there is generation and disappearance of natural entities, but in an uninterrupted sequence of transformations that is based on the continuous transmutation of elements one into another. Aristotle took from Empedocles the concept of the four basic constituents of matter: Earth, Water, Air, Fire. But he defined each by a *pair* of fundamental properties: hot and cold, dry and moist. Fire is hot and dry, Air is hot and moist, Water is cold and moist, Earth is cold and dry. Elements may be transformed into one another through the gain or loss of these qualities, and this occurs more readily, though not exclusively, between two elements that possess a common quality: Air results from Fire through dry transforming into moist, and so on. The Aristotelian cosmos is fundamentally cyclical, since, for example, heavenly bodies follow the same orbits throughout eternity. This is a fundamental transformation in ancient physics. With Aristotle, for the first time, the discourse of physics lost the narrative structure that tied it so closely to Hesiodic narrative. The problem of the absolute origin of all things disappeared, and cosmology became independent of any cosmogony. The human world, however, is embedded in history; Aristotle states more than once in *Politics* that the time of monarchies is past. But this linearity, with which physics is not concerned, is inscribed within a more fundamental circularity, since the human race is periodically decimated by various cataclysms that oblige the survivors to reinvent civilization. Conversely, the first physicists, being interested in the genesis of all things, had included the study of the development of human civilization in their inquiry into nature.

Yet this closed system was not sufficient unto itself: we have here what we might call the second adaptation to Parmenides' criticism. Everything that is moved is set in motion by a mover, which was set in motion, in turn, by another mover. The ultimate of these movers to be set in motion, the one on whose motion all other motions depend, directly or through mediation, is the "first sky," the set of fixed stars that Aristotle thought were affixed to a sphere, the last one in his geocentric and finite Universe. But the first sky itself received its motion from an unmoved mover, which, for Aristotle, was divinity. This paradoxical concept of the unmoved mover shows clearly the status Aristotle accorded physics. Being immaterial and having no other possible activity—that is, no activity compatible with its preeminent dignity as pure act, except for the activity of thinking about itself—the Prime Mover cannot move in a physical sense. The first sky is thus moved by *desire*, because the perfection of the Prime Mover makes it also supremely desirable. The physical world therefore draws its motion, and even its possibility of a beyond-itself, from a reality that is "metaphysical" in the etymological sense of the term. The higher domain of being lies outside the domain of physics.

Thus the unity of the ancient *physis* was not restored. Moreover, in the cosmos itself certain domains of being are inaccessible to physics. This is true for everything connected with human technologies, and perhaps for certain animal behaviors as well. It is also true in the domain of what Aristotle was the first to call the "practical sciences," i.e., those that take actions resulting from human free will as the objects of ethics and politics. It is perhaps justifiable to speak of nostalgia here as well; in opposition to some Sophists, Aristotle upheld the natural basis of politics and certain social ties. Humans assemble naturally in societies that come to form city-states (poleis); family ties and slavery are also natural, for some people are naturally destined to serve. But this naturalness is not enough to make social and political ties the objects of physics; as those ties are based on human free will, they are subject to a different type of scientific discourse. Finally, phenomena that come about fortuitously, and not always or most of the time, remain outside the science of physics, although they cannot be declared unnatural in every case.

It is at the price of such drastic limitations that Aristotle preserves the status of scientific discourse for physics. The regularities on which this discourse depends are certainly not perfect, whence the reservation noted above: the phenomena studied by physics occur "always or most of the time." But the physicist must uncover the *causes* of these phenomena, and display these properties through demonstrative discourse.

The teleological character that Aristotle attributes to natural phenomena—"nature does nothing in vain," "it always produces the best," he repeats incessantly in his treatises on natural philosophy—is the aspect of his physics that has earned him the most criticism, and interpretation of this teleology remains the object of lively argument among scholars to this day. To understand this Aristotelian position, we should perhaps relate it to what was said above concerning Aristotle's cosmos. If the cosmos is eternal and unchangeable overall, it lacks the possibility of *constructing*, in the past, the perfection—all-encompassing but not total—that we see in it. Moreover, being uncreated, the cosmos cannot derive this perfection from the intelligent intention of a demiurge. It must then be good in and of itself, this goodness being the imperfect imitation of the absolute excellence of the Prime Mover.

The fate of Aristotle's physics, and notably his cosmology and its dynamics, is a paradoxical one. At odds with the past and adopted by none of his successors (even the loyal Theophrastus, who succeeded Aristotle at the head of the Lyceum, criticized his master's teleology), this system is undoubtedly the approach to physics that had the most enduring posterity. Its longevity is largely due to the "Christianization" of Aristotle by certain medieval writers.

Later physicists abandoned Aristotle's eternal and immutable cosmos to return to a more cosmogonic conception of the science of nature. Even if their visions of the universe were radically opposed on several important points, Stoics and Epicureans had in common the conception that worlds form, develop, and finally disappear. Stoic teleology took the providentialist form, which was not part of the Aristotelian cosmos, despite some recent assertions to the contrary, while Epicureanism adopted a modified form of Democritean atomism based on chance. But Aristotelianism obviously left traces. On the fundamental point of the structure of physical discourse, for example, we note that Lucretius, following perhaps the order of exposition of Epicurus's treatise *On Nature*, rather than beginning his poem with the creation of the universe and going on to deal with the genesis of the various entities that compose and inhabit it, first outlines the pertinence of atomic theory, deduces from it the various properties of entities, and then moves on to an "application" of the results of this procedure by examining each category of entities.

Physics from then on was a *part* of philosophy. The first Stoics maintained, emphatically enough to make clear that it was no longer accepted by everyone, the idea that the study of physics was necessary for any would-be philosopher. But from the end of the Hellenistic era on, philosophy began to privilege its ethical side. In his *Naturales quaestiones*, a long treatise on natural science exploring subjects that would have come under the heading of inquiries into nature a few centuries earlier, Seneca justifies his enterprise to Lucilius (to whom the work is dedicated) in terms of an apologetic aim: "You say: 'What good will these things do you?' If nothing else, certainly this: having measured god I will know that all else is petty" (I, Preface, 17). In the context of a polemic with the Epicureans for whom the ultimate object clearly relates to the "art of living," the goal is to have Stoic providentialism triumph over Epicurean atomism, which is based on chance.

THE GREAT DEBATES OF ANCIENT PHYSICS

Such, then, are the principal episodes in the development of ancient speculation concerning *physis*. Let us now look briefly at what we might term the great divisions within ancient physics. At the end of antiquity, the drama whose important events we have just described was played out again more or less synchronically: the theories that had grown out of the difficulties of earlier doctrines coexisted alongside the latter, which took on entirely new forms, as we shall see with the Neoplatonist commentators on Aristotelian physics. In this way, too, ancient physicists bequeathed to the Middle Ages and modern times a set of opposing points of view. Even though these oppositions were of course always outside of physics in the modern sense, the "conflicting matrices" still have plenty of meaning for the Postgalileans that we are. Let us look at two of them.

It is a commonplace to say that, unlike the physics of Galileo's day, the ancient physics was not a physics of engineers. Certainly the Greeks, and through them the Romans, possessed a body of technical thought. The authors of technological treatises made reference to physical science, principally Aristotelian, but knowledge of the available physical theories could not have

helped them in the least. No doubt the point was to provide inventions arising from skill and determination with an a posteriori theoretical foundation.
The machines described in these treatises were related to physics only by virtue of being *material:* they were presented as a direct application of mathematics. The same held true for optics and acoustics, aptly described by Aristotle along with mechanics as "the most physical fields of mathematics"
(*Physics* II.2.94a7). It is in the margins of physics, then, and one might say in
the shadow of mathematics, that the speculations that are the most interesting from the point of view of physics in the modern sense arose. As for Archimedes' treatises, which unquestionably constitute for us the most remarkable
and fertile production of physics in antiquity, the ancients unanimously located this work in the realm of mathematical speculation.

These remarks bring us to the first significant opposition, which has to do
with the role of mathematics in physics. This question must be handled with
the greatest caution, because here we run the greatest risk of being misled by
statements by ancient philosophers that have a modern ring. We may recall
once again to what extent the aims of mathematical physics were alien to the
spirit of the ancient physicists; nevertheless, there is a tradition of mathematical analysis of nature that goes back, if not to Pythagoras himself, at least to
the first Pythagoreans. It is difficult to pin down the exact nature of the
affinity they posited between things and numbers. But what interests us here
is that a Pythagorean-Platonist tradition developed a mathematical approach
to natural phenomena from which Renaissance and modern scientists explicitly drew their inspiration. Certain Neopythagorean and particularly Neoplatonic texts, notably those of Iamblichus (ca. 245–ca. 325 C.E.) and Proclus
(412–485), appear to outline a veritable program for the mathematicization
of nature. These texts remained purely programmatic, although it would take
too long to show why this is so. They are all based, in the final analysis, on
Plato's *Timaeus*, where geometric figures (triangles and squares) are the ultimate components of all corporeal entities. Running counter to this tradition is
Aristotle's qualitative approach, adopted by, among others, the Stoics, who
felt, on the one hand, that mathematics concerned objects less ontologically
rich than those of physics, from which they were derived via abstraction of
their sensible qualities, and, on the other hand, that mathematical explanation of the qualities of bodies—as according to the properties of atoms in
Democritus or to those of elementary triangles in Plato—derived color, for
example, from entities that had no connection to it. For Democritus, it was in
fact the form and structural arrangement of atoms that produced color, atoms
themselves being colorless. Aristotle did not reject the use of mathematics
and measurement in physics, since bodies are mixtures of elements in certain
proportions. He even states explicitly in *Physics* (III.iv.202b30) that physical
science is concerned with magnitudes, which are by definition measurable.

298 ❖ THE GREEK PURSUIT OF KNOWLEDGE

But this avenue of research was of no interest to the Aristotelians for various reasons, chief among them being perhaps that in their view the qualities of bodies—colors, odors, and so on—are among their objective properties.

The second great opposition in the history of ancient physics also divided physicists into two camps, albeit with certain exceptions. On one side were the partisans of a finite world, who adopted a continuous conception of matter and space. This world is, in the majority of accounts, full, or if it does contain some emptiness, it does so in small quantity. On the other side were the partisans of an infinite universe, inhabited by innumerable worlds wandering in the intercosmic void; these thinkers professed an atomist theory of matter and posited the chance encounter of atoms as the basis of all reality. Those who belonged to the first camp, of whom Aristotle was the "purest" representative, had a tendency, entirely consistent with their cosmological presuppositions, to view the universe as the product of an intention or, at the least, of final causes, while the atomists criticized this physical recourse to teleology. The study of "mixed" forms is particularly interesting. The Stoics, for example, as partisans of an absolute providentialism and a determinism so strict that they thought that after its destruction the same world was identically reborn, and that the same Socrates would walk on the same day in the same agora an infinite number of times, shared with Aristotle the idea of a spherical and geocentric world. But not only is this world not eternal, although eternally re-created, nor invariant, since it is susceptible of expansion and retraction, it is also immersed in an infinite void.

This second opposition is of much greater historic importance than the first. At the end of antiquity it formed a background to all physical investigation, pitting Aristotelians and Democriteans against one another. Christians would bring crucial reinforcements to the first camp, but not without undermining the actual organization of Aristotelian physics, which required that the world be eternal. And up to the end of antiquity concepts arising from these physical traditions were studied; a remarkable example is furnished by Aristotle's Neoplatonist commentators, whose richness and intellectual audacity we are only now rediscovering. Primacy of place belongs to the two great 6th-century commentators Philoponus and Simplicius. Let us look at the former. The fact that Philoponus was a Christian led him to criticize the overall conception of Aristotle's eternal universe, but he undertook to rectify or replace certain concepts of Aristotelian physics. Thus he developed the notion of internal momentum that is transmitted from the outside, and that would later be termed *impetus*, to explain the persistence of motion in something mobile that is no longer in contact with its mover. This notion allowed Philoponus to posit a unity of the laws of dynamics: although he preserves the Aristotelian distinction between natural and forced motion, the same kind of impetus explains the motion of heavenly bodies, heavy bodies, and animals. In the same vein, Philoponus abolished the difference in nature between the superlunary and sublunary worlds, maintaining that they are made up of the same matter. In both cases, religious considerations led him to these views: impetus derives ultimately from God, and the fact that the stars were no longer divine but created and destined for destruction removed all their divine character. Philoponus pushed the unification of the universe even further by proposing a definition of matter as extension, which has Cartesian overtones. Through polemics of remarkable theoretical force and subtlety, the notions of space and time were very carefully worked out. All later philosophical and scientific tradition could only return to the same oppositions between absolute or relative space and time.

It seems, then, as if this body of research, based on ancient—and particularly on Aristotelian—notions, which commentators at the end of antiquity handed on to the Middle Ages, constituted a reserve of the principal ideas on which modern physics would draw for its own development. Not that there was theoretical continuity between Philoponus and Galileo, but Galileo could have done nothing without the reelaboration by Philoponus, and his friends and adversaries, of the concepts of Aristotelian physics.

PIERRE PELLEGRIN
Translated by Selina Stewart and Jeannine Pucci

Bibliography

Texts and Translations

Anaxagoras. In *The Presocratic Philosophers*, 2nd ed. Ed. G. S. Kirk, J. E. Raven, and M. Schofield. Cambridge and New York: Cambridge University Press, 1983.

Anaximander. *Fragments et témoignages*. Ed. M. Coche. Paris: Presses Universitaires de France, 1991.

Aristotle. *Meteorologica*. Trans. H. D. P. Lee. Loeb Classical Library.

———. *On Coming-To-Be and Passing-Away*. Trans. E. S. Forster. Loeb Classical Library.

———. *Parts of Animals*. Trans. A. L. Peck. Loeb Classical Library.

Empedocles. In *The Presocratic Philosophers*, 2nd ed. Ed. Kirk, Raven, and Schofield.

Parmenides. Ibid.

Plato. *Timaeus*. In *Timaeus; Critias; Cleitophon; Menexenus; Epistles*. Trans. R. G. Bury. Loeb Classical Library.

Seneca. *Naturales quaestiones*. Trans. Thomas H. Corcoran. Loeb Classical Library.

Studies

Brisson, Luc, trans. Introduction and notes to French ed. of Plato, *Timaeus and Critias*. Paris: Flammarion, 1992.

Burnet, John. *Early Greek Philosophy*. London: A. and C. Black, 1930.

Kahn, Charles. *Anaximander and the Origins of Greek Cosmology*. New York: Columbia University Press, 1960; Philadelphia: Centrum Philadelphia, 1985.

Naddaf, Gérard. *L'origine et l'évolution du concept grec de phusis*. Lewiston, N.Y.: E. Mellen Press, 1992.

Sambursky, Samuel. *The Physical World of the Greeks*. Princeton: Princeton University Press, 1956.

Solmsen, Friedrich. *Aristotle's System of the Physical World*. Ithaca, N.Y.: Cornell University Press, 1960.

Sorabji, Richard, ed. *Philoponus and the Rejection of Aristotelian Science*. Ithaca, N.Y.: Cornell University Press, 1987.

Vernant, Jean-Pierre. *Myth and Thought among the Greeks*. London and Boston: Routledge and Kegan Paul, 1983.

POETICS

FROM THE BEGINNING, poetry has been recognized for its power and strength, owing to its capacity to evoke and communicate certain emotions. We can recall in Book 1 of the *Odyssey,* at the start of the suitors' banquet, how unbearable Penelope finds the evocation, by the minstrel Phemius, of the return of the Achaeans from Troy: "Phemius, many other things you know to charm mortals, deeds of men and gods which minstrels make famous. Sing them one of these, . . . and let them drink their wine in silence. But cease from this woeful song which always harrows the heart in my breast, for upon me above all women has come a sorrow not to be forgotten" (337–342).

Similarly in Book 8, during Alcinous's feast, when the Phaeacian minstrel sings a prelude and, at Odysseus's request, begins to recount the city's capture and fall, Odysseus, hearing about his companions and their exploits, cannot hold back his tears. This leads him to betray himself and to reveal his true identity to his hosts. Thus anamnesis or anticipation can lead to tears, and can likewise awaken a truth.

What better homage can we imagine than this double testimony to the affective power woven into the very fabric of the story being told? What is more modern, too, than this reflection in a mirror in which the narrative work naturally comments on itself and justifies itself, even as it gives impetus to the story in progress? Moreover, it is not insignificant that specific testimony to the irrefutable emotional and affective power of poetic diction is brought us by Odysseus and Penelope, the two protagonists of the *Odyssey.*

A second element to which the poets themselves bear witness is the will to style, *Kunstwollen,* conceived as an inseparable component of their expressive undertaking. Theognis of Megara is perhaps the first to speak of it, when he refers to the inimitable "stamp" he has imposed on each of his works: "For the sake of my art, let a seal be placed on these verses, Cyrnus, so no one can steal them or replace the noble original with inferior copy. All will say, 'These are the words of Theognis of Megara, famous everywhere'" (I.19–23). Phocylides, for his part, uses an authentic signature in many of his compositions, in a familiar formulaic hemistich: "Here is this work, another by Phocylides."

Finally, in a different realm, the art of pastiche as Plato practiced it in *Menexenus, Phaedrus,* and the *Symposium,* for example, is like a repeated mirroring of the effect of style, since it constantly refers to another textual image emerging from the text's fabric or framework. Of course we are dealing here with prose and oratory, but, as we shall see, the factors involved in artful prose, like those involved in the psychagogic—and not merely the argumentative—effect of oratory, belong to poetry.

The theories of the Sophist Gorgias of Leontion evoke the same two aspects of poetry when he formulates the rules for speech making. The argumentation, always brilliant and relative, not to say relativistic, must be accompanied, as in Gorgias's *Encomium of Helen*, by more concerted stylistic effects: the quantitative balance among the parts of a sentence *(kola)*, the use in proximity of words with the same root *(paronomasia)*, rhymes or assonances at the end of the phrase *(homoeoteleuta)*, and so on.

As for Plato himself, playwright and stage manager of his own dialogues, how can we take him seriously when he has Socrates say, in Book X of *The Republic*, that Homer must be banished and the poets, guilty of fictions, are to be thrashed? We may be inclined to read this as a muted echo of the philosophical rigorism that, since Xenophanes' day, had stigmatized the "immorality" of the Homeric gods, rather than as a serious and definitive condemnation, though it is often presented as such. Otherwise, how could we account for the subtle, self-directed irony with which its author says, on several occasions, that the ideal model of a just state, as it is sketched out in the ten books we have just read, constitutes nothing less than the exercise of a verbal fantasy, analogous therefore to poetic and literary fictions? Moreover, is there any better apology for poetry and for the poet than *Ion*, confronting the rhapsodist with his inspiration?

In this dialogue, Plato presents the case of a bard reciting Homeric works. Accompanying himself on the *kithara*, he travels from city to city to give public recitals of parts of the *Iliad* and *Odyssey*. The problem raised is the entirely sophistic one of his competence and technical prowess. Must he be a warrior, a hunter, a fisherman, a strategist, or an artisan if he wants to evoke those diverse activities convincingly for us? Or is it enough for him to be a good interpreter of Homer, persuasive by virtue of his enthusiastic verve alone? The second option is obviously the one retained, accompanied and enriched by the clause that has him share in the power of the gods. The Muses, indeed, are the first to express this; they breathe their grace into the poet, while the interpreter, in this case the rhapsodist Ion, and all those who see and hear him, are participants in the strong sense of the term. This is how the rings attracted by Heracleus's stone are linked, Plato comments, resorting to the rightly celebrated metaphor that represents the poetic attraction exercised by the artist over his public as a force analogous to that of magnetism. The problem of competence, necessarily Protean, was thus a false problem, since the only real role for Homer's interpreter is to be available to transmit the poet's message well, a message that comes from the Muses and thus from the gods. As Socrates says to the rhapsodist: "And when you ask me the reason why you can speak at large on Homer but not on the rest, I tell you it is because your skill in praising Homer comes not by art, but by divine dispensation" (*Ion* 536d). When Hesiod invoked the Boeotian Muses of Mount Helicon on the threshold of his work, his request for protection had the same meaning.

Democritus, in his day, had affirmed that poetic form of enthusiasm. To be *entheos*, "full of the god," is a characteristic that the poet shares with other inspired individuals: prophets, bacchantes, pythonesses. As he puts it, "Everything a poet writes inspired by enthusiasm and a sacred spirit becomes a masterpiece" (frg. 18).

This sort of sacred delirium is not without a relationship to poetry, as Plato's *Ion, Symposium,* and *Phaedrus* attest; we may think in particular of the prayer addressed to Pan and the Nymphs that opens and closes this last text, one of Plato's most inspired dialogues, one that also speaks to us of love and true eloquence. Thus poetic "madness" figures, alongside the madness of Eros or of sacred inspiration, as a high ontological value, proceeding both from myth itself and from the underlying truth expressed in myth. Euripides' *Bacchae* offers an exemplary embodiment of this irrational and inspired aspect of the Greek soul. Let us not forget that Dionysus, god of ecstasy, is the source of the dithyramb and of tragedy. As for Orpheus, whose myth is so frequently invoked, he is the very incarnation of lyricism, which complements the orgiastic music proper to the Dionysian cult. The Thracian bard stands out as an initiate as early as the archaic period, since the purity of his song enables him to cross the portals of death. Thus he is the avatar of the Apollonian theme of continuous creation, for his song, capable of charming all the realms of the living, from craggy rocks to the wildest beast, suffices to ensure the cohesiveness of the cosmos and universal harmony.

Pythagoras belongs in the same company; another Apollonian, he measures and calculates the musical gaps between the various tones in the scale and uses them to measure, in equally harmonic terms, the distance that separates and makes proportionate the orbits of the planets that give the world its rhythm as they gravitate around us. The mathematical model thus guarantees the music of the spheres, establishing and justifying every other form of melody, through the adjustment of gaps in sound, and every other form of rhythm, by recurrences, periods, or returns. In every era, poetry and music are hard to dissociate. They both take their authority from the Muses; they are similarly psychagogic and measurable in their prosodic or harmonic manifestations. The separation of the media comes about only with the first prose writers, with Hecataeus or Herodotus, in other words relatively late, at the beginning of the 5th century. Other genres, however, remained faithful to the ancient alliance.

With Aristotle, reflection on poetry ceases to be circumstantial. In more than one youthful hypothetical treatise devoted "to the poets," of which we have a few fragments, the Stagirite is the author of a *Poetics* that we can rightly call the first handbook of literary theory in the history of Western literature. Without naming it, Aristotle even manages to designate the literary reality that is still seeking a name: "the art which uses either plain language or metrical forms (whether combinations of these, or some one class of metres) remains so far unnamed" (Poetics I.7–8).

Thus in his characteristic concern with making distinctions he separates the plastic, musical, and "literary" arts according to the means they use to bring about what he calls imitation. The key term *mimesis* in fact characterizes any artistic production, any figurative representation, whatever the genre. Thus what is at stake is not simply imitation understood as a copy of an external and anterior reality; rather, what is at stake is the very essence of artistic activity. Moreover, when Aristotle tells us that "art imitates nature," he implies that the process of art *(techne)* is analogous to that of nature *(phusis)*. Just as the ancient natural entity of *phusis* ceaselessly produces beings of all sorts and brings them to life, in the same way art produces and creates, bringing into existence a quantity of artifacts that are no less imbued with ontological density than the things that exist "by nature." They may even be considered preferential, owing to their "fabrication" *(poēisis)*, which weighs them down with intellectuality and sometimes saturates them with emotional content. This is how the previously defined literary products appear, for example, and they are clearly distinguished from others. The epic and tragic genres count among these literary products, and the Stagirite speaks of these first of all, at least in the part of his *"ars poetica" (techne poietike)* that has come down to us.

With the initial definitions established relative to the means, objects, and manner of imitation *(mimesis)* or, more precisely, the representation through which literary fiction is exercised, Aristotle is ready to give us his definition of tragedy in chapter VI. Along with *mimesis* we find *katharsis*, the other key term of his aesthetics: the emotional liberation of affects provoked by the dramaturgical act. Here is the rightly celebrated text: "Tragedy, then, is mimesis of an action which is elevated, complete, and of magnitude; in language embellished by distinct forms in its sections; employing the mode of enactment, not narrative; and through pity and fear accomplishing the catharsis of such emotions" (Poetics VI.2–3).

This affirmation of the literary fiction that constitutes the tragic genre, allied to that of the liberating—and properly psychagogic—effect that emanates from it, allows us to rediscover our two elements: style, achieved through appropriate shaping of the text, and emotional impact, here placed under the seemingly ambiguous sign of purification. The term used *(katharsis)* indeed evokes the religious or philosophical lexicon in the sense of lustration and prelude to a ritual or moral purity, and at the same time it refers to the Hippocratic (and more generally medical) vocabulary, in the sense of purge or purgation. In fact, without denying the possibility of multiple meanings, it seems that the term must be endowed here with a meaning sui generis, related to the aesthetic definition of tragedy, the literary genre whose essential and foundational efficacy it represents.

If we return briefly now to the content and outline of *Poetics*, we shall recall that while the treatise posits imitation or representative fiction *(mimesis)* from the outset as the common denominator for all the arts, Aristotle quickly makes his statement more specific, inflecting it in the direction of the arts of speech (I). He spells out the noble subjects that are required by the epic and tragic genres (II) before contrasting narrative and direct action as differential modes of imitative suggestion (III). To complete this fine exordium, he returns to *mimesis*, emphasizing its epistemological role, its hedonic source, and its paradoxical status, which enables us to like even images of corpses (IV).

Next, he evokes comedy and its origins, promising to return to the topic later on. He adds, as if in passing, the theatrical requirement of a fictional action that would take place in the time of one revolution of the sun. He does not return to this point, but his remark leads to the well-known principle of the unity of time (V).

Plunging into the heart of a first argument here, Aristotle seeks to encompass the essence *(ousia)* of tragedy in the definition we have seen, before he goes on to enumerate its component parts: plot, characters, diction, argument, music, staging. From here on, our teacher confines himself to the plan he has outlined, and speaks to us in an orderly fashion of the arrangement of facts *(sustasis tōn pragmatōn)* that will be necessarily unified around a single master action and a single main character (as in the *Iliad*, the *Odyssey*, or *Oedipus the King*). These considerations, which are dealt with in chapters VII through XIV, include important notations such as the indispensable marriage of verisimilitude with internal necessity in plot development (IX), and the differentiation between simple and complex schemas accompanied by vicissitudes and instances of recognition (X–XI). Such dramatic turns of events, arising from the very way the facts are arranged, are designed to produce reactions of pity and fear; as we have seen, these are the hallmarks of the tragic genre (XIII–XIV), whose formal elements (prologue, *parados, stasima,* and so on) have just been reviewed (XII).

We then come to an examination of characters. We are reminded that they are required to be elevated and noble, just as the source is necessarily mythical and aristocratic (XV). Our instructor now goes back to clarify some earlier points. Returning to the subject of recognition (XVI), he distinguishes among its various possibilities, preferring those that arise directly out of the arrangement of the facts. He reaffirms the preeminence of unity of action, the condition for successful staging (XVII), before applying this principle once again to the denouement (XVIII). A proper outcome, as we recall (XIII–XIV), will bring an average—though noble—individual who had once been guilty of a notorious and forgotten crime *(hamartia)* from happiness to unhappiness, as if through an internal necessity of which he alone is unaware. We recognize the shadow of the redoubtable and pitiable Oedipus.

Once the staging has been reduced to its dependence on the play's unitary composition as well as to the result of a good overall visualization (XVII), along with music, which has been sufficiently evoked in the earlier chapters (and it will come up again in the eighth book of *Politics*), all that remains to be considered is argument. Argumentative discourse must be given a logical form according to the places from which the actors are speaking and according to the actors' conditions. Aristotle refers us here to *Rhetoric*.

As for the play's diction, concerning the writing per se and its stylistic effects, the author allows himself an ample digression (XX–XXII) in which he deals in turn with phonetics, linguistics, grammar, and prosody. He then examines effects as such: rare words, ornaments, metaphor. Metaphor is admirably defined (XXI) as a mixture attributable to the passage of a single term into the categories of genre and species, or even to an analogy grouping disparate terms in pairs: thus with reference to Ares, it will be said that the cup is Dionysius's shield, or with reference to the revolution of the sun, that evening is the old age of day, just as old age is the sunset of life. Chapter XXII presents the outline of a series of "problems" in which examples of barbarisms and solecisms are juxtaposed with ingredients of the elevated style, such as extensions, inversions, and insertions of dialectal expressions.

After those three rich and difficult chapters (which cannot be separated from a perfectly explicit development), the author moves on to examine the epic genre. The rhythm of the exposition is amplified even as it is accelerated, from the criteria defining the genre to unity of action (XXIII–XXIV), again passing through the sketch of a series of historical and technical "problems" (XXV) up to the lovely aesthetic comparison of the respective merits of the two genres at issue (XXVI). What results is the preeminence of tragedy, owing to its greater liveliness of presentation and the fact that unity of action is more natural in tragedy: "tragedy possesses all epic's resources (it can even use its metre), as well as having a substantial role for music and spectacle, which engender the most vivid pleasures. Again, tragedy has vividness in both reading and performance. Also, tragedy excels by achieving the goal of its mimesis in a shorter scope; greater concentration is more pleasurable than dilution over a long period: suppose someone were to arrange Sophocles' *Oedipus* in as many hexameters as the *Iliad*" (*Poetics* XXVI.9–13). And the text concludes, a few lines further, with a familiar refrain: "As regards tragedy and epic, . . . let this count as sufficient discussion" (XXVI.16). The developments that were to follow, concerning comedy, dithyrambic verse, and—perhaps—poetic and musical lyricism, seem to be irremediably lost.

Through certain of its technical aspects, especially the examination of specific problems raised by various passages in the *Iliad* and *Odyssey*, Aristotle's

Poetics announced and in part inspired the works of Homeric philology to which we must now turn. As early as the 3rd century B.C.E., in Alexandria, in the context of the Museum and its sumptuous Library, a whole literary school flourished; its principal representatives, following Zenodotes and Callimachus, became specialists in the works of Homer. They produced editions and commentaries of which we have only indirect traces, but these are nonetheless revealing.

The principal scholar of the group was Aristophanes of Byzantium, the author of a critical edition of the two epics; he corrected the texts, which were apparently riddled with errors. In the following century his illustrious successor, Aristarchus of Samothrace, produced the first vulgate of the Homeric text, with its division into books and into the number of verses that would thenceforth be traditional. There is general agreement that traces of this work are present in the principal medieval manuscripts, especially the 10th-century *Venetus* A, and the 11th-century *Venetus* B. The abundant scholia that accompany the text of these manuscripts represent the state of Aristarchus's Alexandrine commentary, especially in the case of *Venetus* A. *Venetus* B is thought to have retained traces of more symbolic commentaries that came from the Pergamene school, a rival of the Alexandrian school. The author is thought to have been one Crates of Mallus, Aristarchus's contemporary and Pergamum's rival.

Thus an entire philological and historical corpus of knowledge developed around Homer, not without some connections to the logical and linguistic preoccupations of early Stoicism. There is evidence of the same preoccupations, moreover, during the imperial period (from Augustus to Hadrian), in authors such as Didymus, Aristonicus, Herodian, and Nicanor. In any event an anonymous text, known as the "Résumé of the Four," was circulated under those four names; this text too found its way in part into the famous scholia of *Venetus* A. Along the same lines, I should also mention the *Homeric Questions* of Porphyrus of Tyr, in the 3rd century C.E.

Let us turn now to two important treatises on literary aesthetics in which we shall once again encounter the two major ideas of style and inspiration. These are Demetrius's *Peri hermeneias (On Style)*, from the end of the 2nd century B.C.E., and an anonymous text entitled *Peri hupsous* (On the Sublime), very probably dating from the 1st century C.E.

The first of these should not be attributed to Demetrius of Phalerum, one of the founders of the Alexandrian Library, but to a less well-known grammarian from Syria who was active in both Alexandria and Athens, where the young Cicero, the future defender of the poet Archias, may have heard him as a very old man. Despite the title, which might be understood as announcing a theory of interpretation, the treatise deals directly with what we term "style." The author offers us four approaches to the topic. He sorts out the various stylistic possibilities and characterizes them briefly, examining typical exam-

ples of each and identifying the forms of excess to avoid. He always uses the
same schema and the same order of presentation. The examples are distributed evenly among the great classical authors, from Homer to Thucydides
and Demosthenes; they include, as Aristotle had proposed, "plain language"
and "metrical forms." We can see that the effect of art in literature decidedly
exceeds the bounds of mere versification or "poetic art" in the restricted sense
of the term.

Thus Demetrius reviews in turn "grand style," warning us against the
coldness it may entail; "elegant style," which charms but must avoid falling
into affectation; "plain style," a sort of "zero degree of writing," occasionally
risking dryness; and, finally, "forceful style," or, more explicitly, "vehement
[deinos] style," which seems to be given preferential treatment by the author.
Of course, the interest of the undertaking lies more in the distribution of
styles than in the examples, which are circumstantial and sometimes repeti-
tive. Thus the work of Sappho, mentioned several times, is celebrated repeatedly under various headings: its hyperbole ("more golden than gold") keeps it
from being cold (127), and its use of anaphor or repetition leads to effects always touched with grace and elegance, whether the poet is speaking to us of
nuptial bonds or addressing the Evening Star (141):

> Evening Star, you bring everything home,
> You bring the sheep, you bring the goat, you bring the child to its
>   mother.

The last characteristic, "vehemence," may be the most difficult of all; it
needs to be defined briefly here, or, rather, its mechanisms need to be spelled
out. The first of these, brachylogy, is entirely Spartan; it must never lapse into
enigma. The best example would be the laconic declaration, "Dionysius, at
Corinth," the goal of which is to recall that the tyrant of Syracuse, defeated
and overthrown, had been reduced to earning his living as a schoolmaster in
Corinth (V.241). Then there are figures such as antithesis, imitative harmony,
anaphora, extreme gradation (klimax), certain compound words, true (non-
"rhetorical") questions, emphasis, and, finally, certain euphemisms or figurative allusions: these are all devices, ways of taking recourse to figures of
speech, that make it possible to approach or achieve a form of the "sublime" that has not yet been articulated, which the author classifies under the
heading of vehemence, or deinotes (251–300). It is clear that the art of
Demosthenes is often invoked as an example or as a representative sampling
of this maniera. The "repulsive style," which would be its negative excess, is
hastily evoked at the end of the treatise, as if in remorse or through anticipation.

As for the sublime, properly speaking, it appears as early as the title of
the anonymous text mentioned earlier. That text was for a long time attrib-

uted to Cassius Longinus, a rhetor from the 3rd century C.E., or, more prudently, to a pseudo-Longinus whom we would do better to put back on the shelf of historical errors or cultural approximations. Boileau may well have believed in him; the occasional imprudent contemporary commentator (certainly not a well-trained Hellenist) may resort to that opinion; still, we shall do better to yield to the arguments of internal criticism as well as to those of cultural coherence. In the authoritative opinion of Henri Lebègue, those arguments indicate that the author of the treatise on the sublime wrote early in Tiberius's reign.

However this may be, and without neglecting the influence of middle Stoicism in the writings of two scholars from Rhodes, Panaetius and Posidonius, we must now turn to the well-documented establishment of this new aesthetic category, the sublime (*to hupsos*, "the highest"). The author of the text begins by defining his object as a devastating force equally present among poets, prose writers, and orators. This force aims more at creating overwhelming delight or ecstasy than at deploying any power of reason or persuasion. It is like a bolt of lightning, he says, which shatters everything (I.4). Its means and its forms then remain to be defined. Loftiness of thought is the first criterion proposed, but to this must be added pathetic effects and expressions of enthusiasm. The vividness of the text's imagery and its power of suggestion guarantee its authenticity. Certain tropes and figures are privileged for creating the effect of surprise: the absence of liaisons (asyndeton), breaks in construction (anacoluthon), the disruption of logical order in phrasing (hyperbaton), augmentative repetition and the effect of accumulation (epanaphoron and amplification), and, finally, hyperbole and apostrophe, which are to be discreet and must hide their effects as much as possible. All this is to be counterbalanced by a major concern with construction, with the unity of the whole, and with the successive order of presentation of terms.

Such textual construction is the principal quality recognized by the author in the beautiful poem by Sappho evoking the torments and physical pains of love, a poem that has been preserved thanks to him. If only on this account, the treatise would deserve to be called "the little golden book," as the humanist Casaubon dubbed it. Here is the excerpt and the accompanying commentary:

> I think him God's peer that sits near you face to face, and listens to
> your sweet speech and lovely laughter.
> It's this that makes my heart flutter in my breast. If I see you but
> for a little, my voice comes no more and my tongue is broken.
> At once a delicate flame runs through my limbs; I see nothing with
> my eyes, and my ears thunder.
> The sweat pours down: shivers grip me all over. I am grown paler
> than grass, and seem to myself to be very near to death.

Here the commentator interrupts: "Is it not wonderful how she summons at the same time, soul, body, hearing, tongue, sight, skin, all as though they had wandered off apart from herself? She feels contradictory sensations, freezes, burns, raves, reasons, so that she displays not a single emotion but a whole congeries of emotions. Lovers show all such symptoms, but what gives supreme merit to her art is, as I said, the skill with which she takes up the most striking and combines them into a single whole" (*On the Sublime* X.2–3).

Moreover, the models the author proposes remain Homer, Thucydides, Plato, Euripides, and Demosthenes, in preference to the orators Lysias, Isocrates, or Hyperides. The latter may be the principal champions of Atticism, but their only merits are their correctness (deemed mediocre) and their seemingly smooth, well-disciplined style, in which all the effects are diluted under the emollient action of overly obvious syntactic links. Even Cicero's ample cadences are only a vast wildfire compared to Demosthenes' phrasing, which strikes like lightning (XXXIV.4).

It is clear that one of the aims of this short treatise was polemic in nature. It was first directed against a certain Cecilius who had, shortly before, spoken ploddingly on the subject, but it also targeted an Atticist tendency, anticipating Dionysius of Halicarnassus, who preferred to the brilliant imperfections of the advocates of the sublime in literature the monotony and impeccable demeanor of works with more modest—not to say more mediocre—ambitions and intonations.

Finally, I shall mention the *Chrestomathy* of Proclus, a writer of the 2nd century C.E. who owes a good part of his celebrity to someone who remains, after the patriarch Photios, his best critic and biographer: Albert Severyns, the learned editor, translator, and commentator of the precious relics of Proclus's work of literary theory. The work is actually a "short course" or "literary handbook" in which the author declares at once that prose and poetry have similar qualities, particularly where style is concerned. Style is of three orders, with no other specification: abundant style, pared-down style, and middle style. However, the surviving summary of the first two books of the treatise deals essentially with poetry. Chronology thus requires that one begin with the epic, in which what is at issue is mainly the content of the various works in the Trojan cycle, from the "Cyprian songs" to the Telegony. Then come definitions and historical evocations of the various poetic genres: elegy, iamb, and lyric.

The latter is subdivided into sacred lyric, including hymns, paeans, dithyrambs, and nome, and secular lyric, covering elogy, epinicia or homage to the conquerors, scholia or alternating songs used in banquets *(symposia)*, and assorted variants of love songs: epithalamia, wedding songs, and other drinking songs. Various choral genres, such as partheneia or daphnephoria, are evoked at the end, before the conclusion of this summary of the first two books of Proclus's "literary handbook"; it leaves us wishing for more.

The summary itself, the work of Photius, contained in codex 239 of his "Library," is an entirely fortuitous windfall. Let us recall that the patriarch, accompanying a Byzantine embassy to the Middle East in the 9th century, had with him a shipment of books; he seems to have spent most of his time drafting summaries of these works for the benefit of his brother, who had remained in the capital, unless he did the work after his return to Constantinople. Although he does not mention any poet by name, the place he reserved for Proclus's handbook has allowed me to discuss it here, with all the respect it is due. This "Library," dating from the first renaissance, was indeed a remarkable and irreplaceable conservatory of Greek and Byzantine letters.

To return to Proclus, another part of his work, which is actually a "life of Homer," has been transmitted to us by the scholia of the medieval manuscripts mentioned above. As anecdotal as one could wish, and highly colorful, this brief *Vita Homeri* gets lost in calculations concerning the place of origin as well as the cause and modalities of the poet's death, before offering, in a few brief pages, the best summaries we have of the now-lost epics of the Trojan cycle: the "Cyprian songs" concerning the most remote prodromes of the Trojan war, going back to the wedding of Peleus and Thetis and to the apparition of Eris that led to the quarrel over the golden apple and the three goddesses. We recall Aphrodite's poisoned gift to Paris: he was to marry the beautiful Helen and incite war. The episode of the pseudo-sacrifice of Iphigenia and her rescue among the Taurians, owing to Artemis's intervention, is very clearly presented, along with Odysseus's feigned madness and the role of Telephus, who guides the fleet to Troy. The other lost epics—which were to give Virgil the inspiration for his *Aeneid*—are also summarized clearly, the "little Iliad" and the "capture of Troy" in particular, where the "traitor" Sinon appears, along with the wooden horse and a certain priest called Laocoon.

Finally, to return to our starting point—namely, to Homer—let me evoke Eusthathius's Byzantine commentary on the two epics, in a text dating from the late 11th or early 12th century, i.e., from the beginning of the second Byzantine renaissance, as well as the statements of his contemporary Tzetzès, whose praise to the poet begins with a good summing up of the great Homeric devotion of his time, echoing our own, at least in its best moments:

> Homer,
> Learned in all things
> Ocean of words replete with nectar
> Entirely free of salt.

PIERRE SOMVILLE
Translated by Catherine Porter and Dominique Jouhaud

Bibliography

Texts and Translations

Aristotle. *Poetics*. Trans. Stephen Halliwell. Loeb Classical Library.

Chiron, Pierre. *Introduction, édition et traduction de "Demetrios, Du style."* Paris: Les Belles Lettres, 1993.

Demetrius. *On Style*. Trans. Doreen C. Innes, based on trans. of W. Rhys Roberts. Loeb Classical Library.

Homer. *Odyssey*. Trans. A. T. Murray, rev. George E. Dimock. 2 vols. Loeb Classical Library.

Lebègue, Henri. *Introduction, édition et traduction de "Du sublime."* Paris: Les Belles Lettres, 1939.

"Longinus" (Dionysius or Longinus). *On the Sublime*. Trans. W. Hamilton Fyfe, rev. Donald A. Russell. Loeb Classical Library.

Somville, Pierre. *Platon: Ion, texte et bref commentaire*, 5th ed. Liège: Dessain, 1974.

Plato. *Ion*. Trans. W. R. M. Lamb. In *The Statesman; Philebus; Ion*. Loeb Classical Library.

Proclus Diadochus. *In Platonis Cratylum commentaria*. Ed. Georgius Pasquali. Leipzig: B. Teubner, 1908.

Theognis. In Mulroy, David. *Early Greek Lyric Poetry*. Ann Arbor: University of Michigan Press, 1995.

Studies

Boyancé, Pierre. *Le culte des Muses chez les philosophes grecs*. Paris: De Boccard, 1937.

Delatte, Armand. *Les conceptions de l'enthousiasme chez les philosophes présocratiques*. Paris: Les Belles Lettres, 1934.

Dodds, Eric Robertson. *The Greeks and the Irrational*. Berkeley: University of California Press, 1968.

Labarbe, Jules. *L'Homère de Platon*. Liège and Paris: Les Belles Lettres, 1949.

Lanata, Giuliana. *Poetica pre-platonica (testimonianze e frammenti)*. Florence: "La Nuova Italia," 1963.

Motte, André. *Prairies et jardins dans la Grèce antique*. Brussels: Palais des Académies, 1973.

Norden, Eduard. *Die antike Kunstprosa*. Leipzig and Berlin: Teubner, 1909.

Schamp, Jacques. *Photios, historien des lettres*. Liège and Paris: Les Belles Lettres, 1987.

Segal, Charles. *Singers, Heroes and Gods in the Odyssey*. Ithaca, N.Y.: Cornell University Press, 1994.

Severyns, Alvert. *Le cycle épique dans l'école d'Aristarque*. Liège: H. Vaillant-Carmanne, and Paris: E. Champion, 1928.

——. *Recherches sur la Chrestomathie de Proclos*. Vols. 1 and 2, Liège: Faculté de philosophie et lettres, and Paris: E. Droz, 1938; vol. 3, 1953: vol. 4, 1963. Repr. Paris: Les Belles Lettres, 1977.

Somville, Pierre. *Essai sur la Poétique d'Aristote*. Paris: Vrin, 1975.

————. "Ironie platonicienne à la fin de la *République*." In *Serta Leodiensia secunda: Mélanges publiés par les Classiques de Liège à l'occasion du 175e anniversaire de l'Université*. Liège: Ulg, 1992. Pp. 445–450.

Vernant, Jean-Pierre, and Pierre Vidal-Naquet. *Mythe et tragédie en Grèce ancienne*. Paris: Maspero, 1972.

RHETORIC

IN THE CONTEMPORARY USAGE of all modern European languages, outside the specialized vocabulary of certain antiquarian and literary critical coteries, the word *rhetorical* is unfailingly pejorative. Rhetoric now roughly connotes the dissembling, manipulative abuse of linguistic resources for self-serving ends, usually in a political context: witness the routine coupling of "rhetoric" with "propaganda" in the dismissal of an opponent's speech. Yet from the time of the Roman republic down to at least the beginning of the 19th century, rhetoric so dominated both general and political culture (albeit with certain periodic eclipses), that a person without rhetorical training could hardly pretend to education at all. What is rhetoric, that it could suffer so curious a fate? During its ascendancy the answer, enshrined in a multitude of handbooks that first appeared in the ancient world and were propagated tirelessly down the centuries, is obvious and uncontentious: rhetoric is "the tool of persuasion," and an education in rhetoric is an education in the elaborate technical expertise needed to produce and appreciate persuasive discourse, oral and written, sometimes stretched to include the visual arts, architecture, and music.

But the great Latin exemplars of the rhetorical tradition, primarily Cicero and Quintilian, did not live and work in a vacuum. As in so much else, the Romans inherited the very idea of rhetoric, at least as a self-reflective concept, from the Greeks. In the classical Greek world there was no consensus on either the nature or the value of rhetoric: instead there was a fierce and profound debate, ignited by the late 5th-century figure Gorgias of Leontini and cast in its enduring form by Plato, whose polemic insists that rhetoric be defined in contrast to philosophy, and seeks to persuade us that the comparison is all to the disadvantage of rhetoric. Since his formulation of the issue so dominates the earliest Greek phase of the history of rhetoric, only an examination first of Gorgias himself, and then of Plato's dialogue named after him, can help us understand what Cicero and ultimately we ourselves inherited, and what was done with it.

Who was Gorgias? Philostratus, a hack writer of the Second Sophistic, reports that Gorgias is the man "to whom we believe the craft of the sophists is to be traced back as it were to his father" (Buchheim, test. 1). Philostratus's mediocrity is precisely what renders his opinion valuable: it reveals how Gorgias typically appeared to later antiquity. But why did he appear as the father of sophistry? First, because of rhetorical innovations at a basic technical level that Gorgias is supposed to have made, involving both structure and ornamentation. Second, and of considerably more interest, because he introduced *paradoxologia*, which embraces both paradoxical thought and paradoxical expression. On the occasion of his famous embassy to Athens seeking military aid for his home city, Leontini, in Sicily, his skill in speaking *extempore* reputedly brought nearly all the leading politicians and intellectuals under his influence. Of the three most striking claims preserved in the largely anecdotal biographical reports, one is that he pioneered improvisation, so that "on entering the Athenian theater, he cried out 'Give me a theme!' . . . in order to demonstrate that he knew everything" (test. 1a); a second, that his pupil Isocrates claims in an apparently neutral tone that Gorgias accumulated relatively great wealth by traveling about unwed and childless, thus avoiding the civic and educational expenses of the paternal citizen (ibid. 18); and the third, that "among the Thessalians 'to orate' acquired the name 'to gorgiasie'" (test. 35).

Clichéd as they are, these fragmentary portraits raise all the important questions about Gorgias. Why is Gorgias a "sophist"? Whatever sophistry might be, is it necessarily connected with rhetoric? Need a sophist/rhetor really claim omniscience? What does the performative aspect of rhetoric (Gorgias impressing his public in the theater) reveal about its nature? Isocrates' denial of familial and civic identity to Gorgias does not sit easily with Gorgias's role in obtaining Athenian aid for his fellow citizens: how, then, does rhetoric connect with political activity? Finally, to compound the confusion, many scholars lengthen the list of characterizations of Gorgias by adding the title philosopher, albeit usually only for the early stages of his career. A reading of Gorgias's immensely provocative texts, *On What Is Not* and *The Encomium of Helen*, will show that this difficulty in classifying him, so far from being a mere pedant's problem, goes to the heart of his unparalleled contribution to the history of rhetoric. But, since Gorgias unmistakably challenges us to react to both works against one specific philosophical background, that of Parmenides' great argument, we must first extract some vital information from the figure dubbed by Plato the father of philosophy, to match Gorgias, the father of sophistical rhetoric.

Parmenides' goddess (the figure of authority in his poem) announces: "You must hear everything, both the unmoved heart of persuasive *alētheiē* and the opinions of mortals, wherein there is no *alēthēs* conviction" (Coxon, frg. 1). *Alētheiē* is conventionally rendered either "truth" or "reality," and often context clearly favors one over the other: the problem here is that Parmenides seems not only to fuse the real with the true but also to suggest that truth/ reality is *objectively* persuasive.

"Never will the strength of conviction permit something extra to come to be from what is not; that is why justice has released neither generation nor destruction by loosening their bonds, but holds them fast" (frg. 8). This later declaration adds the paradoxical dimension that persuasion, standardly opposed to compulsion, actually shares in constraining necessity: thus judicial imagery recurs in the famous claim that "powerful necessity holds what is in the bonds of a limit." Not only that, but rational conviction also seems to act on or at least with what is, as the goddess associates reality with reason ever more intimately.

Yet when she passes from truth to human delusion, the goddess implicitly acknowledges that reality is unfortunately not alone in swaying minds, although she emphatically divorces falsity from conviction: "Now I put an end to persuasive *logos* and thought about reality/truth, and from this point do you learn mortal opinions by listening to the deceptive *kosmos* of my words" (frg. 8). *Logos* here resists translation even more than *alētheiē*. First, although it often means "verbal account," it stands here in polar opposition to the "words," thus highlighting the logical, rational character of truth. Second, and crucially, the debate between philosophy and rhetoric can be formulated as a conflict over the very meaning of *logos*. What is *"kosmos?"* Anything ordered or harmonious, but also, by an obvious extension, anything adorned by virtue of arrangement—hence *cosmetics*. Just as a painted face deceives the onlooker, so the goddess's phrase suggests the disturbing possibility that a *kosmos* of words—a *logos,* perhaps—might mislead precisely in that it wears an attractive appearance of order.

These features of Parmenides' discourse make an essential context for the appraisal of Gorgias, since together they formulate questionable conditions on argument that he deftly exploits. In the first place, even if the goddess insists that it is the force of her *logos* to which the auditor must yield, the fact remains that Parmenides puts his argument into the mouth of an authoritative divine figure. Is this not a rhetorical rather than a strictly philosophical device? Again, Parmenides fuses reality with persuasive truth by way of rational compulsion, but Greek culture traditionally opposes force and persuasion; thus the difficulty in aligning conviction with necessity, as Parmenides does so forcefully. Perhaps no one can simply will to believe (rationally): one must be *made* to believe, ideally by valid argument (cf. Descartes: "I move the more freely toward an object in proportion to the number of reasons that compel me," letter to Mersenne of February 9, 1645). Of course, rational constraint does not necessarily equal compulsion; both Gorgias and Plato will, however, return to the problematic relation between them. Next, when Parmenides contrasts *logos* with (mere) words, he must intend us to understand that the only vehicle of authentic conviction is rational argument, whereas Gorgias will systematically subvert the claims of philosophical *logos* to this monopoly. Finally, the goddess's exhortation to "decide by *logos* the controversial test enjoined by me" (frg. 7) encapsulates in philosophical form the salient competitiveness of Greek culture. Controversy normally entails a victor and a vanquished: does a successful persuader then inevitably victimize his audience?

Gorgias's *On What Is Not* has come down to us in two versions, one preserved by the skeptical philosopher Sextus Empiricus, the other in the Peripatetic mélange *About Melissus, Xenophanes, and Gorgias*. Although we should not believe we have access to the Gorgianic original, we can nevertheless maintain with due caution that what we read is a reasonable extrapolation from *On What Is Not* itself. Our purpose is not to investigate *On What Is Not* in its entirety, but rather to focus on its exemplification of *paradoxologia*, its discussion of communication, and its problematic relation to philosophical thought.

In the very title we confront our first paradox: it actually bears a disjunctive name, *On What Is Not, or About Nature* (Sextus, *Against the Professors* 7.65). Unfortunately the alternatives might both be later impositions, but they could preserve a significant Gorgianic joke. For an ancient philosopher or scientist, "nature" is what really is, so that *On Nature* became the standard designation awarded to Presocratic writings by Hellenistic librarians. If the alternative titles are original with Gorgias, then he is blithely equating what really is with nothing; taken together, the titles constitute a self-negating claim, a saying that unsays itself. This phenomenon of arrested or self-destructive communication, introducing semantic convention only to flout it, will emerge as the hallmark of the entire work. All the same, even if the doubled label is not original it remains of interest, since it then so clearly betrays the difficulty later readers experienced in attempting to pigeonhole Gorgias's text alongside less arresting Presocratic works.

The text begins disconcertingly: "He says there is nothing; even if there is something, it is unknowable; even if it both is and is knowable, nevertheless it is not showable to others" (979a12–13). We shall not pause over the details of Gorgias's "proof" of nihilism and unknowability beyond remarking that it deliberately overturns Parmenides' denial that "is not" is either sayable or thinkable, and that at this early date Parmenides' deduction was the paradigmatic, almost unique, example of logical progression, as manifested in Gorgias's conditional sentence. Parmenides had argued that reality is single and changeless; when Gorgias maintains that reality is not, is he any less credible? If both thinkers marshal deductions to reach contradictory but equally incredible conclusions, what becomes of Parmenides' theme that conviction unfailingly accompanies truth?

"Even if things are knowable," the text continues, "how could someone, Gorgias says, reveal them to another? For how could he say in *logos* what he has seen? Or how could a thing the listener does not see become clear to him? For just as vision does not recognise speech, so neither does hearing hear colours, but rather speech; and the speaker produces a *logos*, not colour or the thing" (980a2–b3). Gorgias is assuming that the sense modalities exclusively apprehend their own objects: a heard *logos* cannot convey anything not aural. The argument is puzzling, because the special object of hearing is surely sound in general, not speech. In fact the word translated as *speech* can, albeit rarely, mean just sound, but this gives rise to a dilemma: if *speech* is widened to *sound*, then the passage presumes that one simply hears *logoi* as one hears any noise, and the essentially meaningful character of *logos* is repressed; if, however, speech *is* what is meant, then Gorgias may well not be repressing the fact that *logoi* have semantic content—but then our simply hearing *logoi* as we see colors loses all plausibility.

"When a person does not have something in his thought, how will he acquire it from another through *logos* or some sign different from the thing . . .? For to begin with, the speaker produces neither noise nor colour, but *logos*; so it is possible to have neither colour nor noise in thought, only to see or hear them" (980b3–8). Gorgias now identifies *logos* as the tool with which we fruitlessly attempt to convey our thoughts to one another (notice that the mere act of hearing or reading and understanding *what Gorgias says* is enough to show that this cannot be true). Two considerations against successful communication are adduced. First, a sign is necessarily different from its object. As experience must (it is assumed) be direct, all symbols, by definition different from what they represent, inevitably fail. As for the (admittedly noncommunicable) *logoi* in our thoughts, these will also presumably be non-representational, for they cannot be signs *of* anything from which they differ. Second, "noise" rather than "sound/speech" is now the proper object of hearing, so that no means remain whereby we might perceive *logoi*. Gorgias caps his case against *logos* as a medium of communication by making it a condition for conveying information that one and the same *logos* be present in both speaker and auditor, which is impossible (980b9–11); thus he assimilates *logos* to a unique physical object that cannot be reproduced.

What are we to make of these amazing propositions? Parmenides' philosophy issues in the "rational" conclusion that all that is, is a unique, homogeneous, timeless entity, but it does not explain how, then, he can engage us in dialogue. In parallel, Gorgias's exercise in argumentation, a reaction to Parmenides, suggests that successfully *saying* that communication cannot occur must lead to self-contradiction and paradox. If *On What Is Not* is a perfectly acceptable piece of philosophy and this is its message, then philosophical *logos* will by itself carry precious little conviction, despite Parmenides' attempt to monopolize persuasion.

But *is* it philosophy? Or is it merely a cerebral joke? (We cannot dismiss it as a game on the evidence of the argumentative flaws I have only partially catalogued, since by that criterion a large proportion of early Greek philosophy would disappear from the canon.) To decide if it really is philosophical requires analysis of its arguments (or pseudo-arguments). But perhaps this analytical response presupposes just what we want to find out. Scholars have claimed too that *On What Is Not* formulates a *theory* of *logos* that liberates both rhetoric and literature from the supposed constraints of representational discourse: if language is not *about* the world, then poets and orators are free to influence us in disregard of the inaccessible facts. This sadly mistaken reading overlooks the most obvious consequence of Gorgias's *paradoxologia:* his message refutes itself, and in consequence, so far from constituting a theory of *logos*, it confronts us with a picture of what language cannot be, with what we must not assume it should aspire to be. I propose instead that the significance of *On What Is Not* resides in our very uncertainty over whether Gorgias is in earnest. As indicated in our reading of Parmenides, philosophy pretends to an impersonal authority deriving from *logos*. But the fact that any honest attempt to determine whether Gorgias's text has the status of "authentic" philosophy seemingly presupposes an affirmative answer to that question suggests that its actual genre is to be discovered only in the obscure intentions and pretensions of its author and not in or from the *logos* itself. That is to make the decision a very personal, contingent matter indeed, and thus to undermine the philosophical drive beyond personal authority. *On What Is Not* seriously threatens philosophy because philosophy cannot tell whether to take it seriously without dangerously compromising its fundamental commitment to a reason that is no respecter of persons. We shall see that Gorgias redeploys the weapon of the joke in *Encomium of Helen,* and that Plato's *Gorgias* hammers away inexorably at the problem of the (im)personal generated by Gorgias's challenge to Parmenides.

In the technical handbooks, rhetoric came to be divided into three main genres, forensic (speeches of defense or accusation before a law court), deliberative (political advice to a legislative and executive body), and epideictic (speeches in praise or blame of some individual or institution). *Encomium of Helen* ostensibly falls in the last category. Although scholars now appreciate that epideictic oratory in the civic context played a prominent role in the construction and maintenance of civic identity in the Greek city-state, a casual attitude toward *Helen* still prevails; since Helen herself is no more than a figure from mythology, it is typically felt that a composition about her could only have been a display piece intended to advertise Gorgias's craft and perhaps to serve as a model for students. In fact *Helen* masterfully complements Gorgias's maneuver to wrest the *logos* out of philosophical control in *On What Is Not,* and it further develops his challenge by uncompromisingly opening up the political dimensions of rhetoric.

Who is Helen? Wife of Menelaus, lover of Paris, she is an adulterous and infinitely desirable anti-Penelope. Even in her first, Homeric incarnation, she arouses profoundly ambiguous feelings. Although in the fourth book of the *Odyssey* she initially appears as a reinstated spouse entertaining Telemachus with stories, Menelaus recounts an unsettling anecdote that casts a shadow on her verbal skill: at the moment of maximum danger, when the Achaean warriors were concealed within the wooden horse, she mischievously imitated the voices of their wives to lure them out. Her association with *logos* is implicit from the beginning: she yielded to the verbal importunity of Paris, and she herself possesses a bewitching, deceptive tongue. So what would it mean to speak in *praise* of Helen? In fact Isocrates in his own *Helen* upbraids Gorgias on this very score, asserting that despite his express intention, Gorgias actually wrote not an encomium, but rather a defense of her (*Helen* 14–15). I shall argue that as concerns Helen, Gorgias's text is indeed forensic, but that it crosses genres by mounting this defense within the scope of its true epideictic purpose, the glorification of *logos*.

At the outset Gorgias announces: "The *kosmos* . . . of *logos* is *alētheia*" (*Helen* 1). All these key words are featured in Parmenides, where, however, deceptive *kosmos* was opposed to *logos* as argument. Will Gorgias, too, seek to persuade us by means of logical reasoning? And does *alētheia* here signify truth, with the implication that Gorgias's *Helen* in particular can achieve the excellence of *logos* only if it tells us a *true* story? If *kosmos* regularly connotes ornamentation and artifice, is there not the danger that a cosmetic *logos* may disguise rather than represent reality?

Gorgias excuses his passing over the events leading up to Helen's departure for Troy by saying that "to tell those who know what they know carries conviction, but conveys no pleasure" (5). Plato's Gorgias will concede that the orator *cannot* communicate knowledge, and that his utterances carry no conviction for knowers. Here, in contrast, the real Gorgias declines to retail common knowledge on the grounds that it brings no pleasure: if his *logos* is to be pleasing, then at the very least it must be novel. Granted, novelty is not incompatible with truth, but commitment to the principle that the criterion of pleasure (at least partially) governs what will be said surely renders problematic Gorgias's other commitment, that to *alētheia* (only a philosopher would even pretend to take pleasure in the truth alone). What we will get are causes making Helen's behavior *eikos*. Perhaps the most important word in Greek rhetoric, *eikos* can be rendered as likely, plausible, probable—often, as here, with the positive normative connotation of reasonable. It is a commonplace of subsequent rhetorical theory that the orator's task of instilling confidence in the likelihood of his case depends on achieving verisimilitude that might, but need not, coincide with the facts. It is because the orator occupies the ineliminable gap between the likely and the true that he can serve flexibly pro or contra. Thus Gorgias's intention to deliver a "likely" *logos* in conjunction with his promise to please distances him yet further from *alētheia* in Parmenides' sense of truth/reality.

Gorgias will exculpate Helen by running through each of the possible causes for her elopement with Paris and suggesting in each case that she cannot be held accountable; thus, if the catalogue is exhaustive, her defense will be successful (it is perhaps to this methodical procedure that he refers when he speaks of the *logismos* in his *logos*). "Helen did what she did through either the wishes of chance and the intentions of the gods and the decrees of necessity, or because she was seized by force, or persuaded by *logoi*, or captured by love" (6). At this stage Gorgias presents force and persuasion as categorically distinct, but his rhetoric will operate to erode this hallowed distinction. "How would it not be *eikos* for a woman forced, deprived of her country, and bereaved of her family to be pitied rather than reviled in *logos*? He acted terribly, but she suffered; thus it is just to feel sorry for her, but to hate him" (7). Here *eikos* must have normative force, as a plea for a *reasonable and just* reaction to the victim's plight from the listener or reader—but the reasonable response is *emotional:* does this mixture of compassion and indignation also afford us the promised pleasure? The opposition of "he acted . . . she suffered" invokes a second fundamental polarity, that between action and passion; when the first opposition between force and persuasion comes under pressure, the scope of the role of sufferer will enlarge to threaten us as well.

The heart of Gorgias's text comes in section 8: "But if *logos* persuaded and deceived her soul, it is also not difficult to construct a defense." Helen went to Troy: if this action was not inherently bad, its consequences indubitably were. A conventional piece of forensic rhetoric would be to plead compulsion on Helen's behalf; if she was forced to go with Paris, she deserves to be exonerated, maybe even pitied. What one therefore anticipates is an argument that she did *not* yield to persuasion. The standard polar opposition of force and persuasion entails that succumbing to a merely verbal seduction is altogether blameworthy. Instead—and here, surely, we find the most illuminating example of the *paradoxologia* to which Philostratus attributed Gorgias's fame—he unnervingly collapses the polarity. The process is begun by simply juxtaposing "persuasion" and "deception," as if persuasion too, by its very nature, victimizes, and by introducing the concept of the soul into the argument, a tactic with the most far-reaching consequences.

"*Logos* is a great *dynastēs,* which accomplishes divine deeds with the smallest and least apparent of bodies; for it is able to stop fear, remove pain, implant joy, and augment pity" (8). With this ringing affirmation the political implications of Gorgias's rhetoric break cover. *Dynastēs,* like *tyrannos* (applied in section 3 to Zeus), need not carry sinister, "tyrannical" overtones, but it certainly can. The rallying cry of Athenian democratic ideology is "free speech": a citizen is supposedly free in that his access to political power is limited only by his ability to persuade his fellows in the Assembly; it is not limited by brute force or by the handicaps of low birth or poverty. But if *logos* confers such power, the chief mechanism for the maintenance of a democratic polity may actually subvert it. Anxiety at this point is deepened in the original by the fact that the verb "is able" in Greek is etymologically related to *dynastēs,* permitting Gorgias a clever word play: verbal ability in and of itself creates political dominance. And the ramifications of this elaborate sentence spread wider still. Another traditional Greek polarity is that between word and deed: Gorgias's claim that *logos* performs superhuman deeds erases it. The illustrations of divine accomplishments, which presumably exemplify persuasion/deceit, are all of emotional rather than intellectual change, and the ability to instill rational conviction is not even mentioned. An almost universal inclination in Greek thought conceives of the emotions as *pathē*, states that happen to us, before which we are passive. In retrospect we realize that Gorgias's own *logos* (which enjoined us to "pity" Helen) may already have exerted an impact on our souls, in which *logos* can "augment pity." If Paris seduced the hapless Helen, by the same token we, in responding emotionally to Gorgias's rhetorical seduction, are equally passive, equally impotent before his active and divine power.

Gorgias's first species of omnipotent *logos* is poetry, which he famously defines as "*logos* with meter" (9): its auditors literally experience "sympathy" with depicted characters when poetic *logoi* cause their souls to "suffer." Later traditions in literary criticism will tend to discriminate among various poetical (especially theatrical) devices, and *not* to attribute to *logos* as such the predominant, let alone exclusive, responsibility for moving the emotions. Gorgias's monistic conception of *logos,* in contrast, should warn us that his definition is not intended to suggest that the emotional power of poetry resides extrinsically in the meter; while Parmenides was at pains to separate superior *logos* from deceptive "words," Gorgias strives to fuse all aspects of *logos,* irrational as well as logical, into a single overwhelming force.

The second species of logos is magic, which also has the ability to change feelings: "Inspired spells working through *logoi* effect the attraction of pleasure and the repulsion of pain; for by coming together with the opinion of the soul, the power of the spell enchants and persuades and moves it by wizardry" (10). The words "coming together" and "moves" strengthen the impression—not to be exaggerated into a theory—of the soul as a quasi-concrete object open to manipulation. That idea that spells work "through *logoi*" makes them into uniquely effective tools, but any choice between *logoi* as meaningful, persuading by their meaningful content, and *logoi* as instruments, shaping by their quasi impact, is rejected by the collocation "enchants and persuades and moves." The reason for this is clear: if a spell contains a linguistic message, it is one addressed to the god or daemon whose aid is being sought, not to the intended beneficiary or victim on whom the spell works. By so artfully intertwining brutely physical and semantic features, Gorgias refuses to admit categorical differences between species of *logos.* He is at work systematically obliterating distinctions between *logoi,* which are all alike in being emotionally manipulative, and different only in mode of operation and, presumably, effectiveness.

In section 12 comes the turning point of the text, where Gorgias explicitly denies the difference between force and persuasion—indeed actually identifies them—so as to complete his defense of Helen: "*Logos* in persuading the soul it persuaded forced it to obey what was said and approve what was done. Therefore in persuading, that is forcing, he commits injustice, but in being persuaded, that is being forced by the *logos*, she wrongly has a bad reputation." In the original Greek, because "*logos*" is grammatically masculine and "soul" *(psyche)* grammatically feminine, an immediate transition can be made from the asymmetric relation between *logos* and soul to that between Paris and Helen: the "he" and "she" in the last sentence refer indifferently to *logos*/Paris and soul/Helen. Grammar is being used not only to persuade us to apply the model to this particular compulsion but also to associate characteristics of one mythological case with the persuasive/compulsive situation in general. All the verbal forms of *logos*/Paris are active, while all the forms of soul/Helen are passive, as we have come to expect. But further, the deliberate feminization of the soul plays on Greek culture's assumption that the female is a passive object shaped at will by a dominating, masculine force. Thus, perhaps, every male citizen who yields to rhetorical *logos* is comparable to a man who suffers the physical violence of another, and whose masculinity is thereby humiliated: the successful orator performs psychic rape.

Gorgias adduces further examples of *logos* "molding" the soul as it wishes: "One should notice . . . necessary contests through *logoi*, in which a single *logos* written with skill, not uttered in truth, pleases and persuades a great crowd; and the conflicts of philosophical *logoi*, in which swiftness of judgment is also shown to make the conviction of opinion readily changeable" (13). These "necessary" conflicts are legal battles, and "necessary" in both a passive and an active sense: such speeches are delivered under compulsion by defendants, but they compel the jury to yield. The opposition of a single *logos* to a great crowd will be turned against rhetoric in Plato's *Gorgias;* and now Gorgias's promise to retail pleasure rather than (known) truth is fulfilled when persuasion results from a misleading pleasure induced by rhetorical skill inimical to truth. In making philosophical argument just another species of *logos*, Gorgias is deliberately ignoring Parmenides' epoch-making insistence that deductive *logos* is sui generis: *all* varieties of *logos* are displays of persuasive contention; despite its pretensions, philosophy does not establish stable, well-founded judgment but only demonstrates the mutability of passive belief as now one, now another participant in philosophical contests gains the upper hand.

"The power of *logos* has the same ratio *(logos)* to the order of the soul as the order of drugs has to the nature of bodies. For just as different drugs expel different humours from the body, and some put a stop to illness, others, to life, so too some *logoi* cause pain, some pleasure, some fear, some induce confidence in the auditors, some drug and bewitch the soul with a certain bad persuasion" (14). This passage assimilates *logos* to an irresistible drug administered either to heal or harm at the whim of the practitioner, and the drug it-self to an occult agent. The same *logos* that, as white magic, gives pleasure, creates pain in the guise of "bad" persuasion/compulsion, but in either case the defenseless soul is drugged, not offered a rational invitation to react. Gorgias elicits an analogy between rhetorician and doctor, *logos* and chemico-magical agent; Plato will both insist on a sharp distinction between healing doctor and amoral wizard, and deny that the rhetorician deserves comparison with the doctor properly understood.

We have hardly plumbed the riches of *Helen*, passing over without com-ment its fascinating account of erotic and visual attraction, but enough has now been assembled to permit meaningful comparison with Plato's *Gorgias* so as to reconstruct the challenges that rhetoric and philosophy presented to each other in ancient Greece. The text ends: "I wished to write the *logos*, an encomium of Helen, but an amusement for myself" (21). Of course what we have is a text in praise of *logos* itself. Too many pedestrian critics take refuge from Gorgias by understanding this sting in the tail as a simple disclaimer: *Helen* is just a harmless joke. But when we recall how *On What Is Not* dislo-cated philosophy by obstinately hovering between "serious" and "playful" intentions, we can recognize that *Helen*'s joke is on us. When we ourselves are made to pity Helen and execrate Paris, are persuaded (perhaps) that per-suasion is manipulation, and enjoy the deception with which Gorgias amuses us even as we discern it, we feel in our own souls the seduction of rhetoric.

Plato's response to Gorgias in his dialogue *Gorgias* is to present us with the most emphatic reaffirmation of the Parmenidean ideal, a scheme of philo-sophical dialectic utterly distinct from and immeasurably superior to rhetoric, which is fiercely castigated as nakedly exploitative emotional manipulation. The terms of the contrast are of course by now thoroughly familiar; what Plato does is to reinstate systematically all the great polarities that Gorgias just as studiously, if with profound ambiguity, chose to occlude. The running theme of our investigation has been the paradoxical skill with which Gorgias encourages us to place his very own words within the scope of his rhetoric about rhetoric. In consistency we must ask how *Gorgias* itself fares according to its author's strictures on the use and abuse of language. Gorgias insists that his *logos* constitutes no exception to the way words work, because they all work to the same purpose, but Plato's writing is informed by an incomparably higher degree of tension, because his Socrates pretends that there is all the difference in the world between a philosopher and a rhetorician. To avoid damning inconsistency, this had better not be just another rhetorical claim.

Gorgias falls little short of *The Republic* in the continuous influence it has exerted on Western intellectual and political history, and it has stimulated vo-luminous scholarship. Largely because in it Socrates propounds his celebrated paradox that no one does wrong willingly, and embarks on the psychological theorizing that attains full expression in *Phaedo*, the majority of its students concentrate on the second two-thirds of the dialogue, in which Gorgias himself does not feature as the chief interlocutor. We shall instead limit our attention to the first portion, where Plato most obviously addresses rhetoric in rhetoric's own terms; even so, our analysis will be highly selective, omitting everything not directly germane to an appreciation of why Gorgias matters so much to the history of persuasion.

In the very first lines of the dialogue Socrates prepares his attack. Depicted as arriving shortly after Gorgias's performance, he asks if he is too late for the "feast," introducing a metaphor that will not lie dormant for long (447a). When he is assured that Gorgias will gladly "display" for him again (the word is cognate with the label "epideictic" for the rhetorical genre exemplified by *Helen*), Socrates requests something else: will Gorgias instead engage in "dialectic," explaining what the "power" of his skill might be (447b–c)? Gorgias readily agrees, confidently making the boast recorded in Philostratus, that no question whatsoever exceeds his ability to answer. After Socrates again discriminates between dialectic and "so-called rhetoric" (448d), Gorgias affirms that rhetoric is to be defined as "knowledge of *logoi*" (449e). But Socrates immediately demands clarification, and elicits the admission that *logoi* concerning matters of health are the exclusive preserve of the doctor, the physician *rather than* the rhetorician. His point hangs on a conception of expertise shared by the Platonic Gorgias that *knowledge* alone confers mastery of a given domain; Gorgias's specialism has already been distinguished from that of his medical brother, Herodicus (448b), disposing of *Helen*'s likening of global *logos* to a physician's enchanting drug.

Under increasing pressure to explain what rhetoric is about *in particular*, Gorgias finally makes the grandiloquent pronouncement that its *logoi* concern "the greatest and best of human affairs" (451d). Socrates objects that this claim is doubly contentious: there is disagreement over what is greatest and best, and there are rival claimants for the role of purveying it, specifically the traditional contenders for the supreme good, health, beauty, and wealth, and their matching specialists, the doctor, the trainer, and the moneymaker. Gorgias's reply is a subtle reworking of the real Gorgias's *logos*, but one endowed by Plato with a newly explicit political emphasis, for rhetoric now imparts freedom to the man who can wield it, together with control over everyone else in his city (452d). (Cf. "A Athènes, tout dépendait du peuple, et le peuple dépendait des orateurs," Fénelon.) Gorgias thus aggressively enunciates the antidemocratic possibilities incipient in "*logos* the great ruler." Rhetoric is the power to persuade with *logoi* people assembled in any *political* gathering whatsoever; it makes "slaves" of all the other experts to the expert empowered to persuade "the masses," who appropriates their products and profits (452e).

Socrates expresses satisfaction with the completeness of Gorgias's disclosure, and quietly encapsulates it in the definition that has echoed down the centuries: rhetoric is "the craftsman of persuasion"; the power of rhetoric is "to produce persuasion in the soul" (453a). Socrates will demolish Gorgias by taking issue with the Gorgianic conceptions of both persuasion and psychology.

Before pushing the argument a stage further, Socrates interjects a methodological aside bearing directly on his attempt to prise apart philosophical dialectic and rhetorical display. He insists that more clarification come from Gorgias, rather than himself, "not for your sake, but for the *logos*, so that it will advance in the fashion best able to render what is under discussion clear to us" (453c). Gorgias had represented rhetoric as an asymmetric, exploitative relation: the active individual uses his *logos* to enslave the passive multitude. Now, while Socrates does not substitute individual concern for his interlocutor—his procedure is not for Gorgias's sake (alone)—the dialectical *logos* does not fall within the scope of a personal pronoun; it progresses through the phases of argumentative development to the intellectual benefit of questioner and answerer together. Dialectic is ultimately for the sake of knowledge. If it appears either to attack or to spare the interlocutor, that is a mere appearance. The *logos* itself is not just our chief but our sole concern: we interact with our partner in the investigation only because and insofar as he contributes to it. By the same token, we do not care about our own dialectical fate as such, that is, whether whatever fragment or figment of truth emerging from the discussion is "ours." Truth on this Socratic conception is not a commodity accessible at some points within a hierarchy at the expense of the occupants of other positions; all participants in the discussion share the truth communally. It hardly needs pointing out that in this remark Plato provides the starkest possible contrast to Gorgias's definition of rhetoric as ideological manipulation for the sake of personal political power.

Socrates suggests that the definition "craftsman of persuasion" is successful only if rhetoric is unique in producing conviction, but as a matter of fact all experts by teaching persuade us of matters falling within their specialty, so that the variety of persuasion to which rhetoric lays claim remains obscure. Gorgias repeats that specifically rhetorical persuasion is aimed at "crowds," and adds that it concerns justice and injustice, a topic embracing deliberative politics as well as legal conflict (454b). His earlier reference to "the masses" could but need not carry pejorative implications, but "crowds" most definitely does. Plato puts in Gorgias's mouth a word unmistakably intended to exacerbate any democrat's suspicions of his indispensable but dubious ally, the orator. "Democracy" means "rule of the *dēmos*," and *dēmos* neutrally means "the common people," as opposed to the affluent and aristocratic few. Only an enemy of the people would designate them "the crowd," a term of opprobrium at home in oligarchic polemics. This is not to pretend that the Platonic Socrates is by any means a democratic champion; in the last portion of the dialogue, he will contentiously disparage the achievements of the greatest Athenian heroes and astonishingly reserve for himself the title of the city's only authentic politician, albeit in his own special sense. Socrates is not at all concerned to deny that the Athenian civic body is a "crowd"; his aim is to demonstrate that Gorgias's advertisement for the omnipotence of rhetoric is indeed justified within a democratic political structure, and thus to damn rhetoric rather than defend democracy. But to jump to the conclusion that he therefore stands revealed as the enemy of freedom would be highly premature. If—a very large "if"—his vision of dialectic as enquiry aimed at shared truth can be sustained, then liberty, if not unqualified equality, is to be found within the limits of philosophical *logos*, and there alone.

Socrates now exploits, lethally, Gorgias's earlier admission that teaching issues in persuasion. He extracts the agreement that learning and conviction are distinct; there is false conviction as well as true, but knowledge is always true. Therefore there are two species of the genus persuasion, one convincing with knowledge, the other without it, and Gorgias volunteers that rhetorical persuasion falls within the latter (454d–e). "Then neither does the rhetor teach juries and other crowds about justice and injustice, but only persuades them; for certainly he could not teach such great matters to so many people in a short time" (455a). Philosophical insistence on knowledge as opposed to mere fallible belief shows that the Gorgianic identification of *logos* with power is falsified by the rhetorician's incapacity to convey knowledge within his special context of adversative debate on political and legal matters before the masses. In *Helen* Gorgias had not ignored philosophers, but there they were yet another type of fighter contending in the battle of *logos*, compelling rather than instructing their passive auditors' souls.

The question of abiding interest to us is not whether the most scathing critique of Athenian participatory political and judicial practice is warranted, but rather whether the category "persuasion without knowledge" has contemporary, worrying, validity. (In passing I note that in Athens a tragedian was conceived of as "teaching" the entire assembled city, and that his production was evaluated by a jury selected on egalitarian principles; Plato's denial in *Gorgias* that instructing a multitude is possible thus effectively robs of all legitimacy an Athenian institution we regard as one of radical democracy's signal triumphs.) Socrates' denigration of democratic decision-making relies on two presuppositions about which we moderns might feel rather differently. The first is the supposed impossibility of "true" education on a mass scale. If anything, subsequent history has given us far greater reason for profound pessimism on this score (and about there being one "true" education for all). But the second is the proposition that there is or could be "instructive persuasion" in politics. Anyone who claims to possess political "expertise" (unless he means Gorgias's antidemocratic power politics) must believe that there is. Thinking democrats, however, should insist that although there is a recognizable sphere of public interest, it does not define a corresponding specialist; no one is *authoritative* about justice. Plato has Protagoras expound how this could possibly be so in his eponymous dialogue. If we wish to resist the second assumption in *Gorgias*, we must be prepared to explain how modern democratic ideology is compatible with the political "expertise" its inaccessible institutions encourage and the propagandistic manipulation they invite.

Socrates goads Gorgias into delivering an extended defense of and panegyric on omnipotent rhetoric by making a deliberately naive claim about the Athenian manner of implementing public programs—surely the advice of the relevant expert, the architect, will prove persuasive, rather than that of the rhetorician? Gorgias retorts that as a matter of verifiable historical fact, it was Themistocles and Pericles who, through rhetoric, were responsible for Athens's imperial projects. He insists that if a competent orator such as himself were to compete against a doctor or other knowledgeable specialist in convincing a recalcitrant individual to submit to painful treatment, or for a civic medical position, the orator would invariably win—"for there is nothing concerning which the rhetor could not speak more persuasively than any other craftsman among the masses" (456c6; the damning "crowds" has now discreetly disappeared). So much for panegyric. His apology on behalf of rhetorical experts, only dubiously consistent with the implications of his former characterization of rhetoric as the means for tapping ultimate political power, rests on the plea that in itself it is a neutral capacity. It can be exploited to good or ill effect, but that is a decision for the individual skilled speaker, not his rhetorical teacher. Rhetoric is intrinsically an amoral weapon. This position is inherently unstable, since Gorgias classes rhetoric together with the maritial arts as a combative skill; surely this entails that it is intrinsically aggressive. The defense is culturally specific and wholesomely conventional. Greek society enthusiastically cultivated expertise in all sorts of competitive physical combat. It is of course no part of the job of the physical trainer to encourage his student to unleash that deadly expertise against friends and family. Gorgias piously assures us that rhetoric analogously is to be used justly, that is, only defensively against enemies and wrongdoers (456e); the worthy rhetorician could but would not rob the physician of his reputation.

Gorgias now pretends that the proper exploitation of rhetorical power is invariably morally correct—the word *just* and its cognates run right through his speech. He nowhere specifies what this actually means, but given his repeated appeal to conventional mores, he must intend to rely on the popular Greek conception of right and wrong, familiar from *The Republic*, that right action benefits or protects members of one's "own" group, not outsiders; harm to enemies is positively encouraged. However, a Greek's sense of his affiliations, the ground for even minimal moral consideration, was notoriously fluid and easily capable of generating unresolvable contradictions; most Athenian political dissension was the direct upshot of individuals' pursuing the ambitions of their "own" clan or class against those of the large body politic.

Thus Gorgias's proviso guarantees very little. It leaves the potentially lethal orator free to speak against the interests of anyone beyond what might prove a desperately narrow social limit. Furthermore, Gorgias's reference to disciples who pervert rhetoric of course concedes that the uninhibited, selfish exertion of rhetorical power is a fact of realpolitik.

Before returning to the attack, Socrates interjects a further declaration of the essential distinction between philosophical and rhetorical conflict: "I am afraid to push through my examination of you, lest you imagine that my purpose in competing is not clarification of the issue, but your defeat . . . I am one of those who would gladly be refuted on saying something not true, gladly refute someone else uttering falsehood, but bearing refutation no less gladly than administering it" (458a). In *Helen* Gorgias had undertaken to refute her slanderers, but his exaltation of a *logos* that pleases and deceives left no room for construing refutation as anything other than personal defeat. Socrates' reaffirmation of truth as the supreme good, falsehood as the ultimate evil, opens a space for unselfish "competition," where dialectical "victor" and "victim" alike share the spoils of discovery.

Socrates' renewed onslaught addresses the implications of the idea that the audience (once again a pejorative "crowd") in the rhetorician's sway is ignorant; if a speaker is more persuasive in this context, this is only because a man who does not know has the advantage over one who does among people as ignorant as he. As the real Gorgias had proclaimed, rhetorical power consists in deception, since it has its effect on the foolish by *appearing* more knowledgeable than expertise (459c). Plato's Gorgias is made to concede the point and with embarrassing fatuity extol the convenience of besting legitimate experts without the inconvenience of learning anything but meretricious rhetoric.

This is the philosopher's damning representation of Gorgias's boast that he can extemporize with equal facility on any topic whatsoever thrown at him in public display. It is mere display, because only the readiness of the ignorant "crowd" to be amused by the equally ignorant blandishments of rhetorical *logos* assures his success. Now, a basic strategy of the real Gorgias in both *On What Is Not* and *Helen* had been playfulness: are these texts *jeux d'esprit*, and any the less effective for it? High Platonic seriousness will brook none of that. But notice how Socrates' indictment turns on a rationalist presumption that comes all too easily to thinkers, such as Parmenides and perhaps Socrates himself, for whom the supposed fact that "*logos* is a great ruler" entails that logic must be omnipresent in discourse and in reality. Of course a *manifest* fool would be unpersuasive in political debate, but that is no reason to conclude that rhetorical authority uniquely appeals, or even pretends to appeal, to the intellect. Political discourse need not mimic ratiocination, as the authentic Gorgias indicated in his global catalogue of *logos;* only in Socrates' wholly rational world would even fools require specious *knowledge* to be impressed.

We shall not pursue Gorgias's discomfiture any further, as Socrates argues that this moralized rhetoric is inconsistent with Gorgias's previous admissions (457e) and constructs a definitive refutation from the impossibility of simultaneously maintaining both that a teacher is not at fault if his students turn morally neutral rhetorical power to evil ends, and that a teacher, such as Gorgias, is capable of imparting ethical and political expertise to his students. Does Socrates win? Most of the premises Plato feeds into the argument would strike most of us as, at best, intensely problematic, since the dialectic depends on an extreme form of Socratic rationalism. It is not just that both Socrates and Gorgias are committed to an intellectualist conception of expertise extending throughout the area of politics. The development of the theme that the rhetorician will "teach" ethics, which is crucial for the refutation, cannot be sustained without the Socratic thesis that true knowledge suffices for virtue. That is a paradox that Plato himself will come to reject as his psychology develops, and accordingly he will modify his vehement rejection of rhetoric as the indefensible manipulation of ignorant emotion.

But the point is not simply the tenability, or otherwise, of the substantive theses of the argument in *Gorgias;* rather, the confrontation with Gorgias takes shape in the very opposition of methods, "display" versus "dialectic," regardless of whether the philosophical method in this particular instance succeeds in divulging truth. Does Socrates "bewitch" Gorgias, does Plato seduce us, into haplessly conceding that the *logos* that is proper argument logically compels a conviction distinct from the psychic impress of a brute force? Later in the dialogue Plato will reanimate the Parmenidean imagery of logical necessity, the necessity that Gorgias in turn had conflated with a uniform persuasion before which our passive souls must yield. If Descartes was right to assert, paradoxically, that the compulsion of reason enhances rather than inhibits freedom, then we should take a stand against both Gorgias and his modern ideological heirs, such as Foucault. Gorgianic psychology is bleakly reductive; Socratic psychology is overweeningly rationalistic. Yet if we are to resist a portrait of ourselves as passive Helens, we cannot allow that species of power reflect mere superficial variations in mode and effectiveness, rather than essential differences in nature.

This introduction to Greek rhetoric works within the narrowest constraints: using the paradigm of Gorgias, it seeks to involve the reader in the *problematic* of the rhetorical tradition rather than to supply a substantive exposition. Nevertheless, a complete omission of Aristotle would be unacceptable, on two grounds: first, and simply, his enormous historical import; second, his intimate connection with the seminal conflict I have sketched between philosophy and rhetoric. One might contend that it is precisely by virtue of that connection that Aristotle occupies his prominent position in the development of rhetoric.

The Socrates of *Gorgias* rejects rhetoric so resolutely and in its entirety because he conceives of it as at once pandering to and exploiting vulgar ignorance; thus his reaction flows immediately from a provocative philosophical psychology of extreme rationalism. This attitude undergoes drastic revision in *Phaedrus*, which, importantly, presupposes and elaborates on the famous division of the soul into three components introduced in *The Republic*. This pluralization of the psyche is, in part, specifically designed to accommodate the genuine occurrence of conflict between reason and passion that Socrates had previously refused to recognize, but, more positively, it also clears a theoretical space for a conception of the passions that need not automatically condemn them, on condition that they obey the dictates of independent reason. Most pertinently, the way is now open for the vindication of at least a properly regimented rhetoric, since the irrational components of the soul are susceptible to distinctive, irrational modes of persuasion. If there is more to a human being than more or less defective rationality, then rhetoric has found its proper voice: it speaks to the emotions in the only accents they can hear.

Thus the evolution of Plato's philosophy of mind exonerates the rhetorical project, if only as an "ideal" and "scientific" rhetoric. But the rehabilitation is hardly unqualified. Even an "ideal" rhetoric, deployed skillfully and with the best intentions, would remain firmly subordinated to philosophy. This follows inevitably from the very condition permitting the partial rehabilitation of rhetoric, the pluralistic model of the soul. If the irrational psychic components are legitimately susceptible to distinctively rhetorical persuasion, by the same token they are deaf to the purely rational, philosophical persuasion that the highest, rational part of the soul heeds. Emotion has independent reality but remains markedly inferior to reason; analogously, rhetoric is authentic but is ranged well below philosophy.

This is the juncture at which Aristotle makes his decisive contribution to the debate. Aristotelian philosophy of mind flatly rejects any Platonic scheme of psychic pluralization. For Aristotle, thought and desire combine in the act of deliberation to constitute the choices that are the precondition for fully rational human behavior. Philosophical analysis detects intellectual and affective aspects in deliberation, but this analytical distinction is just that—it does not reflect a categorical division between reason and passion in the soul.

The consequences for rhetorical theory could not be more radical. Platonic emotions are irrational, not in the sense that they are reducible to, e.g., simple tastes or tactile feelings, but rather because they are, by definition, unmotivated and unmodified by the full-blown, active rationality most evident in philosophical *logos*. In complete contrast, Aristotelian emotions are permeated by reason. When I, for instance, unhappily perceive a state of affairs as unfortunate and react accordingly, I do indeed perceive it *as* unfortunate: cognitive, evaluative, and affective responses are, apart from pathological cases, typically indissoluble. This is not, of course, to pretend that misperception (along any of these dimensions—cognitive, evaluative, affective) does not occur, but it is to insist that emotion as such must not be prised apart from *logos* and then, inevitably, disparaged.

"The *pathē* are those things because of which people change their judgements, and are accompanied by pain and pleasure" (*Rhetoric* II.1)—so Aristotle defines emotion before issuing subtly detailed analyses of the passions, together with prescriptions for arousing and stilling them. Gorgias had refused to discriminate between modes of persuasion; Plato's reaction was to make distinctions with a vengeance, all to the discredit of rhetoric. With characteristic dialectical agility, Aristotle deliberately revives and revitalizes the terms of our primary encounter: "Rhetoric is the power of discovering potential persuasion about everything. This is the function of no other skill; for each of them can instruct and persuade about its own subject, e.g., medicine about health and sickness . . . But rhetoric seems to be able to discover persuasion about any given subject. That is why we say that its expertise does not concern some specific, separate class" (*Rhetoric* I.2). Aristotle here draws from Gorgias not only the conception of rhetoric as power but also the explosive claim of universality. Evidently the assumption that a skill provides persuasive instruction within the field of its proprietary expertise comes straight from *Gorgias*, as witnessed by the perennial example of medicine. Yet, unlike the Platonic Socrates, Aristotle does not infer that such particular expertise precludes the existence of a quite general rhetorical faculty founded on legitimate technique, not ignorance. It is not that Aristotle simply returns to Gorgias: his dialectic achieves a truly novel synthesis. *Rhetoric* hardly suggests that there is nothing to choose between a philosophical argument and a rhetorical plea. But Aristotle does not merely maintain, as does the Plato of *Phaedrus*, that rhetoric is, after all, acceptable in its (unavoidable) place. He further insists that, when in the rhetorical forum we induce emotions in others and, in turn, are emotionally swayed, this is not an unfortunate *pis aller* we follow only under the compulsion of political exigency.

"There are three kinds of persuasive means furnished by the *logos:* those in the character of the speaker, those in how the hearer is disposed, and those in the *logos* itself, through its demonstrating or seeming to demonstrate" (*Rhetoric* I.2). This critical tripartition will play a major architectonic role in *Rhetoric:* Aristotle not only acknowledges that rhetoric includes aspects irreducible to argument (that is, *ostensible* argument) but also recognizes that these divisions enjoy a certain independence. Explicating the second, emotive means of persuasion, he says that "the orator persuades through his hearers, when they are led into emotions by his *logos*" (ibid.), while his metaphorical description of rhetoric as an "offshoot" of dialectic and politics indicates a refusal either to assimilate or to rip asunder reasoning and affective motivation: this intricate scheme is intended at once to divide and to unify. Although rhetoric is a "part and likeness" of dialectic, in general its arguments, even when valid, do not meet the high (and inappropriate) standards of theoretical investigation, but they are *real* arguments for all that. There are also, of course, rhetorical appeals to the emotions, but the orator in arguing and in influencing our feelings is not precariously engaged in disparate activities. Just as the perception of something *as* unfortunate is a unitary state, so my persuading you to see it as so is a single, if highly complex, act of rhetoric.

At the outset I remarked on the curious fate of the word *rhetoric,* suggesting that our negative conception of it displays closer affinities to the original Greek contention in which the very idea of rhetoric was born than to the vast stretch of history in which it came close to epitomizing culture itself. What happened in between? Anything less than a grotesquely oversimplified response would have to mention almost all aspects of Western intellectual and political evolution, but our reflection on the formative battle between rhetoric and philosophy can at least provide a useful hint. Isocrates, that genius of mediocre compromise, synthesized Protagoras's paean to human progress with the Gorgianic conception of *logos:* it is responsible for all civilization, with the telling detail that political concord is maintained by those "we call capable of speaking to the masses" (*Antidosis* 256). Isocrates quite deliberately equates *logos* in the sense of "right reason" with *logos* in the sense of rhetoric, and he is surely challenging Plato when he insists that one and the same man persuades others and judges right for himself, by engaging in an internal discourse (he artfully employs the very word *dialectic,* which the philosopher reserved for his special, rational discourse). Isocrates makes the next move in the game by returning to Gorgias's position that *logos* is unitary, but with the blandly moralistic conception of rhetoric offered by the chastened Platonic Gorgias, rather than with the infinitely more arresting idea of the real Gorgias's *Helen.*

Through the conduit of Cicero this anodyne conciliation of the quarrel achieved an authority that set the seal on rhetoric's official status as universal culture. The Gorgianic boast of universal fluency is a salient topic in the first book of *De oratore.* Cicero prevaricates. He does not affirm that the profession of rhetorical skill promises ability to orate *knowledgeably* on any subject but rather, "elaborately and abundantly." Yet by tempering the Platonic rejection of a rhetorical *scientia universalis* to a commonplace admission of its extreme rarity, he in fact keeps alive the middlebrow Isocratean vision of the political orator who indeed "knows," but only because this knowledge is polymathic competence, rather than the all-demanding, all-conquering *logos* to which Gorgias and Plato alike responded with pure extremism.

The complementary extremism of our century has revitalized the original terms of the quarrel. For us, no issue burns more fiercely than the attempt to impose a civilizing distinction between force and persuasion. If we no longer formulate it precisely as the difference, if any, between rhetoric and philosophy, the fact remains that the primal scene between Gorgias and Plato provides our intellectual and political debates with their fundamental structure, and that meditation on it continues to offer one of our best hopes of under-standing, if not resolution. If we can ultimately accept even a heavily modi-fied version of Aristotelian psychology, we might aspire with him to tran-scend the conflict opposing Gorgias to Plato. For many centuries the verdict went in Aristotle's favor; our age is characterized by its indecision over this issue of the gravest political moment.

ROBERT WARDY

Bibliography

Brunschwig, Jacques. "Gorgias et l'incommunicabilité," in *La communication: Actes du XVe congrès des Sociétés de philosophie de langue française*. Montreal, 1971. Pp. 79–84.

Buchheim, Thomas. *Gorgias von Leontini: Reden, Fragmente und Testimonien, Her-ausgegeben mit Übersetzung und Kommentar*. Hamburg, 1989.

Cassin, Barbara. *L'effet sophistique*. Paris, 1995.

Coxon, A. H. *The Fragments of Parmenides: A Critical Text with Introduction, the Ancient Testimonia and a Commentary*. Assen/Maastricht, 1986.

Desbordes, Françoise. *La rhétorique antique*. Paris, 1996.

Loraux, Nicole. *The Invention of Athens: The Funeral Oration in the Classical City*. Trans. Alan Sheridan. Cambridge, Mass., 1986

Newiger, H.-J. *Untersuchungen zu Gorgias' Schrift über das Nichtseiende*. Berlin, 1973.

Plato. *Gorgias: A Revised Text with Introduction and Commentary*. Ed. E. R. Dodds. Oxford, 1959.

Romilly, Jacqueline de. "Gorgias et le pouvoir de la poésie." *Journal of Hellenic Studies* (1973): 155–162.

Segal, Charles. "Gorgias and the Psychology of the Logos." *Harvard Studies in Clas-sical Philology* (1962): 99–155.

Vickers, Brian. *In Defence of Rhetoric*. Oxford, 1989.

Vlastos, Gregory. "The Socratic Elenchus." *Oxford Studies in Ancient Philosophy* (1983): 27–58.

Wardy, Robert. *The Birth of Rhetoric*. London, 1996.

TECHNOLOGY

A REMARKABLE PASSAGE in Sophocles illustrates the respect that the Greeks reserved for *tekhne*. It is an encomium on skillfulness, an exaltation of the powers of human beings, of the tricks and tools by which these singular animals are able to alter their condition and escape, for better or for worse, the laws common to all species:

Many things are formidable, and none more formidable than man! He crosses the gray sea beneath the winter wind, passing beneath the surges that surround him; and he wears away the highest of the gods, Earth, immortal and unwearying, as his ploughs go back and forth from year to year, turning the soil with the aid of the breed of horses.

And he captures the tribe of thoughtless birds and the races of wild beasts and the watery brood of the sea, catching them in the woven coils of nets, man the skilful. And he contrives to overcome *[kratei mechanais]* the beast that roams the mountain, and tames the shaggy-maned horse and the untiring mountain bull, putting a yoke about their necks.

And he has learned speech and wind-swift thought and the temper that rules cities, and how to escape the exposure of the inhospitable hills and the sharp arrows of the rain, all-resourceful; he meets nothing in the future without resource; only from Hades shall he apply no means of flight; and he has contrived escape from desperate *[amechanon]* maladies.

Skilful beyond hope is the contrivance of his art *[to mechanoen technas]*, and he advances sometimes to evil, at other times to good. When he applies the laws of the earth and the justice the gods have sworn to uphold he is high in the city; outcast from the city is he with whom the ignoble consorts for the sake of gain. (Sophocles, *Antigone* 332–371)

The underlying theme of this hymn, interrupting the initial plot development of *Antigone*, is the ambivalence of human invention: humans are so cunning that their audacity affords them the capacity for good and evil. Once free of nature's constraints, man is at maximum risk, and the laws of the polis may conflict with the unbreakable edicts of the gods. Despite the grave possible consequences of such action, the step is taken and man emancipated. Sophocles gives a comprehensive list of the skills in which material tools coexist alongside the intellectual faculties of speech and law: navigation, agriculture, hunting, domestication, language, social life, and construction.

PRACTICAL INNOVATIONS AND
WRITTEN TRADITIONS

The originality of the Greek contribution probably lies beyond particular inventions or techniques. What is most noteworthy about Greek technology, rather, is a conceptualization of *tekhne*, and the rational principles underlying machines and technical procedures.

Every civilization cultivates its own forms of technical skill, and the principal inventions of which the Middle Ages took increasing advantage derive from many sources. Crucial innovations can very probably be credited to the Greek world, although it is often impossible to disentangle fact from legend. Traditions that are extremely difficult to verify generously attribute notable inventions to the legendary heroes of ancient times. Plato, for example, lists Thales among the *eumekhanoi*, men skillful in invention *(The Republic)*, and the anchor and potter's wheel are attributed to Anacharsis, the screw and the pulley to Archytas, and the arch to Democritus. The figure of Archytas symbolizes the very ideal of the philosopher capable of technological invention.

At a later period various inventions are associated with the name of Archimedes, without definite historical proof, and it is still a matter of dispute whether Archimedes was as great a technician as he was a mathematician. The two principal incidents that illustrate his technical genius, the revelation of the fraud perpetrated by the royal goldsmith and the defense of Syracuse against the Romans, are attested only in much later writings, and we have no precise and reliable text concerning his actual procedures—if they existed.

More precisely and more credibly, the catapult may have been invented around 400 B.C.E. by engineers in the service of Dionysius of Syracuse (Diodorus of Sicily).

Such inventions, often difficult to date or to attribute to a particular inventor with any certainty, are unlikely to represent the principal, original contribution of Greek culture in technical matters. In the field of technology, as in many others, the remarkable fecundity of Greek culture consists largely in the organization of knowledge, and in the sustained and stubborn effort to discover logical principles and present them through written exposition. The Greek world has left behind a rich heritage of theoretical outlines and treatises, transmitted to the West under the names of Aristotle, Philon of Byzantium, Archimedes, and Hero, to name only the most important.

A broad selection of literary works, including the *Iliad* and *Odyssey*, offers all kinds of precious information concerning weaponry, agriculture, metallurgy, the transportation of water, navigation, and so forth. In *Works and Days*, Hesiod mentions in passing the type of wood to be used in plow making, and in *Oeconomika* Xenophon discusses the most appropriate methods of seeding, planting, and harvesting wheat, and compares the characteristics of different soils. Thucydides describes a few war machines, for instance the hollow engine used by the Boeotians for setting fire to the ramparts of Delion during their conflict with the Athenians.

But these isolated instances, while indications of a technical culture, do not constitute a technology per se, that is, an organized discourse on tools and methods. We do, however, find accounts in Greek texts that, linked together, form series of writings that transmit and refine the description of certain instruments or methods. It is these series or written traditions that we shall focus on here: mechanics, optics, and alchemy.

These technical treatises exhibit one remarkable characteristic: they include little or nothing concerning the most vital or basic techniques—nothing about roofing, pottery, textiles, or agricultural work. The texts frequently describe apparatuses without any practical or everyday use: automata for the theater, complex toys, gear systems that are probably unworkable and entirely theoretical, distorting mirrors for the amusement of princesses, stills for a chimerical transmutation of metals. The only apparatuses of any real importance in these texts are the war machines: assault engines, tortoise-shell shields, watchtowers, mines, and catapults.

It is extremely difficult for us, surrounded as we are by technological artifacts, not to project our own habitual categories and classifications onto ancient Greek culture. The Greek categorization of knowledge is different: its tenets are hidden from us. For whom were these treatises on technology (if that is the right word) written? What did the Greeks mean, in different periods, by the term *mechanics*?

Although the texts in question may have had little to do with everyday life and with practical human needs at the time, this is not to say that their impact has been negligible. Historians of technology hypothesize that the Romans put into practice certain Greek innovations (an apparatus consisting of multiple pulleys for use on construction sites, siphon pipes for aqueducts, arch construction); it is possible that certain Greek "machines" that had retained the status of prototypes or fictions were actually constructed within the larger framework of the Roman empire.

But the texts also achieved an even more brilliant and fertile destiny later on. Cardan, Tartaglia, Galileo, and Newton were inspired by the *Problemata mecanicae* of (Pseudo-)Aristotle and by the books of Hero, Pappus, and Vitruvius. Greek mechanics contributed fundamentally to the renewal of the theoretical science of forces in Europe in the 16th and 17th centuries.

THE ARTS OF WAR

One skill not included in Sophocles' list of technological accomplishments is of all the arts perhaps the most favored by those in power and the most productive of innovations: war. The realm of the art of warfare is also one of the best represented in our surviving texts.

The invention of the catapult is an element in the transformation of the martial arts that appears to have taken place about 400 B.C.E., in particular during the campaigns of Dionysius of Syracuse, Philip of Macedon, and Alexander and his immediate successors. The catapult is a kind of enlarged crossbow attached to a pedestal (stationary or mobile); the bow is replaced by two arms that pass through a bundle of twisted fibers, and when the apparatus is stretched, the fibers twist and recoil. Naturally, care must be taken to ensure that the force of the recoil is the same on each side; otherwise, the arrow or stone will fire at an angle.

The use of this new weapon spread widely between 400 and 350; highly effective, the catapult made a strong impression at the time and brought about new methods of attack. At about the same time, we find other indications of a profound alteration in the techniques of warfare (attack, siege, entrenchment), as Herodotus attests somewhat earlier in regard to the Phoenicians' skill in digging a canal for Xerxes' troops. It is hard to say which of these inventions actually did originate with Greek-speaking inventors. The perfecting of military techniques in this period, especially projectile armaments, is echoed in a series of descriptive, more or less theoretical texts by Aeneas Tacticus, Philon of Byzantium, and other authors whose writings are lost (Ctesibius, for one).

At the same time, a class of men who can be termed military engineers began to emerge, especially in the entourages of Philip and Alexander. A passage in Vitruvius (10.16) sets forth the characteristics of this class of military experts and attests to their new importance: the Rhodians dismiss Diognetes, their military architect, who is a native of the island, and allow themselves to be seduced by a newcomer, Callias, who presents them with a superb description (akroasis) of his new machines; Callias claims to be able to withstand the assault towers of Demetrius Poliorcetes, or rather of Epimachus, the military architect in Demetrius's service. But it turns out that Callias's machines do not work, and the previous architect, Diognetes, is recalled and entreated to save his country. Finally Diognetes uses the old hydraulic methods, rerouting water channels so that Demetrius's assault towers become unusable. This example is a clear indication of the new requirements of the city-states and the emergence of the figure of the architect or mechanic, who combines the old architectural capability with more recent know-how involving various machines. Such a man can sell himself to the highest bidder and must be able to convince princes and statesmen of his own expertise and the originality of his techniques: he gives a lecture, provides models, promises a technology superior to that of the enemy (one may wonder whether the arms trade has changed significantly).

In this context, a literature of military technology begins to flourish. The first author whose book has survived is Aeneas Tacticus (about whom we know very little). He left a treatise called *Poliorcetica* (The Art of Siege Warfare), illustrated with allusions to events that took place between 400 and 360 B.C.E. He also mentions other works he had written on the arts of war: a book on supply *(poristika)* and on fortifications or preparations for war *(paraskeuastika)*. The book that has survived describes various aspects of siege tactics: the choice of sites and hours when watches should be set, means of reconnaissance, passwords and secret messages, and precautions to be taken against plots and mutinies. It also describes some technical procedures: the use of mines and countermines, incendiary devices, and so forth. Machines per se occupy little space. There is an apparatus for toppling assault ladders whose description and usage are somewhat unclear.

Shortly after Aeneas, other authors (a certain Diades, for example) wrote works on war machines that have not survived, though some elements appear to have been used by Philon of Athens around 300 in his own (lost) treatise *Poliorcetica*, which Philon of Byzantium used in turn around 225 for a new treatise on the same subject. It was at this point that the field of military technology was expanded and reorganized: Philon also wrote a book on projectile armaments in which he proposed several improvements for catapults (replacing the twisted fibers with metal springs, or even a system of compressed air, inspired by Ctesibius). Thus a corpus of technical texts on the art of war and projectile and siege machines was developed.

FROM MILITARY ARTS TO MECHANICS

With Philon of Byzantium, however, the theory of war machines became part of a larger technical corpus, within what Philon termed a *syntaxis mechanike*—in other words, a treatise based on mechanical procedures. On the basis of the order of Philon's surviving works, A. G. Drachmann has been able to reconstitute the general organization of this "mechanical syntax":

1. preamble
2. levers
3. the construction of ports
4. catapults
5. pneumatics
6. automat theaters
7. the construction of fortresses
8. the siege and defense of cities *(poliorcetica)*
9. stratagems

The book on catapults (4) has been preserved in Greek, as well as portions of those on fortresses (7) and sieges (8); pneumatics (5) exists only in Arabic. Except for a few fragments cited by other authors, the rest has been lost.

The arts of war thus became part of a larger discipline called mechanics, with a more systematic form of presentation. Connections appeared among several branches: new catapults presupposed levers and even pneumatics. Mathematics acquired a privileged position. The element of theory in Philon had rational foundations at least up to a certain point, if what is indirectly attested in the preamble can be believed (Book 1). To calculate the dimensions of a catapult with twice the capacity of a given model, Philon has to solve the problem of the duplication of the cube (Catapults, Book 4); he discusses the conditions for making a tool starting from a different-size model, and proposes using a graduated ruler to effect the change of scale. On both occasions, Philon mentions that he has treated these questions in his preamble. His treatise on mechanics thus opens with the rudiments of applied mathematics. Likewise when he reports on his predecessors and their efforts to construct projectile armaments, Philon reproaches them for being ignorant of the whys and wherefores, and of having proceeded by trial and error without an overall perspective. Aristotle's influence can be felt in Philon's theoretical requirements and even in his vocabulary.

IN SEARCH OF MECHANICS

Thus the arts of war are integrated into mechanics. But what is mechanics? In Europe, from the 18th century on, mechanics meant the science of movements and forces. Previously, between the end of antiquity and roughly the 1700s, mechanics was the theory of machines (sometimes "simple machines"; the same theory is sometimes improperly called "statics"). These simple machines, or "mechanical powers," were listed by Hero of Alexandria: the wheel, the lever, the multiple pulley, the wedge, the screw (Pappus, VIII). This is a quite restrictive interpretation of mechanics, much narrower than that of Philon of Byzantium.

To understand the subject matter of mechanics in the 3rd century B.C.E. we must turn to etymology. We have already encountered the term *mekhane* in Sophocles; if man rules over other living species, if he delves unremittingly and without respect into the venerable earth, if he has created shelters for himself, and cities with their own laws, it is thanks to all kinds of *mekhane*. Here the word is used in a very broad sense, similar to its use in the *Odyssey*, where Odysseus is termed a master of tricks *(polymekhanos)*.

Before it was used to designate a specific body of doctrine (whose outline, moreover, is difficult to trace), *mekhane* referred in general terms to expedients, remedies, artifices, tricks, machinations, and skilled resources—processes or even modes of behavior rather than things. The word has undergone an evolution comparable to that of Old French *engin:* the Latin term *ingenium* became the medieval "engine," trick or machination, and finally came to designate the technological object itself, independent of the mind that "manufactured" or "machined" it.

Mechanics was established as a distinct science before Philon's time; a specific science designated "mechanics" is found in the Aristotelian corpus, for example. It is listed among the "physical components of the mathematical sciences," along with optics, harmonics, and astronomy (Aristotle's two lists in *Physics* III and *Metaphysics* M can be combined). These four disciplines study objects or concrete phenomena, considering them, according to Aristotle, as mathematical objects: the light or visual ray as a geometric line, sound vibration as a relationship between numbers, the movement of stars as a circular orbit. The status of the object of mechanics is more difficult to pin down. What, according to this perspective, is the proper object of mechanics, and in what respect is that object mathematical?

The answer probably lies in a text that belongs, marginally, to the Aristotelian corpus: the *Problemata mecanicae* (*Mechanical Problems*, or simply *Mechanics*), attributed to Aristotle, which was rediscovered in the Renaissance and which stimulated discussions among scientists on the most important questions of physics. Galileo, for example, held the *Problemata mecanicae* in high esteem and drew from it on several important points.

The *Problemata mecanicae* begins with a definition of *mekhane*:

Remarkable things occur in accordance with nature, the cause of which is unknown, and others occur contrary to nature, which are produced by skill *[techne]* for the benefit of mankind. For in many cases nature produces effects against our advantage; for nature always acts consistently and simply, but our advantage changes in many ways.

When, then, we have to produce an effect contrary to nature, we are at a loss, because of the difficulty, and require skill. Therefore we call that part of skill which assists such difficulties, a device *[mechane]*. For as the poet Antiphon wrote, this is true: "We by skill gain mastery over things in which we are conquered by nature."

Of this kind are those in which the less master the greater, and things possessing little weight move heavy weights, and all similar devices which we term mechanical problems. These are not altogether identical with physical problems, nor are they entirely separate from them, but they have a share in both mathematical and physical speculations, for the method is demonstrated by mathematics, but the practical application belongs to physics.

Among the problems included in this class are those concerned with the lever. For it is strange that a great weight can be moved by a small force, and that, too, when a greater weight is involved. For the very same weight, which a man cannot move without a lever, he quickly moves by applying the weight of the lever.

Now the original cause of all such phenomena is the circle. (Aristotle, *Mechanical Problems* 847a10–b16)

Mechanics is similar to the other sciences that are "common" to physics and mathematics (astronomy, optics, and harmonics): its object is material and physical, yet it is considered mathematically. At the same time there is a difference: the movements of stars, light rays, and sound vibrations are considered as simplified mathematical objects—curves, lines, numerical relationships—while in the case of mechanics the object itself remains indefinite, and it is the mode of explanation that is mathematical (mathematics provides the reason).

We learn more about the variety of objects of mechanics by pursuing the thirty-five questions of the collection. First: why are larger scales more accurate? The questions that follow—in an order that is difficult to justify—have to do with standard instruments (the sling, the pulley, the steelyard, forceps), with common technical devices (rowboats or sailboats, bedsprings), with reflections on everyday situations that involve the distribution of force (carrying by several persons, the posture of a person rising), or with natural phenomena (why are pebbles by the seashore round? the study of projectiles and the continuation of movement, whirlpools). There are even questions that might be considered as stemming from pure theory: the study of the composition of movements according to the parallelogram, and the paradox known as Aristotle's wheel. The mixture of everyday, practical situations and speculations in the realm of mathematics or dynamics is striking, and appears to be new in the history of technological literature as we know it.

The unknown author puts forward answers to these questions, often in interrogative form ("Is it because . . . ?"); sometimes he even suggests several responses. The theory of mechanics thus appears relatively "open" and unsystematic. But the majority of machines derive from the lever, which derives in turn from the circle. The initial principle is the following: a larger circle is more powerful than a smaller one because an identical force produces a larger effect if it is less distorted or disturbed, and because the force is distorted to a greater extent if it is exercised on a trajectory that is more sharply curved (see François De Gandt, 1982).

This general foundation of mechanical theory is probably connected to Aristotle's arguments on forces in *Physics* (VII.v). However, it seems exaggerated to deduce from this, as Pierre Duhem did, that Aristotle is the father of rational mechanics.

DEVELOPMENTS IN MECHANICS

As the generations passed, mechanics was enriched, further developed, and refined. In particular, we have an Arabic translation of a book by Hero of Alexandria, who probably lived about 60 C.E.: *Mechanics, or Elevator*. Otherwise the *Mathematical Collection* of Pappus (ca. 300 C.E.) is a precious compilation, containing in its eighth book a collection of propositions on mechanics, drawn from Hero among others. Finally one must mention Vitruvius's treatise *On Architecture*, which despite being composed in Latin (ca. 30 B.C.E. in all probability), passes on elements of mechanics and architecture taken from Greek authors and practitioners, particularly in Book X, which is devoted exclusively to mechanics.

In Hero and Pappus, mechanics is occasionally extremely theoretical (for example, in the calculation of the gearing necessary to raise a given weight with a given force; Hero calls this a *baroulkos,* which would allow—theoretically—a weight of 1,000 talents to be balanced by another of 5 talents). But one also finds remarks dealing with quarries or construction sites, and Hero gives detailed instructions about transportation by wheel bearings, different types of cranes, and even wine and oil presses (Book III).

The sources of the theory are multiple. The authors seem to have hesitated to follow the dynamic reasoning of *Problemata mecanicae,* and here and there they presuppose a different kind of foundation: Archimedes' geometrical theory of levers and centers of gravity, which has nothing to do with the consideration of forces (see, for example, Hero's *Mechanics* I.24 and II.7).

The beginning of Hero's *Pneumatika,* where the author discusses the composition of air and possible explanations for the elasticity of gases, was also influential. Hero envisaged a multitude of tiny voids disseminated throughout matter (this text inspired authors of the Renaissance, particularly Galileo). On the other hand, *Pneumatika* is particularly poorly organized and difficult to read, and one is apt to remember only a few toys or amusing devices, some magic tricks, and an astonishing water organ. Hero's work was held in high regard during the Middle Ages.

OPTICS AND ALCHEMY

The two remaining corpuses of the technological tradition are not very closely related to mechanics or to machines of war or construction; they warrant an overview here.

Greek optics is principally represented by Euclid's *Optica* and his *Catoptrica* (preserved in Greek, edited by Heiberg in 1895 with a Latin translation) and Ptolemy's *Optica* (by indirect transmission, preserved in a Latin translation issuing from a lost Arabic version). In Ptolemy's case, it is difficult to uncover the original argumentation behind the successive versions of the text.

Euclid's *Optica* is a strictly geometrical theory of light rays, presented in axiomatic form and proceeding from definitions. The light ray is thought to originate in the eye, and the object of study is the cone whose summit is in the eye and whose base rests on the contours of the object seen. Euclid dis-

cusses and justifies effects of perspective and the illusions created by distorting mirrors, but makes no physical study of either light or color. (On the status and limitations of this view of optics, Gérard Simon demonstrates that it
would be wrong to confuse the geometrical study of visual rays undertaken
by Euclid with a theory of the propagation of light; it is only with Al-Hazen
in the 11th century that the physiological study of the eye as an optical apparatus begins, opening up new paths for instrumental optics.)

Ptolemy, so far as one can judge from the highly unsatisfactory text that
has come down to us, enters more into physical and psychological considerations, discussing cases of altered vision (myopia, presbyopia) and the role of
the mind in visual illusions. He is interested in reflection and refraction, and
he even presents numerical tables for calculating the angle of refraction starting from the angle of incidence.

The alchemical corpus is completely separate: it consists of later texts written in a far less rational mode than the mechanical ones. A *Collection des
anciens alchimistes grecs* was published by Marcellin Berthelot in the 19th
century, but the choice of manuscripts is somewhat idiosyncratic, and the absence of a commentary makes this edition difficult to use. A more systematic publication has begun at the Editions des Belles Lettres (*Les alchimistes
grecs*, volume 1, covers the Leiden Papyrus, Stockholm Papyrus, fragments
of formulas; edited by R. Halleux). The texts are heterogeneous and fairly
obscure, mixing the theory of matter with blueprints for dyeing, metallurgy, and magic charms. Subsequent volumes will include the writings of
Pseudo-Democritus *(Physica* and *Mystica)*, the *Opusculae* of Zosimus (thirteen texts, edited by M. Mertens), and finally the writings of the commentators Synesius, Olympiodorus, and Stephen of Alexandria.

Alchemists often quote the Presocratics and other philosophers in the
Greek tradition, imbuing them with mystical signification, and it is difficult
to tell which conception of matter is the underlying one. Certain texts are
veiled in figurative language. The intellectual ambiance is that of the magical
and occultist religiosity that is linked to Neoplatonism and Hermeticism
(Zosimus cites Hermes and Zoroaster).

Zosimus, originally from Pannopolis in Egypt (ca. 300 C.E.), is the first in
this chain of authors to be historically identifiable. He is cited as an authority
by his successors, and even as an inspired soothsayer. His writings put forward a symbolics of the liberation of the soul, while describing in enigmatic
form certain operational procedures and apparatuses difficult to reconstruct
exactly (stills, and so on). Metals are made of spirit and body, and matter dies
in order to be reborn. Jung and historians of religion are particularly interested in the "vision of Zosimus" (*Opusculae* X): "I fell asleep, I saw a sacri-
ficer standing before me above an altar"; "the said altar had fifteen steps up to
it" (X.2); "he whom you saw as a man of copper and who vomited his own

flesh, this one is both he who sacrifices and he who is sacrificed" (X.3). These accounts have the strange beauty of dreams or surrealist poems, but interpretation is indispensable for determining what is meant by each symbol (are the fifteen steps the fifteen days of the rising of the moon, the heavenly body that rules over waxings and wanings?). It is too early to form an accurate idea of the content of these texts and to evaluate their subsequent influence.

FRANÇOIS DE GANDT
Translated by Selina Stewart and Jeannine Pucci

Bibliography

Texts and Translations

Aeneas Tacticus. *Poliorcetica*. In *Aeneas Tacticus, Asclepiodotus and Onasander*. Trans. members of Illinois Greek Club. Loeb Classical Library.

Aristotle. *Mechanical Problems*. In *Minor Works*. Trans. W. S. Hett. Loeb Classical Library.

Hero of Alexandria. *Les mécaniques, ou l'élévateur des corps lourds*. Trans. Carra de Vaux. Paris: Les Belles Lettres, 1988.

Pappus of Alexandria. *La collection mathématique*. 2 vols. Trans. Paul Ver Eecke. Paris: Librairie scientifique et technique A. Blanchard, 1982.

Philon of Byzantium. *Traité de fortification, d'attaque et de défense des places*. Trans. Rochas d'Aiglun. Paris: Ch. Tanera, 1872.

Sophocles. *Antigone*. Trans. Hugh Lloyd-Jones. Loeb Classical Library.

Zosimus. *Historia nova*. Trans. Ronald T. Ridley. Canberra: Australian Association for Byzantine Studies, 1982.

Studies

Daumas, Maurice, ed. *Histoire générale des techniques*, vol. 1. Paris: Presses Universitaires de France, 1962.

De Gandt, François. "Force et science des machines." In *Science and Speculation: Studies in Hellenistic Theory and Practice*. Ed. Jonathan Barnes et al. Cambridge and New York: Cambridge University Press, 1982. Pp. 96–127.

Drachmann, A. G. *The Mechanical Technology of Greek and Roman Antiquity: A Study of the Literary Sources*. Copenhagen: Munksgaard; Madison: University of Wisconsin Press, 1963.

Duhem, Pierre. *Les origines de la statique*. 2 vols. Paris: A. Hermann, 1905–1906.

Ferrari, G. A. "Meccanica allargate." In *La scienza ellenistica*. Ed. Gabriele Giannantoni and Mario Vegetti. Naples: Bibliopolis, 1985. Pp. 225–297.

Frontisi-Ducroux, Françoise. *Dédale: mythologie de l'artisan en Grèce ancienne*. Paris: F. Maspero, 1975.

Gille, Bertrand. *Les mécaniciens grecs: La naissance de la technologie*. Paris: Seuil, 1980.

Jacomy, Bruno. *Une histoire des techniques.* Paris: Seuil, 1990.

Rose, P. L., and S. Drake. "The Pseudo-Aristotelian Questions of Mechanics." *Renaissance Culture: Studies in the Renaissance* (1971): 65–104.

Simon, Gérard. *Le regard, l'être et l'apparence dans l'optique de l'antiquité.* Paris: Seuil, 1988.

THEOLOGY AND DIVINATION

HECTOR IN THE *Iliad* has an alter ego, his prudent adviser Polydamas, "who alone saw before and after." Polydamas's counsel is ordinarily full of carefully articulated calculation. But on one occasion he grounds his advice in augury: the portent of an eagle carrying a snake that bites its captor and thus effects its escape. Hector's response is to reject reliance on "long-winged birds." He does not care whether they fly to the right or to the left. His trust is in the plan of mighty Zeus, lord of all mortals and immortals. He sums the matter up in the most famously skeptical remark about divination in all Greek literature: "One omen is best—to fight for one's country" (*Iliad* 12.243).

Augury, oracles, and prophetic dreams are dominant features of the literature of the classical period, and nowhere more so than in the plots of Greek tragedy and the narratives of Herodotus's history. They are usually portrayed as true but ambiguous or unbelievable divine communications, although Herodotus is clear that the Delphic oracle was sometimes subject to political manipulation. When properly explained, they can normally be seen to have encapsulated authoritative advice and correct predictions, but often so obscurely or counterintuitively that those who can interpret them—the wild visionary Cassandra, the blind seer Tiresias—are distrusted and abused.

Despite its troubled prominence in literature, divination probably played a more restricted role in the key decision-making processes of the Greek city-state than it did either in Rome or, for example, among Africa's Azande in Evans-Pritchard's account. Argument in a council or assembly could settle most political issues. But there remained certain momentous choices fraught with uncertainty that required guidance that merely human resources could not supply. Thus the need for favorable auguries in deciding when to join battle was universally accepted. And while the international status of the Delphic oracle placed it outside the institutional framework that defined the civic community, it was nonetheless consulted on matters of state, albeit mostly for specifically cultic questions: e.g., the foundation of colonies, regulations for sacrifices, purificatory procedures for sacrilege or epidemics.

If reason in these various ways limited the scope or questioned the power of divination, there is no evidence of general doubt about *whether* the gods would indicate to humans what they should or should not do, still less about the existence of a divine order itself. The worry was whether humans in general or "experts" in particular really had the ability to decipher what were alleged to be signs of divine intention or approval. This apprehension actually presupposes a belief in divine beings, and that belief was expressed in the complex and disparate religious structures that governed the rhythms of the public calendar of the city-state. The greatest authority on the nature of the many divinities who presided over different aspects of the life of the polis, or the greatest "theologian," as Aristotle calls him, was Homer. For later generations, the *Iliad* (ca. 725 B.C.E.) and *Odyssey* (ca. 700) came to constitute a cultural encyclopedia that, amid other information, told of the names, natures, responsibilities, and interrelations of the gods. Homer is often linked with Hesiod, the contemporary author of a poem entitled *Theogony,* which attempts, in a sequence of creation and succession myths, genealogies, and tales of war in heaven, to bring some order to the bewildering variety of deities and divine forces attested in stories—many newly imported from the Near East—about the gods.

Our first evidence of philosophical speculation dates to the following century: Thales, regarded by the Greeks as its originator, was active in Miletus in the first half of the 6th century. When philosophers started to engage explicitly with the beliefs and practices of traditional religion, what they confronted was the whole structure of polytheism and its claims to make sense of the natural world. And dealing with Homer and Hesiod was a central part of that enterprise.

XENOPHANES

Indeed, Greek philosophical theology begins with a celebrated lampoon: "Homer and Hesiod have attributed to the gods everything that is a reproach among men, stealing and committing adultery and deceiving one another." Like mortals in general, they cast divinities in their own image. The Ethiopians make them black and snub-nosed; the Thracians give them blue eyes and red hair. No doubt lions or horses would represent them as lions or horses if they were capable of art.

This brilliant critique was the work of the traveling philosopher-poet Xenophanes (ca. 570–470 B.C.E.), born in Asia Minor but mostly active in the Greek colonies of southern Italy. It made a deep impact on Plato, who develops its attack on Homeric theology (partially preserved in Xenophanes, frgs. 11, 14–16) in Books 2 and 3 of *The Republic,* and subsequent Greek philosophers were agreed—with the notable exception of Epicurus—that the gods were not to be conceived as anthropomorphic. In place of these traditional conceptions Xenophanes proposed monotheism: "one god . . . in no way similar to men either in body or in thought" (frg. 23). We must rid ourselves of the notion that divinity needs limbs and sense organs. This god causes things to happen by thought alone, without moving a muscle; all of him sees, hears, thinks (frgs. 24–26).

Xenophanes insisted that he did not claim the status of knowledge for his proposal: "No man knows, or ever will know, the clear truth about the gods and about all the things I speak of" (frg. 34). Yet he was doubtless confident that it was eminently more rational than the ideas he was attempting to displace. The same goes for his naturalistic demythologizing explanations of phenomena traditionally associated with divine intervention in the world. Iris, the rainbow, for example, who features as a goddess in Homer, is construed by Xenophanes like other meteorological and celestial phenomena as a particular variety of cloud. It comes as no surprise to find him reported as rejecting the validity of divination.

In other parts of Xenophanes' fragmentary oeuvre evidence survives of prescriptions for moral and religious reform complementing his onslaught on traditional belief. In particular, frg. 1, on the proper conduct of a symposium, focuses on the nature of true piety. After advising cleanliness, purity, and simplicity in all the material aspects of the occasion, the poem turns to what is to be said. "Reverent words and pure speech" hymning the god are to precede talk of virtue, of right and noble deeds—not tales of giants, Titans, and centaurs, nor of conflicts between men in which there is no profit: nothing, presumably, at all like *Theogony* or *Iliad*.

The main elements in Xenophanes' thinking about the nature of divinity and proper religious practice were what remained the dominant ingredients of most later philosophical treatments of these subjects: namely, a radical conception of god or gods; rationalizing explanations of phenomena traditionally explained in religious terms; and new notions of piety.

LATER PRESOCRATICS

So far as we can tell from their surviving fragments, few of the later Presocratic philosophers made theology the explicit focus of their writing and thinking. If we may use modern categories to describe their preoccupations, what primarily concerned them was metaphysics, theory of knowledge, and cosmology and natural philosophy. Their theories might or might not recognize a function for some particular conception of the divine, but understanding the nature of god or gods was not their main purpose.

Anaxagoras (ca. 500–428 B.C.E.) and Diogenes of Apollonia (late 5th century) illustrate the point. With them physics, not metaphysics or epistemology, takes center stage. In their systems god is introduced as first cause: transcendent in Anaxagoras, immanent in Diogenes. Anaxagoras never actually names his first cause "god." He identifies it as mind, unlimited, self-governed, and free from mixture with any other substance (frg. 12). In virtue of these attributes it has the ability to control everything else, and to order nature as it decides. But the language in which Anaxagoras speaks of mind is hymnic, and when Diogenes repeats the same phraseology with reference to his very similar immanent principle (intelligent air) he has no qualms about explicitly identifying it with god (frg. 5), conceived as author of cosmic order, as evidenced, e.g., in the disposition of the seasons of the year (frg. 3). This identification supplied Aristophanes—on the premise that all intellectuals have more or less the same ideas—with ammunition for caricaturing Socratic philosophy as a form of atheistic materialism in his comedy *Clouds* (423 B.C.E.). Even if theological concerns were not uppermost in Diogenes' mind, the radically antitraditional theological consequences of his theory were not lost on his readers. The same goes for Anaxagoras's claim that the heavenly bodies were nothing but incandescent rocks, which prompted his prosecution by the Athenians for impiety around 433. The antireligious reputation he retained throughout antiquity is typified by the anecdote that has him giving an entirely naturalistic explanation of the portent—produced for divinatory diagnosis—of a ram with a single horn in the middle of its forehead.

Heraclitus (probably active around 500 B.C.E.) is closer in time and spirit to Xenophanes. He too lambastes Homer and Hesiod: Homer as a fool, despite his reputation (frgs. 42, 56), Hesiod as one of a number of practitioners of intellectual inquiry who are dismissed as charlatans (frgs. 40, 57). Humans in general are consistently presented as benighted and confused, in their religious practices as elsewhere (e.g., frg. 15). Many of Heraclitus's sayings talk about god or divine understanding or "the one wise willing and unwilling to be called by the name of Zeus" (frg. 32). As this interest in understanding and wisdom indicates, Heraclitus's notion of the divine is geared to the epistemological preoccupations that pervade his fragments. God is for him the complete vantage point, from which every opposition is comprehended as a unity—even if that generally eludes the grasp of human understanding—and indeed the locus of a perspective in which *all* oppositions are simultaneously apprehended in a single vision (frg. 63). Heraclitus has no *theory* about this transcendent perspective: its very transcendence ensures that it cannot be adequately captured or explained in human language. But the *logos* or structure of the universe and of everything in it expresses the unity and identity of opposites, and as such is conceived as conforming to divine law (frg. 114). So the divine perspective apparently exercises a prescriptive function both in cosmic organization and in the human ethical and religious spheres. But those of Heraclitus's remarks on these themes that mention divinities or the divine continue to be informed primarily by epistemological concerns.

The Presocratic who most resembles Xenophanes in the theological and religious orientation of his philosophy, and in his concern with practice as well

as theory, is someone who writes with a passionate commitment as far removed as could be imagined from Xenophanes' coolly critical tone. This is the
extraordinary Sicilian thinker Empedocles (ca. 495–435): philosopher-poet,
political leader, medical man, and magician. In Empedocles, physical and cosmological concerns are fused with intense moral and religious preoccupations.
The life cycles of the biological realm are for him echoed both in an overarch-
ing pattern of disintegration and reconstitution predicated on the universe itself, and in the fall of the soul, its incarnation and successive reincarnations as
an exile from god, and its eventual restoration to peace and harmony. There
can be little doubt that his whole complex system is elaborated ultimately in
an attempt to make sense of the human condition.

Empedocles seems to have introduced talk about some of the principal deities of traditional Greek religion at a fairly early stage in his major poem,
later known as *On Nature*. He offers radical reinterpretations (frg. 6): Zeus is
really one of the four natural elements (probably air), and Hera likewise
(probably earth). Similarly Aphrodite, or Love, is the motive force of harmony at work in the natural world, causing combinations of elements that
then constitute the huge variety of living forms (frg. 17). For his conception
of *true* divinity Empedocles borrows heavily from Xenophanes. He speaks of
a holy mind, "darting through the whole universe with swift thoughts," and
attacks the idea that it might possess limbs, genitals, and the like (frg. 134).
Indeed at the time of most complete cosmic harmony it makes up a perfect
sphere, subsuming into one unit all the diversity of the world with which
we are familiar (frgs. 27, 31). Is Empedocles' god a first cause? Love and the
opposing principle of strife play that role in his system. Perhaps, like
Heraclitus's god, it is rather the locus of perfect understanding.

In a powerful sequence that inspired later writers, such as the Neoplatonist
Porphyry (3rd century C.E.), in their arguments against animal sacrifice and
meat eating, Empedocles imagines a mythical time when Aphrodite ruled
over nature as undisputed queen. Then man and beast lived as friends (frg.
130), and sacrifice involved no bloodshed: Aphrodite was worshipped with
images and incense and gifts of honey, and "the altar was not drenched with
the unspeakable slaughter of bulls" (frg. 128). Implicit in this vision is a deep-
seated belief in the Pythagorean doctrine that all life is akin, which is taken to
dictate a law of nature against bloodshed (frg. 135). Empedocles diagnoses
man's primal sin as the infraction of this law, brought about by "trust in rav-
ing strife" and punished by a sequence of incarnations (frg. 115).

In his later poem *Purifications* he seems to announce his recall from spiritual exile and his transcendence of that gulf between god and man that had
been a powerful theme in Homeric theology: "An immortal god, mortal no
more, I go about honored by all" (frg. 112). This claim echoes the words of
self-disclosure employed by Hermes in the *Iliad* (24.460) and by Demeter in
the Homeric *Hymn to Demeter* (120). But they are deployed in service of a

new form of religion preoccupied with the fate of the individual soul, as in the greeting with which the deceased initiate of the mystery cults is received (apparently by Persephone) in the formula recorded in the "golden plates" recovered at the southern Italian site of classical Thurii: "Happy and blessed one, you shall be a god instead of a mortal."

ETIOLOGY AND ALLEGORY IN
THE AGE OF THE SOPHISTS

The Sophists of the mid- to late 5th century B.C.E. are generally associated in our sources with various forms of theological skepticism. Thus, on record is a famous remark by Protagoras, portrayed by Plato as the leading Sophist of the period (frg. 4): "About gods I cannot know either that they are or that they are not. For many things prevent one from knowing—the obscurity of the question, and the life of man, which is short." This has a Xenophanean ring to it, and indeed the limitations of human understanding are a constant theme of the Presocratics and other early Greek writers. Protagoras's notoriety came from his boldness in focusing agnosticism explicitly on the existence and nature of the gods. A more obscurely celebrated figure, apparently active in Athens at the same time as Protagoras, was Diagoras of Melos, frequently designated "the atheist." Most of the evidence about him is anecdotal. It suggests that he earned his reputation by his expressions of contempt for religious practices, and by his cynicism about the idea that the gods have any concern for human affairs in general and for justice in particular.

Other Sophists were more confident than Protagoras of what to say about religion. Prodicus offered an anthropological account of the origins of belief in gods, as did the atomist philosopher Democritus (born ca. 460 B.C.E.). A sophisticated political explanation—put in the mouth of a character in a fragmentary drama called *Sisyphus*—of how religion was invented as a tool of law enforcement also originated in this milieu. But these theories are antitheological, not exercises in theology, although the line between the two genres became increasingly hard to draw. From around 500 B.C.E. onward, allegorical interpretations of Homer were proposed that represented his understanding of the Olympian deities as much more like that of Prodicus or Democritus than might superficially appear. It was suggested that a distinction should be drawn between what Homer said and the meaning he was conveying by what he said. Thus, for example, when the *Iliad* portrays the gods at war with each other, this is Homer's way of indicating the opposition of fire (Apollo and Hephaestus) and water (Poseidon and Scamander), or again between wisdom (Athena) and folly and desire (Ares and Aphrodite, respectively).

To Plato's disgust, the allegorization of Homer was particularly popular in his time. Its most systematic philosophical exponents in antiquity were the Stoics. The fullest early specimen of the method, belonging probably to the early 4th century B.C.E., is in the Derveni papyrus, which contains extensive fragments of a commentary in this style, although not on Homer but on an Orphic hymn. The poem itself evidently presented a variant of a Hesiodic succession myth, and told of Zeus swallowing an earlier generation of deities. According to the commentator it is not really about creation at all. He explains it as a statement of the philosophy of Anaxagoras (in Diogenes' version): the poem is taken to be expounding how air or mind governs all the things by reason. The author's technique is essentially arbitrary, but interestingly includes appeals to etymology, grammar, common usage, and the principle that one thing can have several different names.

SOCRATES, PLATO, ARISTOTLE

Did Socrates have a theology? According to Xenophon, yes; readers of Plato would infer no. In *Memorabilia* (1.4 and 4.3) Xenophon ascribes to Socrates a set of proofs for the existence of god, including an argument from design, that were later appropriated by the Stoics. But their Socratic credentials are generally disbelieved, as incompatible with his determination to have nothing to do with natural philosophy. What Socrates did introduce—if we are prepared to trust Plato's *Apology*—was a novel and highly individual religious position.

He was charged at his trial with disbelieving in the city's gods and introducing new divinities. The charge was probably correct. At any rate, in *Apology* Socrates represents himself as living his life like a soldier under orders imposed on him by an authority higher than the state. Practicing philosophy and what it entails—submission by himself and others to moral and intellectual examination—"has been commanded me, as I maintain, by the god through oracles and dreams and every other means through which divine apportionment has ever commanded anyone to do anything" (33c). And Plato often has Socrates appealing to the "divine sign" that would restrain him from action. How this conviction of a divine mission so described relates to the austere critical rationality of his ethical method is a matter for debate. It is perhaps significant that the one dialogue of Plato's wholly devoted to a theological question—the early *Euthyphro*, on piety—explores a problem of just this sort: is piety loved by the gods because it has some moral characteristic independent of their loving it, or does it count as piety precisely because it is behavior loved by the gods?

Plato's dialogues are designed to conceal as much as to disclose their author's mind. Nonetheless he evidently writes from a deep sympathy for a religious outlook on life and, particularly in his later works, enunciates a number of strong theological positions, crucial for the moral or theoretical projects being undertaken in the contexts in which they appear, and in the case of *Timaeus* greatly influential in later antiquity and the Middle Ages. Part of the difficulty of evaluating his contribution to theology comes from not knowing whether some uses of the notion of divinity are revolutionary or merely figurative. The Forms in their otherworldly eternity and perfection are often characterized as "divine," and the language of mystic initiation is used to describe the soul's approach to them—*Theaetetus* speaks of "assimilation to god" (176b). The Form of Good, ultimate cause of all there is, has often been thought to function as Plato's supreme deity, notably by the Neoplatonists (3rd to 6th centuries C.E.) in their grand synthesis of Platonic and Aristotelian theology. Another problem is that most of Plato's uncontroversially theistic propositions leave the identity and attributes of the god or gods he speaks of un- (or at any rate under-) determined. At one point he goes so far as to make Socrates insist that we know nothing about the gods (*Cratylus* 400d).

For evidence of Plato as theologian, four dialogues are particularly important. The first chronologically is *Phaedo*, which sees humans as subjects or possessions of the gods, benefiting from their providential care and destined to fall under divine judgment after death. *Phaedo* expresses the wish for a convincing teleological explanation of all things in terms of the dispositions of mind, and this is supplied in *Timaeus*, where Plato argues, first, that as something perceptible the world must have been created, and, second, that its order and beauty are such that its creator must be a "good craftsman," "the best of causes." He is subsequently called "the god" in Plato's comprehensive teleological account of the way the universe is constructed—using relatively sophisticated mathematics—as a living being. Plato stresses the god's goodness and generosity; and goodness and incapacity of deceit are the main attributes of god insisted on in the attack on Homeric theology in *The Republic*.

Book 10 of Plato's last work, *Laws*, deals with the place of religion in the ideal state. Its theological interest consists in the proofs of the existence and providence of gods that Plato presents as weapons to be used against atheist materialists not persuaded of the need for piety. He argues that soul is causally and ontologically prior to body, because only soul is capable of the fundamental form of movement, namely self-motion. The heavenly bodies, as perfect paradigms of self-motion, must therefore be governed by perfect souls. Such causal powers can in fact be exercised only by gods, so the argument effectively demonstrates the existence of gods. But it is important to appreciate that this equation of "souls" with "gods" is for popular consumption. It suffices to refute atheism, not to unlock a true philosophical understanding of the supreme form or forms of deity.

In theology, as in other areas of thought, Aristotle is both at odds with Plato and very close to him. The opposition in their modes of thought comes out very sharply in their approach to divination. While despising the arts of augury and their claims to knowledge, Plato treats as a gift of god those forms of divination that were regarded as divine possession or madness. He construes dreams in particular as giving the irrational part of the soul access to truths, which can only be interpreted, however, when reason returns. Aristotle, by contrast, like Democritus and the Hippocratic treatise *On Regimen*, argues for a completely naturalistic account of dreams. If they came from god, they would be experienced during the day and by the wise. As it is, they resemble the hallucinations of the sick in telling us much more about the physiological or psychological condition of the dreamer than about the future. Sometimes they *are* precognitive: e.g., someone preoccupied with some present or future project may find his waking thoughts causing him dreams on the same subject, and these may in turn become starting points for actions to be performed on rewaking. In this sense some dreams may be "signs and causes." But for the most part any correspondence between a dream and its apparent fulfillment is pure coincidence.

All the same, Aristotle's principal theological arguments have much in common with the ideas of *Laws* 10, although since in his physical system the universe has no beginning, he has no interest in *Timaeus*'s conception of a creator god. The nature and causes of the perfect movements of the heavenly bodies were topics to which he returned again and again, usually with a view to drawing theological conclusions. His final position on these issues is given in Book 12 of *Metaphysics*, where he argues that since everything in the sublunary world sooner or later perishes, that world would eventually collapse if it were not sustained by an eternal motion, namely that of the heavenly bodies, or rather the fixed stars. These he construes in Platonic fashion as self-movers. At this point he diverges from Plato, for he has argued exhaustively in Book 8 of *Physics* that ultimately no self-motion is self-explanatory, but can be caused only by a mover that is not itself moved: by a pure actuality not subject to change of any kind. This is Aristotle's god. He explains that it moves the stars because its mode of being is the object of their desire, and he identifies its activity or life as the self-reflexive exercise of thinking. As Aristotle himself insists, this means that if physics is the study of the changeable, theology—now for the first time formally located on a comprehensive map of the sciences—has to be a quite different discipline, devoted to understanding unqualified being.

EPICUREANS, STOICS, AND SKEPTICS

In the dominant philosophical systems of the Hellenistic age, questions about the existence and nature of gods acquired an established place among the fundamental topics of philosophy. Epicurus believed that without a proper understanding of what the gods were like there was no prospect of attaining the *ataraxia*, freedom from anxiety, to which his whole philosophical teaching was directed. For the Stoics, theology, conceived as cosmology (and so as part of physics), constituted the final and, from some points of view, most important chapter in their favored sequence of philosophical topics.

Both schools summarized the key elements of their teaching on the subject in pithy syllogisms easy to memorize. The first two prescriptions of Epicurus's "fourfold remedy" *(tetrapharmakos)* against anxiety are directed toward allaying fears of divine punishment before or after death. The argument relating specifically to the gods runs as follows (in the version of *Key Doctrines* 1): "That which is blessed and imperishable neither suffers nor inflicts trouble, and therefore is affected neither by anger nor by favor. For all such things are marks of weakness." The Stoics, for their part, produced whole batteries of arguments in this style. Most of those attributed to Zeno of Citium (334–262), founder of the school, aimed to establish pantheism: e.g., "If something generates from itself life and rationality, it is itself alive and rational. But the world generates living rational creatures. Therefore the world is alive and rational." The cosmic *logos* or reason on which the rationality of the world is properly predicated is also conceived as its creator, regularly reconstituting it after periodic destructions, and Chrysippus (ca. 280–206), third head of the school, propounded a cosmological argument for such a divine creator: "If there is something in nature which human mind, reason, strength and power cannot make, what *does* make it must be superior to man. But the things in the heavens and all those whose regularity is everlasting cannot be created by man. Therefore what creates them is superior to man. But what more appropriate name is there for this than 'god'?" Zeno even propounded what has sometimes been construed as the first ontological argument for the existence of god or gods: "It would be reasonable to honor the gods. It would not be reasonable to honor what does not exist. Therefore gods exist."

Epicurean cosmology is constructed on mechanistic principles that leave no room for divine agency in the world. The conclusions reached by physical inquiry therefore turn out to be consistent with the general preconception of the blessedness and invulnerability of the gods on which Epicurus relies in *Key Doctrines* 1. Whether he actually believed in their *existence* was controversial in antiquity and remains so today. Some texts support the idea that Epicurean gods were envisaged as inhabiting interstices between universes, where they would be relatively protected against atomic collisions. Others suggest that they are nothing more than our own instinctive, self-projecting thought constructs. Stoic theology is a more ambitious theoretical undertaking. It too draws on what are claimed to be common notions about the gods, but it builds these into a systematic construction incorporating much earlier philosophical thought. Indeed Stoic theological cosmology can be viewed as a rewriting of *Timaeus*, but with the divine craftsman converted into an immanent principle of creative reason embodied in Heraclitean fire, and with periodic cosmic bonfires replacing the imperishability of the Platonic cosmos. Divine reason "encompasses all the seminal principles whereby everything comes about in accordance with fate": "god, intelligence, fate and Zeus are one."

More original is the Stoics' explication of the concept of providence, to which their commitment was no less fierce than the Epicureans' hostility. Here, three ideas in particular are worth mentioning. First is the Stoic doctrine of the cosmic city. Because, according to the Stoics, humans and gods are unique in *sharing* the capacity to love according to reason, so constituting a community under the same moral law, it must be supposed that the universe and its contents were designed for the sake of men as well as gods—just as cities are designed for their inhabitants. Here the Homeric gulf between god and man has yielded to an outlook that manages to be simultaneously theocentric and anthropocentric. Second, because the gods care for men, we must expect them not only to give us signs serving as premonitions of the future, where this is to our advantage, but also to put in our hands the means of understanding such signs. In other words, disbelief in divination is incompatible with belief in providence, and natural theology itself indicates the necessity of revelation. Third, the Stoics recognized that their belief in providence obliged them to attempt a theodicy, i.e., an explanation of why a deity who cares for humans should allow evil in the world. They seem to have canvassed a number of possible answers, but their favored argument was the contention that there cannot be good without evil. In his *Hymn to Zeus* Zeno's successor Cleanthes (331–232) says: "No deed is done apart from you except what bad men do in their folly. But you know how to make things crooked straight and to order things disorderly. You love things unloved. For you have so welded into one all things good and bad that they all share in a single everlasting reason."

Not surprisingly this and every other doctrine of Stoic theology provoked counterargument and often mockery and parody by opponents, notably from the Skeptic Carneades, head of the Academy in the mid-2nd century B.C.E. Each of the three syllogisms quoted above was attacked. Using arguments parallel with Zeno's, one could prove that the world is not only alive and rational but also a harpist and a flute player; or, again, that since it would be reasonable to honor the wise, wise persons exist—which the Stoics denied. As for Chrysippus, the Academics complained that he relied heavily on notions like "superior," which are hopelessly vague. In making their criticisms they disclaimed atheistic intentions. Custom and tradition were, they said, a sufficient basis for accepting the existence of gods. Reason—especially in its guise as Stoic demonstration—was neither necessary nor sufficient.

Are natural theology and the study of religion the proper province of metaphysics, cosmology, anthropology, or physiology and psychology? The question is still disputed, and the cacophony of answers given by ancient Greek thinkers has not been improved on. Can we know anything about the gods? And if so, by what means? Here, too, it is the variety of incompatible answers proposed by Greek philosophy that constitute one of its most impressive and characteristic legacies to theology.

Agnosticism took different forms: we simply have no means of knowing (Protagoras); reason cannot establish theological truths, but that should not threaten customary belief (Skeptics); we don't know, but we can make reasonable conjectures (Xenophanes). It was no doubt the very existence of articulate agnosticism, and indeed atheism, that prompted the general philosophical project of offering *proofs*—elaborate or otherwise—of the existence of gods: this is explicitly acknowledged by Plato in *Laws* 10. To put the point another way, theology as a specialized philosophical discipline was born from philosophical doubt about the gods. At the same time theistic philosophers, notably Aristotle and the Stoics, were anxious to insist that the common belief in gods, universal among humankind, was already a testimony to their existence. The Stoics seem to have gone so far as to claim that the existence of gods is obvious, as indicated, for example, by the order of the universe in general and the heavenly bodies in particular. We should accordingly interpret philosophical demonstrations of their existence or nature in line with Aristotelian and Stoic theories of science: as attempts to advance us from the bland certainties of belief to true understanding or, more specifically, to articulate common notions in ways that exhibit and analyze the deep truths about the universe that they encapsulate.

Philosophy therefore came to claim for theology and (in the Stoic case) divination a more secure epistemic status than either traditional belief or rational reflection had earlier thought possible. If this historical outcome of the ancient debate about the gods is a dubious achievement, we can at least grant that Greek thinkers identified many of the perennial problems of theology, and pioneered many strategies for handling them that have proved attractive in the long history of inquiry in this field.

MALCOLM SCHOFIELD

Bibliography

Bouché-Leclercq, Auguste. *L'astrologie grecque*. Paris, 1899.

———. *Histoire de la divination dans l'antiquité*. 4 vols. Paris, 1879–1892.

Dodds, E. R. *The Greeks and the Irrational*. Berkeley, 1951.

Dragona-Monachou, Myrto. *The Stoic Arguments for the Existence and Providence of the Gods*. Athens, 1976.

Festugière, A. J. *Epicure et ses dieux*, 2nd ed. Paris, 1968.

———. *La révélation d'Hermès Trismégiste*. 4 vols. Paris, 1944–1954.

Gerson, L. P. *God and Greek Philosophy.* London, 1990.

Kenney, J. P. *Mystical Monotheism: A Study in Platonic Theology.* Hanover, N.H., 1991.

Kirk, G. S., J. E. Raven, and M. Schofield. *The Presocratic Philosophers,* 2nd ed. Cambridge, 1983.

Lloyd, G. E. R. *Magic, Reason and Experience.* Cambridge, 1979.

Long, A. A., and D. N. Sedley. *The Hellenistic Philosophers.* 2 vols. Cambridge, 1987.

Solmsen, Friedrich. *Plato's Theology.* Ithaca, N.Y., 1942.

Vernant, J. P., ed. *Divination et rationalité.* Paris, 1974.

THEORIES OF RELIGION

From its very inception, philosophy thrived by breaking with tradition and—although total respect was the rule in such matters—evaluating cults and beliefs on the basis of innovative criteria that later became entrenched. A reader of the early thinkers discovers a jubilant and stimulating energy that is apparent even in a domain as ordinarily austere as religion. This initial spark gave rise to all subsequent thinking on the subject.

Aside from the usual problems (gaps in sources, length of the period studied, and so on), one difficulty in particular is of concern in the present study: practices and beliefs may have varied from city to city and from epoch to epoch, in ways about which we have no information; thus there is a considerable risk of oversimplification. The main hurdle, however, is methodological. Often, philosophers did not begin by interpreting factual data but took the opposite course: they analyzed or evaluated religion on the basis of their own concept of divinity. As a result, it can be difficult for us to define the role of their own theology with respect to both their analysis of religion and their understanding of it.

Although Homer, Hesiod, and Pindar developed some themes in what amounted to early reflections on religion, it seems preferable here to present only judgments formulated by philosophers; these provide a critical perspective in the very broadest sense of the term. Moreover, the opinions of Greek philosophers, while they do not actually constitute a system, do allow for a methodical approach to religion. After Anaximander, who regarded the gods as natural beings, the Presocratics included them in their investigations, and some examined the validity of beliefs and cults surrounding the gods. This was the beginning of the history of the relationship—often a discordant one—between religion and philosophy. The principal questions, from the outset, concerned the conception of the gods, ritual practices, mythology, and divination.

Xenophanes was the first to articulate a line of thinking that looked at religion objectively. His thinking was based on a particular hypothesis that later became widespread: the impossibility of knowing the divine with certainty. In a famous passage, Xenophanes criticized the anthropomorphism that was the basis of Greek religion: "But if cattle and horses or lions had hands, or were able to draw with their hands and do the works that men can do, horses would draw the forms of the gods like horses, and cattle like cattle, and they would make their bodies such as they each had themselves" (frg. 169). Along the same lines, he also attacked the belief that gods were born and died, and moved around like people; he denounced the myths of Giants and Titans, linked to certain cults, as "pure fiction created in remote times." More broadly, he condemned immoral myths. Finally, he rejected divination entirely. Despite his critique of beliefs, he advocated respect for traditional forms of piety: he recommended prayers and hymns, "holy respect for the gods." Here, too, in his conciliatory language, he was a pioneer. But it would be a mistake to limit Xenophanes' contribution to these few fragments. His scientific interpretation of celestial phenomena took them out of the realm of superstition: for example, he explained rainbows, usually viewed as apparitions of the goddess Iris, as multicolored clouds. In this he was following a path opened up by Anaximander, and he had illustrious successors in Anaxagoras and Democritus. Some forty years after his death, a decree promulgated by Diopeithes in Athens around 433 B.C.E. prohibited "speaking of celestial things," at the risk of being tried for impiety.

Heraclitus's even more radical critique concerned cult itself: "The secret rites practised among men are celebrated in an unholy manner" (frg. 242, p. 209). His well-known statement that cadavers are no more than manure reflects his complete indifference toward funeral rites, which were regarded as most sacred of all. Heraclitus ridiculed official purification rites, the cult of statues, and prayers: "They vainly purify themselves of blood-guilt by defiling themselves with blood, as though one who had stepped into mud were to wash with mud; he would seem to be mad, if any of men noticed him doing this. Further, they pray to these statues, as if one were to carry on a conversation with houses, not recognizing the true nature of gods or demi-gods" (frg. 241, p. 209). In ancient Greece, questioning such official practices was more revolutionary than challenging the beliefs behind them: not only were there no theological dogmas, but the only expression in classical times for belief in gods, *theos nomizein*, originally meant simply to honor the gods as custom (*nomos*) ordained.

By attacking religious customs, Heraclitus demonstrated an audacity paralleled only by that of the Cynics. However, the essential feature of his contribution to the field of religion does not lie in his criticisms, which, considered in isolation from the rest of his theory, might take on a positivist aspect running counter to the spirit in which they were formulated. By striving to adapt religious representations borrowed from traditional beliefs to his own conception of the divine, Heraclitus shed light on those representations. His puzzling statement, "One thing, the only truly wise, does not and does consent to be called by the name of Zeus" (frg. 228, p. 202), goes to the very heart of religious thought. The Greeks in effect measured the distance between the divine and its human representation (or name): they emphasized the ambiguous relationship between gods and men, a relationship symbolized in particular by Apollo Loxias (the Oblique), so called because the meaning of his prophecies was never obvious. For Heraclitus, the "Logos" is "common"; it can be clearly heard. Thus "men should try to comprehend the underlying coherence of things" (frg. 193, p. 186), that which links men objectively to one another, but the very meaning of Logos remains unheard, because "men always prove to be uncomprehending" (frg. 194, p. 187). Clarity and obscurity are thus components of human experience and discourse. This duality applies in particular to religion. An anecdote reported by Aristotle is revealing. A group of foreigners who had come to visit the sage in Ephesus did not dare to approach because they saw that he was "warming himself by the fire" (a euphemism designating a more trivial occupation). Heraclitus encouraged them to come in, saying: "The gods are found here as well." Thus a mysterious aspect of the sacred, echoes of which are found in Greek ritual, is expressed with the greatest clarity by one of the harshest critics of tradition. Heraclitus was also the first to reveal the role of the sign in divination: "The Lord whose oracle is in Delphi neither speaks out nor conceals, but gives a sign" (frg. 244, p. 209). Last, and most important, Heraclitus influenced the understanding of the religious phenomenon itself by showing that what is self-evident, even when it is derived from cult practice, is merely the visible pole of a symbolic system whose meaning the mind cannot encompass as a whole.

Democritus proposed an approach to religion that might be called, anachronistically, anthropological. He tried to account for the origin of the common belief in the gods by adopting an approach that was new in philosophy but pursued also by contemporary Sophists: Democritus did not refer to theology but relied solely on phenomena, although without attributing any truth-value to them. According to a later account, he believed that the experience of celestial phenomena, such as thunder, lightning, and eclipses, so terrified the ancients that they were convinced that only the gods could have caused them. Stobaeus tells us that Democritus imagined hell as a fable inspired by the fear of punishment after death. On the scientific origin of the concept of God, Sextus Empiricus has recorded this explanation: "Democritus says that certain images impinge on men, and of these some are beneficent, others maleficent—whence also he prayed that he might have 'propitious images'—, and these images . . . signify the future to men beforehand, as they are visible and utter sounds. Hence the ancients, on receiving a presentation of these images, supposed that God exists, God being none other than these images, and possessed of an indestructible nature" (*Against the Physicists* I.19). So we have the remarkable conception of a divinity whose only reality consists in images. According to Cicero, Democritus would have approved of the examination of the entrails of animals offered as sacrifices: their shape and color provided "signs" predicting good health or epidemics, or the fertility or sterility of the land (Cicero, *On Divination* I.131). In other words, for Democritus divination rested on the purely natural correspondence between the state of the entrails and that of the place where the animal had lived and grazed.

Rapid though the present survey is, it may seem surprising that the names of several great Presocratics, such as Pythagoras, Parmenides, and Empedocles, are absent from it. However, there are very few fragments on the subject of civic religion that can be attributed to them, no doubt because their conception of the divine was too far removed from popular belief. Their philosophy, on the other hand, had considerable influence in the religious sphere. The Pythagoreans, through many ritual observances, undermined religion. Empedocles took up their condemnation of animal sacrifices on the basis of the following argument, according to Aristotle: "In fact, there is a general idea of just and unjust in accordance with nature, as all men in a manner divine, even if there is neither communication nor agreement between them . . . And as Empedocles says in regard to not killing that which has life, for this is not right for some and wrong for others 'But a universal precept, which extends without a break throughout the wide-ruling sky and the boundless earth'" (*Rhetoric* I.xiii.2.1373b). Here the contract between men and gods—the basis for Greek sacrifice—is called into question.

Ancient tradition often regarded the Sophists as atheists. Only the first sentence of Protagoras's treatise *On the Gods* has survived, and it testifies to his agnosticism. However, he did not reject all forms of popular religion: in a passage from Plato's *Protagoras*, apparently reflecting the thinking of the great Sophist (325a, d), religion is taken as an element of "human virtue," indispensable to civic life. Skepticism and the cultural enhancement of religion have generally gone hand in hand in the Greek tradition. Another Sophist, Prodicus, stated that people regard as divine, and worthy of honor, whatever ensures their livelihood: the sun, the moon, rivers, springs, the fruits of the earth. Among other examples, he cited wine, which takes its name from Dionysus, and water, named after Poseidon, to show that these divinities always correspond to elements of nature. This allegorical method, developed further by Metrodorus of Lampsacus, was to enjoy lasting popularity. In addition, according to Daniel Babut, Prodicus anticipated modern theory concerning the origin of religion by claiming that all religious practices were derived from agriculture and were expressions of man's gratitude for the blessings he received from the earth.

Critias took a decisive step forward in the debate on the origin of the gods when he declared that "a wise and clever man invented fear [of the gods] for mortals, that there might be some means of frightening the wicked, even if they do anything or say or think it in secret. Hence he introduced the Divine saying that there is a God flourishing with immortal life, hearing and seeing with his mind . . . who will be able to see all that is done" (frg. 25, in Free-man, *Ancilla*, p. 158). This view of religion as a factor in political stability was shared and advanced by many others, particularly by historians such as Polybius. According to ancient sources, Critias wrote a satirical play, *Sisyphus* (now sometimes attributed to Euripides); Sextus Empiricus quotes some forty lines of it in which the writer makes fun of theologians and popular beliefs alike. Critias's reputation as an atheist appears to be fully justified.

Thus, at the end of the 5th century B.C.E., the principal lines of thought about religion were established: an anthropomorphic conception of the gods, polytheism, the value of rituals and cults, and their historical origins, along with the historical origins of belief in gods. These themes were addressed by Xenophanes, Heraclitus, Democritus, and the Sophists in particular, but we should also keep in mind the works of the tragic poets in these areas. Their analyses are essential to our understanding of certain key concepts that are derived from ritual, such as notions of purity and impurity. In *Philosophy of Religion*, Hegel grants preeminence to Sophocles for the depth of his re-flection on religion, and in particular for his demonstration of the close con-nection between freedom and necessity. As for Euripides, whose views were close to those of the Sophists, the critique he formulated took into account the diversity of cults and beliefs and thus contributed to a better understanding of them.

The remarkable legacy of Presocratic thought provided the foundation for the subsequent attitudes of philosophers toward religion. These later atti-tudes favored, in a more systematic fashion, three principal options: first, the coexistence of philosophy and religion, either as two separate fields or with certain traditional elements integrated into philosophy; second, the annex-ation of religion by philosophy; and third, the total rejection of religion. Soc-rates may be said to be the pivotal figure in this evolution. Xenophon por-trays him as the systematic defender of religious tradition. Socrates himself appears not to have foreseen the conflict between his rationalist approach in philosophy and a scrupulous respect for tradition. However, it was the ratio-nalist approach that led him to criticize the conception of piety that was gen-erally accepted in Athens at the time, what he called a "commercial technique, governing exchanges between gods and men." In Plato's *Euthyphro* Socrates, on the way to his trial on charges of impiety, shows that the pious gesture is not pious because it is pleasing to the gods, as his interlocutor the priest Euthyphro believes; on the contrary, it is pleasing to the gods because it is pi-ous. This is a crucial distinction, because it affirms the intrinsic value of piety. When, at the end, Socrates declares to his judges: "I will obey the gods rather than you," he breaks the fundamental connection between the gods and the state. Daniel Babut stresses this "striking paradox," pointing out that "Socra-tes, the unconditional defender of traditional state religion, is also the one who first calls into question its fundamental principle." Socrates thus inaugurated two major trends: on the one hand, respect for religion, notwithstanding the triumphs of theoretical knowledge, and on the other hand, the control, indeed the domination, exercised by philosophy over religious thought. Plato was to develop in depth this second trend more than any other.

In his very first dialogues, Plato reveals that the Greek religion of his time suffered from a lack of spirituality, a spirituality that he tries to instill in the ideal religion described in his last work, Laws. However, in earlier works he examines various aspects of the state religion. Thus, in Cratylus, he considers "what kind of correctness" the names of the gods have. He first remarks that "we, if we are sensible, must recognize that there is one most excellent kind [of correctness], since of the gods we know nothing, neither of them, nor of their names, whatever they may be, by which they call themselves, for it is clear that they use the true names. But there is a second kind of correctness, that we call them, as is customary in prayers, by whatever names and patronymics are pleasing to them, since we know no other" (Cratylus 400d–e). Then he goes on to explain at length the etymologies of the names of various gods; these appear to be based on views formed by men in accordance with tradition. But this play on the gods' names that Plato somewhat ironically attributes to Socrates conceals a critique of etymological interpretation. This practice, widespread in ancient Greece, was brought back into fashion by Max Müller with his famous maxim: "Mythology is a disease of language." According to Critias, recourse to myths and the search for aspects of the past appeared quite late, at about the same time as leisure, when some people were able to free themselves from the harsh necessities of daily life. The representation of the gods also conformed to social status. The armed figure of Athena appeared at a time when "the activities of warriors were shared by men and women alike": "The people of that time, in accordance with custom, depicted the goddess armed as a dedicatory offering." This attempt at historical explanation can be seen as the counterpart to a rejection of traditional myths, expressed most notably in the second book of The Republic, as well as a rejection of the rationalization of myths through allegorical method. There is no hidden meaning to be found in mythology that might lead to some Idea of the divine. However, in Phaedrus the value of inspired divination is affirmed: "The greatest of blessings come to us through madness, when it is sent as a gift of the gods" (244b). For Greece, prophecy of this kind "has conferred many splendid benefits" (ibid.). In contrast, Plato sees the art of augury (prophecy based on the flight of birds), which he considers somewhat inferior, as arising out of a purely human rationality. Finally, The Republic and Laws specifically advise consultation of the oracle of Delphi about the cult of the gods and about funeral customs.

Laws accords religion a central position. As Olivier Reverdin points out, religion in Delphi and in the city-states seemed to Plato to be a valuable inheritance that, in the absence of dogma, was at risk of succumbing to the attacks of skepticism, atheism, and foreign superstitions. Plato tried to provide what was lacking and to make religion the basis for moral and civic life in the best of all city-states. But the status of belief, as Plato conceived of it, called into question the role of theology: "For we needs must be vexed and indignant with the men who have been, and now are, responsible for laying on us this burden of argument, through their disbelief in those stories which they used to hear, while infants and sucklings, from the lips of their nurses and mothers—stories chanted to them, as it were, in lullabies, whether in jest or in earnest; and the same stories they heard repeated also in prayers at sacrifices, and they saw spectacles which illustrated them, of the kind which the young delight to see and hear when performed at sacrifices; and their own parents they saw showing the utmost zeal on behalf of themselves and their children in addressing the gods in prayers and supplications, as though they most certainly existed" (Plato, *Laws* 887c–d).

Here Plato affirms that belief in the divine is inherent in cult practice and is transmitted through tales, not unlike fables for children, which constitute a more solid ground for religion than any rational discourse. Denied this naive faith, citizens must be induced to obey religious laws and be threatened with punishment if they disobey.

Cronos, the divine legislator, justified recourse to such measures: he is said to have originally imposed exemplary laws of piety. However, as Plato stresses, the story of Cronos is a myth, whereas the Athenian in *Laws* goes so far as to state that, if there were an individual of pure intellect, it would be a *sacrilege* for him to obey any law, since the intellect is "master of all." How better to suggest that religious obligations and prohibitions serve, above all, to maintain the stability of the city-state? From this political perspective, Plato allows no private cults, thereby denying the fundamental link between public cults and family cults that was essential to Greek religion. Last, in the ideal city-state the legislator prohibited the mystery cults that Isocrates celebrated for offering "the sweetest hopes for the end of life and eternity." Plato, in contrast, feared their excesses, their shadowy, magical character. Thus, following in the footsteps of his master, Socrates, the disciple Plato believed that piety consisted first and foremost of a moral and intellectual attitude. But by giving preeminence to religion in the ideal city-state, he also showed that it provided the best paradigm of Law, and that it offered, through the Olympians, a credible conception of the divine, in a realm where the truth cannot be known. Plato's work therefore marks a decisive turning point in the history of the relationship between philosophy and state religion: it defined for the first time the terms and the stakes in each field, what they had in common, and where they diverged.

Aristotle's approach, in the treatises that have come down to us, is characteristic of the tendency to present religion and philosophy as coexisting independently. The question of the divine is approached through metaphysics with the concept of the "Prime Mover." In *Nicomachean Ethics*, Aristotle states that it would be ridiculous to reproach God for not returning love, since love and friendship exist only among beings of the same species. Nevertheless, Aristotle does not object to the beliefs and institutions of popular religion; on the contrary, he recognizes their necessity. In *Politics*, in his list of the functions that are essential to the life of a state, he includes "a primary need, the service of religion, termed a priesthood" (VII.vii.4.1328b). In *Topica* he asserts that "those who feel doubt about whether or not the gods ought to be honoured and parents loved, need castigation" (I.xi). Following Plato's example, Aristotle too believes that religious festivals are moments of relaxation for the citizens.

This conservatism in religious matters seems to be based primarily on the principle, already recognized by Plato, according to which "what is most ancient is most revered" (*Metaphysics* I.iii.6). Aristotle formulates a new argument favoring belief in the gods, that of universal consensus: "All men have a conception of gods, and all assign the highest place to the divine, barbarians and Hellenes" (*On the Heavens* I.iii.270b). This argument will be heard over and over again. On other subjects, mythology and the anthropomorphism of the gods, Aristotle adopts Xenophanes' position. Finally, he takes up divination in a manner that reflects his own thinking more deeply. In *Parva naturalia*, he challenges the supernatural origin of dreams (*On Prophecy in Dreams*), but, in accordance with tradition, which is "based on experience" (462b), he accepts the truly prophetic nature of some of them. "For quite common men have prescience and vivid dreams which shows that these are not sent by God; but that men whose nature is as it were garrulous or melancholic see all kinds of sights" (468b). Prophecy is therefore natural. If Freud makes room for Aristotle in *The Interpretation of Dreams*, it is because the latter explains religious belief without reference to theology.

The absolute rejection of religion, a view first formulated by Critias, is illustrated by the Cynics. They spared no quarter, neither the conception of the divine, nor mythology, nor the cults (least of all the mystery-cults that provoked Antisthenes' mockery), nor divination. This rejection of popular religion rested on the principle that whatever conforms to custom *(nomos)* is worthless compared to what is natural *(phusis)*; hence the Cynics, and especially Diogenes, modified and intensified an opposition that had been preeminent in the thought of the Sophists.

Then there is Euhemerus (ca. 340–260 B.C.E.), a strange author who defies categorization and whose conception of religion is better known than any other. He held that the gods were divine men. If one judges by the long extract that is preserved in the work of Diodorus of Sicily, his *Sacred History* is a strange tale about a marvelous imaginary island, Panchaea. Various mythi-

368 ◆ THE GREEK PURSUIT OF KNOWLEDGE

cal sites appear in this text along with the ancient descendants of deified men. "There is also on the island [of Panchaea], situated upon an exceedingly high hill, a sanctuary of Zeus Tripylius, which was established by him during the time when he was king of all the inhabited world and was still in the company of men" (Diodorus, VI.I.6). "Around the world, Jupiter spread the sympathy for his cult and provided an example for men to imitate" (Lactantius, *Divine Institutions* I). "Venus established the art of the courtesan" (Quintus Ennius, "Euhemerus," 134–135). In short, all the quotations from *Sacred History* are in the same vein. Perhaps owing to its apparent ingenuousness, Euhemerus's story enjoyed great success not only in Greece but also in Rome, where it was revived and circulated by Ennius.

The Hellenistic period was characterized by profound changes: the accelerated decline of traditional religion, the growth of individualism, and, last, the increasing importance of practical concerns, particularly those relating to the cults. More than ever before, philosophy sought to include religion in its purview. The major systems, such as those of Epicurus and the Stoics, attest to this radicalization. In the Epicurean doctrine, paradoxically, the popular representation of the gods was included and granted some legitimacy. People have a true "preconception" of the gods derived from images, some perceived in dreams (which are the source of belief, according to many philosophers), others appearing by day. These images take the traditional form, and Lucretius's picture of the gods in their "calm abodes" is the same as the picture presented in Homer's *Odyssey*. However, for most people this conception is distorted because of their ignorance of the causes of natural (in particular, heavenly) phenomena. They thus think, mistakenly, that the gods govern the world, and in this way do themselves the greatest harm.

Epicurean doctrine held that, on the contrary, the gods embody the ideal of happiness and the absence of troubles. They can be perceived only through images that strike the mind directly. According to Epicurus, it is the "mind directed toward these images, and concentrated on them" that obtains knowledge of the "blissful and eternal nature" of the divine (Cicero, *On the Nature of the Gods* I.49). Thus, while most philosophical schools tended toward a monotheistic view, the philosophy thought to be most hostile to religion was in fact the only one both to accept Greek polytheism and to supply concrete arguments for the traditional view of the gods. However, Epicureanism repudiates divination and deprives worship of its traditional purpose. Myths, particularly those of the underworld, are rejected: since death means annihilation, myths of the underworld are merely projections of the fears felt by the living. According to Lucretius, the primary function of Epicureanism is to dispel "this terror of mind . . . and this gloom" (*On the Nature of Things* I.146–148). He concludes his description of Iphigenia's sacrifice with a well-known statement about the miseries produced in the name of religion ("often . . . superstition has brought forth criminal and impious deeds," *On the Nature of Things* I.82–83). No ancient author offers a better denunciation than Lucretius of the violence embedded not only in blood sacrifice but also in other rituals. Lucretius exposes the sexual aspect of this violence by revealing the orgiastic displays of the cult of Cybele. In Rome, the connection established between *religio* and *religare* (to tie), according to a commonly accepted "etymology," helped to denounce the alienating character of religion. Neither Epicurus's *Letters* nor the fragments of his other writings reveal the same virulence; he encouraged participation in traditional cults and participated in them himself.

In contrast to Epicureanism stands Stoicism. According to Plutarch, in all their written works the Stoics "railed" against Epicurus, whom they accused of overturning the common view of the gods by eliminating the role of Providence. However, Stoicism, so closely linked to religion, had constructed its own system in this domain as well, which explains the harshness of Stoic criticism of cults and popular beliefs. The Stoics rejected myths, calling them "futile and inconsistent"; they denounced the irrational character of anthropomorphism and the triviality of some of the gods venerated in cult practices. All of these criticisms stem from the Stoics' belief in a single god, the Reason *(Logos)* inherent in the universe. However, by means of etymological explanation, the Stoics tried to identify popular religion with their doctrine. Thus, through a process that was the opposite of Prodicus's approach, the Stoics saw the various divinities as metonyms for a universal god: Demeter is the earth mother *(Ge meter)*, Hera is air *(aer)*, and so on. Most Stoics even defended divination, which became a science based on the Stoic theory of signs. Cicero, in his *On the Nature of the Gods,* not only presented these various aspects of Stoicism but also showed that they were hotly contested, especially by the philosophers of the New Academy. Their spokesman in Cicero's dialogue, taking up Carneades' arguments, accused the Stoics of misinterpreting and perverting religion. As a follower of the Skeptic academy, Cicero accepted tradition without committing himself and recognized some intrinsic value in the cults of different societies. In his view, writers who study myths provide important evidence of the various representations of divinity. A method was thus established for analyzing religious practices and beliefs as sociocultural data. This method was further developed by Plutarch, although in a very different spirit, for he attempted, through allegorical exegesis, to find in religion a nucleus of transcendent truth.

The "challenge" that philosophy posed from its very beginning is particularly applicable to the area of religion. The validity of philosophers' opinions consists in the depth and variety of the points of view presented as much as in the accuracy and coherence—at least within each system—of the methods used to pin down the nature of religion. But cults were rarely analyzed in their own right and on the basis of the details that enable modern scholars to pursue a phenomenological approach to the sacred. Owing in particular to the critical distance required by theology, most Greek philosophers aspired to a general understanding of practices and beliefs. While this was one source of their greatness, it was also a limitation.

JOSÉ KANY-TURPIN
Translated by Elizabeth Rawlings and Jeannine Pucci

Bibliography

Texts and Translations

Aristotle. *Art of Rhetoric*. Trans. J. H. Freese. Loeb Classical Library.
————. *Metaphysics*. Books I–IX. Trans. Hugh Tredennick. Loeb Classical Library.
————. *On the Heavens*. Trans. W. K. C. Guthrie. Loeb Classical Library.
————. *Parva naturalia*. Trans. W. S. Hett. Loeb Classical Library.
————. *Politics*. Trans. H. Rackham. Loeb Classical Library.
————. *Topica*. Trans. E. S. Forster. Loeb Classical Library.
Freeman, Kathleen. *Ancilla to the Pre-Socratic Philosophers: A Complete Translation of the Fragments in Diels*. Oxford: Basil Blackwell, 1948.
Kirk, G. S., J. E. Raven, and Malcolm Schofield. *The Presocratic Philosophers*, 2nd ed. Cambridge: Cambridge University Press, 1983.
Lactantius. *The Divine Institutions*. Trans. Sister Mary Francis McDonald. Washington, D.C.: The Catholic University of America Press, 1964.
Plato. *Cratylus*. Trans. H. N. Fowler. Loeb Classical Library.
————. *Euthyphro*. Trans. H. N. Fowler. Loeb Classical Library.
————. *Laws*, vol. 2. Trans. R. G. Bury. Loeb Classical Library.
————. *Phaedrus*. Trans. H. N. Fowler. Loeb Classical Library.
————. *Protagoras*. Trans. W. R. M. Lamb. Loeb Classical Library.
Sextus Empiricus. *Against the Professors*. Trans. R. G. Bury. Loeb Classical Library.

Studies

Babut, Daniel. *La religion des philosophes grecs*. Paris: Presses Universitaires de France, 1974.
Burkert, Walter. *Greek Religion*. Cambridge, Mass.: Harvard University Press, 1985.
Decharme, Paul. *La critique des traditions religieuses chez les Grecs*. Paris: Picard, 1904.
Détienne, Marcel. *Les jardins d'Adonis: La mythologie des aromates en Grèce*. Paris: Gallimard, 1972.
Morel, Pierre-Marie. "Le regard étranger sur la cité des Lois." In *D'une cité possible: Sur les Lois de Platon*. Ed. J. F. Balaudé. 1. Nanterre: Université Paris X–Nanterre, 1995. Pp. 95–113.
Obbink, Dirk. "Epicurus 11(?): Sulla religiosità e il culto popolare." In *Corpus dei papiri filosofici greci e latini*, vol. 1. Florence: Olschki, 1992. Pp. 167–191.

Pépin, Jean. *Mythe et allégorie: Les origines grecques et les contestations judéo-chrétiennes*. Paris: Montaigne, 1958.

Reverdin, Olivier. *La religion de la cité platonicienne*. Paris: De Boccard, 1945.

Vernant, Jean-Pierre. *Mythe et pensée chez les Grecs*. Paris: Maspéro, 1965; La Découverte, 1985.

———. *Mythe et religion en Grèce ancienne*. Paris: Le Seuil, 1990.

CHRONOLOGY

History	Culture	Science
1270(?)B.C.E.: Trojan War ~1200: First Greek colonization (Asia Minor)		
	Composition of Homeric poems (~850–750 B.C.E.)	
753: Founding of Rome 750: Second Greek colonization (Western and Eastern) 593: Solon's reforms in Athens	Hesiod (~700?) "Milesians": Thales, Anaximander and Anaximenes (~600–550). Anaximander writes the first Greek treatise in prose ~546	~585 B.C.E.: Eclipse predicted by Thales
540: Founding of Elea	Pythagoras teaches (~532?)	
509: Founding of Roman Republic 508–507: Cleisthenes' reforms in Athens 490: Battle of Marathon, defeat of the Persians 481: Alliance between Athens and Sparta (second Persian War) 480: Battle of Salamis, Greek naval victory	Heraclitus (~545–480) Parmenides of Elea teaches (~478) Aeschylus, *The Persians* (472); *Oresteia* (458) ~454: Anaxagoras (500–428) tried for impiety in Athens Empedocles (~492–432) Protagoras (~492–421) Zeno of Elea (~490–454)	510–490: Voyages of Hecataeus of Miletus
443: Pericles General of Athens. Alcibiades (450–404), Athenian political leader, student of Socrates	~450: Herodotus (~484–425), *Histories*. Sophocles, *Antigone* (443)	~440: Leucippus, first expression of the theory of atomism

History	Culture	Science
	~435: Socrates (469–399) teaches in Athens	Hippocrates of Chios (~470–400), *Elements of Geometry*
	Democritus (~460–?)	
	Thucydides (~455–400)	
Peloponnesian War (431–404)	427: Gorgias (~480–376) teaches rhetoric in Athens	
	~423: In *The Clouds*, Aristophanes ridicules the teaching of Socrates	
	Antisthenes (~445–360)	Hippocrates (~460–380)
404: Rule of the Thirty Tyrants in Athens	~405: Euclid of Megara founds the Megarian school	
403: Restoration of democracy	399: Trial of Socrates; death penalty. Aristippus founds a school at Cyrene	
	~390: Isocrates opens a school at Athens and teaches "philosophy" to a large audience	
	Xenophon (~428–354)	
	387: Plato (429–347) founds the Academy	Mathematical works of the Academy (Theaetetus, Eudoxus, Archytas, Leodamas)
		388–315: Work of Heraclides Ponticus (rotation of the earth)
384–322: Demosthenes	Diogenes of Sinope (400–325)	381: Observations of Eudoxus of Cnidus (400–347) in Egypt; epicycloidal movement of the planets (370)
343: Aristotle tutors Alexander the Great	347: Death of Plato; Speusippus succeeds him as head of the Academy	
340: War between Philip of Macedon and Athens		
338: Defeat of Athens at Chaeronea		

History	Culture	Science
336: Accession of Alexander the Great, King of Macedonia	335: Aristotle (385–322) founds the Lyceum in Athens. Pyrrhon (~365–275) accompanies Alexander to Asia	Aristoxenes' theory of harmonics
332: Founding of Alexandria		
323: Death of Alexander at Babylon; formation of separate Hellenistic monarchies	322: Death of Aristotle; Theophrastus succeeds him	
	306: Epicurus (~342–271) founds the Epicurean School	
	~301: Zeno of Citium founds the Stoic School	~300: Euclid's *Elements*
	~295: Ptolemy I founds the Library at Alexandria	
	283–239: Antigonus Gonatas, King of Macedonia, protects philosophers, especially the Stoics	~281: Aristarchus of Samos and heliocentrism
		~270: Herophilus (physician) practices in Alexandria
	268–264: Arcesilaus succeeds Crates as head of the Academy and gives the school a skeptical orientation	~260: Erasistratus practices medicine
	262: Cleanthes succeeds Zeno as head of the Stoic school	
	The Septuagint	250: Teaching of Diophantus (mathematician)
		~245: Eratosthenes (~275–194) librarian in Alexandria

History	Culture	Science
	~232: Chrysippus (~280–207) succeeds Cleanthes as head of the Stoic school	
218: Second Punic War		
217: First War of Macedonia		Archimedes (~287–212) killed by a Roman soldier during the siege of Syracuse
		~200: Work of Apollonius (theory of conics)
	Polybius (208–118)	
169: War between the Seleucids and the Jews of Palestine	167–166: Carneades, Scholarch of the Academy	161–126: Teaching of Hipparchus (origins of trigonometry, excentric and epicyclic systems theory)
	155: Carneades becomes Ambassador to Rome; accompanied by Diogenes of Babylon (Stoic) and Critolaos (Peripatetic)	
148: Macedonia becomes a Roman Province		
146: Greece becomes a Roman Province. Destruction of Carthage by Rome		~150: Hipparchus's geographical map
	110–109: Philon of Larissa becomes Scholarch of the Academy; in 88, flees Athens and seeks refuge in Rome	
~88–86: War of Mithridates		
	~79: Antiochus of Ascalon, Scholarch of the Academy, opens his own school at Athens and moves away from the "skeptical" orientation that lasted from Arcesilas to Philon of Larissa	Posidonius (~135–51) works in geography and astronomy

HISTORY	CULTURE	SCIENCE
	Lucretius, *De Natura Rerum* (~54–53)	
	Cicero, *De Republica* (54–52)	
	Philodemus of Gadara founds a center of Epicurian studies in Naples	
	48: First fire in the Library of Alexandria	
	~40: Andronicos of Rhodes publishes the works of Aristotle	
30: Battle of Actium; Egypt becomes a Roman Province. End of the Hellenistic period	30(?): Epicurian inscription of Diogenes of Oenoanda (dated by some scholars to ~125 C.E.)	
27 C.E.: End of the Republic; beginning of the Roman Empire	29(?)C.E.: Death of Jesus of Nazareth	10–25 C.E.: Strabo, *Geography*
	37–41: Embassy of Philon of Alexandria to Caligula	
54–68: Nero's reign; burning of Rome (64); persecution of Christians	48–65: The Stoic Seneca becomes tutor, then advisor to Nero, before being forced to commit suicide; *Letters to Lucilius*, 63–64	
	60: Teaching of Ammonius, a Platonist in Athens	~60: Heron of Alexandria, *Mechanica*
70: Titus takes Jerusalem	64(?): Death of Saint Paul	
	93–94: Expulsion of the philosophers from Rome by Domitian. Epictetus (55–135) founds a school at Nicopolis, on the Greek coast of the Adriatic	~100: Nicomachus of Gerasa (theory of numbers) and Menelaus (on spheres)
	~110: Plutarch (~46–~120) advisor to Trajan, then Hadrian, for Greek affairs	

History	Culture	Science
	~120: Christian apologists begin to present Christianity as philosophy	~125: Theon of Smyrna (numbers theory)
135: Jewish Diaspora	~133: Earliest evidence of gnosticism (Basilides)	
	~150: *Didaskalikos* (summary of Platonism) of Alcinous	Teaching of Ptolemy at Alexandria: *Almagest* (150); *Geography* (155)
161–180: Reign of Marcus Aurelius in Rome	176: Marcus Aurelius founds chairs in the four principal schools of philosophy at Athens: Platonic, Aristotelian, Stoic, Epicurian	
	~177: Celsus, Platonist and anti-Christian polemicist	Galen (129–200)
	~180: *Stromates* by Clement of Alexandria	
	~190: *Outlines of Pyrrhonism* by Sextus Empiricus, source of information on the arguments of early Skeptics (Agrippa and Aenesidemus)	
	~198: Teaching of Alexander of Aphrodisias (Peripatetic) in Athens	
	200: *Lives and Doctrines of the Philosophers* by Diogenes Laertius	
	244: Plotinus (205–269) opens a school in Rome	Diophantus: *Arithmetica*
	~260: Founding of the School of Antioch	
	263: Porphyry becomes a student of Plotinus; publishes the *Enneads* ~301	
312: Conversion of Emperor Constantine		

History	Culture	Science
313: Edict of Milan allows Christianity in Roman Empire 314: First partition of Roman Empire	~313: Iamblichus (250–325) founds a Neoplatonist school at Apamea Writings of Basil of Caesarea, Gregory of Nazianzus, Gregory of Nyssa	~320: Pappus of Alexandria writes a commentary on Ptolemy and Euclid Theon of Alexandria succeeds Pappus as professor of mathematics
361–363: Reign of Julian the Apostate, Neoplatonist philosopher; reaction against the Christians 380: Christianity becomes official religion of Roman Empire 410: Sack of Rome by Alaric	386: Conversion of Augustine; writes *Confessions*, 400; *The City of God*, 413–426	415: Death of Hypatia, daughter of Theon, scholar and a key figure in Neoplatonist philosophy
476: Fall of the Western Empire	~438: Proclus succeeds Syrianus as head of the Neoplatonist school 520: Damascius succeeds Zenodotus as head of the Neoplatonist school 529: Justinian closes the school of Athens. Seven Neoplatonist philosophers flee to Persia (including Simplicius and Damascius)	

CONTRIBUTORS

Annie Bélis, Centre National de la Recherche Scientifique, Paris
Jacques Brunschwig, Université de Paris I
François De Gandt, Université de Lille III
Michael Frede, Keble College, Oxford
David Furley, Princeton University
Christian Jacob, Ecole des Hautes Etudes en Sciences Sociales, Paris
José Kany-Turpin, Université de Paris XII, Val-de-Marne
Wilbur Knorr, Stanford University
Geoffrey E. R. Lloyd, Darwin College, Cambridge
Anthony A. Long, University of California, Berkeley
Mario Mignucci, Kings College, London; Università di Padova, *emeritus*
Oswyn Murray, Balliol College, Oxford
Carlo Natali, Università di Venezia
Pierre Pellegrin, Centre National de la Recherche Scientifique, Paris
Malcolm Schofield, St. John's College, Cambridge
Pierre Somville, Université de Liège
G. J. Toomer, Harvard University
Robert Wardy, St. Catharine's College, Cambridge

INDEX

Academy, 46–47, 48–49, 54–55, 274
Aeneas Tacticus, *The Art of Siege Warfare*, 338–339
Alcmaeon, 86–87, 270
Alexander of Aphrodisias, 60
Alexandria: and knowledge, 151–152; and language, 197–198, 201, 202; and learning, 56–57; and mathematics, 260; and medicine, 265, 272, 273; and Peripatetics, 56–57; and philosophic schools, 63–64; and poetics, 307
Ammonius, 233, 260
Anaxagoras, 70, 71, 132–133, 288–289, 349–350
Anaximander: and Aristotle, 293–294; and cosmology, 129, 131; and geography, 150–151, 154; and physics, 283, 285, 293–294; school of, 41
Anaximenes, 41, 71, 129, 130
Anthemius of Tralles, 261
Antigonus of Carystus, 51
Antiphon, 246. *See also* Sophists
Apollonius of Perge, 121, 257–258
Apollonius of Tyana, 14
Aratus, 120
Archimedes, 255–256, 336; *Method*, 108; *On the Quadrature of the Parabola*, 109
Archytas, 242, 250, 252, 255
Aristarchus of Samos, 121, 138; *On the Sizes and Distances of the Sun and the Moon*, 115
Aristarchus of Samothrace, 198, 307
Aristides Quintilianus, *Peri mousikes*, 168, 173
Aristophanes, 187–188, 189
Aristophanes of Byzantium, 307
Aristotle: and Anaximander, 293–294; and cosmology, 135, 136–138, 139, 140, 142, 144, 145, 146; and demonstration, 92, 103–106, 111, 112; and Empedocles, 294; and Epicurus, 139, 140; and Galen, 111; and geography, 159; and Gorgias, 332; and knowing, 29, 32, 34–35, 36–38; and language, 194–196; and logic, 205–206, 208–223, 224, 226, 227, 231; and mathematics, 251; and mechanics, 341–342; and medicine, 263, 264, 272–273; and Milesians, 293–294; and observation, 68, 76–80, 85, 90; and Parmenides, 293, 294; and physics, 289, 290, 293–296, 297–298; and physiology, 111; and Plato, 76, 137, 209, 211, 331, 332, 354–355; and poetics, 303–307; and Pythagoras/Pythagoreanism, 97, 239–240; and religion, 354–355, 366–367; and rhetoric, 105, 331–333; and Stoicism, 142, 144, 145, 146; and teaching, 49–50; and Thales, 4, 97; and thought, 23; and wisdom, 9; *Categories*, 76; *Mechanical Problems*, 341–342; *Metaphysics*, 36–38; *Physics*, 76, 77–78, 105; *Poetics*, 303–307; *Posterior Analytics*, 37, 103, 104, 105, 106; *Rhetoric*, 105, 332; *On the Soul*, 23. *See also* Lyceum
Aristoxenus, 164–166, 167, 168, 169, 170, 172, 173, 174–175
Athens: and music, 161; and schools, 47–48, 50, 54, 60, 62, 63; and Sophists, 43–44; and Zeno of Citium, 52–53
Atomism, 132, 133
Autolycus of Pitane, *On Moving Spheres*, 115

Babylon, 81–82, 119, 120, 122, 123, 124, 237–238. *See also* Mesopotamia
Bacchius the Old, 163
Bryson, 246–247

Callippus, 135, 136
Calvenus Taurus, 59
Carneades, 357. *See also* Skepticism
Christianity, 15–16, 63–64
Chrysippus: and cosmology, 145, 147; and logic, 230–231, 232; and religion, 356, 357; and Stoic school, 53; and Zeno, 145. *See also* Stoicism